Sanskrit Syntax

SANSKRIT SYNTAX

J.S. Speijer

With an Introduction by
H. Kern

MOTILAL BANARSIDASS PUBLISHERS
PRIVATE LIMITED • DELHI

*8th Reprint : Delhi, **2018***
First Edition : Leiden, 1886

ISBN : 978-81-208-0482-1 (Cloth)
ISBN : 978-81-208-0483-8 (Paper)

MOTILAL BANARSIDASS
41 U.A. Bungalow Road, Jawahar Nagar, Delhi 110 007
1 B, Jyoti Studio Compound, Kennedy Bridge, Nana Chowk, Mumbai 400 007
203 Royapettah High Road, Mylapore, Chennai 600 004
236, 9th Main III Block, Jayanagar, Bengaluru 560 011
8 Camac Street, Kolkata 700 017
Ashok Rajpath, Patna 800 004
Chowk, Varanasi 221 001

Printed in India

by RP Jain at NAB Printing Unit,
A-44, Naraina Industrial Area, Phase I, New Delhi–110028
and published by JP Jain for Motilal Banarsidass Publishers (P) Ltd,
41 U.A. Bungalow Road, Jawahar Nagar, Delhi-110007

In order to comply with the wishes of Dr. Speijer I take the liberty to introduce his work with the students of Sanskrit.

Indian grammar, which is virtually the same as saying Pâṇini's grammar, superior as it is in many respects to anything of the kind produced among other civilized nations of antiquity, is professedly deficient in its treatment of syntax. As all Sanskrit grammars published by Western scholars are, so far as the linguistical facts are concerned, almost entirely dependent, either directly or indirectly, upon Pâṇini, it cannot be matter for surprise that syntax is not adequately treated in them, although it must be admitted that Professor Whitney's grammar shows in this respect a signal progress.

Some parts of Indian syntax have received a careful treatment at the hands of competent scholars, amongst whom Delbrück stands foremost. All who are grateful to those pioneers will, it may be supposed, gladly receive this more comprehensive work, the first complete syntax of classical Sanskrit, for which we are indebted to the labours of Dr. Speijer. May it be the forerunner of a similar work, as copious and conscientious, on Vaidik Syntax!

H. KERN.

LEYDEN, 13 July 1886.

PREFACE.

This book aims to give a succinct account of Sanskrit Syntax, as it is represented in classic Sanskrit literature, without neglecting however the archaisms and peculiarities of vaidik prose (brâhmaṇa, upanishad, sûtra) and of epic poetry. The facts laid down here have been stated chiefly by my own observations in perusing Sanskrit writings, and accordingly by far the great majority of the examples quoted have been selected directly from the sources, if not, those suggested by the Petropolitan Dictionary or others have, as a rule, been received only after verification. Moreover, valuable information was gained by the statements of vernacular grammarians, especially of Pâṇini, to whose reverenced authority due respect is paid and whose rules are referred to at every opportunity. For some useful intelligence I am indebted to Mr. ANUNDORAM BOROOAH's *Higher Sanskrit Grammar* Calcutta 1879. A welcome and precious assistance were to me some treatises or occasional hints of distinguished European scholars, who, as DELBRÜCK, DE SAUSSURE, WHITNEY, have explored tracks of this scarcely trodden region of Indian philology. But for the greater part of the subjects falling within the scopê of this compilation, monographies and special investigations of a sound philological and scholarlike character are still wanting, and I have felt that want often and deeply. For this reason I am fully aware, that many deficiencies and inaccuracies will certainly be found now or appear afterwards in this first Sanskrit Syntax written in Europe. Notwithstanding, as I felt convinced that my labour, however imperfect, might prove of some profit by facilitating both the access to Sanskrit literature and the study of Sanskrit language, and that on the other hand this work might afford some base for further investigations on special points of Syntax, it is placed before the public with the confidence that it may be judged, what it is, as a first attempt, and an attempt undertaken by a foreigner.

In arranging materials I preferred following, as best I could, the nature and spirit of the language I was working on, rather than clinging too closely to the classification familiar to us by the Syntax of Latin and Greek; in stating facts I have avoided generalizing from such instances as did rest only on my own limited experience, remembering the wise words of Patanjali महान्हि शब्दस्य प्रयोगविषयः..... एतावन्तं शब्दस्य प्रयोगविषयमननुनिशम्य सन्त्यप्रयुक्ता इति वचनं केवलं साहसमात्रम्.

The whole of this Syntax is made up of six Sections.

Amsterdam, July 1886. J. S. SPEIJER.

On p. 34 § 46 R. I wrote. I could adduce no instance of चि with two acc. Afterwards I met with this: R. 3, 42, 31 कर्णिकारानशोकांश्च चूतांश्च मदिरेक्षणा। कुसुमान्यपचिन्वन्ती चचार रुचिरानना.

SECTION THE FIRST.

GENERAL REMARKS ON THE STRUCTURE OF SENTENCES.

---

1. Subject and predicate. The **subject of the sentence** [1]) is put in the nominative case. The **predicate of the sentence** is either noun or verb; अश्वो धावति (the horse runs), तरुणोऽश्वः (the horse is young).

2. Verbum substantivum. To the **noun-predicate** the so called *verbum substantivum* is commonly not subjoined; from a logical point of view it is indeed of no use, and its obligatory employment in modern western languages rather to be called an abuse. Panc. 26 स महात्मा वयं कृपणाः (he is a lord, we are mean people), Nala 1,30 त्वं चापि रत्नं नारीणां नरेषु च नलो वरः, Çâk. I अपि संनिहितोऽत्र कुलपतिः (is perhaps the head of the family near?). It may, however, be added. Panc. 100 अस्माकं स्वामी वैनतेयोऽस्ति, Kathâs. 16, 115 अहमेवापराध्यस्मि (I alone am guilty.) —

---

1) Vernacular grammar has no term to name the subject of the sentence or grammatical subject. The term *kartṛ* signifies the agent or *logical subject.* In the same way *karma* means the *logical object*, whatsoever may be its grammatical function; it thus implies the object of the active verb as well as the subject of the passive or the objective genitive. In such sentences as »the knife cuts", the grammatical subject is both *kartṛ* (agent) and *karaṇa* (instrument).

It must be added, if »to be" means »to exist" or »to be met with;" likewise if the grammatical tense or mood is to be expressed.

Rem. It is even wanting sometimes in such sentences, as contain a predicate in the optative or imperative mood; especially in some current phrases, as नमस्तस्मै (adoration to him), भद्रं ते [sc. भूयात्] hail to you), का कथा (why make mention of —) शान्तम् or शान्तं पापम् (v. a. *malum absit*), etc. Prabodh. III p. 66 the Bauddha monk entreats the Çaiva to let him enjoy the instruction of his doctrines आचार्यस्त्वं शिष्योऽहं प्रवेशय मां पारमेश्वरीं शिक्षाम् (be you my teacher, I your pupil, initiate me into the doctrines of the Çaivâs).

3. Besides अस्ति and भवति, the verbs विद्यते, तिष्ठति, वर्तते and the participle गत may be used more or less as *verbum substantivum*. Schol. on P. 3, 4, 65 [1]) विद्यते भोक्तुम् (there is something to eat), Ven. III p. 94 एष दुर्योधन अस्यां न्यग्रोधच्छायायामुपविष्टस्तिष्ठति (here D. is sitting down under the shade —), Hit. 107 वायसराजो द्वारि वर्तते the king of the crows is at the door). From the given examples it however sufficiently appears that the original meaning of those verbs has not wholly faded. Accordingly it is sometimes not indifferent which verbum subst. to choose. So विद्यते especially denotes the »being met with" fr. *il y a*, likewise अस्ति, but not भवति; गत expresses the »being in or on", as चित्रगतः (v. a. painted); वर्तते comp. Lat. *versatur*.

Rem. By consequence, भवति is the proper verb, if there be laid some stress on the predicate, in other terms, if it be pointed out that the subject is invested with the dignity or possesses the quality predicated of it. Ch. Up. 6, 16, 1 it is said with respect to somebody, seized on account of a theft, apparently committed by him स यदि तस्य कर्ता भवति [not अस्ति]; Panc. III, 57 वनानि दहतो वह्नेः सखा भवति मारुतः (when the fire burns the wood, wind is his mate), Mhbh. 1,89,2. यो विद्यया तपसा जन्मना वा वृद्धः स पूज्यो भवति द्विजानाम्.

4. The same character is exhibited by the predicates

1) विद्यते in this sutra is one of the अस्त्यर्थाः (words meaning *to be*).

made up of a noun and a verb of *becoming*, *growing*, *seeming*, *remaining*, *being called*,-*considered* and the like. Comp. **32**.

5. The noun-predicate itself deviates by no means from the common use of other tongues. It may thus be any kind of noun either substantive or adjective, and is put in the nominative case, provided that it be pointing at the same person or thing as is pointed out by the subject, as शीतला रात्रिः (the night is cold), for in that sentence the subj. रात्रिः and the predicate शीतला are relating to one and the same thing. This we may call the noun-predicate proper. Nothing, indeed, forbids other nouncases, adverbs and the like doing duty of the predicate, as कूपे तोयम् when = „water is in the pit," Pat. 84 अदो यत्रासौ काकः (yonder [house], where that crow is), Mudr. 23 नायशः प्रमार्ष्टुमलम् (he [will] not [be] able to blot out [that] stain), R. 2,42,7 नाहं तेषां न ते मम (I have nothing in common with them nor they with me) and sim.

Noun-predicate.

6. As to the **verb-predicate**, the same action may be expressed as well by the active voice as by the passive. When active, its agent or subject is put in the nominative case and its object in the accusative; देवदत्तः कटं करोति (N. N. makes a mat). In the passive sentence, the object of the action is subject of the sentence and accordingly a nominative; the agent is invariably put in the instrumental. देवदत्तेन कटः क्रियते (the mat is made by N. N.); of स्वपिमि (I sleep) the pass. form is मया सुप्यते (it is slept by me), and so on.

Verb-predicate in the active voice or in the passive.

7. Sanskrit has a decided predilection for the passive

Passive voice.

voice. In translating from that language it is often necessary to transform passive sentences into active. For inst. Panc. 43 चिरकालं श्रुतो मया तवापवादः (it is a long time I hear blame you), Daçak. 133 कयापि दिव्याकारया कन्ययोपास्थायिषि (a maiden of heavenly appearance respectfully approached me), Hit. 43 तत्र तेन मृग एको व्यापादितः। मृगमादाय गच्छता तेन घोराकृतिः सूकरो दृष्टः। ततस्तेन मृगं भूमौ निधाय सूकरः शरेण हतः

Impersonal passives.

8. Since this preference is of course not limited to transitive verbs, nothing can be more common than the use of **impersonal passives**. Hit. 93 केनापि शस्यरक्षकेनैकान्ते स्थितम् (some guardian of the crops was standing aside), Daçak. 18 केसरिणा करिणं निहत्य कुत्रचिदगामि (the lion, after having-slain the elephant, disappeared), Ven. III p. 79 कथमेवं प्रलपतां वः सहस्रधा न दीर्णमनया जिह्वया. Even the verb subst. has occasionally a passive form, cp. **32** *b*).

Impersonal verbs.

Rem. Apart from the said impersonal verbs, we have to record the old and genuine impersonals with active or medial endings and meaning. In classic Sanskrit they are scarcely used, being but remnants of a more widely employed idiom of the elder language. Ait. Br. 1,9,2 तस्यै जनतायै कल्पते यत्रैवं विद्वान्होता भवति (it avails such community, as where is a *hotṛ* knowing this), Açv. Gṛhy. 4,1,1 आहिताग्निं चेदुपतपेदुद्वस्येत् (if a worshipper in the three fires be affected by illness, he should withdraw); — Panc. I यत्ने कृते यदि न सिध्यति (if it does not succeed notwithstanding the effort —). Likewise वर्षति (it rains) = देवो वर्षति (cp. Yâjñ. 1,136 with Kâç. on P. 1,4,89) and so on.

Participles, doing duty of finite verbs.

9. Participles, especially those in त and तवन्त् and the kṛtyâs are frequently employed as if they were finite verbs, without the attendance of the verb subst. In simple prose a great deal of the sentences are moulded in that shape. Hitop. 12 असौ व्याघ्रेण व्यापादितः खादितश्च (the tiger killed him and devoured him), ibid. 7 तस्य विष्णुशर्मणः पुत्रान् समर्पितवान् (he entrusted his sons to the foresaid Vishṇ.), Çâk. I विनीतवेषेण

प्रवेष्टव्यानि तपोवनानि नाम (surely, the hermitages should be entered in modest dress).

Rem. The participles of the present and the future do not partake of this construction, cp. P. 3, 2, 124 with 126[1]).

10. Subject implied. The subject of the sentence is not always expressed. Often it is implied by the verb. For ददामि and ददासि are quite as intelligible as अहं ददामि and त्वं ददासि, and likewise in the third person the sole ददाति suffices, if there can be no doubt as to the giver meant.

Nevertheless, the personal pronouns denoting the subject are not seldom added, even when not required for the understanding, certainly much oftener than in Latin and Greek. See f. inst. Nala 2,19; 3,9; Kathâs. 6,133. But the omission is impossible, if stress should be laid on the pronoun.

Agent implied. In passive sentences, the personal pronouns denoting the agent may be wanting likewise, but of course this is not by far done so often as in active sentences. Panc. 127 इति निश्चित्याभिहितम् [sc. अनेन], ibid. 327 भो मित्र किमेवं पलाय्यते ऽलीकभयेन (say, friend, why do [you] run away thus by false fear?).

The omission is regular with passive imperatives, that are expressive of an injunction or commandment in a softened or polite manner, as गम्यताम् (go), श्रूयताम् hear) Panc. 87 the panther thus addresses the hungry lion, his

---

1) A vârtt. to P. 3,2,124 states an exception for the case, that the negation मा is added to the participle, in order to signify an imprecation. Of this rule applied I know but one instance, Çiçupâl. 2,45 quoted by the Petr. Dict. s. v. मा, V p. 680; but it is not improbable that the author of that poem has done so designedly to show his own skill by applying an out-of-the-way grammatical rule.

master स्वामिन्क्रियतामद्य मम प्राणैः प्राणयात्रा। दीयतामत्तयो वासः स्वर्गे। मम विस्तार्यतां क्षितितले प्रभूततरं यशः

11. But in sentences without a finite verb the personal pronoun denoting the subject cannot be missing. It may be said promiscuously कृतवानस्मि and कृतवानहम्, कृतकृत्योऽसि and कृतकृत्यस्त्वम् and so on. The full forms अहं कृतवानस्मि, त्वं कृतकृत्योऽसि are, of course, also available.

Rem. Occasionally they are wanting even then, provided that it be beyond doubt, which subject is meant. Panc. 214 the crow Sthirajîvin relates to the king of the owls the ill treatment he has endured from his own king, for तेन दुर्जनप्रकोपितेनेमां दशां नीतः [sc. अहम्, as is perspicuous by the context]; ibid. 53 the lover addresses the princess राजपुत्रि सुप्ता [sc. त्वं] किं वा जागर्षि; ibid. 38 वत्स धन्योऽसि यत्प्रथमे वयस्येवं विरक्तिभावः [sc. त्वम्]. Cp. ibid. 137, 13; 154, 10.

12. *General subject.* A general subject may be expressed by using the passive form, as उच्यते (it is said), श्रूयते (it is taught). Likewise by the plural of the 3[d] pers. of the active as आहुः (they say, when = it is said; germ. *man sagt*), विदुः (it is known), आचक्षते it is told). But not seldom also the **singular of the 3[d] pers.** of the active is employed in this manner. Panc. II, 34 कारणान्मित्रतामेति कारणादेति शत्रुताम् (it is not without cause, one becomes a friend or a foe). The pronoun omitted is स (= one, germ. *man*), which is also sometimes added. Panc. I, 216 त्याज्यं न धैर्यं विधुरेऽपि दैवे। धैर्यात्कदाचित्स्थितिमाप्नुयात्सः (one must not lose courage even in distress; by courage one may regain one's position in time).

---

13. The accessory parts of the sentence, such as are to point out the *where*, the *when*, the *why*, the *how* of the fact related, the qualities and other attributes of the persons or things involved, are embodied into speech by the same or nearly the same grammatical apparatus, as serves that purpose in other languages. It is the relative frequency or rareness and the distribution of these instrumentalities of speech, which gives to Sanskrit style its proper and peculiar character, the main features of which may be sketched as follows:

14. Character of Sanskrit style.

Ily. Sanskrit, in comparison with western languages, does not avail itself much of finite verbs. Hence abundance of gerunds, participles, absolute locatives, noun-predicates and a relative scarcity of subordinate sentences. Accumulating short coordinate phrases is likewise avoided by using gerunds. Daçak. 19 बालं शनैरवनिरुह्यादवतार्य वनान्तरे वनितामन्विष्याऽविलोक्यैनमानीय गुरवे निवेद्य तन्निर्देशेन भवदन्तिकमानीतवानस्मि = »I took off the baby from the tree and sought for the fair one in the forest, but not discovering her I carried it to my teacher, and gave it over in his hands. By his order I now have brought the boy to you."

In Sanskrit style the predicate of the sentence is many times expressed by means of a *nomen actionis*, to be translated by a finite verb. Panc. 21 दमनक आह । स्वामिन् किमिह निवृत्यावस्थानम् (Dam. said: why does my master stop and stay here?)

IIly. Abstracts in °ता or °त्व may be made of any noun either simple or compound. Since they are available in all noun-cases, they afford an easy expedient to bring a whole clause into a shape as concise as possible and to express logical relations in the very sharpest and most distinct way. Hence they are often employed in treatises, commentaries and similar works. A more detailed account of them will be given hereafter.

III[ly]. A great and important place in Sanskrit composition is filled up by **compound nouns**. This synthetic expression of thought is applied to the most various and manifold logical relations, but it is especially in the more flowery style of adorned literary composition, that they are used at a considerably large extent. Relative clauses are commonly avoided by them.

IV[ly]. An other characteristic of Sanskrit style is its predilection for the *oratio directa*. Words and thoughts are related just as they have been spoken and thought or supposed to have been, but they are not moulded into the figure of an oratio obliqua. Generally the adverb इति (thus, so) is put behind the words or thoughts related. Accordingly the English sentence *he asked his friend, why he had not left this town* is Sanskrit कस्मादस्मान्नगरान्न प्रस्थितोसीति मित्रमपृच्छत्. So f. inst. Utt. I परिश्रान्तेयमार्या तद्विज्ञापयामि विश्राम्यतामिति (Mylady is tired; for this reason I beg Her to take Her rest).

V[ly]. The system of correlation between relatives and demonstratives, though sufficiently developed as to the number and variety of combinations, has retained a great deal of the unwieldiness and prolixity of its rudimentary stage. It often reminds of the solemn style of old Latin. Mostly the relative clause precedes. Panc. 2 यथा मम मनोरथाः सिद्धिं यान्ति तथानुष्ठीयताम् (act so as to fulfill my wishes), ibid. 70 यः कूपो दृष्टो ऽभूत्तमेव कूपमासाद्य, and the like.

VI[ly]. Sanskrit likes rhetorical interrogations, that is, such as do not put a question, but contain a statement either positive or negative. As this turn is much more employed than in modern languages, such interrogations are often to be translated rather freely. So कः is not rarely an other expression of »nobody" and को न = »every body;" कुतः is frequently = »because." Similarly अथ किम् = »yes," कथम् and ननु = »certainly," cp. the idiom क्व च..... क्व च and other turns, more fully to be dealt with in one of the subsequent chapters. Compare Engl. *why*, when = »now, well," Greek *οὐκοῦν*.

VII^ly. The predilection for the passive construction has been already mentioned (see **7**). It is of course not restricted to the finite verb, but applies also to participles.

15. Order of words. Like all languages, that possess a rich store of inflections, Sanskrit affords a comparatively great freedom as to the order of words in the sentence [1]). Yet, it is frequently not altogether indifferent in what order one puts one's words. We ought to distinguish between the traditional or regular arrangement and the various exceptions caused by the exigencies of style, euphony, metre etc. Therefore though tracing a general scheme, we must keep in mind, that it bears but on the most frequent employment, as it has been observed in perusing the best writers, but it cannot claim to be a set of fixed rules rigorously to be followed throughout.

16. The traditional **order of words** is this. [2])

Traditional. 1. The predicate being verbal, it ordinarily closes the sentence, which is headed by the noun-subject, when expressed. The other elements of the sentence are taken in the midst, but placed so as to make the

1) Compare Pat. I, p. 39, l. 18 संस्कृत्य संस्कृत्य पदान्युत्सृज्यन्ते तेषां यथेष्टमभिसंबन्धो भवति। तद्यथा। आहर पात्रं पात्रमाहरेति।

2) On this subject we have an excellent treatise of Prof. DELBRÜCK *Die altindische Wortfolge aus dem Çatapathabrâhmaṇa* 1878. Yet, of course, it does not go beyond the archaic period of Sanskrit literature.

verb have its object immediately before it, देवदत्तः कटं करोति (N.N. makes a mat), देवदत्तो भ्रातृभिः सह पाटलिपुत्रं प्रस्थितः (N.N. has parted for Pâṭaliputra with his brothers). In a similar manner the attributes and other accessories of nouns precede them. Moreover, as one is inclined in Sanskrit to avoid subordinate sentences by availing one's self largely of participles, gerunds and the like (**14**, I), it often occurs, that the chief sentence is preceded by a greater or smaller amount of accessory elements of the kind, put according to the exigencies of grammar and style either before the subject or subsequent to it. This sentence, taken from Patanjali (I, p. 39, 10) may illustrate the above statement, प्रमाणभूत आचार्यो दर्भपवित्रपाणिः शुचाववकाशे प्राङ्मुख उपविश्य महता यत्नेन सूत्रं प्रणयति स्म. Here the subject preceded by its attribute stands at the head, then follows दर्भपवित्रपाणिः formally a predicative attribute of the subject, but as to its meaning an accessory of the gerund उपविश्य, 3ly the other accessories of the said gerund, 4ly the gerund itself, 5ly the accessories of the chief predicate, finally that predicate itself.

Rem. In passive sentences the agent, as far as I have observed, seems to have the precedence in the traditional order of words, not the nominative of the karma. Panc. 126 तैर्विप्रैः सर्ववस्तूनि विक्रीय बहुमूल्यानि रत्नानि क्रीतानि, Hitop. 92 तैर्वानरैर्वृक्षमारुह्य सर्वे नीडा भग्नाः

2. If the predicate be a noun, it is put before the subject. Panc. 38 असारः संसारोऽयं गिरिनदीवेगोपमं यौवनं तृणाग्निसमं जीवितं शरदभ्रच्छायासदृशा भोगाः स्वप्नसदृशो मित्रपुत्रकलत्रभृत्यवर्गसंबन्धः. Similarly in the passive. Hit. 20 अधुना तवानुचरेण मया सर्वथा भवितव्यम् (now at all events I must be your companion).

Rem. Pronouns, it seems, may be put indiscriminately before or behind their noun-predicate: समर्थोऽहम् or अहं समर्थः

3 Attributes are put before their nouns. But when

doing duty of a so called predicative attribute, they generally follow. Comp. for inst. the proverb स्वयमुपगता श्रीस्त्यज्यमाना शपति (fortune which has arrived spontaneously, grows a curse, when neglected).

Rem. Not seldom they are separated from the noun (or pronoun) they belong to. Daç. 141 मयास्मि जातमात्रः पापया परित्यक्तः; when translating this sentence one should render पापया by the adverb *basely* or *in a base manner*. So Panc. 73 तद् द्रोहबुद्धेरपि मयास्य न विरुद्धमाचरणीयम्; note the disjunction of द्रोहबुद्धेः and अस्य.

4. The vocative generally heads the sentence.

5. The prepositions are commonly preceded by their cases.

6. In sentences linked to the preceding by means of relatives or particles, these words are put first; when enclitical, they are affixed to the first word of the clause they introduce.

17. Modified. As it has been stated above (**15**), this traditional order of words is liable to be modified by various influences of the power to cause the speaker to prefer an other arrangement. Instead of the subject, the word on which stress is laid will head the sentence. In this way the verb or an oblique noun-case or an adverb (especially when of time), are not seldom put first, because of emphasis. Hit. 97 सन्त्येवम्भूता बहवः (of the kind there exist many, indeed), Daç. 132 अथावोचम्। अपसरतु द्विरदकीट एष अन्यः कश्चिन्मातङ्गपतिरानीयताम् (then I said: let this miserable elephant be gone, bring an other, a number 1 of the elephants);" Hit. 110 मम बलानि तावदवलोकयतु मन्त्री; Panc. 39 रात्रौ त्वया मठमध्ये न प्रवेष्टव्यम्; ibid. 53 अद्यैव तया सह समागमः क्रियताम् (meet with her still to-day). Absolute locatives and the like are also placed at the beginning. Bhojap. 8 गृहीते भोजे लोकाः कोलाहलं चक्रुः, Hitop. 131 पश्यतो बकमूर्खस्य नकुलैर्भक्षिताः सुताः, Panc. 54 एवं तस्य तां नित्यं सेवमानस्य कालो याति.

Likewise in connecting sentences it is necessary to

commence a new sentence or a new clause at the word, which relates to somebody or something mentioned in the foregoing. Hence demonstratives often head the sentence. Panc. 37 अस्ति कस्मिंश्चिद्विविक्तप्रदेशे मठायतनं । तत्र — परिव्राजकः प्रतिवसति स्म। तस्य — महती वित्तमात्रा संजाता। ततः स न कस्यचिद्विश्वसिति.

Rem. In general, the manner in which sentences are linked together may be of some influence on the arrangement of words. So the type, represented by Hit. 110 राजा सर्वान्शिष्टानाहूय मन्त्रयितुमुपविष्टः। आह च तान् [instead of तांश्चाह], often occurs, especially in polished style. Cp. f. i. Daç. 139 अहंच.... विषं क्षणादस्तम्भयम्। अपतच्च स भूमौ, Harsha 11 मर्त्यलोकमवातरत्। अपश्यच्च.

On the other hand similar reasons may expel the verb from its place at the rear, substituting for it some other word, required there by economy of style, because the end of a sentence is also fit to give some emphasis to the word placed there. Ratn. III न खलु किञ्चिन्न संभाव्यते त्वयि (in you there is nothing we may not look for), Daç. 97 न चेच्चोरितकानि प्रत्यर्पयसि द्रक्ष्यसि पारमष्टादशानां कारणानामन्ते च मृत्युमुखम् (if you do not restore to the citizens what you have stolen of them, you will know by experience the succession of the eighteen tortures, and at last the mouth of death); Kād. I, p. 292 राजपुत्रि किं ब्रवीमि वागेव मे नाभिधेयविषयमवतरति त्रपया.

There is much freedom, where to put the negations, as will be shown in the chapter, which treats of them.

18. *Poetical.* Sanskrit poets, especially in the more artificial and refined kinds, display a still greater variety in arranging the parts of the sentence. We may account for it partly by the exigencies of versification, but for a good deal it is the effect of their aspiring after an elegant and exquisite diction. Yet, as deviation from the traditional order of words is not striven at for itself, the idiom of the poets is rather characterized by the richness and size of compounds, by the elegancy of words and the melodiousness of sounds, by the elevation and perfection of style, than by an artificially disturbed arrangement of words. Such entangled and intricate structure, as for example characterizes Latin poetry, is an exception in Sanskrit [1]). There it is chiefly displayed in the extraordinary great liberty in placing relatives, interrogatives and negations.

Rem. Rhythmical wants and euphony, of course, may also exercise a greater or smaller influence on the order of words. Especially in the old dialect. Here are some instances. Ch. Up. 4,4,2 बह्वहं चरन्ती (instead of बहु चरन्त्यहम्), Ait. Br. 1,30,9 तस्माद्धस्याग्निं पुरस्ताद्धरन्ति (instead of °अस्य पुरस्ताद्ग्निम्), ibid. 2,37,4 आग्नेयं होता ऽऽज्यं शंसति. The rhythmical disposition of the words is here prevailing on the regular arrangement required by logic, compare the figur *hyperbaton*, so much employed in Greek and Latin. — An other mark of antiquity is separating prepositions from their verbs, chiefly by particles put between them, as Ait. Br. 2, 31, 6 उप वा वदेदनु वा व्याहरेत्.

SECTION II.

SYNTAXIS CONVENIENTIAE AND SYNTAXIS RECTIONIS.

CHAPT. I. **Concord.**

19. A twofold agreement is here to be spoken of, one

---

1) Kathâs. 30,53 may give an instance of poetical arrangement.

सोऽपि शापान्तबद्धाशः कालं मातलिबोधितः
कृच्छ्रात्सहस्रानीकस्तां विनानैषीन्मृगावतीम्.

In prose the words कृच्छ्रात्कालमनैषीत् would not have been separated.

existing between idea and word (I), the other between words standing in the same sentence (II).

Real and grammatical gender and number.

I. As a rule, there is agreement between the real and the grammatical gender and number. As to the number, an exception is to be stated for the collective nouns and some *pluralia tantum*, as आपः (water), प्राणाः and असवः (life), वर्षाः (the rainy season), in the elder language also जत्रवः (collar-bone), ग्रीवाः (neck). 1) Rarely the gender disagrees, as the neuter मित्र »friend," words as भाजन, पात्र »vessel; fit person," f. i. Mhbh. 1,61,3 श्रोतुं पात्रं च राजंस्त्वम् (you are the proper man to hear —) दैवत (n.) and देवता (f.) »deity," etc; — दाराः masc. plur. »wife" is an instance of disagreement in both gender and number [2]).

The diminutives generally retain the gender of their primitives [3]): पुत्रक m. as पुत्र, but पुत्रिका f. as पुत्री.

Rem. Of the collectives some are not always used so; जन f. ex. may as well denote a single individual as a collection of individuals. Accordingly, in the latter case it may be said as well जनः (sing.) as जनाः (plur.). [4]) Similarly लोकः or लोकाः »people, *le monde*, *les gens*," प्रजा or प्रजाः »offspring; subjects."

20. Singularis generalis.

In a general proposition a whole class of individuals may be optionally denoted by the singular or by the

Pâṇ. 1,2,58.

---

1) Still Pâṇini seems to have known it but as a plural, for in teaching taddhitas derived from it, he says ग्रीवाभ्यो [not ग्रीवायाः] ऽण् च 4,3,57. Compare the similar development of Latin *cervix* out of the pl. tant. *cervices*, see Quintilian VIII, 3,35.

2) दार is used as a singular in the Dharmasûtra of Âpastamba (see I, 32, 6; II, 1, 17; 5, 10; 11, 12; 22, 7, etc.).

3) Words in अ have, however, sometimes diminutives in ई. So शस्त्री (a small dagger = असिपुत्री Amar. k.), whereas शस्त्र (n.) more especially »sword."

4) So Nala 6,11 ततः पौरजनाः सर्वे मन्त्रिभिः सह भारत । राजानं द्रष्टुमागच्छन्, but in the subsequent cloka we read ततः सूत उपागम्य दमयन्त्यै न्यवेदयत् । एष पौरजनो देवि द्वारि तिष्ठति कार्यवान्.

plural of the common noun. ब्राह्मणः पूज्यः or ब्राह्मणाः पूज्याः (the brahman [that is, any brahman as far as he is a brahman] ought to be honored). Cp. f. inst. Bhoj. 13 सर्पदष्टं विषव्याकुलं रोगग्रस्तं...... तत्क्षणादेव विगतसकलव्याधिसंचयं कुर्मः [a kâpâlika speaks] »men, bitten by a serpent, or poisoned, or sick, we release immediately from illness."

Plural of proper names.

Rem. Proper names occasionally are employed in the plural number, when signifying one's family or descendants. Ragh. 1,9 रघूणामन्वयं वक्ष्ये (I will celebrate the family of Raghu). — Pâṇ 2,4, 62—70 gives a list of those, that admit of such a plural.

Plural of abstract nouns.

21. The **plural of abstract nouns** is employed in Sanskrit more largely than with us, at least sometimes in phrases, somewhat strange to our feeling. Kâmand. 1,62 जितेन्द्रियस्य नृपतेर्नीतिमार्गानुसारिणः। भवन्ति ज्वलिता लक्ष्म्यः कीर्तयश्च नभःस्पृशः »if a prince, who keeps his senses under control, follows the path of polity, his fortune (*fortunæ*) blazes upward, and his glory (*laudes*) reaches heaven," Çâk. VI शय्याप्रान्तविवर्तनैर्विगमयत्युन्निद्र एव क्षपाः »sleepless he passes his nights, tossing himself to and fro upon his couch," ibid. VII सन्ति पुनर्नामधेयसादृश्यानि, *nominum similitudines*. Of the kind are आपत्सु Mhbh. 1, 123, 77 »in times of distress," भयेषु (= भयकालेषु) R. 3, 4, 9 and the like.

Plural of a people's name.

Pân. 4, 2,81.

22. The plural of a people's name is commonly used to denote the region, where that people dwell. The country, inhabited by the nation called अङ्गाः is also named अङ्गाः; in the same way it is spoken of पञ्चालाः, मत्स्याः, कोसलाः, विदर्भाः etc, if the country of Pancâla, Matsya, Kosala, Vidarbha is meant. Compare Latin *Volsci*, *Parisii*, *Chatti*, Germ. *Polen*, *Hessen*, *Sachsen*, Engl. *Sweden* and sim.

Pluralis majestaticus.

23. The **pluralis majestaticus** is often used in addressing persons or speaking of them in a reverential manner. This applies to all words and epithets, such venerable men are designated with. Çâk. II the king asks the messenger किमम्बाभिः

प्रेषितः (are you sent by my revered mother?). R. 1, 68 king Janaka tells Daçaratha the great exploit done by his sublime son Râma सेयं मम सुता राजन्विश्वामित्रपुरस्कृतैः । यदृच्छयागतै राजन्निर्जिता तव पुत्रकैः (your illustrious child, my king, has won my daughter, as he was come here by chance, a companion of Viçvâmitra).

Rem. Note the much employed metaphor of speaking of »the feet of —" instead of the revered master himself. In that case the name or title is commonly compounded with °पादाः — note the *plural* — as Hitop. 96 एष दुष्टबको ऽस्मद्देशे चरन्नपि देवपादानधिक्षिपति »— insults Your Majesty."

24 Similarly it is a token of great respect, if one is addressed by the plural of the personal pronoun, यूयम् or भवन्तः instead of त्वम् or the polite भवान्. Daç. 69 a girl thus addresses a holy man भगवन्नस्या मे दोषमेषा वो दासी विज्ञापयति (Reverend, she, your servant, tells you of wrong done by me), Çâk. V the ascetic Ç.ngârava says to king Dushyanta श्रुतं भवद्भिः (Your Majesty has heard —), Panc. 71 [Damanaka to the lion] देव संजीवको युष्मत्पादानामुपरि द्रोहबुद्धिः [1]).

25. वयम् = अहम् or आवाम्. Pâṇ. 1, 2,59. The plural of the first person is allowed to be made use of, when meaning a singular or a dual. Here we have not a majestic plural, but almost the same liberty as in Latin, to use *nos* = *ego*. Thus वयम् may have the purport of अहम् and आवाम्, and कुर्मः may be = करोमि or कुर्वः. Instances are very common. Mudr. I Câṇakya thus addresses his pupil वत्स कार्याभियोग एवास्मानाकुलयति, Panc. 41 a monk asks for hospitality with these words भो भद्र वयं सूर्योढा अतिथयस्त्वान्तिकं प्राप्ताः । न कमप्यत्र ग्रामे जानीमः. [2]) Similarly Panc. 58 the

1) Pâṇini does not mention this idiom; did it not exist in his time? Patanjali also is silent about it, but the Kâçika-comm. contains the vârtt. (on P. 1, 2, 59) युष्मदि गुरावेकेषाम्.

2) The given instance does not agree with the statement of some grammarian quoted by Pat. I, 230 अपर आह । अस्मदः सविशेषणस्य प्रयोगो न. Pat. himself allows the plural of the first person even then, unless the proper name or the *yuvapratyaya* be added, thus अहं देवदत्तः, not वयं.

plural is used instead of the dual, किं कुर्मः सांप्रतम् (what shall we do now [you and I]?)

26. Dual. In all periods of the language the **dual** is the proper and sole number by which duality is to be expressed. Pâṇ 1, 4,21 sq.

If the voluminous mass of Sanskrit literature will once be thoroughly examined with respect to syntactic facts, it is not improbable there will be put forward sundry instances of duality expressed by the plural number. But the number of such exceptions cannot be but exceedingly small.[1]. For, though the vulgar dialects and the pali have lost the dual, polished Sanskrit always strictly observes its employment and does in no way offer that confusion of dual and plural, which is so obvious in Attic Greek and already in the dialect of Homer.

27. Sâmânâdhikaraṇya. II. — Concord in case, number, gender and person is in Sanskrit the same, as in all languages with inflections, that is to say, it does exist between all such words, as, while standing in the same sentence, are to point at the same thing. For this reason, the *predicate* does agree with its subject in case and person, the *attribute* with the noun, it qualifies, in case and — if possible — also in number and gender, and so on. It would be superfluous to exemplify this general rule,[2]) which, moreover, is common to all

1) I have noticed three instances, all of them in poetry, and partly fit methinks to be interpreted so as to confirm the general rule. Of them, one R. 2, 22, 23 ऋषयोऽपि भ्रश्यन्ते काममन्युभिः contains a plural, which may be accounted for as denoting either the various kinds of *studium* and *ira* (cp. Manu 7, 45—48) or as pointing at the diversity in time, space and persons of the manifold instances of holiness lost, so the comm. बहुवचनं व्यक्तिबहुत्वात्. — Kathâs. 107,51 श्वश्रूश्वशुराणाम् the majestic plural seems to have been employed. Strange is this passage: Mhbh. 1, 24, 6 चन्द्रादित्यैर्यदा राहुराख्यातो ह्यमृतं पिबन्, there being no room for the scholiast's interpretation आदित्यस्य मूर्तिबहुत्वेन चन्द्रादित्यैरिति बहुवचनम्.

2) Grammatical concord bears with vernacular grammarians the well-

languages It will suffice to notice some more or less remarkable features:

1) Pronouns follow the general rules of agreement. Thus it is Sanskrit to say **स प्रश्नः**, as it is Latin to say *haec est quaestio*, whereas Teutonic dialects always put the pronoun in the neuter sing. Dutch *dat is de vraag*, Germ. *das ist die Frage*. Panc. 63 मम प्राणयात्रेयम् (so is my livelihood), ibid. II, 201 असौ परमो हि मन्त्रः (that is the most important counsel), Câk. VII सिध्यन्ति कर्मसु महत्स्वपि यन्नियोज्याः संभावनागुणमवेहि तमीश्वराणाम् (if officers are successful in weighty affairs, impute it to the virtue of their masters, who honour them with the execution). — Yet there may occur instances, where it would be not possible to observe this rule [1].)

2) Occasionally the verb will agree with the noun-predicate when standing near, instead of agreeing with the subject. Panc. 263 सर्प आह । सांप्रतं त्वं मे मित्रं जातम् [not जातः], M. 9, 294 सप्त प्रकृतयो ह्येताः सप्ताङ्गं राज्यमुच्यते (these [foresaid] seven elements are named together the seven-membered kingdom), ibid. 2,81 महाव्याहृतयः .... त्रिपदा चैव सावित्री विज्ञेयं ब्रह्मणो मुखम् (— and the three-membered *sâvitrî* should be considered as the mouth of *brahma*).

---

chosen name of *sâmânâdhikaranya*, that is »the relation existing between *samânâdhikaranâs* or words, whose substrate (अधिकरण) is the same (समान)".

1) See for inst. Ch. Up. 6, 16, 2 एतदात्म्यमिदं सर्वं तत्सत्यं स आत्मा तत्त्वमसि श्वेतकेतो. Here स आत्मा is rendered by Prof. Max Müller »it is the Self," in a note he subjoins: »The change of gender in *sa* for *tad* is idiomatic. One could not say in Sanskrit *tad âtmâ* it is the Self, but *sa âtmâ*." (Pref. to the Sacr. Books of the East, I, p. XXXVI). Nevertheless, in the words immediately following तत्त्वमसि, that very idiom seems to be neglected, for the neuter तत् is the predicate of the masc. त्वम्. Here the neuter has been preferred, because of *tad* and *tvam* there is not affirmed a full identity, as it is done with respect to *sa* and *âtmâ*, but it is only said, *tvam* is a phenomenal manifestation of *tad*: »*tad* (sc. âtmà) is also in you."

3) Sometimes, in cases of discordance between the grammatical and the real gender or number of a noun, its predicate or attribute will agree with the latter (**constructio ad synesin**) R. 2, 52, 42 त्वां चिन्तयन्तः — निराहाराः कृताः प्रजाः (thinking of thee — the subjects do not take food); here to प्रजाः, though grammatically a fem., is added a participle in the mascul. Note in the example quoted the distance by which the attribute is separated from the noun, it qualifies.

28. If the same predicate belongs to more subjects or the same attribute refers to more nouns at the same time, the idiom of Sanskrit is almost like that of other languages.

Either the common predicate (attribute) agrees with but one and must be supplied mentally with the others, as Prabodh. III आवासो लयनं मनोहरम् cp. the schol. p. 57 ed. Calc. द्वयमपि मनोहरम्; Daç. 135 कान्तिमती राज्यमिदं मम च जीवितमद्यप्रभृति त्वदधीनम् (Kântimatî and this kingdom and my own life are at your mercy from this moment). — This practically has the same effect as applying the Rem. on b.) of the other alternative, recorded on page 20.

or it has a grammatical expression adequate to its character of being common to more substantives at the same time. In that case:

a.) the **number** required is of course the **dual** when relating to two individuals, otherwise the **plural.** रामो लक्ष्मणश्च महावीरौ; — रामः सीता च लक्ष्मणश्च वन उषिताः. Cp. the Rem. on b.).

b.) as to the **gender** there must be distinguished between persons and things. When relating to persons of the same sex, the common predicate or attribute is of the same gender: पिता भ्राता च द्वावपि । माता स्वसा च द्वे अपि. When applying to persons of different sex, it is always put in the masculine: पिता माता च द्वावपि. But when belonging to inanimate things or things and persons mixed, it is neuter. Kâm. 1, 54 मृगया ऽक्षास्तथा पानं गर्हितानि महीभुजाम्; M. 4, 39 मृदङ्गं दैवतं विप्रं घृतं मधु चतुष्पथम्। प्रदक्षिणानि कुर्वीत.

Rem. If neuter words are mixed with words of other gender, it is allowed to put their common predicate or attribute in the neuter of the *singular*. Mrcch. V पक्षविकलश्च पक्षी शुष्कश्च तरुः सरश्च जलहीनं। सर्पश्चोद्धृतदंष्ट्रस्तुल्यं लोके दरिद्रश्च (the bird, whose wings are clipped, the leafless tree, the desiccated pool, the toothless snake are equal in the eyes of men, so the moneyless man).

Pâṇ 1, 2, 69.

c.) as to the **person**. In the case of difference, the first person outweighs the second and third, and the second precedes the third (see Pat. I, p. 352, cp. 240, n° 26, Kât. 3, 1, 4). Patanjali gives these examples त्वं च देवदत्तश्च पचथः। अहं च देवदत्तश्च पचावः। त्वं चाहं च पचावः

29. The type *Tiberius et Gaius Gracchi*, *linguae Latina et Graeca* is also Sanskrit. Ch. Up. 5, 3, 2 पथोर्देवयानस्य पितृयाणस्य च.

30. Occasionally words connected by »with" are construed as if they were copulated by »and." R. 2, 34, 20 तं परिष्वज्य बाहुभ्यां तावुभौ रामलक्ष्मणौ। पर्यङ्के सीतया सार्धं रुदन्तः समवेशयन्. Here the *plural* रुदन्तः समवेशयन् proves that सीतया सार्धम् has the same effect on the construction as सीता च.

PREDICATE AND ATTRIBUTE.

31. The distinction between **predicate** and **attribute** [1]) is chiefly a logical one. Formally both follow the same rules of syntax, and it is but by the context, partly also by the place it occupies in the sentence,

1) The term »attribute" in this book is virtually the same as the term *viçeshaṇa* of Hindu grammarians. It includes therefore the so called »apposition," for I found no reason why I should retain the needless distinction, which is often made between attribute and apposition.

we can learn how to understand a given samânâdhikaraṇa, whether वृद्धः पिता = „the old father" or = „the father is old," etc

As to their meaning, then, we may distinguish five classes, I the simple *attribute*, वृद्धः पिता = „the old father," II the so-called *predicative-attribute*, as पिता वृद्धः (= वृद्धः सन्) „the father, *when* old," III the *noun-predicate of the sentence*, as वृद्धः पिता = „the father *is* old," IV the *noun*, *wanted* by the verb for making up together the predicate of the sentence, as पिता वृद्धः संपद्यते (the father *grows old*), पितरं वृद्धं मन्यसे (you think the father old), V such a noun, as though formally agreeing with the subiect or some other substantive, really serves to qualify the verb, as Daç. 141 मयासि जातमात्रः पापया परित्यक्तः, see above, page 11 Rem

Of them the formal agreement of class I and II is fully made clear in **27**. As to class III see **5**.

om-
ting
ttri-
ute.

32. IV. — The **noun wanted for completing the predicate** is used in many idioms, the most important of which are:

) a
mi-
tive.

a.) it is a nominative, when accompanying verbs of *being*, *seeming*, *becoming*, *growing*, *remaining*, such passives as *to be called*, *held for*, *considered*, *appointed*, *made*, sim. Çâk. I मृग एष विप्रकृष्टः संपन्नः (this deer has become distant), Hitop. 92 पक्षिणः सकोपा बभूवुः (the birds grew angry), Panc. 51 किमेवं त्वमकस्माद्विचेतनः संजातः (why you have swooned so at a sudden?); Priy. p. 14 कस्मात्प्रहृष्ट इव लक्ष्यसे (why do you look so glad?) Panc. 56 स राजा प्राकारशेषः कृतः (the king was reduced to the possession of nothing but his fortress), Panc. III, 152 गृहिणी गृहमुच्यते (it is the wife that is called one's »home").

b.). an instrumental.

b) it is an instrumental, if wanted by a verb of *being*, *becoming*, *seeming* etc. when impersonal passive In this case both subject and noun-predicate are put in the instrumental. Mudr. I मया न शयानेन स्थीयते = अहं न शयानस्तिष्ठामि; Daçak. 18 बालकेन सकलक्लेशसहेनाभावि (the baby was strong enough to endure all this toil).

This idiom is, of course, obligatory with the kṛtya's of भू. Daçak. 164 त्वदनुजीविना राजपुत्रेण भवितव्यम् (the prince deserves to be your attendant), Panc. 21 तस्य च शब्दानुरूपेण पराक्रमेण भाव्यम् (and his strength may be adequate to his voice).

c.) an accusative.

c.) an accusative, when qualifying the object of the verbs of *calling* and *naming*, of *esteeming*, *holding for*, *considering*, *knowing as*, of *making*, *appointing*, *electing* and the like. M. 2, 140 तमाचार्यं प्रचक्षते (him they call a teacher), Nala 3, 22 नलं मां विद्धि (know me being Nala), Mudr. III कौटिल्यो नृपतिमकरोन्मौर्यवृषलम् (Cânakya has made king a çûdra, the son of Murâ), Pat. I, p. 332 तण्डुलानोदनं पचति (he boils rice to a jelly), Panc. 3 एतानर्थशास्त्रं प्रति द्रागयथानन्यसदृशान्विदधासि तथा कुरु.

Concurrent idiom

NB. It is superfluous to give some more instances of that well-known type, but it must be observed, that Sanskrit has also other concurrent idioms, it often prefers. Note in the first place, the nominative with इति, 2ly the instrumental of abstract nouns. Both are equivalent to the nomin. or accus. of the completing predicate. Instead of ब्राह्मणं भवन्तं संभावयामि (I hold you for a brahman), it is also said ब्राह्मण इति भव° or ब्राह्मणत्वेन भव°; the same of course applies to the passive construction. R. 3, 9, 11 वनं दण्डका इति विश्रुतं प्रस्थितस्त्वम् (you have set out for the forest, called Daṇḍaka), Kâç. on P. 1, 1, 1 वृद्धिशब्दः संज्ञात्वेन विधीयते (*vrddhi* is established [here] a grammatical term). A more detailed account of those idioms will be given in the course of this book.

33. In the archaic dialect we frequently meet with *two nominatives* construed with some verbs in the middle voice, viz. such as signify *to call one's self, to consider one's self.* [1]) Rgv. 10, 85, 3 सोमं मन्यते पपिवान् (he thinks himself having drunk *soma*), Ch. Up. 5, 3, 4 किमनुशिष्टो ऽवोचथा यो हीमानि न विद्यात्कथं सो ऽनुशिष्टो ब्रुवीत (why did you say you had been instructed? how could anybody, who did not know these things, claim himself instructed?), Tbr. 2, 3, 8, 2 सो ऽसुरान्सृष्ट्वा पितेवामन्यत (he, after having created the asuras considered himself as if he were a father). [2]) — Similarly it is said in liturgical style रूपं कृ with nom. »to assume the shape of —", Ait. Br. 6, 35, 4 अश्वः श्वेतो रूपं कृत्वा (having assumed a white horse's shape), Tbr. 1, 1, 3, 3 आखू रूपं कृत्वा. [3])

Middle voice attended by two nominatives.

Rem. In classic Sanskrit this idiom seems to have antiquated. »To call —, to consider one's self" is expressed by means of the reflexive pronoun, as आत्मानं मन्ये । आत्मानं ब्रवीमि. Instead of the old type अश्वो रूपं कृत्वा we meet with such compounds as Panc. 326 अश्वरूपं कृत्वा.

34. In the case of a substantive being the attribute or predicate of an other substantive, disagreement of gender or number or of both is possible. R. 2, 115, 15 भरतः शिरसा कृत्वा संन्यासं पादुके (Bh. put on his head *the pledge*, [namely] *the slippers*).

---

1) This nominative has its counterpart in Greek and in modern languages. So says an illustrious German poet (Felix Dahn, *Skaldenkunst* p. 79) »weise wähnt' ich mich, und ach! ein Thor, ein pflichtvergessner Knabe erwies ich mich."

2) In a few passages of the upanishads and epic poetry we meet with such expressions a पण्डितं मन्यमानः »holding one's self a learned man," for ex. Mhbh. 13, 22, 13. They are hardly to be accepted as compounds, like पण्डितंमन्य, सुभगंमन्य and the like (P. 3, 2, 83).

3) See the amount of examples in Weber, Ind. Stud. XIII, 111. — Ait. Br. 5, 7, 2 we have a confusion of the two constructions, the acc. of the pronoun आत्मानम् being used together with the nom. of the noun इन्द्रो वा एताभिर्महानात्मानं निरमिमीत.

Chapter II. **How to denote case-relations.**

35 The manifold relations between nouns and verbs or nouns and nouns are signified by cases, by the periphrase of cases, by compounding. As to the proportional frequency of the said modes of expression, *nude cases* are more freely employed in poetry than in prose, oftener in the earlier periods of Sanskrit than in the latter; whereas *periphrastic expression* strives at extending by the time, the implements of circumlocution increasing in number and variety, the nearer we approach to our own times. But the faculty of signifying case-relations by confining the correlating nouns into the somewhat rudimentary shape of *compounds* has not been overturned nor diminished by time. On the contrary, whether we look at their frequency or at their manifoldness or at their expansibility, the old dialect is by far surpassed by the alexandrinian period of Sanskrit literature.

36. The same *richness* and *abundance* is generally displayed in the several constructions, taken separately. Two or more conceptions of the same case-relation being equally possible in thought, they mostly are also available in speech; there is perhaps no language, where one may be less limited in this respect. Thus we meet side by side with a partitive genitive, a partitive ablative, a partitive locative. Causality may be denoted by means of the instrumental as well as by the ablative or by various periphrase, as हेतोः, कारणेन, कारणात् etc. The person spoken to may be put in the accusative or dative or expressed by means of प्रति, पुरः, अग्रे. The verbs of giving are not only construed with the dative of the person bestowed upon, but also with genitive or locative. The dative of the purpose is interchangeable with many a periphrase (अर्थम्, निमित्तम् etc.) and with infinitives. And so on. — Add to this the many implements for periphrase, *either* prepositions, partly ancient and common to the Indo-european mother-tongue, partly new-formed in Sanskrit, *or* nouncases and verbal forms that have almost the force of prepositions, as सकाशम् समीपम् etc. when = „to," कृते „on account of," वर्जयित्वा or मुक्त्वा = „without," मार्गेण = „by means of", sim. Moreover, in most cases one is free to compound the substantive with those words, for ex. to say जीवितहेतोः instead of जीवितस्य हेतोः (for the sake of life), पाषाणोपरि = पाषाणस्योपरि (over a stone), etc. — Finally it must be kept in mind that in a large amount of cases one has even the *choice* of either expressing the case-relation, or letting it be implied by a compound, made up of the two correlating substantives पुरुषसिंहः = पुरुषेषु सिंहः (a lion *among* men), राजपुरुषः = राज्ञः पुरुषः (the king's attendant), अहिहतः = अहिना हतः (slain *by* a serpent), sim.

37. In consequence, the three general classes, we have set up, — cases, periphrase, compounds — do but represent one and the same logical category and are in practice coordinate. For clearness' sake however, as they cannot be dealt with promiscuously, they require to be treated successively. Accordingly chaptt.

III—VII will contain the syntax of the cases, chapt. VIII the periphrastic expression of case-relations; in chapt. IX the different kinds of compounds — including also dvandva and karmadhâraya, though logically belonging to other categories — will be gone through.

General scheme of the cases.

38. *Scheme of the cases.* The nominative or first case (प्रथमा sc. विभक्तिः) is expressive of the sentence's subject and predicate, see **1** and **5.** Moreover the nominative is employed to denote the noun taken by itself, apart from the sentence, as will be shown hereafter.

The person addressed is put in the vocative.[1]).

1) Though the vernacular grammarians have a proper term for the vocative — *âmantrita* P. 2, 3, 48 — and even two for the vocative of the sing. (the voc. sing. especially is named *sambuddhi*, ibid. 49) it is however not considered a distinct eighth case, but an appendix to the nominative. Pâṇini, after having stated (2, 3, 46) प्रातिपदिकार्थलिङ्गपरिमाणवचनमात्रे प्रथमा »the first case serves only to signify the gender and number of the thing designated by the word's rude form or *prâtipadika*", thus proceeds: संबोधने च (47) साऽऽमन्त्रितम् (48), that is »it serves also to address, then it bears the name of *âmantrita*." — By the way I remark, that in translating P.'s rule on the proper sphere of the first case, I have dissented from the traditional interpretation. According to the commentaries परिमाण means »size" or »measure" — such words as द्रोण, खारी; आढक are given for examples — and वचन is »the grammatical number" so as to make the whole signify: »the first case denotes the mere meaning of the *prâtipadika*, the mere gender, the mere size (or weight), the mere number." See f. ex. the Kâçika on our sûtra. That interpretation cannot be right. In the first place, in the Pâṇinean terminology, it must be observed, *prathamâ* does not mean the word put in the nominative case, but only the suffix of that case, just as *dvitîyâ* names the suffix of the accus., *tṛtîyâ* that of the instrumental and so on. Now, to say in earnest, the prathamâ has the duty of denoting *three* things apart from the purport of the prâtipadika, viz. linga or gender, parimâṇa or measure and vacana or number is unacceptable and almost ridiculous, for the suffix of the nominative cannot give us certain knowledge but as to two of

Of the six others the general purport [1]) may be sketched thus:

1. The accusative or second case (द्वितीया) denotes a.) the *whither*, b.) the object of transitives, c.) an extension in time or space, d.) it is used adverbially.

2. The instrumental or third case (तृतीया

---

them, nl. gender and number; the size or measure of the thing denoted by the prâtipadika is made as little known by declension, as its color or its age. Moreover gender and number are grammatical conceptions, measure, size, weight geometrical ones. It is time to discharge Pâṇini of the absurdity imputed to him by his interpreters, and to show he is here as plain and judicious as that great grammarian is wont to be. The commentators were misled by वचन, which they did accept as expressing »the grammatical number", as, indeed, it very often does. Yet here it must be the *bhâva* of वच् in its original meaning *the naming* or *the being named*, cp. P. 1, 4, 89 आङ्मर्यादावचने (= *âṅ*, when *naming* a boundary), 2, 1, 33 कृत्यैरधिकार्थवचने (= with kṛtyâs, when *denoting* exaggeration), 5, 3, 23 प्रकारवचने थाल्, etc. Therefore it is not वचन, which here is carrying the meaning of *grammatical number*, but परिमाण; for this word may as well be employed in the narrower sense of »size; periphery," as in the larger of »any measure whatever," and accordingly it is also occasionally a synonym of संख्या, (cp. P. 5, 2, 41 and the passages adduced in the Petrop. Dict. IV, p. 540). For these reasons the sûtra, which occupies us, is to be analysed in this way प्रातिपदिकार्थस्य ये लिङ्गपरिमाणे (= ये लिङ्गसंख्ये or ये लिङ्गवचने, for संख्या and वचन are both expressive of the grammatical number) तयोर्वचनमात्रे प्रथमा.

1) Pâṇini has short and well-chosen terms to point out their different provinces. The category of the accusative he names *karma*, that of the instrumental *kartṛ* »agent" and *karaṇa* »instrument," that of the dative *sampradâna*, that of the ablative *apâdâna*, that of the locative *adhikaraṇa*. The duties of the genitive have not found an adequate expression.

With respect to the nominative it must be observed, that Pâṇini's definition (see the preceding note) does ascribe a larger sphere of employment to that case than we do in styling it the case of »the subject and predicate." In this the Indian grammarian is right. Nouns quoted or proffered outside the context of sentences are always put in the *nominative*.

may be called the *with*-case, for it signifies *with what*, *by what*, *how*. According to the various applications of this fundamental notion, there may be set up divers kinds of instrumental. So we have an instrumental of accompaniment — the so-called *sociative* — one of the instrument, one of the agent, of the way, the means, the manner, the quality, of time, of value, and so on.

3. The dative or fourth (चतुर्थी) points out the *direction* of a movement. Mostly it is employed in a metaphorical sense. For the rest, its employment admits of a division into two kinds: a.) the so-called *dative of interest*, b.) the *dative of the purpose*.

4. The ablative or fifth (पञ्चमी) denotes *whence* there is a starting, withdrawal, separation, distance, consequence and the like, it being applied to various categories of thought.

5. The genitive or sixth (षष्ठी) upon the whole may be described as the case, which signifies *cohesion*. It chiefly serves to express relations existing between substantives [1]) and according to the logical varieties of these relations we may distinguish between the *possessive genitive*, the *partitive*, the *subjective*, the *objective* etc. Besides, the sixth case is wanted with some adjectives (as those of likeness, knowing and the contrary) and some verbs (as those of remembering). Sanskrit also has three more kinds of genitive, each of them displaying a particular character, nl. 1. the *genitive of*

---

1) In this book the term *substantive* has not the limited acceptation it has with the etymologist and the lexicographer, but includes any noun that syntactically has the worth of a substantive, as सत्य, when = »truth."

the time, *after which*, 2 the *absolute genitive*, 3. the *genitive*, *which is concurrent with the dative of interest.*

6. The locative or seventh (सप्तमी) signifies the *where* and therefore it generally is to be rendered by such prepositions as in, at, to, on. As its employment is not restricted to real space, but of course also extends to other spheres of thought, there are various classes of locatives, for ex. those of *time*, of *circumstance*, of *motive* (the so-called निमित्तसप्तमी), the *absolute locative.* On the other hand the locative is not limited to the spot, where something is or happens, but it also signifies the *aim reached.*

Rem. 1. All nouns are declinable and put in the said cases, if wanted. This applies also to such conventional terms and signs, as the grammatical roots, affixes, anubandhâs, prâtipadikâs, etc

Rem. 2. Indeclinable are 1ly the adverbs, 2ly some nominal derivations of the verb, namely the gerunds and the infinitives Why they are devoid of declension is quite plain; for they do duty of noun-cases and generally their etymology does agree with their employment.

Chapt. III. **Accusative.**

Acc. denoting the whither.

39. I. The accusative expresses whither something is moving. Panc. स्वगृहं प्रस्थितः (he set out for his home), Nala 1, 22 विदर्भानगमंस्तदा (then they went to the country of Vidarbha), M. 2, 114 विद्या ब्राह्मणमेत्याह (Knowledge came to the Brahman and said —). In the instances adduced the movement is real. But in a metaphorical sense the accusative is likewise available. R. 2, 82, 9 जगाम मनसा रामम्, Daç. 40 तच्चिन्तया दैन्यमगच्छम् (by this solicitude I grew sad).

This obvious construction is not the only one.

The *aim striven at* may also be put in the dative (**79**), the *aim reached* is mostly denoted by the locative (**134**). Moreover various periphrases by means of प्रति, अन्तिकम्, सकाशम्, समीपम्, उद्दिश्य etc are concurrent idioms, see chapt. VIII.

40. From this acc. of the aim the acc. of the object is not sharply to be severed. On the boundary are standing such turns as त्वां श्रयति (he bends to you, rests on you), विद्यां प्रपद्यते (he attains knowledge), ग्राममभिवर्तते (he moves towards the village).

Verbs of *bringing* and the like.

Rem. Verbs of *bringing*, *carrying*, *leading*, *conveying* may be construed with two accusatives, one of the aim and one of the object ग्राममजां नयति हरति कर्षति वहति वा (see Siddh. Kaum. on P. 1, 4, 51); — Daç. 83 त्वां नयेयं त्वत्प्रियतमम् (let me conduct you to your lover), Çâk. V शकुन्तलां पतिकुलं विसृज्य (having dismissed Çak. to the home of her husband).

41. When construed with a passive verb, the accus. of the aim sometimes remains accusative, as in Latin and Greek, sometimes it turns nominative. So it is good Sanskrit to say मया ग्रामो गम्यते, मया ग्रामो गन्तव्यः Kathâs. 25, 210 संप्रति गन्तव्या पुरी वाराणसी मया (now I want to go to the city of Benares), Pat. I, 464 गंस्यते सो ऽर्थः (the meaning will be understood), cp. ibid. 44 कथमनुच्यमानं गंस्यते, ibid. 102 ग्रामो भवता गन्तव्यः [1]).

Acc. of the aim with passive verbs.

---

1) Vernacular grammar makes no distinction at all between aim and object. Both kinds of accusative share the common appellation *karma*. Yet I greatly doubt, whether the acc. of the aim may turn nomin. when attending on the passive of *all* verbs of moving. I, for my part, am not aware of instances of any of them, but for गम्. The transitive compounds (**43**) of course are left aside, likewise such verbs, as the vaidik ईयते, when = »to be asked for —".

Rem. The acc. of the aim is not changed into the genitive, when attending a noun. It is said नेता ऽश्वस्य स्रुघ्नम् (the transporter of a horse to Srughna), with the acc. of the aim and the gen. of the object. Cp. Pat. I, p. 336.

42. Acc. of the object. II. The **acc. of the object.** — Upon the whole, the same category of verbs are transitive in Sanskrit as are elsewhere. Yet, some cases of discrepancy and some idiomatic turns proper to Sanskrit are to be noticed: 1. Verbs of speaking may admit of the accus. of the person addressed, cp. **46**; 2. Many a Sanskrit intransitive, whose English equivalent is likewise intr., may occasionally admit of an object put in the accus.; then the translation will generally differ. Of the kind are:

1. रोदिति	intr. to weep,	tr. to weep for;
2. हसति	» to laugh,	» to laugh at;
3. नन्दति	» to rejoice,	» to rejoice at;
4. शोचति	» to be sorry,	» to pity;
5. वर्षति	» to rain,	» to rain upon;
6. युध्यति	» to fight,	» to fight;
7. चिन्तयति	» to think,	» to think of; to reflcct;

8. Verbs of *rambling*, *erring*, like भ्रम्, अट् are trans. when = »to walk over, to go through", note also such turns as मृगयां धावति (he is a hunting), भैक्षं चरति (he lives by begging). — 9 नमस्करोति, नमति and its compounds, may be construed with the acc. of him to whom respect is shown. A complete list of such verbs is difficult to give. Most of them are to be known by the dictionary.

Rem. 1. As a rule, the said accusatives are not obligatory. So the verbs of *speaking* admit also of a dat. or locat. or प्रति; — नम् and प्रणम् are oftener construed with dat. or gen.; — it is said as well युध्यति शत्रुणा or शत्रुणा सह (समम् etc.) as युध्यति शत्रुम्, and so on.

Rem. 2. Note also the turn एतन्मां भवति (this falls to my share) and the trans. construction of पुष्यति or पुष्णाति शोभाम् (लक्ष्मीम् etc.), see f. inst. Kumâras. 1, 25; 3, 63; Ragh. 3, 22; 4, 11.

Rem. 3. दीव्यति (to play) with the acc. of the wager is an idiom of the brâhmaṇa. P 2, 3, 60.

43. Intr. versb, becoming transitive, when compounded.

Intransitive verbs may become transitive, when being compounded with some preposition[1]; गामनुगच्छति (he goes after the cow), pass. अनेन गौरनुगम्यते. This chiefly applies to verbs, compounded with अति अधि अनु उप प्रति, but also to others Examples: अतिक्रामति (to transgress); अधिशेते अध्यास्ते अधितिष्ठति, cp. P. 1, 4, 46; अनुकम्पते (to pity); अनुभवति (to partake of-, to enjoy); उपजीवति (to live by-), उपवसति (to dwell near-); प्रतिभाति (to appear to-); अवलम्बते and आलम्बते (to rest on, to grasp), आवसति (to inhabit), उत्क्रामति (to neglect), प्रत्युद्गच्छति (to go to meet) etc.

Rem. This influence of the preposition is even seen in the acc. attending on some compound adjectives, as अनुव्रत, उन्मुख (Nala 2, 27 दमयन्तीमनुव्रतः, R. 2, 50, 1 अयोध्यामुन्मुखः).

44. Cognate accusative.

Instances of the so-called etymological or cognate accusative are not wanting Daç. 133 वाष्पयं मधुवर्षमवर्षत्, R. 2, 54, 37 उषिताः स्मो ह वसतिम् (v. a. we have passed the night), ibid. 58, 21 यथान्यायं वृत्तिं वर्तस्व मातृषु (behave yourself properly with respect to your mothers), Mhbh 1, 102, 3 भीष्मः कन्याः शुश्राव वृणवानाः स्वयंवरम्. — An example of its passive construction is this: R. 2, 58, 20 कुमारे भरते वृत्तिर्वर्तितव्या च राजवत्.

Rem. 1. Some of these etymological accusatives touch upon the sphere of the adverb and the gerund in °अम्. Sometimes it is rather difficult in what category to class them. Of the kind are Ch. Up. 3, 15, 2 न पुत्ररोदं रोदिति, Mhbh. 1, 154, 30 पशुमारममारयत् (he killed [him] as one kills a beast), P. 3, 4, 43 पुरुषवाहं वहति, sim.

Rem. 2. The krts in °इञ् are only available when etymol. accus. The Kâçikâ gives these examples: Qu. कां कारिमकार्षीः Answ. सर्वां कारिमकार्षम्; so कां गणिमजीगणः etc. P. 3, 3, 110

45. Some verbs admit of a double construction, which

---

1) Pat. I, p. 107 अकर्मका अपि वै सोपसर्गाः सकर्मका भवन्ति.

Verbs with a double construction.

is the counterpart of the well-known Latin idiom *munus mihi donat* = *munere me donat*. Compare for inst.

विभज्. — Mhbh. (ed. Calc. 3, 17242) धर्मस्तु विभजत्यर्थमुभयोः पुण्यपापयोः (Dharma bestows riches on both good and wicked).

Yâjñ. 2, 114 [पिता] स्वेच्छया विभजेत्सुताञ्ज्येष्ठं वा श्रेष्ठभागेन (a father may either bequeath his sons as he likes best, or he should bestow the best lot upon the eldest).

क्षिप्. — R. (Gorr.) 5, 11, 11 धूर्तप्रलापान्क्षिपन्ति (they utter out beguiling talk).

M. 8, 270 एकजातिर्द्विजातींस्तु वाचा दारुणया क्षिपन् (a not-dvija, when hurting a dvija with harsh words).

लुप्. — लुम्पत्यर्थम् (he robs the money).

लुम्पति स्वामिनम् (he robs the owner).

Both constructions are used side by side in this mantra of Pâraskara (Gṛhy. 2, 2, 7) येनेन्द्राय बृहस्पतिर्वासः पर्यदधादमृतं तेन त्वा परिदधामि.

Rem. The verb यज् *seems* to offer some irregularity of construction, but in fact it is not this verb, which is dealt with in a strange way, but it is the common translation of it, which conceals its proper meaning. One is wont to translate it »to sacrifice," but its real purport must have been some of »worshipping, honouring, feeding" or the like. Accordingly the offering is put in the instrumental, the divinity fed or worshipped in the accusative. One needs must say हविर्भिर्देवान्यजामहे τοὺς θεοὺς ἁζόμεθα θύμασι. — The real equivalent of our »sacrificing" is हु = θύειν; here the divinity is a dative, and the object is *either* the fire or wheresoever the offering is poured into, *or* the offering itself; therefore देवेभ्य अग्निं जुहोमि or देवेभ्य अग्नौ हविर्जुहोमि. — Moreover the etymol. accus. is of course also available as well with यज् as with हु; it may be said यज्ञं यजामहे, अग्निहोत्रं जुहोमि. But the instrum. of the offering with हु is vaidik according to P. 2, 3, 3 (see Pat. on that sûtra, I, p. 444).

46. Now, some verbs have the faculty of admitting t w o o b j e c t s at the same time.

Double object.

It is said as well कथां वक्ति (he tells a story) as त्वां वक्ति (he speaks to you); as well शत्रुं जयति (he vanquishes the enemy) as राज्यं जयति (he conquers a kingdom); as well शिष्यमनुशास्ति (he teaches his pupil) as धर्ममनुशास्ति (he teaches the law). By combining both constructions we obtain 1. कथां वक्ति त्वाम्; 2. शत्रुं राज्यं जयति; 3. शिष्यं धर्ममनुशास्ति.

This double object may attend a.) verbs of *speaking*, as ब्रू, वच्, आचक्ष् etc., *asking*, as याच्, भिक्ष्, प्रार्थयति, पृच्छति and sim., *teaching*, especially अनुशास्ति and अध्यापयति, b.) some others, especially जयति (*to win*), दोग्धि (*to milk*), दण्डयति (*to punish*, *to fine*). See P. 1, 4, 51 with the commentaries.

Examples: *speaking:* Nala 1, 20 ततो ऽन्तरिक्षगो वाचं व्याजहार नलं तदा, R. 2, 52, 31 आरोग्यं ब्रूहि कौसल्याम्; — *asking*, *begging:* Ch. Up. 5, 3, 5 पञ्च मा राजबन्धुः प्रश्नानप्राक्षीत् (that fellow of a râjanya asked me five questions), M. 8, 87 साक्ष्यं पृच्छेदृतं द्विजान्, Kathâs. 1, 31 स वरं मामयाचत (he requested a boon of me), Mhbh. 1, 56, 24 सुवर्णं रजतं गाश्च न त्वां राजन्वृणोम्यहम् (I do not beg gold of you, my king, nor silver, nor cows); — *teaching* R. 2, 39, 27 करिष्ये सर्वमेवाहमार्या यदनुशास्ति माम् (I will do all that, which Mylady enjoins me to do); — जि: Mhbh. 3, 59, 5 निषधान्प्रतिपद्यस्व जित्वा राज्यं नलं नृपम्; — दुह्: Kumâr. 1, 2 भास्वन्ति रत्नानि महौषधीश्च — दुदुहुर्धरित्रीम् (they milked from the earth resplendent gems and herbs of great medicinal power); — दण्डय्: M. 9, 234 तान्सहस्रं दण्डयेत् (he should punish them with a fine of a thousand paṇa).

Rem. Indian grammar adds to them some others, instances of which construed with a double object are scarcely met with in literature, if at all. Of the kind are चि (to gather), रुध् (to check), मुष् (to rob), मथ् (to churn), thus exemplified: वृक्षमवचिनोति फलानि। गामवरुणद्धि व्रजम्। सुधां क्षीरनिधिं मथ्नाति etc. [1]).

47. Yet, with none of the said verbs the double accusative is of necessity. Other constructions are quite as usual, sometimes even preferable, especially in simple prose.

---

1) Here also vernacular grammarians put the two accus., depending on such verbs, as नी, वह्, see **40** R.

The verbs of *asking* are often construed with the *ablat.* or *genit.* of the person addressed. Those of *teaching* admit of acc. of the person + loc. of the thing taught (Priy. p. 11 गीतनृत्यवाद्यादिषु.... शिक्षयितव्या), आदिशति, संदिशति and other verbs of *enjoining* are construed with acc. of the enjoinment + dat. (or its substitutes) of the person. Those of *speaking* are often construed with the dative of the person addressed, or the genitive, or प्रति.

NB. Some verbs as कथयति (to tell), वेदयति (to make known), आदिशति (to enjoin) never comply with the double object.

48. In the passive construction the *person* asked, addressed, defeated etc. turns *nominative*, the *thing* asked for, spoken etc. remains *accusative*. Therefore, though it may be said separately उक्तोऽर्थः as well as उक्तस्त्वम्, पृष्टो वृत्तान्तः as well as पृष्टाः पुत्राः, when combined, we get the type एतमर्थमुक्तस्त्वम् । पृष्टाः पुत्रा वृत्तान्तम्. Examples: Panc. 29 प्रार्थितो मया भवदर्थे स्वाम्यभयप्रदानम् (v. a. I have asked my master to grant you his protection), Kathâs. 27, 142 बाणेन युद्धयोग्यमरिं हरो याचितः (Bâṇa has prayed Çiva for a foe, fit to fight with); — R. 2, 97, 15 न हि ते निष्ठुरं वाच्यो भरतो नाप्रियं वचः; — Daç. 80 मया जितश्चासौ षोडशसहस्राणि दीनाराणाम्; — M. 8, 36 अनृतं तु वदन्दण्ड्यः स्ववित्तस्यांशमष्टमम् (but when bearing false witness, he must be punished with a fine of one eighth of his goods).

This passive construction is often avoided [1]) by employing one of the concurrent idioms, taught in **47**. Therefore उक्तमिदं त्वां प्रति or तुभ्यम्, मयायमर्थस्त्वत्तः पृष्टः or त्वत्सकाशात्, etc.

49. **Accusative with causative verbs.** — If the primitive

---

1) With some verbs it is, if at all, but rarely met with. Upon the the whole, the construction with a double object appears to be the remnant of an old vegetation, which has almost passed away to be succeeded by new stalks and young stems. We may see the same process at work in Latin, Greek and the teutonic languages. In all of them the idiom of the double object loses territory time going.

Double object with causatives.

be an *intransitive* verb, its causative is construed with the accusative of its (the primitive's) subject. Prim. शेते देवदत्तः Caus. यज्ञदत्तो देवदत्तं शाययति. The same applies to verbs of *going*; then we will have occasionally two accusatives, one of the aim and the other, pointing out the primitive's subject. Prim. देवदत्तो पाटलिपुत्रं गच्छति Caus. राजा देवदत्तं पाटलिपुत्रं गमयति.

P. 1, 4, 52.

But if the primitive be a *transitive*, there is diversity of idiom. Often the primitive's subject is in the same manner put in the accusative, when construed with the causative, but often also in the instrumental. In the former case we have of course two accusatives, as Kathâs. 9, 10 मन्त्रपूतं चरुं राज्ञीं प्राशयन्मुनिसत्तमः (the best of ascetics made the queen eat a consecrated porridge), wherewith cp. this instance of the instrumental: Mhbh. 2, 1, 7 न शक्ष्यामि किञ्चित्कारयितुं त्वया (I shall not be able to get anything done by you). The difference of both constructions is determined by the diverse nature of the notions, carried by them. If one wants to say *he causes me to do something, it is by his impulse I act*, there is room for the type मां किञ्चित्कारयति, but if it be meant *he gets something done by me, I am only the agent or instrument through which he acts*, the instrumental is on its place किञ्चित्कारयति मया.

Examples: a.) of two accusatives; Mudr. I, p. 43 अपि कदाचिच्चन्द्रगुप्तदोषा अतिक्रान्तपार्थिवगुणानधुना स्मारयन्ति प्रकृतीः (do not the vices of Candrag. still remind the people of the former kings?), Daç. 144 पितरौ तस्या दारिकाया मां पाणिमग्राहयेताम् (my parents allowed me to wed that girl), Mhbh. 1, 75, 28 स ऋषीन्करमदापयत् (he made the holy men pay taxes), R. 2, 55, 17 रामस्तामध्यारोपयत्प्लवम् (he ordered her to embark), ibid. 2, 94, 2 अत्र दाशरथिश्चित्रं चित्रकूटमदर्शयत्। भार्याम्, Daç. 215

ज्ञापय मां स्ववार्त्ताम्. — So always अध्यापयति कंचित्किंचित्, for this verb at the same time formally is a causative and as to its meaning (*to teach*) it belongs to the category, mentioned in 46.

b.) of the instrumental of the primitive's subject: Daç. 170 सा तस्य साधोश्चित्रवधमज्ञेन राज्ञा समादेशयां चकार (she obtained an order of the king who was unaware [of what had happened before] to put to death this honest man); Mudr. I, p. 37 लेखं शकटदासेन लेखयित्वा (after having got written the letter by Çakatadâsa); Panc. 51 रथकार आप्तपुरुषैस्तं स्वगृहमानाययत् (the cartwright let him bring home by friends), Kumâras. 6, 52 स तैराक्रामयामास शुद्धान्तम् (he [Himavân] suffered his zenana to be entered by them, that is »he opened his zenana to them"), M. 8, 371 तां श्वभिः खादयेद्राजा (her the king should order to be devoured by dogs) [1]).

50. In the passive construction these two types are likewise possible: 1. *the primitive's subject turns nominative, the primitive's object remains accusative*, as Mudr. V, p. 172 परिधापिता वयमाभरणं कुमारेण, the active form of which would be कुमार अस्मानाभरणं परिधापितवान्, 2. *the primitive's subject is instrumental, but the primitive's object turns nominative*, as Mudr. I, p. 22

1) Pàṇini gives a different rule about the construction of the causatives. In his sûtra 1, 4, 52 he teaches that the primitive's subject is the karma of the causatives of a.) all intransitives, b.) the verbs of *going* (*moving*), c.) those of *perceiving* and *knowing* (बुद्धि), d.) those of *feeding*, e.) those of *uttering voice*, and the following rule declares »optionally also with कारयति and हारयति" [and their compounds, see Pat. I, p. 109, l. 10]. With the other causatives, therefore, the primitive's subject is not considered an object (karma), accordingly not put in the accus., but in the instrumental, according to P. 1, 4, 55 compared with 2, 3, 18. Now, to these rules of Pâṇini, which do not take account of the internal difference existing by necessity between the two conceptions, but simply set up some outer marks, I have substituted the description expounded in the context. Mr. Anandoram Borooah has preceded me in this way. Moreover I have tested Pâṇini's rule in numerous instances, but found it deficient now and then even when paying due respect to the modifications made in it by the different vârttikas on our sûtras (1, 4, 52 sq.), whereas the same enquiry confirmed the exactness of the rule as it has been laid down in the context.

विषकन्यया राक्षसेन घातितस्तपस्वी पर्वतेश्वरः active विषकन्यया राक्षसो घातितवान्तपस्विनं पर्वतेश्वरम् (R. has killed the unhappy Parv. by means of a *vishakanyâ*). The latter type appears to be rare [1]), the former is the general one and is applied even in such cases, as would not admit of two accusatives in the active form.

Examples of type 1. — Mudr. VII, p. 222 शकटदासस्तपस्वी तं कपटलेखं मयैव लेखितः, Kull. on M. 8, 287 यावान्व्ययो भवति तमसौ दापनीयः (he must be caused to pay as much as has been expended), Daç. 164 अहञ्च कोशदासेन स्नानभोजनादिकमनुभावितोऽस्मि (Koçadâsa made me enjoy a bath, food etc.), Hitop. 90 ततस्तेन [sc. शशेन] स यूथपतिः प्रणामं कारितः (then he [the hare] commanded the chief elephant to make his prostration), R. 2, 62, 1 राजा राममात्रा श्रावितः परुषं वाक्यम्.

Example of type 2. Mâlav. I, p. 15 अथावश्यमेव माधवसेनो मया पूज्येन मोचयितव्यः (v. a. His Majesty, indeed, has it in his own power to make me release Mâdhavasena).

51. When having got a more or less figurative sense, the causatives may change their construction. So with दर्शयति (to show) and श्रावयति (to tell) the person who is caused to see and to hear is sometimes put in the acc. as attending on a causative, but it is more common to use the gen. or dat., because they in fact range with the verbs of *showing* and *telling*. So वेदयति and its compounds are never construed with the acc. of the person to whom something is made known.

52. Accusative depending on nouns. The accusative of the object is not restricted to the finite verbs, but affects also some active verbal forms, which are grammatically classed among the nouns. In the first place all participles, gerunds and infinitives with active signification must have their object put in the accusa-

---

1) Apart from the two examples adduced in the context I do not remember having met with any. In both of them the object and the agent are persons.

tive. Hitherto there is no difference between the syntax of Sanskrit and of its sister-languages. But the accusative is also wanted with some classes of verbal nouns, commonly not reckoned among the participles etc., [1]) nl. *a.*) with those in उ, made of desiderative verbs; this class of adjectives has indeed almost the nature of participles, *b.*) with some in इष्णु of kindred signification, *c*) with those in अक, when having the worth of a partic. of the future, *d.*) with some kṛts in °इन् [2]), *e.*) with the kṛts in °तृ, when barytona.

P. 2, 3, 69 sq.

Examples: *a.*) M. 1, 8 सिसृक्षुर्विविधाः प्रजाः (wishing to create the manifold creatures), Mhbh. 1, 167, 48 सर्वयोषिद्वरा कृष्णा निनीषुः क्षत्रियान्क्षयम्; — *b.*) Daç. 25 तेषां भाषणपारुष्यमसहिष्णुरहम् (as I could not bear the harshness of their words); — *c.*) Kâç. on P. 2, 3, 70 कटं कारको व्रजति (he goes to make a mat) [3]); *e.*) see 53.

Rem. 1. Those in उक are also mentioned by Pâṇini as agreeing with acc., but this construction has antiquated. Instances of it are met with in the archaic dialect. Taitt. S. 6, 1, 6, 6 कामुका एनं स्त्रियो भवन्ति य एवं वेद, Ch. Up. 5, 2, 2 लम्भुको ह वासो भवति (surely, he obtains a dress).

Rem. 2. Note also the acc. with the adj. अर्ह (worth, deserving). As far as I know, this idiom is restricted to the epics. Mhbh. 1, 63, 4 इन्द्रत्वमर्हो राजायं तपसा (this king is by his penance worth of

---

1) See SIECKE, de genetivi in lingua sanscrita imprimis vedica usu, p. 17 sqq.

2) Especially, if a debt be the object, P 2, 3, 70. Kâç. शतं दायी.

3) Examples in literature are scarce. WHITNEY (Grammar § 271 *c.*) quotes Mhbh. 3,73,25 भवन्तमभिवादकः, but the example is doubtful, for the whole sentence runs thus: आगतो ऽस्मि भवन्तमभिवादकः, where it is also possible to accept the acc. as the aim of the verb आगतः. — R. 3, 10, 15 तदर्थमानान्रक्षाभिर्दण्डकारण्यवासिभिः। रक्षकस्त्वं would afford an instance of रक्षक, construed with the accusative, if it were not probably a bad reading; रक्षकस्त्वम् is to be changed in रक्ष नस्त्वम्.

Indra's rank), R. 1, 53, 12 न परित्यागमर्हेयं मत्सकाशात् (she is not worth being given up by me) [1]).

Rem. 3. In the ancient dialect of the vaidik mantras many more kinds of verbal nouns may agree with acc. So for inst. Rgv. 6, 23, 4 बभ्रिर्वज्रं पपिः सोमं ददिर्गाः. Mhbh. 1, 113, 21 we have even an acc. depending on a nomen actionis जिगीषया महीं (by his desire to conquer the earth) पाण्डुर्निरक्रामत्पुरात्; likewise ibid. 1, 167, 3 द्रोणं प्रतिचिकीर्षया (by his wish to retaliate Droṇa).

53. The acc. with the barytona in °तृ though not rare in the earlier period, seems to protract but an artificial life in classic Sanskrit, as it is met with only in refined style and even there side by side with the genitive [2]). Daç. 199 it is said of a good king, that he was संभावयिता बुधान्प्रभावयिता सेवकानुद्भावयिता बन्धून्न्यग्भावयिता शत्रून् (honouring the wise, making his attendants mighty, raising his kinsmen, lowering his foes); comp. Panc. III, 71 नरपतिर्नेता प्रजाः (a king, who rules his subjects). -- On the other hand, the examples given by Kâç. on P. 3, 2, 135 prove that at the time, they were applied at first, the construction with the acc. was obvious and natural. So मुण्डयितारः श्राविष्ठायना भवन्ति वधूमूढाम् (the Çrâvishṭhâyanâs have the custom to shave the hair of the young-married woman.) Cp. Âpast. 1, 3, 15.

54. *Acc. of space and time.* III. The **accusative of space or time** serves to denote a continuity of either; it expresses therefore *what space is occupied* or *during what time* the action is *P. 2, 3, 5.*

---

1) In the classical language अर्ह् complies with genitive. So Priyad. 39 उपविशत्वर्हेयमर्धासनस्य (let her sit down, she is worth half of my seat). Likewise अनर्ह.

2) Pâṇini explicitly states (P. 3, 2, 134 sq.), that the barytona in °तृ are restricted to the denoting of lasting and inherent qualities. But he nowhere affirms that the oxytona are not to be employed in that sense. Indeed, a genitive with nouns in °तृ, even when expressing lasting qualities, is very common in classic Sanskrit. In the same passage Daç. 199, the example in the context has been borrowed from, we read परोक्षिता सर्वाध्यक्षाणाम् and सद्यः प्रतिकर्ता दैवमानुषीणामापदाम्.... मनुमार्गेण प्रणेता चातुर्वर्ण्यस्य. Comp. the list of epithets in Kâd. I, p. 2 कर्ता महाश्चर्याणाम् etc.

going on. Compare the *acc. spatii* and *temporis* in Latin, Greek, German etc.

Examples: *a.*) space R. 2, 91, 29 बभूव हि समा भूमिः समन्तात्पञ्चयोजनम् (for the soil became flat over an extent of five yojana's in every direction), Mhbh. 1, 153, 40 निगृह्य तं... चकर्ष ह तस्माद्देशाद्धनूंष्यष्टौ (he seized him and dragged him along over a space of eight bow-lengths).

Rem. When naming the dimensions of a thing, one does not use this accus., but avails one's self of bahuvrîhi-compounds.

b.) time Panc. 165 एतावन्ति दिनानि त्वदीयमासीत् (for so many days it was yours), Daç. 96 भद्रकाः प्रतीक्ष्यतां कञ्चित्कालम् (gentle sirs, please, wait a moment).

Rem. 1. Now and then the acc. of time denotes the time *at which*. R. 2, 69, 1 यामेव रात्रिं ते दूताः प्रविशन्ति स्म तां पुरीम्। भरतेनापि तां रात्रिं स्वप्नो दृष्टो ऽयमप्रियः, Daç. 153 सो ऽपि विटः...... तदहरेव स्वगृहे स्नानभोजनादि कारयित्वोत्तरेद्युः...... मामनुगम्य...... विसृज्य प्रत्ययासीत्. Cp. Ait. Br. 1, 22, 12; Mhbh. 1, 63, 40; ibid. 1, 121, 34; Âpast. 1, 5, 12.

Rem. 2. Sometimes यावत् is put behind the acc., when denoting the time, *during which*. Hitop. p. 51 मया माससेकं यावद्गौरीव्रतं कर्तव्यम् (I am bound to perform during a month a vow for Durgâ).

Rem. 3. The acc. of time remains unchanged in the passive; see Daç. 96 quoted above. But occasionally it is dealt with, as if it were the object. R. 2, 88, 2 इह तस्य महात्मनः शर्वरी शयिता भूमौ (= here the noble hero has passed the night on the naked earth) instead of शर्वरीं शयितम्[1]).

55. Adverbial accusative. IV. As a rule, the accusative neuter of any adjective noun may do duty for an adverb, शीघ्रं गच्छति (he goes swiftly), मृदु भाषते (he speaks gently),

1) Comp. such Latin expressions, as Caes. B. G. 5, 39, 4 *aegre is dies sustentatur*, and the interesting discussion on the matter Pat. I, p. 445 sq. From Patanjali's words it is sufficiently plain, that to say आस्यते मासः। शय्यते क्रोशः is as good as आस्यते मासम्। शय्यते क्रोशम्. From another passage of the same book (I, p. 338, vârtt. 9) it results, that some made the kâlakarma-verbs range with the *akarmaka* or intransitives.

छन्नं विहरति (he amuses himself secretly), सबहुमानं सत्करोति (he entertains respectfully).

The acc. of the subst. नाम (name) is used as a particle = »namely," sometimes also it answers to Greek ὄνομα »of name." Nala 1, 1 आसीद्राजा नलो नाम.

56. A great number of prepositions and the like agree also with the accusative, see chapter IX. Of the interjections, धिक् is often attended by accusative.

CHAPTER IV. Instrumental.

57. The third case has been styled **instrumental** after its most usual employment of expressing the instrument or means or agent [P. 2, 3, 18 cp. 1, 4, 42]. Yet its starting-point is rather the conception of *accompaniment*, and it is for this reason some claim for it the name of sociative.[1]) Nor can there be any doubt, the suffixes, by which the third case is made, viz. *bhi* and *á*, convey the meaning of accompaniment, simultaneousness and nearness

58. I. **Sociative.** — The instrumental is the equivalent of our *with = together with*, *accompanied by*. In this manner the third case is used f. i. Panc. I, 305 मृगा मृगैः सङ्गमनुव्रजन्ति गावश्च गोभिस्तुरगास्तुरङ्गैः। मूर्खाश्च मूर्खैः सुधियः सुधीभिः (deer seek after the comradeship with deer, so kine with kine and horse with horse, the fool with the fool and the wise with the wise).

Instrumental, when sociative.

a.) with prepositions.

Upon the whole however, the instrumental, when sociative, is accompanied by some word expressive of

1) This tenet has been laid down by B. DELBRÜCK in his pathmaking treatise *Ablativ*, *Localis*, *Instrumentalis*, 1867.

the notion of *being together* viz. 1° the adverbs सह, समम्, सार्धम्, साकम् which may then be considered prepositions, as रामः सीतया सह; 2° such participles as सहित, सङ्गत, युक्त, अन्वित and the like, as रामः सीतया सहितः or compounded सीतासहितः Or the notion of the sociative is expressed by a compound, the former part of which is स° (or सह°) as रामःससीतः. Occasionally the gerund आदाय (having taken) is also used in the meaning of *with*.

The prepositional adverbs सह etc. are likewise added to the instrumental for the sake of denoting relations between different parties as *to converse with*, *to meddle with*, *to fight with*, *to contend with*, sim.

Examples: *a.*) सह etc. expressive

1. of concomitancy. Mṛcch. X, p.372 अपि ध्रियते चारुदत्तः सह वसन्तसेनया (are Cârudatta and Vasantasenâ still alive?), Mhbh. 1, 113, 20 स ताभ्यां व्यचरत्सार्धं भार्याभ्यां राजसत्तमः । कुन्त्या माद्र्या च राजेन्द्रः, Panc. 127 तेन सममेव स्वदेशं प्रति प्रस्थिताः, Kathâs. 4, 136 अहं जनन्या गुरुभिश्च साकम्...... अवसम्;

2. of mutual relations. Panc. 78 तैः सहालापं न करोति; ibid. 257 कस्तेन सह तव स्नेहः (v. a. how are you his friend?), ibid. 281 मित्रेण सह चित्तविश्लेषः (disagreement with a friend), Kathâs. 47, 88 स तेन विदधे समं युद्धम् (he fought with him), Panc. V, 66 चारणैर्वन्दिभिर्नीचैर्नापितैर्बालकैरपि । न मन्त्रं मतिमान् कुर्यात्सार्धम्. Note the phrase तेन सह दर्शनम् (Panc. 137, 13; 178, 1) and the type, represented Panc. 43 तां स्थूणाया सह दृढबन्धनेन बद्ध्वा (after having *fastened* her *to* the pile with a strong fetter).

b.) सहित and the like: Kathâs. 13, 110 स्वगृहं भृत्यसहितः पलाय्यैव ततो ययौ (he fled from this spot to his home with his attendance), R. 2, 52, 91 Sîtâ prays पुनरेव महाबाहुर्मया भ्रात्रा च संगतः [that is: *with* his brother and me] अयोध्यां वनवासात्प्रविशतु.

Rem. An elegant paraphrase of the sociative is occasionally °द्वितीय used as the latter part of a bahuvrîhi. So in the verse quoted Pat. I, p. 426 असिद्वितीयोऽनुससार पाण्डवम् = »alone but for his good sword, he went after the Pâṇḍava," Daç. 159 एकान्ते भवानुत्कण्ठित इव परिवादिनीद्वितीयस्तिष्ठति (you stand aside as if longing for some you love, alone with your lute), Panc. 159 राजकन्या सखीद्वितीया.

59. *b*) without prepositions. Yet the sole instrumental will not rarely suffice. In the old vedic dialect, the brâhmaṇas included, it is very common, denoting as well concomitancy as mutuality of relations. But in classic Sanskrit it is restricted to the language of poetry and poetical prose and to some typical expressions.

Examples: *a.*) from the archaic dialect. Ṛgv. 1, 1, 5 देवो देवेभिरागमत् (may the god come with the gods), ibid. 8, 85, 7 मरुद्भिरिन्द्र सख्यं ते अस्तु; — Ait. Br. 1, 6, 3 अश्नुते प्रजया ऽन्नाद्यम् (he enjoys food with his family), Ch. Up. 5, 10, 9 आचरँस्तैः (conversing with them).

b.) from classic poetry, etc.: 1. concomitancy R. 2, 27, 15 साहं त्वया गमिष्यामि वनम् (I shall go to the forest with thee), ibid. 2, 68, 2 असौ मातुलकुले..... भरतो वसति भ्रात्रा शत्रुघ्नेन; — 2. mutuality of relations Daç. 175 तयापि नववध्वा द्वेषमल्पेतरं बबन्ध (he took a great aversion to his young wife), ibid. 91 तया बन्धक्या पणाबन्धमकरवम् (with this courtesan I made a bargain), R. 3, 18, 19 क्रूरैरनार्यैः सौमित्रे परिहासः कथञ्चन न कार्यः (Laxmaṇa, one should make no joke at all with cruel and vile people), Panc. V, 62 न ताभिर्मन्त्रयेत्सुधीः (a wise man does not keep counsel with women). It is often said विरुध्यते शत्रुणा without सह, etc.

Rem. 1. Note the turn, instances of which are afforded by Mudr. III, p. 116 मया स्वजीवनमात्रेणैव स्थापितौ (I have left them nothing but life) and Prabodh. V, p. 103 अचिरादसौ शरीरेणैव न भविष्यति (in short he will part with his body).

Rem. 2. Note कलह (quarrel) with the sole instrum. Panc. V, 74 मेषेण सूपकाराणां कलहः (the cooks' quarrel with the ram).

60. Compound nouns or verbs, whose former part is सं, स or सह, 2ly many words expressive of the notions of *uniting*, *combining*, *mingling* are often construed with the sole instrumental, even in prose. This construction is the regular one with युज् and its derivates.

Examples: *a.*) compounds, commencing by सं etc. Daç. 79 अक्षधूर्तैः समगंसि, Hitop. p. 16 यस्य मित्रेण संलापस्ततो नास्तीह पुण्यवान् (there is not in this world a man more happy, than he, who has a friend to converse with), Çâk. IV, vs. 12 चूतेन संश्रितवती नवमालिका (a jasmine, clinging to a mango-tree). Mrcch. I, p. 34 रत्नं रत्नेन संगच्छते.

b.) other verbs of uniting, mingling, combining. — M. 1, 26 द्वन्द्वैरयोजयच्चेमाः सुखदुःखादिभिः प्रजाः, Panc. 274 सोऽपि स्वजात्या मिलितः (mixed with his kinsmen), Çâk. I, vs. 30 वाचं न मिश्रयति मद्वचोभिः (she does not join her voice to mine).

Rem. 1. योजयति is often = Lat. *afficere alqum alqua re.* So Mhbh. I (Paushyap.) शिष्यान्क्लेशेन योजयितुं नेयेष (it was not his intention to harass his pupils), cp. R. 2, 75, 57. Many times it is = »to bestow something upon somebody", f.i. Panc. 3 अहं त्वां शासनशतेन योजयिष्यामि (I will bestow a hundred of grants upon you).

Rem. 2. P. 2, 3, 22 mentions the verb संज्ञा, complying with acc. or instrum., but instances of that idiom seem to be wanting in literature; Patanjali gives the example पितरं or पित्रा संजानीते, but it is not plain what is here the meaning of संज्ञा. — A similar instrum. depending on a compound verb, commencing by सं, is taught by Pâṇ. 1, 3, 55 and his commentators, see Pat. I, p. 284. According to them it is said दास्या संप्रयच्छते । वृषल्या संप्रयच्छते »he makes presents to a servant-maid, to a female of low-caste, etc." the instr. being used only in the case of illicit intercourse.

61. Instrum. or genitive with adjj. of *likeness*, *equality*, etc.

The instrumental attends on the adjectives of *equality*, *likeness*, *identity* and the like, as सम, समान, सदृश, तुल्य. Here however the genitive is a concurrent construction, just as in Latin. It is said promiscuously पितुः or पित्रा समः पुत्रः [P. 2, 3, 72.]

Examples: R. 2, 118, 35 शक्रेण समः (equal to Indra), Hit. I, 22 पशुभिः समानाः (like beasts), Hit. p. 118 अनेन सदृशो लोके न भूतो न भवि-

व्यति, Mâlav. I, p. 21 अयं न मे पादरजसापि तुल्यः (he is not even equal to the dust of my feet); Pat. I, p. 327 तैः साम्यं गतवान्भवति (he has become their equal). — If »to compare with" is to be expressed by some metaphor, the instrumental will often be of use, so for ex., when it is denoted by the image of putting on a balance, cp. Kumâras. 5, 34. — Compare also such expressions as Daç. 130 सोऽहमप्येभिरेव सुहृद्भिरेककर्मा (and I having the same business as these friends of mine here).

of a genitive: Mhbh. 1, 139, 16 अर्जुनस्य समो लोके नास्ति कश्चिद्धनुर्धरः; R. 2, 23, 5 बभौ क्रुद्धस्य सिंहस्य मुखस्य सदृशं मुखम् ([his] face shone like the face of an angry lion).

62. Instrumental with words of separation. As the instrumental is the exponent of the notion of *accompaniment* and *simultaneousness*, so it is also available with words expressive of the very contrary, namely *separation* and *disjunction*. In the same way as it is said त्वया सहितः, त्वया युक्तः „with you," one is allowed to say त्वया रहितः, त्वया वियुक्तः „without you." [1]) The proper case for expressing separation, the ablative is however also available. In some phrases the instrumental is more frequently employed, in other again the ablative. The instrum. prevails with वियुज् and most of the compounds, beginning with वि°, also with रहित and हीन, but the ablative with such as मुच्, भ्रंश्.

Examples: Panc. 84 प्राणैर्न वियुक्तः (he was not deprived of life),

1) Delbr. l. l. p. 71 »Der begriff *trennung* ist zwar logisch der gegensatz von zusammensein, liegt ihm aber desshalb psychologisch sehr nahe." Or, to speak more exactly, it is not the conception of separation, that is expressed or signified by the instrumental, but the notion of *mutuality* underlying both union and separation, finds in it its adequate expression. We have here therefore the same kind of instrum., which is spoken of in **59**, *b* 2. Accordingly words of separation may also be construed with सह etc. Panc. 57 ममानया सह वियोगो भविष्यति. Compare English *to part with*.

Daç. 172 तुषैरखण्डैस्तण्डुलान्पृथक्चकार (she peeled the grains of rice of their husks, so [cleverly] as to keep them entire), Kathâs. 15, 82 सीतादेव्या रामो विषेहे विरहव्यथाम् (R. forbore the grief caused by his separation from Sîtâ), R. 2, 96, 27 कलुषेण महता मेदिनी परिमुच्यतां (let the earth be freed from a great stain).[1]

Rem. The adjectives रहित, हीन, विहीन, वियुक्त sim. often are = »without."

63. Instrumental, the how-case. II. By extending the notions of concomitancy, accompaniment, simultaneousness from space and time to all sorts of logical categories, we may understand how large a sphere of employment the third case occupies in Sanskrit syntax. Generally spoken, it is always used, when it is wanted to express the circumstances, instruments, means, ways, properties accompanying the action and qualifying it. In other terms, the instrumental has the duty of telling the *how* of the action or state, expressed by the verb or verbal noun, it depends on.

For clearness' sake the most striking types of this instrumental will be severally enumerated: 1ly and 2ly it is expressive of the instrument (karaṇa) and the agent (kartṛ). These two kinds of instrumental are practically the most important, for they are the most wanted for. Examples of the former दात्रेण लुनाति (he cuts with a knife), पद्भ्यां गच्छति (he goes on foot); of the latter मया तत्कृतम् (it is done by me) (**57**).

---

1) M. 2, 79 affords an instance of instrum. and abl. depending on the same verb. The latter half-çloka runs thus महतोऽप्येनसो मासात्त्वचेवाहिर्विमुच्यते (after a month he is released even from a great sin likewise as a snake from its skin). Here the abl. एनसः and the instr. त्वचा are coordinate. Compare the like coincidence of *abl.* and *instr. causae.*

Thirdly, the instrum. denotes *accompanying circumstances* and *qualities*, like Latin abl. modi and qualitatis. M. 4, 3 अक्लेशेन शरीरस्य कुर्वीत धनसंचयम् (he must make money, but without giving toil to his body), Panc. 129 दमनकसाचिव्येन पिङ्गलको राज्यमकरोत् (Ping. exercised his royalty with Dam. as his minister).

Fourthly, it declares the test, to measure by; फलेनैतज्ज्ञास्यसि (you will know it by its fruit).

Fifthly, it expresses the price or value, something is rated at, bought, sold, hired for, the thing, some other is taken for in exchange, sim. Panc. 158 रूपकशतेन विक्रीयमाणः पुस्तकः (a book sold for a hundred rupees).

Sixthly, it denotes the way, by which one goes; Çâk. III अनया बालपादपवीथ्या सुतनुरचिरं गता (the tender girl has passed a little before along this row of young trees).

Seventhly, the instrumental denotes the *cause*, *motive* or *reason*, by which something is done or happens to be; धनेन कुशलः (prosperous by wealth), विद्यया यशः (fame by learning), मदाज्ञयागतोऽसौ (that person has arrived by my order), प्रीत्या दानम् (v. a. a present).

64. *Instrum. compared to English* with. It should be kept in mind, however, that these and similar distinctions are but made for argument's sake and do not answer to sharply separated real divisions. Properly speaking, there is but *one* instrumental in all of them, just as in English it is the same word *with*, which is used in phrases as distant from one another as *I go with you*, *I cut with a knife*, *he with his black hat*, *he is content with me*. For this reason on the one hand nothing impedes increasing the number of divisions and subdivisions according to the manifold logical variety of its employment, but on the other hand no system of division will exhaust it, and more than once we may be at a loss under which head to enregister a given instrumental.

Rem. The being implied of so various logical conceptions by an implement for expression as small, as a case-ending is, has by the time become inconvenient. Instead of the simple instrumental, therefore, a more explicit mode of expression, signifying more precisely which kind of logical relation is meant in every instance, is often made use of, namely the periphrase by such words as मार्गेण, द्वारेण, योगेन, मुखेन, कारणेन etc. Its relative frequency is one of the most striking features of modern, compared to ancient, Sanskrit.

65. Fuller account of them. Some fuller account on the different kinds of instrumental will be given now.

1. instrument or karaṇa. — Examples: Pat. I, p. 119 रज्ज्वायसा वा बद्धं काष्ठम् (a piece of wood, tied with a rope or with iron), Mṛcch. I (p. 54) अनेन प्रावारकेण छादयैनम् (cover him with this cloth), Panc. 148 एतेन वंशेन भिक्षापात्रं ताडयामि, Mhbh. 1, 144, 18 प्रायाद्रासभयुक्तेन स्यन्दनेन (he started on a chariot, drawn by asses), ibid. 1, 120, 19 यज्ञैस्तु देवान्प्रीणाति स्वाध्यायतपसा मुनीन् । पुत्रैः श्राद्धैः पितृंश्चापि आनृशंस्येन मानवान् (by sacrifices he propitiates the gods, by study and penance the munis, by [procreating] sons and [performing] the funeral rites the fathers, by [practising] mildness he propitiates men).

Persons, when being instruments, are likewise put in the third case; consequently the Sanskrit instrumental of a person answers as well to Lat. *per* as to Lat. *a*. Prabodh. VI, p. 132 मया च प्रणिधानेन विदितम् = Lat. compertum est *a* me *per* speculatorem.

66. 2. agent or kartṛ. — In this meaning the instrumental attends *a.*) on passive verbs, to denote the subject of the action, as has been pointed out **6**, —*b*) on verbal nouns, as Mâlav. I, p. 28 तितिक्षमाणः परेण निन्दाम् (forbearing the blame of others), for परेण निन्दाम् = परेण कृतां निन्दाम्. In the latter case the so-called subjective genitive is a concurrent construction, which is even generally preferred unless ambiguity would result from its employment, cp. **114**.

Agent of a kṛtya. P. 2, 3, 71.

Rem. *Likewise both instrumental and genitive are available to denote the agent with a kṛtya.* As a rule the instrumental is required, if the verbal sense prevail, but the genitive, if the krtya have the value of a noun adjective or substantive. Examples: instr. Panc. 167 मयावश्यं देशान्तरं गन्तव्यम् (I am obliged to emigrate), Mâlat. II किमत्र मया शक्यम् (what can I help here?), Vikram. I अवहितैर्भवितव्यं भवद्भिः (v. a. the audience are requested to listen with attention); — gen. Panc. I, 450 मूर्खाणां पण्डिता द्वेष्या निर्धनानां महाधनाः । व्रतिनः पापशीलानामसतीनां कुलस्त्रियः (the learned are an object of dislike to the ignorant, the wealthy to the poor, the virtuous to the wicked and honest women to such as are of a loose conduct), ibid. p. 268 वयं ग्राम्याः पशवो ऽरण्यचारिणां वध्याः (we, domestic animals, are a prey for wild beasts). Hence, when compounded with अ, दुः or सु, they are construed with gen., Panc. 176 दर्शय किञ्चिद्गम्यं स्थानं लुब्धकानाम्, Mṛcch. IV (p. 144) गुणेषु यत्नः पुरुषेण कार्यो न किञ्चिदप्राप्यतमं गुणानाम्.

67. 3. Quality etc. P. 2, 3, 21.

3. quality, attribute, circumstance[1]). — When denoting a quality or attribute it is = the abl. qualitatis of Latin grammar, but the restrictions as to its employment in Latin do not exist in Sanskrit. So it is said (Kâçikâ) अपि भवान्कमण्डलुना छात्रमद्राक्षीत् (have you seen a disciple with a pitcher?), ibid. on P. 2, 3, 37 यो जटाभिः स भुंक्ते; so Hitop. 125 कोषः स्वल्पव्ययेन (a treasury with little expenses) comm. स्वल्पव्ययेन विशेषणे तृतीया; R. 3, 7, 3 विविधैर्द्रुमैः काननम् (a forest with manifold trees).

Examples of its attending a verb. — Then it has the nature of Lat. abl. modi or circumstantiae. R. 2, 64, 47 स तु दिव्येन रूपेण स्वर्गमध्यारुहत्क्षिप्रम्, Panc. 161 वरो महता वाद्यशब्देनागच्छति (a bridegroom approaches with a great noise of music), ibid. 28 तस्य सकाशं गत्वा भ्रातृस्नेहेनैकत्र भक्ष्यपानविहरणक्रियाभिरेकस्थानाश्रयेण कालो नेयः [sc. त्वया] (go to him and while living brotherly with him on the same spot,

---

1) Pâṇ.'s sûtra is इत्थंभूतलक्षणे [sc. तृतीया], which is expounded by Kâç. = इत्थंभूतस्य लक्षणे »to name the laxaṇa or mark, which makes known somebody or something as possessing such quality, property, nature etc." It includes therefore the notions *quality*, *attribute*, *circumstance*.

spend the time with eating, drinking, walking together), ibid. 162 अनेन वार्त्ताव्यतिकरेण रजनी व्युष्टा (while discoursing thus, the night passed away).

Rem. 1. Note वर्तते with instrum. »to behave in such a manner," Panc. 56 त्वं मर्यादाव्यतिक्रमेण वर्तमानमालोक्य.

Rem. 2. Such instrumentals have often the character of adverbs and may be considered so (77). Among others we mention compounds in °रूपेण and °क्रमेण, when = »as, by the way of." Mṛcch. V, p. 187 द्रवीभूतं मन्ये पतति जलरूपेण गगनम् (methinks, the firmament dissolves and falls down as rain).

Rem. 3. In some turns the instrumental of circumstance may show something of the fundamental character of the sociative. So R. 2, 37, 18 लक्ष्मणेन सहायेन वनं गच्छस्व पुत्रक (*with L. as your companion* go to the forest, my son), ibid. 2, 30, 27 न देवि तव दुःखेन स्वर्गमप्यभिरोचये (I should forsake even heaven, my queen, if its attainment would be *joint with* grief of you). Similarly Panc. 309 जालहस्तधीवराः प्रभूतैर्मत्स्यैर्व्यापादितैर्मस्तके विधृतैरस्तमनवेलायां तस्मिञ्जलाशये समायाताः (the fishermen arrived...... with a great number of fishes they had killed and bore on their head). Here we are, indeed, on the very boundary of the sociative and the instr. of quality.

68. This instrumental is by far not so frequent as its equivalents in Latin and Greek, the attributes or accompanying circumstances generally finding their adequate expression in the bahuvrîhi-compound, see chapt. X. Qualities and dispositions of temper and mind are also signified by compounds, beginning with the particle स°, as सरोषम्, सबहुमानम्, cp. **185.** R. 1, occasionally by periphrase, as Kâm. 3, 3 समन्वितः करुणया परया दीनमुद्धरेत् (with the utmost compassion he must succour the distressed).

69. Test. 4. test or criterion. — Examples: Ragh. 15, 77 अन्वमीयत शुद्धेति शान्तेन वपुषैव सा (her chastity was inferred from her pure body), R. 3, 12, 23 औदार्येणावगच्छामि निधानं तपसामिदम् (by the dignity of his person I conceive him a vessel of penance and self-control). Cp. Lat. *magnos homines virtute metimur.*

70. Price. 5. price or value. — Examples: Panc. 318 ततोऽहमाभिः प्रभूता गा ग्रहीष्यामि गोभिर्महिषीर्महिषीभिर्वडवाः, Kâç. on P. 2, 3, 18 सहस्रेण पशून्क्रीणाति,

Panc. 3 नाहं विद्याविक्रयं शासनशतेनापि करोमि, R. 2, 34, 40 अपक्रमणमेव सर्वकामैरहं वृणे (I choose exile, were it at the price of all my wishes).

Likewise the instrum. is used to denote that, which is given in exchange for something: Panc. 152 गृह्णातु कश्चिद्लुञ्चितैर्लुञ्चितांस्तिलान् (who takes [from me] peeled sesam in exchange for unpeeled?)

Rem. 1. The last but one example admits however also of an other interpretation, as सर्वकामैः may signify »above all my wishes." There are a good deal of instances proving, that Sanskrit had, especially in the ancient dialect, an instrum. *of the thing surpassed* of the same power as the so called *ablativus comparationis*. More on this subject see **107**.

P. 1, 4, 44.

Rem. 2. The verb परिक्री (to hire) may be construed either with the *instrum.* or with the *dative* of the wages; शतेन or शताय परिक्रीतः Both conceptions are logically right.

71. 6. Way, by which.

6. way, by which. — Panc. 212 कतमेन मार्गेण प्रणष्टाः काकाः (in what direction the crows have disappeared?). By a commonplace metaphor मार्गेण, पथा sim. are also used to signify the manner, in which one acts. Panc. I, 414 नराधिपा बुधोपदिष्टेन पथा न यान्ति ये.

72. 7. Causality (*instrumentalis causae.*)

P. 2, 3, 23.

7. cause, motive, reason. — Examples: Daç. 198 कोऽपि कुमारः क्षुधा तृषा च क्लिश्यन् (some boy, vexed by hunger and thirst), Ch. Up. 4, 10, 3 स ह व्याधिनाऽनशितुं दध्रे (from sorrow he was not able to eat), Çâk. IV भर्तुर्विप्रकृतापि रोषणतया मा स्म प्रतीपं गमः (even when injured by your husband you should not oppose him from wrath).

Causality is also expressed by the *ablative*, and in some cases the latter is to be employed exclusively. But commonly both constructions are promiscuous and occasionally found together in the same sentence. Panc. IV, 34 नामृतं न विषं किञ्चिदेकां मुक्त्वा नितम्बिनीं। यस्याः सङ्गेन जीव्येत म्रियेत च वियोगतः (nothing is ambrosia and poison at the same time, woman alone excepted, by whose union one lives, and the separation of whom causes death), Kathâs. 29, 25 हर्षेण नष्टास्याः क्षुन्न रोगतः (it is from joy she has no appetite, not from illness).

P 2, 3 24 sq.

Rem. The ablative is forbidden and accordingly the instrumental is of necessity, if 1ly the cause or motive be at the same time the agent, see **102**, 2ly if it be an abstract noun of the *feminine* gender, expressing a quality.[1]) It may thus be said वीर्येण or वीर्यान्मुक्तः (released by heroism), but only भिया पलायितः (he fled from fear). Hence often the abl. of a masc. and neuter and the instr. of the feminine range together, as R. 2, 70, 25 बभूव ह्यस्य हृदये चिन्ता सुमहती तदा । त्वरया चापि दूतानां स्वप्नस्यापि च दर्शनात्, or Prabodh. II, p. 31 बालः खल्वसि मया द्वापरान्ते दृष्टः । संप्रति कालविप्रकर्षाद्वार्धकग्रस्ततया च न सम्यक्प्रत्यभिजानामि (as you were a boy, forsooth, I have seen you at the end of the Dvâpara-age, now by length of time and by my being vexed by old age I did not recognise you exactly). In scientific and philosophical works, commentaries and the like, ablatives in °त्वात् alternate with instrumentals in °तया in order to denote the cause or the moving principle.

73. *Instrumentalis partis.* Next to the instrumental of causality comes that, which signifies *by what side*. Like the Latin abl. partis it commonly depends on adjectives, but may also be the complement of the whole predicate. It is especially used to point out the *points of comparison* with verbs or nouns, which denote superiority or inferiority, likeness or difference.

Examples: R. 1, 1, 55 रूपेण विकृतः (disfigured), Ch. Up. 2, 11,2 महान्प्रजया पशुभिर्भवति महान्कीर्त्या, Daç. 77 कलागुणैः समृद्धो वसुना नातिपुष्टोऽभवत् (he was rich in various kinds of knowledge and in good qualities, but not very bulky in earthly goods), Panc. 274 किमहमेताभ्यां शौर्येण रूपेण विद्याभ्यासेन कौशलेन वा हीनः (am I inferior to both of them either in valour or in outer appearance or in study or in cleverness?), Daç. 177 अभिजनेन विभवेन राजान्तरङ्गभावेन च सर्वपौ-

1) P. 2, 3, 25 perhaps admits of two interpretations. The words विभाषा गुणेऽस्त्रियाम् may signify »optional, when expressing a quality, provided this quality is no feminine" or »*optional*, when expressing a quality; *not at all*, if [the motive be] a feminine." Moreover the term *strî* may denote as well *all* feminines, as only such, as have special feminine endings. — At all events, in practice, when signifying causality, the ablative with the special femin. ending °आः is always avoided.

रानतीत्य वर्तते (he is surpassing all his citizens by his birth, his wealth and his being the king's confident), Çâk. V अनुभवति हि मूर्ध्ना पादपस्तीव्रमुष्णं शमयति परितापं छायया संश्रितानाम् (the tree does tolerate the ardent glow of the sun on its summit to assuage by its shade the heat of those who come to it for shelter). In the last example, the instr. छायया may also be accepted as the instrument. In practice, indeed, the different shades of the how-case do not show themselves so sharply, as they are exhibited by the standard-types, cp. **64**.

Rem. 1. Concurrent idioms denoting the side by which, are the ablative and the locative, especially if it be wanted to express the points of comparison. It is even allowed to use them side by side. So R. 1, 17, 13 two instrumentals are used together with an abl. (तेजसा यशसा वीर्यादत्यरिच्यत), Mhbh. 1, 16, 9 they range with a locative (द्वौ पुत्रौ विनता वव्रे कद्रूपुत्राधिकौ बले । तेजसा वपुषा चैव).

P. 2, 3, 20.

Rem. 2. The instrumental is of necessity, when naming the part of the body, by which one suffers, as अक्ष्णा काणः (blind of one eye), पाणिना कुणिः, पादेन खञ्जः. Ch. Up 2, 19, 2 य एवं वेद नाङ्गेन विहूर्छति (he who knows so, is not crippled in any limb).

Rem. 3. With comparatives and the like the instrumental is equivalent to the Latin ablativus mensurae. Daç. 73 केनांशेनार्थकामातिशायी धर्मः (by how much is duty superior to interest and pleasure?), Utp. on Varâh. Brhats (translation of Kern p. 7) अमुको ग्रह एतावद्भिर्योजनैर्भूगोलादुपरि भ्रमति (such a planet moves so many yojanas above the terrestrial globe).

74. Special construction.

The instrumental is used in many idiomatic turns, most of which belong to the general heads described in the preceding paragraphs. Of them the most important are:

1. *to honour-, to favour-, to attend on with* Çâk. I कालिदासग्रथितवस्तुना नवेन नाटकेनोपस्थातव्यमस्माभिः (we want to wait upon you with a new drama etc.), Panc. III, 139 स्वैर्मांसैर्निमन्त्रितः [sc. कपोतेन शत्रुः].

2. *to swear-, to conjure by*. R. 2, 48, 23 पुत्रैरपि शपामहे (we swear; even by our children); Mrcch. III (p. 126) अस्मच्छरीरस्पृष्टिकया शापितोऽसि;

Mhbh. 1, 131, 46 सत्येन ते शपे. — Likewise तेन सत्येन, an elliptical phrase = यथा मयोक्तं सत्यं तेन सत्येन (as I have said the truth, by that truth), cp. Ch. Up. 3, 11, 2; Nala 5, 17—20.

3. *to boast on.* Mhbh. 2, 64, 1 परेषामेव यशसा श्लाघसे त्वम्.

4. *to live by.* M. 3, 162 नक्षत्रैर्यश्च जीवति (v. a. an astrologer), Çâk. VII प्राणानामनिलेन वृत्तिः

5. *to rejoice, to laugh, to wonder etc. at.* Mhbh. 1, 138, 71 प्रीये त्वयाहम् (you make me glad), Mudr. VII p. 221 गुणैर्न परितुष्यामो यस्य (with whose virtues I am not content), Kathâs. 20, 43 जहास तेन स नृपः (the king laughed at it). Cp. साधु (bravo, well done) with instr. Mâlat. I (p. 8) साधु वत्से साध्वनेन मत्प्रियाभियोगेन.

Rem. In the case of 4. and 5. the ablative may occasionally be made use of. That आजीव्, उपजीव्, हस्, नन्द्, शुच् may be transitives, has been stated 43 and 42, 4; the last (शोचति) is commonly construed so, and does but rarely comply with the instr.

Rem. 2. With रम्, क्रीड् and the like the instrum. may be either the sociative proper (then सह, समम् etc. may be added) or the karaṇa. Ch. Up. 8, 12,3 gives a fair instance of its standing on the bordering line of both acceptations जक्षत्क्रीडन्रममाणः स्त्रीभिर्वा यानैर्वा ज्ञातिभिर्वा (laughing [or eating], playing and rejoicing with women, carriages or relatives).

6. *to fill with.* Panc. 317 तेन भिक्षार्जितैः सक्तुभिर्भुक्तशेषैः कलशः संपूरितः (what was left of his store of barley, he had earned by begging, therewith he filled his bowl), Mudr. V p. 184 ते पांसुभिः पूर्यन्ताम्. — The *genitive* with words of filling is also met with, yet the general use prefers the instrumental, at least with पूरयति.

7. *to vanquish in (a battle, etc.).* Panc. 291 तं रिपुं युद्धेन परिभूय.

8. *to carry -, to keep -, to bear on (in, with.)* Panc. III, 202 रथकारः स्वकां भार्यां सजारां शिरसावहत् (the cartwright carried his wife with her paramour on his head), Daç. 140 मत्पितुरुत्तमाङ्गमुत्सङ्गेन धारयन्ती.

Rem. In the cases of 7 and 8 the locative is the concurrent idiom. It is said promiscuously युद्धे and युद्धेन जितम्, स्कन्धे or स्कन्धेन धृतम्. Cp. Kumâras. 3,22 भर्तुराज्ञामादाय मूर्ध्ना मदनः प्रतस्थे with Kâd. I, p. 29 शिरसि कृत्वाज्ञाम्. But always तुलया धृ »to hold on the balance", v. a. »to weigh, to compare."

9. It is said अक्षैर्दीव्यति and अक्षान् (he plays at dice). Cp. also R. (Gorr.) 3, 30, 4 रुधिरधाराभिर्वर्षन्तो मेघाः with Mhbh. 13, 148, 2 पर्जन्यो ववृषे निर्मलं पयः, Lat. *pluit lapides* or *lapidibus*. — Similarly शपथं शपति and शपथेन (to swear an oath).

Rem. In the old dialect of the Vedic mantras the instrum. attends on पत्यते and भुज् just as the abl. on Latin *potiri* and *fungi*, see DELBR. Abl. Loc. Instr. p. 65. To the instances adduced there I add the mantra in Âçv. Grhy. 1, 23, 19 तन्मावतु तन्माविशतु तेन भुक्षिषीय.

75. 10.) the set phrases किं प्रयोजनम् (or कार्यम्), कोऽर्थः sim., or in a negative form न प्रयोजनम् etc. are construed with the instr. of that, which „does not matter." Or even it is said simply किं तेन (what matters this?). He, whom it does not matter, is put into the genitive. Examples: Panc. 285 किं मदीयेन रथकारत्वेन प्रयोजनम् (what profit have I being cartwright?), Mâlav. III (p. 81) न मे मालविकया कश्चिदर्थः (I have nothing to meddle with M.), R. 2, 73, 2 किं नु कार्यं मम राज्येन (what matters me the kingdom?), Daç. 140 न मेऽनयास्ति चिन्तया फलम्, Mudr. I (p. 21) अप्राज्ञेन च कातरेण च गुणाः स्यात्सानुरागेण कः (what profit may be derived from an unwise and coward [officer], though he be faithful?), Pat. I, p. 7 किं न एतेन (what matters us this?), Çâk. V किं पितुरुत्कुलया त्वया.

In the same way it is said किं करोमि तेन *quid faciam eo?* Panc. 276 किं व्याधिग्रस्तेन मया करिष्यसि.

Rem. 1 Like अर्थ, its derivative अर्थिन् complies with instrum., when = »wanting-, being eager for -, coveting." R. 3, 18, 4 भार्यार्थी (he wants to be married), Mudr. V (p. 166) एतेषां मध्ये केचिदरेः कोषदन्तिभ्यामर्थिनः केचिद्विषयेण (some of them long after the foe's treasures and elephants, some others are coveting his domains).

Rem. 2. Note परवन्त् with instrum. »dependent on, in the power of," R. 3, 18, 9 परवान्भ्रात्रा, Mâlat. VI (p. 97) परवानस्मि साध्वसेन. Yet gen. and loc. are also available, cp. आयत्त 124.

76. 11.) with अलम्, अस्तु, कृतम् the instrum. expresses a prohibition or an invitation to cease or to stop.

Vikram. I अलमाक्रन्दितेन (stop your cries), Çâk. I अथवा कृतं संदेहेन (well, no hesitation more), Mahâv. II (p. 25) अस्तु दुरासदेन तपसा (cease your unparalleled penance).

77. Many instrumentals have more or less the character of adverbs, as प्रायेण (mostly), सुखेन (easily), दुःखेन and कृच्छ्रेण (hardly), सर्वात्मना (with all my heart), etc. So R. 1, 13, 34 अवज्ञया न दातव्यं कस्यचिल्लीलयापि वा (one should not bestow a gift in a disdainful manner nor in jest), Panc. II, 204 मित्राणि करोत्यत्र न कौटिल्येन वर्तते (he makes friends and does not converse with them falsely), Mrcch. VII (p. 237) क्षेमेण व्रज बान्धवान् (auspicious be your way to your kinsmen), Mâlat. X (p. 165) कामन्दक्यापि नातः परं वत्सावियोगेन जीवितव्यम् (nor can K. live longer either without her daughter).

78. *In-strum. time.* III. The **instrumental of time** serves to denote *in what time* something is accomplished. Not rarely this conception coincides with that of the *time*, *after which* something is happening. मासेनानुवाकोऽधीतः (the chapter was learned in (after) a month). *P. 2, 3, 6.*

The same applies to space. क्रोशेनानुवाकोऽधीतः [1]).

Examples: Panc. 2 द्वादशभिर्वर्षैर्व्याकरणं श्रूयते (v. a. grammar requires twelve years to be mastered), ibid. 237 कतिपयैरेवाहोभिर्मयूर इव स बलवान्संवृत्तः (in a few days he [the crow] grew strong like a peacock), Daç. 159 ततोऽल्पीयसा कालेन राज्ञः प्रियमहिष्येकं पुत्रमसूत (after some time the king's chief queen was delivered of a son), R. 1, 13, 35 ततः कैश्चिदहोरात्रैरुपयाताः महीक्षितः, Panc. 282 तयोर्व्रजतोर्योजनद्वयमात्रेणाग्रतः काचिन्नदी समुपस्थिता (as they went on, after no more than two yojanas the couple came in sight of some river). So दिनैः, दिवसैः etc. = »in process of time."

---

1) The difference between this *instrum. of time* and the above mentioned *acc. of time* (**54**) is illustrated by these examples of the Kâçikâ: It is said मासेना(क्रोशेना)नुवाकोऽधीतः, but मासमधीतोऽनुवाको न चानेन गृहीतः, for »if the subject ceases the action before having reached its aim, the instrumental may not be employed."

Rem. 1. The fundamental conception seems here to be that of concomitancy. Hence it may be explained, how the third case occasionally denotes even *at what time*, as R. 1, 72, 12 एकाह्ना (at one and the same day) राजपुत्रीणां चतसृणां पाणीन्गृह्णन्तु चत्वारो राजपुत्राः, and such standing phrases as तेन कालेन, तेन समयेन, which are especially frequent in Buddhistic and Jain books.

P. 2, 3, cp. 4, 2

Rem. 2. The naxatra or constellation, under which something occurs, may be put indifferently in the third or the seventh case: पुष्येण or पुष्ये पायसमश्नीयात्. Examples of the instrum. Âçv. Gṛhy. 3, 5, 1 अथातोऽध्यायोपाकरणमोषधीनां प्रादुर्भावे श्रवणेन..... हस्तेन वा, Pat. I, 231 कतरेण तिष्येण गतः

Chapter V. **Dative.** [1]

General employment of the dative.

79. The dative or fourth case serves to point out the *destination*, and therefore it generally does answer to English *to* and *for*, Latin *ad* or *in* with acc. Yet, if it be wanted to express the destination of a real going or moving, the accusative (**39**) or locative (**134**) are commonly preferred, although the dative may be used even then, **ग्रामाय गच्छति** being as correct as **ग्रामं गच्छति**. So Ragh. 12, 7 वनाय गच्छ, Daç. 76 नगरायोदचलम्, Mudr. II कुसुमपुराय करभकं प्रेषयामि (I will send Karabhaka to Pâtaliputra), Kathâs. 47, 92 संहृत्य युद्धं ययतुः स्वनिवेशायोभे बले (after ceasing the battle both armies retired to their encampments). — With causative verbs of moving, as those of *bringing*, *throwing*, *casting*, this kind of dative is frequent. R. 3, 25, 27 प्रासाञ्शूलान्परश्वधान्। चिक्षिपुः परमक्रुद्धा रामाय रजनीचराः, Mâlav. III (p. 76) अशोकाय पदं प्रहिणोति (she lifts up her foot to the açoka-tree), Mhbh. 1, 114, 2 विदुराय चैव पाण्डुः प्रेषयामास तद्धनम्.

P. 2, 3,

Dat. with words of *moving*.

Rem. The aim, reached, attained is never put in the dative (**39**) [2].

---

1) Compare Delbrück's monography on the employment of the dative in the Ṛgvedasanhitâ in Kuhn's *Zeitschr.* XVIII, p. 81—106. Monographies on the syntax of the dative in classic Sanskrit are not known to me.

2) Cp. Pat. I, 448, vârtt. 4 on P. 2, 3, 12.

80. Dat of the destination

In the great majority of cases the destination purported by the dative, has an acceptation more or less figurative. The different kinds of datives, which display this character, may be arranged in two distinct groups, viz I, the so-called *dative of concern or interest*, II, the *dative of the purpose*. The former has almost the same functions as the dative of modern european languages, the sphere of the latter is that of the dativus finalis in Latin.

Both are but varieties of the fundamental notion, as will be made plain by these examples, which contain some datives of the kind I and II, construed with the verb *to go*. I. Hitop. p. 42 न देवाय न विप्राय न बन्धुभ्यो न चात्मने। कृपणस्य धनं याति वह्नितस्करपार्थिवैः (the riches of the miser go neither to a god nor to a brahman, nor to his family nor to himself, because of fire, thieves, the king). II. R. 1, 46, 7 इत्युक्त्वा तपसे ययौ (after these words he set out to penance, viz. in order to do penance), Veṇ. II (p. 39) गच्छ त्वमात्मव्यापाराय (go to your business).

81. Dat. of concern.

I. The **dative of concern** denotes the person or thing concerned by the action, in whose behalf or against whom it is done, or who is anyhow interested by it [1]).

It is put 1) to transitive verbs, as *a.*) those of *giving* and *offering*, *b.*) of *showing*, *c.*) of *telling*, *speaking*, *announcing*, *promising*, etc., *d.*) of *doing* or *wishing* good or evil, and the like, for expressing the so-called „remote object "

Remote object.

Examples: *a.*) R. 2, 40, 14 वासांस्याभरणानि च सीतायै श्वशुरो ददौ; Panc. 173 राजपुरुषो वित्तमुपभुक्तधनाय समर्पयामास (the king's officer gave the money to Upabhuktadhana), Çâk. III दर्भान्नृत्विग्भ्य उपहरामि, Mṛcch. I (p. 21) कृतो मया गृहदेवताभ्यो बलिः; — *b.*) Kathâs. 29, 32 अदर्शयत्पित्रे सखीम् (she presented her friend to her father); — *c.*) Ch. Up. 3,

---

1) Cp P. 1, 4, 32 कर्मणा यमभिप्रैति स संप्रदानम् and Patanjali on that sûtra I, 330.

11, 4 तद्वैतद्ब्रह्मा प्रजापतय उवाच प्रजापतिर्मनवे मनुः प्रजाभ्यः; Kathâs. 53, 139 बालाय.... तदूचे (the matter was told to the boy), Çâk. VII तत्तस्यै कथयति (he tells her so); Âçv. Gṛhy. 1, 22, 10 तदाचार्याय वेदयीत (he should deliver to his teacher [the alms he has received]); Nala 3, 1 तेभ्यः प्रतिज्ञाय नलः करिष्य इति (he promised them, he would do so); — *d.*) Mudr. I (p. 44) प्रीताभ्यः प्रकृतिभ्यः प्रियमिच्छन्ति राजानः; Mhbh. 1, 3, 178 तस्मै प्रतिकुरुष्व (requite him this).

2.) to intransitives as those of *pleasing*, *bowing* and *submitting*, *appearing* etc. So Panc. 282 रोचते मह्यम् (it pleases me), Çâk. V यथा गुरुभ्यो रोचते; Nala 5, 16 देवेभ्यः प्राञ्जलिर्भूत्वा; R. 2, 25, 4 येभ्यः प्रणमसे पुत्र ते च त्वामभिरक्षन्तु (and may those, to whom you bow, my son, preserve you); Nir. 2, 8 तस्मै देवता.... प्रादुर्बभूव (a deity appeared to him).

82. Concurrent idioms. In these and similar instances it is not the use of the dative, which should be noticed, *but the faculty of employing in a large amount of cases instead of it some other case, mostly a genitive or a locative* (cp. **129** and **145**). Some words even seem wholly to avoid the dative of concern; so विक्री (to sell) is generally construed with the locative of the purchaser, क्षम् (to pardon) with a genitive, adjectives as प्रिय, अनुरूप, उचित, युक्त are as a rule construed with a genitive, etc.

83. Special cases of the dat. of concern. In some special cases the use of the dative is enjoined by vernacular grammarians; of the kind are:

1. The dat. with हित (good for). Cp. Pat. I, 450; Pâṇ. 5, 1, 5 तस्मै हितम्. Even here the gen. may be used, see f. i. R. 3, 36, 24.

2. The dative of the creditor with धारयति (to owe). P. 1, 4, 35.

3. Some utterances of ritual, almost = „hail" to — as नमः, स्वाहा, स्वधा, वषट् — likewise most phrases of blessing and salutation. They are construed with a dative, but

some of them [1]) either with dat. or with genitive. नमो रुद्राय, स्वाहा देवेभ्यः, स्वधा पितृभ्यः, स्वस्ति प्रजाभ्यः, आयुष्यं तुभ्यम् or तव भूयात्, कुशलं देवदत्तस्य and देवदत्ताय. Vikram. p. 62 स्वागतं देव्यै. In the ninth act of the Mṛcch. Cârudatta greets the judges with an अधिकृतेभ्यः स्वस्ति, wherea the chief judge answers him स्वागतमार्यस्य. But R. 3, 24, 21 स्वस्ति is construed with a gen. स्वस्ति गोब्राह्मणानां च लोकानां च.

P. 2, 3, 16; 2, 3, 73.

4. Verbs of *anger*, *jealousy*, *injuring*, *discontent* agree with the dative of the object of the animosity. Mhbh. 1, 3, 186 नृपतिस्तक्षकाय चुकोप ह (the king felt angry towards Taxaka), Kathâs. 17, 44 नास्यै चुक्रोध, Âpast. 1, 1, 14 तस्मै न द्रुह्येत्कदाचन (him he should never offend), Ait. Br. 8, 23, 11 तस्मादेवं विदुषे ब्राह्मणायैवं चक्रुषे न क्षत्रियो द्रुह्येत्, Kâd. I, 217 असूयन्ति सचिवोपदेशाय (they find fault with the advice of their ministers), Mahâv. I (p. 18) स्पृहयामि राज्ञे दशरथाय (I am jealous of king Daçaratha).

P. 1, 4, 37.

Rem. Yet with असूयति (to find fault with) and द्रुह्यति (to hurt) the acc., with those of anger and jealousy the gen. and loc. or प्रति are also available. When compounded, द्रुह् and क्रुध् must agree with acc. देवदत्ताय क्रुध्यति but देवदत्तमभिक्रुध्यति.

P. 1, 4, 38.

5. Some other verbs, enumerated by Pâṇini, viz. श्लाघ् (to praise), ह्नु (to conceal), शप् (to swear, to conjure) and स्था. Here the dative is required of him, whom it is wanted to inform of something, f. i. देवदत्ताय श्लाघते »he praises to N.N." [here N.N. is the person addressed], Prabodh. III, p. 66 बुद्धेभ्यः शतशः शपे (I swear a hundred times to the Buddhas), Naish. 1, 49 अपह्नुवानस्य जनाय निजामधीरताम् (concealing from the people his unsteadiness). — As to स्था, it is not plain, what meaning it has here. By comparing P. 1, 3, 23 with the examples adduced there by Kâçikâ, तिष्ठते with a dat. may be = »he presents or he discovers himself to [2])," but

P. 1, 4, 34.

---

1) Viz. आयुष्य, मद्र, भद्र, कुशल, सुख, अर्थ, हित and their synonyms (vârtt. on P. 2, 3, 73).

2) The examples of Kâç. on 1, 3, 23 are तिष्ठते कन्या छात्रेभ्यः। तिष्ठते वृषली ग्रामपुत्रेभ्यः; here तिष्ठते is said to be = प्रकाशयत्यात्मानम्.

स्था with a dat. may also have had the meaning »to have faith in —, affection to," Çvetâçv. Up. 3, 2 एको हि रुद्रो न हि द्वितीयाय तस्थुः, Naish. 7, 57.

6. P. 1, 4, 41 enjoins a dat. with the compound verbs अनुगृणाति and प्रतिगृणाति, being technical terms of the ritual »to utter [a certain formula] after —, in reply to another." [1]).

7. P. 1, 4, 39 mentions a dat. with verbs of *casting one's nativity* etc., like राध्, ईक्ष्, to denote him, on whose behalf this is done. We have here an instance of the dative of profit, treated in the following paragraph.

84. Dat. *commodi* and *incommodi*. Sometimes the dative involves the notion of some profit or damage caused by the action (*dativus commodi et incommodi*). Ch. Up. 6, 16, 1 अपहार्षीत्स्तेनमकार्षीत्परशुमस्मै तपत (he has taken something, he has committed a theft, heat the hatchet *for him*), Kâm. 3, 9 आधिव्याधिपरीताय अद्य श्वो वा विनाशिने। को हि नाम शरीराय धर्मापेतं समाचरेत् (for who, indeed, would do wrong *for the sake* of his body, a thing beset by sorrow and disease and destined to die some day or other?), Daç. Uttar. page 19 of the ed. of Ḍamaruvallabhaçarman अस्यै दास्यमद्यप्रभृत्यभ्युपेतं मया (from this day I have come in bondage of her), Çâk. III अहमपि तावद्वैतानिकं शान्त्युदकमस्यै गोतमीहस्ते विसर्जयिष्यामि.

Here, as in **82**, it is not the dative, that is remarkable, but the faculty of substituting for it the genitive, as Çâk. III कस्येदमनुलेपनं मृणालवन्ति च नलिनीपत्राणि नीयन्ते (whom this ointment and these lotus-leaves are sent for?). The dat. commodi is often periphrased by अर्थम्, अर्थे, कृते sim.

85. Dat. with words of counterpoising etc. Verbs and nouns of *befitting*, *suiting*, *counterpoising* are construed with the dative. So the verbs कल्पते, संपद्यते [vârtt. 2 on P. 2, 3, 13], राध्यति, प्रभवति, the nouns प्रभु, अलम् and the like

1) The old language seems to have allowed more of such datives with compound verbs, so as to be the counterpart of Latin *instat hosti*, *occurrit mihi* and the like. So Âpast. I, 14, 15 विषमगतायागुरवे नाभिवाद्यम्, ibid. II, 11, 3 राजा दण्डाय प्रतिपद्येत [instead of दण्डं प्र°]. A curious dative of the same kind, it seems, is Daç. 149 यावदायुरत्रत्यायै देवतायै प्रतिशयिष्यामि.

[P. 2, 3, 16 and Pat. on this sûtra I, p. 450, vârtt. 2]. So Daç. 73 श्रेयसेऽनल्पाय कल्पते (he is fit for a considerable share of heavenly blessing); Çâk. VI कल्पिष्यमाणा महते फलाय वसुन्धरा; R. (Gorr.) 5, 25, 7 तस्य नैर्ऋतराजस्य भार्यायै किं न कल्पसे (why should you not suit to be the wife of the king of the infernal regions?); Âpast. 1, 12, 13 नरकाय राध्यति (he becomes fit for hell); Kumâras. 6, 59 भवत्संभावनोत्थाय परितोषाय.... नाङ्गानि प्रभवन्ति मे (my body is not strong enough to bear the joy, you have caused me by your homage); Vas. Dh. adhy. 8 अलमग्न्याधेयाय नानाहिताग्निः स्यात् (if he have the wealth to perform the *agnyâdheya* sacrifice, he must keep the fires); Pat. अलं or प्रभुर्मल्लो मल्लाय (one athlete is a match for another).

Rem. With some adjectives of *competency* the genitive may also be used, especially with पर्याप्त and शक्त, as Var. Brh. 32, 4 शक्तोऽहं नास्य खेदस्य, R. 3, 38, 9 रामान्नान्यद्दू ब्रलं लोके पर्याप्तं तस्य रक्षसः

86 Old datives. It is likely, that the genitive had not encroached so much on the dative's sphere of employment in the dialect of the brâhmaṇas and of ancient epic poetry, as afterwards. In some instances the dative is no more used in the classical language, after having been employed so in the archaic dialect.

Of the kind are *a.*) the dative of the agent of krtyas. It seems to be restricted to the oldest dialect, that of the vedic mantras. Rgv.I, 31, 5 उद्यतस्रुचे भवसि श्रवाय्यः (you are worshipful to him who holds the spoon uplifted). Cp. DELBR.'s monography, p. 90.

b.) the dative with the adjectives of friendship and the contrary. Ṛgv. 7, 36, 5 इदं नमो रुद्राय प्रेष्ठम्. The classic construction is here gen. or locative. See Delbr. l.l. p. 90.

c.) the dative with श्रद्धा (to have faith, to trust), श्रु (to listen), see Delbr. l. l. p. 84.

In classic Sanskrit the person trusted is put in the gen. or loc., the thing believed in the acc., and when = »to approve" or »to welcome," श्रद्धा is of course a transitive, as Kathâs. 5, 114; 46, 136. On the classic construction of श्रु see **95**, 4°, **126** *b*). Its desiderative शुश्रूषते (to listen) is construed with a dat. in the Chândogya Upanishad (7, 5, 2) तस्मै शुश्रूषन्ते, but in classic Sanskrit it is mostly a transitive, even when meaning *to obey*, Çâk. IV शुश्रूषस्व गुरून्

d.) a dative with substantives, to denote *the possessor*, cp. English »a son *to* me." Rgv. 1, 31, 2 विभुर्विश्वस्मै भुवनाय (ruler of the whole universe); Ch Up. 4, 3, 6 यस्मै वा एतदन्नं तस्मा एतन्न दत्तम् (you have not given the food to him, to whom it belongs). — This construction has long subsisted in the case of the possessor being a personal pronoun, especially in epic poetry. Mhbh. 1, 51, 5 पिता मह्यम्, R. 1, 54, 11 बलं मह्यम् instead of मम; Mhbh. 1, 151, 39 नानुज्ञां मे युधिष्ठिरः प्रयच्छति वधे तुभ्यम् (Yudh. refuses me the permission of killing you), ibid. 1, 111, 14 दर्शनं मह्यम्, R. 1, 13, 4; 2, 32, 8, etc.

NB. In the brâhmana-works it is sometimes impossible to decide whether a dative or a genitive has been employed. Both cases may formally coincide in the singular of the feminines in °आ, °ई, °ऊ (°इ, °उ). In the dialect of these books the gen. and abl. of the singular may end in °ऐ, just as the dative does; स्त्रियै in the brâhmana-works = classic स्त्रियै or स्त्रियाः. See Kuhn, *Zeitschr.* XV, p. 420 sqq., Aufrecht p 428 of his edition of the Aitareyabrâhmaṇa.

87. Dat. of the purpose.

II. The **dative of the purpose or aim** is of very frequent occurrence. It may be made use of always, if one wants to denote *either* the thing wished for *or* the action intended. Of the former kind are such datives as फलेभ्यो याति (he goes out for fruits), यूपाय दारु (wood for a sacrificial stake), कुण्डलाय हिरण्यम् (gold for a ring), Hitop. 95 उपायो जीवनाय.

In the latter case the *nomen actionis* itself is put in the dative and has the power of an infinitive. Çâk. I आर्तत्राणाय वः शस्त्रं न प्रहर्तुमनागसि (your weapon serves to protect the afflicted, not to hurt the innocent). Here of two actions equally aimed at, one is expressed by the dative of a nomen actionis, the other by an infinitive. The third concurrent idiom is using periphrase by means of such words as अर्थम्, निमित्तम् = „for the sake of." Prabodh. V, p. 100 वेदसंरक्षणाय नास्तिकपक्षप्रतिक्षेपार्थं च शास्त्राणां सांहत्यमस्ति (the systems [of philosophy] keep together for the sake of guarding the Veda and combating the party of the atheists).

Other examples of the infinitive-like dative. — Panc. 58 युद्धाय प्रस्थितः, Prabodh. V, p. 113 इदानीं ज्ञातीनामुदकक्रियायै भागीरथीमवतरामः (now, let us plunge into the Ganges for the bathing-ceremony for our kinsmen), Hitop. 7 एतेषामस्मत्पुत्राणां नीतिशास्त्रोपदेशाय भवन्तः प्रमाणम् (you have full power to instruct these my sons in the doctrine of politics so as you like best), Veṇ. I, p. 24 त्वरते मे मनः संग्रामावतरणाय, Kathâs. 26, 33 दिष्ट्या सास्त्येव नगरी तत्प्राप्त्यै चायमेव मे...... विहगो वाहनीकृतः (thank God, that is the town, for attaining which I have placed myself on the back of this bird), Mâlat. VI, p. 87 जागर्ति दंशाय..... भुजङ्गी, Kâm. I, 66 गुरुस्तु विद्याधिगमाय सेव्यते, Mṛcch. VII (p. 238) एवं पुनर्दर्शनाय (—till we meet again).

88. Some idioms, though implied by the general description, given in the preceding paragraph, are worth special notice.

1. The datives of abstract nouns, when expressing „to serve to, to conduce to." They often make up the whole predicate. — Examples: Pat. I, 11 नैव तद् दोषाय भवति नाभ्युदयाय (v. a. it is neither good nor evil), Panc. III, 103 परोपकारः पुण्याय पापाय परपीडनम्, ibid. p. 192 लघूनामपि संश्रयो रक्षायै भवति (even if weak people keep together, it may afford protection). Cp. the marriage-mantra in Âçv. Gṛhy. 1, 7, 3 गृभ्णामि ते सौभगत्वाय हस्तम् (I take your hand for happiness'sake). — Compare Latin *haec res tibi est laudi.*

Similarly संपद्यते with dat. = »to turn, to change into", कल्पते (to suit) see **85**.

Rem. 1. A vârtt. on Pâṇ. 2, 3, 13 gives a special rule on the dative, when serving to explain a prognostic as वाताय कपिला विद्युदातपायातिलोहिनी। पीता वर्षाय विज्ञेया दुर्भिक्षाय सिता भवेत्.

Rem. 2. The person, to whom something will conduce to good, evil etc., is put in the genitive: तवैतद्यशसे (this will be to your glory), cp. **130**. — In the archaic dialect, however, we have two datives, one of the concern and one of the aim, just as in Latin. A. V. 1, 29, 4 राष्ट्राय मह्यं बध्यतां सपत्नेभ्यः पराभुवे (let I put it on [viz. the *mani*], for acquiring my kingdom for myself and defeat for my rivals); Rgv. 2, 5, 1; Ait. Br. 2, 3, 3 देवेभ्यो वै पशवोऽन्नाद्यायालम्भाय नातिष्ठन्त (the sacrificial victims did not stand still to the gods for the sake of being used as food and immolated).

Rem. 3. With मन्यते (to hold for) the predicative dative *may* be used instead of the acc. (**32**, *c*), if contempt is to be expressed; names of animated beings are excepted and should therefore be put exclusively in the acc. So Pâṇini (2, 3, 17). Kâç. न त्वा तृणं or तृणाय मन्ये। बुसम् or बुसाय; yet it allows the dat. of श्वन्; न त्वा श्वानं or शुने मन्ये. Instances of this dative in literature I have but found for तृणाय, see Petr. Dict. s. v. and Daç. 88 कुबेरदत्तस्तृणाय मत्वार्थपतिम् »Kub. *does not çare a straw for Arth.*"

89. 2ly. The dative of the aim aspired after with verbs of *wishing*, *striving*, *endeavouring*, sim. P 1, 4, 36.

Examples: R. 2, 95, 17 नायोध्यायै न राज्याय स्पृहये (I do not long for Ay. nor for the kingdom), Spr. 128 तथापि रामो लुलुभे मृगाय (nevertheless R. aspired after the deer), Çâk. V मनोरथाय नाशंसे (I do not hope for [the fulfilling of] my wish), R. 1, 18, 57 इच्छाम्यनुगृहीतोऽहं त्वदर्थं परिवृद्धये (it is in your behalf I wish to grow mighty), Mâlav. I, p. 15 तदन्वेषणाय यतिष्ये (I will try to find her out)

Rem. All these verbs of course admit also of accusative, if some thing, and of infinitive if some action be aimed at; इच्छति स्त्रियम्। इच्छति भोक्तुम्

90. 3ly. The infinitive-like dative with verbs of *beginning*, *resolving*, *being able* (f. i. शक्) and with those of *ordering to* and *appointing to*.

Examples: Daç. 157 राजमन्दिरद्वारे चिताधिरोहणायोपक्रमिष्यसे (you shall begin to ascend the funeral pile at the gate of the king's palace), ibid. 126 प्रावर्तत शपथाय (he commenced to take an oath), Prab. V p. 102 तेन जीवोत्सर्गाय व्यवसितम् (he has resolved to die), Daç. 192 सा चेयं कथा क्षत्रियस्याकर्षणायाशकत् (and this tale was fit to win the warrior), Kumâr. 4, 39 देहविमुक्तये स्थिता रतिः (Rati, being ready to give up life); — Çâk. I दुहितरमतिथिसत्काराायादिश्य (having charged his daughter with the reception of guests), Kathâs. 15, 82 रावणोच्छित्तये देवैर्नियोजितः (he was appointed by the gods to destroy Râvana).

Even with verbs of *promising*. Prabodh. II, p. 24 प्रतिज्ञात सामात्येन विवेकेन प्रबोधचन्द्रोदयाय (Viveka and his minister have engaged themselves to rouse the moon of enlightening).

91. In short, in Sanskrit datives of nomina actionis (*bhâvavacanâni*) do often duty of infinitives. As they, however, are always felt as noun-cases, they agree with the genitive of their object. But in the ancient dialect many of them had verbal construction. More ample information about them will be given in the chapter on the infinitive.

92. Time-denoting dative: Time-denoting datives may serve for expressing a time to come, when a limit of something to be done. Mâlav. V, p. 139 मया..... वत्सराय निवर्तनीयो निरर्गलस्तुरङ्गमो विसर्जितः (I have set at entire liberty the horse, that it might be brought back after a year).

Of a similar nature is this dative in R. 2, 62, 17 (Kausalyâ speaks) वनवासाय रामस्य पञ्चरात्रोऽत्र गण्यते यः शोकहतहर्षायाः पञ्चवर्षोपमो मम »we count now on R.'s exile but five nights, which seem to me as many years."

CHAPTER VI. **Ablative** [1]).

93. The fifth case or ablative serves to denote the *whence*,

1) Comp. DELBRÜCK *Ablativ, Localis, Instrumentalis*, p. 1—27.

General view of the ablative.

and is therefore the very opposite of the dative. Nevertheless both cases are formally identical in the dual and the plural. [1]) In the singular the form of the ablative often coincides with that of the genitive. It is but the ablatives in °अात्, that are exclusively expressive of the fifth case. Moreover those made by means of the adverbial suffix °तः are not seldom preferred to the regular ablatives of the singular, ambiguousness being wholly excluded from them.

For easiness' sake we will treat of this case under four general heads, I abl. of separation, II abl. of distance, III abl. of origin and cause, IV abl. expressing „on what side." In all of them, however, the unity of the fundamental conception is evident, and sometimes one may account for the same ablative in more than one way.

94. Ablative expressive of the *whence, from, out of.*

P. 1, 4, 24.

I. The ablative, then, is wanted to express, *from* or *out of* what place there is a starting and moving [2]):

a.) in its proper sense, as Panc. 21 अहमस्माद्वनाद्गन्तुमिच्छामि (I wish to get out of this forest), Kâdamb. I, 21 क्षितिपतिरास्थानमण्डपादुत्तस्थौ (the king got up from his hall of audience), Panc. p. 42 स्वसखीं ग्रामादभ्यागताम् (— returning from the village), Kathâs. 29, 179 वल्लभीतः समागता, Çâk. I स्थानादनुच्चलन् (without moving from

---

1) In the dual the same form discharges even the functions of three: abl., instr. and dative. As we cannot doubt, that -*bhyâm* and -*bhyas* contain the same element -*bhi*, which is in the suffix -*bhis* and Greek -φι, it is, upon the neuter territory of the instrumental, that the two contrarious conceptions of abl. and dat. must have met together.

2) Pânini, in his lively way, gives this definition of the sphere of the ablative: ध्रुवमपाये ऽपादानम् »if there be a withdrawal, that which stays is *apâdâna*."

the place), ibid. III न च निम्नादिव सलिलं निवर्तते मे ततो हृदयम् (and my heart does not come back from thence as little as water from below), Kathâs. 72, 175 निरगान्नगर्याः, Daç. 29 आन्दोलिकाया अवतीर्य (descending from the swing).

95. *b.*) in its manifold applications to kindred conceptions. Of the kind are:

1. *to see, hear, speak* etc. *from* a spot. R. 2, 7, 2 अयोध्यां मन्थरा तस्मात्प्रासादादन्ववैक्षत (Mantharâ let go her looks over Ay. from the platform) [1]).

2. *to fall from, to waver from, to swerve from etc.* यूथाद्भ्रष्टः »a beast that has swerved from its flock". Var. Brh. 9, 44 पतति न सलिलं खात् (no water falls down from heaven). So often with metaphor. Ch. Up. 4, 4, 5 न सत्यादगाः (you have not swerved from the truth), Kathâs. 25, 179 निश्चयान्न चचाल सः (v. a. he did not give up his purpose), Mudr. III, p. 126 चाणक्यतः स्खलितभक्तिमहं सुखेन जेष्यामि मौर्यम् (I will easily vanquish the Maurya, for he has withdrawn his affection from C.). Compare the Latin *causa cadere.*

3. *to take, to receive from.* M. 4, 252 गृह्णीयात्साधुतः सदा (he never must accept but from an honest man), Panc. 48 क्षुरभाण्डात्क्षुरमेकं समाकृष्य (he took a razor from his box), ibid. 286 कुतोऽपि धनिकात्किंचिद् द्रव्यमादाय (— raised some money from a money-lender), Kathâs. 29, 47 मया चैतान्यवाप्तानि तातात्. Likewise *to marry from:* Kathâs. 24, 152 न ह्यहं परिणेष्यामि कुलाद्यादृशतादृशात्.

4. *to get information -, to hear -, to learn from.* P. 1, 4, 29. Panc. 216 स्वजनेभ्यः सुतविनाशं श्रुत्वा, Daç. 68 कुतश्चित्संलपतो जनसमाजादुपलभ्य (— learnt from a group of conversing people), Ch. Up. 1, 8, 7 हन्ताहमेतद्भगवत्तो वेदानि (well, let me know this from the Reverend) [2]).

5. *to ask, to wish from.* Kathâs. 25, 137 केनाम्भो याचितं भूपात् (who has asked the king for some water?), Kâm. 1, 41 लुब्धकाद्गीतलोभेन मृगो मृगयते वधम् (by its eagerness for music the deer seeks

---

1) See vârtt. 1 and 2 on P. 2, 3, 28 in Pat. I, p. 455.

2) The commentaries explain the rule of Pâṇ. 1, 4, 29, so as to make an artificial distinction between the constructions with gen. and with abl., not thought of by Pâṇini himself.

death from the hunter), Mhbh. 1, 159, 17 याचमानाः परादन्नं परिधावेमहि श्ववत्.

6. the so called partitive ablative, see **116** R. 1.

NB. In the cases 3—6 the genitive is the concurrent idiom, with those of *asking* also the accus. (**46**).

96. *Ablative of separation.* The ablative also attends words of *separation* and *disjoining* to denote from whence there is a withdrawal, as Kathâs. 72, 13 भवद्भ्यो वियोजितः (separated from you). As we have shown above (**62**), the instrumental is here the concurrent idiom.

The following examples may illustrate the various applications of this employment.

a.) *to draw off, to sever; to disagree with.* Panc. 50 संजीवकं प्रभोर्विश्लेषयामि, Mudr. IV p 136 चन्द्रगुप्तादपरक्ताः सन्तः (being disinclined to C.) — b.) *to release of.* Panc. 45 तां बन्धनाद्विमुच्य, Mahâv. I, p. 9 सेयमद्य तस्मादेनसो निरमुच्यत (she has now been released from that sin), — c.) *to deprive of.* R. 2, 8, 25 असावत्यन्तनिर्भग्नस्तव पुत्रो भविष्यति सुखेभ्यश्च राजवंशाच्च (he will be wholly spoliated [lit. disinherited], your son, of enjoyments, yea, of all connection with the royal family), M. 5, 161 सा.... पतिलोकाच्च हीयते, Panc. II, 117 स्वर्गाद्भ्रश्यते (he forfeits heaven), cp. **95**, **2**., — d.) those of *desisting from, stopping, ceasing.* Kumâr. 3, 58 योगादुपरराम (he desisted from his exertions), Daç. 132 विरम कर्मणो ऽस्मान्मलीमसात्, Kumâr. 5, 73 निवर्तयास्मादसदीप्सितान्मनः (turn away your mind from this bad design).

Rem. 1. Note वञ्चयति (to cheat of) [1]) with abl. Kathâs. 42, 75 अहं सुतप्राप्तेः सपत्न्या वञ्चितैतया (she, my fellow-consort, has by trickery taken away my obtaining a son), Panc. III, 117 वञ्चयितुं ब्राह्मणं छागलात् (to cheat a brahman of his he-goat).

Rem. 2. With प्रमाद्यति and the like, the thing *neglected* is put in the ablat. (vârtt. on P. 1, 4, 24). Taitt. Up. 1, 11, 2 स्वाध्यायान्मा प्रमदः, Pat. I, p. 326 धर्मात्प्रमाद्यति, धर्मान्मुह्यति (he neglects his duty).

---

1) Literally »to cause to tumble out of," for वञ्च् वच् (cp. वक्र) is akin to lat. *văcillare*, germ. *wanken*, dutch *waggelen*.

97. Likewise the ablative joins verbs or verbal nouns of *keeping off*, and kindred notions. Of the kind are:

with verbs of keeping off

1. those of *restraining*, *preventing*, *excluding from*, as माषेभ्यो गा वारयति (he keeps the cows from the beans); 2. those of *protecting*, *guarding*, *securing from*, as चौरेभ्यो रक्षति (he protects from thieves); 3. those of *being afraid of* and *suspecting*, especially भी and उद्विज्, f. i. चौरेभ्यो बिभेति. Examples: 1. — Kâm. 16, 15 वृथा कोलाहलाडास्याद् द्यूतात्पानाच्च वारितः, Mahâv. I, p. 10 मातामहेन प्रतिषिध्यमानः स्वयंग्रहात् (as his mother's father prevented him from taking her [viz. Sîtâ] by violence). 2. — Panc. 298 त्वया पुत्रो ऽयं नकुलाद्रक्षणीयः, Mhbh. 1, 82, 21 अधर्मात्पाहि मां राजन्, Mâlav. V, p. 135 इमां परीप्सुर्दुर्जातेः (eager for defending her from the wicked [aggressor]). 3. — Panc. 179 लुब्धकाद् बिभेषि (you are afraid of the huntsman), Mudr. III, p. 102 भेतव्यं नृपतेस्ततः सचिवतो राज्ञस्ततो वल्लभादन्येभ्यश्च ([a king's servant] must not stand in awe of his master only, but of the king's minister, of the king's favourite and of others), M. 2, 162 संमानाद् ब्राह्मणो नित्यमुद्विजेत विषादिव (a brahman should always shun marks of honour, as if they were poison), Mhbh. 1, 140, 61 अशङ्कितेभ्यः शङ्केत शङ्कितेभ्यश्च सर्वशः (he should mistrust those, who are worth mistrusting and those, who are not so), Kâç. on 1, 4, 28 उपाध्यायादन्तर्धत्ते (he conceals himself from his teacher).

being afraid off

P. 1, 4, 27. P. 1, 4, 25. P. 1, 4, 25; 28.

NB. The verbs, mentioned sub 3., admit also of the genitive, see 126 *c*).

Rem. Note जुगुप्सते (to shrink from, to shun, to despise) with abl. according to a vârtt. on P. 1, 4, 24. Instances are met with in the archaic literature. In modern Sanskrit it seems to be exclusively construed with accus. — The verb निर्विद्यते (to be disgusted with) is construed with abl. or instr., sometimes even with acc. and gen.

98 II. The point from whence a distance is counted (*terminus a quo*), is expressed by the ablative. Pat. I, p. 455

Ablative, the terminus a quo.

गवीधूमतः सांकाश्यं चत्वारि योजनानि (from Gavîdhûma to Sânkâçya four *yojanas*). Hence the ablative joins *a.*) such prepp. as आ, प्रभृति, etc., *b.*) the names of the cardinal points and those in °अस्, as प्राक् *c.*), all words meaning *far*, as दूरे and the like.

Examples: — of *a.*) see in chapter IX.

b.) Daç. 156 तीर्थस्थानात्प्राच्यां दिशि (east from the *tîrth*), Pat. I, p. 475 see Rem. 1. on this paragraph.

P. 2, 3, 29.

c.) Mṛcch. VII, p. 234 अहो नगरात्सुदूरमपक्रान्तो ऽस्मि, Mhbh. 1, 152, 1 अविदूरे वनात्तस्मात्, ibid. 1, 151, 44 नातिदूरेण..... वनादस्मात्, Âpast. 1, 31, 2 आराद्वसथान्मूत्रपुरीषे कुर्यात् (he shall void excrements far from his house).

Rem. 1. With derived adverbs of the species दक्षिणातः, उत्तरतः[1]) the genitive should be employed, not the ablative [P. 2, 3, 30], with those in °एन the accusative [ibid. 31]. Hence it is said for ex. R. 3, 4, 27 प्रवभ्रमखनंत्पार्श्वतस्तस्य (he dug a hole by his side), Pat. I, p. 475 कः पुनरार्यवर्तः। प्रागादर्शात्प्रत्यक्कालकवनाद्दक्षिणेन हिमवन्तमुत्तरेण पारियात्रम् (what is Âryavarta? The country east of Âdarça, west of Kâlakavana, south of the Himavat and north of Pâriyâtra), Çâk. I दक्षिणेन वृक्षवाटिकमालाप इव श्रूयते. — But the genitive with those in °एन is also allowed [see Kâç. on P. 2, 3, 31], as R. 3, 13, 21 उत्तरेणास्य (north of this place).

Rem. 2. Pâṇini [2, 3, 34] allows optional construing with abl. or gen. all words, meaning *far* and *near*, दूरं ग्रामात् or ग्रामस्य। अन्तिकं ग्रामात् or ग्रामस्य. As far as I have observed, an ablative with those of

---

1) P. षष्ठ्यतसर्थप्रत्ययेन. — Kâç. gives as instances also पुरस्तात्, उपरि, उपरिष्टात् That on the other hand the abl. is available, even if the adverb itself have the ending of that case, is exemplified by this çloka quoted by Pat. I, 457.

दूरादावसथान्मूत्रं दूरात्पादावसेचनम्
दूराच्च भाव्यं दस्युभ्यो दूराच्च कुपिताद्गुरोः

nearness — except compounds of दूर — will be scarcely met with in literature.

99. When d e n o t i n g t i m e, the ablative carries the meaning of *from*, *since*, *after*. Commonly it is attended by prepositions, as आ, प्रभृति, ऊर्ध्वम्, अनन्तरम्, but there are instances enough of the single ablative. So मुहूर्तात्, क्षणात् (after a while) = मुहूर्तेन, क्षणेन. Likewise चिरात्, अचिरात्, दीर्घकालात्, etc. and cp. **128**. — Kâç. on P. 2, 3, 54 quotes the verse एति जीवन्तमानन्दो नरं वर्षशतादपि (even after hundred years a man may enjoy happiness); Mhbh. 1, 170, 3 ते त्वगच्छन्नहोरात्रात्तीर्थम्, M. 8, 108 यस्य दृश्येत सप्ताहादुक्तवाक्यस्य साक्षिणः । रोगः (if a witness, who has borne evidence, fall ill after a week).

Rem. 1. This kind of abl. is meant by P. 2, 3, 7, when he enjoins the use of a fifth or seventh case to denote an interval of time or space, f. ex. अद्य भुक्त्वा देवदत्तो द्व्यहे द्व्यहाद्वा भोक्ता (D. has eaten now and will not eat but after two days), इहस्थोऽयमिष्वासः क्रोशे (or क्रोशात्) लक्ष्यं विध्यति. Cp. **144**.

Rem. 2. Âpast. 1, 9, 6 and 1, 15, 19 are instances of the single ablative = आ + abl., when signifying »till."

100. Ablative of the origin and the former state. III. The ablative serves to express *from what origin* there is a rising or issuing. In the first place it joins words of being *born*, *proceeding* etc.;

2ly it denotes the *former state or shape*, *out of which* some other state or shape proceeds or is produced;

3ly it signifies the *model* or *pattern*, something is imitated, borrowed, measured from.

Examples: of 1. — Ch. Up. 1, 9, 1 सर्वाणि ह वा इमानि भूतान्याकाशादेव समुत्पद्यन्ते (all these things proceed from ether alone), M. 1, 8 शरीरात्स्वात्सिसृक्षुर्विविधाः प्रजाः (desiring to create the manifold beings out of his body), Kathâs. 25, 43 वाताहताच्च जलधेरुदतिष्ठन्महोर्मयः (big waves rose from the ocean, as it was swept by the wind); Mhbh. 1, 115, 5 पाण्डोः शप्तस्य समुत्पन्ना दैवतेभ्यः पुत्राः पञ्च — here the name *Pâṇḍu* is

P. 1, 4, 30; 31.

put in the genit., for the five sons did belong to him, but the *deities*, who had *procreated* them, are put in the ablative.

So often with verbs of *being born* the name of the father is put in the abl., that of the mother in the locative, R. 2, 107, 2 जातः पुत्रो दशरथात्कैकेय्याम्, M. 10, 64 शूद्रायां ब्राह्मणाज्जातः. Yet, the father may also be a gen. commodi (**132**) or an instrumental.

Note such phrases as (Pat. I, 455) कुतो भवान्। पाटलिपुत्रात् and (Kathâs. 25, 55) ब्राह्मणः शक्तिदेवाख्यो वर्धमानपुरादहम् (I am the brahman Çaktideva from the town of Vardhamâna).

2. — Mhbh. I, (Paushyap.) स समावृत्तस्तस्माद्गुरुकुलवासाद्गृहाश्रमं प्रत्यपद्यत, Daç. 141 जनयितापि मे नरकादिव स्वर्गं तादृशाद् व्यसनात्तथाभूतमभ्युदयमारूढः (and my father, who had come from such a distress to as great a happiness, as if he had risen from hell to heaven), Ratn. I, p. 16 उत्सवादुत्सवान्तरमापतितम् (v. a. we have festival after festival). — So *to heal* or *recover from* illness: Panc. V, 91 त्रयोऽप्यन्यायतः सिद्धाः (all three of them were healed from their infirmity).

3. — Mrcch. IV, p. 135 अयं तव शरीरस्य प्रमाणादिव निर्मित अलङ्कारः (this ornament has been made, as if it were, according to the measure of your body), Mâlav. IV p. 91 विभवतः परिवारः (attendance according to her rank). Cp. **69**.

101 In short, the ablative is available in any case, it is wanted to express the *side*, something has come *from*, whether contained in the foresaid categories or not. So R. 2, 26, 31 सा] त्वत्तः संमानमर्हति (she deserves respect from your side), Mhbh. 1, 145, 9 तान्राज्यं पितृतः प्राप्तान्धृतराष्ट्रो न मृष्यते (Dhr. cannot bear them having obtained the royalty because of their father), Panc. 262 सर्प आह। कस्मात्ते परिभवः। स आह। दायादेभ्यः (from the side of my kinsmen).

Rem. The last example is at the same time an instance of the abl. which denotes him, by whom one is defeated or overthrown [P. 1, 4, 26]; cp. Kathâs. 28, 49.

102. Hence, the *cause*, *reason*, *motive by which*, is likewise expressed by the ablative namely as far as it is con-

Ablative of causality.

ceived as the origin or starting-point, from whence some consequence has resulted [1]).

The instrumental, as we have seen formerly (**72**), may likewise serve that purpose, and in the case of feminine nouns of quality it is even obligatory. For the rest, ablative and in tr. of causality are generally interchangeable, and not seldom they are used side by side. So Kathâs. 29, 25 हर्षेण नश्नास्याः नुन्न रोगतः (it is from joy she does not eat, not from illness), Mṛcch. I, p. 44 अन्यजनशङ्कया खल्विदमनुष्ठितं न दर्पात् (surely, it has been done by taking her for somebody else, not by insolence). But, if the efficient cause be some *obligation* or other binding motive *by virtue of which* some effect is produced, the ablative alone is to be used [2]). Nothing impedes concrete nouns to be put in the *abl. of cause* [3])

---

1) How easily this transition is made, will be plain by this example: Mâlav. V, p. 140 वीरसूरिति शब्दो ऽयं तनयात्त्वामुपस्थितः. Literally these words signify »the name of mother of a hero" touches you *from the part of* your son," but as to their meaning they should be rather translated thus »now you deserve the name »m. of a h." *because of* your son." In other terms the abl. of origin is at the same time an abl. of cause.

2) Pâṇini's rule, which contains this statement, is too narrowly interpreted by the commentaries. His words अकर्तर्यृणे पञ्चमी [P. 2, 3, 24] are explained thus: the abl. [alone] is to be used, if the cause be a *debt*, provided it be not at the same time the agent; examples of which are adduced as शताद्बद्धः (he is confined for a debt of 100), whereas one must say शतेन बन्धितः. But why should we restrict *ṛṇa* to its special sense of a »debt of money" and not take the more general meaning of »obligation" and »duty"? If it could be proved that ऋण implies also the notion of *necessity*, ἀνάγκη, the rule would be quite correct, for in the case of direct and unavoidable consequence of an efficient cause the ablative alone is to be used, even of feminine words.

3) Speaking plain, neither the ablat. of bhâvavacanâni nor that of concrete nouns is allowed by Pânini's rules. The sûtras 2, 3, 23 –25 name

but often they are expressed by periphrase, especially by means of हेतोः (**192**).

Examples. — Kathâs. 27, 76 दिव्याः पतन्त्येव शापान्मानुषयोनिषु (by consequence of a curse celestial beings are borne among men), Panc. 202 कपिञ्जलः शालिभक्षणादतीव पीवरतनुः, Panc. 49 स्त्रीधर्षणाद्वध्यः (he is to be put to death for having insulted a woman), Hit. 96 भयादिदमाह (from fear he spoke thus), Veṇ. II, p. 39 अयं....प्रीतोऽभिमन्योर्वधात् (he is glad on account of Abh.'s death), Mṛcch. I, p. 45 उत्तिष्ठामि समयतः (I will stand up, on condition —), Kathâs. 30, 112 नाज्ञायत यदा चौरस्तदा ज्ञानिप्रसिद्धितः। आनाययामास नृपो हरिशर्माणमाशु तम् (as the thief was not found, the king sent forthwith for H. on account of the reputation of his knowledge), Panc. I, 180 दुर्मन्त्रान्नृपतिर्विनश्यति यतिः सङ्गात्सुतो लालनात्। विप्रोऽनध्ययनात्कुलं कुतनयात् (by bad counsel a prince comes to ruin, a holy man by wordliness, a son by spoiling, a brahman by not-studying, a family by a bad son), Çâk. I, vs. 22 वयं तत्त्वान्वेषान्मधुकर हताः (to seek after the truth [liter. by seeking —], it is I, who have been annoyed by the bee). The examples have been selected so as to show, that the different shades of the notion of causality — *cause*, *motive*, *reason* — are promiscuously signified by the ablative.

Many ablatives of causality have assumed the character of adverbs, see **104**.

103. *Ablative expressive of the side, on which.* IV. Sanskrit, just as Latin, uses the ablative not only for the sake of signifying *from what side*, but also *on what side*. Here the ending °तः is employed, it seems,

---

the instrumental as the regular case to denote cause or motive, but with these exceptions, 1° that if the cause be a quality (गुणे) the ablative *may* be used too, but for feminines [or rather — as the term स्त्री is an ambiguous one — only such as have been made by the fem. endings °ई, °आ], 2° that the cause being an *ṛṇa*, the abl. *must* be used, and not the instrum. Now, these rules do not leave any room for neither bhâvavacanâni nor concrete nouns, something very strange, because really both classes of words are put in the ablative of cause as often and as well as the guṇavacanâni. See the examples adduced in the context.

by preference, at least in the case of indicating space and direction. So it is said दक्षिणतः (at the right), वामतः (at the left), पार्श्वतः (at the side), पृष्ठतः (at the back) etc. — In figurative sense this abl. is likewise used, as Ch. Up. 4, 17, 4 यद्यृक्तो रिष्येत्.... यदि यजुष्टः.... यदि सामतः (if [the yajña] would be vicious on account of an ṛc, a yajus, a sâma), Âpast. 1, 1, 15 स हि विद्यातस्तं जनयति (v. a. for he is his spiritual father), Mâlav. I, p. 25 मध्यस्था भगवती नौ गुणदोषतः परिच्छेत्तुमर्हति (Your Reverence is even-handed; be you, then, the umpire to judge us with respect to our qualities and our shortcomings).

Vârtt. on P. 5, 4, 44.

In its metaphorical application this *ablativus partis* not rarely touches upon the *abl. causae*, treated in **102.** So f. i. with the *points of comparison*, as R. 2, 34, 9 गाम्भीर्यात्सागरोपमः (in depth like the ocean = »by its depth" or »as to its depth").

104. Ablatives of the cause and of the side often have the the characterofad verbs (**77**); especially when ending in °तः. So स्वभावात् or °वतः (by disposition), अनुलोमतः (in due order), प्रतिलोमतः (in inverse order), स्ववीर्यतः (through one's own exertion), शक्तितः (with all one's power), आदरात् (out of respect), अकस्मात् (without motive; on a sudden), and so on. P. 2, 3, 33 gives a special rule for the ablatives कृच्छ्रात्, स्तोकात्, कतिपयात्, अल्पात् being interchangeable with the instr. कृच्छ्रेण etc.; both sets have the character of adverbs, as अल्पेन or अल्पान्मुक्तः (he was released easily).

Rem. Note दूरात् in comparisons = »by far." Panc. II, 170 दूराद्वरम् (by far better).

105. **Ablative of comparison.** — The ablative expressive of the notion *on what side, with respect to* — is frequently applied in comparisons to signify the thing compared with, provided there be superiority or inferiority or discrepancy [1]).

Ablative of comparison.

It joins 1st comparatives; then the abl. = our „than."

1) For in the case of identity, likeness, equivalence the instrum. or gen. is required (**62**) and the dat. also in the case of counterpoise (**85**).

Panc. 56 नास्त्यन्यो धन्यतरो लोके मत्तस्त्वत्तश्च (there is no happier man in the world than you and I), cp. Lat. *nemo te felicior*;

2ly positives of any adjective. Daç. 141 भगवतो मघवतो ऽपि भाग्यवन्तमात्मानमज्ञीगणत् (he considered himself fortunate, even in comparison with Lord Indra);

3ly words, expressing superiority or inferiority, such as वरम् (lit. „the better thing," = better than), अधिक (exceeding), पूर्व (superior), अतिरिच्यते (to excel), परिहीयते (to be inferior), sim. Mudr. I, p. 53 सेनाशतेभ्यो ऽधिका बुद्धिर्मम (my mind is outweighing hundreds of armies);

4ly all words, meaning *other* or *different*, as अन्य, इतर, अपर, भिन्न Panc. 208 षाड्गुण्यादपरो ऽभिप्रायो ऽस्ति (there is some other contrivance, besides the well-known six expedients).

Here are some more examples. Of 1. — Ṛgv. 8, 24, 20 वचो घृतात्स्वादीयो मधुनश्च (utterance by voice being sweeter, than ghee and honey); Ch. Up. 3, 14, 3 एष म आत्मान्तर्हृदये ऽणीयान्व्रीहेर्वा यवाद्वा सर्षपाद्वा श्यामाकाद्वा श्यामाकतण्डुलाद्वा। एष म आत्मान्तर्हृदये ज्यायान्पृथिव्या ज्यायानन्तरिक्षाज्ज्यायान्दिवो ज्यायानेभ्यो लोकेभ्यः (he is the Self within my heart, smaller than a corn of rice, smaller than a corn of barley, smaller than a mustard seed, smaller than a canary seed or the kernel of a canary seed. He is the self etc., greater than the earth, greater than the sky, greater than heaven, greater than these worlds); Âpast. 1, 13, 19 एतेन ह्यहं योगेन भूयः पूर्वस्मात्कालाच्छ्रुतमकरवम् (by this way I have got more learning, than formerly).

of 2. — Panc. 285 भार्या सर्वलोकादपि वल्लभा भवति (v. a. one's wife is beloved more than anybody else); Hit. 16 त्वत्तो नास्तीह पुण्यवान् (compared with him nobody is happy here); Utt. II, p. 29 वज्रादपि कठोराणि मृदूनि कुसुमादपि। लोकोत्तराणां चेतांसि को नु विज्ञातुमर्हति॥

of 3. — R. 2, sarga 95*, 53, एकाङ्गहीनं क्षस्त्रेण जीवितं मरणाद्वरम् (to live, deprived of one member by your weapon, is better than death), Panc. 142 त्वत्तोऽधिकः परमं सुहृत्, Mhbh. 1, 89, 2 पूर्वो वयसा भवत्तः (your superior by age), R. 2, 8, 18 कौसल्यातो ऽतिरिक्तं च मम शुश्रूषते बहु (he listens much to me, and more than to the Kausalyâ), Kathâs. 53, 10 लक्षादूनं न दातुं स जानाति स्म किलार्थिने (indeed, he did not know how to give less than a *laxa* to an indigent), M. 2, 95 प्रापणात्सर्वकामानां परित्यागो विशिष्यते (giving up all desires exceeds obtaining them). Compare this instance from the archaic literature: Ait. Br. 7, 17, 4 गवां त्रीणि शतानि त्वमवृणीथा मत् (you have chosen three hundred of cows instead of me).

of 4. — Rgv. 10, 18, 1 पन्था] इतरो देवयानात् (the other path, which is not the path of the gods), Ch. Up. 1, 10, 2 नेतो [= न + इतो] ऽन्ये विद्यन्ते (nor are there others but these), Panc. II, 12 साहाय्यं मित्रादन्यो न संदधे, Prabodh. III, p. 61 जगन्मिथो भिन्नमभिन्नमीश्वरात् (the creatures so different among themselves, yet not different from God).

106. Observations on the abl. of comparison.

Rem. 1. Our »than" with the comparative is to be rendered in Sanskrit by the ablative. Such restrictions, as for instance limit the faculty of using the abl. of comparison in Latin, do not exist in Sanskrit. It is impossible to say in Latin *dat tibi plus me* = »he gives to you more than to me," but it must be said *plus quam mihi*. In Sanskrit nothing impedes such sentences as तुभ्यं ददाति मत्त अधिकम्. So Mâlat. X, p. 164 स्नेहो मातुर्मयि समधिकस्तेन युक्तस्त्वयापि (hence, you must bear more affection towards me, than towards your own mother).

Rem. 2. Note the abl. with such words as: double, treble etc. sim. M. 8, 289 मूल्यात्पञ्चगुणो दण्डः (a fine of five times the value).

Rem. 3. If it is to be said *no other than*, *nobody but*, any phrase with the meaning »but for" may be used instead of the abl. Panc. 176 त्वां मुक्त्वान्यो न ज्ञास्यति (no other but you will know it), ibid. 160 त्वद्वर्जमन्यो भर्ता मनस्यपि मे न भविष्यति॥ — Then, the ablative may also be used even without अन्य, as Kumâras. 6, 44 यस्मिन्नान्तकः

कुसुमायुधात् »where there is found no [other] death but the god with the flowery arrows [no other Mâra but Mâra = Kâma]."

In Patanjali I have met with some instances of a rather pleonastic idiom, the neuter अन्यद् with abl. = »but for" put before the ablat., though the adj. अन्य precedes, f. i. Pat. I, 279 को ऽन्यो द्वितीयः सहायो भवितुमर्हत्यन्यदत उपसर्गात् (what else ought to accompany it, if not this preposition), cp. p. 445, line 2; p. 447, line 4; p. 323, line 6. This adverbial use of अन्यद् (cp. Greek ἀλλά, and such phrases as οὐδὲν ἄλλο.... ἀλλ' ἤ) is confirmed by its being named among the nipâtâs in the gaṇa स्वरादि (Kâç. I, p. 17, line 10).

Rem. 4. Çâk. VII मघवतः सत्क्रियाविशेषादनुपयुक्तमिवात्मानं समर्थये (I do not hold myself for deserving the extraordinary honour bestowed upon me by Indra) is an instance of this abl. with the negative अनुपयुक्त (not fit); the abl. would be impossible here, but for the negation.

107. Instrumental of comparison.

In the archaic and epic dialect an **instrumental** of comparison is sometimes used instead of the ablative. — So R. 2, 26, 33 प्राणैः प्रियतरौ मम instead of प्राणेभ्यः, ibid. 2, 48, 36 सुतैर्हि तासामधिको ऽपि सो-ऽभवत् (he was to these women even more than their own sons), comm. सुतैः। तृतीयार्थे, ib. 1, 54, 15 न त्वया बलवत्तरः। विश्वामित्रः

Genitive of comparison.

Rem. Such passages as R. 6, 24, 28 इष्वस्त्रे ऽप्यधिको राज्ञः कार्तवीर्यस्य लक्ष्मणः (and in archery L. even exceeds king K.), Panc. 28 [and R. 1, 47, 22] नास्ति धन्यतरो मम, Panc. IV, 7 काचिन्ममैवापरा (any woman else but I) show that even a *genitive* of comparison has been used.

108. The ablatives in °तः

In the foregoing the ending तः has been considered as if it possessed the full worth of the regular case-endings of the ablative. Yet a full and complete identity between them may alone be stated for the pronouns. Pâṇini gives some rules about °तः affixed to nouns, which show that its sphere of employment, though mostly coinciding with that of the ablative, is sometimes a different one. (P. 5, 3, 7.)

1ly With हीयते and रुह् it is forbidden to express the »whence" by the forms in °तः. Therefore स्वर्गाद्धीयते। पर्वतादवरोहति, not स्वर्गतो हीयते, पर्वततो ऽवरोहति· P. 5, 4, 45.

2ly Excelling or being weak *in*, blaming *on account of*, wickedness *with respect to* is to be denoted by the instrumental, or by °तः, not by the ablative proper. — For this reason, in the verse quoted by Pat. I, p. 2 दुष्टः शब्दः स्वरतो वर्णतो वा (a word, wrong on account of its accent or of its sound), स्वरतः and वर्णतः are interchangeable with स्वरेण and वर्णेन, not with स्वरात् and वर्णात्. Likewise, in Ch. Up. 4, 17, 4 — quoted page 77 of this book — ऋक्तः। यजुष्टः। सामतः are synonymous with the instrum., and the abl. ऋचः। यजुषः। साम्नः would not be allowed. P. 5, 4, 46; 47.

Rem. It should however be remembered, that this rule does not apply neither to the points of comparison — f. i. गाम्भीर्यात्सागरोपमः — nor to the ablative of comparison.

3ly If the ablative is to express the »*whence*" — except in the case recorded sub 1 — तः is equivalent with the regular case-endings. The same applies to the abl., depending on the prepos. प्रति. P. 5, 4, 45. P. 5, 4, 44.

Rem. Pânini does not give any rule about using the abl. in तः with such adverbs and pronouns as ऋते, विना, अन्य. Now, ablatives of that kind are certainly not expressing the *apâdâna*, as they are taught in the third chapter of the 2d adhyâya, not in the fourth of the 1st. Accordingly it would not be allowed using °तः with them. Yet practice is not wholly consistent therewith, f. i. आ मूलतः = आ मूलात्.

4ly In two cases °तः is interchangeable with a genitive, but not with an abl. *a.*) when expressing the standing *on one's side* देवा अर्जुनतो (or अर्जुनस्य) ऽभवन्, *b.*) if denoting the *disease*, *against which* one applies some remedy or cure: प्रवाहिकातः [or °कायाः] कुरु (give something against diarrhoea). P. 5, 4, 48. P. 5, 4, 49.

Chapter VII. **Genitive.** [1]

109. The fundamental notion of the genitive or sixth

1) On the genitive in Sanskrit, especially in the dialect of the Ṛg-vedamantras, there exists a monography of Dr. Siecke *de genitivo in lingua Sanscritica imprimis Vedica usu*, Berlin, 1869.

General view of the genitive.

case is to mark the *belonging to*, *partaking of*. In Sanskrit, it is employed in so manifold and so different ways as to make it very difficult to give a satisfactory account of all of them [1]). — The absolute genitive will be treated in the chapter on participles.

110. Its employment with substantives.

I. With **substantives**, the genitive serves to qualify them, as राज्ञः पुरुषः (the king's man), दमयन्त्याः स्वयंवरः (the self-choice of Dam.), शत्रोर्बलम् (the enemy's strength), मित्रस्यागमनम् (the friend's arrival), समुद्रस्य शोषणम् (the drying up the ocean), यज्ञस्यावयवः (a part of the sacrifice), युद्धस्यावकाशः (the opportunity of fighting). These examples show 1st that the genitive, at least in prose, commonly precedes the substantive, it is depending upon, 2ly that, like in Latin and Greek,

1) Kâç. on P. 1, 1, 49 बहवो हि षष्ठ्यर्थाः स्वस्वाम्यनन्तरसमीपसमूहविकारावयवाद्याः. — Pânini seems to have not sharply defined the genitive's sphere of employment, at least if we explain his sûtra (2, 3, 50) षष्ठी शेषे with the Kâç. as meaning »*in all other instances* [namely if none of the other cases, taught 2, 3, 1—49, be available], one should use the sixth case." But then it is strange, P. has not said inversely शेषे षष्ठी (cp. his constant use 1, 4, 7; 1, 4, 108; 2, 2, 23; 3, 3, 151; 7, 2, 90). Now, Patanjali gives a somewhat different explication (I, p. 463) कर्मादीनामविवक्षा शेषः »the sixth case is required, if the categories object and the rest are not to be distinctly expressed" but tacitly implied. I am rather inclined to suppose, that *either* in framing that sûtra Pâṇini had in view his definition of the employment of the nominative, which immediately precedes; then शेषे would be said in opposition to the प्रातिपदिक ...... मात्रे of s. 46 (note on **38**) and mean »something else, apart from the gender and number of the conception, signified by the prâtipadika", *or* शेषे may mean »accessory" (see Petr. Dict. *s. v.* 1, *b*); then the sûtra enjoins the use of the genitive if the conception, signified by the prâtipadika, is accessory of some other conception. But, which of these acceptations should prove the correct one, the intrusion of the term शेषे in the following sûtras (51, etc), as is done by Kâç. and others, is to be blamed.

the most different *logical* relations will find their expression by it. When dividing the whole of its dominion by setting up such categories as the *possessive* gen., the *subjective*, *objective*, *partitive*, that of *origin*, *matter*, *quantity* etc., it must not be overlooked, that these divisions have been made for clearness' sake and do not affect the unity of the grammatical duty discharged in all these cases by the genitive. For the rest, not rarely the ordinary logical distinctions may fall short of classifying some given genitive, as in the case of युद्धस्यावकाशः, or Utt. II, p. 28 अगस्त्याश्रमस्य पन्थाः (the way to the hermitage of A.) etc.

Concurrent constructions are 1. compounding the gen. with the subst., it qualifies राजपुरुषः = राज्ञः पुरुषः, see **214**, 2. using instead of the gen. the derived adjective, as शात्रवं बलम् = शत्रोर्बलम् or शत्रूणां बलम् etc. Of these substitutions the latter is comparatively rare, when contrasted with the utmost frequency of the former.

Rem. The so called *appositional* or *epexegetic* genitive is not used in Sanskrit. It is said पुष्पपुरं नगरम्, not as in English »the city *of* Pushp." R. **2**, 115, 15 शिरसि कृत्वा संन्यासं पादुके (Lat. *pignus soccorum*, the pledge [represented by] the slippers).

111. When pointing out the genitive as the case to put in such substantives as are wanted to qualify other substantives, it is by no means said that no other construction may be used for the same purpose Verbal nouns often retain the verbal construction. So, if a moving to or from some place is to be expressed, nouns must be construed just as verbs; it is said पुरात्प्रवासनम्, पुरं गमनम् not पुरस्य. Cp. Rem. on **41**.

Thus we meet with instrumentals as वियोगो भवादृशैः »the separation from men as you are," कन्यया शोकः »sorrow on account of a girl;" — ablatives as पतनाद्भयम् »fear of falling;" — datives as यूपाय दारु »wood for a stake," समयो यौवराज्याय »the fit time for being heir-apparent;" — locatives as विषयेषु सङ्गः »attachment to the world, worldliness;" — prepositions as मां प्रति कोपः »anger towards me," तस्योपरि पक्षपातः »partiality for his sake," समं शक्तिमता युद्धम् »a contention with a mighty one."

Rem. Pâṇini has a special rule about the nouns ईश्वर (lord), स्वामिन् (owner), अधिपति (chief), दायाद (heir), साक्षि (witness), प्रतिभू (bail) and प्रसूत (born) as agreeing with a locative as well as with a gen. So गवां स्वामी or गोषु; cp. Kathâs. 18, 144 त्वमस्माकं स्वामी with ibid. 6, 166 स्वामी विषये. So Mrcch. X, p. 384 पृथिव्यां सर्वविहारेषु कुलपतिरयं क्रियताम् (let he be appointed prior of all the monasteries of the land). P. 2, 3, 39.

112. *Possessive genitive.* The **possessive genitive** has nothing remarkable. As in other languages, it may be the predicate of the sentence. M. 7, 96 यो यज्जयति तस्य तत् (what one conquers, is one's own), ibid. 7, 91 the vanquished warrior surrenders himself with these words तवास्मि (I am yours); Mhbh. I, 154, 3 कस्य त्वम् (»whose are you?" that is »of what family?"); Mudr. III, p. 103 स्थाने खल्वस्य वृषलो देवश्चन्द्रगुप्तः (duly, forsooth, the Çûdra-king Candragupta is his = is but an instrument in his [Câṇakya's] hand), R. 2, 42, 7 (Daçar. to Kaik.) ये च त्वामनुजीवन्ति नाहं तेषां न ते मम (and those, who are your attendance, do not belong to me, nor I to them). That it may also denote the *party*, of which one is an adherent, is stated above (**108**, 4).

113. *Genitivus materiae and originis.* The gen. of the *material*, something is made of, and that of the *origin* are not very frequent. Examples: Pat. I, 112 अस्य सूत्रस्य शाटकं वय (weave a cloth of this thread), Ch. Up. 6, 12, 2 तं होवाच यं वै सौम्यैतमणिमानं न निभालयस एतस्य वै सौम्यैषोऽणिम्न एवं महान्यग्रोधस्तिष्ठति (he said to him: my dear, that subtile essence, which you do not perceive there, of that subtile essence this so great nyagrodha-tree exists); — Mhbh. 1, 100, 47 कन्या दाशानाम् (a fisherman's daughter).

Rem. In sûtra-works there is also a gen. of the authority, according to whom something is stated. So often एकेषाम् »according to some," P. 3, 4, 111 शाकटायनस्यैव »according to Ç. alone." This gen. depends on the word मते not expressed »according to the opinion of."

114. Subjective genitive. The **subjective genitive** is interchangeable with the instrumental of the agent (**66**). According to Pâṇini, the latter is *necessary*, if the verbal noun be attended by its subject and its object at the same time. In this manner two genitives are avoided, as गवां दोहो गोपेन [not गोपस्य] (the milking of the cows by the cow-herd). We may fairly extend this observation, it seems, to all such instances, as where the subjective genitive would be used together with some other sixth case. R. 3, 6, 23 विप्रकारमपाक्रष्टुं राक्षसैर्भवतामिमम् (in order to put and end to the harm caused to you by the râxasas), Mâl. VIII, p. 133 एकाकिनो बहुभिरभियोगः[1]); Mhbh. 1, 145, 17 यदा.... कार्यमस्माकं भवद्भिरुपपत्स्यते (if there will occur something to do by you for us) [not कार्यमस्माकं भवताम्, an accumulation of gen. subj. and commodi];

P. 2, 3 66.

Rem. Some vârttikâs on this sûtra of Pâṇini contest the exactness of it. With some krts the subjective genitive is said to be obligatory, even when being used together with an objective genitive, as चिकीर्षा विष्णुमित्रस्य कटस्य (V.'s desire of making a mat). According to some, the gen. of the agent is nowhere forbidden.

[1]15 [Ob]jec[tiv]e genitive. The **objective genitive** is occasionally interchangeable with a locative or with prepp as प्रति, उपरि, etc. Sometimes it may be used in turns too concise to be rendered without periphrase. Mrcch. I, p. 44 शङ्कया तस्याः (by supposing, it was she).

1) But Mudr. I, p. 49 न मर्षयिष्यति राक्षसकलत्रप्रच्छादनं भवतः, for here nothing impedes using the genitive of the agent, the other being avoided by compounding.

116. Partitive genitive. The **partitive genitive** denotes *either* the whole, a part of which is spoken of, as अर्धं नगरस्य (half of the town), यज्ञस्यावयवः (a part of the sacrifice), Kâd. I, p. 21 अम्बरतलस्य मध्यम् (the middle of the sky) *or* it carries the notion of selecting out of a multitude as Nir. 1, 12 वैयाकरणानामेके „some of —, among the grammarians". In the latter case, the genitive is interchangeable with the locative: मनुष्याणां (or मनुष्येषु) क्षत्रियो शूरतमः

Examples: of genitive Ait. Br. 1, 5, 25 श्रेष्ठः स्वानाम् (the foremost of his kin), Kathâs. 29, 69 धुर्यो धनवताम् (the foremost among the wealthy), Panc. III, 222 स एवैको ऽत्र सर्वेषां नीतिशास्त्रार्थतत्त्ववित्; — of locative Kathâs. 24, 47 दृष्टा पुरी युष्मासु केनचित्; M. 5, 18 श्वाविधं शल्यकं गोधां खड्गकूर्मशशांस्तथा। भक्ष्यान्पञ्चनखेष्वाहुरनुष्ट्रांश्चैकतोदतः

From the examples given it will be plain, that in Sanskrit, as elsewhere, the partitive cases may not only attend substantives, but all kind of nouns and pronouns.

Rem. 1. If there be meant a „taking out of," the *ablative* is to be used, cp. **95**, 2°. — R. 1, 2, 15 क्रौञ्चमिथुनादेकमवधीः (you have killed one out of the couple of plovers), cp. Kathâs. 13, 144; 24, 176; Prabodh. V, p. 102 अग्नेः शेषमृणाच्छेषं शत्रोः शेषं न शेषयेत् (one should not leave a remnant of fire, of a debt, of a foe). 1)

Rem. 2. It is very common, especially in simple prose, to periphrase the partitive cases by °मध्ये (= gen. or loc.) and °मध्यात् (= abl.). See **191**.

Rem. 3. The partitive construction is unfit to be employed, if

---

1) This is the very ablative, enjoined by P. 2, 3, 42. Kâç. is wrong interpreting the sûtra otherwise; Patanjali's view (I, p. 459) is correct.

the conception of a part selected out of a whole be wanting. »All of them" = ते सर्वे both of us" आवामुभौ [1]).

117. Some turns, relating to the partitive construction, are to be noticed:

1. option between two things is variously expressed:

a.) both are put in the gen. M. 7, 53 व्यसनस्य च मृत्योश्च व्यसनं कष्टमुच्यते (liter. »of both vice and death, vice is called the worse").

b.) both are put in the abl. Mṛcch. I, p. 18 दारिद्र्यान्मरणाद्वा मरणं मम रोचते न दारिद्र्यम् (v. a. I prefer death to poverty).

c.) both are nominatives. Mhbh. 1, 161, 6 ब्रह्मवध्यात्मवध्या वा श्रेयानात्मवधो मम (v. a. I hold suicide to be preferable to the killing a brahman).

Note the standing prolixity of such phrases.

2. Of a partitive gen., depending on some word not expressed, there are some instances. Âçv. Gṛhy. 4, 4, 11 आदित्यस्य वा दृश्यमाने प्रविशेयुः (or they must enter [the village] while there is still visible ever so a little part of the sun), Kâç. on P. 2, 1, 8 यावदमत्रं ब्राह्मणानामामन्त्रयस्व (invite of the brahmans according to the number of vessels). The partitive gen., that attends verbs (**119**), may be explained in this way.

3. One, two, three times a day, a week, etc. is expressed by the partitive gen., as M. 3, 281 श्राद्धं त्रिरब्दस्य निर्वपेत्, Pâr. Gṛhy. 1, 3, 31 असकृत्संवत्सरस्य. Likewise M. 5, 21 संवत्सरस्यैकमपि चरेत्कृच्छ्रं द्विजोत्तमः (a pious twice-born man should perform at least one »strong penance" a year). P. 2, 3, 64.

4. A partitive gen., depending on the neuter of an adjective, is rare, even in the old language. Ait. Br. 2, 15, 8 महति रात्र्याः. In the Ṛgvedasanhitâ there are even such gen. as इदा अह्नः, प्रातरह्नः, which remind of Lat. *id temporis* and the like; cp. Siecke p. 65.

118. II. Several verbs are construed with a genitive.

Genitive with verbs.

1. A *possessive genitive* is put to some verbs of *owning* and

1) Yet Mhbh. 1, 37, 8 I have found सर्वे नः = »all of us," just as in English.

ruling, viz. प्रभू, ईश् [P. 2, 3, 52], the vedic राज्. Comp Greek ἄρχειν τινός. — So Ṛgv. 1, 25, 20 त्वं विश्वस्य मेधिर दिवश्च ग्मश्च राजसि; Çat. Br. 5, 1, 5, 4 एकः सन्बहूनामीष्टे. — M. 5, 2 कथं मृत्युः प्रभवति वेदशास्त्रविदाम् (how is it, that Death has power over such as have mastered the veda and the sciences?), Mâlat. II, p. 38 प्रभवति प्रायः कुमारीणां जनयिता दैवं च, cp. ibid. IV, p. 70, l. 2, Mâlav. V, p. 143. — This construction is rare in classic Sanskrit; ईश् with a gen. seems to be wholly obsolete.

119. 2. A *partitive genitive* is frequently employed in the elder literature, and had not yet entirely disappeared in the days of Pâṇini. But in classic Sanskrit such phrases as अमृतस्य ददाति (he gives of the ambrosia), सर्पिषो नाथते (he desires of the butter) are out of use.

In mantra, brâhmaṇa and upanishad it is often attending verbs of *giving*, *begging*, *eating*, *drinking* and the like [1]). Ṛgv. 10, 85, 3 सोमं यं ब्रह्माणो विदुर्न तस्याश्नाति कश्चन (of the soma, the brahmans know, nobody eats), ibid. 9, 70, 2 स भिक्षमाणो अमृतस्य चारुणः (he, begging [a share] of the delightful ambrosia), Ch. Up. 1, 10, 3 एतेषां मे देहि (give me of these), TBr. 2, 2, 9, 3 समुद्रस्य न पिबन्ति (they do not drink of the ocean), Ait. Br. 1, 22, 6 त्रयाणां ह वै हविषां स्विष्टकृते न समवद्यन्ति (of three oblations they do not cut off for the Svishṭakṛt).

Rem. To this belong the rules of P. 2, 3, 61 and 63, which enjoin the genitive of the oblation *a.*) in certain formulae, uttered at the moment of offering it to the deity, *b.*) with यज्. So f. i. Çat. Br. 3, 8, 2, 26 अग्निषोमाभ्यां छागस्य वपायै [gen. = वपायाः **86** NB.] मेदसो ऽनुब्रूहि (announce to Agni and Soma [their shares] of the epiploon and the fat of the he-goat), Ṛgv. 3, 53, 2 सोमस्य त्वा यक्षि (I have worshipped thee [with your share] of soma), Ait. Br. 2, 9, 5.

120. 3. The genitive serves to denote the objects of some verbs: *a*) स्मृ (to remember), *b.*) दय् (to have mercy), *c.*) अनुकृ (to imitate), *d.*) some verbs of *longing for*. With all of them, however, the accusative is also available. P. 2, 3, 52

Examples: *a.*) Mudr. II, p. 71 हा देव नन्द स्मरति ते राक्षसः प्रसादानाम् (ah, king Nanda, Râxasa is well aware of your marks of kindness),

---

1) See SIECKE p. 33—37.

Daç. 60 स्मर तस्या हंसकथायाः. Compare with those genitives these accus. Mâlav. III, p. 63 अपि स्मरेदस्मदभ्यर्थनाम् (should she perhaps remember our suit?), Çâk. V स्मरिष्यति त्वां न स बोधितोऽपि सन्. The verb विस्मृ (to forget) is construed with acc. [1])

b.) Daç. 97 एते भद्रमुखास्तव दयन्ताम् (may these dear men show mercy towards you). It is often construed with acc.

c.) The person whose deeds etc. are imitated is generally put in the genitive. Mrcch. VI, p. 222 भीमस्यानुकरिष्यामि बाहुः शस्त्रं भविष्यति, Mâlav. V, p. 141 ननु कलभेन यूथपतेरनुकृतम् (v. a. the apple falls not far from the tree).

Rem. 1. Comp. अनुवदते (to speak after), which is construed similarly by Kâç. on P. 1, 3, 49, and अनुहरति (to take after). Pat. I, 393 पितुरनुहरति (he takes after his father).

Rem. 2. According to P. 2, 3, 53 compared to 6, 1, 139 उपस्कुरुते (to take care of) may admit of a genitive.

d.) Here the acc. is the regular construction, and the gen. but scarcely met with, as M. 2, 162 अमृतस्येव चाकाङ्क्षेदवमानस्य सर्वदा (he must always long for being insulted as if it were ambrosia), Mhbh. 3, 12630 नाथन्तः सर्वकामानाम्, Mâlat. V, p. 72 अपि भवानुत्कण्ठते मदयन्तिकायाः (do you long for Madayantikâ?); R. 3, 47, 30 gen. with स्पृहयति.

121. 4. In the archaic dialect many more verbs may be construed with the gen. of their object. Pâṇini prescribes its being used with *a*) *all* verbs of remembering [2]); *b*) नाथ् when = »to desire, to hope," cp. 120, *d*; *c*) five verbs of injuring viz. जासयति, नाट्, निप्रहन्, क्रथ्, पिष्, *d*) the verbs of *illness* — fever excepted — as चौरस्य रुजति. As he does not add that the gen. with them is restricted to the holy texts, it is likely, that it was used so in his days, but that it has antiquated afterwards. SIECKE p. 50—52 of his treatise on the vedic genitive has given some examples of its being used in the

P. 2, 3, 55.

P. 2, 3, 56.

---

1) Yet Bhaṭṭ. 17, 10 it complies with a gen., see Petr. Dict. *s. v.* p. 1386. So in a prâkrt passage of the Uttararâmacaritra p. 19 विसुमरिदा अम्हे महाराअदसरहस्स रामभद्देण »Râma has made us forget king Daçaratha."

2) Pâṇini (2, 3, 52) speaks of अधीगर्थ, that is »all, which mean *to think of*." In classic Sanskrit I greatly doubt instances will be found of any other verb but स्मृ.

Rigvedasanhitâ with such verbs as अधी, अधिगा, चित्, मन् etc. With विद् (to know; to be aware of, to experience) it often occurs in the brâhmana-works. Ait. Br. 2, 39, 11 प्राणो वै जातवेदाः स हि जातानां वेद. As to the foresaid verbs of injuring, in the Râmâyana also स्पृश् (to touch) is construed with a gen., 2, 75, 31 गवां स्पृशतु पादेन, likewise 3, 66, 6 [1]).

Rem. According to P. 2, 3, 51 the verb ज्ञा is construed with the gen. of the instrument (*karaṇa*), then ज्ञा must not be equivalent with विद्. Kâç. gives this example सर्पिषो जानीते = सर्पिषा करणेन प्रवर्तते. It is not sufficiently plain, what is here the meaning of ज्ञा [2]).

122. 5. The *wager* with verbs of playing or betting, the *purchase-money* with those of buying and selling is to be put in the gen., according to P. 2, 3, 57—60, thus exemplified by Kâç. शतस्य व्यवहरति or पणते or दीव्यति. Instances of this rule applied in literature if they occur at all, must be scanty. [3]) With the compounds of दिव् the gen. is told to be optional — शतस्य or शतं प्रदीव्यति —, in the brâhmana the simple दिव् is construed with the acc. of the wager, see P. 2, 3, 60 with comm.

---

1) Cp. the Greek τυγχάνειν, θιγγάνειν and sim. For the rest, objective genitives with verbs of *touching*, *desiring*, *remembering* are common to the whole Indo-germanic family and the most probable explication, which may be given of them is to consider them as having had at the outset the character of *partitive* genitives. Their fate has been the same in Sanskrit as in its sister-tongues. In the ancient literature they are relatively common; but gradually they decrease by time both in frequency and in extent, and modern Sanskrit has but retained a few remnants of that old and once widely-spread idiom.

2) So the Kâçikâ. It proffers also a different explication, according to which ज्ञा with gen. = »to ween, to fancy," for मिथ्याज्ञानमज्ञानमेव. Patanjali has not expounded the sûtra. For the rest, as it runs thus ज्ञोऽविदर्थस्य करणे, nothing impedes reading it rather ज्ञो विदर्थस्य करणे. Then it is said just the contrary: ज्ञा when = विद् complies with a gen. and in fact, in the ancient dialect ज्ञा was not rarely construed so.

3) A prâkṛt passage in Mṛcch. II, p. 68 दशसुवण्णाह लुडु जूदकरु [= Skr. दशसुवर्णस्य रुद्धो द्यूतकरः] (this player is detained for 10 *suvarṇas*) may afford an instance of it.

123 6. Verbs of *fulness*, *repletion*, *satisfaction*, as पूरयति, तृप्, तुष् are often construed with a genitive, but more commonly with the instrumental. Cp. Latin *vas plenum vini vel vino* [1]). Examples of the genit. Suçr. 1, 116, 14 वक्त्रमापूर्यते ऽश्रूणाम् (the face is bathed with tears), Panc. I, 148 नाग्निस्तृप्यति काष्ठानां नापगानां महोदधिः। नान्तकः सर्वभूतानाम् (fire gets not satiated of wood, nor the ocean of rivers, nor death of mortal beings).

NB. But the gen. of the *person*, towards whom kindness is shown with तुष्यति, तुष्ट, प्रसीदति and other similar words is of a different kind (**131**). Mhbh. 1, 229, 32 तुतोष तस्य मुनेः (he became well-disposed to this brahman), Panc. 314 तुष्टस्तवाहम् (I am satisfied with you), R. 1, 33, 13 तस्यास्तुष्टो ऽभवद्गुरुः [2]).

Rem. 1. Vedic mantras contain many instances of other similar verbs — as प्री, मद्, कन् etc. — being construed so. Siecke, p. 44 sq.

Rem. 2. With तृप्यति the loc. is also available. Daç. 174 सर्वेष एवान्धस्यतृप्यत (he ate it all).

7. With several verbs the genitive does the duty of an ablative. See **126**.

8. With several verbs the genitive does the duty of a dative. See **131**, **132**.

124. III. A g e n i t i v e w i t h a d j e c t i v e s is frequently used. When attending adjectives akin to transitive verbs, it is an objective gen., as Kathâs. 29, 55 जरा विनाशिन्यस्य रूपस्य (old age, which will destroy this beauty). Among them are to be especially noticed:

Genitive with adjectives.

---

1) Both gen. and instrum. seem to be old idioms. Yet it will seem, that the gen. with words of *fulness* has got out of use nowadays. R. 2, 89, 17 अभिपूर्णा being construed with a gen. — नारीणामभिपूर्णास्तु काश्चित् [sc. नावः] काश्चित्तु वाजिनाम् — the commentary deems it necessary to explain the idiom: नारीभिः पूर्णा इत्यायर्थः. Cp. the similar process in Latin (Quintil. 9, 3, 1).

2) So Kathâs. 27, 206 तुष्टोऽस्मि वाम्; the interpunction in Brockhaus, edition is here wrong.

1. Those of *knowledge*, *skill*, *experience* and the contrary (as अभिज्ञ, अनभिज्ञ, कोविद् and उचित (*wont to*). Mudr. I, p. 34 साधु वत्स अभिज्ञः खल्वसि लोकव्यवहाराणां (bravo, my child, you are well acquainted with the practice of the world), R. 1, 20, 24 संग्रामाणामकोविदः (not skilled in battles); — R. 2, 51, 3 उचितो जनः क्लेशानाम् (people who are accustomed to trouble).

Examples with others: Mudr. IV, p. 146 श्रीः] असहा भरस्य (impatient of the burden), Kâm. 3, 22 गिरं विसृजेत्] ह्लादिनीं सर्वसत्वानाम् (he must speak so as to rejoice all beings).

NB. With the adjectives of *knowledge* and *skill* and with some others the locative is also used (**142**).[1]

P. 2, 3, 40.

2. आयत्त (depending on) and सक्त (clinging to). Panc. 231 त्वदायत्तः स प्रतीकारः (that remedy depends on you), ibid. 277 यत्तवास्य सक्तं किञ्चिद्गृहीतमस्ति तत्समर्पय (give up that, which you have taken belonging to him).

3. पूर्ण (full) and its compounds. See **123**.

4. Those of *likeness* and *equality*. See **61**.

---

1) The Kâçikâ errs interpreting this sûtra so as to take आयुक्त and कुशल, as if they meant *but these two words*, though it is evident, that *two categories* of words are meant by Pâṇini, that of »occupation" (आयुक्त) and that of »skill" (कुशल). The rule given 1, 1, 68 — स्वं रूपं शब्दस्याशब्दसंज्ञा — is commonly interpreted in too narrow a sense. It does not purport that any word occurring in Pâṇini's text, but for a *sanjñâ*, does signify but the word itself, not its synonyms — if this were so, we should have to enregister its violation every moment — but simply this: with the exception of such algebraical signs, as वु = अक, ढ = एय, घ = the suffixes of the grades of comparison, sim., the sounds and words of which the vyâkaraṇa-sûtra is made up, are to be understood such as they are uttered. But it is left to the common sense of the reader to infer in each separate case, whether the word contained in the grammatical rule is meant as to its outer shape or as to its meaning, whether it is to denote but one or a whole class of words of the same purport, as आयुक्त and कुशल evidently do here.

For the rest, the vernacular grammarians themselves are obliged to admit of exceptions on their own interpretation of P. 1, 1, 68. See but the vârtt. on that sûtra.

Rem. Note द्वितीय with gen., when subst. = »the match, the counterpart" Pat. I, 445 अस्य गोर्द्वितीयेनार्थः (an other ox is wanted like this), Kathâs. 25, 178 अहमेवानयाम्यस्य द्वितीयं नूपुरस्य ते (I will fetch you myself the match of this foot-ornament).

5. A great number of adjectives admit of the dative-like genitive, see **129**.

ABLATIVE-LIKE GENITIVE.

125. Ablative-like genitive. IV. Sometimes the genitive is available in such cases as do properly belong to the category of the ablative, if there be at the same time room for the conception of „belonging to" and that of „proceeding from." Of the kind we have already mentioned two instances, viz. 1. the genitive of origin (**113**), 2. that of the starting-point (**98**, R. 1 and 2). The latter is not limited to the cases, mentioned above, but is sometimes used side by side with the ablative even with such nouns as उत्तर, दक्षिण etc., Vishṇup. 2, 3, 1 उत्तरं समुद्रस्य (north of the ocean).

Concurring with the ablative

126. On this account we may understand how the genitive is sometimes used instead of the ablative with *a*) verbs of *asking*, *wishing*, *taking*, *receiving* etc., *b*) of *hearing*, *learning*, *c*) of *being afraid of*.

a). The abl. is here the regular idiom; the gen. not frequent, as Râjat. 1, 131 राज्ञस्तस्य..... व्रजतो विजयेश्वरं।ययाचे काचिदबला भोजनम्, R. 1, 28, 10 प्रतीच्छ मम (accept of me), M. 4, 87 राज्ञः प्रतिगृह्णाति लुब्धस्योच्छास्त्रवर्तिनः (— accepts of a king, who is avaricious and a transgressor of his royal duty), Panc. 225 अहमस्य ब्राह्मणस्य गोयुगमपहरिष्यामि. So already in the archaic dialect. Gaut. 17, 1 प्रशस्तानां स्वकर्मसु द्विजातीनां ब्राह्मणो भुञ्जीत प्रतिगृह्णीयाच्च (a brahman is allowed to eat and to accept presents from twice-born men of good behaviour);

b) R. 6, 31, 2 चाराणां रावणः श्रुत्वा प्राप्तं रामम् (Râvaṇa after having heard from his spies the arrival of Râma), ibid. 3, 3, 4 निबोध मम (be informed from me). So sometimes with शुश्रूषते (cp. **86** *c*), as R. 2, 100, 7 कच्चिच्छुश्रूषसे पितुः

c) R. 2, 29, 4 तव सर्वे हि बिभ्यति (all are afraid of you), Panc. III, 195 या ममोद्विजते नित्यम् (she, who has always an aversion to me). R. 3, 46, 29—31 affords an instance of *both* constructions *together*: इह शाखामृगाः सिंहाः.... कथं तेभ्यो न बिभ्यसे।....कुञ्जराणां तरस्विनां कथं.... न बिभेषि.

Rem. Compare निर्विण्ण (disgusted with) with a gen. Panc. 171 मूषकमांसस्य निर्विण्णाहम् (I am disgusted with the flesh of mice), cp. **97**, R.

Spreading of its employment with modern writers.

Now and then this abl.-like genitive seems to have been extended beyond its limits by abuse, especially of modern writers[1]).

127. Note the genitive being used in some turns of phrase, which might be put as well in the category of the ablative as in that of the genitive.

---

1) But not exclusively. The older literature does not lack of instances, as R. 3, 51, 27 बद्धस्त्वं कालपाशेन क्व गतस्तस्य [instead of तस्माद्] मोक्ष्यसे; cp. 3, 66, 11. — A very striking example is Bhâg. Pur. 8, 6, 21 अमृतोत्पादने यत्नः क्रियतामविलम्बितम्। यस्य पीतस्य वै जन्तुर्मृत्युग्रस्तो ऽमरो भवेत्; here the gen. is abusively employed instead of the abl. यस्मात्पीतात्. M. De Saussure, from whose valuable treatise *de l'emploi du génitif absolu en Sanscrit* I borrow this example (see his note on p. 10), proves the impossibility of accounting for that gen. in a satisfactory way, when starting from the absolute construction. Hereby it is however not said that the presence of the participle पीत has not moved the author of the Bhâgavata to employ the genitive instead of the ablative. Likewise I scarcely believe Kalhaṇa would have used a gen. with याच् (Râjat. 1, 131, see **126** *a*), if the noun were not attended by a participle. Similarly with श्रु the gen. is preferred, if it be wanted to express the *hearing somebody say or utter something*, as Mhbh. 1, 141, 18 शृणु वदतो मम. In short, it is likely, that the relative frequency of genitives of participles in Sanskrit style, especially if compared to the rareness of similar ablatives, has favorized the spreading of the ablative-like genitive.

It may also be noticed, that in most of such cases pronouns are concerned.

1° a gen. with verbs of *speaking* etc. to denote him, *about whom* something is said, as Panc. 82 ममादोषस्याप्येवं वदति (so he speaks of me, who am however guiltless [1]).

2° with संभावयति and the like = »to expect *of*, to suppose *of*.” Mṛcch. IX, p. 297 सर्वमस्य मूर्खस्य संभाव्यते (that blockhead is capable to everything), Panc. 34 न तादृक्पुरुषाणामेवंविधं चेष्टितं संभाव्यते (of such men one must not suppose such conduct). But the locative is here also available.

3° with क्षम् (to forbear of) etc. R. 1, 15, 7 सर्वं तस्य क्षमामहे, Pat. I, p. 40 एतदेकमाचार्यस्य.... मृष्यताम्. — When without object, the gen. with क्षम् may be considered a dative-like one, as Mhbh. 1, 79, 9 शिष्यस्याशिष्यवृत्तेस्तु न क्षन्तव्यं बुभूषता (a man who wishes his wellbeing should not forbear a scholar, who does not behave as such).

128. Time-denoting genitive. The **time-denoting genitive** is likewise standing on the ground of the ablative, for it does always express *after what time* something is happening. It is usually restricted to some fixed terms, as चिरस्य or चिरस्य कालस्य = चिरात्, मुहूर्तस्य = मुहूर्तात् etc. Çâk. VII इमामाज्ञाकरीं वो गान्धर्वेण विधिनोपयम्य कस्यचित्कालस्य [»after a while”] बन्धुभिरानीतां स्मृतिशैथिल्यात्प्रत्यादिशन्नपराद्धोऽस्मि, Mhbh. 1, 47, 14 कतिपयाहस्य (after some days), R. 2, 118, 44 सुदीर्घस्य तु कालस्य राघवोऽयं.....यज्ञं द्रष्टुं समागतः

Rem. 1. It is very rare, that a not-time-denoting word is put in this gen., as Veṇ. I, p. 14 मम शिशोरेव = मम शिशुकालादेवारभ्य (since my very infancy).

Rem. 2. A time-denoting word may be attended by the *genitive of a noun + participle.* By this is denoted the time »since” some action has come to pass. Mṛcch. V, p. 172 चिरः खलु कालो मैत्रेयस्य वसन्तसेनायाः सकाशं गतस्य (it is indeed a long time, Maitreya is gone to V.), Mudr. IV, p. 134 अद्य दशमो मासस्तातस्योपरतस्य (it is to day just the tenth month since father died), Veṇ. I, p. 25 आर्य का खलु वेला तत्रभवत्याः प्राप्तायाः किंतु...आर्येण न लक्षिता (Sir, it is some time Mylady stays

---

1) See De Saussure l.l. p. 54 N.

here, but you have not noticed her), Panc. 303 क्रियान्कालस्तवैवं स्थितस्य, Utt. IV, p. 72; R. 3, 50, 20 [1]).

DATIVE-LIKE GENITIVE.

129. *Dative-like genitive or genitivus commodi et incommodi.* V. The genitive serves also to denote him, who is concerned by the action or fact, the so-called *remote object.*

This kind of genitive, as it stands on the same ground as the dative, I name **dative-like genitive.** Partly it may be substituted to the dative, but in a great number of cases the dative would even be unavailable, at least in classic Sanskrit, especially, if the person concerned is to be expressed *in such sentences, as where the predicate is nominal* (*substantive or adjective*). In such turns as Kathâs. 29, 98 इहामुत्र च साध्वीनां पतिरेका गतिः (for virtuous wives the only path to follow here and hereafter is their husband), Panc. II, 58 कोऽतिभारः समर्थानां किं दूरं व्यवसायिनाम्। को विदेशः सविद्यानां कः परः प्रियवादिनाम् (what is too heavy for the vigorous? what danger does exist for the audacious? what is a foreign country for the learned? who is unattainable for the flatterer?) the genitive is the regular idiom, and the dative out of use. Likewise the genitive — not the dative — is to be employed, with adjectives of *friendship* and *enmity*, *fitness* and *unfitness*, *good* and *evil* etc., as Panc. 331 अस्य मत्स्यामिषं सदा प्रियम् (a fish-dinner is always welcome to him), ibid. 213 न युक्तं भवतः (it does not suit you).

---

1) This idiom extends also to *adjectives, used as participles.* Utt. III, p. 57 देव्या शून्यस्य जगतो द्वादशः परिवत्सरः (it is now the twelfth year, that the world is destitute of its queen).

Examples: Kumâr. 3, 10 के मम धन्विनोऽन्ये (who are other archers to me?), Mrcch. VIII p. 246 मदनः] सत्पुरुषस्य...... भवति मृदुर्नैव वा भवति (the God of Love is either mild for an honest man or he does not exist for him), Mhbh. 1, 141, 36 अविज्ञाता भविष्यामो लोकस्य (we shall be unknown to the people), Panc. 200 यथार्थवादिनो दूतस्य न दोषः करणीयः (one must not take it ill of a messenger, if he speaks plain), Çâk. IV भर्तुर्विप्रकृतापि रोषणतया मास्म प्रतीपं गमः (do not oppose your husband by anger, even when offended).

With adjectives, as प्रिय etc.

Among the adjectives, which comply with a gen., note such as अनुरूप, अनुकूल and प्रतिकूल, प्रिय and विप्रिय, योग्य, युक्त — and even the verb युज्यते (to suit) — and their synonyms. So Nala 1, 19 करिष्यामि तव प्रियम्, Panc. III, 104 आत्मनः प्रतिकूलानि परेषां न समाचरेत् (one should not do to others, what is grievous to one's self), Mrcch. I, p. 58 अयोग्यमिदं न्यासस्य गृहम् (this house is not fit for a deposit), ibid. X, p. 355 न युज्यते तव प्राणपरित्यागः, Mâlav. IV, p. 96 शीतक्रिया चास्या रुजः प्रशस्ता (and cold is excellent against this ailment), Mhbh. 1, 15, 4 समः सर्वस्य लोकस्य (the same to all beings), Mâlav. IV, p. 88 क एवं विमुखोऽस्माकम् (who is so disinclined to me?), ibid. III, p. 75 पर्याप्तमेतावता कामिनाम् (so much suffices for persons in love).

So सदृश and उचित, when = »becoming to, suiting." R. 2, 30, 41 सर्वथा सदृशं सीते मम स्वस्य कुलस्य च । व्यवसायमनुक्रान्ता कान्ते त्वमतिशोभनम्; Çâk. I उचितमेवैतत्पुरुवंशप्रभवनरेन्द्रप्रदीपस्य. As to अर्ह and अनर्ह cp. the foot-note on p. 40 of this book. Note also अनघ, अनृण etc. with a gen. = »guiltless towards", as R. 2, 49, 7 प्रजानामनघः, M. 9, 106 पितॄणामनृणः (having paid his debts to the *pitaras*).

Rem. 1. Pâṇini teaches, that with participles in °त the genitive must be used, and not the instrum. of the agent, if the participle is employed as a present one. Such genitives as राज्ञां मतः (approved by the kings), राज्ञां पूजितः (honored by the kings) fall within the limits of this rule. See Mhbh. 1, 141, 36 and Çâk. IV quoted above, and cp. Çâk. II विदितो भवानाश्रमसदामिहस्थः (your staying here is known to the hermits).

P. 2,3, 67.

Rem. 2. On the genit. with kṛtyâs see **66** R. According to P. 2, 3, 69 the genitive is forbidden with the kṛts खलर्थे, that is such as सुलभ, ईषत्कर (cp. P. 3, 3, 126 sq.). Kâç. gives as examples

ईषट्करो भवता कटः (the mat is scarcely to be made by you), ईषत्पानः सोमो भवता. So R. 3, 5, 23 कर्म ह्यनेन कर्तव्यं महदन्यैः सुदुष्करम्. In fact, however, सुकर, दुष्कर, सुलभ, दुर्लभ are often construed with the genitive. Daç. 72 द्वितीयस्तु सर्वस्यैव सुलभः, R. 2, 97, 7 नेयं मम मही दुर्लभा, Kathâs. 24, 65 किं नाम कितवस्य हि दुष्करम्.

130. *Dative-like gen. = to have.* When used with the verb substantive expressed or implied, the dative-like genitive is not seldom equivalent to our verb *to have.* Pat. I, 427 one asks the other कति भवतः पुत्राः। कति भवतो भार्याः (how many children have you? how many wives?). Cp. the Latin phrase *est mihi filius.* Ait. Br. 7, 13, 1 तस्य ह शतं जाया बभूवुः, Çâk. I अस्ति नो ऽन्यदपि प्रष्टव्यम् (I have something else to ask you about), Panc. 166 अन्यत्र गतानां धनं भवति (men make money, if they go abroad). Likewise in such terms as किं तवानेन (what have I [to meddle, to do] with him?), cp. **88** R. 2.

131. *Dat.-like genitive with verbs.* The dative-like genitive attends even on verbs. Mrcch. X, p. 375 किमस्य पापस्यानुष्ठीयताम् (what is to be done to this wicked man?) and ibid. X, p. 384 किमस्य भिक्षोः क्रियताम् (what is to be done for this monk?) are striking examples of the sixth case used so. It is especially verbs of *doing good or evil* (as उपकृ, प्रसद्, अपकृ, अपराध्), विश्वस् (to trust), क्षम् (to forbear) and some others which partake of this idiom, its concurrent construction being the locative, rarely, if at all, the dative [1]).

Examples: R. Gorr. 4, 38, 47 मित्राणामुपकुर्वाणो राज्यं रक्षितुमर्हसि (you

---

1) As to अपराध्, उपकृ, अपकृ, विश्रवस्, I do not remember having met with any instance of their agreeing with a dative; क्षम् governs a dative Bhaṭṭ. 4, 39. Upon the whole, the dative of profit and damage within its narrower limits is very scarce in Sanskrit, cp. **84**.

must guard your kingdom by doing well to your friends), ibid. 3, 1, 16 रामस्य सत्कृत्य (offered hospitality to R.), Panc. 289 किं मया तस्यास्तवापि चापकृतम् (in what have I injured her or you?), Çâk. VII अपराद्धोऽस्मि तत्रभवतः कण्वस्य (I have sinned against the reverend Kanva), Panc. 38 स न कस्यचिद्विश्वसिति (he trusts nobody), Mhbh. 1, 23, 26 प्रसीद नः प्रयाचताम् (be merciful to us, who beseech thee), Mâlat. VII, p. 126 वायुर्यूनामभिनववधूसंनिधानं व्यनक्ति (the wind declares to the young men the nearness of young women).

Rem. In Latin, with such turns as *adimo vestem servo* or *servi*, *civium* or *civibus dolor auctus est*, the dative and the genitive are both available. Sanskrit invariably uses the genitive. Panc. II, 141 उद्यमेन हि सिध्यन्ति कार्याणि न मनोरथैः। न हि सिंहस्य सुप्तस्य प्रविशन्ति मुखे मृगाः (it is by exertion, that enterprises are successful, not by wishing, deer do not enter the mouth of a sleeping lion), ibid. p. 145 हिरण्यकोऽपि मन्थरकस्य प्रणामं कृत्वा (H. made his reverence to M.), ibid. 137 मम महती प्रीतिः संजाता (I have got great pleasure).

132. *Genitive of the remote object.* Finally, the genitive *is allowed* to attend all verbs, as are commonly construed with the dative of concern. Such a genitive may be not without affectation [1]), it is

1) So at least is the opinion of ANANDORAM BOROOAH (§ 212 of his »*Higher Sanskrit Grammar*") —and his opinion may be considered to hold good nowadays in India with Sanskrit-writing people — »the gen. is also occasionally used for the Dat. or Indirect Object, especially by pedantic writers" and »it will be seen from the above examples that such use besides being pedantic, is very ambiguous." The ambiguity, however, cannot be very great, for as a rule the context will show us how to accept such genitives, and in such cases, as where the context would not enable us to understand him plainly, a good writer will avoid *all* ambiguous constructions. That the dative-like genitive has been known and employed in India of old — though not to the extent, it has got in the classic dialect — may be seen from some of the examples quoted above. As with other concurrent idioms, there is many an instance of both cases used together, as R. 2, 34, 6 द्वारि तिष्ठति ते सुतः। ब्राह्मणेभ्यो धनं दत्त्वा सर्वं चैवोपजीविनाम्, schol. उपजीविनां च तेभ्यश्च दत्त्वा. In the comment of Kâç. on P. 3, 3, 111 the printed

of frequent occurrence in literature[1]). So it is found with 1. verbs of *giving*, *offering*, 2. of *telling*, *speaking*, 3. of *carrying*, *sending*, 4. of *showing*, 5. of *enjoining*, 6. of *promising*, 7. of *pleasing*, 8. of *being angry*, 9. of *bowing*, *prostrating one's self*, etc.

Examples: 1. Ch. Up. 2, 22, 5 प्रजापतेरात्मानं परिददानि (let me surrender myself to Pr.), Panc. 85 मया तस्याभयं प्रदत्तम् (I have granted him safety), Çâk. I सुतस्याभरणानि धनुश्चोपनीयार्पयति, Mrcch. II, p. 80 अन्यान्तावद् दश सुवर्णानस्यैव प्रयच्छ (give but to this very fellow ten other pieces of gold).

2. Mhbh. 1, 12, 6 चख्यौ पितुः (he told his father —), Panc. 292 कथयास्माकं देशान्तरवृत्तान्तम् (relate us of your adventures in foreign countries), Mrcch. I, p. 45 यदीमं वार्त्तामार्यचारुदत्तस्य नाख्यास्यसि, Panc. 246 ततस्तैः सर्वैरेव गत्वा दर्दुरराजस्य विज्ञप्तम् (then they went all and addressed the king of frogs), ibid. 62 स तदाकर्ण्यान्येषामपि जलचराणां तत्तस्य वचनं निवेदयामास.

3. Çâk. III कस्येदमुशीरानुलेपनं मृणालवन्ति च नलिनीपत्राणि नीयन्ते (to whom are carried —?), ibid. IV तामद्य संप्रेष्य परिगृहीतुः (having sent her now to her husband).

4. Kathâs. 29, 18 अदर्शयत्तस्याः पुत्रिकाः (she showed her the puppets).

5. Panc. 289 तेन च मम समादिष्टम् (and he prescribed me), Çâk. IV भगिन्यास्ते मार्गमादेशय (show the way to your sister).

---

text has ऋणं यत्परस्य धार्यते, the other reading परस्मै is mentioned in a foot-note.

1) In the vulgar dialects the dative has got obsolete, and the genitive has been substituted to it, the few traces of a dative in Prâkrit literature being owed to the artificial language of dramatic poetry. See LASSEN *Inst. linguae pracriticae*, p. 299, VARARUCI *Prâkṛtaprakâça* 6, 64. KUHN *Beiträge zur Pali Grammatik*, p. 70 sq. gives an account of the remnants of the dative in Pali, which are more considerable, than in the other prâkrts, and contain both infinitives in °*tave* and datives in °*âya*, especially *atthâya* = skṛt *arthâya*; as a rule, the pali dative serves to denote the *purpose*. The same process has been at work in Modern Greek. SCHINAS, *Grammaire élémentaire du grec moderne*, Paris, 1829 p. 90: »le génitif sert de régime indirect aux verbes et remplace le datif: δῶσε μου ψωμί donne-moi du pain, λέγω τοῦ κριτοῦ τὴν ἀλήθειαν je dis au juge la vérité."

6. M. 9, 99 अन्यस्य प्रतिज्ञाय पुनरन्यस्य दीयते (she has been promised to one and given to another).

7. Panc. 235 किं तव रोचत एष (does he please you?).

8. R. 2, 100, 33 भृता भर्तुः कुप्यन्ति (servants are moved with anger against their master), Çâk. VII ममानतिक्रुद्धो मुनिः

9. Var. Yog. 2, 32 एकस्य प्रणमन्ति मर्त्याः (people bow to one), R. II, sarga 96*, 47 न्यपतत्काको राघवस्य महात्मनः (the crow prostrated himself to the magnanimous Râma).

Rem. Even श्रद्धा (to believe) is met with gen. Ait. Br. 1, 6, 11 न बहूनां चनान्येषां श्रद्दधाति he does not believe others, however many).

132*. The dative of the purpose is not interchangeable with the genitive [1])

---

1) In the prâkṛts even then. It is singular, that an observer as accurate, as Pâṇini is, should have overlooked the important function of the dative-like genitive. A rule of his, indeed, mentions the sixth case चतुर्थ्यर्थे बहुलम् (2, 3, 62), but the word छन्दसि added and the examples proffered by tradition show that according to the vulgar interpretation we have here a very special enjoinment, closely connected to the preceding sûtra (61), not one of general bearing. Yet I greatly doubt the exactness of that explication, by which the word चतुर्थ्यर्थे is quite superfluous, as देवतासंप्रदाने needs must be repeated from s. 61, and this suffices for the vulgar interpretation. Perhaps we may remove the technical difficulty by an other distribution of the words, that make up sûtra 61—63. When read *uno tenore*, we get प्रेष्यब्रुवोर्हविषो देवतासंप्रदाने चतुर्थ्यर्थे बहुलं छन्दसि यजेश्च करणे. It would be convenient both to the internal probability and to the simplicity of the interpretation, if they are divided in this but slightly different manner: 61. प्रेष्यब्रुवोर्हविषो देवतासंप्रदाने, 62. चतुर्थ्यर्थे बहुलं, 63. छन्दसि यजेश्च करणे. According to this partition, Pâṇini, after having given in 61 a special rule about the gen. being employed in some formulae of sacrificing, adds in 62 the general enjoinment *that in many cases, where the dative is required* — mark चतुर्थ्यर्थे, which encompasses by far more than संप्रदाने — *the genitive is likewise available, either by preference, or optionally, but not in all.* For thus is the meaning of बहुलम्:

क्वचित्प्रवृत्तिः क्वचिदप्रवृत्तिः क्वचिद्विभाषा क्वचिदन्यदेव
विधेर्विधानं बहुधा समीक्ष्य चतुर्विधं बाहुलकं वदन्ति

(see Boethlingk *Pâṇini* II, p. 82). — As to sûtra 63 छन्दसि यजेश्च करणे, it offers no difficulty in itself, but disturbs the methodical arrangement

Chapter VIII. **Locative** [1]).

133. Locative of the spot where. The seventh case or locative serves to signify the scene of the action. Its power is expressed by English prepositions, as *in*, *on*, *at*, *among*, *with*, *by*, *near*. It has not only the duty of pointing out the spot where, but also the spot whither. In other terms, sometimes it answers Lat. *in* with abl, sometimes *in* with accus.

A. **Locative of the spot where.** — Here we must make the following distinctions.

a.) the locative conveys the notion of being *within*, *in*. M. 1, 9 तस्मिञ्जज्ञे स्वयं ब्रह्मा (in this [egg] Brahman himself was born), Daç. 156 गङ्गाम्भसि विहरन् (sporting in the water of the Ganges), ibid. 179 कस्यचिच्चित्रकरस्य हस्ते चित्रपटं ददर्श.

b.) it denotes a surface, trodden or touched: *on*, *upon*, *over*, *at*. Panc. 307 रासभः कश्चित्तत्र श्मशाने दृष्टः (an ass was seen on that cemetery), R. 3, 5, 10 व्यजने] गृहीते वारनारीभ्यां धूयमाने च मूर्धनि (courtesans, holding fans, waved them over his head), Panc. 331 ते च मत्स्या वह्नौ पाचनाय तिष्ठन्ति (and those fishes are being boiled over

---

of the rules which treat of the employment of the genitive (2, 3, 50—73). For this reason I consider it an additional rule, interpolated at an unproper place — we had rather expected it between s 51 and 52 — so as to obscurate by its close following the sûtra 62, the right understanding of the latter. That there are several rules in our Pâṇini, which did not belong to the original work, but were at the outset vârttikâs, which afterwards have been taken up in the text, is a fact now universally acknowledged. As concerns the s. 63, I remark, that many other vaidik gen. partitives with verbs (**119**) are not mentioned by Pâṇini, and that the seeming anomaly of यज् (cp. **45** R.) must have drawn special attention for all that regarded that verb; in a time as early as Patanjali, it was already considered to have something peculiar, see his comment on P. 1, 4, 32 = Pat. I, p. 331 (in the Kâçikâ his words are wrongly indicated as if they were a vârttikâ).

1) See Delbrück *Ablativ*, *Localis*, *Instrumentalis* p. 27—49.

the fire), **Daç.** 140 पिता मे विविक्तायां भूमौ स्थितोऽभूत् (my father laid down on the naked earth), ibid. 141 शिरसि जिघ्रन्ती·

c.) it signifies the dominion or territory: *in*, *at*, *on*, Latin *apud*, *in*. Panc. 1 अस्ति दाक्षिणात्ये जनपदे महिलारोप्यं नाम नगरम्, ibid. 319 राजगृहे मेषयूथमस्ति (in the royal palace there was a flock of rams), Kumâras. 5, 60 फलं दृष्टं द्रुमेषु (fruits are seen on the trees). So पञ्चालेषु (in the country of the Pancâlâs), काश्याम् (at Benares), Mhbh. 1, 31, 18 अयमिन्द्रस्त्रिभुवने कृतः (he has been made Lord over the three worlds); cp. **111** R.

d.) it indicates something very near, though not directly touched: *near*, *on*, *about* [1]). Mhbh. 1, 170, 3 आसेदुर्गङ्गायां पाण्डुनन्दनाः (Pâṇḍu's sons pitched tents near the Ganges), Hitop. 29 नो चेदनाहारेणात्मानं तव द्वारि व्यापादयिष्यामि (otherwise I will kill myself by starvation at your door). So Kâd. I, p. 39 यत्र is used, while meaning »about which spot."

e.) it is expressive of *among*, *amid*. Nala 1, 13 न देवेषु न यक्षेषु तादृग्रूपवती क्वचित्। मानुषेष्वपि चान्येषु दृष्टपूर्वाथ वा श्रुता (neither among devas nor yakshas nor men nor among other beings such a beauty has been seen nor heard of anywhere), Daç. 124 अभ्रमच्च पौरजानपदेष्वियं वार्त्ता (this report spread among the townsmen and the countrymen). Cp. **116**.

All these variegations are mixed up in the general notion, carried by the seventh case. Greater precision, if wanted, may be obtained by using periphrasing turns, as the prepos. अन्तः (within), or such words as मध्ये, तले, पृष्ठे, एकदेशे, संनिधौ, etc. See **165**, **190**, **192**.

134. B. **Locative of the spot whither.** It attends of course on verbs and verbal nouns of moving, such as *to go*, *to start*, *to lead*, *to send*. Ch. Up. 2, 24, 5 एष वै यजमानस्य लोक एतास्मि (I shall go to the world of him, in whose behalf the sacrifice is performed), Panc. 321 स अटव्यां गतः (he set out to the forest), ibid. 41 समीपवर्तिनि नगरे प्रस्थितः, ibid. 269 शोभनस्थाने त्वयाहं नीतः

Locative of the spot whither.

1) This is the so called सामीप्ये सप्तमी·

(you have conducted me to a fine spot), R. 1, 11, 24 पौरेषु प्रेषयामास दूतान् (he sent messengers to the citizens), R. 2, 7, 26 अपवाह्य...... भरतं तव बन्धुषु after having removed Bharata to your kinsmen —).

to enter. Panc. 283 मत्स्यो नद्यां प्रविवेश, ibid. 52 त्वया सह वह्नौ प्रविशामि (with you I will go into the fire).

to fall on or *in.* R. 3, 18, 25 पपात भूमौ, Çâk. I रेणुः पतति..... आश्रमद्रुमेषु (the dust falls on the trees of the hermitage).

to submerge in. Kumâras. 1, 3 एको हि दोषो गुणसंनिपाते निमज्जतीन्दोः किरणेष्विवाङ्कः (for [that] one defect disappears in the contact with his virtues, like the moon's spot submerges in its beams).

to throw in. Daç. 61 सर्वमेव कुटुम्बकं बन्धने क्षिप्त्वा, Panc. 124 तं नदीगुहायां प्रक्षिप्य.

to place —, to put in, upon. Mudr. III, p. 91 न्यस्तं मूर्ध्नि पदं तवैव जरया (old age has set its foot on your head), Panc. 146 तत्रैव भिक्षापात्रे निधाय (— put it in that very beggar's bowl), Mhbh. 1, 40, 21 तस्य स्कन्धे मृतं सर्पं क्रुद्धो राजा समासजत्, Âpast. 1, 15, 21 खट्वायां च नोपदध्यात् (nor shall he put [fire] under his bedstead). Metaphor: Prabodh. V, p. 112 यदादिशति भगवती मूर्धनि निवेशिताः सर्वा एवाज्ञाः

to ascend Kathâs. 29, 129 तरौ..... आरूढा तत्र राक्षसी (the râxasî climbed into the tree). Metaphor: Panc. I, 266 यस्मिन्..... चक्षुरारोपयति पार्थिवः (he, on whom the king fixes his looks).

to strike, to hit. Çâk. I आर्तत्राणाय वः शस्त्रं न प्रहर्तुमनागसि, Kathâs. 28, 31 तस्मिन्खड्गेन प्राहरन्मुनौ (he stroke the holy man with his sword), Mṛcch. II, p. 83 घोणायां मुष्टिप्रहारं ददाति, Panc. 295 तं शिरस्यताडयत्. And so on.

Rem. Note कृ with loc., a very common turn = »to put in or on," as स्कन्धे, हस्ते, पाणौ [1]), धुरि कृ (to put at the head), sim.

1*. The spot reached may also be denoted by the *accusative*. Compare with the above examples these: Ch. Up. 5, 3, 1 समितिमेयाय (he came at the meeting), Panc. 143 स्वपृष्ठमारोप्य माम् (after having put me on your back), Çâk. I तपोवनं तावत्प्रविशामि etc. etc.

1) Cf. P. 1, 4, 77, where it is taught, that हस्तेकृत्य पाणौकृत्य are to be used when = »having married", but हस्ते कृत्वा »having put in the hand, — taken by the hand."

So with verbs of *going*, *bringing*, *carrying*, *sending*, *ascending*, *entering*. Those, however, of *falling*, *throwing*, *placing*, *putting* — as पत्, क्षिप्, न्यस्, निवेशयति, स्थापयति — seem to be construed with the locative exclusively. On the other hand the accusative is obligatory, if „to come to" is the metaphorical expression of „to become" (**236**), and in some other standing turns, as तुलामारोहति.

135. Noun-qualifying locatives. According to what has been said **111**, it is plain, that nothing impedes locatives qualifying a noun. Such phrases as कूपे सलिलम्। नद्यां नौका are as good Sanskrit as „water in the pit," „a boat on the river" are good English. — Here the genitive is concurrent.

In some turns the locative is standing, as in divisions of literary works as इति श्रीमद्रामायणे वाल्मिकीय अरण्यखण्डे प्रथमः सर्गः, we say, the first sarga *of* the Âranyakhaṇḍa *of* the Râmâyaṇa of Valmîki.

136. Locative in idiomatic phrases. II. Both kinds of locative are applied in so many and in so manifold ways, as to make it hardly practicable to enumerate them all distinctly and completely. It may suffice to mention the most important and the most striking idioms:

1. *to drink from* etc. 1. We will notice in the first place some peculiar phrases. Of the kind are:

to drink from. Panc. I, 327 लोकः पिबति सुरां नरकपालेऽपि (men drink strong liquor even from a man's skull)[1]).

to feed on. Daç. 174 सशेष एवान्धस्यसावतृप्यत (he feasted on the rice, without leaving anything). In metaphorical sense तृप्यते and the like may also be construed with a locative. Mhbh. 1, 84, 2 न तृप्तोऽस्मि यौवने. Cp. **123**.

1) See DELBRÜCK l.l. p. 33.

to be born from; *to beget with*. The mother is put in the locative. Cp. **100**, 1. Kumâras. 1, 22 सा तस्यामुदपादि.

to reckon among. Daç. 199 अगण्यतामरेषु (he was reckoned among the gods).

137. *2. to stay with.*

2. The locative in which is put the person, with whom one *dwells*, *stays*. Prabodh. VI, p. 123 अनाथाहं त्वयि वस्तुमिच्छामि (I am without protector and wish to stay in your house), Mhbh. 1, 74, 12 नारीणां चिरवासो हि बान्धवेषु न रोचते, Mudr. VII, p. 229 वयं मलयकेतौ किञ्चित्कालान्तरमुषिताः (I have stayed for some time with Mal.). So especially गुरौ वसति (he dwells with his spiritual father), Ch. Up. 4, 4, 3 ब्रह्मचर्यं भगवति वत्स्यामि (v. a. I will be the pupil of the Reverend).

138. *3. मते तिष्ठति etc.*

3. स्था or वृत् with loc. = „keeping close to", that is *observing*, *obeying* one's precept, principle, judgment etc. Çâk. VI न मे शासने तिष्ठसि (you do not obey my order), Daç. 72 मातुर्मते वर्तस्व (comply with the wish of your mother). Cp. Lat. *stat promissis*, *stat sententiâ* and Kâç. on P. 1, 3, 23 मयि तिष्ठते (it rests on me = I am to decide.)

139. *4. Locative of the thing touched.*

4. The locative, which serves to denote the thing touched. It is used with *a*) verbs of *fastening at* — especially बन्ध् — as well in their proper as in a figurative sense; likewise with the others, *b*) those of *clinging*, *adhering to*, as लग्, श्लिष्, सञ्ज् etc., *c*) of *leaning on*, *relying on*, *trusting*, *d*) of *seizing by*, *e*) of *falling at one's feet* — and in other similar locutions, as f. i. Ragh. 1, 19 मौर्वी धनुषि चातता (and the string, bent on the bow), Çâk. VI शृङ्गे कृष्णमृगस्य वामनयनं कण्डूयमानां मृगीम् (an antelope's female, rubbing her left eye against the horn of her male companion).

with verbs of fastening.

Examples: *a*) Panc. 238 तत्र वृक्षे पाशं बबन्ध, ibid. 286 दासेरकग्रीवायां महती घण्टा प्रतिबद्धा, Pat. I, p. 40 नौर्नावि बद्धा, Bhâg. Pur. 4, 27, 10

विषयेष्वबध्यत (he was attached to wordliness), Ragh. 3, 4 अभिलाषे तथाविधे मनो बबन्ध (she bent her mind to such a desire).

of clinging and adhering. *b*) Panc. V, 8 आढ्ये रज्यन्ति जननिवहाः (crowds of people cling to a rich man), ibid. 307 कश्चित्तस्य ग्रीवायां लगति (one [of them] falls on his neck), Daç. 75 तस्यामसौ प्रासजत् (he fell in love with her), Ch. Up. 4, 14, 3 एवंविदि पापं कर्म न श्लिष्यति (no evil deed clings to him, who knows so), Panc. II, 131 व्यसनेष्वसक्तं शूरम् — (a hero, not addicted to vices).

c) 1. *to lean on.* R. 2, 46, 27 न.... स्वपेयुर्वृक्षमूलेषु संश्रिताः (lest they should sleep, lying down on roots of trees). — With श्रि and its compounds, likewise with अवलम्ब्, the accus. is the regular construction, not the loc., especially in the metaph. sense »to apply one's self to somebody, to implore one's aid." — 2. *to rely on.* Panc.

of relying on and trusting. II, 194 न मातरि न दारेषु न सोदर्ये न चात्मजे। विश्रम्भस्तादृशः पुंसां यादृङ्मित्रे निरन्तरे, Çâk. I बलवदपि शिक्षितानामात्मन्यप्रत्ययं चेतः (even these who possess strong learning, mistrust themselves). So with आशंस् (to hope on), विश्वस् (to trust), sim. Çâk. II आशंसन्ते सुराः..... अस्याधिज्ये धनुषि विजयं पौरुहूते च वज्रे (the gods have confidence in his bent bow and in Indra's thunderbolt), Panc. II, 48 विश्वसिति शत्रुषु. Cp. 131.

of seizing by. of falling at one's feet. *d*) Panc. 161 पाणौ संगृह्य (seized by the hand —), Mṛcch. I, p. 39 रदनिकां केशेषु गृहीत्वा, Kathâs. 29, 3 कण्ठे जग्राह (she laid her hand on her neck).

e) पादयोः पतति is a standing phrase. See f. i. Çâk. IV पितुः पादयोः पतति.

140. *5. Locative in abstract sense.* 5. The locative, when used in the same way as English „*in him* I see much skill." So Mhbh. I सर्वं संभावयाम्यस्मिन्नसाध्यमपि साधयेत् (I may expect all of him, he can do impossibilities), Çâk. II दृष्टदोषा मृगया स्वामिनि (hunting is reckoned to be vicious in a prince), Prab. V, p. 109 आर्तानामुपदेशे न दोषः (there is no sin in giving a good counsel to the afflicted), R. 2, 7, 10 आचचक्षेऽथ कुब्जायै महतीं राघवे श्रियम् (and she told Kubjâ of the great happiness of Râma).

Rem. 1. When used as the predicate of the sentence, this locative is occasionally carrying the notion of »suiting, befitting." Panc. I, 305 समानशीलव्यसनेषु सख्यम् (friendship suits similar characters and inclinations), ibid. p. 251 नयत्यागशौर्यसंपन्ने पुरुषे राज्यम् (the royal dignity befits a man accomplished in political science, liberality and gallantry).

Locat. = »in the meaning of."

Rem. 2. Synonyms explaining the meaning of some word, are put in the locative, which accordingly = »in this meaning." Amarak. कलापो भूषणे बर्हे तूणीरे संहतावपि (the word *kalâpa* may have the meaning of *bhûshaṇa* ornament, *barha* a peacock's tail, *tûṇîra* quiver and *saṃhati* mass or heap), Kâm. 2, 17 विदिर्ज्ञाने निरुच्यते (*vid* is explained as meaning: to know), Âpast. 1, 5, 1 नियमेषु तपः शब्दः

141. 6. Locat. with words of excellence, weakness etc.

6. The qualities, arts, science etc. *in* which one excels or is weak, equal or unequal, when put in the locative. R. 1, 1, 17 समुद्र इव गाम्भीर्ये स्थैर्ये च हिमवानिव। विष्णुना सदृशो वीर्ये क्षमया पृथिवीसमः। धनदेन समस्त्यागे सत्ये धर्म इवापरः, Mhbh. 1, 88, 13 प्रभुरग्निः प्रतपने भूमिरावपने प्रभुः। प्रभुः सूर्यः प्रकाशित्वे. Here the ablative and instrumental are concurrent idioms.

142. 7. With nouns of *ability*, *skill*, etc.

7. The seventh case attending nouns of *ability*, *skill*, *knowledge* and the like. Here the genitive is the concurrent construction (**124**, 1°).

Examples of the locative: Ch. Up. 1, 8, 1 त्रयो होद्गीथे कुशला बभूवुः (three men were well-versed in the Word), Kathâs. 24, 187 रत्नादिष्वनभिज्ञस्य (of one, not being a judge of jewelry), Mâlav. V, p. 131 कस्यां कलायामभिविनीते भवत्यो (what art the ladies are acquainted with?), Nâgân. I, p. 2 नाट्ये दक्षा वयम् (we are skilled in dramatic representations). — It attends also verbs of that meaning. Pat. I, p. 280 विद्यासु शिक्षते। धनुषि शिक्षते.

Rem. 1. Vârtt. 1 on P. 2, 3, 36 gives a special rule for adjectives in °इन् made of participles in °त, complying with locative. The examples given by Pat. I, p. 458 अधीती व्याकरणे (well read in grammar), आम्नाती छन्दसि (knowing the theory of metrics) prove that kind of locative to belong to the general class of words of ability and skill. Cp. Daç. 157 देव स एष मे जामाता..... अधीती चतुर्ष्वाम्नायेषु गृहीती षट्स्वङ्गेषु.

Rem. 2. P. 2, 3, 44 teaches the promiscuous use of locative and instrumental with the adjectives प्रसित and उत्सुक (caring for, solicitous).

8. Locative of time and circumstances.

143. 8. The locative, which denotes the *circumstances, under which* the action comes to pass So आपदि „in time of distress", काले „in due time," भाग्येषु „in fortune" and the like. This kind of locative has a very great extension and encompasses also the **locative of time** as well as the **absolute locative.** The former denotes the time *at* which, the *when*, as दिनेदिने (every day), वर्षासु (in the rainy season), निशायाम् (at night), प्रत्यूषे (at daybreak), एषु वासरेषु (in these days), आदौ (at the beginning) etc. Ch. Up. 3, 16, 2 एतस्मिन्वयसि (in this age).

The latter occurs, if the *circumstance under which* is signified by two nouns, one of which is the predicate of the other. As the said noun-predicate generally is expressed by a participle, it is to the chapter on participles we refer for a full account of the absolute locative. Here it may suffice to point out by an evident example its close connexion with the locatives of circumstance and time. Mudr. IV, p. 147 त्वय्युत्कृष्टबले ऽभियोक्तरि नृपे नन्दानुरक्ते पुरे
चाणक्ये चलिताधिकारविमुखे मौर्ये नवे राजनि
स्वाधीने मयि मार्गमात्रकथनव्यापारयोगोद्यमे
त्वद्वाञ्छान्तरितानि सम्प्रति विभो तिष्ठन्ति साध्यानि नः

thus freely translated by WILSON: »But let Your Highness weigh | *these circumstances* also..... your forces are collected, | yourself, the heir legitimate of kings, | your adversary but a base usurper; | his very capital is hostile him, | in me you have a faithful guide at least; | and all appliances and means to boot | provided; nought remains but your command" [1]).

---

1) Compare such locatives, which denote a circumstance by a single word, as in the proverb छिद्रेष्वनर्था बहुलीभवन्ति (v. a. misfortune never comes singly), Panc. V, 103 नैकः सुप्तेषु जागृयात्. They cannot be styled absolute locatives, but serve just the same purpose as those.

144. (9. Locat. of distance.) 9. The locative denoting, *at which distance* one thing or fact is from another. Ait. Br. 2, 17, 8 सहस्राश्वीने वा इतः स्वर्गो लोकः (heaven, indeed, is from here at a distance of a thousand journeys on horseback), R. 3, 4, 20 इतो वसति..... अध्यर्धयोजने महर्षिः, Kathâs. 28, 188 इतो मे षष्टियोजन्यां [1]) गृहम् (my house is at sixty yojanas from here). Cp. **99** R. 1.

Rem. Pat. I, p. 455 mentions the promiscuousness of the turns गवीधूमतः सांकाश्यं चत्वारि योजनानि or चतुर्षु योजनेषु. But if an interval of time is to be signified, the locative alone is available: कार्त्तिक्या आग्रहायणी मासे (the full moon of Âgrahâyanî is a month after that of Kârttikî).

145. (Dative-like locative.) III. **Dative-like locative.** In **134** it has been shown, that the locative is used with verbs of *putting in* or *on*, *placing* etc. Sanskrit extends that idiom to many kindred conceptions, and often uses the locative with verbs of *giving*, *promising*, *buying*, *selling*, *telling* etc., so as to make it concur with the dative or the genitive of the remote object. Cp. English *to bestow upon*.

Examples of the dative-like locative: R. 1, 68, 16 संप्रदानं सुतायास्तु राघवे कर्तुमिच्छति, ibid. 1, 51, 5 राम उपाहरत्पूजां मम माता, ibid. 1, 75, 7 सहस्राक्षे प्रतिज्ञाय (promised it to Indra), Mudr. V, p. 159 शरीरं विक्रीय धनवति (having sold himself to a rich man), Mhbh. 1, 30, 6 नाम चक्रुर्महाखगे (they gave a name to the great bird), Kathâs. 28, 34 एतत्कृतं त्वयि (this is done to you). Cp. R. 2, 96, 28 मोक्ष्यामि शत्रुसैन्येषु कक्षेष्विव हुताशनम्.

146. In several phrases the locative may even be a concurrent idiom of the *dativus finalis*, especially of the infinitive-like dative. It is namely put to *a*) words of *striving after*, *wishing*, *resolving*; *b*) to verbs of *appointing to*, *ordaining*, *enjoining*, *permitting*, as स्थापयति, आदिश्,

---

1) So is the good reading. Brockhaus' edition has *shashṭiyojanyaṃ gṛham.*

नियुज्, *c*) to words meaning *able*, *fit* and the like.

Examples: *a*) Mhbh. 1, 138, 69 प्रयतितं राज्ये मया तव (I have coveted your kingdom), Panc. IV, 26 सर्वस्वहरणे युक्तं शत्रुं..... तोषयन्त्यल्पदानेन (an enemy, who ha sprepared himself to take off the whole, may be appeased by a small gift), Mâlat. III, p. 50 महत्त्वारोपणे यत्नः (endeavours to attain at greatness), Mhbh. 1, 141, 2 दहने बुद्धिमकारयत् (he made up his mind to burn [the Pâṇḍavas]), R. 3, 4, 4 वेगं प्रचक्रतुर्वधे तस्य (both made speed to kill him).

b) M. 1, 28 कर्मणि न्ययुङ्क्त (he has appointed to a task), Çâk. I इमां वल्कलधारणे नियुङ्क्ते (v. a. he obliges her to wear a dress of bark), Kathâs. 25, 123 स राजा मल्लस्य युद्धे तस्य समादिशत्..... तम् (the king designated him to fight the athlete), ibid. 29, 29 अनुज्ञा त्वत्पार्श्वगमने (permission to go to you). — In the same way one says राज्ये स्थापितः (he is appointed to the kingdom), पतित्वे वरयामास तम् (she chose that man to be her husband), Panc. 162 तं यौवराज्ये ऽभिषिक्तवान् (he anointed that [young man] heir-apparent) and the like.

c) R. 3, 13, 20 भवान् शक्तः परिरक्षणे (you are able to guard), Panc. 156 असमर्थोऽयमुदरपूरणे ऽस्माकम् (he is not able to supply us with food), Mhbh. 1, 148, 3 कालं मन्ये पलायने (it is time, methinks, to run away).

147. *Nimittasaptamî.* IV. **Nimittasaptamî.** As the locative often denotes the spot, towards which there is some movement, so it may be used at a very large extent to signify the person or thing, *towards which* some action is directed, in other terms, that *on account of which* something is done. Speaking exactly, the dative-like locative, we have dealt with in the last two paragraphs, is but a consequence of this general faculty to denote that, *about which* one is engaged. Here are some examples of this idiom: Kâç. on P. 2, 3, 36 चर्मणि द्वीपिनं हन्ति दन्तयोर्हन्ति कुञ्जरं। केशेषु चमरीं हन्ति सीम्नि पुष्कलको हतः (the panter is killed on account of its skin, the elephant for its tusks, yaks for their tails and the musk-deer on account of its musk-gland), Kâç. on P. 1, 3, 47 क्षेत्रे विवदन्ते (they are at law on account of a field), Panc. 288 युक्तमिदं स्वामिनो निजभृत्येषु

(this is convenient for a lord with respect to his attendants), M. 3, 107 उत्तमेषूत्तमं कुर्याद्धीने हीनं समे समम्.

148. This kind of locative is sometimes bordering on that, taught in **140.**

The *nimittasaptamî* (locative of the motive; locative of reference) often serves to qualify such substantives as सौहृद, भक्ति, वैर, अभिलाष, आदर, अनादर, अनुक्रोश, अवज्ञा, कृपा, विश्वास and the like. The genitive is here, of course, the concurrent construction.

Examples: Daç. 89 तस्योदारके वैरमभ्यवर्धयत् (he fomented his enmity towards Ud.), Mhbh. 1, 155, 9 अर्हसि कृपां कर्तुं मयि (you must have pity on me), Çâk. I अस्यामभिलाषि मे मनः (my heart longs for her), R. 2, 103, 22 रामे दृढभक्तिमान्, Hitop. 9 कथं त्वयि विश्वासः, R. 1, 50, 24 महाधनुषि जिज्ञासा, Panc. 251 न च लघुष्वपि कर्तव्येषु धीमद्भिरनादरः कार्यः (a wise man must not be careless about business, however small).

It also attends on several adjectives, part of which likewise comply with a genitive, as प्रिय, युक्त, भक्त and the inverse of them, रत (fond of), निरत (delighting in) etc. Mâlat. X, p. 172 प्रीतो ऽस्मि जामातरि, Çâk. II अनुकारिणि पूर्वेषां युक्तरूपमिदं त्वयि, Panc. V, 65 नार्यः केवलं स्वसुखे रताः

149. Locative expressive of a disposition towards. In general, the locative may denote a disposition *towards somebody*. Then it is synonymous with the prepos. प्रति, as देवदत्तः साधुर्मातरि or मातरं प्रति (N. N. is good for his mother). P. 2, 3 43.

Examples: Daç. 144 प्रतिनिवृत्तो युष्मासु यथार्हं प्रतिपत्स्ये (when I shall be returned, I shall deal with you as you deserve), Câk. I कथं यथा वयमस्यामियमप्यस्मान्प्रति यथा स्यात् (how, can it be, that she feels towards me, as I towards her?), Panc. IV, 72 उपकारिषु यः साधुः साधुत्वे तस्य को गुणः। अपकारिषु यः साधुः स साधुः सद्भिरुच्यते (if one is good for those, who have done well to him, what is his merit? only *he* is named good by the virtuous, who does well to his enemies), Çâk. IV भव दक्षिणा परिजने (be kind to your household).

150. Locatives as adverbs. Many locatives have the character of adverbs, as आदौ (in the beginning), रहसि (secretly), एकान्ते (apart), अग्रे (at the head), etc., especially such as denote time or space[1]).

CHAPTER IX. Periphrastic expression of case-relations.

151. The apparatus for periphrasing case-relations may be classed into three main categories, viz. 1. prepositions, 2. noun-cases, 3. verbal forms. The boundary between the first class and the second is in some degree unsettled and floating; of the noun-cases concerned here a great deal, indeed — viz. such words as अन्तरेण, समम्, ऋते, प्रभृति, those in °तः etc. — are construed in the same way as the old and genuine prepositions, whereas others are always felt as nouns and construed accordingly — of the kind are निमित्तेन, बलात्, वशात्, हेतोः, द्वारेण, मध्ये, etc.

The third class is made up of gerunds — as आरभ्य, आदाय, उद्दिश्य, आस्थाय, मुक्त्वा, अधिकृत्य, etc. — or participles in °त — viz. युक्त, सहित, रहित, हीन, गत and the like.

152.

I. PREPOSITIONS[2]).

Sanskrit prepositions should rather be styled „post-

---

1) Mhbh. 1, 140, 49 the loc. एकस्मिन्, it seems, does duty of an adverb = »singly, alone." The chacal has artfully removed his competitors, and now he eats up all the flesh, alone.

एवं तेषु प्रयातेषु जम्बुको हृष्टमानसः
खादति स्म तदा मांसमेकस्मिन्मन्त्रनिश्चयात्

Cp. Dutch: in zijn eentje.

2) Indian grammar, which does not possess, as we do, that hetero-

Prepositions. positions," as they are generally put behind the nouns, they are construed with, आ being the one, that is always put before. As a rule, they are also allowed to be compounded with their nouns; in that case, the preposition is generally the former member[1]).

153. The archaic dialect used more prepositions and used them oftener, than the classic language does. The more we go back in time, the greater the number and the variety of idioms. So for instance, in the days of Pâṇini some prepositions — अधि, अभि, उप, परि — seem to have been in common use, but in classic literature they are, if at all, rarely met with.

Rem. The vaidik mantras contain accordingly a still greater number of prepp. and are displaying a still greater variety and manifoldness in employing them. So the old words सनितुः (without) preceded by an acc., its synonym सनुतः preceded by an abl., सत्रुः (with) construed with instrum., do not occur but in the mantras, likewise तिरः and परः, see **160.** — The upasargas अव, निः, वि do not do duty of karmapravacanîya, but for a few passages; Pânini does not mention them in his list of karmaprav., nor are they used so in the liturgical books of the Veda. The once pre-

---

geneous set of terms styled *parts of speech*, has no term exactly answering to our »prepositions," but it calls them by different names according to their phonetical, etymological or syntactical properties. When compounded with roots, so as to make up compound verbs and the like, they are styled *upasarga*. But the same particles will be styled *karmapravacanîya*, when separate words. For this reason, the karmapravacanîya-class does not comprise such prepp., as उपरि, पुरः, सह, but on the other hand it contains some particles, which cannot at any rate be called »prepositions," as अपि, सु. Cp. P. 1, 4, 58; 59; 83—98.

1) It is wrong to say that the noun-case, attending on the prepos., is *governed* by it, for it is not the preposition, that causes the case, but it is the general bearing of the case, which is qualified and limited by the preposition.

positional employment of नि: is proved by compounds of the type निष्प्रवाणि (fresh from the loom), निष्कौशाम्बि (from Kauçâmbi), if compared with अनुगङ्गम्, अतिखट्व (P. 2, 2, 18 with vârtt.) etc.

154. The old prepositions are, in alphabetical order:

1. अति *[1]
2. अधः
3. अधि *
4. अनु *
5. अन्तः
6. अप *
7. अभि *
8. आ *
9. उप *
10. उपरि
11. तिरः
12. परः
13. परि *
14. पुरः
15. पुरा
16. प्रति *
17. बहिः
18. विना
19. सह

Of them, nine (the n°s 1, 3, 6, 7, 9, 11, 12, 13, 15) are obsolete or at least used extremely seldom in the classic dialect.

a.) OBSOLETE PREPOSITIONS.

155. अति. 1. अति is rarely used as a prepos., however frequent, when mere adverb = »exceedingly, very." When prepos. it agrees *with accus.* Ait. Br. 4, 6, 13 अति वै प्रजात्मानमति पशवः (offspring, indeed, and cattle have the precedence above the husbandman himself); Mhbh. 1, 110, 1 Bhîshma says इदं नः प्रथितं कुलम्। अत्यन्यान्पृथिवीपालान्पृथिव्यामधिराज्यभाक् (our renowned family deserves the sovereignty over the earth above other princes). P. 1, 4, 95[2])

Rem. When being compounded with its noun, the compound is adverb: अतिनिद्रम् (beyond one's sleep). P. 2, 1, 6.

156. अधि. 3. अधि is of frequent occurrence in the archaic and old epic writings. In the classic dialect it is still used to express the relation between the ruler and the ruled, as well the ruling *over* P. 1, 4, 97.

1) Those marked by an asterisk are *karmapravacanîya*, see foot-note on p. 114. Hence the other (n°. 2, 5, 10, 11, 12, 14, 15, 17—19) do not share the appellation *upasarga*, even when put close to a verb.

2) The Kâçikâ gives no example of अति being employed as a preposition; it does illustrate but its being = »too much" or = very well." Pâṇini, however, must have thought also of the preposition अति. — Patanjali does not comment on this sûtra.

as the standing *under*; then it is construed with a locative. It is said either अधि पञ्चालेषु ब्रह्मदत्तः (Brahmadatta [ruling] over the Pancâlâs) or अधि ब्रह्मदत्ते पञ्चालाः (the P. under Br.). So Daç. 112 अद्यैव प्रहारवर्मण्यधि विदेहा जाताः [1]).

When put twice, it agrees with the accusative (**171 R.**)

When compounded with its noun, the compound is an adverb and is equivalent to the simple locative of the noun, especially to the nimittasaptamî (**147**): अधिस्त्रि (with respect to women), अधिदैवतम् (with respect to the deity), etc. P. 2, 1, 6.

Rem. In the older dialect अधि is joined by loc., abl. and acc. *With loc.* it indicates the surface »on," as in the old verse quoted by Pat. I, p. 4 भद्रैषां लक्ष्मीर्निहिताधि वाचि (holy bliss is seated on their tongues). — *With abl.* it signifies the coming »from". — *With acc.* it is = »over, on [a surface];" so it is often met with in mantras, sometimes in the brâhmaṇas. Çat. Br. 1, 1, 4, 3 कृष्णाजिनमधि दीक्षन्ते.

157. अप. 6. अप *with ablat.* is mentioned by Pâṇini (1, 4, 88; 2, 1, 12; 2, 3, 10). The standing example of his commentators is अप त्रिगर्तेभ्यो वृष्टो देवः (it has rained outside Trig.). No other instances are known.

158. अभि and परि. 7. अभि and 13. परि, both *with acc.*, are almost synonymous, cp. Greek ἀμφί and περί.

They had of old the meaning »round, about," when in metaphorical sense, also »concerning, on." In literature examples of परि are extremely rare, if they occur at all; it seems to have soon antiquated. Instances of अभि are met with, especially in the archaic dialect. Kâç. on P. 2, 1, 14 अग्निमभि — or अभ्यग्नि [compound adverb] — शलभाः पतन्ति (the fire-flies hover round the fire); Ch. Up. 4, 6, 1 अभि सायम् (about the evening); Kaṭh. 1, 10 वीतमन्युर्गौतमो मामभि (G. feels no anger against me).

---

1) According to P. 1, 4, 98 in the case of अधिकृ (to appoint over) it may be said optionally either अत्र मामधि करिष्यति or अत्र मामधिकरिष्यति (he will put me over it). The Petrop. Dict. — I, p. 142 *s. v.* अधि 2) *a*) *β*) — wrongly takes माम् for the word construed with अधि. It is not the acc. माम् but the locat. अत्र, which stands in construction with the preposition, as is plainly shown by the meaning of the sentence.

Rem. 1. Pânini (1, 4, 90)[1]) teaches a fourfold employment of परि: *a.*) it denotes a mark, *b.*) it expresses a quality, *c.*) it signifies that which falls to one's share, *d.*) it is used in a distributive sense. The same is stated for अनु and प्रति; also for अभि, save that it cannot be karmapravacanîya in the case *c.*). The Kâçikâ illustrates this rule by these examples: *a.*) वृक्षं परि - or प्रति or अनु or अभि - विद्योतते विद्युत् »the lightning flashes round the tree;" *b.*) साधुर्देवदत्तो मातरमभि - or अनु or प्रति or परि - »N.N. is good for his mother;" *d.*) वृक्षंवृक्षमभि - or अनु or प्रति or परि - सिञ्चति »he waters one tree after another,"[2]) whereas *c.*) यदत्र मां परि - or प्रति or अनु - स्यात्तद्दीयताम् »give me whatever be my share of it," but यदत्र मामभिष्यात्, here अभि is upasarga not karmapravacanîya. P. 1, 4, 91

In the dialect of the vaidik mantras, indeed, both अभि and परि display this large sphere of employment, almost the same as that of प्रति in classic Sanskrit, see **179**. With अभि cp. the like use of Greek ἀμφί, Germ. *um*, Dutch *om*.

Rem. 2. To the obsolete अभि and परि classic Sanskrit has substituted their derivatives अभितः and परितः, which however are only used of space. See **186**.

Rem. 3. An *ablative* is taught with परि, when = अप (**157**). Then the prepos. should be put twice: परि परि त्रिगर्तेभ्यो वृष्टो देवः In literature, however, परि with abl. is as little met with as अप, except the vaidik mantras, but there it has a larger employment, being = Lat. *ex* or *ab*. P. 2, 3, 10. P. 8, 1, 5.

159. उप. 9. उप is frequent in the vaidik mantras, afterwards rare. P. 1, 4, 87 classes it among the karmapravacanîya, 1. to denote a »going beyond," then it is construed with a locat. उप निष्के कार्षापणम् (by a karshâp. more than a nishka), 2. to denote inferiority, then it complies with the acc. उप शाकटायनं वैयाकरणाः P. 2, 3, 9.

1) P. 1, 4, 90 लक्षणेत्थंभूताख्यानभागवीप्सासु प्रतिपर्यनवः
» » 91 अभिरभागे.

2) When used in a distributive sense, अनु, अभि, परि are rather to be considered adverbs; वृक्षं वृक्षमनु सिञ्चति is literally = »he waters tree tree successively," similarly °परि or °अभि सिञ्चति »he waters tree tree roundabout." Cp. such passages as R. 3, 47, 10 अयाचतार्थैरन्वर्थैः »he entreated [her] by [offering her] grants after grants" lit. grants grants successively.

Rem. 1. According to the commentaries on P. 2, 1, 6 उप, like अभि, expresses *nearness*, when compounded with its noun: उपकुम्भम् (near the pot). So Daç. 99 उपकन्यकापुरम् (near the zenana).

Rem. 2. In the vaidik mantras उप is construed with acc., loc., instr. and is expressive of nearness. Rgv. 1, 23, 17 अमूर्या उप सूर्ये याभिर्वा सूर्यः सह· — *With accus.*, I have met with this instance in epic poetry. R. 3, 37, 21 Mârîca dissuades the rapture of Sîtâ on account of the irresistible power of great Râma दूष्टश्चेत् त्वं रणे तेन तदन्तमुप जीवितम् (if he will meet you [Râvaṇa] in battle, then your life is on its end).

160. तिरः 11. तिरः — in form and meaning = Lat. *trans* — does duty of a prepos. in the archaic dialect of the brâhmaṇas etc. It is found partly *with acc.* = »athwart, through, beyond," partly *with abl.* »beyond, out of reach of:" Çat. Br. 3, 3, 4, 6 तिर इव वै देवा मनुष्येभ्यः Cp. the ablat. with तिरस्करोति and other words of *concealing* (97).

12. परः (beyond) with instrum., abl. or acc. is restricted to the vaidik mantras.

13. परि see 158.

161. पुरा· 14. पुरा *with ablative* is a time-denoting prepos. of the archaic and epic dialect. It means »before." Âçv. Gṛhy. 1, 15, 1 पुरान्यैरालम्भात् (before his being touched by others), Ch. Up. 2, 24, 3 पुरा प्रातरनुवाकस्योपाकरणात् (before the beginning of the prâtaranuvâka). Cp. 175.

Rem. Sometimes पुरा may have expressed separation. Rgv. 8, 44, 30 पुरा ऽग्ने दुरितेभ्यः पुरा मृध्रेभ्यः कवे प्र ण आयुर्वसो तिर (extend our life, Agni, keeping it, wise being, far off from misfortune etc.), Ait. Br. 2, 6, 14 पुरा नाभ्या अपिशसो वपामुत्खिदतात् (he must cut out the omentum without hurting the navel).

b). PREPOSITIONS STILL EXISTING.

162. The other ten are still in common use, though not all of them are equally frequent. We will treat of them in alphabetical order, adding moreover to each such younger prepositions as are more or less its synonyms.

163. अधः and अधस्तात्. [2.] **अधः** (below, under). Its synonym is **अधस्तात्**, a derivative of it. Both are construed *with preceding genitive*. Çâk. I नीवाराः... भ्रष्टास्तरूणामधः, Panc. 211 अस्यैव न्यग्रोधस्याधस्तात्प्रक्षिप्य माम्.

Rem. 1. Sometimes it complies with abl. Panc. 145 वृक्षादधः Compare 171 R.

Rem. 2. To denote a lower place or state the old dialect possessed also the adverbs अवः and अवस्तात्[1]). Çat. Br. 9, 3, 1, 6 अवस्ताद्धि दिव आदित्यः

164. अनु. [4.] **अनु** *with accusative* „after." Like its Latin counterpart „secundum" it is used in various senses: *a.*) of space and rank, *b.*) of time, *c.*) = „according to," *d.*) = „adhering to one's side," sim. Mostly, at least in prose, it is put behind the noun-case as **तदनु** (thereafter), **तमनु** (after him).

Its manifold employment may be illustrated by these examples: 1. *after* - in space, time, rank - R. 2, 90, 3 जगामानु पुरोहितम्, Panc. 203 अहमपि तावनु प्रस्थितः, Kâç. on P. 1, 4, 86 अन्वर्जुनं योद्धारः (warriors inferior to A.); — 2. *along* R. 2, 83, 26 निवेश्य गङ्गामनु चमूम् (he encamped his army on the banks of the Ganges); — 3. »following" = »adhering to" Mhbh. 3, 12, 45 यस्त्वां द्वेष्टि स मां द्वेष्टि यस्त्वामनु स मामनु; — 4 »after" = »according to" R. 2, 58, 19 अनु राजानमार्यां च कैकेयीं कारय; — 5. *about* Nir. 12, 1 प्रकाशीभावस्यानुविष्टम्भमनु (about the gradual advancing of dawn); — 6. *concerning* Ch. Up. 4, 17, 9 एवंविदं ह वा एषा ब्रह्माणमनु गाथा (concerning the brahman who knows so, it is said in a verse —).

Rem. 1. अनु may be compounded with its noun. Mhbh. 1, 170, 14 अनुगङ्गं चरन् (rambling along the Gangâ), Kathâs. 28, 26 अनुजाह्नवि.

---

1) Comp. the upasarga अव and *lacus Avernus*, the Latin designation of the regions below.

If अनु have a distributive meaning, compounding is obligatory: अन्वहम् (day after day), अनुज्येष्ठम् ([all ranged] according to the eldest).

Rem. 2. In epic poetry अनु is sometimes found with the ablative. The instances, I know, are Mhbh. 1, 99, 38 शप्ता यूयम्.... अनु[1]) संवत्सरात्सर्वे शापमोक्षमवाप्स्यथ (you are cursed, but after a year you will be released of the curse); ibid. 14, 71, 6 — the Pâṇḍavas enter Hastinâpura and make their compliments to Dhṛtarâshtra — धृतराष्ट्रादनु च ते गान्धारीं... कुन्तीं च... विदुरं पूजयित्वा etc.; R. Gorr. 6, 10, 23 लोको भजते कारणादनु (v. a. men's destiny is in proportion to the cause, whence it has sprung)[2]).

Rem. 3. Pâṇini treats of अनु in four sûtras: I, 4, 84—86 and 90 The last, which sums up the meanings of अनु when = परि and प्रति, is quoted **158** R. 1.

165. अन्तः [5.] **अन्तः**, a very old particle. It is *added to a locative* for the sake of specifying its meaning „within" (**133**, *a*). But often also noun + **अन्तः** are compounded into an avyayîbhâva. — Examples: *a*) of अन्तः with locat. M. 7, 223 शृणुयादन्तर्वेश्मनि (he must give audience within doors), Panc. I, 32 निवसन्नन्तर्दारुणि वह्निः (the fire, dwelling within the wood), Kathâs. 4, 57 सोऽपि नीतस्तमस्यन्तः पुरोहितः (and the purohita was likewise led into the darkness); *b*) of अन्तः compounded. Panc. 144 अहं सलिलान्तः प्रविष्टः (I entered the water), ibid. 277 ब्राह्मणास्तया कूपान्तः पातितः, Kâd. I, 47 क्रोडान्तर्निहिततनयाः ([birds] which have put their young ones between their wings).

Rem. अन्तः occasionally complies with a genitive. Yâjñ. 2, 104 सर्वभूतानामन्तश्चरसि, Kumâras. 2, 5 अपामन्तरुप्तं बीजम्.

166. अन्तरा and अन्तरेण. Kindred forms of **अन्तः** are the particles **अन्तरा** and **अन्तरेण**, petrified instrumentals. Both agree *with the accusative*. They are 1st = „between," 2ly = „without,"

1) The Petr. Dict. reads अनुसंवत्सरात् as a compound.

2) The Petr. Dict. gives also some instances of अनु with a *genitive* See I, p. 197 *s. v.*

3ly = „save, but for;" 4ly अन्तरेण may signify „with respect to, concerning." — Like अन्तः, they are allowed to make up a compound with their noun, then the noun is the former member.

Examples: of 1. — Çâk. III यावद्विटपान्तरेणावलोकयामि (meanwhile I will look *between* [= *through*] the foliage). When construed with two nouns, the prepos. precedes, and च is put twice. Pat. I, 45 अन्तरा त्वां च मां च कमण्डलुः (the pitcher is *between* you and me), Çat. Br. 1, 1, 1, 1 अन्तरेणाहवनीयं च गार्हपत्यं च [1]); — 2. Pat. I, 8 अन्तरेणापि मन्त्रमग्निः कपालानि संतापयति (even *without* the uttering of mantras fire heats the plates), R. 2, 11, 18 तत्र त्वां च्यावयच्छत्रुस्तव जीवितमन्तरा (there the enemy threw thee down lifeless); — 3. Panc. 60 नूनं स लुब्धो नोपायमन्तरेण वध्यः स्यात् (I am sure that voracious beast cannot be killed *but* by a stratagem), R. 3, 19, 7 नहि पश्याम्यहं लोके यः कुर्यान्मम विप्रियम्। अन्तरेण... महेन्द्रम् (none *but* Mahendra); — 4. Çâk. V. तदस्या देवीं वसुमतीमन्तरेण महदुपालम्भनं गतोऽस्मि (therefore I have incurred a heavy reproof from her *with respect to* queen Vasumatî) [2]).

Rem. 1. Occasionally a genitive is found instead of the acc. with अन्तरेण, as Mhbh. 5, 16, 29. — Cp. Pat. I, 59 वृषलकुलमनयोरन्तरा (between these two [families of brahmans] there dwells a family of çûdras), here अन्तरा complies also with the gen., it seems.

Rem. 2. Difference between is expressed not by a preposition, but by means of two genitives. R. 3, 47, 45 यदन्तरं सिंहशृगालयोर्वने यदन्तरं स्यन्दनिकासमुद्रयोः। सुराग्र्यसौवीरकयोर्यदन्तरं तदन्तरं दाशरथेस्तवैव च (what differente there is between lion and chacal in the forest, between a rivulet and the ocean, between ambrosia and the beverage of the Sauvîras, that is the difference between the son of Daçaratha

---

1) Comp. a somewhat similar idiom in Latin, f. i. Horat. Epist. I, 2, 11 Nestor componere lites । *inter* Peliden festinat *et inter* Atriden.

2) So in this prâkṛt passage of the Mâlavikâgnimitra IV, p. 89 तदो ताए.... भवदो अविणअं अंतरेण परिगदत्था किदा.

and you), Mhbh. 12, 8, 15 विशेषं नाधिगच्छामि पतितस्याधनस्य च. As to the dvandva-compounds in the first example see **207**.

167. A synonymous prepos. with acc. = »between, through" is मध्येन. R. 2, 98, 15 द्रुमजालानि मध्येन जगाम. It may be compounded with its noun. Panc. 151 चापकोटिर्मस्तकमध्येन निष्क्रान्ता.

168. आ. [8] आ always agrees *with the ablative*, and is put before its noun. It serves to denote the boundary or limit, either the terminus a quo or the terminus ad quem, mostly the latter. It is available both in space and in time, and may be rendered accordingly now by „since" and „till", now by „from" and „to." M. 2, 22 is an example illustrative of its signifying the two termini आ समुद्रात्तु वै पूर्वादा समुद्रात्तु पश्चिमात्। तयोरेवान्तरं गिर्योरार्यावर्तं विदुर्बुधाः (the wise know Âryâvarta to be the country between the said mountains *from* the eastern ocean *to* the western).

Other examples: 1. *term. a quo.* Çâk. I आ मूलाच्छ्रोतुमिच्छामि (I wish to hear it from the root); Kathâs. 24, 186 आ बाल्यात्तापसो ऽभवम् (since my childhood I was an ascetic);

2. *term. ad quem.* Mhbh. 1, 163, 8 आ कर्णाद्भिन्नवक्त्रः (having his mouth split up to the ears), Çâk. IV ओदकान्तात्स्निग्धो जनोऽनुगन्तव्य इति श्रूयते; — Çâk. V आ प्रसवादस्मद्गृहे तिष्ठतु (let her stay with us till her delivery), Âçv. Gṛhy. 1, 19, 5 आ षोडशाद् [viz. वर्षाद्] ब्राह्मणस्यानतीतः काल आ द्वाविंशात्क्षत्रियस्या चतुर्विंशाद्वैश्यस्य (until the sixteenth year the time is not passed for the brahman, etc.). — In a figurative sense f. i. Çâk. I आ परितोषाद्विदुषां न साधु मन्ये प्रयोगविज्ञानम् (I do not approve the skill of performing a representation, unless the connoisseurs be contented).

आ is often compounded with its noun into an avyayîbhâva. Daç. 175 आकण्ठं पपौ (he drunk his fill, liter. »till his throat"), Kathâs. 5, 103 आसंसारं जगत्यस्मिन्नेका नित्या ह्यनित्यता (for, since the world exists, there is but one thing steady in the Creation, namely unsteadiness); Panc. I, 39 आमरणं भिक्षा (a lifelong beggary).

Rem. In the vaidik mantras आ is of the utmost frequency, and is put to different cases, sometimes before, sometimes behind. In most instances it is rather a mere adverb. [1]).

169. Other prepositional words = „till, until; since" are यावत्, आरभ्य and प्रभृति.

यावत्. यावत् is mostly attended by the accus., sometimes by the abl. Utt. I, p. 6 कियन्तमवधिं यावत् (till how long?); Kathâs. 54, 47 असौ त्वया प्राप्यतां स्वगृहं यावत् (— as far as his house); Mhbh. 1, 95, 12 प्राचीं दिशं जिगाय यावत्सूर्योदयात्.

Rem. As यावत् is properly no prepos., but the acc. of the neuter of a pronoun, used as an adverb »as long as, as far as," it is plain that it may also signify »*during* some time." Panc. 198 कदाचिन्महत्यनावृष्टिः संजाता प्रभूतवर्षाणि यावत्. Cp. **54** R. 2.

170. आरभ्य and प्रभृति. आरभ्य and प्रभृति *with preceding ablative* are very common. The former is properly a gerund = „beginning-, starting from," प्रभृति is construed with abl. by so-called syntactic analogy, see Rem. 2.

Examples of आरभ्य = since. Panc. 238 मम शिशुकालादारभ्याशीतिर्वर्षाणि समभूवन्; Mâlat. VI, p. 88 मालत्याः प्रथमावलोकनदिनादारभ्य (since the day I have seen M. for the first time).

Examples of प्रभृति = since. Panc. 51 बाल्यात्प्रभृति सहचारिणौ; Mâlat. III, p. 50 मन्मथोद्यानयात्रादिवसात्प्रभृति (since the day of the procession in the garden of Kâma); Mudr. II, p. 70 आज्ञापय कुतः प्रभृति कथयामि.

Rem. 1. They may also be used of space. Hit. 132 नकुलविवरादारभ्य सर्पविवरं यावत्; Kumâras. 3, 26 असूत सद्यः कुसुमान्यशोकः स्कन्धात्प्रभृत्येव.

---

1) In a period as early as Yâska, आ with loc. had antiquated, for this exegete deems it necessary to interprete the mantric expression अभ्र आ अपः (water in the cloud) by अपो ऽभ्रे ऽधि (Nir. 5, 5). In a subsequent time the very gloss of Yâska would have required another, for अधि with loc. in this meaning being obsolete (**156**), classic Sanskrit would have employed अन्तः or °मध्ये or have said अभ्रगता अपः

Rem. 2. प्रभृति is originally a feminine, meaning »origin, commencement" and like its synonym आदि, it is often used at the ends of bahuvrîhis (**229**, 1°). At the outset, therefore, such a term as तत्कालप्रभृति was said in the very same acceptation as तत्कालादि, viz. meaning स कालः प्रभृतिर्यस्य तत्. By the time, however, the noun प्रभृति ceased to be employed as a separate word, and one commenced to look upon the adverbial compounds, ending in °प्रभृति, as if they were ending in some preposition, meaning »since." By this mistake it happened that प्रभृति assumed even the character of a self-existent particle construed with ablative, by analogy of आरभ्य and the like. Hence f. i. the compound जन्मप्रभृति »since his birth" (M. 8, 90) represents an older idiom than जन्मनः प्रभृति. In such turns as तदाप्रभृति (since then), यदाप्रभृति (since when), अद्यप्रभृति, the true nominal nature of प्रभृति is plain, and it is again a misunderstanding to write them as two words तदा प्रभृति etc.

171. उपरि. [10] उपरि (above, over, on, upon) is the very opposite of अधः, see **163**. As a rule, it is construed with preceding *genitive* [1]), unless it makes up the latter part of a compound: तस्योपरि or तदुपरि. Its employment is various, as it is used *a.*) of space, *b.*) of time »upon = immediately after," *c.*) of rank, *d.*) = »on, upon about, concerning, with respect to," then उपरि is concurrent with प्रति and with the *nimittasaptamî*, *e.*) = »before, under the eyes of."

Examples: *a.*) Kâç. on P. 8, 1, 7 उपरि शिरसो घटं धारयति (he carries a jar upon his head), Panc. 125 राज्ञो वक्षःस्थलोपरि मक्षिकोपविष्टा, Kathâs. 25, 228 स राजा तद्धेमाब्जं स्थापयामास.... कलशोपरि, Panc. 112 कोपात्तस्योपरि पपात (moved by anger he made a bolt at him). — Metaphorically f. i. Panc. I, 166 देशानामुपरि क्ष्माभृदातुराणां चिकित्सकाः etc. »the king lives *on* his dominions, physicians *on* the sick," R. 3, 54, 23 क्रोधो

1) So it is taught by Pâṇini, as must be inferred by comparing P. 2, 3, 30 with 5, 3, 27—34.

ममापूर्वो धैर्यस्योपरि वर्धते (the fresh anger grows over my forbearance, that is: goes beyond my forb.);

b.) Kâç. on P. 3, 3, 9 उपरि मुहूर्तस्योपाध्यायश्चेदागच्छेत् (if the teacher arrives after a moment) [1]);

c.) Kathâs. 6, 167 तां देवीनामुपरि कृतवान् (he honoured her above his queens);

d.) Panc. 142 विरक्तिः संजाता मे सांप्रतं देशस्यास्योपरि (I have now taken a dislike to this country), Mudr. III, p. 105 अहो राजपरिजनस्य चाणक्यस्योपरि विद्वेषपक्षपातः (well, the king's attendance are not friendly disposed towards Câṇakya), Panc. 116 किं तव ममोपरि चिन्तया (what have you to care for me?), ibid. 26 न दीनोपरि महान्तः कुप्यन्ति;

e.) Panc. 266 प्राणत्यागं तवोपरि करिष्यामि (I will kill myself before your eyes). Comp. **177.**

Rem. Occasionally उपरि is construed with a locative. Kathâs. 3, 58 उपर्यन्तःपुरे सा च रत्नमित्यभिरक्ष्यते. — With ablative it is also sometimes met with, as in the passage of Utpala, quoted by Kern in his translation of Varâham. Brh. I, p. 7, which has been adduced **73** R. 3 [2]). Even the *accus.* with उपरि is not forbidden. Pâṇ. 8, 1, 7 teaches उपरि, अधि and अधः being put twice, when denoting a close nearness, as उपर्युपरि ग्रामम्। अध्यधि ग्रामम्; here the accus. is standing (see the kârikâ quoted by Kâç. on P. 2, 3, 2). Çiçup. 1, 4 नवानधोऽधो बृहतः पयोधरान्, Mhbh. 1, 120, 9 उपर्युपरि गच्छन्तः शैलराजम् [3]).

72. उपरिष्टात्, a derivate of उपरि, is construed, when prepos., with

---

1) In full, the example given by the Kâçikâ, is ऊर्ध्वं मुहूर्तादुपरि मुहूर्तस्य etc. In the bad excerpt of the Calcutta edition of Pâṇini these words have been mutilated into मुहूर्तादुपरि, which has deceived Boethlingk in his edition of Pâṇini and in his Petr. Dict. (I, p. 968).

2) The example of the Petrop. Dict. (*s. v.* V, p. 1191), Kathâs. 53, 125 यावत्स्वर्गादुपर्यगात् is not convincing. It is rather probable, that the abl. should be construed with यावत् [**169**], उपरि being a mere adverb = »upward." — For the rest, it is not strange that the wavering between abl. and gen. in construing adjectives and adverbs of space and time (**125**) appears also in the syntax of prepositions. Cp. **173** R. 1.

3) It is no exception, that Nala 1, 2 the gen. is used उपर्युपरि सर्वेषाम्, since the repetition does not imply here the notion of proximity, the meaning being »[standing] high above all men."

preceding genitive, and generally signifies »above, upon" in space. The archaic dialect did use it also as a time-denoting word = »after" [cp. उपरि, **171** *b*)]. — In the Çat. Br. it sometimes complies with the accusative.

Rem. ऊर्ध्वम् = »above" is not frequent. M. 1, 92 ऊर्ध्वं नाभेर्मेध्यतरः पुरुषः परिकीर्तितः. But it is frequent, when of time = »after," see **174**.

173. परम्, परस्तात्, परतः, परेण. [12]. Akin to the old and obsolete परः [**160**] classic Sanskrit possesses **परम्, परस्तात्, परतः** and **परेण**, all of them expressive of the notion *beyond*. When denoting space, they serve also to signify the *passing by* — especially **परेण** with accus. — and the *surpassing* — espec. **परस्तात्** with genit. When denoting time, they are = „after" and comply with *ablative*.

Examples: *a.*) of space and rank. Ait. Br. 8, 14, 3 ये के च परेण हिमवन्तं जनपदाः (all countries *beyond* the Himâlaya); Mhbh. 1, 232, 11 परेणास्मान्प्रेहि (»*pass by* us", v. a. »do not harm us"); Kâm. 5, 61 लक्ष्मीरेवान्वयो लोके न लक्ष्म्याः परतोऽन्वयः (— nor does noble extraction *go beyond* wealth), Malâv. I, p. 1 यः पर ायतीनाम् (who surpasses all ascetics).

b.) of time: »after." M. 2, 122 अभिवादात्परम् (after the salutation), Panc. V, 58 मुहूर्तात्परतः (after a moment), Utt. III, p. 38 स्तन्यत्यागात्परेण (after leaving the breast). So the frequent phrases अतः परम्, ततः परम् and the like.

Rem. 1. Occasionally they occur, when being attended by a genit., even while time-denoting. M. 8, 223 परेण दशाहस्य [Kull. = दशाहादूर्ध्वम्], Ait. Br. 2, 33, 5 संवत्सरस्य परस्तात्.

Rem. 2. As परम् etc. answer to Latin *ultra*, so अर्वाक् is the equivalent of Lat. *citra*, denoting the side next to us. When time-denoting, अर्वाक् contrasted with परम् and the like is accordingly = »before;" then it may be construed with the ablative. M. 8, 30 प्रनष्टस्वामिकं रिक्थं राजा त्र्यब्दं निधापयेत्। अर्वाक् त्र्यब्दाद्धरेत्स्वामी परेण नृपतिर्हरेत् (property the owner of which has disappeared, must be guarded by the king for three years. Before that term, the owner may reclaim it; afterwards it falls to the king).

174. ऊर्ध्वम् and अनन्तरम्. „After" in time is often expressed by ऊर्ध्वम् or अनन्तरम् *with ablative*. Of them, अनन्तरम् commonly makes up the latter part of a compound adverb. Kumâras. 6, 93 त्र्यहादूर्ध्वम् (after three days), Ragh. 3, 7 पुराणपत्त्रापगमादनन्तरं लता (a creeper at the time it has lost its old foliage), Panc. 52 तस्या दर्शनानन्तरम् (after having seen her). So तदनन्तरम् (after this) and the like.

That the single ablative may occasionally express »*after* what time" has been stated above (**99**).

175. पश्चात्. Another word for „after" is पश्चात्. When prepos., it complies *with a genitive* generally preceding, and is mostly used of space and rank. Kathâs. 6, 134 अहं प्राविशं मम पश्चाच्च शर्ववर्मा; Panc. 181 अस्य पश्चान्न न्यः सुहृन्मे (no friend I put after him).

Rem. »After" in space may also be denoted by words meaning »west of" as प्रत्यक्, by पृष्ठे (at the rear) and जघनेन (back). The last seems to be restricted to the old liturgical dialect.

176. पुरः, पुरतः, पुरस्तात् and अग्रे, अग्रतः etc. [14]. The very opposite of पश्चात् is the old adverb पुरः = *before* and its synonyms: *a*) the kindred पुरतः, पुरस्तात्, *b*) अग्रे and अग्रतः (literally „at the top, at the head"). When prepositions, they comply *with genitive* or are compounded. They are employed both of space and of time.

Examples of पुरः etc. applied to space. Çâk. V ततः प्रविशन्ति मुनयः पुरश्चैषां कञ्चुकी पुरोहितश्च; Âçv. Grhy. 1, 11, 6 तस्य [पशोः] पुरस्तादुल्मुकं हरन्ति (before the victim they bear a blazing stick); Panc. 286 तस्या अग्रे निचिक्षेप [sc. पल्लवानि] (he cast the young shoots down before her). — As to their application to time see **178**.

177. They are also often used to denote „in the presence of, under the eyes of" = Lat. *coram*. In the same way

समक्षम् and प्रत्यक्षम्. Moreover words, meaning „in the vicinity of" as संनिधौ etc.

Note the frequent employment of this turn with verbs of *saying*, *telling*, *promising*, even with those of *going*, *bringing*, *appearing* und the like. It is virtually the same to say तस्याग्रे —, तस्य पुरतः, समीपे etc. कथयति (प्रतिशृणोति etc.) or तस्मै —, तस्य —, तं प्रति कथयति (प्रतिशृणोति etc.)

Examples: 1. — पुरः etc. = Lat. *coram*. Daç. 96 सा तान्पुरुषान्सामपूर्वं मम पुरस्तादयाचत; Ratn. III, p. 67 ह्रिया सर्वस्याग्रे नमति [1]) वदनम् (for shame she lowers her face before everybody); Kathâs. 4, 79 सत्यं समक्षमस्माकमनेनाङ्गीकृतं धनम् (forsooth in our presence he has avowed [as to] the money); Daç. 176 तस्याः पुरो रुरोद (— wept before her eyes).

2. — पुरः etc. with verbs of *saying*, *telling*, *bringing* etc. Kathâs. 27, 27 स राज्ञः पुरतः सर्वमब्रवीत् (he told the king all); Panc. 274 तौ पित्रोरग्रतो विहसन्तौ ज्येष्ठभ्रातृचेष्टितमूचतुः; ibid. 25 the chacal says to the lion किं स्वामिपादानामग्रे ऽसत्यं विज्ञाप्यते; Nala 1, 15 तस्याः समीपे तु नलं प्रशशंसुः.... नैषधस्य समीपे तु दमयन्तीं पुनःपुनः; Kathâs. 25, 211 एतत्प्रतिज्ञातं स्वयं नरपतेः पुरः.... मया (I myself have promised so to the king). Panc. 277 पेटा राज्ञाग्रे नीता (the basket was brought to the king), Mahâv. I, p. 18 रामभद्रस्य पुरतः प्रादुर्भवतु तऊनुः = रामभद्राय [or °द्रस्य] प्रादुर्भवतु.

Rem. The inverse of Lat. *coram*, viz. *clam* »at the back of, without the knowledge of" is expressed by परोक्षम् or °क्षे, पृष्ठे, पृष्ठतः sim. Kathâs. 29, 73 सा स्नुषां.... पुत्रस्य परोक्षमकदर्थयत् (she illtreated her daughter-in-law without the knowledge of her son). [2]).

---

1) So I have mended the bad reading of mss. and edd. नयति.

2) In the brâhmaṇas परोक्षम्, °क्षात् when = *clam*, is also construed with instrum. Çat. Br. 1, 5, 2, 7 यज्ञमानेन परोक्षम्, Ait. Br. 3, 36, 5 अहिना बुध्न्येन परोक्षात्.

178. When of time, पुरः etc. agree likewise with a genitive [1]). Yet „before" in time is commonly not expressed by them, but rather by प्राक् or पूर्वम्, both complying with the ablative.

Examples *a.*) of time-denoting पुरः etc. Çâk. VII happiness is said to be the consequence of the favour of mighty persons तव प्रसादस्य पुरस्तु संपदः (but your favour is anticipated by happiness), Mhbh. 1, 232, 1 पुरतः कृच्छ्रकालस्य धीमाञ्जागर्ति पूरुषः; — *b.*) of प्राक् and पूर्वम्. Çâk. V प्रागन्तरिक्षगमनात्स्वमपत्यजातमन्यैर्द्विजैः परभृता खलु पोषयन्ति; Ragh. 12, 35 अभिगमनात्पूर्वम् (before approaching).

179. प्रति. [16] प्रति *with accusative* is, relatively speaking, the most common among the so called prepositions. It generally denotes the direction towards, and for this reason it often is a concurrent idiom of the sole accusative, dative and locative. It is used *a*) with words of movement to signify the „whither," *b*) in such turns, as *speaking to*, *bowing to*, *striving to*, *love* —, *hatred* —, *anger to* and the like, *c*) like the nimittasaptamî (**147**) to express „with respect to, on account of, concerning, about, on", *d*) = „about," to denote nearness in space or time, *e*) it has a distributive sense, in what case one is wont to compound प्रति with its noun, as प्रत्यहम् (every day).

As a rule, प्रति is put behind its noun, at least in prose.

Examples: *a*) Panc. 42 गृहं प्रति प्रतस्थे (he set out homeward), Daç. 30 गच्छन्निजदेशं प्रति; — methaphor. R. 2, 107, 11 गयेन यजमानेन

---

1) Note the ablative with अग्रे: M. 3, 114 अतिथिभ्यो ऽग्र एवैतान्भोजयेत् »he must entertain them even before his guests" [Kullûka अतिथिभ्योऽग्रे पूर्वमतिथिभ्यः]

पितॄन्प्रति (by Gaya, as he directed his worship to the *pitaras*).

b). Panc. 159 भणितं त्वां प्रति तया; — R. 2, 52, 79 नदीं तां सह सीतया प्रणामत्प्रति संतुष्टः; — Mudr. I, p. 22 तद्ग्रहणं प्रति यत्नः; — Çâk. III एवमुपालब्धस्य ते न मां प्रत्यनुक्रोशः; — Çâk. VII सहधर्मचारिणं प्रति न त्वया मन्युः कार्यः; — R. 3, 54, 23 वैरं रामं प्रति; — Çâk. I मन्दोत्सुक्योऽस्मि नगरगमनं प्रति.

c.) M. 8, 245 सीमां प्रति समुत्पन्ने विवादे (if a contest have arisen *about* some boundary); Nala 2, 6 चिन्तयामास तत्कार्यं सुमहत्स्वां सुतां प्रति (— *concerning* his daughter); Mâlat. IX, p. 154 प्रियां तु मालतीं प्रति निराशो ऽस्मि; Panc. 3 Vishnuçarman engages himself to make the king's sons नयशास्त्रं प्रत्यनन्यसदृशान्; Çâk. I किं नु खलु यथा वयमस्यामेवमियमप्यस्मान्प्रति स्यात् (should she perhaps be disposed towards me, as I am to her?).

Rem. Note the phrase मां प्रति »in my opinion, for my part," fr. *selon moi*. In full मां प्रति प्रतिभाति (it looks-, seems to me). Hitop. 100 तेन विना सकलजनपूर्णोऽप्ययं ग्रामो मां प्रत्यरण्यवत्प्रतिभाति.

d.) Mhbh. 1, 8, 7 अप्सरा मेनका.... तं गर्भम्.... उत्ससर्ज यथाकालं स्थूलकेशाश्रमं प्रति (— *about* the hermitage of Sth.); M. 7, 182 मार्गशीर्षे शुभे मासि यायाद्यात्रां महीपतिः। फाल्गुणं वाथ चैत्रं वा मासौ प्रति.

e). Panc. 286 तस्य वर्षं प्रति करभमेकं प्रयच्छति (he gives him one camel a year); Yâjñ. 1, 110 यज्ञं प्रति (at every sacrifice). — Compounded f. i. Çâk. I प्रतिपात्रमाधीयतां यत्नः (let each actor do his duty), Bhojapr. 14 तस्मै राज्यं ददौ निजपुत्रेभ्यः प्रत्येकमेकैकं ग्रामं दत्त्वा. A concurrent idiom is mentioned **158** R. 1.

180. Pâṇini enjoins also the *ablative* with प्रति, in two cases viz, when pointing out *a*) one's match or substitute, *b*) something given in exchange. The Kâçikâ illustrates our rule by these examples: *a*). प्रद्युम्नः कृष्णात् or कृष्णतः प्रति (Pr. the match or substitute of K.), *b*). तिलेभ्यः प्रति यच्छति माषान् (in exchange of sesam he gives beans). I have nowhere met with instances of that construction in literature, but for one, I borrow textually from the Petr. Dict., viz. Mhbh. 3, 13287 उक्षाणं पक्त्वा सह ओदनेन अस्मात्कपोतात्प्रति ते नयन्तु. Yet there are several instances in the ancient Vedic dialect as well as in classic Sanskrit of an *accus*. with प्रति, when signifying the »match." Rgv. 2, 1, 8 त्वं सहस्राणि शता दश प्रति (you are equal to

P. 1, 4, 92; cp. 2, 3, 11.

thousands etc.), Kathâs. 45, 400 न च शक्तस्त्वमिमं प्रति (nor are you a match for him).

181. बहिः [17] **बहिः** (outside, out) is the very opposite of **अन्तः** **(165).** It is more used as a mere adverb than as a preposition. In the latter case it complies with preceding *ablative.* Panc. 176 त्वं जलाद् बहिर्भव (get out of the water), ibid. 291 तद्गृहाद् बहिर्निष्क्रान्तः. Or it may be the latter part of a compound: Utt. IV, p. 73 आश्रमबहिः.

Rem. Daç. 77 बहिः is construed with a genitive: अद्राक्षं च मार्गाभ्यासवर्तिनः कस्यापि क्षपणकविहारस्य बहिः.... कमपि क्षपणकम्.

182. विना. [18] **विना** (*without*) is construed with *instrumental*, *accusative* or *ablative.* In prose it is commonly put behind its case[1]), in poetry it often precedes (P. 2, 3, 32.)

Examples: with instrum. Panc. 266 अहं त्वया विना नात्र वस्तुं शक्नोमि (I cannot live here without you); — with accus. Panc. 269 सा पुनर्न शक्ता त्वां विना स्थातुम् (but she cannot stay without you), R. 3, 9, 20 न विना याति तं खड्गम् (he does not go abroad without that sword); — with ablat. Daç. 141 तादृशाद् भाग्यराशेर्विना (without such a store of happiness), Var. Bṛh. 44, 17 स जयति तदा नरेन्द्रः शत्रूनचिराद्विना यत्नात्.

Rem. 1. Occasionally विना may have the meaning of »save, if not". Panc. I, 42 विना मलयमन्यत्र चन्दनं न प्ररोहति, ibid. p. 244 न च रक्ताक्षं विना धीमान् (there is nobody wise but Raktâxa).

Rem. 2. Just as विना are construed पृथक् and नाना »apart from." (P. 2, 3, 32.) Of नाना, when a prepos., I can quote no instance from literature, of पृथक् only with an ablat. Bhojapr. 27 राजधर्मः पृथग्विद्वद्धर्मात् (the king's duty lies outside the duty of the scholar), Prabodh. II, p. 34, Mudr. I, p. 48.

---

1) But not always. Mudr. VII, p. 223 f. i. विनैव युद्धादार्येण पराजितम् it precedes, stress being laid upon it »*even without* striking a blow Your Excellence has vanquished."

183. Separation is expressed by some more prepositions, as अन्तरेण, अन्तरा, अन्यत्र, ऋते, moreover by verbal periphrase (**202**, 2°). About अन्तरा and अन्तरेण see **166.**

अन्यत्र and ऋते.

अन्यत्र *with ablative* is „except, save," in interrogative and negative sentences = „but;" ऋते is likewise construed *with ablative* and generally it is also = „except, save," sometimes = „by default of," rarely = „without."

P. 2, 3, 29.

Examples: of अन्यत्र. Mhbh. 1, 147, 20 न चैनानन्वबुध्यन्त नरा नगरवासिनः। अन्यत्र विदुरामात्यात्तस्मात्खनकसत्तमात् (and nobody among the citizens did know them, but —); Ch. Up. 6, 8, 4 तस्य क्व मूलं स्यादन्यत्रान्नात् (and where could be its root except in food?). The proper meaning of अन्यत्र being of course »elsewhere," the ablat., which attends on it, is that of comparison (**105**).

of ऋते. 1. = save, except. Bhojapr. 27 कालिदासादृते ऽन्यं कविं न मन्ये, Çâk. III किं नु खलु मे प्रियादर्शनादृते शरणमन्यत् (what other relief is there for me, except beholding my sweetheart?); -- 2. = by default of. R. 2, 66, 27 ऋते तु पुत्राद् दहनं महीपतेर्नारोचयन् (they did not approve burning the king's body, no son of his being present); Yâjñ. 2, 117 it is said that after the death of the mother her daughters must have the succession ऋते ताभ्यो ऽन्वयः (by default of them, the descendants); — 3. Ch. Up. 5, 1, 8 कथमशकततें मज्जीवितुम् (how did it forbear to live without me?).

Rem. Sometimes ऋते is construed with the *accusative*, especially in epic poetry. Nala 4, 26 प्रविशन्तं च मां तत्र न कश्चिद् दृष्टवान्नरः। ऋते तां पार्थिवसुताम्.

184. [19] Of सह „*with*" and its synonyms समम्, सार्धम्, साकम् a full account has been given in the chapter on the instrumental (**58**). Mostly they precede the instrumental, they are complying with, but they may also be put behind or be separated from it by one or more

सह and its synonyms

interjacent words [1]). As they are, when without noun-case, adverbs meaning „together," it is, exactly speaking, a pleonasm to put them to the instrumental, as the notion of concomitancy is already carried by that case.

Rem. Occasionally सह with instr. may even be expressive of the *instrument*. Kathâs. 37, 62 प्रज्वाल्याग्निं सहेन्धनैः (after having inflamed the fire by combustibles). This idiom, though not of frequent occurrence in literature, must be very old, as it is met already in the Ath. Veda, see f. i. 8, 1, 11 दिव्यस्त्वा मा धाग्विद्युता सह (lest the Celestial burn thee with his lightning).

185. Compounding सह with its noun is allowed. Yet in most cases to सह° one substitutes स°, either of them being the former member of the compound. It is exactly the same to say रामः ससीतः or रामः सह सीतया. An instance of interchanging सह° and स° may be Veṇ II, p. 43 सहभृत्यगणं सबान्धवं सहमित्रं ससुतं सहानुजं। स्वबलेन निहन्ति..... पाण्डुसुतः सुयोधनम्.

सह° and स° in compounds.

P. 6, 3, 82.

Rem. 1. Some cases are taught by Pâṇini, where सह is required to be the compound's former member, not स, some others in which on the contrary स must be used. Thus सह° is wanted *a*) in time-denoting adverbs as सहपूर्वाह्णम् (the forenoon included), *b*) in blessings as अस्मै सहपुत्राय स्वस्ति भूयात् (hail to him with his son). Yet the phrases सवत्साय -, सगवे -, सहलाय स्वस्ति भूयात् are admitted as equally good as सहवत्साय and the rest.

P. 6, 3, 81.

P. 6, 3, 83.

But स° — not सह° — is required *a*) in all compound adverbs, not expressive of time, therefore exclusively in such terms as सरोषम् (with anger), सबहुमानम् (respectfully), Daç. 84 सलज्जञ्च सहर्षञ्च ससंभ्रमञ्च मामभाषत (he addressed me in a manner adapted to his shame, to his joy and to his excitement) and so often; — *b*) in some special phrases, as सकलं ज्योतिषमधीते — not सहकलं —, वेदः सवेदाङ्गः, and the like.

P. 6, 3, 78-81.

Rem. 2. सार्धम् and समम् are seldom compounded with their noun.

---

1) So f. i. Daç. 156 सह विहृत्य राजकन्यया, Ait. Br. 1, 13, 18 तैरेवैनं सहागमयति, R. 2, 95*, 29 गिरिपुत्र्या पिनाकीव सह, etc.

If this be the case, they make up the latter member. Panc. 276 वाक्समसमेव च ब्राह्मणी जीविता सा (with these very words the wife of the brahman was restored to life).

186. 1. समया, निकषा 2. अभितः etc. Finally we must mention some prepositions, not spoken of in the foregoing, viz. 1st समया and निकषा, both = „near, about," 2ly अभितः, परितः, सर्वतः, समन्ततः (round, about, on all sides), उभयतः (on both sides). All of them agree with the *accusative*. Vârtt. on P. 2, 3, 2

Examples: 1. Daç. 146 समया सौधभित्तिं.... प्रसुप्तमङ्गनाजनमलक्षयम्;

2. Kathâs. 33, 113 अभितः क्षेत्रं पाशान्दत्त्वा; R. 2, 103, 21 सीता पुरस्ताद्व्रजतु त्वमेनामभितो व्रज; Kathâs. 18, 5 तं सामन्ताः परितो ध्रुवं ग्रहगणा इव (on his sides his vassals marched, like the hosts of stars round the polar-star).

Rem. 1. A genitive with अभितः, समन्ततः is rare, but it seems it is regular with समन्तात्. Panc. 185 तस्य न्यग्रोधस्य समन्तात्परिभ्रमति.

Rem. 2. In modern writings विष्वक् with gen. = „on all sides."

II PERIPHRASE BY MEANS OF NOUN-CASES.

187. Periphrase by means of noun-cases. In the preceding paragraphs we have already dealt with such noun-cases as have got more or less the character of prepositions. Those, we will look upon now, have still retained as much of their original and proper significance as to consider them as nouns even from a syntactical point of view. Of course all of them comply with the genitive or may be the latter part of compounds.

188. अन्तिके, समीपे and other words of *proxi-* In the first place: the loc., acc. and abl. of nouns, meaning *proximity*, *vicinity*, *neighbourhood* (as अन्तिक, समीप, सकाश, संनिधि) or the *side* (पार्श्व) and similar, are a means for expressing „near; to, towards; from."

ity, when expressive of „towards," and the like

This periphrase is especially employed to signify a moving towards or from a *person.* „He has come to me" मदन्तिकं [or °के] आगतः or मत्सकाशम्, मत्समीपम्, मत्पार्श्वम् etc., „he is gone from me" मत्पार्श्वादपयातः etc.

Examples: 1. moving *to a person.* Accus. and locat. of the periphrasing noun. — *antika:* Daç. 19 बालं.... भवदन्तिकमानीतवानस्मि, Panc. 269 तवान्तिके तमानेष्यामि; — *sakâça:* Mrcch. III, p. 125 मैत्रेय गच्छ वसन्तसेनायाः सकाशम् (M., go to V.), Panc. 262 अहं त्वत्सकाशे मैत्र्यर्थमागतः (I have come to you for friendship); — *samîpa:* Hit. 22 अस्य समीपमुपगच्छामि, Panc. 178 भूयोऽपि सत्वरं चित्राङ्गसमीपे गतः; — *pârçva:* Panc. 257 वानरपार्श्वमगमत्, ibid. 55 भगवान्नारायणः कन्यकापार्श्वेऽभ्येति; — *saṃnidhi:* Daç. 133 आदाय चैनं मम पित्रोः संनिधिमनैषम्; — *nikata:* Kathâs. 24, 66 ब्राह्मणं तं विसृष्टवान्.... दुहितुर्निकटं तदा (then he allowed that brahman to go to his daughter), Bhojapr. 60 राज्ञनिकटे नीतः; — *abhyarna:* Daç. 36 वनितां.... मत्पितुरभ्यर्णमभिगमय्य (conducted the woman to my father and —); — *upakaṇṭha:* Daç. 39 तदुपकण्ठमुपेत्य. This list may easily be enlarged. From the archaic dialect I add an instance of अर्ध being equivalent with पार्श्व. Ch. Up. 5, 3, 4 स हायस्तः पितुरर्धमेयाय (he went sorrowful to his father).

2. moving *from a person.* Ablat. of the periphrasing noun. — Kathâs. 10, 26 श्रीदत्तः सह तैर्मित्रैस्तत्समीपादपासरत् (Çrîd. with his friends withdrew from him), Ragh. 5, 24 रघोः सकाशादनवाप्य कामं। गतः (gone from Raghu, without having obtained his desire), Mrcch. X, p. 375 अपनीयतामयं चारुदत्तपार्श्वात्.

3. Staying *near.* Locat. of the periphrasing noun. — Âçv. Gṛhy. 1, 18, 7 स्थित्वाहःशेषमाचार्यसकाशे वाचं विसृजेत, Panc. 277 कूपोपकण्ठे विश्रान्तो ब्राह्मणः, ibid. 160 धवलगृहपार्श्वे = »near the white house." When attending on persons, the periphrasing nouns may of course be = »in the presence of," thus being synonymous with पुरः, अग्रे and the like (177). Hence they may occasionally denote the person addressed to. R. 3, 10, 9 इति मया व्याहृतं द्विजसंनिधौ (so I have spoken to the brahmans).

Rem. 1. By so called syntactic analogy सकाशात् is occasionally construed with the abl. instead of the gen. of the noun, it qualifies.

Varâh. Brh. 104, 12 चौरकुमारकेभ्यो भौमः सकाशात्फलमादधाति (Mars takes away the fruit of thieves and princes).

Rem. 2. Kathâs. 25, 129 we have अन्तिकेन = »near," श्मशानस्यान्तिकेन स.... अशृणोद्गिरम्.

Rem. 3. पार्श्वतः, समीपतः, सकाशतः sometimes have the worth of ablatives, but sometimes also that of locatives, f. i. Kathâs. 32, 99 अस्तीहेक्षुमती नाम पुरी तस्याश्च पार्श्वतः। नदी (— and at its side a river), cp. Nala 6, 4.

189. सकाशात्. Moreover **सकाशात्** — and also, but not so often, अन्तिकात् and पार्श्वात् — serves also to periphrase many other kinds of ablative, especially if = „from the side of *a person*". So Panc. 28 स्वामिनः सकाशादभयदक्षिणा दापयितव्या [sc. त्वया] (you must procure me safety from the side of your master), ibid. 137 भोश्चित्रग्रीवस्य मया तव सकाशात्पाशमोक्षणं दृष्टं। तेन मम महती प्रीतिः संजाता। तत्कदाचिन्ममापि बन्धने जाते तव पार्श्वान्मुक्तिर्भवति (well, I have seen how you have loosened Citragrîva of his fetters, and I was much pleased at this, for I too, if perchance I should get into captivity, may be released from your side); — to receive from: Mṛcch. X, p. 341 इच्छाम्यहं भवतः सकाशात्प्रतिग्रहं कर्तुम्; — to ask from: Panc. 75 मया त्वत्सकाशाद्भोजनमर्थनीयम्; — to learn from: M. 2, 20 एतद्देशप्रसूतस्य सकाशादग्रजन्मनः। स्वंस्वं चरित्रं शिक्षेरन्पृथिव्यां सर्वमानवाः; — to buy from: M. 9, 174 क्रीणीयाद्यस्त्वपत्यार्थं मातापित्रोर्यमन्तिकात्। स क्रीतकः सुतस्तस्य (he whom somebody has bought from his parents that he might be instead of a son, is called his *bought son*); — to be borne from: Panc. 318 मम कन्यां दास्यति तत्सकाशात्पुत्रो मे भविष्यति (he will give me his daughter, of her I shall have a son). — Abl. of comparison: Panc. 271 अतस्तं संमानादिभिः सर्वेषां राजपुत्राणां सकाशाद्विशेषप्रसादेन पश्यति (from this time he looked on him with favour above all rajputs, showing his grace by marks of honour and the like), Vajracched. p. 16 अस्य खलु पुण्यस्कन्धस्यान्तिकादसौ पौर्वकः पुण्यस्कन्धः शततमीमपि कलां नार्हति (forsooth, if compared to the foresaid bulk of good works, this second bulk of good works is not equal to the hundredth part of it).

190. मध्ये, अन्तरे. In the same way the loc., acc. and abl. of **अन्तर**, **मध्य**, sim. may periphrase the being or the getting „within," the moving „from within."

a.) being within. Panc. 259 अस्ति समुद्रान्तरे अस्मद्गृहम्; ibid. 67 कूपमध्य आत्मनः प्रतिबिम्बं ददर्श; — *b.*) getting within. Panc. 246 ब्राह्मणानामन्तरमपक्रान्तः (he disappeared in a crowd of brahmans); ibid. 39 रात्रौ मठमध्ये न प्रवेष्टव्यम्; — *c.*) coming from within. Panc. 38 नक्तंदिनं कक्षान्तरात्तां मात्रां न मुञ्चति (never at day nor at night he draws the money out of his belt), ibid. 70 ततः प्रतिशब्देन कूपमध्याद् द्विगुणतरो नादः समुत्थितः (then, the echo caused a noise twice as heavy to go up from the interior of the pit).

Rem. अन्तरे may occasionally be = »with respect to, concerning." So R. 2, 90, 16; cp. the same meaning of अन्तरेण **166**, 4°. As to मध्येन see **167**.

191. मध्ये and मध्यात् are often used in a partitive sense; then they are concurrent idioms of the partitive cases, see **116**, Rem. 2. Panc. 120 आवयोर्मध्ये यश्चौरस्तं कथय; ibid. 86 तेषां मध्यात्काकः प्रोवाच (among them, the crow spoke).

मध्ये and मध्यात्.

192. The locative denoting „*on* or *in* what spot", is often specified by means of such words as °देशे, °उद्देशे, °तले, °तटे, °पृष्ठे sim. When translating such tatpurushas, these latter members must generally be rendered by prepositions: *in*, *upon*, *over* etc. Pat. I, 123 धूमः स आकाशदेशे निवाते नैव तिर्यग्गच्छति नावागवरोहति (that smoke being in the atmosphere, it does not go athwart, if the air be calm, nor falls down), Daç. 169 कमप्यवनिपृष्ठे विचेष्टमानं पुरुषमद्राक्षीत् (he saw somebody moving on the earth).

°देशे serving the periphrase of the locative.

Rem. Likewise विषये may periphrase the metaphorical sense of the locative, as Bhâg. Pur. 1, 4, 13 मन्ये त्वां विषये वाचां स्नातम् (I think you are accomplished in grammar), Panc. 173 धनविषये संतापो न कार्यः (one must not be grieved for the sake of earthly goods). So often अत्र विषये »in this respect."

193. Several periphrasing words may signify *for the sake of*, *because of*, *for*, viz. 1 कृते, used almost as a real

कृते, हेतोः; अर्थ, निमित्त, कारण etc., expressive of cause, motive, aim.

preposition, 2. हेतोः the ablative [1]) of हेतु „motive," 3. अर्थम्, अर्थाय and अर्थे, the acc., dat. and loc. of अर्थ (matter, sake), 4. the instrum., accus. and abl. of निमित्त and कारण „cause, motive." They are construed with *preceding* genitive, if they do not make up the latter part of a compound.

Examples: 1. कृते. — Panc. IV, 29 न स्वल्पस्य कृते भूरि नाशयेत् (one must not spend much for the sake of little); Mṛcch. IV, p. 131 मया खलु मदनिकायाः कृते साहसमनुष्ठितम्; Panc. IV, 51 वाक्कृते रासभो हतः (the ass was killed for his voice).

2. हेतोः. — Bhagavadgîtâ 1, 35 एतान्न हन्तुमिच्छामि.... अपि त्रैलोक्यराज्यस्य हेतोः किं नु महीकृते (them I would not kill.... not even for the sake of the realm of the three worlds, how much less for the possession of land); Çâk. V स्वसुखनिरभिलाषः खिद्यसे लोकहेतोः (while not caring for your own pleasure, you tire yourself for the sake of your people); Ragh. 2, 47 अल्पस्य हेतोर्बहु हातुमिच्छन्विचारमूढः प्रतिभासि मे त्वम् (you seem to me a thoughtless fool, that you desire to give up much for a trifle); Mâlat. IV, p. 65 जीवितत्राणहेतोः = जीवितत्राणाय. — Note कस्य हेतोः (why?), कस्यापि हेतोः (for some motive) and the like.

1) It is not quite plain, how Pâṇini did account for हेतोः. Yet, his commentators and followers consider it a *genitive*, and it is very likely, he has thought so himself. At least, we may draw the inference. After having taught in his sûtra 2, 3, 26 षष्ठी हेतुप्रयोगे, that is »the genitive is required [instead of the instrum. of causality] when employing हेतु", he adds this clause (s. 27) सर्वनाम्नस्तृतीया च »but in the case of a pronoun of the class *sarva* etc., either the gen. or the instrum." With the said pronouns it is therefore allowed to use two idioms promiscuously — f. i. कस्य हेतोः and केन हेतुना —, but for the rest the only idiom available is that, which is exemplified by पुरुषस्य हेतोः. Now, as केन and हेतुना are *both* instrumentals, it is but consistent that of कस्य हेतोः, the parallel idiom, *both* elements are meant as genitives. Then, of course पुरुषस्य हेतोः must also be considered as genitives both. The very words of Pâṇini do not admit of another interpretation.

3. *a.*) अर्थम्. — Panc. 169 जलार्थं तदेव पुलिनमवतीर्णः (he is gone to the same bank for water), ibid. 212 उलूकाधिपो वायसवधार्थं प्रचलितः (— set out in order to kill the crows), Mrcch. III, p. 116 मदनिकाया निष्क्रयणार्थं वसन्तसेनागृहं गच्छामि, R. 3, 35, 34 अमृतानयनार्थं चकार मतिम् (he made up his mind to fetch the amrta). It is plain, that अर्थम् is in all such phrases the equivalent of a final dative. Cp. 87.

b.) अर्थाय. — Mhbh. 1, 144, 17 न गर्हयेयुरस्मान्वै पाण्डवार्थाय कर्हिचित् (they will not reprove us for the sake of the Pâṇḍavas); Panc. III, 178 एक एव हितार्थाय तेजस्वी पार्थिवो भुवः (no ruler but a monarch promotes the welfare of his country), here हितार्थाय is = हिताय, cp. Nala 13, 19.

c.) अर्थे. — Mṛcch. III, p. 116 गणिकार्थे ब्राह्मणकुलं तमसि पातितम्, Panc. 325 आपदर्थे धनमित्रसंग्रहः क्रियते (it is for evil days, that wealth and friends are sought after), R. 2, 118, 53 ऊर्मिला भार्यार्थे लक्ष्मणस्यापि दत्ता (U. has been given to L. to be his wife) [भार्यार्थे accordingly = भार्यायै or भार्या, cp. ibid. 3, 34, 21; Mhbh. 1, 14, 7].

4. निमित्तम् etc. — Daç. 25 महीसुरनिमित्तं गतजीवितोऽभूत् (he has died for a brahman), Panc. 228 घृततैललवणतण्डुलादिक्रयनिमित्तं सपरिवारा गता, Mhbh. 12, 342, 23 अहल्याधर्षणनिमित्तं हि गौतमाद्धरिश्मश्रुतामिन्द्रः प्राप्तः (it is because of his adultery with Ahalyâ, that Indra got a reddish

---

But however great the authority of Pânini may be, as it is, when he states facts and describes phenomena, there is no plausible reason to follow it, where his explication of them is wrong. To him, who did not know but one language, हेतोः could appear as a genitive, but for us, who have the opportunity of comparing similar idioms in different languages, f. ex. Latin *causâ* and *gratiâ*, English *because of*, it is impossible not to take हेतोः for an *ablative of causality*. By doing so we account for the idiom in question in a quite satisfactory manner. Therefore कस्य हेतोः is to be compared with Latin *cujus rei causa*, not with *qua de causa*, the Sanskrit equivalent of which is कस्माद्धेतोः.

कस्माद्धेतोः reminds me of the vârtt. on P. 2, 3, 27 निमित्तकारणहेतुषु सर्वासां प्रायदर्शनम्. This precept is strictly true by itself — the word प्राय shows sufficiently that it must not be urged too much — but it cannot be said with some reason, Pânini has left out this rule, as he did not want to enjoin it at all.

beard from the side of Gautama); — R. 2, 90, 12 नियुक्तः स्त्रीनिमित्तेन पित्रासौ (he, being enjoined by his father because of a woman —); — Nala 4, 4 विषमग्निं जलं रज्जुमास्थास्ये तव कारणात् (for you I will take poison etc.)

194. The foresaid apparatus for expressing the *purpose*, the *aim*, the *motive*, the *sake*, though the most common, is not the sole, अर्थ, निमित्त, कारण, मूल, हेतु etc. serving also for this purpose, when being part of a bahuvrîhi. Daç. 75 f. i. विस्मयहर्षमूलः कोलाहलो लोकस्योदजिहीत (from astonishment and joy people burst out into clamour). A fair sample of manifoldness of expression we have in these lines from the Râmâyaṇa

न शोभार्थाविमौ बाहू न धनुर्भूषणाय मे
नासिराबन्धनार्थाय न शराः स्तम्भहेतवः (2, 23, 31),

in each *pâda* a different way has been followed to signify the aim. In the first अर्थ is the latter member of a bahuvrîhi, in the fourth हेतु, in the second the dative of the aim has been used, and the third has periphrase by means of अर्थाय. Cp. R. 3, 43, 17; Nala 14, 19.

Rem. It is plain that datives as अर्थाय, निमित्ताय, हेतवे will signify but the *purpose* or *aim*, whereas ablatives as कारणात्, instrumentals as निमित्तेन, compounds in °मूल are only expressive of the *cause*. But in some of the foresaid implements for periphrase, as कृते, अर्थम्, निमित्तम्, हेतोः, the contrast, which does logically exist between the conceptions »aim" and »cause" is not to be found. Strictly speaking, they are standing on the neuter territory of the »motive" which partakes of both. See the examples given.

195. वशात् and बलात्. The *cause* — either material or efficient — is moreover often periphrased by वशात् (or वशेन) liter. „by the rule of" and बलात् (or बलेन) liter. „by the power of." Panc. 43 कथं मद्यपानवशादप्रस्तुतं वदसि, ibid. 327 दैववशात्संपद्यते नृणां शुभाशुभम्; Var. Brh. 2, 4 आसादयेदनिलवेगवशेन पारम् (he may perhaps reach the other side by the strength of the wind); Kathâs. 12, 59 आत्मनः।

अदर्शनं युक्तिबलाद् व्यधाद्यौगन्धरायणः (Yaug. made himself invisible by sorcery).

196. The *agent*, *instrument*, *means* may be periphrased by such words as द्वारेण (by means of), मार्गेण (by way of), परम्परया (by a continual line of), मुखेन and वचनेन or मुखात्, वचनात् (by mouth of), योगेन or योगात् (by exercising, practising), अनुसारेण (agreeably to), sim.

Periphrase of agent, instrument, means.

Prabodh. II, p. 35 तेन [sc. चार्वाकेण] च शिष्योपशिष्यद्वारेणास्मिँल्लोके बहुलीकृतं तन्त्रम् (and he has spread his doctrine *by* his disciples and the disciples of them); Panc. 239 आकाशमार्गेण प्रायात् (he went off *through* the sky); Mrcch. VIII, p. 255 यदि पुनरुद्यानपरम्परया नगरीमुज्जयिनीं प्रविशावः (but if we entered the city of U. by following the line of groves); Panc. 56 स राजा देवीमुखेन तां दुहितरमुवाच; Çâk. II रक्षायोगादयमपि तपः प्रत्यहं संचिनोति (he too [the king] earns *tapas* day after day by his giving protection); Panc. 126 कोपि विप्रो महाविद्वान्परं पूर्वजन्मयोगेन चौरो वर्तते (— but *because of* deeds, done in a former existence he was a thief); Bhojapr. 3 वदामि स्वमत्यनुसारेण (I speak *according to* my opinion).

III. PERIPHRASE BY MEANS OF PARTICIPLES, GERUNDS AND THE LIKE.

197. Some participles in °त may serve the want of periphrase, as:

गत

1. गत, often used as an equivalent of the locative, as it may be rendered by *in*, *into*, *to*, *towards*, Panc. 155 आवयोर्हस्तगतं जातम् (it has come *into* our hand), Mâlav. I, p. 12 गवाक्षगता तिष्ठति (she stands *at* the window), M. 2, 218 गुरुगतां विद्यां शुश्रूषुरधिगच्छति, here गुरुगता विद्या = गुरौ विद्या »the wisdom which dwells in his teacher.” Panc. 272 a lion takes up the helpless young of a chacal holding it between his teeth दंष्ट्रामध्यगतं कृत्वा = दंष्ट्रामध्ये कृत्वा. Likewise R. 3, 46, 6 जनस्थानगता द्रुमाः = जनस्थाने सन्तो द्रुमाः »the trees in Jan.”

Examples of गत, periphrasing the nimittasaptamî (**147**). R. 3, 43, 48 पश्य लक्ष्मण वैदेह्या मृगत्वचि गतां स्पृहाम् (Laxmaṇa, look how fond Sîtâ is of the skin of the antelope), Çâk. I सखीगतं किमपि पृच्छामः (I will ask something concerning your friend).

Rem. Occasionally संश्रित, आश्रित and the like are used in this manner. See f. i. R. 3, 11, 65 and 3, 54, 26.

198. other participles = „with" and „without." 2. Such as are expressive of *concomitancy* or the contrary of it, as सहित, युक्त, when = „with," रहित, हीन, when = „without." It is a matter of course, that we have the right of speaking of them as periphrasing case-relations only in such cases, as where the original and proper meaning of these participles has faded away in so far as not to admit of their being translated by English participles. With them may be remembered the adjective सनाथ, which is often almost equivalent to our »with," as Panc. 62 अस्ति.... नातिदूरे प्रभूतजलसनाथं सरः (a lake with much water).

Rem. To them we may add वीत, अपगत, विगत and the like, when being the first members of bahuvrîhis as अपगतभय = »fearless," Daç. 25 वीतदयः »pityless."

3. Some participles in the neuter gender may be met with occasionally, used as adverbs with a prepositional function. Mhbh. 1, 115, 11 अज्ञातं धृतराष्ट्रस्य (without the knowledge of Dhṛ.); Panc. 272 तेन भूभुजा स कुम्भकारः प्रस्तावानुगतं पृष्टः (in the course of the conversation the king asked the potter). Cp. Kathâs. 39, 167.

199. अभिमुख, उन्मुख, संमुख. To them we may subjoin, as they do duty of participles, the adjectives अभिमुख, उन्मुख, संमुख, when pointing out the direction of a movement. Then their proper meaning „[having] the face [turned] to" has dwindled down to a mere *to* or *towards* = प्रति. They are often used so, either as adjectives, or adverbially. — Examples of adjective: Panc. 208 स्वपुराभिमुखः प्रतस्थे which is identical with स्वपुरं (or स्वपुरं प्रति) प्रतस्थे; ibid. 299 मातुः संमुखो गतः = मातुः सकाशे गतः; — of adverb: Panc. 64 सा स्वगृहाभिमुखं प्रतस्थे.

200. उद्दिश्य. A similar periphrase is exhibited by the gerund उद्दिश्य, as it is expressive of the aim the action is pointing at. Therefore उद्दिश्य may serve almost the same purpose as प्रति, and is available as well in figurative as in literal sense. So Panc. 210 स्वगृहमुद्दिश्य प्रपलायितः (he fled to his home), Mudr. I, p. 8 ब्राह्मणानुद्दिश्य पाकः (the cooking for the brahmans). In the former instance the mere accus. स्वगृहम् would suffice, in the latter the gen. or dat. ब्राह्मणानाम् or °णेभ्यः.

Other examples: R. 3, 11, 44 रामः] प्रतस्थेऽगस्त्यमुद्दिश्य (- *to* Agastya), Kâd. I, p. 19 राजानमुद्दिश्यार्यामिमां पपाठ ([the bird] pronounced this âryâ with regard to the king), R. 3, 38, 13 यज्ञमुद्दिश्य दीक्षितः, Panc. 82 निमित्तमुद्दिश्य प्रकुप्यति, (he is angry for some cause), Çâk. V किमुद्दिश्य भगवता काश्यपेन मत्सकाशमृषयः प्रेरिताः स्युः (for what purpose —?), etc.

Rem. Like उद्दिश्य it is also said समुद्दिश्य or one makes use of kindred nouns, as उद्देशेन, समुद्देशेन, उद्देशात् all = »with regard to."

201. Gerunds, expressive of »about in regard of" sim., as अधिकृत्य, पुरस्कृत्य etc. Some other gerunds, as पुरस्कृत्य, मध्येकृत्य, अधिकृत्य, आश्रित्य, उपेत्य, संख्याय may be used in a similar way, viz. to signify *in regard of*, *with respect to*, *concerning*, *about* sim.

Examples: Panc. IV, 70 मित्रतां च पुरस्कृत्य किंचिद्वक्ष्यामि तच्छृणु (I will say something about the friendship, hear it); Çâk. II अहं तु तामेव शकुन्तलामधिकृत्य ब्रवीमि (but I say so only in regard of the foresaid Ç.), ibid. I ग्रीष्मसमयमधिकृत्य गीयताम् (sing of the hot season); R. 2, 9, 60 उवाच कुब्जा भरतस्य मातरं हितं वचो राममुपेत्य चाहितम् (Kubjâ spoke well as far as her words regarded the mother of Bharata, but not well with respect to Râma); ibid. 2, 40, 14 वनवासं हि संख्याय वासांस्याभरणानि च। भर्तारमनुगच्छन्त्यै सीतायै श्वशुरो ददौ (in regard of the life in the forest, her father-in-law gave to Sîtâ —).

202. Among the other gerunds, which may in some degree or other do duty of prepositions, we notice:

other gerunds.

1. those, expressing concomitancy, as आदाय and गृहीत्वा, when = „with;"

2. such as are expressive of separation, as मुक्त्वा, वर्जयित्वा, परित्यज्य sim., as they are = „save, except, but for;"

3. such as serve to denote the instrument, means, manner, in short, to periphrase the third case, as आस्थाय, द्वारीकृत्य, अवलम्ब्य, अधिष्ठाय;

4. विहाय and अतीत्य when = Lat. *prae* „in preference to;"

5. आरभ्य „since."

आदाय, गृहीत्वा. Examples: of 1. — Çâk. III ततः प्रविशति कुशानादाय यजमानशिष्यः (enters a sacrificer's disciple with kuçagrass); Panc. 173 वित्तमादाय समायातः (he came with money); R. 3, 24, 12 गृहीत्वा वैदेहीं .... गुहामाश्रय (retire with Sîtâ into a cavern). — They are especially of use to point out the attributes or tools one takes along. Panc. III, 143 स [लुब्धकः] पञ्जरकमादाय पाशं च लगुडं तथा। नित्यमेव वनं याति; Kathâs. 21, 134.

मुक्त्वा, वर्जयित्वा, परित्यज्य. of 2. — Panc. 203 धर्मं मुक्त्वा नान्या गतिरस्ति (there is no other path, *except* duty); R. 1, 67, 19 निपेतुश्च नराः सर्वे तेन शब्देन मोहिताः। वर्जयित्वा मुनिवरं राजानं तौ च राघवौ (and all the people fell down, confounded by that sound, *save* Viçvâmitra, Janaka and the two Raghuides); Panc. 273 मयाद्यैनं शृगालशिशुं परित्यज्य न किञ्चित्सत्त्वमासादितम् (I have caught to day not a single animal *except* this brat of a chacal).

वर्जम्. NB. Another implement of the same purport as मुक्त्वा etc. is °वर्जम्, always making up the latter part of a compound adverb. Var. Bṛh. 47, 28 यद्विस्तरेण कथितं मुनिभिस्तदस्मिन्। सर्वं मया निगदितं पुनरुक्तवर्जम् (all that has been told at large by the old seers, I have explained, save the repetitions).

आस्थाय. of 3. — R. 1, 16, 2 उपायः को वधे तस्य राक्षसाधिपतेः सुराः। यमहं तं समास्थाय निहन्यामृषिकण्टकम् (what way, ye gods, may lead to the death of that prince of Râxasas, *by* which means I may kill the disturber of holy men?); Mudr. IV, p. 136 न वयममात्यराक्षसद्वारेण [cp. **196**] कुमारमाश्रयामहे किं तु कुमारस्य सेनापतिं द्वारीकृत्य (we do not approach the Prince by the interference of Minister Râxasa but by that of the Commander of the Prince's Army); Mâlav. II, p. 45 राज्ञा। दाक्षिण्यमवलम्ब्य = सदाक्षिण्यम् »courteously".

Likewise the participle आस्थित. Panc. I, 243 नृपतिर्लोकान्पालयेद्यत्नमास्थितः = यत्नेन लोकान्पालयेत्.

विहाय, अतीत्य. of 4. — Çâk. II. मूर्ख अन्यमेव भागधेयमेते तपस्विनो निर्वपन्ति यो रत्नराशीनपि विहायाभिनन्द्यते (fool, these holy men strew about a quite different tribute, which has a greater value than even heaps of precious stones); R. 2, 94, 26 अतीत्यैवोत्तरान्कुरून्। पर्वतश्चित्रकूटो ऽसौ बहुमूलफलोदकः (Mount Citrakûta has even more roots, fruits and water than the land of the Hyperboreans).

of 5: have been given already **170**.

Rem. This list is not complete. It may happen that some more gerunds are occasionally to be rendered by English prepositions or prepositional phrases. So अनादृत्य may admit of the translation »in spite of," अवष्टभ्य may be = Lat. *ob*, as R. 3, 18, 15 where Çûrpaṇakhâ speaks so to Râma इमां विरूपां..... वृद्धां भार्यामवष्टभ्य न मां त्वं बहु मन्यसे (it is for that old and ugly wife you do not esteem me), etc.

अनादृत्य. अवष्टभ्य, etc.

203. In determining the site of some locality gerunds are often used, which admit of being rendered by prepositions. R. 2, 80, 21 जाह्नवीं तु समासाद्य [राजमार्गः] (the highway is along the Ganges). Kâçikâ on P. 3, 4, 20 [1]) gives these instances: अप्राप्य नदीं पर्वतः स्थितः। अतिक्रम्य तु पर्वतं नदी स्थिता (the mount is before the river, but the river is beyond the mount).

Chapter X. Compounds.

204. In western languages compounds are not considered a topic of Syntax. The fact of their being made up

1) The rule of Pâṇini treats only of this idiom when expressive of the notions »beyond" and »before."

Compounds a topic of Syntax.

of two or more self-existent words — however important for the etymologist — has little or nothing to do with their employment in speaking or writing. In Sanskrit it must be otherwise. Keeping apart such compounds as have got any special meaning, which stamps them to unities [1], there exists in that language an almost illimited freedom of expressing any kind of relations, grammatical or logical, by the way of compounding. Every moment the speaker and especially the writer of Sanskrit may have the opportunity of substituting compounds to the analytical mode of expression For this reason, Sanskrit Syntax has to deal with compounds, as far as regards giving an account of the part they are acting in the phraseology and of the modes and ways how to employ them, whereas it is a topic of Sanskrit Etymology to expound their structure and their outer shape.

The three great classes of compounds, set up by vernacular grammar, are d v a n d v a, t a t p u r u s h a, b a h u v r î h i. They include nearly all varieties as well of the simple compounds, which are made up of but two non-compound words, as of those, which are most intricate and of an immoderate length. Outside of them, there remains only the class of such compounds as are produced by putting together the preposition + the noun-case depending on it, as आकण्ठम् etc. (**152**) [2]); in most cases

1) Such as हिमालय when the name of the mountain, महात्मन् »noble," भूसुर »brahman," सप्तर्षय: the well-known constellation, अबला »woman," and the like.

2) Whitney *Sanskrit Grammar* § 1310 calls them »prepositional compounds."

this fourth class coincides with the avyayîbhâva of vernacular grammar [1]).

1. Dvandva.

205. Dvandva. P. 2, 2, 29. The **dvandva** serves to express concatenation and addition. Two or more nouns linked to another by „and" may be united into a dvandva. So instead of saying रामो लक्ष्मणश्च we may use the dvandva रामलक्ष्मणौ, instead of स्त्रियो बालाश्च वृद्धाश्च it may be said स्त्रीबालवृद्धाः.

Rem. In the archaic dialect the freedom of making dvandvas was very little. At least in the vaidik writings dvandvas are almost bound to set formulae and do never consist of more than two members. Most of them are dvandvas of divinities, especially in the mantras, such as मित्रावरुणा, इन्द्राग्नी. See Whitney, *Sanskrit Grammar* § 1255 and 1256.

206. [I]s gender [a]nd number. The dvandva has the gender of its last member. Its number is determined by the real number of the persons or things, comprised by it. Panc. I, 4 अजातमृतमूर्खेभ्यो मृताजातौ सुतौ वरम् (from the three classes of sons: 1 not born at all, 2 sons died, 3. blockheads, the first and second classes are to be preferred), ibid. p. 195 प्राणान्तिकं सदैव वायसोलूकानां वैरम् (there always is a deadly hatred between crows and owls), Harshac. p. 28 नृत्यगीतवादित्रेष्वबाह्याः (no strangers to dancing, singing and playing

1) All *compound adverbs*, the former member of which is an indeclinable word, are comprehended by the general appellation **avyayîbhâva** (P. 2, 1, 5—16). Moreover this category contains some few kinds of compound adverbs, whose former member is a noun-case or an adj.; they are summed up by Pâṇini (2, 1, 17—21). — But *compound adjectives* are never styled avyayîbhâva, even if their former member be an indeclinable word. So for example when saying रामः ससीतः, we have a »prepositional compound" indeed, ससीतः being = सह सीतया, but not an avyayîbhâva.

on instruments). As the number of the members is illimited, we may have such long dvandvas as f. i. Nala 1, 28 वयं हि देवगन्धर्वमानुषोरगराक्षसान्द्रष्टवन्तः etc.

But if the dvandva is to represent a real unity or if not individuals but categories are linked together, it generally is á neuter and á singular. So it is said **पुत्रपौत्रम्** (children and grandchildren), **गवाश्वम्** (kine and horses), **आराशस्त्रि** (awl and knife).

Rem. 1. A full and exhaustive account on this subject is given by Pâṇini (2, 4, 2—17) and his commentators. They distinguish between those cases where the dvandva must be a singular and a neuter, those where it must not be so, and those in which it is allowed to use either idiom optionally. So, among others, the singular of the neuter is of necessity with dvandvas signifying parts either of the body or of musical instruments or of [P. 2, 4, 2.] the army, as पाणिपादम्, रथिकपादातम्, likewise if names of rivers and countries, when of different gender, are linked together, as [P. 2, 4, 7.] गङ्गाशोणम्, कुरुकुरुक्षेत्रम्. On the other hand, dvandvas made up of nouns denoting animate beings are not allowed to be put in the singular number, save *a.*) very small animals, as दंशमशकम्, *b.*) such [P. 2, 4, 8.] as by their nature are living in eternal mutual enmity, as मार्जारमूषकम्, गोव्याघ्रम्, *c.*) classes of çûdras, not considered abject [1]), as [P. 2, 4, 9.] [P. 2, 4, 10] तक्षायस्कारम्, *d.*) some others as गवाश्वम्, पुत्रपौत्रम्, श्वचण्डालम्, स्त्रीकुमारम्. — Dvandvas of contrasting qualities or things are optionally [P. 2, 4, 11] put in the singular or in the dual, as सुखदुःखम् or °खे, शीतोष्णम् or °ष्णे. And so on. [P. 2, 4, 13]

Rem. 2. It is forbidden to compound a genus with its species. See Pat. I, p. 252.

Rem. 3. Instead of the dvandva मातापितरौ the simple पितरौ may be used (so f. i. Ragh. 1, 1 जगतः पितरौ वन्दे पार्वतीपरमेश्वरौ. Likewise [P. 1, 2, 70 and 71.] श्वशुरौ is synonymous with श्वश्रूश्वशुरौ, see f. i. Kathâs. 58, 89. —

---

1) P. 2, 4, 10 शूद्राणामनिरवसितानाम्. Kâç. यैर्भुक्ते पात्रं संस्कारेणापि न शुध्यति ते निरवसिताः

Dvandvas = »brother and sister," »son and daughter" are not used, here भ्रातरौ, पुत्रौ are of necessity. — Cp. Latin *soceri* = *socer et socrus*, *fratres* = *frater et soror*. P. 2, 1, 68.

Rem. 4. As to the order, to be followed in putting together the links of a dvandva, fixed rules cannot be given. Yet it is common to put at the head either the themes ending in इ or उ, or those commencing by a vowel while ending in अ, or the shortest. P. 2, 2, 32-34.

207. Its significance. Besides its most common duty of expressing coordination, the dvandva is also available, if „and" connects persons or things standing in mutual relation with one another. Another species is the distributive dvandva.

Examples of the dvandva of relationship. — R. 3, 27, 10 स संप्रहारस्तुमुलो रामत्रिशिरसोस्तदा। संबभूवातिबलिनोः सिंहकुञ्जरयोरिव (then a wild battle began between Râma and Triçiras, both of extraordinary strength, as if between a lion and an elephant), Mâlav. I, p. 21 अत्रभवतः किल मम च समुद्रपल्वलयोरिवान्तरम् (forsooth, there is as great a difference between you and me, as there is between a pond and the ocean), Harshac. 5 निसर्गविरोधिनी चेयं पयःपावकयोरिवैकत्र धर्मक्रोधयोर्वृत्तिः (and like water and fire, so righteousness and anger, [when meeting] at the same place, by their proper nature combat each other).

Examples of distributive dvandva. — Mâlav. V, p. 137 तौ पृथग्वारदाकूले शिष्टामुत्तरदक्षिणे। नक्तं दिनं विभज्योभौ शीतोष्णकिरणाविव (let them rule severally the banks of the Varadâ, one the northern bank, but the other the southern, as moon and sun share their sway over night and day); Mudr. I, p. 19 द्वितयं] फलं कोपप्रीत्योर्द्विषति च विभक्तं सुहृदि च (I have bestowed the double fruit of my wrath and my affection on foe and friend); Kathâs. 25, 229: Açokadatta by his utmost bravery has conquered a golden lotus and presents it to the king his master, who puts the precious flower in a silver vase; on that account the poet makes this comparison उभौ कलशपद्मौ च शुशुभाते सितारुणौ। यशःप्रतापाविव तौ भूपालाशोकदत्तयोः (and both the vase and the flower shone, one white, the other red, as if they were that splendour and that glory combined, which adorned one the king, the other Açokadatta).

208. Dvandvas of adjectives are relatively seldom, if compared with the frequency of those made up of substantives.

Dvandvas of adjectives.

So Kathâs. 25, 6 संप्राप सोऽथ विन्ध्यमहाटवीं विवेश च.... तां गहनायताम् (thick and long), Kumâras. 1, 35 वृत्तानुपूर्वे च नातिदीर्घे जङ्घे (legs round, well-proportioned and not too long), Kathâs. 25, 229 सितारुणौ see **207**, Malâv. V, p. 137 उत्तरदक्षिणो see **207**. — Panc. I, 204 व्याकीर्णकेसरकरालमुखा मृगेन्द्राः (lions with dishevelled mane and frightful mouth) may be an instance of a dvandva of two adjectives, either of which is a compound itself.

---

209. Two kinds of compounds are reckoned by vernacular grammar among the tatpurushas, which by their meaning should rather be considered dvandvas:

Combination of participles: 1. कृताकृत and the like; 2. दृष्टनष्ट and the like.

1. Such as अशितानशित (eatable and not eatable), कृताकृत (done and undone; wrought and unwrought), कृतापकृत, गतप्रत्यागत. Cp. Kathâs. 27, 1 नमितोन्नमितेन शिरसा (by turns lowering and raising his head).

P. 2, 1, 60 with vârtt.

2. Those made up of two participles in °त, the compounding of which declares the two actions being done immediately one after another. The former in time is also the former member. Of the kind are दृष्टनष्ट (as soon lost as it is seen), स्नातानुलिप्त (after bathing and anointing one's self). Çâk. IV अथ प्रविशति सुप्तोत्थितः शिष्यः (enters a disciple, just arising from his couch), Ragh. 4, 37 कलमा इव ते.... उत्खातप्रतिरोपिताः (like stalks of rice dug out and forthwith replanted), Panc. I, 5 जातप्रेतः (died soon after birth), ibid. V, 7 वित्तविहीनाः] सततं जातविनष्टाः पयसामिव बुद्बुदाः पयसि. Kathâs. 29, 141 an illness (रोगः) is said to have been ज्ञातापनीतः »as soon driven out as its nature had been recognised."

P. 2, 1. 49.

2. Tatpurusha.

210. The **tatpurusha** serves to express in a condensed shape a noun — substantive or adjective — together with some other noun qualifying it, as तत्पुरुषः = तस्य पुरुषः (his man), अहिहतः = अहिना हतः (bitten by a serpent), नवयौ-

Tatpurusha.

वनम् = नवं यौवनम् (the first youth). The noun qualifying is the former member of the tatpurusha; the noun qualified, which is at the same time the main element, its latter member [1]).

Rem. The efficient elements of a tatpurusha are not of necessity self-existent words. The former part may be such a particle as सु°, दुः°, अ°, see **218**. The latter may be a kṛt, not otherwise used but in compounds, as °ज, °ग, °स्थ, °ज्ञ, °भुज्, °भाज्, °शय, °कृत्, °कारिन्, °भोजिन्, °हारिन् etc. Many of these compounds have got a special meaning so as to make them indissoluble unities, as अण्डज »bird," कुम्भकार »potter," किंकर »servant." Yet free compounding is also allowed. So Panc. I, 103 कौशेयं कृमिजम् may be analyzed into कौ° कृमेर्जातम्, ibid. p. 28 प्रसादसंमुखो नः स्वामी वचनवशगश्च [= वचनवशे गतः], Bhojapr. 2 लोकोऽयं मां सर्वज्ञं वक्ति, Panc. 41 समीपवर्तिनि नगरे [= समीपे वर्तमाने न°].

211. The former member may be either = a noun-case (as in तत्पुरुषः, अहिहतः), or = an adjective (as in नवयौवनम्). In the latter case, there exists grammatical concord between the two members; such tatpurushas bear the special appellation of **karmadhâraya.**

karma-dhâraya.

The faculty of combining adjectives with their substantives into karmadhârayas is theoretically almost unrestricted, but in practice not all possible combinations are used [2]). Most karmadhârayas are terms often recurring which *either* have got some special meaning,

---

1) Pat. I, p. 392 उत्तरपदार्थप्रधानस्तत्पुरुषः. In the same way the dvandva is styled उभयपदार्थप्रधानः, the bahuvrîhi अन्यपदार्थप्रधानः, and the avyayîbhâva पूर्वपदार्थप्रधानः.

2) Pâṇini's rule 2, 1, 57 विशेषणं विशेष्येण बहुलम् plainly shows not all combinations of the kind to be allowed.

or are wont to be much employed though nothing impedes expressing them by the two elements severed. Of the former kind are such as परमात्मा (the highest soul), युवराजः (heir apparent), of the latter such as कृष्णासर्पः (a black serpent), पक्वान्नम् (cooked rice), and the great class of compounds, a full account of which is given by Pâṇini in the first adhyâya of his second ashtakam (see espec. the sûtras 49, 58, 61, 67 and 70), containing those, the former member of which is a pronoun as सर्व, एक, पूर्व, अपर, स्व, and such adjectives as नव, पुराण, महा°, मध्य, मध्यम, सत् (good) etc. To them we may add such words as नित्य, मुख्य, प्रधान, and even such as begin by सु°, दु°: and the negation अ°, as सुजनः (an honest man), दुर्जनः (a bad man), अकोविद् (not skilled).

212. Yet there are instances enough of a freer employment. Panc. 327 किमेवं पलाय्यते ऽलीकभयेन (why do you run away thus by a false fear?), Pat. I, p. 2 शाष्कैधः = शाष्कमेधः, Panc. 30 अनुचितस्थान उपविष्टः, Mâlav. I, p. 3 वर्तमानकवेः कालिदासस्य (of the living poet K.), Harshac. 6 शैलूष इव वृथा वहसि कृत्रिमोपशमम् (like an actor you are displaying in vain a fictitious tranquillity of mind), Bhoj. 28 प्राक्तनकर्मतो दारिद्र्यमनुभवति (in consequence of his deeds in a former existence he is now poor), Panc. 37 त्वदीयवचनम् (your orders), Mâlav. I, p. 28 यस्यागमः केवलजीविकायै (to whom his learning serves only for a livelihood), Kathâs. 39, 131 दत्त्वा वराश्वम् (— gave a best horse).

Upon the whole, such freer karmadhârayas are used in a greater extent in poetry, also when being themselves but a member of some large compound, as f. i. Panc. 37 अनेकसाधुजनदत्तसूक्ष्मवस्त्रविक्रयवशात् (by selling fine clothes given to him by many pious people), in analyzing which we get अनेकसाधुजनै[karm.]र्दत्तानां सूक्ष्मवस्त्राणां [other karm.] विक्रयस्य वशात्.

Rem. In the case of such words as पापनापितः, there seems to exist a slight difference between the karmadh. and the analytical construction of the same purport; पापनापितः is »a bad barber" who knows his art badly, but पापो नापितः »a barber of a bad temper." See P. 2, 1, 54.

213. We will insist on some species:

a.) such as are made up of a title + the noun of its bearer, as आर्यचाणाक्यः (Sir Câṇakya), अमात्यराक्षसः (Minister Râxasa). So Utt. II, p. 30 कुमारलक्ष्मणः (Prince L.), Mâlav. I, p. 24 पण्डितकौशिकी खलु भवती (you are the learned Kauçikî, are not you?), Mṛcch. III, p. 115 अहं हि गणिकामदनिकार्थमकार्यमनुतिष्ठामि, but some lines after (p. 116) we read in inverse order मदनिकागणिकार्थे, cp. Panc. 59 अनेन विष्णुशर्मामातृप्रभावेण सर्वे शत्रवो निहताः, here the proper noun विष्णु is followed, not preceded by its epithet. In some cases the latter idiom seems to be the regular one, as विन्ध्याचलः (Mount Vindhya).

b.) those ending in °जन, the former part being a subst., as स्त्रीजनः, दुहितृजनः, गुरुजनः. Here जन has sometimes the power of a collective, sometimes it denotes the individual (19 R), स्त्रीजनः may be = »womankind," »women" or even one »woman," and so on;

c.) the type अर्धपिप्पली (half a pepper). It is not allowed to say पिप्पल्यर्धम्, but पिप्पल्या अर्धम्; when compounded it must be अर्धपिप्पली. [1]) P. 2, 2, 1 and 2. So f. i. Ragh. 7, 42 अर्धमार्गे (halfway), Panc. 203 अर्धपादस्पृष्टभूमिः (touching the earth with the half of his foot). The same applies to पूर्व, अपर, अधर, उत्तर, etc. when denoting: the fore-part, the part behind, the lower- and upper part. Therefore it is said पूर्वकायः (the fore-part of the body), पूर्वाह्णः (fore-noon), अपररात्रः (the latter part of the night), उत्तमाङ्गम् (head), प्रथमरात्री (the fore-night), and the like. So मध्य in मध्याह्नः = मध्यमह्नः. We have here the same adjectival conception as in Latin *summus mons*, *media urbs*, Greek *μέση ἡ πόλις* etc.

Rem. 1. अर्ध, like our »half," is also compounded with a participle or some other adjective, as अर्धोदितः सूर्यः (the sun, half-risen), Panc. 9 अर्धस्फाटितो दारुमयः स्तम्भः.

Rem. 2. As to compounds, commencing by द्वितीय, तृतीय, चतुर्थ P. 2, 2, 3. or तुर्य, when = »half, the third —, fourth part," one may say as well द्वितीयभिक्षा as भिक्षाद्वितीयम् (half an alms) and the like. The same may be stated of अग्र (top, edge, extremity), as it is said as well अग्रनख (the edge of a nail) as नखाग्र (see Petr. Dict. *s. v.* and the passages adduced there *s. v.* अग्र).

---

1) But it is allowed to say पिप्पल्यर्धः (a *portion* of a pepper). Pat. I, 407 states अर्ध to be a neuter, when meaning »half," but a masculine, when = »portion, part:" समप्रविभागे नपुंसकलिङ्गो ऽवयववाची पुँल्लिङ्गः

214. Compounds in °भूत and the like, the former member of which is a predicate.

A proper species of tatpurushas is made up by those, whose latter member is a verbal noun, the noun predicate of which is signified by the former member. The commonest instances of the kind are adjectives in °भूत (being, making up, behaving as). Pat. I, 39 प्रमाणभूत आचार्यः (the teacher, who is [the pupil's] authority), Daç. 176 तस्याहमस्म्युदाहरणभूता (I am an example thereof), M. 1, 5 आसीदिदं तमोभूतम्. Moreover there is a class of much used compound verbs, whose former part is a noun, whereas the latter is the verb कृ or भू; they carry the conception of something transformed from one state into another. They will be dealt with when treating of the Syntax of the Verb; see **308**.

Among other similar tatpurushas we notice *a.*) those ending in उक्त, समाम्नात, मत, समाख्यात, कृत etc. Daç. 61 स च..... अम्बालिकायामबलारत्नसमाख्यातायामतिमात्राभिलाषः (he, being passionately in love with Ambâlikâ surnamed: the jewel of womankind); *b.*) those in °ब्रुव (having but the name of) and °मानिन् and °मन्य (thinking one's self —), as ब्राह्मणब्रुवः »one who claims himself a brahman" [on account of his birth, but who does not behave as such], पण्डितमानी (wise in one's own opinion), Atharvav. 15, 13, 6 अव्रात्यो ऽव्रात्यब्रुवः, R. 3, 21, 17 शूरमानी न शूरस्त्वम्, Daç. 99 धन्यंमन्यः [1]).

P. 2, with co[...] P. 3,

Rem. Somewhat different is the nature of those, the former part of which is not the predicate, but the predicate's attribute, as उत्तानशय and अवमूर्धशय given as examples by the comm. of vârtt. 3 on P. 3, 2, 15 and पूर्वसर (going at the head) see P. 3, 2, 19.

215. Tatpurusha, consisting of noun-case + noun.

Among such tatpurushas as are made up of *a noun-case + the noun qualified by it*, by far the most common are those, whose former part is to be periphrased by a genitive, as राजपुरुषः = राज्ञः पुरुषः, शत्रुवधः =

---

1) With them may in some degree be compared such tatpurushas as Kathâs. 9, 48 आमिषशङ्कया (holding [her] for a piece of raw flesh), Hit. 93 व्याघ्रबुद्ध्या (taking [him] for a tiger). Here the former member is the predicative object of the verbal noun, which is the latter member.

शत्रोर्वधः or शत्र्वोः or शत्रूणाम्. As this type is met with on every page, it is useless to quote instances from literature. Another frequent type is that, represented by अहिहतः = अहिना हतः. Panc. 118 गुरुजनानुज्ञातः = गुरुजनेनानुज्ञातः, ibid. V, 93 राक्षसेन्द्रगृहीतः (seized by the prince of giants), Bhojapr. 7 सोऽपि तदाकर्ण्य वज्राहत इव भूताविष्ट इव ग्रहग्रस्त इव.

For the rest, any noun-case may become the former part of a tatpurusha, as मासकल्याणः = मासं कल्याणः (happy for a month), मातृसदृशः = मात्रा or मातुः सदृशः (resembling his mother), यूपदारु = यूपाय दारु (wood for a sacrificial stake), वृकभयम् = वृकात् or वृकेभ्यो भयम् (fear of a wolf or of wolves), स्थालीपाकः = स्थाल्यां पाकः (cooking in a pot).

216. Yet, there are some restrictions. For this reason, Pânini when treating of compounds made up of a noun-case + noun, gives a detailed account of them. The summary of which runs in this way:

[f]ormer [mem]ber is [ge]nitive.

I. As a rule, any genitive may be compounded (*shashthîsamâsa*). Some cases are excepted. Among others it is not allowed to use compounds, made up of a genitive + a participle or a gerund or a kṛtya or an infinitive, nor those consisting of a genitive + comparative or superlative or ordinal noun of number, nor such as where a genitive is compounded with some noun in °तृ or °अक. Therefore, such phrases as मनुष्याणां शूरतमः (the most heroic of men), छात्राणां पञ्चमः (the fifth of the disciples), अपां स्रष्टा (the creator of the waters), ब्राह्मणस्य कुर्वन् or कृत्वा or करणीयम् or कर्तुम् (doing etc. for the benefit of a brahman) are unfit for compounding. Partitive genitives are likewise excluded, nor is the dative-like genitive (**129**), it seems, as a rule, fit for being compounded. —

P. 2, 2, 8.

P. 2, 2, 11.

P. 2, 2, 15.

As little, so we learn from Pâṇini's commentators [1]) an objective genitive in such cases, as विचित्रा सूत्रस्य कृतिः पाणिनिना, here it is not allowed to say सूत्रकृतिः पाणिनिना, since both the subject and the object of the action conveyed by the noun कृतिः are expressed, for nothing impedes using the compound सूत्रकृतिः = सूत्रस्य कृतिः, if the agent is not expressed. [2]).

---

1) See Kâç. on P. 2, 2, 14; Pat. I, p. 415, vârtt. 6. Pat. himself rejects the interpretation given there.

2) The *shashṭhîsamâsa* is treated by Pâṇini in the second adhyâya of his 2d book (2, 2, 8—17), some statements are also scattered in the third book, see f. i. 3, 3, 116. Additions ad corrections on them are of course made in the commentaries. But now and then the cavillations of the commentators have rather obscured the good understanding of some rules. So the Kâçikâ is wrong loosening sûtra 2, 2, 14 from its adhikâra क्तेन and interpreting this rule — कर्मणि च — as if it taught something concerning the objective genitive. Now, as the sûtra could in no way be explained so as to contain a prohibition of compounding any objective genitive whatever, as such compounds are very common indeed, the Kâçikâ was obliged to add a clause of its own उभयप्राप्तौ कर्मणीति षष्ठ्या इति ग्रहणम्, which statement certainly will be correct by itself, but not the smallest trace of which is to be found in Pâṇini. In fact, Pâṇini has here not thought of an *objective genitive.* When reading the sûtras 12, 13, 14 at a stretch and without prejudice, one sees plainly that कर्मणि of 14 qualifies क्तेन of 12. Sûtra 14 prohibits compounding a *genitive* + a participle in °त with *passive* meaning. It is not allowed to say तद्दर्शितम् instead of तस्य दर्शितम् (shown *to* him), whereas Pâṇini allows it, when representing तेन दर्शितम् (shown *by* him), cp. 2, 1, 32.

The following sûtras 15 and 16 — तृजकाभ्यां कर्तरि । कर्तरि च — afford a fair sample of absurd hairsplitting. In s. 15 Pâṇini had given a rule about the words in °तृ and °अक when denoting the agent; with them a genitive cannot be compounded, save the few instances mentioned 2, 2, 9. Accordingly it is prohibited by Pâṇini to say वज्रभर्ता instead of वज्रस्य भर्ता (bearer of the thunderbolt) or ओदनपाचकः instead of ओदनस्य पाचकः (one who cooks rice). But some schoolmaster, who commented on our great grammarian, discovered Pâṇini to have omitted some kind of words in °अक, which though not-denoting the agent are likewise forbidden to be compounded with a preceding genitive, as भवतः शायिका (your lying down) cp. P. 3, 3, 111. In order to make our sûtra comprise even them, an accusative; II. compounding the accusative is allowed: P.2,1,29.[1])

a) when being one of time as मासकल्याणः. So R. 2, 71, 18 सप्तरात्रोषितः पथि, Mâlat. I, p. 14 बहुदिवसोपचीयमानमिव मन्मथव्यथाविकारमुपलब्धवानस्मि;

b) with some participles in °त, with active or intransitive meaning, as ग्रामगतः (gone to the village), नरकपतितः (fallen to hell), कष्टश्रितः (come to hardship), सुखप्राप्तः [2]) sim. In practice, there are more. So f. i. the restriction of खट्वारूढ (P. 2, 1, 26) to a reproachful term does not imply the prohibition of compounding आरूढ otherwise. See but Panc. 51 करेणुकारूढा, ibid. 30 गृहायातः P. 2, 1, 24. P. 2, 1, 26.

an instrumental; III. compounding the instrumental is allowed:

a) if denoting the agent or instrument + some verbal noun, as अहिहतः. The participles in °तवन्त् are excepted, compounding अहिना + हतवान् therefore not allowed. — Some proverbial locutions are explicitly named by Pâṇini, as काकपेया नदी, श्वलेह्यः कूपः, but P. 2, 1, 32. P. 2, 1, 33.

---

the well-known *yogavibhâga*-expedient was taken recourse to, and our sûtra was split up in two. One made the discovery that the word कर्तरि admitted of two acceptations, according to its being construed either with तृजकाभ्याम् or with the general adhikâra षष्ठी; in other terms, P. could mean either *any genitive + agent in* तृ *or* अक or *the subjective genitive + any noun in* तृ *or* अक. By combining both and assigning to either an own sûtra the ἀπορία felt by the commentator found its λύσις. See but the artificial interpretation of both in the Kâçikâ. How Patanjali interpreted the rule we do not know, a comment of his on s. 15 and 16 being wanting; from vârtt. 2 on I, p. 415 it appears he was acquainted at least with s. 15.

In 2, 2, 11 it seems strange, that a special prohibition — that concerning the ordinal nouns of number — is enjoined immediately after the general one (2, 2, 10) which includes also that special case.

1) The preceding sûtra 28 is too artfully interpreted by Pat. and Kâç. to have been interpreted well. It is likely, we have here again an instance of distortion by *yogavibhâga*. I am sure, Pâṇini himself has given but *one* rule काला अत्यन्तसंयोगे च. Patanjali's defence (I, p. 384) is not persuasive.

2) I agree with Boethlingk and Whitney in explaining प्राप्तजीविक and the like as bahuvrîhis. Pâṇini brings them under the tatpurushas, see 2, 2, 4. Inversely such compounds as सुरापीत, मासजात which P. 6, 2, 170 understands as bahuvrîhis, are to be recognised as tatpurushas.

from this it should not be inferred that it is wholly forbidden to make up any other compound of instrumental + kṛtya. Panc. 327 त्वङ्कृत्यो ऽयं मानुषः = त्वया भ°. Yet such compounds are not frequent.

b) if the latter member is a word expressive of *likeness*, *equality*, *superiority*, *want* [1]), see **61** and **73**. Of the kind are such compounds as पितृसमः (equal to his father), मातृसदृशः (resembling his mother), मासपूर्वः and मासावरः (earlier —, later by a month), M. 8, 217 अल्पोनं कर्म = अल्पेनोनं कर्म (*v. a.* work, almost finished), Panc. 23 स्वामिसदृशा एव भवन्ति भृत्याः; P. 2, 1, 31.

c) the instrum. + the words कलह (quarrel), निपुण (clever), मिश्र (mixed), श्लक्ष्ण (lax). Kâç. gives these examples: असिकलहः, वाङ्निपुणः, गुडमिश्रः, आचारश्लक्ष्णः. When extending the rule to all words of the same purport, as we may do (see above p. 92 N.), the frequent compounds in °मिलित, °अन्वित, °युत, °युक्त, °उपेत etc. are included, also many of those, the former part of which is an *instrumentalis partis* (**73**). P. 2, 1, 31

d) in the case of compound adjectives, the former part of which is an instrumental of causality, illustrative of the adjective it is joined to [2]). So R. 3, 16, 13 निःश्वासान्ध आदर्शः (a mirror tarnished by exhalation), ibid. 3, 55, 20 वीर्यसमः (equal by strength), ibid. 2, 118, 4 गुणश्लाघ्यः (praiseworthy by his qualities), Panc. I, 39 ज्ञात्यादिमहोत्साहा नरेन्द्राः = ज्ञात्यादिना महोत्साहा नरेन्द्राः, Kumâras. 3, 12 तपोवीर्यमहत्सु (men, great by their heroic penance). — Of the same kind are the compounds, made up of instrum. + अर्थिन् (75 R. 1), as Panc. 10 किं P. 2, 1, 30

1) In Pânini's text पूर्वसदृशसमोनार्थ° अर्थ is of course to be construed with each of the members: पूर्वार्थ, सदृशार्थ, समार्थ, ऊनार्थ, cp. p. 92 N.

2) Sûtra 2, 1, 30 is ill-handled by the commentaries. They expound तृतीया तत्कृतार्थेन गुणवचनेन, as if तत्कृतार्थेन were a dvandva = तत्कृतेन + अर्थेन. How they have come to this contorted interpretation I did not understand before perusing Patanjali; from him I have seen, that his very cavillations (I, 384 sq.) must have provoked it. Yet the aim of the author of our sûtra is unmistakable. He allows the instrumental to be compounded with any adjective (गुणवचनेन), which has its justification by that instrumental: तत्कृतार्थेन = यस्यार्थस्तया तृतीयया कृतः स्यात्तेन. So in निःश्वासान्ध आदर्शः the instance, I have quoted from the Râm., it is the exhalation that causes the mirror to be qualified a tarnished one.

भवानाहारार्थी केवलमेव (are you desirous of nothing but food?), Kathâs. 24, 176 etc.

e) in the case of food dressed with some ingredient or by mixing two materials, as दध्योदनः, गुडधानाः. Likewise Daç. 139 विषान्नम् (empoisoned food). P. 2, 1, 34 and 35.

dative; IV. the dative may be compounded:

a) the dative of the aim in such cases as यूपदारु = यूपाय दारु, कुण्डलहिरण्यम् = कुण्डलाय हिरण्यम्; P. 2, 1, 36.

b) the dative of the remote object with the words बलि (offering to), हित (good for), सुख (pleasant for), रक्षित (kept, guarded for) and the like, as विष्णुबलिः, गोहितम्, Panc. I, 47 सा सेवा या प्रभुहिता, etc. — With them is named अर्थ »purpose, aim, scope." On the compounds in °अर्थ we have treated **194**. P. 2, 1, 36.

ablative; V. the ablative:

a) with words expressive of *fear*, as वृकभयम् (fear of wolves), R. 3, 27, 20 व्याधत्रस्ता मृगाः (deer, afraid of the hunter); P. 2, 1, 37.

b) with some participles, which signify a withdrawal [1]). Daç. 89 नृत्योत्थिता सा प्रातिष्ठत (she rose from the dance and went away), M. 2, 89 सावित्रीपतितः (one who has forfeited the *sâvitrî*), R. 3, 25, 24 चिच्छिदुर्बिभिदुश्चैव रामबाणा गुणाच्युताः.

locative. VI. the locative:

a) with such nouns as are construed with a locative of reference, as those of *attachment*, *skill* and the like (**148**). R. 3, 19, 22 मानुषौ शस्त्रसंपन्नौ (two men, accomplished at arms), Panc. I, 18 भाण्डक्रयविचक्षणाः (skilled in the commerce of merchandises); P. 2, 1, 40.

b) in some cases, when denoting a time or a place. Of the kind Pâṇini names compounds in °सिद्ध (prepared, dressed), °शुष्क (dried), °पक्व (cooked), °बन्ध, also parts of the day or night + कृत, as सांकाश्यसिद्ध (prepared in Sânkâçya), आतपशुष्क (dried in the sun), पूर्वाह्णकृत (done in the forenoon); P. 2, 1, 41. P. 2, 1, 45.

c) in some standing phrases and proverbial locutions, see P. 2, 1, 42—44; 46—48.

217. This list of possible kinds of tatpurushas, made up of noun-

---

1) These compounds are not frequent अल्पशः (P. 2, 1, 38).

additions to the rules of Pâṇini thereabout.

case + noun, is however not complete, as will soon appear, if one undertakes to systematize the tatpurushas occurring in fact in some literary work. [1]) So, among others, Pâṇini does not mention the abl. of comparison, compounded with अन्य and इतर; the instrumental + words expressive of plenty; the accus. with the participial adjectives in °उ. Then, many more participles, whose former part is some noun-case, are in common use, though not necessarily, if at all, implied by the foresaid rules.

1. abl. of comparison + अन्य, especially, if the former part be a pronoun, as Hit. 30 भवदन्यो मया कः सुहृत्प्राप्तव्यः, Panc. I, 12 trade is said to be the best means for making money, तदन्यः [sc. उपायः] संशयात्मकः (any other but this is dangerous).

2. abl. of compar. + इतर. — Such compounds are an elegant paraphrase, while calling something: the contrary of its opposite. So दक्षिणेतर = सव्य »left," सुलभेतर उपायः (a difficult expedient), Daç. 175 तया नववधूा द्वेषमल्पेतरं बबन्ध (he bore his newly married wife a heavy grudge).

3. instrum. + word expressive of plenty. Of the kind are those in °आढ्य, °प्रचुर, °समाकुल etc Panc. 319 ऊर्णाप्रचुरोऽयं मेषः, ibid. 7 सिंहव्याघ्रसमाकुलेऽस्मिन्वने.

4. accus. + adjective in °उ derived of a desiderative. Panc. 3 नाहमर्थलिप्सुः, M. 7, 197 युध्येत जयप्रेप्सुरपेतभीः.

5. Instances of noun-cases + participles are manifold and often met with. First, such as where the former part represents a sociative instrumental, as Panc. I, 164 संमानसंयुक्ताः सेवकाः, ibid. I, 229 भार्या परसंगता (a wife, who holds illicit intercourse with another). — Then, such as are expressive of separation (**62**). Panc. I, 35 सेवाविवर्जितः (abstaining from attendance), ibid. p. 1 पुत्रा विवेकरहिताः (sons, deprived of discernment), ibid. I, 189 संमानविहीनः cp. **198**. — Further locatives + स्थित, गत (cp. **197**), जात, उत्पन्न etc., as R. 3, 31, 2 जनस्थानस्थिता राक्षसाः (the râxasas, staying at Janasthâna), Panc. I, 128 सदैवापद्गतो राजा भोग्यो भवति मन्त्रिणाम् (when being in distress, a king

---

1) It would be indeed an interesting subject-matter for investigation to compare on a large scale these statements of Pâṇini with the facts offered us by the extant Sanskrit literature.

is always the prey of his ministers), ibid. I, 104 मूषिका गृहजातापि हन्तव्या, Kathâs. 42, 149 अङ्घ्रिपतित: (fallen at their feet). — Or the former member is a dative or loc. of purpose: Panc. I, 125 राज्यलाभोद्यतो वृत्रः (Vrtra, striving for obtaining the royalty); an accusative: ibid. p 37 संजीवकानुरक्तः (attached to S.); an abl. of origin: ibid. p. 2 कुलप्रसूतस्य (of one born from a respectable family); a loc. of reference: ibid. I, 15 गोष्ठिककर्मनियुक्तः. And so on.

6. As to the compound adjectives, they may generally be said to be comprised by the rules of Pâṇini, as their former part is a genitive or may be accepted as such. Among them are to be noticed योग्य, अनुरूप, उचित, समर्थ, those of skill and ability as विचक्षण, अभिज्ञ, कोविद्, then such as सदृश, सम (cp. **216**, III *b*). Panc. 17 राजा भृत्यानुत्तमपदयोग्यान् हीनाधमस्थाने नियोजयति, ibid. 21 तस्य च शब्दानुरूपेण पराक्रमेण भाव्यम् (his strength will be in proportion to his voice), ibid. 27 भवान्वचनपटुर्दृश्यते, ibid. 13 कथमहं सेवानभिज्ञः. Even indubitable dative-like genitives are compounded with the adjectives, which they qualify. Panc. p. 1 राजा तान् शास्त्रविमुखानालोक्य (as the king understood they were averse to the çâstras —). Panc. p. 1 affords even this instance of a tatpur., made up of a dat. of interest + subst., when calling some king सकलार्थिकल्पद्रुमः (v. a. a blessing for all the indigent).

7. Compounds made up of a genitive + agent in °तृ, though explicitly interdicted by Pâṇini, are in fact met with. Panc. I, 2 नमोऽस्तु नयशास्त्रकर्तृभ्यः, ibid. p. 7 तस्य मङ्गलवृषभौ धूर्वोढारौ स्थितौ (two splendid bulls drew his chariot).

8. Finally we may set up a category apart for such tatpurushas, the former part of which is a noun-case, doing more or less duty of an adverb. Panc. 21 न युक्तं स्वामिनः पूर्वोपार्जितं वनं त्यक्तुम्, here पूर्वोपार्जित = पूर्वमुपार्जित »acquired before," Kathâs. 29, 82 व्याजसप्रणयैर्वाक्यैर्वञ्च्यते (— is deceived by words falsely kind), Panc. 63 स्नेहसंभाषः (a friendly discourse), Mhbh. 1, 152, 34 सुखसुप्तान्वने भ्रातॄन्.... न बोधयिष्यामि (I will not awake my brothers who are sleeping quietly in the forest), Kathâs. 42, 149 पर्यायालिङ्गितः (embraced by turns). In all but the first of these examples the former part is an *instrumentalis modi*, used almost as an adverb (**77**). Cp. the following paragraph.

218. The former part of a tatpurusha may also be an adverb or a particle. Panc. 59 प्राग्वृत्तान्तः (the matter of late), Kathâs. 6, 165 प्रतिवसतिपताकाः (flags, waving from every house), ibid. 25, 29 सा [viz. पुरी] च मे ऽवश्यगन्तव्या (and I have to go from necessity to that town), Kumâras. 3, 4 नितान्तदीर्घैस्तपोभिः (by very long penance).

ne former member is an adverb or a particle.

Among the particles several are noticed by Pâṇini, viz. स्वयम् [2, 1, 25], सामि [ibid. 27], the negation अ° [2, 2, 6], ईषत् [2, 2, 7], किम् [2, 1, 64], क, the particles styled »gati" and such particles as प्र, अव, आ when meaning »a little," सु, दुः, अति [2, 2, 18][1]) cp. 210 at the end. — So स्वयंमृतः (died of himself), सामिकृत (half done), अब्राह्मणः »no brahman" or »none but a brahman," ईषदुन्नत (a little elevated), प्रपितामहः (a great-grandfather), सुजनः (a good man), दुर्जनः (a wicked man), etc.

219. Some relative pronouns and adverbs are likewise fit for being compounded with some noun, especially **यथा** and **यावत्**. Those beginning with **यथा** are the most common, they are *either* adverbs of the type **यथाकालम्**, **यथावयः** (according to time, — to age), *or* their second member is a participle in °**त** as **यथोक्त** (as said)[2]). Examples: Mhbh. 1, 145, 16 निवर्तध्वं यथागृहम् (go back, each to his own house), ibid. 1, 149, 1 यथासंप्रत्ययं..... प्रेषयामास पूरुषम् (he sent a man, as was agreed before); — R. 3, 13, 25 यथोपदिष्टेन पथा (on the way, as has been pointed out), Daç. 151 इममर्थं लब्धक्षणो यथोपपन्नैरुपायैः साधयिष्यति (when having got the opportunity he will discharge this affair by such means, as are fit), Panc. 295 यथानिर्दिष्टः क्षपणकः सहसा प्रादुर्बभूव.

P. 2, 1, 7 and 8.

ne former member is यथा or यावत्.

Examples of यावत्. — Panc. 276 इतः प्रभृति यावज्जीवं मयात्मा भवते दत्तः (from this day, I have given my own self to you for my whole lifetime), Kâç. on P. 2, 1, 8 यावदमत्रं ब्राह्मणानामामन्त्रयस्व (invite of the brahmans according to the number of the vessels), Panc. 54 यावद्वात्स्यायनोक्तविधिना (conformably to the rules, taught by Vâtsyâyana).

---

1) As to सु, दुः, ईषत्, in सुकर (easy to be done), दुष्कर (hard to be done) and the like, see P. 3, 3, 126-130.

2) Pâṇini (2, 1, 7) mentions only the former type.

220. Comparison expressed by tatpurushas.

The tatpurusha serves also to express comparison. Such compounds are partly adjectives, partly substantives. The former are of the type घनश्याम (cloud-black), इन्द्रनील (sky-blue). The latter are made up of the thing's real name + the image, under which it is represented, as पुरुषव्याघ्रः, राजसिंहः, दोर्दण्डः, करकिसलयः.

Examples of the former type. Kâm. 3, 12 जलान्तश्चन्द्रचपलं जीवनम् (life, as fickle as the moon, that shines in the water), Daç. 174 हिमशिशिर° (as cold as ice), R. 3, 23, 1 गर्दभारुणः (red-grey as the colour of an ass), Mhbh. 1, 152, 2 °प्रावृड्जलधरश्यामः (as dark as a cloud in the rainy season), Mâlav. V, p. 122 परिघगुरुभिर्दोर्भिः, etc.

The latter type is adapted to signify either praise or blame. Generally the metaphors used are conventional ones. In this way a resolute, energetic character is called पुरुषसिंहः, a beautiful face मुखपद्मम्, आननारविन्दम् sim., eloquent speech वाङ्मधु, heavy sorrow is by a standing comparison शोकसागरः which ocean it is difficult or impossible to pass, and so on. In ancient literature this rather allegorical style is still employed with moderation and within certain limits. But the flowery compositions of medieval India are full of them so as not rarely to make the image appear an appendix wholly meaningless, if not to please the ear of the reader and to display the vaidagdhya of the author. The accumulation of such allegorical designations becomes tedious indeed, unless good taste direct their employment.

Sometimes the metaphor is worked out. Then we may have a set of homogeneous images, expressed by compounds. So Panc. I, 241 गोपालेन प्रजाधेनोर्वित्तदुग्धं शनैः शनैः। ग्राह्यम्, here गोपाल is »king" but at the same time it conveys the meaning of »cow-herd," as गो is = »cow" and = »earth," »he must draw the वित्तदुग्धम् (money-milk) of his प्रजाधेनोः (subject-cow) by degrees" v. a. »a king must draw the money of his subjects by degrees, just as the cowherd draws the milk from his cow." Mrcch. IV, p. 138 इह सर्वस्वफलिनः कुलपुत्रमहाद्रुमाः। निष्फलत्वमलं यान्ति वेश्याविहगभक्षिताः (young gentlemen often come to poverty, being spoiled by courtesans, like great trees, the fruits of which are eaten out by birds). Kathâs. 29, 188 a faithful wife is thus compared to a warrior — her conjugal faith is her chariot, duty her charioteer, good behaviour her armour, wit her weapon भर्तृभक्तिरथारूढाः शीलसंनाहरक्षिताः। धर्मसारथयः साध्व्यो जयन्ति मतिहेतयः.

Rem. 1. According to vernacular grammar, this class of compounds is to be considered a subdivision of the karmadhârayas, there being sâmânâdhikaranya between both members. This explication cannot be right, for it does not account for the inverse order of the two members; one should f. i. expect रत्नस्त्री instead of स्त्रीरत्नम्, as in the karmadhâraya the qualifying noun is of course put first. In fact, we have here no karmadhârayas, but shashthîsamâsas. The former member is a genitive, but it does not bear everywhere the same character. Sometimes it is a partitive one, as पुरुषसिंहः = पुरुषाणां (or पुरुषेषु) सिंहः, राजापसदः »an outcast *among* the kings," cp. the compounds in उत्तम (best) and अधम (worst, lowest). Sometimes, too, it is a genitive of the kind represented by our »a jewel of a woman," »a hell of a fellow," Lat. *scelus hominis*; so गृहभूतिः (Mudr. III, p. 102) »a beauty of a house," सहायसंपत् (Mudr. III, p. 121) v. a. »excellent helpers," भार्याचिल्लम् (P. 6, 2, 126) »a slut of a wife." Not rarely both acceptations are alike probable; स्त्रीरत्नम् f. i. may be as well = स्त्रीषु रत्नम् »a jewel among women" as = »a jewel of a woman."

Rem. 2. Pâṇini treats the said compounds severally, see 2, 1, 53; 56; 62; 66; 6, 2, 126 sq. — Note °कीट and °अपसद expressing blame, and °रत्न, °पाश, °रूप signifying admiration.

221. Tatpurushas, made up of three or more stems, are always dissolvable into two members, either of which may be a compound itself Mṛcch. III p. 125 सुखदुःखसुहृद्भवान्, here the former part is a dvandva सुखदुःखयोः सुहृद्भवान् = सुखे च दुःखे च. Panc. 323 मत्कण्ठस्थिता [viz. रत्नमाला], here the former part is a tatpurusha itself, मत्कण्ठस्थिता being = मत्कण्ठे, that is मम कण्ठे, स्थिता. — Panc. II, 153 स्त्रीवाक्याङ्कुशविक्षुण्णाः (stirred by the sting-like words

Tatpurushas made up of three or more themes.

of a woman), here त्रिजुपणा is the latter member, the former being a tatpurusha of comparison, the former member of which स्त्रीवाक्य is itself an ordinary shashthîsamâsa. — Mhbh. 1, 155, 24 पुष्पितद्रुमसानुषु = पुष्पितद्रुमेषु सानुषु, here the former part of the tatpurusha is a bahuvrîhi. — Kâm. 2, 43 नियतविषयवर्ती (one firmly attached to wordliness) is illustrative of the species of those, whose latter member is a compound, the analysis being नियतं विषयेषु वर्तमानः.

3. Bahuvrîhi.

222. [margin: ...ure and ...racte... ...ics of bahu... ...îhi.] The difference between the tatpurusha and the bahuvrîhi is an essential one. The former implies no more than is purported by its constituent elements, but the bahuvrîhi always adds something tacitly understood, generally the conception of „having, possessing." इन्द्रशत्रुः when tatpurusha = इन्द्रस्य शत्रुः „Indra's foe," when bahuvrîhi it means „having Indra for foe, one whose foe is Indra;" सूर्यवर्णः, when tatp. = सूर्यस्य वर्णः „the colour of the sun," when bahuvr. it denotes „one having the colour of the sun." The bahuvrîhi, therefore, is invariably an *adjective*, referring to some substantive [1]). Pâṇini then is quite right, when he defines the bahuvrîhi as „a complex of elements serving to qualify some other word [2]).

---

1) By this it is however not asserted, that a bahuvrîhi cannot be used as a substantive, but only this: when used so, they are to be considered just as any other adjective, that does duty of a subst. महात्मा when = »a noble-man" is to be compared with such a word as शुचिः when meaning »an honest man" or बालः when = »boy."

2) P. 2, 2, 23 sq. बहुव्रीहिरनेकमन्यपदार्थे. According to that definition, Indian grammar does by no means make restriction as to the number of the elements out of which a bahuvrîhi is made up. This is distinctly expressed in a metrical rule of the *Kâtantra* (2, 5, 9)

Like other adjectives, the bahuvrîhis may be used as adverbs, when put in the accus. of the neuter singular, see **240**.

223. *Its members are to be called predicate and subject.* From a syntactic point of view, the bahuvrîhi, it may be made up of three, four or more elements, does contain but *two* members, virtually identical with the subject and the predicate of a full sentence, just as the tatpurusha represents a main noun with its attribute. And, as within the tatpurusha the attribute is put at the head and the main noun behind (**210**), so within the bahuvrîhi the predicate precedes, the subject is the latter member. When analyzing f. i. the bahuvrîhi महावीर्यः we get the clause यस्य वीर्यं महत् „he whose strength is great," similarly सूर्यवर्णः = यस्य वर्णः सूर्यस्येव „he whose colour is like the sun's," भूतलन्यस्तलोचनः is an epithet of somebody, whose eyes are fixed on the earth यस्य भूतले न्यस्ते लोचने. In these examples, the words वीर्य, वर्ण, लोचन are the subjects within the bahuvrîhis, that which precedes them being the predicates.

The predicate precedes, the subject is the latter member.

In treating of the tatpurushas we have distinguished between 1. the karmadhârayas, 2. those the former mem-

---

स्यातां यदि पदे द्वे तु यदि वा स्युर्बहून्यपि
तान्यन्यस्य पदस्यार्थे बहुव्रीहिः etc.

Nevertheless, in analyzing even intricate bahuvrîhis it will appear that, logically, there are but two members — predicate and subject — either or both of which may be compounds themselves, even if it would not always be allowed to use such compounds by themselves as separate words. Pâṇini himself knows »a class of compounds only allowed for the sake of being used as the former part of other compounds" [P. 2, 1, 51].

ypes of uvrîhis.

ber of which represents some noun-case, 3. where it is a particle. In an analogous way we may speak of three types of bahuvrîhis: *a.*) those, where there is grammatical concord between subject and predicate, *b.*) such, whose predicate is a noun-case, *c.*) such, where it is a particle.

Type *a.* — Here the predicate is mostly an adjective or a participle, as इन्द्रशत्रुः „having Indra for foe." When adjective, the bahuvrîhi has generally the worth of Latin *gen.* or *abl. qualitatis*, or *abl. modi.* So वीरो व्यूढोरस्कः = *heros lato pectore*, Panc. 62 सरः स्वल्पतोयम् = *lacus exiguae aquae.* When participle, the bahuvrîhi not rarely concurs with the gerund, the absolute locative and the like It may as well be said त्यक्तनगरो ऽरण्यायाहं प्रातिष्ठे as नगरं त्यक्त्वा or त्यक्ते नगरे° (I left the town and set out for the forest).

Those belonging to type *b.*) are such as अश्वमुखः (having a horse's face), Panc. 71 संजीवको युष्मत्पादानामुपरि द्रोहबुद्धिः (Sanj. meditates of doing harm to Your Majesty), here द्रोहबुद्धिः = यस्य द्रोहाय (or द्रोहे) बुद्धिः „whose mind is to do harm."

Those belonging to type *c.*) are such as अधोमुख (having one's face cast down), अन्तःसत्त्व (pregnant), एवंप्रभावो राजा (a king of such a power). Very common are those, commencing by अ°, सु°, दुः°, as अपुत्रः (having no sons), सुपुत्रः (having a good son or good sons).

Type *a.*) and *c.*) are much more common than type *b*).

224. Examples of bahuvrîhis. Type *a.*) Nala 1, 5 तथैवासीद्विदर्भेषु भीमो भीमपराक्रमः. R. 3, 16, 11 मृदुसूर्याः पटुशीताः.... दिवसा भान्ति सांप्रतम् (now the days are appearing with a mild sun, much fog and a sharp cold). Hit. 90 असौ पापाशयः (he is of a wicked disposition). Panc. 150 तेन [sc. क्रोडेन].... दंष्ट्राग्रेण पाटितोदरः पुलिन्दो गतासुर्भूतले ऽपतत् (the Pulinda fell down *lifeless* on the earth, *having his belly split up* by the edge of the teeth of the boar). Mâlav. I, p. 14 राजा। अनुवाचितलेखममात्यं विलोक्य (*as* the minister *has finished his lecture of the letter*, the king looks on him). Panc. 71 संदह्यमानहृदयः स्वयमेवाभ्यागतो वक्तुम् (*as it stung my mind*, I myself am come to tell you of it).

Nothing impedes, of course, both the subject and the predicate being concordant substantives. Bhoj. 17 राजानः कोशबला एव विजयिनो नान्ये (no other kings are successful in their wars but those, whose power is a treasury), Panc. 185 तत्र वायसराजोऽनेककाकपरिवारः प्रतिवसति स्म [the bahuvr. = यस्यानेके काकाः परिवारः »whose attendance are many crows"], Daç. 82 अर्यवर्यः कुबेरदत्तनामा (a great merchant, whose name is Kub.), R. 3, 19, 22 मानुषौ चीरकृष्णाजिनाम्बरौ.

Rem. 1. In such bahuvrîhis, as have an adjective behind, that adjective does duty of a subst. So f. i. Çâk. I अभिरूपभूयिष्ठा परिषत् (the assembly is for the greater part made up of distinguished people) here the bahuvr. = यस्या अभिरूपा भूयिष्ठाः »most of which are अभिरूपाः," Mâlat. I, p. 2 उदितभूयिष्ठ एष भगवान्तपनः »the sun has almost risen," R. 2, 40, 17 सीतातृतीयानारूढान्दृष्ट्वा (— saw them mounted, having Sîtâ as the third), R. 3, 55, 15 सहस्रमेकं मम कार्यपुरःसरम् (thousand men whose *main object* [पुरःसरम्] it is to carry out my orders).

Rem. 2. A proper kind of bahuvrîhis are such as असिकर (having a sword in one's hand), अश्रुकण्ठ (sobbing, liter. »one having tears in his throat"). In analyzing them, the latter part turns out a locative, for असिकरः = यस्यासिः करे स and अश्रुकण्ठः = यस्याश्रूणि कण्ठे स. For the rest, we have here no exception to the general rule on the arrangement of the two members of a bahuvrîhi. It is असि and अश्रु which are predicated, not करे nor कण्ठे, for the intention is to say not that Mr. so and so has a hand or a throat, but what it is, he keeps within. [1]) R. 3, 51, 9 Sîtâ has the epithet बाष्पलोचना »having tears in her eyes." Comp. WHITNEY § 1303.

Rem. 3. In some bahuvrîhis the order of the members is optional. One may say promiscuously आहिताग्निः and अग्न्याहितः (one who keeps the holy fires), जातपुत्रः or पुत्रजातः (one having children). Of the kind are दन्तजात or जातदन्त, see M. 5, 58 with Kull., गुडप्रिय and प्रियगुड (fond of sweetmeats) [2]), R. 2, 119, 5 मुनयः कलशोद्यताः (hermits with uplifted pitchers). Participles in °त must be put behind, if the predicate be a weapon, therefore अस्युद्यतः (with uplifted sword), see vârtt. on P. 2, 2, 36.

P. 2, 2, 37.

Rem. 4. The type *a.*) of the bahuvrîhi in its outer form is often identical with a karmadhâraya, for the discrepancies in the accentuation are not heeded. In practice, one avoids to use as bahuvrîhis such compounds as are wont to be karmadhârayas, as सर्वजन, महर्षि, कलरव, and inversely such as महाबाहु, बहुश्रुत, कृतकार्य will not have to be otherwise accepted than as bahuvrîhis. [3]) Yet, it often is only the context which will enable the reader how to accept a given compound.

225. Type *b.*). Panc. 24 कदाचिद् दमनकोऽयमुभयवेतनो भूत्वा ममोपरि दुष्टबुद्धिः

---

1) Cp. vârtt. 4 of Pat. on P. 2, 2, 36.

2) As to प्रिय, Pat. vârtt. 2 on P. 2, 2, 35 teaches the option. But it seems better to explain गुडप्रिय as being a tatpurusha, because 1st प्रिय may be not only = »beloved," but also = »loving," see Petr. Dict. IV, p. 1161 *s. v.* 1 *c*), 2ly as Pâṇini somewhere else [P. 6, 2, 15 sq.] mentions some *tatpurushas* in °प्रिय. The same may apply to some of the participles in °त, if not to all. Since पीत may sometimes have an active signification and sometimes a passive one, it is plain we are allowed to compound as well the tatpurusha क्षीरपीतः = *lac potus*, as the bahuvr. पीतक्षीरः = *lacte poto.* Comp. what has been said p. 157 N. 2.

Panc. 283 affords a specimen of a kind of compounds, in which two types are confounded: काचिच्छृगालिका मांसपिण्डगृहीतवदना, here the author seems to have blended promiscuously two bahuvrîhis मांसपिण्डवदना and गृहीतमांसपिण्डा, either of which would have sufficed. Comp. Hariv. 5814 चक्रोद्यतकरः.

3) See CAPPELLER *Vâmana's Stilregeln: Kâvyasamaya* 7 and 8.

स्यात्, here उभयवेतन is the epithet of one »who accepts wages from both parties," Kathâs. 72, 186 हंसद्वन्द्वरूपं किंचित्सिद्धद्वयम् (two siddhas, who bore the shape of flamingos), Mâlav. I, p. 24 कौशिकी यतिवेषा (K. wearing the dress of an ascetic).

Rem. Comparison is sometimes expressed by them, as R. 3, 69, 43 कौ युवां वृषभस्कन्धौ (who are you, whose shoulders are like those of a bull?). R. 5, 17, 10 Râxasawomen bear the epithet गजोष्ट्रहयपादाः (with the feet of elephants, camels and horses). — But also by type *a.*) as राजीवलोचनः (having lotus-eyes), चन्द्राननः (moon-faced).

225*. Type *c.*) Prabodh. V, p. 103 देवी मामेवमवस्थं न समाश्वसयति (the queen does not comfort me, who am in such a state), Panc. I, 137 अन्तःसारैः..... मन्त्रिभिर्धार्यते राज्यम् (a kingdom is upheld by pithy ministers), Kumâras. 3, 14 the gods bear the epithet उच्चैर्द्विषः (whose adversaries are mighty). — Apart from the very common employment of अ, सु, दुः as the predicate in bahuvrîhis, several particles and prepositions may be used so, as उत्, निः, वि, अति, अव etc., as नीरस (sapless), उदञ्जलिः »one with folded hands," Ragh. 2, 74 पुरमुत्पताकम् (a flagged town), Daç. 137 उदायुधः (with uplifted weapon), Harsha 9 तरुर्विपल्लवः (a leafless tree), Bhoj. 8 खड्गमपकोशं कृत्वा जगाम.

Rem. Compounding with स°, सह° and the like has the same power, as English -*ful*, similarly English -*less* is expressed by compounds, beginning with अ°, निः°, वि°, विगत°, वीत° etc. [1]).

---

1) Patanjali enumerates also different species of bahuvrîhis: *a*) those, the members of which are samânâdhikarana as चित्रगु, *b*) the former part of which is an avyaya, as नीचैर्मुख, *c*) whose former part is a locative or something compared as कण्ठेकाल, उष्ट्रमुख, *d*) where it is a *gen. generis* or a *gen. materiae* as केशचूड (with one's hair tied up, liter. »[bearing] a knot of hair"), सुवर्णालङ्कार (wearing golden ornaments), *e*) whose former part is one of the gana प्रादयः [P. 1, 4, 58] as प्रपर्ण (unleaved), *f*) negation + noun, as अपुत्र. In the case of *c*) an ellipsis is stated of a middle element, कण्ठेकाल representing कण्ठेस्थः कालोऽस्य and उष्ट्रमुख being = उष्ट्रमुखमिव मुखमस्य. As to *e*) and *f*) Patanjali states the option between saying in full प्रपतितपर्णो वृक्षः and the abridgment प्रपर्णो वृक्षः, likewise between अविद्यमानपुत्रः and अपुत्रः Cp. f. i. Daç. 35 उद्गतबाष्पलोचनं तमपृच्छम् with ibid. 176 सा..... उद्बाष्पोवाच; here the full उद्गत°लोचन and the short उद्बाष्प are synonymous.

226. As bahuvrîhis of three and more members are excessively frequent, we will adduce some instances of them.

rge bahuvrîhis.

1. the subject is a compound. Panc. 322 त्यक्ताहारक्रियः (abstaining from taking food) here the subject of the bahuvr. is आहारक्रिया, a tatpurusha; Vâr. Yog. 1, 8 क्षपितधनराष्ट्रो भवति (he loses his wealth and his kingdom) here the subj. is a dvandva धनराष्ट्रे »wealth and kingdom;" Daç. 78 a Jaina monk is thus qualified प्रकीर्णमलपङ्कः प्रबलकेशलुञ्चनव्यथः प्रकृष्टतमक्षुत्पिपासादिदुःखः (v. a. covered with dust and mud, enduring a heavy pain by pulling out his hair, suffering very much from hunger, thirst and the like) here the subjects of the three bahuvr. are respectively the dvandva मलपङ्कौ, the tatp. केशलुञ्चनव्यथा and the tatp. क्षुत्पिपासादिदुःखम् and of them the two tatpurushas are themselves made up of more than two themes, as it is the compound केशलुञ्चन which qualifies व्यथा, and similarly the compound क्षुत्पिपासादि, which is the cause of दुःखम्.

2. the predicate is a compound. — Instances of this category are very often met with, especially such bahuvrîhis as exhibit this type: qualifying noun-case + adjective or participle + substantive. Panc. 42 तद्भर्ता मदविह्वलाङ्गः = मदेन विह्वलान्यङ्गानि यस्य सः; Kathâs. 72, 180 प्रापार्कसंतप्तसिकतां मरुभूमिम्, here the bahuvr. is to be analyzed अर्केण संतप्ताः सिकता यस्यां सा [मरुभूमिः]. But also other types, as: Mudr. III, p. 124 vultures (गृध्राः) have the epithet दीर्घनिष्कम्पपक्षाः, here the analysis is येषां दीर्घा निष्कम्पाश्च पक्षाः, the predicate, therefore, is an adjective-dvandva (208). Çâk. VII a curse is said to be अङ्गुलीयकदर्शनावसानः = यस्याङ्गुलीयकस्य दर्शनमवसानं स शापः.

3. both subject and predicate are compounds. Kâd. I, p. 46 तत्र विस्रब्धविरचितकुलायसहस्राणि..... शुकशकुनिकुलानि प्रतिवसन्ति स्म (crowds of parrots and [other] birds were dwelling there, building confidently thousand(s) of nests), here विस्रब्धविरचित is the predicate and कुलायसहस्र the subject of the bahuvrîhi, the analysis of which is of course येषां विस्रब्धं विरचितानि [°तं] कुलायानां सहस्राणि [°स्रम्].

227. In the case of non-compound words, adjectives carrying the notion of *having*, *possessing*, as is taught in Sanskrit etymology, may be made by putting some

Suffixes, denoting, possession as °इन्, °इत.

derivative suffixe as °मन्त्, °वन्त्, °मय, °इत, °इन् etc. to the substantive, as अग्निमन्त् (fiery), पुत्रिन् (having a son) and the like. Of these suffixes, °इन् is very common[1]). Kathâs. 24, 9 किरीटी कुण्डली दिव्यः खड्गी चावातरत्पुमान् (a divine person descended wearing a diadem, earrings and a sword), cp. R. 3, 50, 21. They may also be put to dvandvas. Mhbh. 1, 126, 21 जटाजिनी (wearing tresses and a deer-skin), Pat. I, p. 1 सास्नालाङ्गूलककुदखुरविषाणिनां संप्रत्ययो भवति स [गो]शब्दः.

P. 5, 2, 128.

sometimes added even to bahuvrîhis.

Now, sometimes, these suffixes are added even then, if they are in no ways necessary for the understanding. So R. 3, 15, 11 पद्मैः सुरभिगन्धिभिः..... रम्या पद्मिनी (a pond charming by its sweet scented lotuses), likewise Panc. 53 the weaver, who has assumed the attributes of Vishṇu, is said to be विष्णुचिह्नितः = विष्णोश्चिह्नैरन्वितः, Bhoj. 2 a brahman is said सकलविद्याचातुर्यवान् = सकलासु विद्यासु चातुर्येण युक्तः. In these cases no suffix was required, for the bahuvrîhis सुरभिगन्ध, विष्णुचिह्न, सकलविद्याचातुर्य would be quite regular and plain. Compare Panc. I, 46 सुवर्णपुष्पिता पृथ्वी = सुवर्णपुष्पा पृथ्वी. This rather pleonastic idiom is especially used in some standing compounds. Grammarians teach and practice confirms °इन् being readily added to compounds in °शोभा, °शाला, °माला, °धर्म, °शील, °वर्ण.

P. 5, 2 132.

Typical compounds.

228. Typical compounds.

So I call such compounds whose latter element is almost used in a **typical** sense, which is more or less remote from their primitive meaning. By them the great importance of compounding for Sanskrit composition appears best. Such among them, as are fit for periphrasing case-relations, have already been dealt with in Chapter IX, especially **188—196**. Of the others the most remarkable are: 1. those in आदि,

1) See P. 5, 2, 115; 116; 128 with the vârttikas on them.

°आद्य, °आदिक, °प्रभृति, which are expressive of „and so on," 2. those in °पूर्वम् and °पुरःसरम्, which may serve to make adverbs of manner, 3. those in °पूर्व = „formerly —," 4. those in °मात्रम्, which does duty of a limitative particle, वाङ्मात्रम् being nearly the same as वागेव, 5. those in °कल्प, °देश्य, °देशीय, °प्राय, to express „nearly, almost," 6. those in °रूप, if रूप may be rendered by „namely," 7. those in °अन्तरम्, when having the worth of „some" or „other." And so on.

229. °आदि etc. To give a fuller account of them, we will treat of them separately.

1. Those in °आदि, °आदिक, °आद्य, °प्रभृति are bahuvrîhis, meaning properly »the beginning of which is —," as is still plain f. i. in M. 1, 50 एतदन्तास्तु गतयो ब्रह्माद्याः (the existences, at the head of which stands Brahmâ, end here). Commonly they are expressive of »etc.; and the like." Panc. 8 तस्यौर्ध्वदेहिकक्रिया वृषोत्सर्गादिकाः सर्वाश्चकार (he performed in his honour all the funeral rites, viz. the vṛshotsarga etc.), Hit. 123 सुवर्णवस्त्रादि प्रसाददानं क्रियताम् (bestow on them presents of the king's favour, gold, clothes and so on), Panc. 62 सर्वे मत्स्यकच्छपप्रभृतयस्तं पप्रच्छुः (all [aquatic animals], fishes, tortoises etc. —). In these examples the compounds are adjectives, but often they are used as substantives too [see note 1 on p 165], as Bhoj. 64 अहमपि ब्राह्मणपुत्रः। त्वामत्र शयानं वीक्ष्य कमण्डलूपवीतादिभिर्ब्राह्मणं ज्ञात्वा भवदास्तरासन्न एवाहं प्रसुप्तः, Panc. 27 अद्यप्रभृति प्रसादनिग्रहादिकं त्वयैव कार्यम् (from to-day it is you by whom favour, punishment, etc. are to be administered.)

°पूर्व, पुरःसर. 2. When adjectives, those in °पूर्व and °पुरःसर may have the same purport as those in °आदि etc. Panc. 20 व्याघ्रद्वीपिवृकपुरःसराः सर्वे (all of them, tigers, panters, wolves and the rest). When adverbs, the latter member is almost meaningless: प्रीतिपूर्वं भाषते = सप्रीति भाषते. Hit. 7 तस्य बहुमानपुरःसरं पुत्रान्समर्पितवान् (respectfully he gave over his sons to him).

3. भूतपूर्व and the like.

3. Those in पूर्व may also signify »having been *formerly* so and so," but now being so no more: आढ्यपूर्वः »one who once has been rich," भूतपूर्वः (of old). N. 1, 13 न क्वचिद् दृष्टपूर्वा (never seen before), Çâk. VI सत्यमूढपूर्वा तत्रभवती रहसि शकुन्तला (indeed, I once have wedded secretly the Lady Çak.)[1]).

4) °मात्रम्.

4. α) Compounds in °मात्रम् are bahuvrîhis, used as substantives of the neuter, and properly have the meaning »the exact measure (मात्रा) of which is —." Yet, as a rule they are used as if their latter member were some limitative particle and °मात्रम् may be translated by »but, only." Prabodh. I, p. 13 किंवदन्तीमात्रमेतत् (it is but a vain rumour), Panc. 192 कोऽपि ते वाङ्मात्रेणापि सहायत्वं न करिष्यति (nobody will make you his friend only on account of your voice), R. 3, 71, 22 नाममात्रं तु जानामि न रूपं तस्य रक्षसः. This transla ion, however, does not suit all instances. Sometimes °मात्रम् signifies, that the whole class is meant, not single individuals belonging to it. Pat. I, p. 242 ब्राह्मणो न हन्तव्यः सुरा न पेयेति ब्राह्मणमात्रं न हन्यते सुरामात्रं च न पीयते (since it is said: »one may not hurt a brahman, nor drink strong liquor", one does not hurt anybody, that is named brahman, nor drinks anything, to which the appellation »strong liquor" is applicable). Comm. on R. 2, 12, 100 कैकेयीदौर्जन्यं दृष्ट्वा राजा शोकेन स्त्रीमात्रं निन्दति (the king seeing the foul conduct of K., by his sorrow chides the whole

°जातम्

feminine sex). — In this meaning °जातम् is almost synonymous, as Daç. 22 चौडोपनयनादिसंस्कारजातमलभत (he obtained the cauda, the upanayana, in short the whole set of sacraments), Bhoj. 62 अखिलेष्वपि कोशेषु यद्वित्तजातमस्ति तत्सर्वं देवेन कविभ्यो दत्तम्.

β) Adjectt. in °मात्र.

β) °मात्र is also put to participles; then it is an adjective and signifies »as soon as —." Panc. III, 3 जातमात्रं शत्रुं प्रशमं नयेत् (one must abate a foe, as soon as he has arisen), ibid. p. 58 भगवता नारायणेन स्मृतमात्रो वैनतेयः संप्राप्तः, Kathâs. 36, 111, etc.

Rem. The adjectival employment of those in °मात्र is however

1) One is wont to analyze भूतपूर्वः by पूर्वं भूतः and so on, see f. i. Kâç. on P. 5, 3, 53, but that analysis does not give a satisfactory account of the nature of the compound. If the adverb पूर्वं were compounded with the noun भूत, one would expect पूर्वभूत in the same way, as f. i. M. 9, 267 पूर्वतस्कराः» people who have formerly been thieves."

not restricted to the case that the former member is a participle. See but Panc. II, 95 नाममात्रा न सिद्धौ हि धनहीनाः... नराः (poor people do but bear the name of men, as they are of no use whatsoever).

°कल्प, °देश्रीय, °प्राय.

5. »Almost, nearly, like" is signified by °कल्प, °देश्य, °देशीय, °प्राय, which have almost got the nature of pure formal suffixes, and, indeed, the former three are taught as such by Pâṇini (5, 3, 67). Of them, those in °कल्प and °प्राय are the most frequent. R. 3, 16, 39 वाक्यान्यमृतकल्पानि (speech like ambrosia), Kumâras. 3, 14 कार्यं त्वया नः प्रतिपन्नकल्पम् (you have nearly engaged yourself to do our affair), Kathâs. 6, 51 छन्दोगः कश्चिदित्युक्तो विटप्रायेण केनचित् (some Sâmavedin was thus addressed by somebody like a rake), Mâlat. IX, p. 149 एवं पर्यवसितप्रायैव नः प्रत्याशा (in this manner all my hope is almost gone), Panc. 202 पक्वशालिप्रायं देशं गतः (gone to a country, where a good deal of the paddy was ripe), Daç. 78 विप्रलम्भप्रायमिदमधर्मवर्त्म (this way of unrighteousness, full of deception). Those in °प्राय are, indeed, bahuvrîhis, to be analyzed thus: »the greater part of which is —," just as those in °कल्प properly are = »the manner or mode of which is —."

6. °रूप.

6. Those in °रूप are likewise adjectives. As रूपम् means not only »shape, form" in general, but also »a beautiful shape, a beauty," so the bahuvrîhis ending in it admit of either acceptation. Pâṇini (5, 3, 66) mentions the latter, when teaching such compounds as ब्राह्मणरूपः, पचतिरूपम् to be praise-denoting.[1]) But, in practice, those in °रूप are not often met with in this meaning, by far oftener they are employed for the sake of qualifying some general kind by describing its species. Then we may often translate them by means of »f. i.; viz." Instances are chiefly found in commentaries and the like. Sây. on Ait. Br. 2, 37, 1 [p. 272 ed. Aufrecht] रथभङ्गरूपो व्यामोहः.

---

1) Pâṇini speaks of °रूप as of a taddhita. Kâç. when commenting on our sûtra shows °रूप to be used to signify the highest pitch of a quality, as वृषलरूपोऽयं यः पलाण्डुना सुरां पिबति. Blame, inversely, is expressed by compounds in °पाश (P. 5, 3, 47), as in this verse of Bhojapr. (p. 7) स्वाम्युक्ते यो न यतते स भृत्यो भृत्यपाशकः (the attendant, who does not exert himself, when ordered by his master, is a bad attendant).

7. °अवधि. 7. Bahuvrîhis in °अवधि (limit) may be synonymous of यावत् in both of its acceptations (169 with Rem.). See f. i. Kathâs. 4, 100 प्रत्यागमावधि (till I shall have come back); 52, 146.

8. °विशेष. 8. Tatpurushas in °विशेष, when meaning »excellent species," are expressive of something »first-rate, excellent." See f. i. Ragh. 2, 7.

9. °अन्तर. 9. Tatpurushas in °अन्तरम् are often to be rendered by »some" or »other." Properly speaking, अन्तरम्, विशेषः and भेदः mean variety, species," and as a »variety of something" is »something different", the transition of meaning may easily be accounted for. — Mâlav. III, p. 60 पूर्वस्मादवस्थान्तरमुपारूढा तत्रभवती (v. a. the lady has changed her former attitude to another), Panc. I, 132 शुभाशुभफलं सद्यो नृपाद्दैवाद्भवान्तरे (the fruit of good and evil deeds comes instantly, when from the king, but in some other existence, when from Destiny), ibid. p. 83 लघूनामपि दुर्जनानां मध्ये वस्तुं न शक्यते। उपायान्तरं विधाय ते नूनं घ्नन्ति (one cannot dwell among wicked people, for they will hurt you by some means or other). The proper meaning of °अन्तरम् is not rarely transparent, as in the example quoted first. Likewise Panc. 248 भर्तान्यमार्गान्तरेणागत्य, Panc. 205 युवयोर्भाष्यान्तरं सम्यङ्न शृणोमि (I do not hear distinctly, of what kind of things you speak).

10. °विधि. 10. Tatpurushas in °विधिः may denote, that the action spoken of is done »in due form." Panc. I, 335 प्रदानविधिना..... संप्राप्यते फलम्, Daç. 80 तदगारेऽत्युदारमभ्यवहारविधिमकरवम् (in his house I gave a stylish dinner).

This list may be easily enlarged.

Final observations.

230. Any Sanskrit compound belongs to one of the great classes mentioned before. Now, as not only the members of a compound but even their constituent elements may be compounds themselves, hence arises an almost unlimited freedom of enlarging compounds by taking up into them all sorts of nouns or adverbs serving to qualify the whole of the compound or part of it. In this way, very large and very intricate compounds are atricate mpounds. available, and in fact they often occur, albeit that the field of combinations and images is in some degree limited by conventional usage and by the examples of the best authors. For the rest the frequency and the nature of those intricate and bulky compounds will much depend on the style of the literary work. It requires, therefore, a good deal of training to catch forthwith the purport of many an intricate compound.

A few instances will suffice. Kâdamb. I, p. 15 the king, it is said, saw a lady कुपितहरहुताशनदह्यमानमदनधूममलिनीकृतामिव रतिम् »who was like Rati, stained by the smoke of Kâma burning by the fire of angry Çiva," for when analyzing the complex, we get कुपितस्य हरस्य हुताशनेन दह्यमानस्य मदनस्य यो धूमोऽभूत्तेन मलिनीकृताम्, apparently a tatpurusha, the former member of which is also a tatpurusha the former member of which is also a tatp. and so on. Now a bahuvrîhi. In the same Kâd. (p. 39) a forest अरण्यम् bears the epithet दशरथसुतनिशितशरनिकरनिपातनिहतरजनीचरबलबहुलरुधिरसिक्तमूलम् (where the roots [of the trees] had been moistened by the abundant blood of the army of the Râxasas killed by the shots of the crowd of sharp arrows [discharged] by the son of Daçaratha), here मूलम् is the subj. of the bahuvrîhi, the preceding complex being its predicate, an intricate tatpurusha, as it is thus to be analyzed दशरथस्य सुतस्य निशितानां शराणां निकरस्य निपातैर्यन्निहतं रजनीचराणां बलं तस्य बहुलेन रुधिरेण सिक्तम्. This whole clause is comprehended within one compound. And so often.

231. **Case-nouns standing outside the compound** are very often to be construed with it or with one of its members. This is but consistent with the whole spirit, which pervades Sanskrit composition. A great liberty is left to the speaker to prefer either a rather synthetical or a rather analytical mode of expression. He has the opportunity of enlarging compounds by making enter within them any noun or adverb serving to qualify the

Case-nouns tanding ıtside the mpound, t to be nstrued with it.

whole or any part of it. But on the other hand nothing compels him to do so. The qualifying noun may as well be a self-existent word having its own nóun-case.[1]) So Çâk. V हिमवतो गिरेरुपत्यकारण्यवासिनः (dwelling in the forests on the slope of mount Himavân), here हिमवतो गिरेः stands outside the compound as to its form, but belongs to it by its meaning, as it qualifies the member उपत्यका. Panc. 42 a weaver returns home to his wife, प्रागेव कर्णपरंपरया तस्याः श्रुतापवादः »having heard evil report on her account;" when using a mere analytical expression, the author of the Pancatantra would have said तस्या अपवादं श्रुत्वा or श्रुते तस्या अपवादे etc., when a mere synthetical one श्रुततदपवादः, but he has here availed himself of a mixed idiom. — Mâlav. V, p. 140 सगरः पौत्रेण प्रत्याहृताश्वः (S., who had the horse brought back by his grand-son); Kumâras. I, 37 एतावता नन्वनुमेयशोभि..... [अस्या] अङ्गम्, here एतावता qualifies अनुमेय the former member of the compound; Mahâv. I, p. 6 प्रकृत्या पुण्यलक्ष्मीकौ कावेत, here प्रकृत्या also is intimately connected with the compound. These few examples will suffice, as the idiom is met with on almost every page of Sanskrit.

232. By this equivalence, and to a certain extent also, promiscuousness of analytical and synthetical expression it is also explained that there must be some freedom in using the so called figure of e l l i p s i s even in compounds. Nala 1, 13 the beauty of Damayantî is said to surpass that of all other women, even of time past, न..... तादृग्रूपवती क्वचित्.... दृष्टपूर्वाथवा श्रुता, here श्रुत is of course = श्रुतपूर्वा. By a similar abridgment Malâv. V, p. 137 moon and sun are named शीतोष्णकिरणौ »the hot- and the cold-rayed[2])."

---

1) I wonder, what reasons may have induced WHITNEY (§ 1316) to speak of this idiom as something irregular. On the contrary, nothing can be more regular.

2) A striking example is afforded by R. 3, 20, 12, if I am right reading there राक्षसास्ते चतुर्दश। ऊचुर्वाचं सुसंक्रुद्धा ब्रह्मघ्नाः शूलपाणयः। संरक्तनयना घोरा

SECTION III.

ON THE DIFFERENT CLASSES OF NOUNS AND PRONOUNS.

CHAPT. I. **Substantive. Adjective. Adverb.**

233. Adjective and substantive. In ancient languages the difference between adjective and substantive is generally not so strongly marked as in modern ones. So especially in Sanskrit. Both classes of nouns have the same declension, and a great number of them have sometimes an adjectival meaning, sometimes they are substantives They are only different as to their gender, substantives being nouns of one gender, but adjectives of three, as they must take the gender of the nouns they qualify [1]): शुक्लो वर्णः, शुक्ला सुधा, शुक्लं वासः.

Adjectives proper, when used as substantives, may be distinguished thus: *a*) the substantivizing results from

---

रामं संरक्तलोचनं। परुषा मधुराभाषं दृष्टादृष्टपराक्रमम्; the Bomb. edition has हृष्टा-दृष्टप°. There is antithesis between the परुषा: [in full परुषाभाषा:] Râxasas and Râma मधुराभाष:, and likewise between them दृष्ट[पराक्रमा:] and Râma who was अदृष्टपराक्रम:. The *saṃdhir ârshaḥ* दृष्टा[:] [अ]दृष्टपराक्रमम् is admitted in the Râmâyana, see f. i. 2, 51, 8; 74, 13; 3, 64, 23.

1) By this way we may account for the fact, that Indian grammar, full as it is of accurate and minute observations and of acute and sharp distinctions, does not possess proper terms expressive of categories of words as common and as indispensable to Western grammar as »adjective" and »substantive." The *guṇavacana* of the vernacular grammarians encompasses more than our »adjective"; neither the *dravyâṇi* nor the *jâtayas* are the exact equivalent of our »substantives". The term *viçeshaṇa*, used by Pâṇini himself, comprises both the apposition and the attributive adjective. The only term adopted to point out the adjective as such is नाम त्रिलिङ्गम् »noun of three genders."

the ellipsis of the concordant subst., as शीताः [viz. आपः] „cold water," पलिताः [viz. केशाः „grey hairs;" *b*) they are substantives when having got some special meaning, as तनु adj. „thin," subst. fem. „body;" हरि adj. „brown," subst. masc. „lion; monkey; Indra; Vishnu;" *c*) they are used as substantives while retaining their general signification, as प्रियः when meaning „a or the beloved one," पापः „a (the) wicked man." The last category is the sole regarding us here, for any adjective may in this way turn substantive. The diversity of the endings for the different genders and numbers enables to express by one single word such phrases as „a rich man," „a young woman," „a business of weight," resp. आढ्यः, तरुणी, महत्. The plural of course, if a plurality of things is meant; hence तानि „that" when = those things, Lat. *ea*, भद्राणि Lat. *fausta*, बहूनि *multa*, etc.

Like other substantives, the substantivized adjectives may be an element in compounds. Hit. 94 हीनसेवा न कर्तव्या कर्तव्यो महदाश्रयः (one must not serve a weak [master], but join a mighty one), ibid. 102 अलमनेनातीतोपालम्भेन (enough of this chiding the past).

Abstract nouns.

234. *Abstract nouns.* Abstract nouns are much used in Sanskrit composition. They are partly derivates of verbs, partly of nouns. The **verbal abstracts** are not rarely to be paraphrased in translating, especially if the predicate of the sentence be made up by them. Then, our language generally prefers finite verbs. R. 3, 2, 11 the man-eater says to Râma

कथं तापसयोर्वां च वासः प्रमदया सह (and how is it, that you dwell with a woman, being ascets?), Daç. 101 अमुना मन्मोचनाय शपथः कृतो मया च रहस्यानिर्भेदाय (he took an oath, he would release me, and I, not to reveal the secret), ibid. 95 शीलं हि मदोन्मादयोरमार्गेणाप्युचितकर्मस्वेव प्रवर्तनम्, Mṛcch. I, p. 32 न पुष्पमोषमर्हत्युद्यानलता (the garden-creeper does not deserve to be stripped of its flowers), Mudr. V, p. 180 (Malayaketu to Râxasa) आर्य तातेन धृतपूर्वाणामाभरणविशेषाणां विशेषतश्चन्द्रगुप्तहस्तगतानां वणिग्भ्यः क्रयादधिगम इति न युज्यत एतत् (sir, it is inconsistent, that by purchase from merchants you should have come by precious jewels, once worn by my father, especially as they have passed into the hands of Candr.).

235. Of the **nominal abstracts** the most important are those in °ता, °त्वम् and °भावः, as they may be derived of any noun. Of मृदु (weak) the abstract „weakness" is not only मार्दवम् or म्रदिमा (see P. 5, 1, 122), but also मृदुता, मृदुत्वम् and मृदुभावः. Nothing, too, impedes making them of compounds, as श्रेष्ठ्यपत्यता or °त्वम् or °भावः „the being the child of a *set*" or चतुर्मुखत्वम् (°ता, °भावः) „the having four mouths" [1]). Hence the abstracts in °ता and °त्वम् and their synonyms are a fit means for expressing clauses and the like in a concise form, especially when attended by a subjective genitive. So देवदत्तस्य श्रेष्ठ्यपत्यत्वम् = „the fact of N.N.'s being a merchant's son," ब्रह्मणश्चतुर्मुखता „the four-facedness of Brahma."

Here are some examples of this widely used idiom: Panc. I, 222 कन्यापितृत्वं खलु नाम कष्टम् (it is a calamity to be father to a daughter);

---

1) The suffixes for making these abstracts are taught by Pâṇini 5, 1, 119—136. Those in °भाव are evidently tatpurushas, भाव meaning »the state, the being." For this reason Pâṇini is right not mentioning them.

ibid. p. 71 दृष्टा मयास्य पिङ्गलकस्य सारासारता (I have scrutinized the good qualities of P. as well as his vices); Kumâras. I, 48: if animals felt shame, the female yaks, it is said, when seeing the beautiful hair of fair Umâ, would have abated their pride of their tails कुर्युर्बालप्रियत्वं शिथिलं चमर्यः; Daç. 36 प्रवहणस्य मग्नतया सर्वेषु निमग्नेषु (as all were drowned because of the ship's foundering); Panc. 73 त्वयास्य सचिवत्वात्सर्वोऽपि राजधर्मः परित्यक्तः (by having him as your friend you have neglected the whole of your royal duty); Çâk. II: king Dushyanta, as his presence is wanted at different places at the same time, says कृत्ययोर्भिन्नदेशत्वाद् द्वैधीभवति मे मनः; Utt. II, p. 35 घनविरलभावः »the density and the being scattered," that is »the relative density;" Comment. on R. 3, 42, 10 पत्तननगरयोरराजधानीराजधानीत्वेन भेदः (the difference between the words *pattana* and *nagara* is this that the former does not signify the king's residence, the latter does). The last example shows also the fitness of this idiom for the sake of explaining and demonstrating. By grasping the different links of a sentence into one single word, scientific or philosophical matters may be treated in the very clearest and plainest manner, complex ideas being rendered by complexes of words, whereas the relation of the abstract noun with the other words of the sentence is sufficiently pointed out by its case-ending.

236. Idiomatic employment of them.

Some idiomatic employment of the abstracts — chiefly those in °ता and °त्वम् — must be insisted upon.

I. Verbs of *going* and *reaching* with the accus. of an abstract noun.

I. Their **accusative** with verbs of going and coming is often used to express the passing from one state to another, cp. **39**. Hitop. 94 महानप्यल्पतां याति (even a mighty one may become mean), Prabodh. IV, p. 78 quotes the verse प्रायशः कृतिनां कार्ये देवा यान्ति सहायताम् (— become helpers), Var. Brh. 2, 17 दैवज्ञत्वं प्रपद्यते (he becomes an astrologer), Panc. 38 तदेनं मायावचनैर्विश्वास्याहं छात्रतां व्रजामि (— I will become his disciple), ibid. 62 सरः शीघ्रं शोषं यास्यति (the lake will soon grow dry), Bhoj. 28 जलदो वल्लभतामेति सर्वलोकस्य.

237. II. Their **instrumental**, may signify *in what quality* somebody or something acts (**67**). Then it may be

The in-
ımental
an ab-
act noun
pressive
in what
uality;
„as.”

rendered by means of „as.” So Hitop. 103 कश्चिद्बको द्वितीयत्वेन प्रयातु (let some other heron go with him *as* [his] *second*), Ratn. IV, p. 114 अयि प्रिये किमद्यापि मध्यस्थतया वर्तसे (why, my dear, do you behave *as if you were indifferent* even now?).

This idiom is much used with verbs of *acting-*, *behaving-*, *being as*; *knowing-*, *considering as*, *taking for*; *calling-*, *signifying as*; *treating as* and many others. Instead of the phrase ब्राह्मणं त्वां जानामि संभावयामि व्यपदिशामि one may say ब्राह्मणत्वेन त्वां जानामि etc.

Examples: Kathâs. 26, 8 कर्णधारतया स्थितः (being steersman); Prabodh. IV, p. 81 तस्य कामः प्रथमो वीरस्तस्य प्रतिवीरतयास्माभिर्भवानेव निरूपितः (Kâma is his chief warrior, it is you we have looked for *as his match*); Daç. 76 ऋषिमुक्तश्च रागः संध्यात्वेनास्फुरत् (and the glow [of passion], which had been loosened from the holy man, [now] shone *as twilight*); Ragh. 14, 40 छाया हि भूमेः शशिनो मलत्वेनारोपिता शुद्धिमतः प्रजाभिः (on spotless moon people have thrown earth's shade *by way of a spot*); Daç. 112 मां तु न कश्चिदिहत्य ईदृक्तया जनो जानाति (nobody here *knows* me *as such*); ibid. 93 त्वया नियतमस्मि तदागतित्वेनाहमपदेश्यः (you cannot but *denounce* me *as the person*, you have got it from); ibid. 144 इयं .... तवैव जायात्वेन समकल्प्यत (she has been *destined a wife* for you); ibid. 94 स एव तपस्वी तस्करत्वेनार्थपतिरग्राहृत (it was the unhappy Arth. who *was seized as the thief*); Pat. I, p. 399 when treating of the karmadhâraya कृष्णतिलाः, says तिलाः प्राधान्येन विवक्षिता भवन्ति कृष्णो विशेषणत्वेन; Kathâs. 52, 60 दासीत्वेनाश्रयामि राजपुत्रम्; Mhbh. 1, 43, 24 गच्छध्वं यूयमव्यग्रा राजानं कार्यवत्तया. [1]).

---

1) The germ of this much used idiom is found already in the Ṛgveda-mantras, in such phrases as पुरुषता (instr. = skrt पुरुषतया). Ṛgv. 10, 15, 6 मा हिंसिष्ट पितरः केन चिन्नो यद्व आगः पुरुषता कराम (do us no injury, fathers, on account of any offence, that we, after the manner of men [as being men], may have committed against you).

Rem. In the instances quoted the abstracts are ending in °तया and °त्वेन. But although these suffixes are the most employed ones, any other abstract has the same effect. Daç. 15 तदीयार्भकयोर्यमजयोर्धात्रीभावेन परिकल्पिताहम् (I was appointed nurse of the twins, his children); Kâç. I, p. 16 स्वमिति ज्ञातिधनयोः संज्ञारूपेण वर्तते (*sva* is used as a designation of kinsmen and property); Pat. I, p. 230 इमानीन्द्रियाणि कदाचित्स्वातन्त्र्येण विवक्षितानि भवन्ति तद्यथा। इदं मेऽक्षि सुष्ठु पश्यति। कदाचित्पारतन्त्र्येण। अनेनाक्ष्णा सुष्ठु पश्यामि. For this reason, different abstracts made from one noun are as a rule promiscuous; compare f. i Kathâs. 13, 132 प्रयाति स्म दूतया with Hit. 97 प्रयातु दौत्येन, both दूतया and दौत्येन signifying »in the quality of a messenger."

238. Other similar idioms: Occasionally — but not often — an ablative will do the same duty as the instrumental of **237**. R. 3, 6, 10 त्वामासाद्य महात्मानम्.... अर्थित्वान्नाथ वक्ष्यामः (— we will address you, Lord, as supplicants), cp. Kathâs. 72, 165.

Locative. The locative of the abstracts may also be used so, as R. 3, 36, 17 शृणु तत्कर्म साहाय्ये यत्कार्यं वचनान्मम (be informed of the matter, which you must perform *as my helper* on my order). It is especially used with verbs of *appointing*, *choosing*, *designing* to some rank or dignity. Panc. 26 स्वामी यदि कथयति ततो भृत्यत्वे नियोजयामि (— I will make [him] your attendant); Nala 3, 23 तेषामन्यतमं देवं पतित्वे वरयस्व ह (choose one of those devas for your husband); Hit. 91 स पक्षिराज्ये ऽभिषिक्तः.

Note that of abstracts of the feminine gender the ablative and locative are not used so, only the instrumental (cp. **102**).

239. Dative. The dative of the abstracts with verbs of appointing etc. will occasionally occur. Mhbh. 1, 139, 1 यौवराज्याय स्थापितो धृतराष्ट्रेण युधिष्ठिरः, Kathâs. 38, 153 वृतवान्मित्रत्वाय नृपो नृपम्.

Rem. In the ancient liturgical books we met with two datives, one of the person and one of the abstract noun, both attending on the same verb, especially स्था and कल्प्. Ait. Br. 4, 25, 8 इन्द्राय वै देवा ज्यैष्ठ्याय श्रैष्ठ्याय नातिष्ठन्त (the devas did not yield to Indra as to the eldest and most excellent [of them])। सो ऽब्रवीद् बृहस्पतिं याजय मा द्वादशाहेनेति। तमयाजयत्। ततो वै तस्मै देवा ज्यैष्ठ्याय श्रैष्ठ्यायातिष्ठन्त etc., cp. T. S. 2, 2, 11, 5. Ait. Br. 7, 17, 7 Viçvâmitra thus addresses his sons शृणोतन..... ये के च भ्रातरः स्थन। अस्मै ज्यैष्ठ्याय कल्पध्वम् (— attend on him [Çunaḥçepha] as your eldest), cp. 7, 18, 8. Note the attraction in this idiom. — Cp. a similar employment of the locative: Ait. Br. 4, 25, 9 समस्मिन्स्वा श्रेष्ठतायां जानते »his kin acknowledge his authority."

ADVERBS.

240. Adverbs. Sanskrit adverbs, as far as they are not old words of uncertain and forgotten origin — as मुहुः, द्राक्, मृषा, मङ्क्षु, अलम् and the like — are noun-cases either distinctly felt as such or in some degree petrified. The accusative of the neuter singular is as a rule employed, if adjectives be wanted to act as adverbs [1]) (**55**).

Bahuvrîhis, like other adjectives, may do duty of adverbs, when put in the accus. of the neuter. Daç. 169 अमुं च..... आत्मनिर्विशेषं पुपोष (and he took no less care for him as for himself); Panc. 55 इति वदत्यां मातरि राजपुत्री भयलज्जानताननं प्रोवाच (as her mother spoke thus, the princess lowered her head for fear and shame and said); Çâk. I ग्रीवाभङ्गाभिरामं मुहुरनुपतति स्यन्दने दत्तदृष्टिः ([the stag] runs on casting now and then a look on the chariot so as to cause to turn its neck ever so neatly); Âçv. Gṛhy. 1, 9, 1 पाणिग्रहणादि गृह्यं परिचरेत् here the first word is an adverb »from his marriage, beginning with his marriage."

When derived from substantives, the adverbs are mostly modal instrumentals and ablatives (**77, 104**). Daç.136 स्मरसि किमयाप्यायथातथ्येन मयोक्तपूर्वम्, here आयथातथ्येन = »falsely;" R. 3, 61, 20 निखिलेन »wholly". Likewise पर्यायेण »alternately," लीलया »jokingly," etc., and ablatives, as हठात्, स्वभावात्.

241. Adverbs in °वत्. For the sake of comparison one uses adverbs in °वत्. They may be made of any noun, and are to be rendered

1) Adverbs are styled क्रियाविशेषणानि »attributes of verbs." The acc. neuter of an adjective, when used adverbially, is named कर्म क्रियाविशेषणम्, see f. i. Kâç. on P. 2, 3, 33.

by „as" or „like." When paraphrased, they are = यथा or इव with any noun-case wanted by the context, therefore सिंहवत् may be = सिंह इव or सिंहमिव or सिंहायेव and so on. — R. 3, 45, 5 सौमित्रे मित्ररूपेण भ्रातुस्त्वमसि शत्रुवत् [= शत्रुरिव] (in the shape of a friend, Laxmaṇa, you are like a foe to your brother); Mhbh. 1, 148, 15 शुचीन्पाण्डुदायादान्दाहयामास शत्रुवत् [= यथा शत्रून्] (the innocent Pâṇḍavas he did burn as if they were his enemies); Kâm. 3, 31 पूजयेद् देवताः सदा। देवतावद्गुरुजनमात्मवच्च सुहृज्जनम् [= देवता इव and आत्मानमिव]; Mhbh. 1, 159, 4 तरध्वं प्लववन्मया [= प्लवेनेव] (pass over by me as if by a vessel); Hit. 10 मातृवत्परदारेषु परद्रव्येषु लोष्टवत् आत्मवत्सर्वभूतेषु यः पश्यति स पण्डितः (he who looks on the wife of another as on his mother, on the goods of another as on clay, on all creatures as on himself, such one is a wise man).

Rem. 1. Compare with them Latin adverbs as *regaliter*, when meaning »kingly, like a king." Mhbh. 1, 145, 1 पाण्डवाः..... भीष्मस्य पादौ जगृहुरार्तवत् (*suppliciter*).

Rem. 2. Like other compounds, the adverbs in °वत् may have their former member standing in construction with some other word outside the compound. Panc. I, 260 अभिमुखो नाशं याति वह्नौ पतङ्गवत् = यथा वह्नौ पतङ्गो याति.

242. Adverbs in °शः involve the dissolution of a whole into many parts. Mâlat. VIII, p. 135 लवशः एनां निकृत्य दुःखमरणां करोमि (I will cut her into pieces and cause her to die a miserable death).

As to those in °धा see **302** R.

243. Adjectives doing duty of adverbs. Sometimes — but not so often as in Latin and Greek — adjectives are used, where one might expect adverbs. Of the kind are f. i. विवश = Lat. *invitus*, केवल (mere). Kathâs 28, 70 रम्भा विवशा सा तिरोदधे (R. disappeared against her will); Kathâs. 29, 120 यन्न मुक्तासुभिस्तत्र कारणं केवलो विधिः (that she did not die, the cause thereof was nothing but Destiny, Germ. *nur das Schicksal*). Likewise others, which in fact serve to qualify the verb, though they do formally agree with some substantive (**31**, V). R. 3, 60, 25 मम विस्रब्धः कथयस्व (tell it me confidentially), M. 3, 101 तृणानि भूमिरुदकं

वाक् चतुर्थी च सूनृता (grass, earth, water, and fourthly, friendly speech). Compare these more instances, taken from the ancient language: Ait. Br. 1, 7, 13 उत्तमामदितिं यजति (finally he worships Aditi), Ch. Up. 6, 6 .स ऊर्ध्वः समुदीषति (it rises upwards), Âçv. Grhy. 1, 11, 5 उदञ्चं नयन्ति (they lead [the victim] to the north.

Degrees of comparison.

244. Comparative. Of two persons or things, possessing the same quality, the **comparative** is to point out that which is endowed with the *higher degree* of it: साधुतरस्तयोः (the better of these two), वचो मधुनः स्वादीयः (words, sweeter than honey). Even if the person or thing compared with, be implied, not expressed, the comparative may be used. We then translate it by „tolerably, rather[1])." Daç. 159 ततोऽल्पीयसा कालेन राज्ञः प्रियमहिषी पुत्रमसूत (not very long hereafter —), Prabodh. II, p. 30 मया स्वगृहिणी प्रियस्यपि प्रोज्झिता (I have abandoned my wife, though I loved her very much), Panc. 35 तच्छ्रुत्वा पिङ्गलकः सादरतरं तमुवाच (after hearing this, P. addressed him in a rather respectful manner). — Occasionally the comparative may even express »too." Mhbh. I (Paushyaparva) Upamanyu, when asked by his master why he looks fat though every opportunity of getting food has been intercepted to him, answers he has drunk the foam, given back by the calves after having drunk the milk of their mothers. But even that livelihood displeases his spiritual teacher, for एते त्वदनुकम्पया गुणवन्तो वत्साः प्रभूततरं फेनमुद्गिरन्ति। तदेषामपि वत्सानां वृत्त्युपरोधं करोषि (these virtuous calves give back *too much* foam, for pity on you, for this reason you prevent also their being fed).

P. 5, 3, 57.

245. Superlative. The **superlative** expresses not only the „highest" but also a „very high" degree, just as in Latin and Greek. पापिष्ठ may be sometimes = *very bad*, sometimes = *the worst*. When denoting the highest degree, there is ge-

---

1) Cp. *Vâmana's Stilregeln* by Cappeller, ch. *Çabdaçuddhi*, s. 62.

nerally some word added, as सर्वेषाम्, लोके etc. Mhbh. 1, 143, 3 अयं समाजः सुमहान्रमणीयतमो भुवि (this great assembly is the móst pleasing on earth). But for the rest it signifies excellency among three or more, the comparative being destined fór denoting it between twó. Of twó bróthers óne is the ज्यायान्, the óther कनीयान्, of more one the ज्येष्ठः, anóther the कनिष्ठः.

246. Careless-ness in their em-ployment. Yet carelessness in the employment of comparative and superlative is not rare in Sanskrit.[1]) Sometimes the comparative is used instead of the superlative. Pat. I, p. 77 यथा तर्हि बहुषु पुत्रेष्वेतदुपपन्नं भवत्ययं मे ज्येष्ठः पुत्रोऽयं मे मध्यमोऽयं मे कनीयानिति — instead of कनिष्ठः. Panc. I, 408 it is said that of the shâdgunya the daṇḍa is the worst expedient, here we find पापीयान्, not पापिष्ठः, ibid. p. 305 among four individuals one is said the ज्येष्ठतरः[2]).

Sometimes again the superlative is used instead of the comparative. Kathâs. 43, 23 of two brothers one calls himself कनिष्ठ, and his brother ज्येष्ठ. Panc. 113 स्वाम्यमात्ययोरेकतमस्य विनिपातः (a mischief of either king or minister). Cp. ibid. V, 36 विद्याया बुद्धिरुत्तमा (judgment is better than learning), here the superl. is of necessity, as the comp. उत्तर does not purport the meaning of excellency. For a different reason प्रथम a superl. as to its form, is the equivalent of both »first" and »former." So f. i. Mâlav. II, p. 35 अत्रभवतोराचार्ययोः कतरस्य प्रथमं प्रयोगं द्रक्ष्यामः (of whom of these two honourable professors shall we see the performance the first?).

247. The suffixes °तर and °तम may be put even to substantives. Instances are scarce in the classic language[3]). Panc. 326 स च सर्वनि-

---

1) Further investigation will decide for how much of that seeming irregularity we are indebted to the faults and the sloth of copyists, and how much of it is really good Sanskrit.

2) As to the form cp. R. 2, 12, 26 भूयस्तरम् and WHITNEY *Sanskr. Grammar* § 473, al. 4.

3) They are somewhat more frequent in the ancient dialect, see WHITNEY § 473, al. 1. Classic Sanskrit possesses some, which have a special meaning, as अश्वतरः (mule), वत्सतरः (Ragh. 3, 32) »an older calf."

अश्वानवलोक्य तं राक्षसमश्वतमं विज्ञायाधिरूढः (and he [the horse-thief] examined all the horses, saw that the râxasa [who had assumed the figure of a horse] was the best of them [liter. »the most horse"] and mounted him).

48. The comparative and superlative being wanted to do duty of adverbs, they are put in the accus. of the neuter, just as is done with all other adjectives (**55**). So भूयः is adverb of भूयान्, प्रथमम् of प्रथमः, etc. Pat. I, p. 10 ननु ये कृतयत्नास्ते साधीयः शब्दान्प्रयोक्ष्यन्ते (will they, who have studied [grammar], apply words the better?); Çâk. IV भूयिष्ठं भव दक्षिणा परिजने.

49. Degrees of comparison may be made from undeclinable words; then they end in °तराम् and °तमाम् as उच्चैस्तराम् (higher). Mâlav. II, p. 36 अतितरां कान्तम् (exceedingly charming), cp. P. 1, 2, 35.

Such comparison is made also of forms, belonging to the finite verb. Instances of comparatives, made from the 3d person of the present not rarely occur in literature. R. 2, 64, 72 हृदयं सीदतेतराम् (my spirits almost lower). Prabodh. IV, p. 87 विनाशो लब्धस्य व्यथयतितरां न त्वनुदयः (to lose something gained before grieves more than having gained nothing at all). Vikram. V, p. 178 प्रभवतितरां..... भुजङ्गशिशोर्विषम् (even of an infant-snake the poison is rather strong). Ratn. III, p. 74 रमयतितराम्. — Kathâs. 102, 35 we meet °तराम् put to a 3d person of the perfect: अदूदधेतराम्. P. 5, 3, 56.

Instances of the superlative I do not recollect having met with, but they must be or have been not less allowed, as both degrees are equally taught by Pâṇini.[1]).

0. *Than* with the comparative is expressed by the ablative, see **105**. But the particles न, न च, न तु, न पुनः are also used for that purpose, especially with वरम्.

1) Whitney § 473, al. 3 says that both compar. and superl. of verbal forms are »barbarous forms;" for what reason, I do not understand. Is it perhaps, because Kalidâsa wrote barbarous Sanskrit, or because Pâṇini did not know well the idioms of his language?

Kathâs. 29, 113 मृत्युर्मम श्रेयान्न पुनः शीलविप्लवः (death is better for me than parting with my virtue); Panc. 213 वरमनारम्भो न चारम्भविघातः (not beginning at all is better than ceasing after having commenced); ibid. I, 451 पण्डितोऽपि वरं शत्रुर्न मूर्खो हितकारकः (a wise foe is even preferable to a foolish friend [1]).

251. A high degree may be expressed also by several other idiomatic phrases, as:

Concurrent idioms, expressive of high degree.

1. by °कल्प [2]), °देश्य, °देशीय, °प्राय, see **229**, 5th inasmuch as they are a concurrent idiom of the comparative in one of its meanings:

2. by putting बहु° or परम° before. Panc. I, 191 जनापवादे जगति बहुचित्रे (slander being rather manifold in the world); R. 3, 53, 1 जनकात्मजा दुःखिता परमोद्विग्ना; Mâlav. I, p. 10 some female is said to be परमनिपुणा मेधाविनी च. Properly बहु° means »tolerably, nearly" see P. 5, 3, 68, परम° »exceedingly."

3. by such phrases as प्रियात्प्रियतरम् (liter. »dearer than dear" = the very dearest), सुखात्सुखतरम्; Mahâv. I, p. 21 प्रियात्प्रियतरं नः (we are exceedingly rejoiced at it); Panc. 326 वेगाद्वेगतरं गच्छति (**247**).

4. by putting the word twice, see **252.**

5. by adding °रूप, see **229**, 6th.

252. For different reasons **a word may be put twice**, *either* when put two times as a separate word, as शनैः शनैः, *or* when making up some kind of compound, as पटुपटुः [3]).

Putting a word twice.

---

1) In a well-known passage of the Hitop. (p. I, 3) वरम् is construed with न च but not followed by a nomin., as one might expect, but by the *instrumental*:

वरमेको गुणी पुत्रो न च मूर्खशतैरपि
एकश्चन्द्रस्तमो हन्ति न च तारागणैरपि·

The instrum. must be that, which expresses: equivalent to; exchangeable for. »Better is one virtuous son, and [»not to be given up for," that is] outweighing even hundreds of stupid ones; one moon dispels the darkness, outweighing even crowds of stars." Cp. **70**.

2) पचतिकल्पम् and the like are among the examples of the commentaries on P. 5, 3, 67. Cp. **249**.

3) Pâṇini deals with this idiom at the commencement of his eighth

1. Adjectives may be put twice, the two making but one word, in order to signify our „—like," „rather." Daç. 149 क्षामक्षामापि देवतानुभावादनतिक्षीणवर्णावकाशा सीमन्तिनी (a woman, who though [of a] rather thin [aspect] had by divine power not too much lost of the brightness of her colour), R. 3, 67, 14 तं दीनदीनया वाचा..... अभ्यभाषत, Panc. II, 50 भीतभीतः पुरा शत्रुर्मन्दं मन्दं विसर्पति (in the beginning a foe sneaks along very slowly, as one being rather afraid). So एकैक, when = »alone," and cp. such phrases, as पूर्वंपूर्वं पुष्प्यन्ते, प्रथमंप्रथमं पच्यन्ते (they blossom-, they ripen the very first) 1). Instances of adverbs put twice are not rare, as शनैः शनैः (slowly, by degrees), मुहुर्मुहुः (repeatedly), पुनःपुनः (again and again), etc. Daç. 172 शालीन्.... मृदु मृदु घर्षयन्ती.

2. In the same way substantives, gerunds, participles when put twice, may indicate the non-interruption of some time or action. R. 3, 10, 5 कालकालेषु (in uninterrupted time), Mâlav. IV, p. 105 पथि नयनयोः स्थित्वा स्थित्वा तिरोभवति क्षणात् (at the very moment she is standing on the path of my looks, P. 8, 1, 4.

---

adhyâya (8, 1, 1—15). In interpreting sûtra 9, the commentaries are wrong accepting it as teaching the formation of the word एकैक. The sûtra एकं बहुव्रीहिवत् cannot have this purport; its literal sense is »if a unity, [it is] bahuvrîhilike." If Pâṇini had meant the *word* एकैक, he would have written एकस्य, not as he does एकम्; cp. the constant genitives in sûtras 5—8. Our sûtra refers to the cases, mentioned by s. 4—8. There the employment is taught of the »*two* (द्वे)" spoken of in 8, 1, 1. Sûtra 9 teaches, how these two are to be accepted, for it says: »[but these two may be] one; then the whole is *as if a bahuvrîhi*", likewise in the case of s. 10. But from s. 11 the unity is *as if a karmadhâraya*. Pâṇini's words in 9—11 are: एकं बहुव्रीहिवत्। आबाधे च। कर्मधारयवदुत्तरेषु. From the conclusion of Kâç. on P.'s sûtra 9 I infer that the right interpretation had been proposed by somebody, but that it has been objected to by Patanjali. On the other hand, such forms with distributive sense as पूर्वपूर्वः being by necessity instances of the idiom, taught P. 8, 1,4 afford some evidence for my own acceptation.

1) See vârtt. 7 on P. 8, 1, 12 in the commentary of the Kâçikâ. Cp. also P. 8, 1, 13, which teaches to say सुखसुखेन and प्रियप्रियेण, when = »with all one's heart."

she suddenly disappears), Daç. 95 अहं रागमञ्जर्याः..... सानुनयं पायितायाः पुनः पुनः प्रणयसमर्पितमुखमधुगण्डूषमास्वादमास्वादं मदेनास्पृश्ये.

3. Moreover, putting a word twice is also often a proper means for signifying a distributive sense (*vípsá*). Instances of this idiom are frequent. Kâç. on P. 8. 1, 4 पुरुषः पुरुषः निधनमुपैति (every man is mortal), Panc. 42 पदेपदे प्रस्खलन् (stumbling at every footstep), Daç. 99 अहरहश्च नवनवानि प्राभृतान्युपहरन्ती (offering [her] always new presents day after day), ibid 216 षण्मासे षण्मासे पिच्छमेकैकं परित्यजन्ति (every sixth month they lose one single feather); R. 2, 91, 53 अप्येकमेकं पुरुषं प्रमदाः सप्त चाष्ट च समापेतुः (singulos viros septenae vel octonae mulieres appetierunt), Âpast. Dh. 1, 13, 18 संवत्सरे संवत्सरे द्वौ द्वौ मासौ समाहित आचार्यकुले वसेत्, M. 2, 20 स्वं स्वं चरित्रं शिक्षेरन् (they must learn every one his own duty). So दिशि दिशि (in every region), अहरहः (day after day) and so on. This idiom is as old as the Vaidik dialect. It is also used of gerunds. Pat. I, p. 44 मण्डूका उत्प्लुत्योत्प्लुत्य गच्छन्ति.

P. 8, 1, 4.

Here as a rule the case-endings of the former member remain.

253. Sanskrit likes juxtaposition of different grammatical forms of the same word or of kindred words. Hence the type *manus manum lavat* is of course very common in Sanskrit. Mṛcch. I, p. 34 रत्नं रत्नेन संगच्छते (pearls string with pearls), Vikram. II, p. 31 तप्तेन तप्तमयसा घटनाय योग्यम्; Pat. I, p. 233 वासो वासश्छादयति (one cloth covers the other), Panc. 322 वनाद्वनं पर्यटति (he rambles from forest to forest), ibid. 267 पदात्पदमपि प्रचलितुं न शक्नोति, Daç. 61 करिणः करिणमवप्लुत्य (jumping from one elephant's back on another).

[...]e type [...]us ma- [...]lavat [...]l the [...]ike.

254. Of a somewhat different nature is the type represented by R. 2, 12, 8 किं कृतं तव रामेण पापे पापम् (what *evil* has Râma done to you, *evil-minded woman?*); cp. the Greek κακὸς κακῶς ἀπόλοιτο. Here the inclination towards homophony is still more pronounced than in the idiom of **253**. Compare Mhbh. 1, 145, 14 तांस्तथावादिनः पौरान्दुःखितान्दुःखकर्शितः । उवाच (tristes tristis est allocutus cives); Kathâs. 38, 153 नरसिंहः.... तं.... वृतवान्मित्रत्वाय नृपो नृपम्.

It is here not the place to expatiate upon this predilection of

Sanskrit for bringing together words kindred in sound and playing with the different meanings inherent to them. Nearly all literary documents from the Vedas to our days afford the most ample evidence of it. For this reason, one must always be prepared to have to deal with riddles and the most various kinds of quibbles and puns. More information on this subject is to be given by works ı Sanskrit rhetoric and Sanskrit literature.

255 *ttingtl· ·rds y·· ·hâsam· ·khyam* It may be of some use to mention here the figure *yathâsam·khyam*[1]), as it is employed not rarely and as its nature should be called rather grammatical than rhetorical. By it a series of substances named together with a series of attributes or predicates are so to be understood that the first substance is to be construed with the first predicate or attribute, the second with the second and so on successively. R. 3, 40, 12 अग्नेरिन्द्रस्य सोमस्य यमस्य वरुणस्य च। औष्ण्यं तथा विक्रमं च सौम्यं दण्डं प्रसन्नताम्। धारयन्ति महात्मानो राजानः (the kings possess the qualities of the five devas, Agni etc., viz. the glow [*aushnya*] of Agni, the strength [*vikrama*] of Indra, etc.), Âpast. Dh. 1, 5, 8 यत्किं च मनसा वाचा चक्षुषा वा संकल्पयन्ध्यायत्याहाभिविपश्यति वा = यत्किं च मनसा संकल्पयन्ध्यायति वाचा वा सं° आह चक्षुषा वा सं° अभिविपश्यति (whatsoever he, desirous to accomplish it, thinks in his mind or pronounces in words or looks upon with his eye).

Chapt. II. Pronouns.

1. Personal pronouns and their possessives.

256. *·ersonal ·onouns.* The personal pronouns are less used, than in English and many other modern tongues, as they are often not expressed, especially when implied by the personal endings of the verb (**10**). Nor are their oblique cases always wanted in Sanskrit, when undispensable in English. So in this sentence Hit. 24 ततो दिनेषु गच्छत्सु पक्षिशावकानाक्रम्य कोटरमानीय प्रत्यहं खादति, the word पक्षिशावकान् is at the same time object of आक्रम्य, of आनीय, of खादति; it is of course put once, but

---

1) I borrow that designation from P. 1, 3, 10, which s. may be compared.

the pronouns referring to it are omitted as being easily supplied by the mind, whereas the English translator is bound to say »she [the cat] reached the young birds, took *them* to her hole and devoured *them*." Cp. ibid. 96 भगवन्तं चन्द्रमसं प्रणम्य प्रसाद्य च [sc. एनम्] गच्छ, Mhbh. 1, 154, 30 निष्पिष्यैनं बलाद्भूमौ पशुमारममारयत्, where the pronoun एनम् though being construed with two verbs is put but once, Daç. 152 अहं च तत्र संनिहितः किञ्चिदस्मेषि [1]) संनिधिनिषण्णास्तु मे वृद्धविटः कोऽपि ब्राह्मणः शनकैः स्मितहेतुमपृच्छत्, sc. माम्, as is plain by the foregoing अहम् and मे.

Likewise the possessive pronouns may be omitted, if there can be no doubt as to the possessor, especially of course when referring to the subject. Hit. 7 तस्य विष्णुशर्मणः पुत्रान् [sc. स्वान्] समर्पितवान् [2]).

257. Their enclitic forms. **1st and 2d person.** — The short forms of the acc., gen., dat. [3]) are enclitic, and used therefore if there is no stress to be laid on the pronoun. It is useless to give examples of them, as they are met with on almost every page. The acc. मा and त्वा are however not so frequent as the other enclitic forms [4]).

---

1) By a common error the printed text has अस्मैषि.

2) So was already taught by Patanjali (I, p. 62) मातरि वर्तितव्यं पितरि शुश्रूषितव्यमिति। न चोच्यते स्वस्यां मातरि स्वस्मिन्वा पितरीति संबन्धाच्चैतद्गम्यते या यस्य माता यश्च यस्य पिता.

3) Epic poetry affords sundry instances pointing to the fact, that the short forms of the gen. and dat. were once, it seems, available for all oblique cases. At least, R. 3, 43, 49 ते is doubtless = त्वया, and Mhbh. 1, 230, 15 नः = अस्मासु. The former passage runs thus अप्रमत्तेन ते भाव्यमाश्रमस्थेन (you must keep watchful in the hermitage), the latter मा त्वं.... स्नेहं कार्षीः सुतेषु नः Cp. *Vâmana's Stilregeln* ch. *Çabdaçuddhi*, s. 11.

4) As मा and मां, त्वा and त्वां are easily exposed to be confounded in manuscripts, it is possible that the enclitical forms have sometimes disappeared in our texts, if the following word commenced by a consonant. At all events, they seem to occur oftener in the ancient dialect than afterwards.

They are of necessity unavailable, if some emphasis of the pronoun be wanted. For this reason they are forbidden: *a*) when heading a sentence, or in poetry even a pâda, *b*) when immediately after a vocative, which heads the sentence, *c*) when followed by some particles, that give them some emphasis, viz. च, वा, ह, अह, एव. See P. 8, 1, 18; 20; 24; 72. Mhbh. 1, 229, 24 त्वामेकमाहुः कवयस्त्वामाहुस्त्रिविधं पुनः [here त्वा would not be allowed]; Kâç. on 8, 1, 18 रुद्रो विश्वेश्वरो देवो युष्माकं कुलदेवता [वः instead of युष्माकम् cannot be, as it heads the pâda]; Hit. 110 राजाह। मन्त्रिन्ममोत्साहभङ्गं मा कृथाः [मम not मे, according to *b*)]; R. 3, 55, 22 भजस्व सीते मामेव (— none but me); Mâlav. I, p. 21 अत्रभवतः किल मम च [not: मे च] समुद्रपल्वलयोरिवान्तरम्.

Rem. According to P. 8, 1, 25 they are also forbidden with verbs of seeing, when used in a metaphorical sense.

258. *Their plural.* The plural of the first person may refer either to a plurality of speakers at the same time or in most cases to *we = I + others with myself.* Similarly the plural of the 2d person may be used, even when addressing one, for the sake of signifying *you and others with you.* Panc. 258 the monkey, being invited by the makara to go with him, declines, for says he वयं वनचरा युष्मदीयं च जलान्ते गृहम् (we monkeys are living in the forest, and your abode is in the water). Mhbh. 1, 152, 26 Hidimbâ says to the single Bhîmasena अहं प्रेषिता भ्रात्रा..... बिभक्षयिषता मांसं युष्माकम् »I have been sent hither by my brother, who is eager to devour the flesh of all of you [viz. of your mother, your brothers and yours]."

259. *त्वम् and भवान्.* The pronoun of the 2d person is used without respect to social relations; the singular त्वम् is applied to superiors as well as to equals and to inferiors. The only case of यूयम् denoting a single individual is mentioned before (24).

Yet, when addressing in a polite manner, one avails one's self of भवान्, f. भवती, plur. भवन्तः, f. भवत्यः — being a popular reduction both in form and meaning of

भगवान् „Lord". Like Spanish *Usted*, Italian *Ella*, भवान्, though being exponent of the second person, does agree with the 3d person of the verb, therefore किं करोति भवान्(भवती), when addressing one, किं कुर्वन्ति भवन्तः (भवत्यः), when addressing more [1]).

Rem. Both modes of expressing the 2d person, either by the pronoun त्वम् or by the title भवान् may be used promiscuously. It is very common to see them used alternately. Panc. 73 Damanaka says to the lion संजीवकः शष्पभोजी भवान्मांसादस्तव प्रकृतयश्च ([the bull] Sanj. is an herbivorous animal, but you [भवान्] and your [तव] subjects feed on flesh); Kathâs. 30, 17 गान्धर्वविधिना] भार्यां कुर्याद्भवानिमाम्। एवम्.... असौ तव.... सेत्स्यति (make her your wife by the Gândharva-rite, in this way she will become yours). In the first book of the Hitopadeça (p. 35 of B. K. Vidyâratna's ed.) the sly cat thus addresses the blind vulture युष्मान्धर्मज्ञानरतान्विश्वासभूमय इति पक्षिणः सर्वे सर्वदा ममाग्रे प्रस्तुवन्ति। अतो भवद्भ्यो विद्यावयोवृद्धेभ्यो धर्मं श्रोतुमिहागतः [अहम्], as to the plural युष्मान्, भवद्भ्यः see **24**.

260. By pointing out भवान् as the proper term for addressing in a polite manner, it is by no means said it is the sole. Many other titles, such as signify *sir*, *lord*, *reverend*, *master* are used according to duty, custom, dignity, age. So holy men are duly addressed by भगवान्, f. भगवती, kings by देवः, respectable merchants and the like by आर्यः, matrons by आर्या, the wife duly addresses her husband by आर्यपुत्रः, the charioteer his prince by आयुष्मान् etc. As a rule a greater respect is shown by such titles than by using the general term भवान् (vocat. भोः). Another difference is this: they may as well denote the 3d person as the 2d, whereas भवान् is only fit for denoting the 2d person.

Moreover there are some general terms, made up of भवान् pre-

---

1) Instances of भवान् construed with the 2d person of the verb are extremely rare and the idiom undoubtedly vicious. So Çânkh. Gṛhy. 2, 2, 8 ब्रह्मचार्यसि भवान्ब्रूहि, instead of ब्रवीतु or ब्रूताम् »say, you are a *brahmacârin*."

ceded by some pronominal prefix, viz. अत्रभवान्, तत्रभवान्, सभवान्. As सभवान् and तत्रभवान् point at somebody absent, but the अत्रभवान् is always present, so the former two cannot refer but to a 3d person, but अत्रभवान् may denote as well the person spoken of as the person addressed. Utt. I, p. 1 the director thus *addresses* the spectators अद्य खलु.... आर्यमिश्रान्विज्ञापयामि। एवमत्रभवन्तो विदांकुर्वन्तु, but Çâk. VII Dushyanta when *speaking of* Çakuntalâ says अये सेयमत्रभवती शकुन्तला.

261. Third person, how expressed. For the **third person** Sanskrit does not possess a proper personal pronoun, like our *he*, *she*, *it*. Its duties are discharged by demonstratives. When wanted to be emphasized, by स, अयम्, असौ, otherwise by the oblique cases derived from the pronominal roots अ, अन, एन, or what is practically the same, in the acc. by एनम्, एनाम्, एनत्, plur. एनान्, एनाः, एनानि, in the other cases by the forms belonging to अयम्. The nomin. is not expressed but with some emphasis. See **274**.

262. Possessive pronouns. The **possessive pronouns** are relatively less used than the genitives of the personal ones. One will oftener meet with मम सूनुः, सूनुर्मे or मत्सूनुः (a *shashthîsamâsa* **216**, 1°) than सूनुर्मदीयः.

The difference, which exists in English between *my* and *mine*, *your* and *yours* etc., is not known in Sanskrit; मदीयं or मम पुस्तकम् may be as well „my book" as „a book of mine," also „the book is mine;" मत्पुस्तकम of course cannot have the last meaning, for subject and predicate are by necessity unfit for being compounded.

Rem. 1. Apart from the regular possessives of the 2d person त्वदीय and युष्मदीय, there exists also भवदीय

derived from the polite **भवान्**. Panc. 168 भवदीयसाहसेनाहं तुष्टः [= भवतः साह° or भवत्साह°].

Rem. 2. The possessive of the 3d person is तदीय (if wanted एतदीय), but here too the genitive of the demonstrative or a shashthîsamâsa are generally preferred.

263. Reflexives. The **reflexive pronouns** **स्व** and **आत्मन्** refer to all persons. — 1. **आत्मा**, acc. **आत्मानम्**, instr. **आत्मना** etc. is the proper equivalent of English *myself*, *yourself*, *himself*, *herself*, *itself*, *one's self; ourselves*, *yourselves*, *themselves*. It is always a masculine and a singular, even when referring to a plural or a not-masculine. Properly it is a subst. meaning »soul, spirit, individuality" and in this meaning it has always remained in common use. But even when pronoun, its origin is more or less perceptible. Occasionally it may be rendered as well by a pronoun as by a subst. [1]).

2. **स्व** generally — though not always — does duty of a possessive; it does denote the subject being possessor and may be rendered, according to sense, by *my*, *your*, *his*, *her*, *our*, *their*. Often it is compounded with its noun.

264. Examples of आत्मन्, when a refl. pronoun. — *a*) 3d person: Panc. 263 सर्पस्तेनात्मना स्वालयं नीतः (he *himself* brought the serpent to his dwelling); Var. Yog. 1, 19 शत्रोर्वधाय सचिवं शुभदैवयुक्तं। आज्ञापयेन्नृपतिरात्मनि दैवहीने (if the king be himself not favoured by Destiny, he should charge his minister, who is, to destroy his enemy); Mâlat. II, p. 38 वासवदत्ता राज्ञे संजयाय पित्रा प्रत्तमात्मानमुदयनाय प्रायच्छत् (Vâsav., though betrothed by her father to king Sanj., gave *herself* to Udayana); R. 2, 64, 29 तौ पुत्रमात्मनः स्पृष्ट्वा तपस्विनौ (both of them touched [the body of] their son); Panc. 184 पुनर्जातमिवात्मानं मन्यमानाः (they..... feeling *themselves* as if they were born again); —

1) Compare the similar use though less developed of Latin *animus*, आत्मानं विनोदयामि = *animum oblecto*. Panc. 160 मयात्मा प्रदत्तोऽयम् (I have given him my heart = myself).

b) 1st and 2d person: Hit. 107 आत्मनः किमुत्कर्षं न साधयामि (why should I not elevate *my own* rank?), Çâk. I पुण्याश्रमदर्शनेन तावदात्मानं पुनीमहे (in the meanwhile, let us purify *ourselves* —), Çâk. IV भर्तारमात्मसदृशं सुकृतैर्गता त्वम् (by your good actions you have got a husband becoming to *yourself*); — *c*) referring to a general subject: Panc. III, 174 यः करोति नरः पापं न तस्यात्मा ध्रुवं प्रियः (who does evil, certainly does not love himself).

As appears from the instances quoted, the gen. आत्मनः or आत्म° in compounds are used to denote the reflexive possessive. There exists even a possessive आत्मीय, as Kâd. I, 19 तदयमात्मीयः क्रियताम् (take him [the parrot] as yours).

Rem. 1. It is plain, that स्व आत्मा is said in the same meaning as आत्मा. R. 2, 6, 21 राजा] ज्ञात्वा वृद्धं स्वमात्मानं रामं राज्ये ऽभिषेक्ष्यति.

Rem. 2. The instrum. आत्मना when added to the reflexive lays stress on the fact, that the subject is acting by himself. Mhbh. 1, 158, 30 तारयात्मानमात्मना (help yourself); Panc. 276 न शक्नोम्यात्मानमप्यात्मना वोढुम् (I cannot bear my own self); R. 3, 47, 1 सीता] शशंसात्मानमात्मना (Sîtâ named herself [to her guest])[1].

265. Examples of स्व. — *a*) 3d person: Nala 3, 13 आक्षिपन्ती..... प्रभां शशिनः स्वेन तेजसा (scorning as if it were at the moon's splendour by *her own* brightness); Panc. 230 अथासौ प्रत्यूष उत्थाय स्वगृहान्निर्गतः (then at daybreak he rose and went out of *his* house); Çâk. I एतास्तपस्विकन्यकाः स्वप्रमाणानुरूपैः सेचनघटैः etc. (these girls of the hermitage, with watering-pots as to suit *their* size); — *b*) 1st and 2d person: Panc. III, 177 देहं स्वं..... शोषयिष्याम्यहम् (I will dry up *my* body); Hit. 137 अस्माकं परभूमिष्ठानां स्वदेशगमनमपि दुर्लभं भविष्यति (when residing abroad it will be hard for us to go to *our own* country); Çâk. VI त्वमपि स्वं नियोगमशून्यं कुरु (and you, do *your* duty without fault); Vikram. I, p. 2 स्वेषु स्थानेष्ववहितैर्भवितव्यं भवद्भिः (you are requested to listen with attention on *your* seats).

Yet स्व is not necessarily a possessive. It may also be equivalent to आत्मा. Hit. 109 स्वस्य राजानं प्रणतवान् = आत्मनो रा°; Panc. 305 नास्मै स्वोपार्जितं दास्यामि (I will not give him, what I have earned

---

1) आत्मना may even stand alone. Kathâs. 25, 133 गच्छाम्यहमात्मना (I will go [by] myself); Kumâras. 2, 54.

myself), here स्वोपार्जितम् = स्वेनोपा° = आत्मनोपा°; Schol. on R. 2, 40, 39 रामो मातरं राजानं च स्वमनुगतौ ददर्श (R. saw his mother and the king following after himself). This idiom is less frequent in classic literature than in commentaries and the like[1]). Note स्वतः »by one's self" f. i. Kathâs. 34, 56; 37, 49.

As स्व may be = आत्मा, it has also a possessive; viz. स्वीय. Panc. 162 स्वीयपितृमातरौ.

Rem. 1. स्वक, poss. स्वकीय, is a deminutive of स्व and स्वीय as to its form, but there is scarcely any difference of meaning. Nala 5, 40 उष्य तत्र यथाकामं नैषधः... जगाम नगरं स्वकम्, Panc. 233 स्वकीयामेव योनिं बहुमन्यसे (it is but your own kin you take regard of).

Rem. 2. Like Latin *suus*, स्व also signifies »one's relations," »one's property,"[2]) therefore, स्वजनः »one's kindred, one's family, attendance," स्वम् »one's goods," सर्वस्वम् »one's whole property."

266. As a third reflexive we may consider **निज** „own," as it may not rarely be rendered by the possessive pronoun. Panc. 56 the king says to his daughter संबोध्योऽद्य त्वया निजभर्ता यथा मम शत्रून्व्यापादयति (you must to day exhort your husband, that he may destroy my enemies). Inversely स्व may also be = »own:" Kathâs. 39, 53 स्वसुखं नास्ति साध्वीनां तासां भर्तृसुखं सुखम्.

267. The reflexives are not bound to refer exclusively to the grammatical subject. In passive sentences they often refer to the agent, in clauses and the like to the main subject. Instances hereof have already been given in **264** and **265**, viz. Panc. 263; Panc. III, 174; Kâd. I, 19; Hit. 137; Vikram. I, p. 2. Here are some more: Panc. 24 न शोभनं कृतं मया यत्तस्य विश्वासं गत्वात्माभिप्रायो निवेदितः, here आत्माभिप्रायः is of course ममात्मनोऽभिप्रायः; R. 2, 11, 22 वाङ्मात्रेण तदा राजा कैकेय्या स्ववशे कृतः sc. कैकेय्या वशम्.

Rem. On the other hand, one may meet with instances of pronouns not-reflexive, in such cases as where one might expect

---

1) As it is good Sanskrit, it makes doubtful how to explain स्व° in such compounds as स्वगृहम्, स्वधर्मः, whether = स्वस्य गृहम् or = स्वं गृहम्.

2) *Çâçvatakoça* ed. Zachariae, vs. 187 स्वशब्दो वदति ज्ञातिमात्मात्मीयधनानि च.

reflexives. So R. 3, 62, 3 त्वमशोकस्य शाखाभिः..... आवृणोषि शरीरं ते [not स्वम् or आत्मनः]; Kathâs. 36, 102.

268. The indeclinable **स्वयम्** does nearly the same duty as Latin *ipse*. It may be added to some other pronoun. Mhbh. 1, 161, 8 न त्वहं वधमाकाङ्क्षे स्वयमेवात्मनः (nor am I desirous of my own death).

स्वयम्

269. The **reciprocal pronouns** अन्योन्य, परस्पर, इतरेतर have almost assumed the character of adverbs. As a rule, they are used in the acc. of the masc. अन्योन्यम् etc. while being applied to every gender and every case-relation. Çâk. I उभे [सख्यौ] परस्परमवलोकयतः (the two friends look at each other); Vikram. I, p. 18 अन्योन्यं हस्तं स्पृशतः (they shake hands); Panc. 216 एवं च परस्परं द्वैधमुत्पन्नम् (and in this manner discord arose between them); Daç. 151 उभौ..... त्रपया साध्वसेन वान्योन्यमात्मानं न विवृणवाते (both, either by shame or by confusion, do not open their soul to each other); Çank. on Ch. Up. p. 42 समानमितरेतरं प्राणादित्यौ (the principle of life and the sun are identical to one another); Pat. I, p. 426 सार्थिकानामेकप्रतिश्रय उषितानां प्रातरुत्थाय प्रतिष्ठमानानां कश्चित्परस्परं संबन्धो भवति. Cp. also Kâm. 2, 42; Mâlav. I, p. 24; Kathâs. 2, 41 etc.

Reciprocal pronouns: अन्योन्य etc.

Yet they admit also of other case-endings, f. i. Panc. III, 200 परस्परस्य मर्माणि ये न रक्षन्ति जन्तवः (they who do not observe the weak points of each other); Harshac. 2 तेषामन्योन्यस्य विवादाः प्रादुरभूवन् (disputations arose between them). So Nala 5, 32 तौ परस्परतः प्रीतौ. Nala 1, 16 the acc. अन्योन्यम् is depending on the prep. प्रति. And so on. See Kâç. on P. 8, 1, 12 vârtt. 9 and 10; vârtt. 10 teaches the optional employment of forms in °आम्, if feminine and neuter words are concerned f. i. इतरेतराम् [or °रम्] इमे ब्राह्मणकुले — इमे ब्राह्मण्यौ — भोजयतः.

The same meaning is carried by the adverb **मिथः** (mutually), which is not less used.

2. Demonstratives, Relatives, Interrogatives.

270. In ancient language the **demonstratives** are often

Demonstratives: general remarks.

indicating the things they are to point at in a more significant manner than in modern tongues. For this reason, when translating from the Sanskrit, it is many times indispensable to render demonstrative pronouns otherwise, f. i. by the pronoun *he*, *she*, *it*, by *the*, by adverbs (*here*, *there*), sometimes even by putting instead of them the very noun, they are referring to. In the same way, indeed, the demonstratives of Latin and Greek must be translated.

We will dispense here with adducing instances exemplifying each of the somewhat freer translations, as have been named. It will suffice giving a few samples of Sanskrit demonstr. pronouns to be rendered by English adverbs. Panc. 204 भो भो कपिञ्जल एष नदीतीरे तपस्वी धर्मवादी तिष्ठति (say, woodcock, *here* on the river-side a holy devotee stands); Vikr. I, p. 15 the king says to his charioteer सूत इदं तच्छैलशिखरम् (— *here* is that mountain-top); Çâk. IV Kaṇva asks »where are Çârngarava and Çâradvata," they answer भगवन्निमौ स्वः (Reverend, here we are). From the Vaidik writings I add Ath. V. 1, 29, 5 उदसौ सूर्यो अगादुदिदं मामकं वचः (*there* the sun has risen and *here* has my spell).

271. Difference of employment between them.

Of the four demonstratives, used in classic Sanskrit, अयम् and एष are opposite to स and असौ. Their different nature is well described by a vernacular grammarian, when pronouncing that एष is expressive of *nearness* but असौ of *remoteness*, and that अयम् implies *presence* but स *absence* [1]). Indeed, both एष and अयम् point at something near to the speaker or his time, whereas

1) See the kârikâ, quoted in a foot-note on p. 188 of Çrîrâmamaya-çarman's edition of Mrcchakaṭî (Majumdâr's series):

इदमः प्रत्यक्षरूपं समीपतरवर्ति चैतदो रूपम्
अदसस्तु विप्रकृष्टं तदिति परोक्षे विजानीयात्.

असौ and स indicate something remote either by space or by time. Therefore, the latter couple may be compared to Lat. *ille* and *iste*, Gr. ἐκεῖνος, Engl. *that*, the former to Lat. *hic*, Greek οὗτος and ὅδε, Engl. *this*.

The difference between them will appear better when perusing Sanskrit texts, than from instances detached from the context they are taken out. Yet, here are several, which may give some idea of it.

1. एष and अयम्. — Vikram. I, p. 14 Purûravas points with his hand to Urvaçî her attendance: एताः says he सुतनु मुखं ते सख्यः पश्यन्ति (Lat. *hae amicae* —); Nala 3, 4 Indra declares to Nala the name of himself and his comrades: अहमिन्द्रो ऽयमग्निश्च तथैवायमपां पतिः।.... यमोऽयमपि पार्थिव (Lat. *ego Indrus*, *hic Agnis* etc.).

2. असौ and स. — Nala 3, 2 Nala asks the devas, for what purpose they wish him to be their messenger कश्चासौ यस्याहं दूत ईप्सितः।किं च तद्वो मया कार्यम्, here both असौ and तत् answer to Latin *iste*; — Mudr. II, p. 77 the minister Râxasa, when hearing from his spy that the physician, whom he had despatched to empoison king Candragupta, had been prevented from performing that plot by the vigilance of Cânakya, exclaims शठः खल्वसौ बटुः। अथ स वैद्यः कथम्, here both असौ and स are = Lat. *ille*.

3. Examples of *this* and *that* in opposition to one another. — Ch. Up. 2, 9, 1 असुमादित्यमुपासीत..... तस्मिन्निमानि सर्वाणि भूतान्यन्वायत्तानि (let him meditate on *that* sun..... it is on *that* all *these* beings [here on earth] are depending upon) ibid. 1, 3, 2 समान उ एवायं चासौ चोष्णोऽयमुष्णोऽसौ (this breath here and that sun there are indeed the same, this is hot and that is hot); Utt. II, p. 27 अयमसावध्ययनविघ्नः *hoc illud studiorum impedimentum* »that well-known hindrance now presents itself." — In the first act of the Mudrarâxasa the minister Cânakya, after having put the jeweller Candanadâsa into prison, thus expresses his contentment: हन्त लब्ध इदानीं राक्षसः।कुतः

त्यजत्यप्रियवत्प्राणान्यथा तस्यायमापदि
तथैवास्यापदि प्राणा नूनं तस्यापि न प्रियाः

तस्य refers to Râxasa, अयम् and अस्य to Candanadâsa. In Latin one would say likewise: ut *hic* in *illius* re adversa suae vitae jacturam facit, sic profecto et *ille* vitam pro nihilo putabit in *hujus* calamitate. — In the Vikramorvaçî king Purûravas designates his beloved Urvaçî by the pronoun अयम्, as long as he knows her present and sees her (1st act), but in the second act, when thinking her absent, he speaks of तस्या आसनम्, expresses his disappointment about her female attendant coming सख्या विरहिता तया, and says on account of her पर्युत्सुकां कथयसि प्रियदर्शनां ताम्।आर्तिं न पश्यसि पुरूरवसस्तदर्थाम् — whereas in the first act, when looking at her face, he admires इदं रूपम्, exclaims नेयं तपस्विनः सृष्टिः, is uneasy, as अस्या भयकम्पः is noticed by him.

272. Though एष may be styled the emphatic अयम्, both pronouns are sometimes used almost promiscuously. Mhbh. 1, sarga 154 Kuntî asks Hidimbâ, who she is: »are you a deity of this forest?" अस्य वनस्य देवता, Hidimbâ answers यदेतत्पश्यसि वनम् etc. In the second act of the Vikramorvaçî the king offering a seat to Citralekhâ says एतदासनमास्यताम्, in the first act of the Mudrarâxasa Cânakya to Candanadâsa इदमासनमास्यताम्.

273. अयम् — not एष — is the proper word, if the speaker wishes to denote something belonging to himself by a demonstrative rather than by the possessive of the 1st. person. अयं बाहुः may signify „this arm of mine," ὅδε ὁ πῆχυς, hoc bracchium. Vikram. II, p. 46 Purûravas laments हृदयमिषुभिः कामस्यान्तः सशल्यमिदम् — viz. मम, Mṛcch. IV, p. 141 न खलु मम विषादः साहसेऽस्मिन्भयं वा (I feel no remorse nor fear on account of the rash deed, I have committed).

अयम् referring to the 1st person.

Rem. Hence अयं जनः a modest phrase to designate the speaker himself, cp. Greek ὅδε ὁ ἀνήρ. Vikram. II, p. 56 the king when taking his leave from Urvaçî says स्मर्तव्योऽयं जनः; Mṛcch. VII, p. 238 Cârudatta tells his friend, he longs for Vasantasenâ सखे मैत्रेय वसन्तसेनादर्शनोत्सुकोऽयं जनः; Daç. 164 सोऽयमर्येणाज्ञाकरो जनोऽत्यर्थमनुगृहीतः (my lord has much gratified his most obedient servant).

274. Pânini teaches, there is some difference in the flexion of अयम् according to its being used *either* when referring to somebody or something already spoken of before, *or*

P. 2, 32-3

when pointing at or showing. In the former case 1. the cases, derived from the root अ are treated as enclitics, 2. the accus. is एनम्, एनाम्, एनत् in the singular, एनान्, एनाः, एनानि in the plural, एनौ, एने in the dual, 3. the instr. of the sing. एनेन, एनया, 4. the loc. of the dual is एनयोः. It is in such instances of *anvâdeça* (reference to something already named before), that the pronoun bears almost the character of our *he*, *she*, *it*. — 1. अस्य etc. enclitic: Mrcch. I, p. 55 यदा तु भाग्यक्षयपीडितां दशां नरः कृतान्तोपहितां प्रपद्यते। तदास्य मित्राण्यपि यान्त्यमित्रताम् (if a man has by Destiny been reduced to poverty, then even his friends become enemies to him), Çâk. I एतास्तपस्विकन्यकाः.... इत एवाभिवर्तन्ते। अहो मधुरमासां दर्शनम् (these girls of the hermitage approach hither, it is pleasant to look on them), Vikram. I, p. 2 परिषदेषा पूर्वेषां कवीनां दृष्टरसप्रबन्धा। अहमस्यां कालिदासग्रथितवस्तुना नवेन त्रोटकेनोपस्थास्ये; — 2. instances of एनम् etc. Mhbh. I, Paushyap. तमुपाध्यायमुपतस्थे प्रोवाच चैनम् (he made his compliment to his teacher and spoke to him), Vikram. III, p. 72 अये। इत एव प्रस्थितो देवः.... यावदेनमवलोकनमार्गे प्रतिपालयामि, Nala 13, 24 तां प्रासादगतापश्यद्राजमाता जनैर्वृताम्। धात्रीमुवाच गच्छैनामानयेह ममान्तिकम् (her the king's mother saw from the balcony, as she was followed by the crowd, and said to the nurse: »go and bring her to me"), Mhbh. 5, 16, 29 Indra receives a deputation of devas, rshis etc., and after being addressed by them उवाच चैनान्प्रतिभाष्य, Ait. Br. 1, 29 treats of the two हविर्धाने (carts in which the soma-herb is carried) in § 6 देवयन्तो ह्येने मानुषाः प्रभरन्ति, ibid. 1, 30, 3 एनौ refers to अग्नीषोमौ, mentioned before.

anvâdeça.

NB. The instr. एनेन and एनया seem to be extremely rare; अनेन at least and अनया are regularly used, when *anvâdeça* is required. Mâlav. I, p. 14 the minister of king Agnimitra reads a letter from the king of Vidarbha; when asked about its contents, he answers to Agn. इदमिदानीमनेन [not: एनेन] प्रतिलिखितम्. And so often.

275. The pronoun स and its employment.

स likewise points at somebody or something known, and therefore, like अयम्, it is fit for doing duty of the pronoun *he*, *she*, *it*. Yet, they are not synonymous. Like Greek, especially Homeric, ὁ, ἡ, τό, it signifies, that the person or thing referred to is well-known, or has been named just before, or will be named forthwith. It is therefore never an enclitic, and is sometimes = Lat. *ille*, sometimes = *is* „the afore said.'' Hence its fitness to be rendered by „the.'' When referring to the relative य, it may be equivalent to „he,'' German *derjenige*. It is also used to indicate the changing of the subject, f. i. स आह or सोऽब्रवीत् = „the other said, answered.'' Yet it may as well point at the same throughout a succession of sentences, in which case one is inclined to put it at the head, as Daç. 12 वामदेवनामानं तपोधनं जगाम। तं प्रणम्य तेन कृतातिथ्यस्तस्मै कथितकृत्यस्तदाश्रमे..... कंचित्कालमुषित्वा.... मुनिमभाषत; Nala 1,5 Bhîma king of Vidarbha has been named, it follows स प्रजार्थे परं यत्नमकरोत्..... तमभ्यगच्छद् ब्रह्मर्षिर्दमनो नाम..... तं [viz. दमनं] स भीमः [the aforesaid Bh.] प्रजाकामस्तोषयामास..... तस्मै प्रसन्नो दमनो वरं ददौ. Cp. also the examples adduced **271**, 3°.

Examples: 1. of स = *ille* (the well-known, the famous). Çâk. VII तत्कोटिमत्कुलिशमाभरणं मघोनः (the *renowned* thunderbolt, Indra's attribute, Lat. fulmen *illud* Jovis).

2. स = »the afore said.'' Çâk. IV Kanva says to Çakuntalâ ययातेरिव शर्मिष्ठा भर्तुर्बहुमता भव। पुत्रं त्वमपि सम्राजं सेव पूरुमवाप्नुहि, here सेव »as she'' means of course Çarmishthâ; Kathâs. 27, 109 उपाध्यायस्य कस्यचित्। ब्राह्मणास्याभवन् शिष्याः सप्त ब्राह्मणपुत्रकाः। (110)स तान् शिष्याानुपाध्यायो धेनुं दुर्भिक्षदोषतः। गोमतः श्वशुरादेकां याचितुं प्राहिणोत्ततः। (111)ते च गत्वान्यदेशस्थं दुर्भिक्षक्षामकुक्षयः। तं तद्गिरा तच्छ्वशुरं तच्छिष्या गां ययाचिरे। (112)सोऽपि वृत्तिकरीमेकां धेनुं तेभ्यः समर्पयत् (some teacher of the brâhmana class had seven disciples, brâhmanas they too. Once because of famine

he despatched these disciples to beg one cow from his father-in-law, who was rich in cows. They set out, suffering much from hunger, to the foreign country, where dwelled that man, and begged a cow of the father-in-law of their teacher, in his name. The father-in-law gave them one, fit to procure [them] a livelihood). Here we have several instances of स referring to something mentioned before, and even such accumulation as in vs. 111 ते... तं तद्गिरा etc., ते pointing at the disciples, तं at the father-in-law, तत्° at the teacher. It is, indeed, always allowed to employ स many times in the same sentence, though pointing at different persons or things, f. i. Mhbh. 1, 2, 395 यो गोशतं कनकशृङ्गमयं ददाति। विप्राय वेदविदुषे च बहुश्रुताय। पुण्यां च भारतकथां शृणुयाच्च नित्यम्। तुल्यं फलं भवति तस्य च तस्य चैव, the last words mean: »of the one as well as of the other."

3. स when adj. = »the." R. 3, 35, 27 a tall fig-tree is described, whose branches are of enormous size: तत्रापश्यत्..... न्यग्रोधम्..... समन्ताद्यस्य ताः शाखाः [»*the* branches of which]" शतयोजनमायताः; Utt. II, p. 29 one asks अथ स राजा किमाचारः संप्रति (but what is *the* king doing now?) another answers तेन राज्ञा क्रतुरश्वमेधः प्रक्रान्तः (*the* king has commenced an açvamedha).

4. स in correlation with य = Germ. *derjenige*. Mhbh. 1, 74, 40 सा भार्या या गृहे दक्षा सा भार्या या प्रजावती. Generally the relative clause precedes, see **452**, 2d and **455**.

Rem. Now and then स refers to persons or things not expressed, but only implied by the foregoing. Mhbh. 1, adhy. 157 it is told, that Kuntî and her strong son Bhîmasena hear cries of distress in the house of the worthy brahman, whose hospitality they are enjoying of. Though the family of the brahman has not been named in the foregoing, vs. 10 introduces them by the pronoun तान्. The same idiom exists in Latin.

276. **स** may point at a general subject, see **12**. Occasionally it may be rendered by „such a one." Mhbh. 1, 158, 31 धर्मज्ञान्राक्षसानाहुर्न हन्यात्स च मामपि (râxasas, it is told, know the dharma, nor would such a one kill me); Kumâras. 5, 83 न केवलं यो महतो ऽपभाषते। शृणोति तस्मादपि यः स पापभाक् (not only he, who speaks evil of the mighty, but likewise he, who listens to a such, commits a sin).

Rem. When put twice, स means »manifold, various, all sorts of —." R. 3, 9, 31 आत्मानं नियमैस्तैस्तैः कर्षयित्वा प्रयत्नतः। प्राप्यते निपुणैर्धर्मः, Kathâs. 29, 169 महादेवी च तैस्तैस्तामुपचारैरुपाचरत् (— with all sorts of civilities —) For the rest स put twice is mostly met with in the apodosis after a double यः preceding. Nala 5, 11 यंयं हि ददृशे तेषां तंतं मेने नलं नृपम् (287). This repeated स has accordingly a distributive meaning, see **252**, 3°.

277. स एव = „the same." With **एव** added to it, **स** = „the very," often „the same," Lat. *idem*. For the rest comp. **398**.

Panc. 172 तावेव द्वौ पुरुषौ मियो मन्त्रयतः (*the same* two men keep counsel together); ibid. V, 26 तानीन्द्रियाण्यविकलानि तदेव नाम। सा बुद्धिरप्रतिहता वचनं तदेव॥ अर्थोष्मणा विरहितः पुरुषः स एव। बाह्यः क्षणेन भवतीति विचित्रमेतत् (his senses are the same, without defect; his name is the same; his is the same vigour of mind, the same speech; yet — how curious it is — the self-same man, when having lost the splendour of his wealth, becomes forthwith a stranger). The latter example shows, that if स is plainly conveying the meaning »the same," एव may be omitted, cp. Ch. Up. 5, 4, 2 तस्मिन्नेतस्मिन्नग्नौ.

278. **स** may be added to other demonstratives, to personal pronouns, to relatives. As to the last combination **यः स**, see **287**.—**सोऽयम्, स एष** and the like, **सोऽहम्, सा त्वम्**, etc. mostly are to express the worth of a conclusive particle„ therefore, for this reason, then," as will be shown further on, when describing the connection of sentences, see **445**.

279. Demonstratives, when first members of compounds. Some other observations on the demonstratives. — 1 In compounds, तत् and एतत् are considered as the themes, which represent स and एष; likewise मत्, त्वत्, अस्मत्, युष्मत्[1]) are respectively the thematic shapes of अहम्, त्वम्, वयम्, यूयम्. — अयम् and

1) By this orthography here and elsewhere I follow the rules of Sanskrit euphony; etymological reasons would rather require to write तद्, एतद्, etc.

असौ are seldom used in compounds, if they are, the neuter (इदम्, अदः) is employed. But, as a rule, एतत् and तत् are substituted for them. In other terms: in compounds, एतत् has the meaning of Lat. *hic* and तत् that of Lat. *is* or *ille*. Mṛcch. I, p. 3 the director informs the public यदिदं वयं मृच्छकटिकं नाम प्रकरणं प्रयोक्तुं व्यवसिताः..... एतत्कविः etc., while speaking of the poet of the piece he has named. Kathâs. 64, 25 अवार्यत पान्थेन तद्वधात् (he was prevented from injuring them by a passer-by), here तद्वधात् refers to अमीभिः.. लोमशैः [sc. तापसैः] in vs. 24.

Idiom: *is pavor = ejus rei pavor.*

2. The idiom, represented by Latin *is pavor = ejus rei pavor* 1) is not unknown in Sanskrit. Mhbh. 1, 6, 11 Agni says बिभेति को न शापान्मे कस्य चायं व्यतिक्रमः, here अयं व्यतिक्रमः = अस्य [शापस्य] व्यति° (who is not afraid of my curse, who has an escape from it?). Panc. 158 a boy has been turned out of doors by his father गृहान्निःसारितः. The author proceeds स च तेन निर्वेदेन देशान्तरं गत्वा, apparently तेन निर्वेदेन is here = तस्य [निःसारणस्य] निर्वेदेन »by despair caused by this expulsion". Cp. Kumâras. 3, 17, Kathâs. 1, 39.

असौ in formulae.

3. In formulae one uses असौ as significative of the proper name of him, whom the formula is to be applied to. When employing them, the proper name is substituted for it. See f. i. Pâr. Grhy. 1, 18, 3 असौ जीव शरदः शतम्, Âçv. Grhy. 1, 20, 5.

neuters of demonstratives, used as adverbs.

4. In the archaic dialect, especially in the liturgical books, the acc. of the neuter singular of demonstratives is often used adverbially. Ait. Br. 1, 9, 6 सर्वैर्वै छन्दोभिरिष्ट्वा देवाः स्वर्गं लोकमजयंस्तथैवैतद्यजमानः.... स्वर्गं लोकं जयति, here एतत् means »in this case." Cp. ibid. 1, 4, 2; 1, 15, 4, Ch. Up. 4, 2, 1 तद् = »then," etc. etc. The classic language has retained adverbial functions of तत् and यत्, see 444 and 463.

280. The **interrogative pronoun** is क. Its comparative कतर and its superlative कतम are likewise used. The po-

---

1) See f. i. Livy 21, 46, 7 Numidae ab tergo se ostenderunt. Is pavor perculit Romanos. Cp. Virg. *Aen.* 1, 261, Nepos *Lys.* 3, 1.

Interrogatives. sitive क simply asks „who?" „what?" „which?", कतर, like Lat. *uter*, arch. Eng. *whether* „which of the two?", कतम „who etc. of many?" They are wanted both in direct questions and in the so-called indirect questions. One says, therefore, को भवान् (who are you?), देवदत्त एतयोः कतरः (which of these two is Devadatta?), Vikram. I, p. 5 परिज्ञायते कतमेन दिग्विभागेन गतः स जाल्मः (is it known, in what direction the rascal has departed?). Cp. **411**.

If wanted, क may be the former part of a bahuvrîhi. Daç. 30 एतत्कटकाधिपतिः किंनामधेयः (what is the name of the chief of this encampment?); ibid. 74 — an ascetic speaks — अर्थकामवात्तानभिज्ञा वयं ज्ञेयौ चेमौ किंरूपौ किंपरिवारौ किंफलौ.

Rem. 1. The distinction between क, कतर and कतम is not always strictly observed. Râm. 1, sarga 38 Râma asks Viçvâmitra, which of the two, Kadrû or Vinatâ will have one illustrious son, and who sixty thousand sons एकः कस्याः सुतो ब्रह्मन्का बहूञ्जनयिष्यति, here क is used, not कतर. — Panc. 284 सामादीनामुपायानां मध्ये कस्यात्र विषयः (for which of the six well-known expedients, *sâma* etc., it is now the fit time?) here कस्य is used within the proper sphere of कतम. — R. 2, 85, 4 Bharata asks Guha कतरेण गमिष्यामि भरद्वाजाश्रमं पथा, though the country is wholly unknown to him, and he, therefore, does not want to be informed »whether" but »which" of the many ways will conduct him to Bharadvâja [1]).

Rem. 2. On the faculty of putting in the same sentence two or more interrogative pronouns referring to different things, see **409**, 2°

281. At the outset क was both an interrogative and an indefinite pronoun, cp. Lat. *quis*, Gr. τίς and τὶς. In classic Sanskrit it has occasionally still the function of an indefinite; yet, as a rule, क is then combined

---

1) Cp. **246** and the foot-note 1) on page 188 of this book.

Indefinites. with some particle: चित् or अपि or चन. Hence कश्चित्, कश्चन, कोऽपि are the proper **indefinite pronouns**, expressing *some(any)body*, *some(any)thing*; *some*, *any*. To them we must add एक, for this word, properly meaning „one," does not rarely duty as an indefinite, and is to be rendered by „some" and even by the so-called article „a."—सर्व is „every; all."

कश्चित्, etc. and एक. Instances of कश्चित्, कश्चन, कोऽपि [1]) it is superfluous to give. As to एक = »a." R. 2, 63, 32 अहं चैकेषुणा हतः (I am hit by an arrow), Daç. 25 कदाचिदेकस्मिन्कान्तारे मदीयसहचरगणेन जिघांस्यमानं भूसुरमेकमवलोक्य (once in some forest I saw some brahman being about to be hurt by the crowd of my companions). Even कश्चित् etc. may be = »a": Daç. 132 सा कंचित्सुतं सूतवती (she was delivered of a son). It is consistent, that एक may also be combined with some other indefinite. Kathâs. 27, 89 कस्याप्येकस्य वणिजः साधुः कर्मकरो गृहे (an honest servant in the house of some merchant), Panc. 9 एकस्य कस्यचिच्छिल्पिनः.

Kathâs. 1, 56 may be an instance of the sole क, bearing the character of an indefinite: नान्यो जानाति कः (and nobody else knows it). Cp. R. 2, 32, 42 वृणीष्व किं चेदपरं व्यवस्यसि (choose something else, if you have made up your mind).

विश्व. Rem. 1. The old dialect possessed a synonym of सर्व, viz. विश्व; in the classic language it is no more used, save in some standing phrases as विश्वे देवाः, being the name of some special class of deities, विश्वं जगत् or simply विश्वम् »the Universe."

सर्व. Rem. 2 सर्व is = »every" and »each," सर्वः »everybody," सर्वम् »everything." Nala 20,6 सर्वः सर्वं न जानाति सर्वज्ञो नास्ति कश्चन (not everybody does know everything, nobody is omniscient).

---

1) According to the Petrop. Dict. the indefinite pronoun कोऽपि was made in a latter period than the other combinations, as it does not occur in the older literature, Manu included (see II, p. 6 *s. v.* क). Yet in the Mahâbhârata and the Râmâyaṇa कोऽपि and such adverbs as क्वापि, कथमपि are as well met with as those in °चित् and °चन. R. 2, 52, 45 क and अपि are separated by च, अहं किं चापि वक्ष्यामि.

282. By adding to the foresaid indefinite pronouns the negation न one expresses the negative indefinites „nobody, nothing, no, none." It is indifferent at what place one puts the negation. Nala 3, 24 प्रविशन्तं न मां कश्चिदपश्यत् (nobody saw me, as I entered), Hit. 95 कोऽप्युपायोऽस्माकं जीवनाय नास्ति (we have no livelihood), M. 9, 26 न विशेषोऽस्ति कश्चन (there is no difference), Kathâs. 34, 120 दरिद्रशब्द एकस्य नासीत्तत्र (there nobody could be named poor).

It is not only said न कश्चित् and न कोऽपि, but also न कश्चिदपि. Panc. 71 न किञ्चिदप्युक्तवान् (he said not a single word).

283. „Other" how expressed. There are several words for „other", viz. अन्य, अपर, पर, इतर. Of these अन्यं is the most common and has the most general meaning.

1. अन्य generally denotes »somebody or something else." In such phrases as अन्यस्मिन्नहनि, »once on a day" it is almost = कश्चित्. Yet it may also signify »the other." So Hit. 102 when a messenger wishes to speak secretly to the king, the king removes his attendance ततो राजा मन्त्री च स्थितौ तत्र। अन्ये ऽन्यत्र गताः (— *the others* withdrew).

2. अपर properly means »the subsequent, the following;" hence it has got also the meaning of »other," but commonly it retains its proper nature of signifying what is named in the second place. Mrcch. I, p. 55 इयं सा रदनिका। इयमपरा का (this is Radanikâ, but this other, who is she?).

3. पर is etymologically related to our *far*, and accordingly it serves also to denote the opposite of स्व. Hence it displays all shades of meaning, as are directly opposite to the notion of »own, proper." It may be sometimes = »strange" and »stranger," sometimes = »enemy," sometimes also when used in a broader sense = »other." Nala 3, 8 कथं नु जातसंकल्पः स्त्रियमुत्सहते पुमान्परार्थमीदृशं वक्तुम् (how should a man bear to speak in this way for the sake of another to a woman, whom he desires for himself?). Mrcch. I, p. 55 न युक्तं परकलत्रदर्शनम् (it does not become a man to look on the wife of his neighbour). Its adjective परकीय = *alienus*. Çâk. IV अर्थो हि कन्या परकीय एव (a daughter is a possession one cannot call one's own).

4. इतर, the comparative of the pronominal root इ, bears a strong affinity to Latin *alter*. It is used, indeed, to signify »the one" and »the other" of two. Bṛh. Âr. Up. 1, 4, 4 ऋउवेतराभवदृषवृष इतरः, cp. M. 4, 137, Kathâs. 19, 50. When dual or plural, it denotes the other of two parties. Mṛcch. I, p. 33 ब्रह्मक्षत्रविशस्तरन्ति च यया नावा तयैवेतरे, Mudr. V, p. 184 तेषां मध्ये ये त्रयः प्रधानतमा मदीयां भूमिं कामयन्ते ते....।इतरौ तु द्वौ हस्तिबलकामौ हस्तिनैव घात्येताम्. — Cp. 217, 2.

Rem. 1. To the foresaid pronouns we may add भिन्न »different," as it sometimes may be rendered by »other." Kâç. on P. 2, 3, 29 भिन्नो देवदत्तात् = अन्यो देवदत्तात्.

Rem. 2. अपर and अन्य, when qualifying some noun, may be used in a somewhat particular manner., Panc. p. 77 contains the story of the jackal who, being hunted by a band of dogs, fled to some dyer's and there jumped into a pot filled with dye. As he got out, he had got a blue colour, तत्रापरे सारमेयास्तं सृगालमजानन्तो यथाभीष्टदिशं जग्मुः. Here अपरे सारमेयाः means »the other, namely the dogs," not »the other dogs." Compare ibid. p. 83 कस्मिंश्चिद्वनोद्देशे सिंहः प्रतिवसति स्म।तस्य चानुचरा अन्ये द्वीपिवायसगोमायवः सन्ति. Here अन्ये does not mean »other panters etc.," but »others, namely a panter, a crow and a jackal." Cp. R. 2, 71, 61 अन्या विधवा = »some widow," Schol. अन्येत्यस्य विवरणं विधवेति. — The same idiom exists in Latin and Greek, f. i. Od. β, 411 μήτηρ δ'ἐμὴ οὔ τι πέπυσται, οὐδ' ἄλλαι δμωαί.

284. „Either," Lat. *alterutter*, is expressed by एकतर. Mudr. IV, p. 146 तयोर्द्वयोरेकतरं जहाति.

एकतर and एकतम.

एकतम denotes »one out of many," cp. कतम (280). Panc. 12 संधिविग्रहयानासनसंश्रयद्वैधीभावानामेकतमेन संविधास्ये (I will arrange it by means of one of the six expedients: *saṁdhi*, *vigraha* etc.). Likewise अन्यतम, »see f. i. Daç. 101.

How »neither" is to be expressed, may appear from these examples. Ch. Up. 5, 10, 8 अथैतयोः पथोर्न कतरेण चन तानीमानि भूतानि भवन्ति (on neither of these two ways these foresaid beings are moving), Panc. 50 तौ द्वावपि न ज्ञास्यतः (neither of them will know it).

285. For denoting „one.... another" one may repeat अन्य or कश्चित् or एक, or use them alternatively; अपर may also be used, except in the first link. If

अन्य... अन्य and the like. there are more links, they may alternate in various manners. As to एकम्.... अपरम् = „first.... secondly" see **439.**

Examples: 1. of अन्य.... अन्य. R. 2, 108, 15 यदि भुक्तमिहान्येन देहमन्यस्य गच्छति (if what is consumed by one, goes into the body of another —), Mhbh. I Paushyap. 174 अन्यस्मिन्करणीये तु कार्ये पार्थिवसत्तम। बाल्यादिवान्यदेव त्वं कुरुषे (you do other things, my prince, than what you should have done). — 2. of एक, कश्चित्, etc. Panc. 297 तेऽपि ताड्यमाना एके मृता अन्ये भिन्नमस्तकाः फूत्कर्तुमुपचक्रमिरे (and as he struck them, some of them died, some others had their heads broken and began to cry violently), M. 9, 32 आहुः.... केचिदपरे... विदुः, — 3. of more links connected. Varâh. Bṛh. 32, 1 क्षितिकम्पमाहुरेके बृहदन्तर्जलनिवासिसत्त्वकृतम्। भूभारखिन्नदिग्गजविश्रामसमुद्भवं चान्ये। अनिलोऽनिलेन निहतः क्षितौ पतन्सस्वनं करोत्येके। केचित्त्वदृष्टकारितमिदमन्ये प्राहुराचार्याः (»some say that an earthquake is caused by some huge animal living in the midst of the waters; others, however, that it arises when the elephants of the quarters, being tired of the earth's load, are taking breath; a wind falling down upon earth with noise, as if struck by another wind, say some; others, however, maintain that it is ordained by unseen powers; other masters again narrate the following," p. 140 of KERN's translation). Cp. Nala 12, 87.

286. Relative pronoun. The **relative pronoun** is य. A full account of its employment will be given in the Section, in which there will be treated of clauses and relative sentences. Here it suffices to point out that य and स are standing complements of one another.

Rem. The comp. and superl. यतर, यतम are restricted to the archaic dialect.

287. How generalized. The relative pronoun may be generalized in various ways: *a*) by putting य twice, then यो यः = „whosoever," and it requires स स in the apodosis; *b*) by adding to it one of the indefinite pronouns so as to make up the combination यः कश्चित्, यः कश्चन or यः कोऽपि; *c*) by putting together य and स in the same case, gender and number, यः सः = „whosoever it may be, any." For the rest, cp. **453**.

Examples of *a*). Nala 5, 11 is quoted **276**; Bhojapr. 36 यंयं नृपोऽनुरागेण संमानयति संसदि। तस्य तस्योत्सारणाय यतन्ते राजवल्लभाः (the king's favourites always plot to the ruin of whomsoever the king loves and honours in his court).

b.) Mudr. IV, p. 158 यः कश्चिन्मां द्रष्टुमिच्छति स त्वया प्रवेशयितव्यः (whosoever it may be, that wishes to see me, you must admit him), Nala 4, 2 अहं चैव यच्चान्यन्ममास्ति किञ्चन (myself and whatsoever belongs to me). This idiom is used so as to be synonymous with the simple indefinite pronoun, as Hitop. 10 सुवर्णकङ्कणं यस्मै कस्मैचिद् दातुमिच्छामि (I desire to give the golden bracelet to whomsoever); Schol. on R. 3, 10, 19 यस्मै कस्मा अपि प्रतिज्ञां प्रतिज्ञाय न जह्याम्.[1]).

Rem. The archaic dialect used also यः कश्च = यः कश्चित्. So f. i. Ch. Up. 3, 15, 4 प्राणो वा इदं भूतं यदिदं किंच (*prâṇa* means all whatever exists here), Ait. Br. 2, 6, 5 यस्यै कस्यै च देवतायै पशुरालभ्यते सैव मेधपतिरिति. It occurs also sometimes in epic poetry. So Hit. 20 the verse यानि कानि च मित्राणि कर्तव्यानि शतानि च proves by its very language to be borrowed from some ancient epic poet.

c.) Kathâs. 27, 208 इत्थं क्रियासु निवसन्त्यपि यासु तासु। पुंसां श्रियः प्रबलसत्त्वबहिष्कृतासु (in this way fortune dwells in *any* action, done by men, when carried out with vigorous energy).

288.

3. Pronominal Adverbs.

The pronominal adverbs may be divided into four main classes: 1. those in °त्र, doing duty as locatives, 2. those in °तः, mostly doing duty as ablatives, 3. those

---

1) यः कोऽपि seems to occur much less than the other combinations. The Petr. Dict. gives no instance of it, Anundoram Borooah does not mention it.

Pronominal adverbs. in °दा expressive *of time*, 4. those in °था significative *of manner*. They are derived of the roots क(कु), अ, इ, त, य, अन्य, एक, सर्व etc. and display the same differences of meaning and employment as the pronouns, which they are made from; they are therefore interrogatives or demonstratives or relatives or indefinites.

1. Those in °त्र are: Interr. कुत्र (where?); Dem. अत्र (here), तत्र (there), अमुत्र (yonder); Rel. यत्र (where); Indef. अन्यत्र (elsewhere), एकत्र (1. at one place, 2. somewhere); सर्वत्र (everywhere), etc. To these we must add two of a similar meaning, but made with different suffixes, viz. Interr. क्व = कुत्र and Dem. इह (here).— By putting °चित्, °चन or °अपि to the interrog., one gets the indefinites क्वचित्, कुत्रचित् etc. „somewhere, anywhere;" यत्र क्वचित् (or कुत्रचित् etc.) = „whereso-ever" (**287** *b*).

2. Those in °तः are: Interr. कुतः (whence?); Dem. अतः (hence), इतः (hence), ततः (thence), अमुतः (from yonder); Rel. यतः (whence); Indef. अन्यतः (from some other place), एकतः (from one place, etc.), सर्वतः (from every place), and so on. — By putting °चित्, °चन or °अपि to the interrog., one gets the indefinites कुतश्चित्, कुतोऽपि, कुतश्चन; of course यतः कुतश्चित् etc. = „from whatever place." (**287** *b*).

3. Those in °दा are Interr. कदा (when?); Dem. तदा (then); Rel. यदा (when); Indef. अन्यदा (at some other time), एकदा (once), सर्वदा (always). Besides, the dem. तदानीम् is the emphatic „then," इदानीम् and अधुना = „now." — By putting °चित्, °चन or °अपि to the interrogative, one gets the indefinites कदाचित् etc. = „at some time;" यदा कदाचित् etc. = „whenever." (**287** *b*).

An other set of temporal adverbs are कर्हि (when?), तर्हि, एतर्हि, यर्हि, यर्हि कर्हिचित्. Of these, all but तर्हि are restricted to the archaic dialect and even in the epics they are seldom used, except the phrase न.... कर्हिचित् (nowhere).

4. In °था there are: Dem. तथा (so); Rel. यथा (as); Indef. अन्यथा (otherwise), सर्वथा (in every manner at all events). The Interr. is slightly different, being कथम् (how?). Demonstr. are also एवम्, इत्थम् and इति = „thus, so, in this manner." — By putting °चित्, °चन or °अपि to the interrog., one gets the indefinites कथंचित् etc. = „somehow;" of course यथा कथञ्चित् etc. = „howsoever." (**287** *b*).

Rem. 1. The archaic idiom यः कश्च (**287** R.) is of course also represented in the adverbs of the ancient dialect. Âçv. Gṛhy. 1, 3, 1 यत्र क्व च होष्यन्त्स्यात् (wheresoever he may intend to make oblations), Ait. Br. 2, 23, 7 तस्य यत एव कुतश्च प्राश्नीयात्.

Rem. 2. The adverbial suffixes are not limited to the adverbs, enumerated above. So it is said परत्र »in the world to come" (f. i. Panc. 39), अपरत्र (f. i. R. 3, 11, 25), पूर्वत्र; सदा (always), नित्यदा (f. i. R. 3, 5, 18), etc.

Rem. 3. A negation added to the indefinites क्वचित्, कुतश्चित्, कदाचित्, कथञ्चित् and their synonyms, serves to express »nowhere,"

»from no place," »never," »in no ways," cp. **282**. Kathâs. 3, 57 चिन्ता मे पुत्र यद् भार्या सदृशी नास्ति ते क्वचित् (I am anxious that nowhere there is a fit wife for you to be found); Nala 4, 19 दोषो न भविता तव राजन्कथंचन (at any rate, you will incur no sin, my king); Panc. 34 मया.... कदापि चिर्भटिका न भक्षिता (I never have eaten cucumbers); ibid. 149 न मया तव हस्तलग्नया क्वचिदपि लब्धं सुखम् (since I am depending on you, I have nowhere enjoyed pleasure).

Rem. 4. The idiom यः सः = »whosoever, any" (**287** *c*) has of course its counterpart in the adverbs derived from the roots य and त. Mrcch. X, p. 360 सुरपतिभवनस्था यत्र तत्र स्थिता वा (staying at the king of the gods, or anywhere).

Rem. 5. कथञ्चित् and कथमपि have also got the sense of Lat. *vix*. Panc. 71 चेतनां समासाद्य कथमपि (after having scarcely recovered his spirits). With emphasis, one says even कथंकथमपि. — Similarly कदापि etc. may be used almost synonymous with our »perhaps." Panc. 200 एवमभिहिते श्रद्धेयवचनात्कदापि निवर्तते (if one speaks thus [to the king of the elephants] he will perhaps withdraw by the force of so trustworthy speech).

Rem. 6. अन्यथा may signify »wrongly, falsely." Hit. 95 उद्यतेष्वपि शस्त्रेषु दूतो वदति नान्यथा. Likewise Çâk. I अलमस्माननन्यथा संभाव्य (do not take me for another person, as I am). As to अन्यथा when = »otherwise" see **485** R. 2.

289. *Pronominal adverbs in त्र and तः doing duty as locatives and ablatives.* The adverbs in °त्र and °तः are not restricted to the denoting of space. Their province is the same, as that of the locative and ablative [1]). Such words as अतः and ततः have the value of the ablatives अस्मात्, तस्मात् etc., that is of the ablat. of the stems अ and त in all *P. 5, 3, 7 sqq.*

1) °तः is a common suffix expressive of the abl., and accordingly put also after nouns (**108**). Locatives in °त्रा made of nouns are taught by P. 5, 4, 55 sq. But such forms as ब्राह्मणत्रा, देवत्रा, मर्त्यत्रा are only met with in the archaic dialect. Yet, though obsolete in the classic period of Sanskrit literature, they must have been in common use in the time of Pâṇini.

genders and numbers. Similarly अत्र, तत्र are identical with the locatives अस्मिन्, तस्मिन् etc. For this reason, like the real ablatives and locatives, they express not only space, but also time and circumstances, and refer equally to persons and things. When pointing to a singular, they may even be used as attributes of ablatives and locatives of substantives. The adverbs क्व and इह, though not made with the suffix °त्र, have similarly the functions of the locative of the stems क and इ in all genders and numbers.

Examples: 1. of their not referring to space. Kathâs. 4, 20 वर्षस्य शिष्यवर्गो महानभूत्। तत्रैकः पाणिनिर्नाम जडबुद्धितरोऽभवत् (Varsha had a great crowd of disciples; among them there was —). Mudr. IV, p. 145 किमिदानीं चन्द्रगुप्तः स्वराज्यकार्यधुरामन्यत्र मन्त्रिण्यात्मनि वा समासज्य — (why has Candrag. now put the yoke of government on [the shoulders of] some other minister or his own....?). Çâk. III अयं स ते तिष्ठति संगमोत्सुकः। विशङ्कसे भीरो यतोऽवधीरणाम् (he, from whom you are apprehending a refusal, that man stands here longing to meet you). Kumâras. 2, 55 इतः स दैत्यः प्राप्तश्रीर्नेत एवार्हति क्षयम् (it is from this man [me, cp. 273] that the Daitya has obtained his glory, therefore it is not I, who must kill him). Mudr. II, p. 86 अमात्यनामाङ्कितेयं मुद्रा। तदितो बहुतरेणार्थेन भवन्तममात्यस्तोषयिष्यति (this ring is engraved with the name of the minister; for this reason, he will reward you with more than [is the worth of] this [ring]). Cp. Nala 13, 44.

2. of their qualifying some substantive. — Panc. 273 तत्र वने भ्रमन् (rambling in that forest), ibid. IV, 71 परस्मिन्निह लोके च (in the other world and in this), ibid. p. 146 भिक्षाशेषं च तत्रैव भिक्षापात्रे निधाय (— put the rest of the alms in that very begging-bowl), ibid. 147 एकत्र कुशसंस्तरे द्वावपि प्रसुप्तौ (they slept both on one couch of kuça-grass), Kathâs. 27, 4 प्रसङ्गे कुत्रापि (at some emergency), Daç. 80 अहसं च किञ्चित्प्रमाददत्तशारिके क्वचित्कितवे (and I laughed somehow at some player making a rash move); — Panc. 308 ततः स्थानात्स्वदेशं

गताः (from that place they went to their country), ibid. 286 कुतोऽपि धनिकात्किञ्चिद् द्रव्यमादाय (he took some money from a moneylender), Prabodh. I, p. 6 कुतोऽपि कारणावशात् (by some cause), Daç. 96 मां कदाचिदनर्थादितस्तारयिष्यति (perhaps, it will rescue me from this misadventure).

Rem. 1. It must be mentioned, that in the case of the *anvâdeça* (**274**) अत्र and अतः are enclitics. So neither इह nor इतः can be used. P. 2, 4, 33.

Rem. 2. Instances of the adverbs in °त्र and °तः denoting time, are not rare. So one uses अतः परम् = »afterwards " ततः = »then," क्वचित्..... क्वचित् may be = »sometimes.... sometimes."

290. There is no proper adverbial suffix for the category of the „whither." Nor is it necessary. For the locative being expressive of the aim and scope with the words of *going*, *arriving*, *entering* and the like (**134**), it results, that one says क्व गच्छामि, तत्र प्रतस्थे and so on, as well as नगरे गच्छामि, नगरे प्रतस्थे. On the other hand, since the adverbs in °तः may have the meaning of „on the side of," cp. **103**, कुतः may be „on what side?" इतः „on this side" etc. Moreover they may even signify „in what direction," f. i. ततः = „towards that place."

a) Panc. 154 अचिन्तयं च किं करोमि क्व गच्छामि, ibid. 289 यदि कश्चिदिह व्याघ्रः समायाति (if some tiger come hither), Mhbh. 1, 163, 4 भीमसेनो ययौ तत्र यत्रासौ पुरुषादकः.

b) Mâlav. I, p. 17 इत आस्यताम् (sit down on this side).

c) M. 2, 200 गन्तव्यं वा ततोऽन्यतः (or you must go *from* that place *to* another), Kull. तस्माद्वा देशाद् देशान्तरं गन्तव्यम्; — Çâk. I एतास्तपस्विकन्यकाः.... इत एवाभिवर्तन्ते (— are moving on in this direction).

4. Pronominal Adjectives.

291. Pronominal adjectives. Pronominal adjectives are: I. कियन्त् (how great, *quantus*), Dem. इयन्त्, तावन्त् and एतावन्त् (*tantus*), with the relat. यावन्त् „[as great] as."

II. कीदृश (*qualis?*), Dem. ईदृश, तादृश, एतादृश (*talis*, such), Rel. यादृश „[such] as", Indef. अन्यादृश „like another." They are also made of personal pronouns: मादृश (somebody like me), त्वादृश, भवादृश etc. — All of them may end also in °दृश् and in °दृक्ष.

II. कति (how many?), Rel. यति „[as many] as," Indef. कतिचित् (some, any). Like the kindred Latin *quot*, *aliquot*, they are indeclinable.

The Dem. तति is not used.

292. Observations on the pronominal adjectives.

1. The mutual relations and combinations of the different classes: relatives, demonstratives, etc., are the same as with the pronouns. In this way it may f. i. be observed, that इयन्त् and ईदृश are to तावन्त् and तादृश, what अयम् is to स; that यावन्त् and यादृश require an apodosis with तावन्त् and तादृश; that such a combination as यादृश-स्तादृशः = »of whatever quality" (Panc. I, 420 उपदेशो न दातव्यो यादृशे तादृशे जने); that यति कतिचित् = »however many," etc.

2. Those of Group I may be the former member of compounds in °दूरम्, °चिरम्, °वारम् and the like. F. i. कियद्दूरम् »how far?," कियच्चिरम् »how long?," कियद्वारम् »how many times?" Bhoj. 28 राजा कियद्वारं मम मनोरथमपूरयत्, Panc. 63 कियद्दूरे स जलाशयः, Kathâs. 13, 137 इयच्चिरं मया धर्मो न ज्ञातः.... अयम् (for so long a time I did not know this duty), Panc. 56 कियन्मात्रास्त्वेते तव पितुः शत्रवः (but how insignificant are these enemies of your father).

3. Instances of कति, कियान् and its adverb कियत् used as indefinites [281] are now and then met with. Panc. 211 कति व्यापादयति कति वा ताडयति (he kills some of them, some others he wounds). — Note the compound कतिपय = »several, sundry."

Chapt. III. On nouns of number.

293. As Sanskrit grammars not only teach, which are the different nouns of number for the unities, decads

Expressing nouns of number by various combinations

etc., but also how to make the interjacent ones (see f. i. WHITNEY § 476 and 477), this point may be passed over here. It will suffice to give some instances of the most usual idioms for expressing numbers higher than 100. So Varâh. Brh. 11, 5 शतमेकाधिकम् = 101, Ch. Up. 3, 16, 7 षोडशं वर्षशतम् »116 years" [liter. a hundred of years, determined by sixteen]. — Of addition, as f. i. पञ्च दश च = पञ्चदश, instances are found very often, especially in poetry. — Expressing numbers by multiplication is not rare, either by saying f. i. द्विः पञ्च instead of दश, or by using the type तिस्रो ऽशीतयः = 240 [lit. three eighties], cp. **295**. Mhbh. 1, 32, 24 नवत्या नवतीर्मुखानां कृत्वा (having made 8100 mouths) we have an instance of multiplication expressed by the instrumental of the multiplicator.

Cp. P. 5, 2, 45.

Rem. 1. A very singular manner of denoting numbers between 200 and 1000, mentioned by WHITNEY § 480, is met with now and then in the dialect of the liturgical books and in epic poetry. Çânkh. Br. 3, 2 त्रीणि षष्टिशतानि संवत्सरस्याह्नाम्, the meaning of which is »360 is the number of the days of a year," not, as one would infer from the very form, 3 × 160. Çânkh. Çr. 16, 8, 9 द्वे अशीतिशते = 280. So R. 2, 39, 36 त्रयः शतशतार्धा मातरः are not = 3 × 150, but = 350, cp. ibid. 2, 34, 13, where the same number is thus expressed: अर्धसप्तशताः = half-seven hundreds, that is $3\frac{1}{2} \times 100$.

Rem. 2. In the ancient dialect cardinal nouns of number show in some degree a tendency to become indeclinable words. See WHITNEY § 486 *c*), who gives instances from vaidik works. But classic Sanskrit disapproved that loss of flexion and checked it [1]).

294. How the nouns of number are construed.

From 1—19 the cardinal nouns of number are adjectives, but 20 and the rest are properly substantives. So विंशतिः does not signify „twenty" fr. *vingt*, but „a number of twenty," fr. *une vingtaine*. For this reason, विंशतिः and the rest, शतम्, सहस्रम् etc. are not only

1) As a rest of it we may consider, that M. 8, 268 and Kathâs. 44, 77 the nom. पञ्चाशत् does duty of an accusative.

singulars having a gender of their own, but they are also construed with the genitive. Yet, this construction is not used exclusively. By a false analogy side by side with the regular construction, as त्रिंशतिः पुराणाम्, शतं पुराणाम्, one says also त्रिंशतिः पुराणि, शतं पुराणि, instr. विंशत्या पुराणाम् or पुरैः, शतेन पुराणाम् or पुरैः, etc. The same applies of course to the compounds in °विंशतिः, °शतम् etc., expressive of the interjacent numbers. — It is a matter of course, that instead of using the genitive, it is allowed to compound the substantive with the noun of number.

Examples: 1. *a*) of a genitive depending on the noun of number: Varâh. Bṛh. 54, 75 विंशत्या पुरुषाणाम् (by 20 men); Ragh. 3, 69 इति क्षितीशो नवतिं नवाधिकां महाक्रतूनां.... ततान (thus the king performed 99 great sacrifices); R. 2, 54, 31 शरदां शतम्; Mhbh. 14, 88, 35 यूपेषु नियता चासीत्पशूनां त्रिशती तथा (300 animals were then fastened to the sacrificial piles); Kathâs. 18, 124 ददौ.... विदूषकाय सहस्रं ग्रामाणाम्; Daç. 142 सुभटानामनेकसहस्रमस्त्येव. — *b*) of compounding: Râj. 1, 311 स वर्षसप्ततिं भुक्त्वा भुवम् (after having reigned seventy years), M. 8, 237 धनुःशतम् (a hundred bow-lengths), Kathâs. 44, 77 उष्ट्रपञ्चशती (500 camels).

2. of विंशति etc. concording in case with their substantives. — R. 3, 14, 10 प्रजापतेस्तु दक्षस्य बभूवुः.... षष्टिर्दुहितरः, Gaut. 8, 8 चत्वारिंशता संस्कारैः संस्कृतः (purified by 40 sacraments), M. 3, 40 जीवन्ति शतं समाः, ibid. 4, 87 याति.... नरकानेकविंशतिम्, Kathâs. 10, 39 वयं दैत्यपतेर्बलेः पौत्र्यो दशशतम् (we are 1000 granddaughters of the chief of Daityas, Bali); Mhbh. 1, 16, 8 वव्रे कद्रूः सुतान्नागान्सहस्रं तुल्यवर्चसः.

Higher numbers, as अयुतम्, लक्षम्, कोटिः, are substantives, and always construed with the genitive of the object numbered. R. 1, 53, 21 ददाम्येकां गवां कोटिम् (I give a crore of cows); Panc. I, 251 न गजानां सहस्रेण न च लक्षेण वाजिनाम्। यत्कृत्यं साध्यते राज्ञां दुर्गेणैकेन सिध्यति (designs of kings, that do not succeed by a thousand elephants nor by a hundred thousand horse, are successful by one stronghold).

Rem. 1. The double construction of विंशति etc. is as old as the Ṛgveda. Cp. f. i. Ṛgv. 2, 18, 5 चत्वारिंशता हरिभिः with Ṛgv. 5, 18, 5 ये मे पञ्चाशतं ददुरश्वानाम्.

Rem. 2. In epic poetry one meets occasionally with a plural of the decads instead of the singular. Nala 26, 2 पञ्चाशद्भिर्हयैः (with fifty horses) instead of पञ्चाशता हयैः.

On the other hand, a singular of the substantive construed with शत and सहस्र occurs now and then, as Hariv. 1823 सहस्रेण बाहुणा [instead of बाहुभिः or बाहूनाम्], Bhâg. Pur. 4, 29, 24 वर्षं शतम् [1]).

295. Multiples of **विंशति** and the rest are denoted by putting them in the plural. R. 2, 31, 22 कौसल्या बिभृयादार्या सहस्रान्मद्विधानपि (the princess Kausalyâ might entertain even thousands of men such as I am) [2]); R 3, 53, 24 राक्षसा निहता येन सहस्राणि चतुर्दश (by whom fourteen thousand Râxasas have been killed); M. 11, 221 पिण्डानां तिस्रो ऽशीतीः.... मासेनाश्नन् (eating in a month 3 × 80 balls); Mhbh. 13, 103, 14 गृष्टीनां शतानि [3]); — Panc. 253 प्रयत्नशतैरपि (even by hundreds of endeavours); Mhbh. 9, 8, 41 दश चाश्वसहस्राणि (and ten thousand horse); Kathâs. 35, 96 नव काञ्चनकोटीश्च विप्रेभ्यः प्रतिपाद्य सः.... तपस्तेपे.

296. Numbers, given approximately, are expressed by such compounds as **आसन्नविंशाः** (nearly twenty), **अदूरत्रिंशाः** (not far from thirty), **उपदशाः** (almost ten), **अधिकचत्वारिंशाः** (more than forty). P. 2, 2, 25.

»Two or three" is द्वित्राणि, »three or four" त्रिचतुराणि, »five or six" पञ्चषाः. Comp. Daç. 94 the compound adverb द्वित्रिचतुरम् »twice, three-, four times."

---

1) Another singular idiom occurs R. 1, 18, 8 ऋतूनां षट् समत्ययुः (the six seasons passed), as if षट् meant »a hexad," not »six." Cp. *Verz. der Berliner Sanskrithandschriften*, n°. 834.

2) सहस्र is masc. or neuter. See the gaṇa अर्धर्चादि on P. 2, 4, 31.

3) An irregular plural is Kâm. 15, 11 तुरङ्गमानां परिकल्पितानामेको गजः षष्टिशतानि हन्ति instead of either षष्टिशतम् or षष्टिं शतानि.

297. Note the use of the words द्वयम् and त्रयम्, or द्वितयम् and त्रितयम् = »couple" and »triad;" »tetrad" is चतुष्टयम्. They are often the last members of compounds. M. 2, 76 वेदत्रयम् (the three Vedas), Utt. III, p. 37 ततः प्रविशति नद्योद्वयं तमसा मरला च.

298. *अपि after cardinals and सर्व.* Putting अपि after a cardinal expresses the completeness of the number. So द्वावपि „both of them," त्रयोऽपि „all three of them." One says even सर्वेऽपि, सकला अपि etc. = »all of them." Bhoj. 91 बहुभिः कपिभिर्जम्बूफलानि सर्वाण्यपि चालितानि.

299. *Nouns of number, being members of compounds.* Cardinals may often be the latter members of compounds, see **294** and **296**.

When former members, they may make up with their latter members the so-called **dvigus**. This term is applied to two different kinds of compounds, viz. 1. the collective compounds, made up of a cardinal + a noun subst., and employed in a collective sense; they must be of the neuter gender, as चतुष्पथम् (juncture of four roads), but themes in °अ may be feminines in °ई as well as neuters in °अम्, as त्रिलोकम् or त्रिलोकी (the three worlds); 2 compound adjectives, which rank with the bahuvrîhis, but the notion inherent to which is not that of „possession," but some other. So the word द्विगु itself, meaning „bought for [having the value of] two cows." Ait. Br. 1, 1, 6 एकादशकपालः पुरोडाशः (a cake *dressed on* eight plates).

P. 2, 1, 23

P. 2, 1, 52.

Beside this special use, the cardinals may be parts of the general tatpurushas and bahuvrîhis, especially the latter. Such bahuvrîhis as दशास्यः (having ten faces), विंशतिबाहुः (with twenty arms), are, in practice, by far more frequent than the adjectival dvigus. Yâjñ. 2, 125 चतुस्त्रिद्व्येकभागाः स्युर्वर्णशो ब्राह्मणात्मजाः (the sons of a brahman *own* according to the caste [of their mother] four, three, two and one portions), Pat. I, p. 62 त्रिपदोऽयं बहुव्रीहिः (this bahuvrîhi *is of* three elements).

300. Ordinal nouns of number, when latter members of a bahuvrîhi, are of course used as substantives (cp. **224** R. 1). So R. 2, 40, 17 सीतातृतीयानारूढान्दृष्ट्वा (after seeing them mounted, having Sîtâ *as the third*, that is: them two with Sîtâ). — Note the phrase आत्मतृतीयः (himself with two others), आत्मपञ्चमः (himself with four others) and the like, cp. Greek *αὐτὸς τρίτος (πέμπτος)*. An instance of the same phrase, but in analytic form, may be Mahâv. IV, p. 74 आत्मना तृतीयेन गन्तव्यमित्यम्बाया आदेशः. — As to °द्वितीय almost = »with" cp. **58** R.

301. Fractions, how expressed. **Fractions** are expressed, as with us, by ordinal numbers, *either* accompanied by some word meaning »part," as in the proverbial phrase कलां नार्हति षोडशीम् (see f. i. Panc. II, 61, M. 2, 86), Ragh. 2, 66 उपभोक्तुं षष्ठांशमुर्व्याः (to enjoy the sixth part of the earth), *or* put alone, when substantives of the neuter gender M 8, 398 ततो विंशं नृपो हरेत् (the king must take the twentieth part of it).

Moreover, they may be denoted also by compounds made up of a cardinal number + such a word as भाग, अंश etc. M. 8, 140 अशीतिभागं गृह्णीयात् (he may take $^1/_{80}$); ibid. 304 धर्मषड्भागः (a sixth part of the virtue); Kumâras. 5, 57 त्रिभागशेषासु निशासु (when but a third part of the night is left); Varâh. Brh. 53, 25 पञ्चांशः = $\frac{1}{5}$ [1]).

Very common are अर्धम् = $\frac{1}{2}$ and पादः = $\frac{1}{4}$. They are substantives and accordingly construed with a genitive, but often also compounded. Note such turns as Bhoj. 48 सपादशतं गजेन्द्राः (125 tall

1) This mode of designating fractions is however not free from ambiguousness, as त्रिभाग may denote also »three parts." See Mallin. on Kumâras. 5, 57. Nor are compounds, beginning with अर्ध° always exempt from it. So f. i. अर्धशतम् may be = half a hundred that is 50, or = a hundred + half of it, that is 150. R, 2. 34, 13 अर्धसप्तशताः: is explained in the Petr Dict., as being 750, but Gorresio is right in accepting it = 350.

elephants, lit. a hundred + a fourth of it), R. 2, 39, 36 अर्धसप्तशताः प्रमदाः = half seven-hundred women, that is 350. Râj. 1, 286 तत्सूनुस्त्रिंशतं सार्धां वर्षाणामन्वशान्महीम् (— reigned 45 years —). Such numbers as $1\frac{1}{2}$, $2\frac{1}{2}$ etc. are signified by the compounds अर्धद्वितीय, अर्धतृतीय etc., that are adjectives and bahuvrîhis, literally meaning »the second, third etc. being [but] half" [1]). M. 4, 95 युक्तश्छन्दांस्यधीयीत मासान्विप्रो ऽर्धपञ्चमान् (for $4\frac{1}{2}$ month a brahman must study the vedic texts). »One and a half" is also अध्यर्धम् [literally = »with a half more"], as अध्यर्धशतम् = 150.

Rem. How the interest of money is denoted, may appear from this passage of Manu (8, 142): द्विकं त्रिकं चतुष्कं च पञ्चकं च शतं समम्। मासस्य वृद्धिं गृह्णीयाद्वर्णानामनुपूर्वशः (he may take 2, 3, 4 and $5^0/_0$ a month according to the caste).

302. Other remarks. By being repeated, cardinals or ordinals acquire a distributive meaning, see **252**, 3°. Panc. 194 त्रिभिस्त्रिभिर्गुप्तचरैः = *per ternos speculatores*, Vâr. Yog. 2, 35 पञ्चमे पञ्चमे ऽह्नि (every fifth day). The same duty may be done by adverbs in °शः, especially by बहुशः, शतशः, सहस्रशः »by hundreds, by thousands," also »in hundred, thousand ways, manifold", गणशः (by crowds), f. i. Çat. Br. 14, 4, 2, 24, etc.

The proper employment of the adverbs in °धा is to indicate a real division of a whole into so and so many parts. M. 7, 173 द्विधा बलं कृत्वा (divided his forces in two parts), Kathâs. 106, 133 तदा ते शतधा मूर्धा विदलिष्यति (— into a hundred pieces).

Our adjectives in —*fold*, etc. are represented in Sanskrit by compounds in °गुण — see the dictionary — as द्विगुण (twofold, double), त्रिगुण, चतुर्गुण, सहस्रगुण. The standard of comparison is here of course put in the ablative, cp. **106** R. 2.

---

1) On this subject see the disputation of Patanjali I, p. 426 who, as is often the case, rather obscures than illustrates the subject which he treats.

SECTION IV.

SYNTAX OF THE VERBS.

CHAPT. I. General remarks Kinds of verbs. Auxiliaries. Periphrase of verbs.

303. Syntax of the verb. The verbal flection, which plays a prominent part in books on Sanskrit Grammar, has not that paramount character in Sanskrit Syntax, at least within the limits of the classic dialect. In days of old, the full value and the different properties of the rich store of the various verbal forms were generally much better understood and more skilfully displayed in literature, than in and after the classic period. The history of the syntax of the Sanskrit verb is a history of decay. Some verbal forms get wholly out of use, others become rare or are no more employed in their proper way. In this manner the conjunctive mood (लेट्) has been lost between the Vedic Period and Pâṇini, and in post-Pâṇinean times the differences between the past tenses are disappearing, and upon the whole the tendency of substituting participles and verbal nouns for the finite verb — see **9**; **14**, 1°; **234** — is increasing. Similarly the faculty of expressing by means of mere flection, not only tenses, moods and voices, but also newly framed verbs: causatives, desideratives, intensives, denominatives, has been much impaired in practice, though it has never ceased to be recognised by theory. In fact, it is only the causatives that have retained their old elasticity and are still made of any verbal root, but the desideratives and denominatives are as a rule employed within a little circle of forms often recurring, and the intensives have almost fallen out of use.

304. Causatives. The **causatives** are expressive of such actions, whose subject is not the agent, but he at whose prompting the agent acts, as देवदत्तः कटं कारयति (N. N. gets the mat made). They are much used both in the active and in the passive voice. Their special construction has been dealt with in full (**49**–**51**). P. 3, 1, 26.

On the middle voice of causatives see **318**, espec. c.).

Rem. Occasionally the causatives are used without a causative meaning, as if they were primitives [1]). R. 1, 5, 9 पुरीमावासयामास (he inhabited the town); Prabodh. II, p. 43 वृत्रमघातयत्सुरपतिः; here अघातयत् is quite synonymous with अहन्.

Panc. 168 किं मामुपालम्भयसि = उपालभसे, ibid. 257 भो मित्र किमद्य चिरवेलायां समायातो ऽसि। कस्मात्साह्लादं नालापयसि [= नालपसि]. Thus often in the prâkṛts. Sometimes the primitive and its causative are used promiscuously, as धरति and धारयति, both »to bear." Sometimes there is some idiomatic difference, as in the phrase राज्यं कारयति (to exercise the royal power), here the primitive is not used. Sometimes the primitive having got obsolete, the causative has been substituted for it, as विवाहयति (to wed) instead of the archaic विवहते; of which primitive it is only the participle व्यूढ that is used in the classic dialect. In special cases refer to a dictionary.

305. Desideratives. The **desideratives** are expressive of the „wish of doing" the action, which is denoted by the verbal root: चिकीर्षति = कर्तुमिच्छति (he wishes to do), लिप्सते (he wishes to obtain). Sometimes they simply denote the „being about:" पिपतिषति फलम् (the fruit is about to fall). It is stated in express terms by native grammarians, P. 3, 1, 7.

1) This employment of the causatives is termed by vernacular grammarians स्वार्थे णिच्.

that the employment of the desideratives is optional [1]) whereas the causatives cannot be periphrased. Accordingly, desideratives are less frequent in literature than causatives. They are not only met with when being finite verbs and participles, but also their derivatives in ॰आ (subst.) and ॰उ (adj.), which may be made from any desiderative, as **चिकीर्षा** (the wish of doing), **चिकीर्षु** (wishing to do).

Examples: Daç. 90 इयमर्थनिरपेक्षा गुणेभ्य एव स्वं यौवनं विचिक्रीषते कुलस्त्रीवृत्तमेवानुतिष्ठासति (she does not care for wealth, it is for virtues alone that she wishes to sell her charms and she is desirous of behaving herself like a respectable lady), ibid. 25 मदीयसहचरगणेन जिघांस्यमानं भूसुरमेकमवलोक्य (as I perceived some brahman, whom the crowd of my attendants were about to kill), Kathâs. 29, 157 राजा ... मुमूर्षुर्व्याधितः (the king being about to die of illness).

306. Intensives. The **intensives** are not frequent in literature. In the brâhmaṇas and in the great epic poems they are more to be met with than in younger texts. The participles of them seem to be more employed than the finite verbs.

Examples: Mhbh. 1, 90, 4 नरकं ते पतन्ति लालप्यमानाः, R. 2, 95, 10 पोप्लूयमानानपरान्पश्य. Kathâs. 81, 17 the glow of the sun at the hottest part of the day is thus described एष हि संप्रति। देदीप्यते स्फुरदूष्मशिखाजालो ऽह्नांपतिः. In Panc. V, p. 321 the ram, that flees into the stable, after having been driven away by the cook with a blazing stick, is called जाज्वल्यमानशरीरः.

307. Denominatives. Various classes of **denominatives** are explained by Pâṇini (3, 1, 8—21; 25; 27—30). Among these, some verbs are very common in literature, as आकर्णयति (to hear), मिश्रयति (to mix), शब्दायते (to cry), but they have nothing remarkable from a syntactic point of view, since the speaker uses them ready made and may use them even

---

1) P. 3, 1, 7 धातोः कर्मणः समानकर्तृकादिच्छायां वा sc. सन्, to be understood from s. 5. But in P. 3, 1, 26, which sûtra teaches the form and employment of the causatives, the particle of optionality is wanting.

without being aware of their etymology. The denominatives which concern us here, are those which one can frame by one's self, if wanted, such as पुत्रीयति intr. (he wishes a son), पुत्रीयति trans. (he treats as a son), श्येनायते काकः (the crow behaves as if he were a falcon) and the like. Examples of them are occasionally met with in literature. Panc. I, vs. 5 इह लोके हि धनिनां परोऽपि स्वजनायते। स्वजनोऽपि दरिद्राणां सर्वदा दुर्जनायते (here on earth even non-relatives behave towards the wealthy, as if they were their kinsmen, but to the poor even their own family are rather bad), Kâd. I, p. 30 सर्वमेव देवीभिः स्वयं करतलोपनीयमानममृतायते (everything which is given [to me] by the queen herself in her own hand, is as ambrosia), Bhoj. 61 सोमनाथेन त्वद्गृहभिक्षुणाद्य मयि कल्पद्रुमायितम् (Somanâtha..... has become a cornucopiae to me).

P. 3, 1, 12.

Inchoatives and Factitives.

Some of those in °आयते convey the notion of coming into some state out of another quite opposite, as भृशायते (to become frequent [after having been infrequent], दुर्मनायते (to grow sorry), शीघ्रायते, मन्दायते. But the number of these *inchoatives* is limited, see Kâç. on P. 3, 1, 12. — Cp. 308.

308. **Inchoatives** may be made of any noun, by compounding it in a special manner with the verb भू (Whitney § 1094), as भृशीभवति (to become frequent), शुक्लीभवति (to become white). The same compounds, when made up with the verb कृ, signify „to bring something into a state, the reverse of that, in which it was before[1])" as शुक्लीकरोति (to make white), कृष्णीकरोति (to make black). These inchoatives are very common. Some of them have got some special meaning, as स्वीकृ (to get possession of), अङ्गीकृ (to allow), क्रोडीकृ (to embrace) see f. i. Nâgân. IV, p. 62.

P. 5, 4, 50.

P. 7, 4, 26, 2[illegible] and 3[illegible]

1) Kâç. on P. 5, 4, 50 अशुक्लः शुक्लः संपद्यते शुक्लीभवति। तं करोति शुक्लीकरोति।

Examples: Daç. 59 सकलमेव कन्यान्तःपुरमाकुलीबभूव, Çâk. II कृत्ययोर्भिन्नदेशत्वाद् द्वैधीभवति मे मनः; — Prabodh. II, p. 42 Krodha says अन्धीकरोमि भुवनं बधिरीकरोमि (I make the world blind and deaf), Mrcch. VIII, p. 256 दुष्करं विषमौषधीकर्तुम् (it is difficult to change poison into medecine).

Rem. Pânini allows even inchoatives, made with the verb अस्ति. From the examples given by Kâç. it is likely, they do exist only in the optative: शुक्लीस्यात्. As far as I know, instances are not found in literature.

309. Another mode of making inchoatives is putting the suffix °सात् to the noun and adding भवति, resp. करोति. This class is, however, limited to substantives, for the suffix °सात् expresses the complete transition of one thing into another, as अग्निसाद्भवति (it vanishes in fire), भस्मसात्करोति (he lays in ashes). According to **308** one may say likewise अग्नीभवति, अग्नीकरोति, अग्नीस्यात्, etc. — Mhbh. 1, 33, 7 स तूर्णं भस्मसाद्भवेत्, Kathâs. 5, 100 राज्ञा हतं निशम्य त्वामुपकोशाग्निसाद्वपुः। अकरोत्. P. 5, 4, 52

Rem. 1. In the case of partial transformation one likewise uses °सात् करोति, भवति and also °सात् संपद्यते f. i. अस्यां सेनायामुत्पातेन सर्वं शस्त्रमग्निसात्संपद्यते (in this army all weapons become fiery by a miracle). See Kâç. on P. 5, 4, 53. P. 5, 4, 53.

Rem. 2. The same idioms °सात् + करोति, भवति, संपद्यते may also signify »to make —, resp. to become the property of:" राजसाद् भवति (संपद्यते) »it becomes the king's." Kathâs. 38, 157 ब्राह्मणसात्कृत वसतिं स्वाम् (she bestowed her estate on the brahmans), Panc. I, 224 परसात्कृता [दुहिता] (given into marriage). P. 5, 4, 54.

Rem. 3. Panc. 45 °सात् is construed with the verb नी. It is written there [देवा] मां भस्मसान्नयन्तु.

309*. The upasarga प्र° prefixed to the verb has sometimes the power of denoting the beginning of the action. Kâç. on P. 1, 2, 21 प्रद्योतितः or प्रद्युतितः (he commenced to shine), Panc. I, 195 हसन्तं प्रहसन्त्येता रुदन्तं प्ररुदन्त्यपि (if he laughs, they begin to smile at him, if he weeps, they shed tears).

310. Periphrase of verbs by means of a general verb *to do* with an object denoting the special action meant, is not uncommon. It is chiefly कृ that is used for this purpose. So कथां करोति = कथयति, नादं करोति = नदति, अध्ययनं करोति = अधीते, प्रसाधनं करोति (to make one's toilet). In the same way the verbs, expressive of *being*, *becoming* etc. are employed for representing nominal predicates. Of the kind are भवति, अस्ति, वर्तते, तिष्ठति, संपद्यते and the like, cp. **3** and **4**. It is proper to call them **auxiliaries**. But the same appellation should be shared by कृ which, in reality, is the causative of the former ones: ग्रन्थः शिथिलो भवति —, संपद्यते (the knot is —, gets loose), ग्रन्थं शिथिलं करोति (he loosens the knot).

Examples: 1. of भू and its synonyms. Çâk. I एष मृगो विप्रकृष्टः संवृत्तः (this deer has got out of reach), Panc. 51 किमेवं त्वमकस्माद्विचेतनः संजातः (why did you swoon thus on a sudden?), Nala 9, 19 त इमे शकुना भूत्वा वासोऽप्यपहरन्ति मे (they, having turned birds, bereave me even of my garment).

2. of कृ. — Çâk. I कथमिदानीमात्मानं निवेदयामि कथं वात्मनः परिहारं करोमि (— or shall I conceal myself?), R. 3, 25, 25 आर्तस्वरं चक्रुः.... निशाचराः, Kumâras. 1, 48 कुर्युर्वालप्रियत्वं शिथिलं चमर्यः (the female yaks would abate of their pride on account of their tails), ibid. 4, 41 अभिलाषमुदीरितेन्द्रियः स्वसुतायामकरोत्प्रजापतिः, Panc. 58 Vishnu says कौलिकशरीरे प्रवेशं करिष्यामि [= प्रवेक्ष्यामि]. Kathâs. 27, 160 आनाययत्स तौ पुरुषौ..... बद्धौ चकार च [= बन्धयामास च]. Çank. on Ch. Up. p. 71 explains **वदामः** by वादं कुर्मः. And so on.

Rem. Other verbs of similar, though less frequent and more limited employment, are ददाति, दधाति, वहति, बध्नाति. One says कर्णं दा »to listen," हस्ततालं दा »to clap hands," अर्गलं दा »to bolt the door;" वृत्तिं वह् »to behave" (cp. R. 2, 12, 8) and the like. Vikr. II, p. 38 नोपवनलतासु..... चक्षुर्बध्नाति धृतिम् ([your] eye does not rest on the creepers in the garden); Mhbh. 1, 74, 101 कपटं न वोढुं त्वमि-

हार्हसि (you ought not to use deceit); Hariv. 531 नारायणो दधे निद्रां ब्राह्मीं वर्षसहस्रकम् (Nar. was asleep —), Ragh. 2, 7 राजलक्ष्मीं दधानः; Mudr. IV, p. 137 अमात्यराक्षसश्चाणाक्ये बद्धवैरः (R. is at enmity with C.); Daç. 19 महदाश्चर्यं बिभ्राणः (being much astonished). And so on.

311. *अस्मि and its employment.* The verb substantive has been dealt with in the opening of this book (2 and 3). Here some remarks may be added:

1. The negation put to भवति or अस्ति may signify »not to exist at all, to be lost or dead." Mudr. VI, p. 197 येषां प्रसादादिदमासीत्त एव न सन्ति (those, by whose favor I enjoyed all that glory, are now dead); R. 3, 31, 31 सीतया रहितो रामो न..... भविष्यति. Even the mere negation without verb may have this meaning. R. 3, 41, 19 Mârîca dissuades Râvaṇa from carrying off Sîtâ, saying आनयिष्यसि चेत्सीतामाश्रमात्सहितो मया। नैव त्वमपि नाहं वै नैव लङ्का न राक्षसाः.

2. अस्ति, the 3d pers. of the present, may be used almost as a particle in the beginning of tales and the like. 1) It is then the very first word. Kathâs. 1, 27 Çiva begins to tell a story: अस्ति मामीक्षितुं पूर्वं ब्रह्मा नारायणस्तथा..... हिमवत्पादमूलमवापतुः, here अस्ति may be rendered by »well." 2) Sometimes it has the force of »it happens that," as Pat. I, p. 48 अस्ति पुनः क्वचिदन्यत्राप्यपवादे प्रतिषिद्ध उत्सर्गोऽपि न भवति (but it happens also elsewhere that —), ibid. p. 444 अयमग्निहोत्रशब्दोऽस्त्येव ज्योतिषि वर्तते..... अस्ति हविषि वर्तते.

3. अस्मि, the first person, is now and then used instead of अहम्. See Petr. Dict. I, p. 536 *s. v.* अस् 6). — Daç. 158 सोऽहमस्मि सुहृत्साधारणश्रमणाकारणः सुह्मेषु..... महान्तमुत्सवसमाजमालोकयम्, here अहमस्मि seems to be quite the same as अहम्. Likewise असि and त्वमसि may

---

1) Cp. the *imperatives* अस्तु and भवतु, which are used to express the necessity or suitableness of yielding to some outward circumstance, like Greek εἶεν. But the *present* अस्ति represents, that the request of him who wishes the tale to be told, is actually complied with.

2) The frequent employment of this idiom may be inferred from this. In the *Pancatantra* ed. Jîvânanda there are 71. numbered tales Of them, 45 begin with अस्ति, and though in most of them no finite verb is found in the first sentence -- in 14 cases there is — yet in the great majority, if not in all, अस्ति is not necessary for the understanding. But in all of them, the tale is told at the request of somebody, likewise in the two passages from the Kathâsaritsâgara, quoted by the Petr. Dict., viz. 1, 27 and 22, 56.

be occasionally used = त्वम्, as is mentioned by Vâmana; see *Vâmana's Stilregeln* by Cappeller, *Çabdaçuddhi* s. 12.

312. कृ, भू and अस् are also auxiliaries in another sense, in as far as they help to form periphrastic tenses, as the periphrastic perfect (**333**), the future in °तृ, the durative (**378**), etc. The same may be said of some others as तिष्ठति, वर्तते, आस्ते, when signifying the durative, see **378**.

313. Tmesis. The ancient dialect had the faculty of severing preposition and verb in compound verbs, the so-called **tmesis**[1]). The sacred texts from the mantras up to the sûtras abound in examples. The greatest freedom is of course found in the sanhitâs. Ait. Br. 1, 21, 7 उपाश्विनोः प्रियं धाम गच्छति = अश्विनोः प्रि° धा° उपगच्छति, Ch. Up. 5, 3, 1 कुमारानु त्वाशिषत्पिता = कु° अन्वशिषत्त्वा पिता, Âpast. 1, 25, 10 एते त्रिभिर्वर्षैरप पापं नुदन्ते.

Classic Sanskrit has lost this faculty[2]).

Chapt. II. On voices.

314. The three voices of the Sanskrit verb. The Sanskrit verb has three voices: the active (परस्मैपदम्), the medial (आत्मनेपदम्) and the passive. Of these, the active is formally different from the other two, but the medial and passive voices have many forms in common. The perfect चक्रे may be = „he made [for himself]" as well as „he was made," the future धरिष्यते is either „he will bear [for himself]" or „he will be

---

1) P. 1, 4, 80—82 ते प्राग्धातोः। छन्दसि परेऽपि। व्यवहिताश्च »these [viz. the *upasargas* and *gatis*] are put before the root; but in sacred texts (*chandas*) also behind and separated from it by other words."

2) Perhaps something like a remnant of the antique tmesis may occasionally be met with. In my notes, I find two passages regarding us here: Mudr. I, p. 20 तं गच्छन्त्यनु and R. 2, 9, 28 सोऽर्थो न त्वा क्रमेदति.

borne.[1])" But in the present and its system (present, imperfect, potential or optative, imperative, participle of the present) each voice has a different formal expression, कुरुते etc. serving exclusively for the medium but क्रियते again having exclusively a passive meaning.

315. The participle in °त may have a passive, an intransitive and a transitive meaning, as will be shown afterwards. See **360**.

Passive aorist in °इ and the tenses derived from it.

Apart from the system of the present, it is but one single form, viz. the 3d pers. of the sing. of the aorist — as अकारि, अस्तावि — which exclusively serves for the passive.

Rem. At the outset even this aorist in °इ was a medial tense. See WHITNEY § 845 and DELBRÜCK *Altind. Tempuslehre* p. 53 अचेति, p. 54 अदर्शि etc. Pâṇini teaches an intransitive employment for अपादि (has arisen, — come forth), अदीपि (has shone), अजनि (was born), अबोधि (has awaked), अपूरि (has grown full), अतायि (has extended), अप्यायि (has grown big). In classic literature अपादि is not rare. Kathâs. 42, 134 रक्षो व्यपादि तत् (the giant died).

P. 60.

316. From this 3d person in °इ, however, it is allowed to derive several passive tenses of all such roots, as end in a vowel, moreover of ग्रह्, दृश् and हन्, see WHITNEY § 998 d. So f. i. दृश्यते, the

P.

1) Cp. f. i. Mhbh. 1, 159, 6 the future परित्रास्ये (I shall rescue) with Daç. 96 परित्रास्येते (those two will be rescued) or Mhbh. 1, 188, 18 जगृहे चार्जुनो धनुः (and Arjuna took the bow) with Kathâs. 71, 34 स तया कण्ठे जगृहे (he was embraced by her). It would be an interesting subject-matter for inquiry to draw a statistical account of the common forms of the *âtmanepadam* with respect to their being used with a medial and with a passive meaning. It seems, indeed, that of several verbs these forms, especially the perfect, have the tendency of conveying exclusively a medial meaning, whereas some others seem to be exclusively passives. Before, however, such an account from standard authors will have been made, it would be premature to state something with certainty on this head.

common future âtman. of दृश्, may sometimes have a passive meaning, sometimes it is medial, but the future दर्शिष्यते — derived from अदर्शि — cannot be used except in a passive sense In practice, these tenses of an exclusively passive meaning seem to be very rare. Daç. 132 मन्त्रिणाहमभ्यधायिषि (I was addressed by the minister), ibid. 133 कयापि दिव्याकारया कन्ययोपास्थायिषि.

317. Difference between the active voice and the medial. The difference between the active voice and the medial is for the greater part only a formal one, at least in the classic language. Many verbs are used in the parasmaipadam, but not in the âtmanepadam, and inversely. The special rules, given for this by grammar (P. 1, 3, 17 sqq.), do not belong to Syntax. Even if the same root is employed in both voices, it is not always difference of meaning, that discriminates them; in poetry, for inst., particularly in epic poetry, an other voice than the legitimate one is often admissible for metrical reasons.

Compare the fact, that sometimes the same verb is a parasmaip. in one tense and an âtmanep. in another. So म्रियते (he dies), but the future is मरिष्यति.

318. Nevertheless, the original difference between active and medial is not lost. Not only the grammarians, who have invented the terms *parasmai padam* and *âtmane padam*, but the language itself shows, it is well aware of it. Several verbs may be employed in both voices in this way, that one avails one's self of the medial especially to denote „the fruit of the action being for the subject," f. i. देवदत्तः पचते „N. N. cooks for himself," but पचति, when it is to be told, he cooks for others. Of the causatives the medial voice serves always for that purpose: कटं कारयते „he orders a mat to be made for his own behalf."

P. 1, 3, 72 foll.

P. 1, 3, 74.

Proper sphere of the medium.

Within this proper sphere of the medium some distinctions may be made. The action may be done *a.*) by the subject himself in his own behalf, as Âpast. 1, 25, 10 एते त्रिभिर्वर्षैरप पापं नुदन्ते (they remove the sin from themselves —), *b.*) by order of the subject, likewise for himself; of the kind is the medium of यज्. यजते is said of the patron, who makes the priests officiate for himself and who obtains the fruit of the sacrifice, whereas the officiating priests यजन्ति, *c.*) so that the same person is both subject and object, as Ch. Up. 4, 4, 2 सत्यकाम एव जाबालो ब्रवीथाः (you must name yourself —). Compare with *a.*) such Greek medial verbs as πορίζομαι „I acquire for myself," with *b.*) such as παιδεύομαι τὸν υἱόν „I have my son instructed," with *c.*) such as καλύπτομαι „I wrap myself." Those in *c.*) are mere reflexives.

Instances of medial meaning conveyed by medial forms seem to be found especially in the older texts, yet they are not wanting in the classic literature.

a.) Pâr. 1, 4, 12 a marriage-mantra contains the words परिधत्स्व वासः (put on the garment [yourself]), for परिधेहि would mean »put it on another;" Ait. Br. 2, 11, 1 देवा वै यज्ञमतन्वत [for their own benefit]; Kathâs. 42, 201 अवृणीत कामार्ता तं विद्याधरकन्यका (she chose him [for her husband]) and in this meaning regularly वृणुते, f. i. Kumâras. 6, 78; R. 1, 61, 21 राजपुत्र नयस्व माम् (prince, take me with you); Kathâs. 25, 232 — the king, being presented with a golden lotus, puts it into a silver vase, and says: I would I had another similar lotus to put it into the other silver vase — आस्थापयिष्ये चामुष्मिन्द्वितीये कलशेऽपि तत्; — Pat. I, p. 281 उत्तपते पाणी (he warms his hands), ibid. p. 282 आयच्छते पाणी (he stretches his hands); — Panc. 64 राज्ञोऽन्तःपुरं जलक्रीडां कुरुते (the king's zenana are sporting in the water); Mhbh. 1, 175, 33 सा गौः..... विश्वामित्रस्य तत्सैन्यं व्यद्रावयत सर्वशः.

b.) R. 2, 4, 22 Daçaratha says to his son Râma तत्र पुष्येऽभिषिञ्चस्व

(have yourself anointed —), and so always with this verb;

c.) Âpast. 1, 6, 3 न चैनमभिप्रसारयीत (he shall not stretch out [his feet] towards him); Mhbh. 1, 121, 31 दर्शयस्व नरव्याघ्र (show yourself, gallant prince); R. 1, 75, 3 महद्धनुः। पूरयस्व शरेणैव स्वबलं दर्शयस्व च.

Rem. 1. If a reflexive pronoun be added, one may use the active as well as the medial voice. P. 1, 3, 77.

Rem. 2. P. 1, 3, 68 teaches the use of the medial causatives भीषये and विस्मापये when meaning: »I cause [you] to fear (wonder at) myself," whereas the regular forms भाययति, विस्माययति have no reflexive meaning.

Rem. 3. Reciprocity may be denoted by compound verbs beginning by व्यति°. These must be generally medial verbs. See P. 1, 3, 14—16 and Pat. I, p. 277.

319. *Passive voice.* The **passive voice** is much used in Sanskrit both personally and impersonally, as has been pointed out **7** and **8**. P. 3, 1, 87.

Moreover it serves to signify such intransitive actions as *the rice boils*, *the wood splits* पच्यत ओदनम्। भिद्यते काष्ठम्[1]), whereas „I boil the rice, I split the wood" is expressed by the active voice ओदनं पचामि। काष्ठं भिनद्मि[2]). Pat. II, p. 14 कूलस्य पिपतिषतो लोष्टाः शीर्यन्ते (from a river-bank, which is about to give way, lumps of earth are breaking off), Kumâras. 4, 5 न विदीर्ये (v. a. my heart does not break), Kathâs. 25, 45 वहनं समभज्यत (the vessel burst), Çat. Br. 1, 5, 4, 5 प्र वनस्पतीनां फलानि मुच्यन्ते (the fruits fall down from the trees). Of the kind are दृश्यते (to appear, to seem), उपचीयते (to increase), अपचीयते (to decrease), युज्यते (to suit, to be fit) and the like.

---

1) The passive, when personal, is styled कर्मणि (expressive of the object), when impersonal, भावे (express. of the state), see P. 1, 3, 13; 3, 1, 67. When having an intransitive or reflexive meaning, it is styled कर्मकर्तरि (express. of both subject and object).

2) Yet one likewise says f. i. साधु स्थाली पचति (the pot boils well), cp. Kâç. on P. 3, 1, 87.

Rem. 1. It is not allowed, however, to use that intransitive passive of all verbs. Pâṇini excepts the roots दुह्, स्नु and नम्. One says दुग्धे - not दुह्यते - गौः स्वयमेव, नमते - not नम्यते - दण्डः स्वयमेव »the cow is milking; the stick bends." Patanjali extends the exception to others, especially to all causatives, and mentions a vârttika of the Bhâradvâjîyas which enumerates even a larger list of exceptions. This statement of the Bhâradvâjîyas has been accepted by the Kâçikâ. At all events, this much is certain, that of several verbs the medial voice has also an intrans. meaning. A concurrence of medial and passive is taught by P. 3, 1, 62 and 63 for the aorist of roots ending in a vowel and also of दुह्; with intransitive meaning it may be said अकारि or अकृत, अदोहि and अदुग्ध, f. i. अकारि or अकृत कटः स्वयमेव.

P. 3. 1, 88.

On the other hand, the pure reflexive — **318** *c*) — is occasionally expressed by a passive; especially मुच्यते »to release one's self." R. 3, 69, 39 परिमुच्यस्व राघव.

Rem. 2. Note the idiom तप्यते तपस्तापसः, a passive with etymological object. See f. i. M. 2, 167.

P. 3, 1, 89.

320. Intransitives how expressed.

Intransitives are often expressed also by the verbs of the so-called *fourth* class of conjugation, which chiefly comprises roots with intransitive meaning, as क्रुध्यति, हृष्यति, सिध्यति, भ्रश्यति. For the rest, intransitive meaning is by no means restricted to a special set of forms and may be conveyed by any. So f. i. स्वप् „to sleep" is formally an active स्वपिति, शी „to lie" a medial शेते, मृ „to die" a passive म्रियते.

The difference of accentuation which exists between the verbs of the 4th class and the passives, must not blind us to the incontestable fact of their close connection. At the outset, there is likely to have been one conjugation in °यति °यते with intransitive function, whence both the 4th class and the passive have sprung. Nor is it possible, even in accentuated texts, to draw everywhere with accuracy the boundary-line between them, see Whitney § 761, especially *b.*) and *c.*) and **762**, cp. also the rule of P. 6, 1, 195. — The old language, especially the dialect of the Mahâbhârata, affords many instances of passive forms with the endings of the parasmaipadam, even with passive meaning. See f. i. Mhbh. 1, 24, 15; 38, 13; 51, 9; 102, 23; Nala 20, 31 etc.[1]).

CHAPT. III. **Tenses and moods.**

321. The Sanskrit finite verb comprises the following tenses and moods: 1. the *present* (लट्), 2. the *imperfect* (लङ्), 3. the *perfect* (लिट्), 4. the *aorist* (लुङ्), 5. and 6. the *future* in स्यति (लृट्) and the *periphrastic future* (लुट्), 7. the *imperative* (लोट्), 8. the *potential* or *optative* (लिङ्), 9. the *precative* (लिङाशिषि), 10. the *conditional* (लृङ्). To them we must add for the archaic dialect the *conjunctive* (लेट्), for the classic language the *participles in* °त and °तवन्त्, as far as they do duty for finite verbs. Of these, 1—6 and the said participles constitute that, which we are wónt to call „the indicative mood;" the other moods are represented by 7—10 and by the लेट्.

Vernacular grammar makes no distinction between tenses and moods, which is, indeed, less developed in Sanskrit, than it is in Latin and Greek.[2])

1) P. 3, 1, 90 mentions two roots, which are verbs of the 4th class, parasmaipada, when being used as intransitive-reflexives, whereas they are otherwise conjugated, when transitives. But Pânini expressly states that the eastern grammarians teach so, the passive of them may, therefore, be also employed, f.i. कुष्यति or कुष्यते पादः स्वयमेव (the foot strikes), रज्यति or रज्यते वस्त्रं स्वयमेव (the garment is dying). Utt. V, p. 102 नेत्रे स्वयं रज्यतः.

2) In Pânini's grammar the 10 or 11 tenses and moods form *one* category,

322. Of the tenses, which constitute the indicative mood, the present is represented by *one*, the future by *two*, the past by *four* (aorist, imperfect, perfect, participles). Of the two futures, that in °स्यति is the general exponent of the future. Likewise the aorist and the participles are the general exponents of the past. The other past tenses and the other future have but a limited sphere of employment. We may remark that those limits are quite different from what one would expect judging from the names, by which Sanskrit tenses have been termed by European scholars. Sanskrit imperfect and perfect have nothing in common with their cognominal tenses in Latin or French or Greek, and the difference f. i. between the employment of Skr. लेखितास्मि and लेखिष्यामि can in no way be compared with that which exists between Lat. *scripturus sum* and *scribam*.

Rem. Sanskrit makes no distinction between absolute and relative tenses. Hence, if one wants to denote what *was* about to be done in the past [1]), one employs the same tense which is expressive of what *is* about to be done now, viz. the future. Similarly, the same past tenses, which signify that which *is* accomplished *now*, may serve also for the expression of the action, which *will be* accomplished at some future point of time. Nâgân. III, p. 55 प्रिये गच्छ त्वमात्मनो गृहमहमपि मित्रावसुं दृष्ट्वा त्वरितमागत एव, here the past tense आगतः has the value of the so-called futurum exactum of Latin, *ego advenero*.

For this reason too, the present does also duty for the durative of the past (**327**) and the past tenses are also significative of the remote past (**339**).

---

but do not bear a common appellation. The *Kâtantra* names them विभक्ति, by the same term which is used for the »cases" of the nouns. See Kât. 3, 1, 11—34 with commentary.

1) This was at the outset the duty of the so-called conditional, but in classic Sanskrit this employment having fallen out of use, it is the future that is to express *scripturus eram* as well as *scripturus sum*. Cp. **347** R.

Present. (लट्).

323. The **present tense** is in Sanskrit what it is everywhere, the expression of facts present or represented as such. The notion „present" has of course the utmost elasticity. It applies to any sphere of time of which ourselves are the centre and it may have as small or as great a periphery as possible. Accordingly, facts which are represented as happening always and everywhere are put in the present. It is superfluous to illustrate this by examples.

Present.

324. Further, the present may denote a near past or a near future. P. 3, 3, 131.

Present, denoting a near future.

1. The *present denoting a near future* may be compared with such phrases as: I am going on a journey next week, instead of: I shall go. So कदा भुङ्क्ते = कदा भोक्ष्यते, etc. P. 3, 3, 5 and 6.

Bhoj. 42 यदि न गम्यते श्वो राजसेवका अस्मान्निःसारयन्ति (if we do not go, the king's attendants will turn us out to-morrow), R. 3, 68, 13 क्षिप्रमेव विनश्यति (he will die soon), Panc. 143 धन्योऽहं यद्भवता सह तत्र कालं नयामि (I am happy, I shall pass the time there with you).

In subordinate sentences the present is very often employed in this manner, especially in final and consecutive clauses, as will be shown afterwards.

Rem. 1. Pânini gives a special rule concerning the present denoting the future with यावत् and पुरा. Example of यावत्: Panc. 286 एतौ यत्नेन रक्षणीयौ यावदहं समागच्छामि (— till I come back). As to पुरा, it may be 1. an adverb »erelong." 2. a conjunction = Lat. *priusquam*. The rule holds good for both. Daç. 136 क्षिणोति च पुरा स कृतघ्नो भवन्तम् (and that ungrateful man will erelong kill you); R. 2, 116, 19 पुरा.... शारीरीमुपहिंसां तपस्विषु। दर्शयन्ति हि दुष्टास्ते त्यक्ष्याम P. 3, 3, 4.

इममाश्रमम् (before those wicked beings inflict any corporal injury upon the ascets, we will leave this hermitage).

Rem. 2. Another consequence of its fitness for denoting a near future is exhibited by its doing duty for a conjunctive (**356**).

325. Present denoting a near past. — P. 3, 3, 131.

2. *The present denoting a near past.* It may be said अयमागच्छामि „I arrive" by one, who has just arrived. Utt. I, p. 3 धर्मासनाद्विशति वासगृहं नरेन्द्रः (the king has just retired from his seat of justice to his inner apartments). — Of this kind are the rules given by Pâṇini (3, 2, 120 and 121) for the employment of present and aorist in answers. If one asks »have you made the mat?", the answer may be, when using न, न करोमि or नाकार्षम् »no, I have not," or if an interrogation, »have I not?" Likewise with नु, अहं नु करोमि or, न्वकार्षम्. But with ननु exclusively the present: ननु करोमि »indeed, I have." [1]).

Rem. Inversely, it may happen that a Sanskrit aorist is to be rendered by an English present, see note 1 on page 253 of this book.

236. Historical present. — P. 3, 2, 118 and 119.

Moreover, the present is often used in relating past actions. Then we may call it historical present. Properly it is distinguished by the particle स्म added, but स्म is occasionally wanting. Nala 3, 18 न तास्तं शक्नुवन्ति स्म व्याहर्तुमपि किंचन (they could not utter a single word to him), Kathâs. 1, 33 इति वक्ति स्म पार्वती। प्रत्युवाच ततो भर्गः (thus spoke Pârvatî, and Çiva answered), Panc. 201 a story ends thus: शशकाश्च तद्दिनादारभ्य सुखेन स्वेषु स्थानेषु तिष्ठन्ति स्म (and since that day the hares lived happily in their dwellings); — Kumâras. 3, 13 व्यादिश्यते भूधरतामवेक्ष्य कृष्णेन देहोद्वहनाय शेषः (Çesha has been appointed —).

327. The present is the durative tense *par excellence.*

But the most common employment of the historical present is that of expressing facts when „going on." As Sanskrit imperfect (लङ्) has not the character of a durative, like the imperfect in Latin and French,

1) A vârttika, expounded and agreed to by Patanjali finds fault with this rule of Pâṇini क्रियासमाप्तेर्विवक्षितत्वात्. See Pat. II, p. 122.

अभरम् may be both a synonym of Latin *ferebam*, and of *tuli* [1]). But the present भरामि is by its nature a durative tense, and for this reason it is eminently adapted to signify the durative, even of the past. Of course, स्म may be added in that case (**326**), but it is not necessary and is generally wanting in the body of a narration. Accordingly, भरामि is often = Lat. *ferebam*.

Examples: Panc. 165 a new story begins in this manner अस्ति कस्मिंश्चिदधिष्ठाने सोमिलको नाम कौलिको वसति स्म (*habitabat*)। स च.... पार्थिवोचितानि सदैव वस्त्राण्युत्पादयति (*is vestes conficiebat*)। परं तस्य.... न भोजनाच्छादनाभ्यधिकं कथमप्यर्थमात्रं संपद्यते (*fiebat*); Ch. Up. 1, 2, 13 स ह नैमिषीयानामुद्गाता बभूव (*fuit*)। स ह स्मैभ्यः कामानागायति (*incantabat*); Mhbh. 1, 157, 5 निवेदयन्ति स्म तदा कुन्त्या भैक्षं सदा निशि (at that time they delivered the food begged to Kuntî every night); Pat. I, p. 5 पुराकल्प एतदासीत्। संस्कारोत्तरकालं ब्राह्मणा व्याकरणं स्माधीयते (*discebant*)..... तदद्यत्वे न तथा; Bhoj. 40 तदाप्रभृति न निद्राति नच भुङ्क्ते न केनचिद्वक्ति केवलमुद्विग्नमनाः स्थित्वा दिवानिशं प्रविलपति (from that time he did not sleep or take food or converse with anybody, but with a heavy mind he lamented night and day); Panc. 145 begins the story of some monk, who did inhabit (प्रतिवसति स्म) some monastery, his ordinary life is described by a set of present tenses without स्म (समाचरति.... स्वपिति.... समाज्ञापयति). — A past tense and the present may even be put close together. R. 2, 63, 14 Daçaratha relates to his queen देव्यनूढा त्वमभवो

---

1) In the brâhmanas the present with स्म, according to Delbrück *Altindische Tempuslehre* p. 129, is always = Lat. imperfect, never = Lat. perfect: »Das Präsens mit sma steht im Sinne der Vergangenheit, jedoch — so viel ich sehe — nicht so dass damit ein einmaliges vergangenes Ereigniss bezeichnet würde. Vielmehr drückt das Präsens mit sma dasjenige aus, was sich öfters, besonders was sich gewohnheitsmässig ereignet hat.”

In the classic dialect, however, भरति स्म is both = *ferebat*, and = *tulit*. Plenty of instances may be drawn from classic literature. Only see the examples to P. 3, 2, 118; 119, and Kathâs. 1, 33 quoted **326**.

युवराज्ञो भवाम्यहम् (at the time you were not married and I was heir-apparent).

Rem. Pâṇini especially mentions the freedom of employing the present instead of a past tense with पुरा (formerly, before). So Panc. 202 the crow says कस्मिंश्चिद्वृक्षे पुराहं वसामि. Here the present is used, but the aorist f. i. Kathâs. 25, 74 पुराभूत्सुमहाविप्रः, the imperf. f. i. ibid. 24, 19 अभवत्पुरे..... पुरा राजा and Pat. I, p. 5 quoted above.

Past tenses.

328. *Actual past and historical past.* In defining the employment of the past tenses one must distinguish between such past facts, as have not lost their actuality, and such as have, and therefore belong to history. The historical past may be expressed by any past tense, but the actual past not. In other terms, as a rule, English *he did* and *he had done* may be rendered by Sanskrit aorist, imperfect, perfect or the participle (कृतवान्, कृतमनेन), but English *he has done* only by the aorist or the participle, not by the imperfect or by the perfect.

Historical past expressed by any past tense. I. For expressing the **historical past**, the four past tenses are used almost promiscuously, and the historical present (**326, 327**) may be added to them as a fifth.

Examples: Kathâs. 24, 10 it is told, one asked (अपृच्छत् imperf.), vs. 11 the other replied (अवादीत् aor.), vs. 13 the former asked again (पप्रच्छ perf.). Ibid. vs. 214 (भयान्न ते। यदा तस्याशकन्वक्तुं दूतान्विससृजुस्तदा। ते च.... तमब्रुवन् »as they could not tell it him [themselves], they sent messengers, who told him") is an other instance of aor., perf. and imperf. used promiscuously and without the slightest difference of meaning. Panc. 276 we have this succession of facts: ब्राह्मणो भार्यामभिहितवान् (participle)..... इत्यभिधाय प्रायासीत् (aorist)। अथ तस्यां पुष्पवाटिकायां पङ्गुर्गीतमुद्गिरयति (histor. pres. with durative meaning »was singing)"। तच्छ्रुत्वा तयाभिहितम् (partic.)..... पङ्गुरब्रवीत् (imperf.) and so on. In an other story Panc. 51, we have this succession of facts: a weaver and a cartwright dwelled (प्रतिवसतः स्म) in the same town and lived always together (कालं नयतः). One day a great festival took place (संवृत्तः) and a procession, in the midst of which they beheld (दृष्टवन्तौ) a maiden of great beauty. On seeing her, the weaver fell in love with her and swooned (सहसा भूतले निपपात). His friend the cartwright got him carried home (स्वगृहमानाययत्) and by proper treatment he soon recovered (सचेतनो बभूव). — Upon the whole, there seems to be a tendency to alternate the past tenses in literary compositions.

329. *Imperf. and perfect restricted to the expression of the historical past.* Now, the **imperfect** and the **perfect** are restricted to that sphere of employment. They cannot be used except of such facts as have lost their actuality for the speaker [1]. Both of them are only available for the historical past. They are to be rendered by our past tense, both अकरोत् and चकार being = „he did."

Both of them are equally applied to facts, that have happened but once (Lat. perfectum historicum), and to actions repeated or continuous (Lat. imperfectum). [2]).

330. *Difference between imperfect and perfect.* There is, however, a difference between the perfect and the imperfect. It is taught by Pâṇini in express terms, that *the perfect* (लिट्) *is restricted to such facts as have not been witnessed by the speaker*, and the practice of good authors is generally in accordance with this statement. It is somewhat uncommon to meet with a per- P. 3, 2, 115.

---

1) This is meant by Pâṇini, when he teaches लङ् (and, as it stands under the same adhikâra, also लिट्) to be used अनद्यतने. P. 3, 2, 111.

2) Cp. Kathâs. 24, 214 दूतान्विससृजुस्तदा। ते च तमब्रुवन् = nuntios *miserunt*, iique ei *dixerunt*, with Mhbh. 1, 68, 9, which verse describes the happiness of the subjects of Dushyanta during his reign स्वधर्मै रेमिरे वर्णाः.... आसंश्चैवाकुतोभयाः = hominum ordines suis quisque officiis *delectabantur*, *erantque* ab omni parte tuti.

fect when expressive of an action the speaker has witnessed himself.

Good authors, accordingly, avoid using the perfect tense, if the facts narrated have been witnessed by the speaker. The *Dacakumâracarita* abounds in stories of adventures, told by the very persons who have experienced them; all past tenses are employed promiscuously, only perfects are wanting. But, in the same work, if the author himself is speaking, or if any of his heroes is relating a fable of olden times, the perfects make their appearance side by side with the other past tenses [1]). The same observation may be made with respect to the Kathâsaritsâgara [2]).

Yet, from this one must not infer, that on the other hand the imperfect is *restricted* to the relation of past facts witnessed by the speaker [3]). Even, if Pâṇini had taught

---

1) So there is not a single perfect in the whole story of Apahâravarma, as he relates his own adventures; for the same reason perfects are wanting in the stories of other princes. The sixth ucchvâsa, *Mitraguptacaritam*, has no perfects, while Mitragupta tells all what has happened to himself, but as soon as he is narrating to the giant the four little tales of Dhûminî etc., perfects abound.

2) Exceptions may, however, occasionally be found. Daç. 110 and 111 prince Upahâravarma, when relating his own adventures, says twice रुरोद, while speaking of a woman, who wept before his eyes. R. 3, 67, 20 the vulture Jatâyu informs Râma, how Râvana सीतामादाय वैदेहीमुत्पपात विहायसम्. Kathâs. 6, 43 the clever merchant, who has made his fortune by trade, uses the perfect ददौ, while relating, that each woodcutter gave him two pieces of wood, as he presented them with a fresh draught. Likewise Nâgân. V, p. 77 पपात instead of the aor. of a fall, which the speaker has seen on the same day and with his own eyes. But, I repeat, such deviations are upon the whole very rare, at least in good authors.

3) The term परोक्ष for the sphere of the perfect, is a point of dispute with the commentators. It is asked, what kind of actions may be said to fall under this category, and as the term, when strictly interpreted, signifies »beyond the reach of the eye," it has been deemed necessary to give an additional rule in express terms, that »well-known facts falling within the speaker's sphere of observation are to be put in the imperfect — not in the perfect — even if they have in fact not been

so [1]), such a rule would be in direct opposition to the constant practice of Sanskrit literature up to the Vedas. The imperfect is always and everywhere used both of past facts which are within the compass of the speaker's experience, and of those which are not.

---

witnessed by him." This vârttika seems to be as old as Kâtyâyana, it is expounded by Pat. II, p. 119.

1) It is not quite sure, that he has. Still, when looking closely at Pâṇini's own words about the employment of लङ् and लिट् and at the commentaries and disputes of his scholiasts, we may consider it a tenet of the grammarians, that लङ् is not available within the sphere set apart for लिट्. From 3, 2, 116 हशश्वतोर्लङ् च »with ह and शश्वत् (forsooth) — cp. **397** R. 3 — लङ् may also be used within the sphere of लिट्", cp. s. 115, we can draw no other inference, than even this, that in any other case one would be wrong in using लङ् परोक्षे. But it is possible, that this sûtra 116 did not belong to the original work of Pâṇini. Indeed setting this sûtra apart, the very arrangement of the rules which treat of the suffixes and tenses of the past, would rather induce us to suppose Pâṇini having taught the employment of लङ् both अपरोक्षे and परोक्षे. From 3, 2, 84 up to 123 भूते is adhikâra, the suffixes taught there are accordingly expressive of »the past." Now, from 84—110 this »past" is not specialized and comprises *any past whatever*. With s. 111 the first restriction makes its appearance, it is stated that the imperfect (लङ्) is used अनद्यतने »denoting the not-actual past." From there अनद्यतने remains adhikâra till s. 119, but s. 115 a second restriction is added to the first: the suffixes are not only expressive of the past अनद्यतने but also परोक्षे. Now the question is simply this: Has Pâṇini meant sûtra 111 (employment of लङ्) to be an *exception* to 110 (employment of लुङ् »aorist") and likewise 115 (employment of लिट्) an *exception* to 111 — or is each of these rules to be interpreted separately and considered by itself? According to the former acceptation, the aorist is taught to be *restricted* to past actions that have happened to-day, the imperfect *restricted* to past actions before to-day, but witnessed by the speaker; according to the latter, the aorist is expressive of any past both actual and historical, and the imperfect of any historical past both witnessed and not-witnessed by the speaker. The former acceptation is that of Sanskrit grammarians up to Patanjali and the author of the vârttikas, the latter is in accordance with the practice of Sanskrit literature.

Rem. 1. In putting questions, the difference between perfect and imperfect vanishes, and it seems, also that between those tenses and the aorist. If I rightly understand P. 3, 2, 117, the employment of both perf and imperf. in putting questions is prescribed by Pâṇini, even if the past action be »near in time" आसन्नकाले. Kâç. exemplifies this rule कश्चित्कंचित्पृच्छति। अगच्छद् देवदत्तः। जगाम देवदत्तः. R. 3, 19, 6 Khara asks his sister Çûrpaṇakhâ कोऽयमेवं महावीर्यस्त्वां विरूपां चकार ह (what strong man has disfigured you thus?). Cp. Ch. Up. 4, 14, 2 quoted **345.**

Rem. 2. Another rule of Pâṇini — 3, 3, 135 — forbids the imperfect, the perfect and the present with स्म [1]) in two cases: क्रियाप्रबन्धसामीप्ययोः. According to the gloss of the Kâçikâ *kriyâprabandha* is »uninterrupted action," *sâmîpya* »the time which immediately adjoins the time of the speaker." In these cases the aorist and the participles are stated to be employed, not the other past tenses. Kâç. gives these examples यावज्जीवमन्नमदात् (as long as he lived he distributed food [to the poor]), येयं पौर्णमास्यतिक्रान्तैतस्यामुपाध्यायोऽग्नीनाधित (at the next full moon the teacher worshipped the holy fires). I do not know how far this injunction is confirmed by the evidence furnished by Sanskrit literature. For the rest cp. **341** R.

331. The perfect of the archaic dialect.

P. 3, 2, 105.

At the outset, the perfect had not the restricted function, which it has in the classic dialect. In the old vedic mantras, like the aorist, it may denote every shade of the past, and occasionally it has even the power of a present tense, in the same way as for instance Greek ἕστηκα οἶδα, Latin *memini consuevi*, Gothic *vait mag*, sim. So Rgv. 5, 60, 3 बिभाय »is afraid," ibid. 1, 113, 3 तस्थुः »they stand still" and the other instances to be found in Delbrück *Altindische Tempuslehre* p. 103 sqq.

Perfect, when a present tense.

The classic language has but two perfects, expressive of the present, viz. वेद (he knows) and आह (he says); the latter may also be used of the past. [2]) From the litur-

1) Though not mentioned either by Kâç. or by Patanjali, the लिट् and the लट् स्मे must needs be implied in the prohibition, for the adhikâra अनद्यतने implies them too.

2) My notes contain, however, two other instances. Panc. 246 आजगाम

gical writings — where, for the rest, the employment of the perfect is already confined within the same limits as afterwards, see DELBRÜCK *l. l.* p. 131 — we may adduce moreover ईशे »he rules" (f. i. Ait. Br. 1, 30, 3), जागार »he is awake" Ch. Up. 4, 3, 6 and perhaps some others, see f. i. Ait. Br. 2, 41, 4.

332. From the above it is sufficiently clear, that the 1st and 2d person of the perfect are hardly met with in classic Sanskrit, except of वेद and आह. — For the 1st person, Patanjali is at a loss, how to employ it, unless to relate facts done while being asleep or drunk. [1]) That the 2d person of the plural is not used, is evident from a passage of the commencement of the *Mahâbhâshya;* there it is observed, that such forms as ऊष, तेर, चक्र, पेच exist in theory only, as one does not say क्व ऊष but क्व यूयमुषिता: See Pat. I, p. 8, l. 23; p. 9, l. 11.

333. Periphrastic perfect. There is no syntactical difference between the perfect simple and that, which is made by periphrase with आस, चकार med· चक्रे, and बभूव.

In the brâhmaṇas चकार and चक्रे are almost exclusively used for this purpose. [2]) Nor does Pânini teach other auxiliaries. [3])

---

is used in the sense of Greek ἥκω. The serpent declares to the frogs ततो ऽहं युष्माकं वाहनार्थमाजगाम (by this [viz. the curse of the brahman, whose son he had bitten to death] I have come to you in order to be your carrier). In the Gaurî recension of the Çâkuntala, V, p. 109 of the 2d ed. of Tarkavâgîça (Calc. 1864) Çârngarava says to Dushyanta यन्मिथ: समयादिमां मदीयां दुहितरं भवानुपयेमे तन्मया प्रीतिमता युवयोरनुज्ञातम्. In both instances the perfect is rather expressive of an action finished, than of an action past.

1) The example given is मत्तो — or सुप्तो — ऽहं किल विललाप. — Another case of its employment is in strong denials, as when one asks दक्षिणापथं प्रविष्टोऽसि and the other answers नाहं दक्षिणापथं प्रविवेश. See vârtt. on P. 3, 2, 115 in Patanj. II, p. 120; the instance given there is evidently a quotation from some literary work.

2) In the Aitar. Brâhm. the periphr. perfect with आस is used but once. See the edition of AUFRECHT, p. 429.

3) To interprete P. 3, 1, 40 कृञ:, as if it were a pratyâhâra of कृ + भू + अस्, is, not to mention other objections, too artificial and too subtle,

But even in the epic poems all of them are used, especially आस, which seems also afterwards to be the most frequent, whereas बभूव is the rarest.

334. Aorist. II. The **aorist** (लुङ्) is expressive of any past, either historical or actual; अकार्षम् may be = „I did," and = „I have done." Examples of the historical aorist have been given **328**.

When denoting the actual past, that is such past acts as are so recent as not to have lost their actuality at the time of their being related, the aorist is used side by side with the participles in °तवत् and °त; neither imperf. nor perfect are then available. „I have seen the man" is अद्राक्षं पुरुषम् or दृष्टवानस्मि [not अपश्यम् nor ददर्श].

Examples of the aorist denoting the actual past. Ait. Br. 1, 6, 11 तस्मादाचक्षाणमाहुरद्रागिति। स यद्यदर्शमित्याहाथास्य श्रद्दधति (for this reason, one says to an eye-witness: have you seen it? for if he says »he has," they believe him); R. 2, 89, 5 Bharata has spent the night with Guha, the next morning his host asks him कच्चित्सुखं नदीतीरे ऽवात्सीः काकुत्स्थ शर्वरीम् (have you past the night well?); Mhbh. 1, 167, 23 king Drupada having lost half his kingdom to Drona, goes to some brahman, who may procure him a means for avenging himself, and says द्रोणः पराजैष्ट माम्; Daç. 27: it has been predicted to the brahman Mâtanga that he will soon meet with a prince, now, when he really meets with a prince, he tells him this prediction and adds these words तदादेशानुगुणमेव भवदागमनमभूत् [neither अभवत् nor बभूव are here admissible]; Çâk. VII Mâtali congratulates Dushyanta on finding back his wife with his son, the king replies अभूत्संपादितस्वादुफलो मे मनोरथः (my desire is gone

---

to be true. Pâṇini knew, or at least approved, no other periphrastic perfect, than that which is made with कृ.

into sweet fulfilment); Kathâs. 40, 108 तुभ्यं मया राज्यमदायि (v. a. I have made you king); Panc. 16 the jackal begs permission to appear before the lion, the doorkeeper grants it him with the words यथावादीइवान्[1]).

Rem. In the archaic dialect of the brâhmanas etc. the aorist seems to serve *exclusively* for this actual past[2]). The contrast between the historical tenses and the aorist is so striking there that it cannot possibly be overlooked by anybody who peruses these writings. The most instructive passages are such, as mention the same fact twice, first when told by the author, afterwards when put into the mouth of one of the actors. Then we invariably find the imperfect or the perfect in the historical account, the aorist in the *oratio directa*. Ait. Br. 7, 14, 5 तस्य ह दन्ता जज्ञिरे। तं होवाचाज्ञत वा अस्य दन्ताः..... तस्य ह दन्ताः पेदिरे। तं होवाचापत्स्वत वा अस्य दन्ताः (then he got teeth; then he said to him: »he has, indeed, got teeth".... then his teeth dropped out, then he said to him: »his teeth, have, indeed, dropped out"). Ch. Up. 5, 3 the following story is told: Çvetaketu once came (एयाय) to the meeting of the Pancâlas. To him the xattriya Pravâhaṇa said (उवाच): »has your father instructed you?" (अनु त्वाशिषत्पिता)[3]). The other answered: »yes, Sir." Then Pr. put five questions to him successively, none of which he could solve, and said: »why have you said (अवोचथाः) yourself instructed, as you do not know these things?" Then Çvetaketu, being sad with grief, came (एयाय) to his father and said (उवाच): »why did you say (भगवानब्रवीत्) I

---

1) We may translate here the aorist by a present: »as you say." Cp. Çâk. II, p. 38 ed. Tarkavâgîça सखे तावदेनां न ज्ञानासि येन त्वमेवमवादीः (you do not know her, since you speak thus). Cp. Greek τί ἐγέλασας; »why do you laugh?" and the like.

2) DELBRÜCK *Altind. Tempusl.* p. 128 »Niemals steht der Aorist [in this kind of works] im erzählendem Sinne, wie etwa das Imperf. oder Perf." Yet, Ait. Br. 2, 23, 3 the aor अक्रत is, indeed, used in a historical sense.

3) Such passages as this plainly show, methinks, that the system of the grammarians, according to which »past facts done *on the same day* as they are related" must be put in the aorist, but when done before that day, in the imperfect (resp. perfect), is refuted by the very facts.

have instructed you (अनु त्वाशिशम्), a simple xattriya has put (अप्राक्षीत्) five questions to me and I could not (नाशकम्) answer even one." So in the story of Uçasti Câkrâyaṇa Ch. Up. 1, 10 etc. the perfect is used while the author himself is speaking, but 1, 11, 2 when the king excuses himself to Uçasti, that he has not chosen him to be his officiating priest, the aorist appears भगवन्तं वा अहमेभिः सर्वैरार्त्विज्यैः पर्यैषिषं भगवतो वा अहमवित्त्यान्यानवृषि (I have looked for you, for all these sacrificial offices, but not finding [1]) Your Reverence, I have chosen others). Cp. ibid. 6, 13, 1 etc. DELBRÜCK, *Altindische Tempuslehre* p. 117 etc. has given a great number of instances from the Çatapatha and the Aitareya.

335. The aorist is used throughout Sanskrit literature in both its acceptations, actual and historical. Instances of the historical aorist occur as early as the Ṛgveda-sanhitâ, though, I confess, not many are recorded [2]); and afterwards it is no less frequent than the other historical tenses. For the rest, it may be observed that in easy proseworks and in compositions of rather simple style, the aorist is comparatively rare, and mostly limited to certain verbs often occurring, as अभूत्, अगमत्, अवादीत्. Yet, in more elegant style, in the works of such writers as Daṇḍin, Bâna, Somadeva, the aorist is employed as often and with as much ease as the other past tenses. [3]).

336. The **participles of the past** in °त and °तवन्त् may

---

1) Construe भगवतो..... अवित्त्या, instr. of अवित्ति. The reading is good, and needs no correction.

2) A prayer-book, indeed, is not the fittest document from which to learn the historical style of a language. In epic poetry the historical aorist is common.

3) For this reason, I am astonished at the statement of WHITNEY (§ 532 of his Sanskrit grammar), that the aorist is »seldom" employed in classic Sanskrit.

The participles in °त and °तावन्त् doing duty as a past tense.

do the same duty as the aorist, whether they are attended by the verb substantive, or without it (9). They are expressive of facts done, finished, and it makes no difference, whether these facts belong to the historical past or have been done of late and have not yet lost their actuality. In both acceptations they are of the utmost frequency. They represent the younger idiom, the aorist the elder one.[1]) Accordingly they are rarely, if at all, thus employed in the archaic dialect.[2]).

1. Examples of the historical past. — *a.*) partic. in °त. Kathâs. 4, 36 यावत्किञ्चिद्गता तावन्निरुद्धा सा पुरोधसा (when she had gone some steps, the purohita stopped her); Panc. 51 कदाचित्..... यात्रामहोत्सवः संवृत्तः (once it happened that a religious feast with a procession took place); Daç. 111 स राजा.... चिरं प्रयुध्य बद्धो देवी च बन्धनं गमिता; — *b*) partic. in °तवन्त्. Panc. 148 कंचिद् ब्राह्मणं वासार्थं प्रार्थितवान् (he asked a brahman for lodging); R. 1, 56, 14 ब्रह्मास्त्रं क्षिप्तवान्गाधिनन्दनः (the son of Gâdhi threw the *brahma*-weapon); Hit. 109 शुकः..... स्वदेशं ययौ ततो विन्ध्याचलं गत्वा स्वस्य राजानं चित्रवर्णं प्रणतवान् (— made his obeisance to his king Citravarṇa).

2. Examples of the actual past. — *a.*) partic. in °त. R. 3, 17, 24 Çûrpaṇakhâ says to Râma राम त्वा.... समुपेतास्मि (R., I am come to you); Kathâs. 42, 100 अनागसौ कथं पित्रा गमितौ स्वो दशामिमाम् (how is it that our father has brought us that are guiltless, into this state?); Çâk. I [the charioteer to the king] एष मृगो विप्रकृष्टः संवृत्तः; — *b.*) partic. in °तवन्त्. R. 1, 76, 2 श्रुतवानस्मि यत्कर्म कृतवानसि भार्गव (I have heard, what deed you have done); Çâk. IV Kaṇva to Anasûyâ अनसूये गतवती वां सहधर्मचारिणी (Anasûyâ, the friend and companion of both of you has departed); Mudr. III, p. 107 Câṇakya to Candragupta वृषल सम्यग्गृहीतवानसि मदाशयम्.

1) Hence commentators often explain aorists by participles.

2) I do not recollect having met with them doing duty as finite verbs, in brâhmaṇas and upanishads. But, as I have not yet made a special inquiry into this subject, I refrain from affirming their entire absence from that class of works.

337. The participle in °त may be sometimes expressive of the present (361). सुप्तः कुमारः »the boy is asleep, is sleeping" as well as »he has just awaked from sleep" (actual past) or »he slept" (historical past). To remove all ambiguousness, one derives participles in °तवन्त् even from *intransitives*, as गतवान्, जातवान्, सुप्तवान्; such participles serve exclusively for the past. — Vikram. V, p. 173 यः सुप्तवान्मदङ्के..... तं मे प्रेषय शिखिनम् (— the peacock, that has slept on my bosom), Panc. I, 224 जननीमनो हरति जातवती, Kathâs. 81, 51 प्राविशत् सा च तत्रैव.... सत्त्वशीलोऽप्यसौ तस्याः पश्चात्तत्र प्रविष्टवान्, Çâk. IV गतवती see **336**, 2°, Hit. 109 प्रणातवान् see **336**, 1°.

But if the participle in °त has a passive meaning, that in °तवन्त् is its corresponding active: उक्तम् (it is said, — has been said, — was said), उक्तवान् (he has said, he said) More about them **360**.

338. Old participles of the past. The old and genuine participles of the perfect, as तस्थिवान् (f. तस्थुषी) or चक्राणः, had the same function as those in °तवन्त् and °त, which have almost wholly superseded them in the classic dialect (359, 2°). In the epic poems and in kâvyas several of them — at least in the active voice — also do duty as finite verbs; they are then expressive both of the actual past, as R. 1, 58, 2 उपेयिवान् (you have gone to —) and the historical, as R. 2, 12, 6 नराधिपः। मोहमापेदिवान्. Cp. Kathâs. 35, 41 and Çiçup. 1, 16.

339. Remote past. Sanskrit lacks a special tense for the so-called r e m o t e p a s t or plusquamperfectum. The general past tenses are used even then. It must accordingly be inferred exclusively from the context, in what case a Skr. past tense answers to our »remote past." That f. i. Kathâs. 25, 180 the words यत्रैव तमवाप्तवान्..... तत्रैव mean »on the very spot, where he *had* got it," can only be shown by reproducing the whole story, from which they are quoted. — R. 2, 26, 3 Râma has told his mother the cruel order he has just received from his father, to retire into the forest; now he goes to Sîtâ, who did not know anything about it वैदेही चापि तत्सर्वं न शुश्राव तपस्विनी (the unhappy princess *had* not yet *heard* anything of it). — Daç. 92 स खलु विमर्दकः..... तदहरेव

प्रातिष्ठत = »Vimardaka *had* indeed already *departed* that very day." It is plain, that gerunds are especially fit to signify the remote past.

Future tenses.

340. Future in °ता. Sanskrit has two future tenses, 1. the so-called periphrastic future (लुट्): कर्तास्मि, 2. the future made with °स्य° (लृट्): करिष्यामि.

The former is a compound tense, being made up of a noun in °तृ + a formal element, expressive of the person, signified either by the auxiliary (अस्मि etc.), or by the personal pronoun [1]): Yet for the third person neither is wanted and the simple noun in °तृ may suffice: one says कर्तास्मि or कर्ताहम्, कर्तासि or कर्ता त्वम्, but in the 3d person the simple कर्ता is available. In the dual and in the plural °ता remains unchanged, when attended by the auxiliary, therefore कर्तास्वः, कर्तास्मः, but in the 3d person कर्तारौ, कर्तारः, and

1) Pâṇini does not mention the 1st and 2d person formed by simply putting together the noun in °ता and the personal pronoun. Accordingly this mode of formation has been excluded from the official paradigms of the periphrastic future. Yet वक्ताहम् is quite as correct and as much used as वक्तास्मि. That Pâṇini left it unnoticed, may be due to his system of explaining grammatical forms. To him वक्तास्मि, वक्तास्मः are forms to be dealt with, because by the union of both elements a new word arises, bearing one accent, but वक्ता + अहम् and the like are units syntactically only, not so from a formal point of view. Hence, to Pâṇini the noun in °ता is not even the nomin. of a noun, but a simple stem to which the personal suffixes are to be added. Upon the whole, the information to be got from him about this future, is scanty, see P. 3, 1, 33; 2, 4, 85 and 7, 4, 50—52, cp. Boethlingk's note on 7, 4, 52.

of course also कर्तारावावाम्, कर्तारो वयम्, sim. Both pronouns and auxiliaries are occasionally severed from the verbal noun; the pronouns may precede as well as follow. Even the auxiliary sometimes precedes in poetry.

Examples: 1st and 2d person: Kathâs. 26, 31 गन्तास्मि (I shall go), R. 3, 69, 40 अधिगन्तासि वैदेहीमचिरेण, Mâlav. I, p. 15 मोक्ता माधवसेनं ततोऽहम् (then I shall release M.), R. 2, 118, 10 तथावृत्तिश्च याता त्वं पतिशुश्रूषया दिवम् (— you will go to heaven), Mudr. V, p. 175 पञ्चभैरहोभिर्वयमेव तत्र गन्तारः (— ourselves shall start), Mhbh. 1, 136, 39 किं ददानि ते। प्रब्रूहि राजशार्दूल कर्ता स्म्यस्मि तथा नृप, ibid. 1, 120, 26 अपत्यं गुणासंपन्नं लब्धा प्रीतिकरं ह्यसि.

3d person: Ch. Up. 4, 6, 1 अग्निष्टे पादं वक्ता (Agni will tell you a fourth part [of it]), Mhbh. I, Paushyap. 56 अश्विनौ स्तुहि। तौ देवभिषजौ त्वां चक्षुष्मन्तं कर्तारौ, Bhojapr. 55 न जाने यातारस्तव रिपवः केन च पथा, Nala 7, 5 नलं जेता भवान्हि सहितो मया.

Rem. 1. The future in °ता may be also used with a feminine subject — R. 1, 38, 8 एका जनयिता पुत्रम् —, but occasionally the fem. in °त्री is used, at least भवित्री, see f. i. Kathâs. 35, 105. — Some kṛts in °इन्, fem. °इनी, especially भाविन्, are also significative of a future tense (see 359). Vikram. V, p. 181 सुरासुरविमर्दो भावी (a quarrel between gods and demons wil. take place).

Rem. 2. The medial endings of this future — or rather, of the auxiliary — are scarcely met with in the archaic dialect (WHITNEY, *Sanskr. Gramm.* § 947). In the classic language they seem to be no more employed. Without auxiliary, there is of course no formal distinction between the active and the medial voices. One says अध्येता (he will study) from the medial अधीयते, Panc. 161 अहं परित्राता from परित्रायते, as well as f. i. द्रष्टा or वक्ता. Even a passive meaning may be conveyed by this future. Kirât. 3, 22 एते.... उन्मूलयितारः कपिकेतनेन (they will be eradicated by Arjuna), R. 3, 56, 5 यद्यहं.... त्वया वै धर्षिता बलात्। शयिता त्वं हतः संख्ये (if I shall be violated by you perforce, you will perish in battle). Of such roots, as may have special passive aorists, futures, etc. (316), a special passive form is accordingly available, »he will be killed” may be either हन्ता or घानिता, »it will be given" either दाता or दायिता, see Kâç. on P. 6,4, 62 = II, p. 311 of the Benares-edition.

Rem. 3. Mhbh. 3, 176, 20 this future is construed with an objective genitive भूयो द्रष्टा तवास्मि (I shall see you again). Likewise Nâgân. IV, p. 65 कस्त्राता तव पुत्रक, the meaning of which, as appears from the context, is »who will protect you, my son?" As a rule, however, the object is put in the accusative.

341. Employment of the two future tenses. As regards its function, the tense in °ता cannot be used of every future, but only of such actions, as will not occur soon, in other terms which have not yet actuality. It is, therefore, a *remote future.* The future in °स्यति, on the other hand, is the *general future*, and may be used of any future action, whether intended or not, whether actual or remote. Hence, for the future in °ता one may everywhere substitute that in °स्यति, but not inversely. P. 3, 3, 15.

That the future in °स्यति may express also purpose, intention etc. will be shown hereafter, see **344.**

The grammarians make the same distinction between लृट् and लुट् as between लुङ् and लङ्. Both imperfect (लङ्) and लुट् are restricted to the अनद्यतन [1]).

---

1) Commentators explain the term अनद्यतने भविष्यत् as meaning »future facts, not to happen to-day, but to-morrow and afterwards." According to them, that which will happen to-day cannot be signified by लुट्. When exemplifying this tense, they are wont to add श्वः. The Kâtantra names it even श्वस्तनी. Yet, this explication of अनद्यतन is no less narrow as regards the future, as it has been shown to be for the past, see note 1 on p. 249 and note 3 on p. 253 of this book. Nor are instances wanting from literature of लुट् denoting facts to happen on the same day. Panc. 161 some bride has been left alone by her bridegroom and the whole marriage-train, who have fled at the threatening approach of a wild

Rem. The past अनद्यतने, as has been stated above (330 R. 2), is to be expressed by the *general* past tenses in two cases. Similarly the future अनद्यतने finds its expression by the *general* future in °स्यति in the same cases, viz. »uninterrupted action" and »the time adjoining immediately that of the speaker," therefore यावज्जीवमन्नं दास्यति [not दाता], येयमामावास्यागामिन्येतस्यामुपाध्यायोऽग्नीनाधास्यति (at the next new moon the teacher will worship the holy fires). Some additional remarks are made by P. 3, 3, 136—138 to exclude लुट् in a few other cases; but nothing, he says, prevents the use of लुट्, if the time be exactly defined by a word meaning »day" or »night." The employment of लुट् together with such words is proved, indeed, by instances, drawn from literature.

P 3, 3, 135.

341*. In most cases, therefore, it is indifferent, what future is employed. Often both alternate. R. 1, 70, 17 वक्ता..... वसिष्ठः, but in the following çloka एष वक्ष्यति वसिष्ठः, cp. R. 1, 38, 8 and 2, 8, 22. This alternation is most apparent in conditional sentences; then either लुट् is used in both protasis and apodosis (Ait. Br. 1, 27, 1), or in the apodosis only, but लृट् in the protasis (Kathâs. 28, 131 सोऽस्य..... यदि वक्ष्यति। तस्यापि भविता मृत्युः), or conversely (Kathâs. 1, 60 यदा तस्मै कथामिमां। पुष्पदन्त प्रवक्तासि तदा शापाद्विमोक्ष्यसे), or the future in °स्यति in both (Kathâs. 39, 67). In putting questions, in uttering prophecies the future in °ता is, indeed, often employed [1]), but the future in °स्यति is even there more frequent.

---

elephant; then a young man comes to her rescue, takes her by the hand and says मा भैषीरहं परित्राता. Prabodh. VI, p. 134 Purusha exclaims सायंगृहो मुनिरहं भवितास्मि सद्यः. Inversely, the other future is used even with श्वः, f. i. Mâlav. II, p. 46 त्वदीयमुपदेशं श्वो द्रक्ष्यामः.

1) Delbrück, *Altindische Wortfolge* p. 6—8, treats the future in °ता, as far as it is employed in the Çatapathabrâhmaṇa. He concludes that it is the »objective future, denoting the certainty of the future fact, apart from any wish or desire on the side of the subject." Though this will hold good in the majority of cases, it is not always supported by facts. A strong desire, an intention, etc. are occasionally also denoted by लुट्. R. 1, 20, 3 Daçaratha offers to Viçvâmitra to fight, himself and his army, against the demons: अनया [viz. सेनया] सहितो गत्वा योद्धाऽहं

341** According to the vernacular grammarians the general future in °स्यति may even be expressive of the past in this case, if a verb of *remembering* be added to the past action related. The imperfect, then, is forbidden and the future to be employed instead of it. Kâç. gives this instance अभिज्ञानासि देवदत्त कश्मीरेषु वत्स्यामः, likewise स्मरसि, बुध्यसे, चेतयसे..... वत्स्यामः = »do you remember, that we dwelled —?" But this substitution of the future cannot be, if the action remembered or reminded is introduced by यत्. A third rule of Pâṇini on this head is explained as allowing both imperf. and future, if the verb of remembering introduces two or more past actions, of which the preparatory action is first named, the main action afterwards. See Pat. II, p. 119.

P. 3, 2, 112. P. 3, 2, 113. P. 3, 2, 114.

Of this strange and rather awkward idiom I know no other instances but those, adduced by grammarians or such authors, as aimed at exemplifying the rules of Pâṇini [1]).

CHAPT. IV. Tenses and moods (*continued*).

342. Subjunctive mood. The subjunctive mood is expressed in Sanskrit by four tenses: 1. लिङ्, called by some **optative,** by others **potential**, 2. आशिषि लिङ् the **precative** or **benedictive**, 3. लृङ् the **conditional**, 4. लोट् the **imperative.** The dialect of the Veda (mantra and brâhmaṇa) has moreover a fifth tense called लेट् by vernacular,

---

तैर्निशाचरैः।..... अहमेव धनुष्पाणिर्गोप्ता समरमूर्धनि; when he then adds यावत्प्राणान्धरिष्यामि तावद्योत्स्ये निशाचरैः, he must needs use the other future, as the action is a permanent one, cp. **341** R.

1) In fact, I cannot persuade myself, that Pâṇini's words have been well understood by the commentators. Especially the phrase अभिज्ञावचने is likely to mean something different. If it could be proved, that Pâṇini used अभिज्ञा in the sense of »purpose" अभिप्राय, all difficulty of interpretation would be removed. Then, indeed, Pâṇini would simply teach the future in °स्यति doing duty as a future's past (**322** R.), वक्ष्यति = *dicturus erat.*

conjunctive by European grammarians, which was already obsolete in the days of Pâṇini. The duties of the missing tense are performed by the imperative, partly also by the present (लट्). Nor is the present the only tense, which apart from its expressing the indicative, may sometimes have the force of a subjunctive; for the future in °स्यति — and, in prohibitions, even the aorist — is occasionally concurrent with लिङ् and लोट्. That the conditional (लृङ्) was at the outset an indicative tense, appears sufficiently not only from its outer form, but also from its original employment. Upon the whole, the boundaries between indicative and not-indicative are less marked in Sanskrit than in Latin and Greek.

The लिङ् (*optative* or *potential*) is the general exponent of the subjunctive mood.

343. The subjunctive mood finds its general expression in the tense termed लिङ् by Pânini, and which one is wont in Europe to name either **optative** or **potential**, though it is not restricted to the expression of both wishes and possibility. In fact, any shade of meaning, inherent to the Latin conjunctive, may be imported by it. Its manysidedness entails the great variety of its translation. According to sense कुर्याम् may be = *I can* (*could*) *do*, *I may* (*might*) —, *will* (*would*) —, *shall* (*should*) —, *must do*, *let me do*, sim.

Its subdivisions.

We may make some main distinctions:

a.) लिङ् is used in exhortations and precepts: hortative.

b.) it is expressive of wishes: optative.

c.) it is a potential, that is, it may purport a

possibility, or a probability, on the other hand also uncertainty and impossibility or improbability.

d.) it is used in hypothetical sentences.

e.) it may be used in such relative sentences, as bear a general import.

f.) it may be used in subordinate sentences expressive of a design or of inevitable consequence.

a.) hortative. P. 3, 3, 161.

a.) Ch. Up. 7, 3, 1 मन्त्रानधीयीय (let me study the mantras), कर्माणि कुर्वीय (let me do sacrificial acts); Panc. V, 103 एकः स्वादु न भुञ्जीत नैकः सुप्तेषु जागृयात्। एको न गच्छेदध्वानं नैकश्चार्थान्प्रचिन्तयेत् (one must not take sweetmeats alone, nor wake alone among sleeping people, nor must one walk alone nor consider one's affairs alone); Kumâras. 4, 36 ज्वलनं.... त्वरयेर्दक्षिणवातवीजनैः (you [Spring] must inflame the fire by the breezes of the southwind); Daç. 152 एषा चाहं पितुस्ते पादमूलं प्रत्युपसर्पेयम् (and now, I might return to your father). — From these examples it appears, that the hortative लिङ् is expressive of any kind of exhortation. भवानधीयीत may be = »you must study" or »you may," »you might," »you are allowed to study," »it is your duty, the due time —" etc. See P. 3, 3, 161; 163; 164 with comm.

b) optative. P. 3, 3, 157 and 159.

b.) R. 3, 19, 20 Çûrpaṇakhâ utters this wish तस्यास्तयोश्च रुधिरं पिबेयमहमाहवे (o, that I might drink their blood). To this pure optative often the particle अपि is added or अपि नाम. Mudr. II, p. 89 अपि नाम दुरात्मनश्चाणक्यहतकाच्चन्द्रगुप्तो भिद्येत; R. 2, 43, 9 अपीदानीं स कालः स्यात्..... पश्येयमिह राघवम् (if that time were already present and I should see Râma here). — The verb of »wishing" being added, it may also be put in the लिङ्. One says either इच्छामि भुञ्जीत भवान् or इच्छेयं भुञ्जीत भवान्. Cp. R. 3, 58, 5. P. 3, 3, 160.

c) potential.

c.) The potential लिङ् comprises various kinds:

1. *possibility* and *ability*, as Panc. 226 कदाचिदयं ब्राह्मणो गोशब्देन बुध्येत (perhaps this brahman will awake by the lowing of the cows), Mṛcch. VII, p. 238 पश्येयुः क्षितिपतयो हि चारदृष्ट्या (for princes can see through the eye of their spies), Kathâs. 2, 37 सकृच्छ्रुतमयं बालः सर्वं चाधारयेद्धृदि (this boy is able to retain by heart all he has heard but once).

2. *probability.* Mṛcch. VIII, p. 268 the rake says अथवा मयि गते नृशंसो हन्यादेनाम् (in my absence the cruel man will kill her), Kathâs. 25, 24 जानीयात्स वृद्धो जातु तां पुरीम् (that old man, methinks, will know that town);

3. *doubt.* Çâk. V किमुद्दिश्य भगवता काश्यपेन मत्सकाशमृषयः प्रेरिताः स्युः (for what reason may the Reverend K. have sent holy men to me?), Panc. I, 215 एकं हन्यान्न वा हन्यादिषुर्मुक्तो धनुष्मता। बुद्धिर्बुद्धिमतोत्सृष्टा हन्ति राष्ट्रं सनायकम् (the arrow shot by an archer may hit one individual or may not hit him, but the wit of a witty man hits a [whole] kingdom with its ruler);

4. in negative and interrogative sentences लिङ् may express *improbability* or *impossibility.* Daç. 92 निपुणमन्विष्यन्नोपलब्धवान् [sc. एनम्]। कथं वोपलभ्येत (he sought carefully, but did not find him; how could he?), Mṛcch. VII, p. 236 अपि प्राणानहं जह्यां न तु त्वां शरणागतम् (I had rather forsake my life, than you who are a supplicant to me), R. 2, 37, 32 लोके नहि स विद्येत यो न राममनुव्रतः;

5. A special kind is the लिङ् being employed for asserting one's power »he may even do this." R. 3, 49, 3 Râvana boasts उद्वहेयं भुजाभ्यां तु मेदिनीमम्बरे स्थितः। आपिबेयं समुद्रं च मृत्युं हन्यां रणे स्थितः। अर्कं तुद्यां शरैस्तीक्ष्णैर्विभिन्द्यां हि महीतलम् (I am able to lift up the earth with my arms, drink up the ocean etc.). So often with अपि (or उत) see P. 3, 3, 152. — But if one says »he may even do this," in order to express blame on that account, the present is necessary, and the लिङ् is forbidden (P. 3, 3, 142). Kâç. gives this example अपि — or जातु — तत्रभवान् वृषलं याजयति (he is even able to officiate for a çûdra).

P. 3, 2, 154.

d.) hypothetical.

d.) the hypothetical लिङ् is used, if it is wanted to say, what will happen or would happen, if some other fact occur or should occur. It is used in the protasis as well as in the apodosis of hypothetical sentences. Mhbh. 1, 82, 21 Çarmishṭhâ says to Yayâti त्वत्तोऽपत्यवती लोके चरेयं धर्ममुत्तमम् (if I had offspring from you, I would walk in the highest path of duty), Pat. I, p. 2 यो ह्यजानन्वै ब्राह्मणं हन्यात्सुरां वा पिबेत्सोऽपि मन्ये पतितः स्यात् (for he, who should kill a brahman or drink strong liquor without knowing it, even such a one would be an outcast, methinks), Panc. III, 203 यदि

स्यात्पावकः शीतः प्रोष्णो वा शशलाञ्छनः। स्त्रीणां तदा सतीत्वं स्याद्यदि स्याद् दुर्जनो हितः. Cp. **489** and **470** R. 3.

लिङ् [d in] [rel]ative [sen]ten[ce]s of [gen]eral [im]port. *e.*) लिङ् used in relative sentences of general import. Âçv. 1, 3, 1 यत्र क्व च होष्यन्स्यात् (wheresoever one has the intention of performing oblations), Panc. I, 165 कालातिक्रमणं वृत्तेर्यो न कुर्वीत भूपतिः। कदाचित्तं न मुञ्चन्ति भर्त्सिता अपि सेवकाः (the king who duly observes the time of paying the wages to his officials, him —), ibid. I, 271 अर्धराज्यहरं भृत्यं यो न हन्यात्स हन्यते.

लिङ् [use]d in [fi]nal [a]nd [co]nse[cu]tive [cl]auses. *f.*) लिङ् expressive of a design or a consequence. Kathâs. 36, 106 हरिं शरणमाश्रये येन स्यां नैव दुःखानां पुनर्भाजनमीदृशाम् (I betake myself to Hari, in order that such grief may never again befall me), R. 3, 13, 11 आदिश मे देशं..... यत्र वसेयम्, ibid. 3, 50, 18 स भारः सौम्य भर्तव्यो यो नरं नावसादयेत् (one must bear only such a burden, as will not exhaust its bearer).

Rem. मा — in epic poetry also न — with लिङ् = »lest.” Cp. **405** R. 1.

It needs no argument, that the subdivisions laid down here and other similar ones are somewhat arbitrary. It is one and the same लिङ् that is involved in all of them, and it is only for the sake of developing the variety of the logical relations, which are signified by that so-called „optative” or „potential,” that we have tried to distinguish at all.

344. [T]he [idi]oms, [co]ncur[r]ent with [लि]ङ्. Apart from the many-sidedness of its employment, it is to be observed, that the लिङ् is in most cases not indispensable. The imperative, the present, the future, the krtyas are often concurrent idioms, occasionally the conditional. The imperative in the subdivisions *a*), *b*) and *c*), as will be shown hereafter (**348**–**352**), the present in the subdivisions *e*) and *f*), as will plainly appear when we treat of subordinate sentences (**458** *b*,

468, 471)[1]). On the kṛtyas see **357**, on the conditional **347**.

Especially the future in °स्य-ति.

But it is especially the **future** in °स्यति that often is employed so as to express a kind of subjunctive mood. The difference which logically exists between the positive statement of some future fact on one hand and the utterance of an exhortation, a wish, a doubt, a supposition, sim. on the other, is not so strong a bar practically as to keep wholly apart the functions of the future tense and the subjunctive mood. Occasionally the same grammatical form may do duty for both. As far as Sanskrit is concerned, we may even state that in the majority of cases there is no boundary between the two. Indeed, the future in °स्यति is available in almost every subdivision, belonging to the department of the लिङ्, save the hypothetical mood.

Examples of the future = subjunctive mood.

a.) *exhortation* and *precept.* R. 1, 61, 2 दिशमन्यां प्रपत्स्यामस्तत्र तप्स्यामहे तपः, from the context it is evident that these words mean: *let* us go to another region, *let* us do penance there. Kathâs 43, 86 तद्गच्छ पार्श्वं तस्याद्य प्रभाते द्रुतमेष्यसि (— you shall return quickly at daybreak).

b.) *wish.* R. 2, 96, 21 अपि नौ वशमागच्छेत्कोविदारध्वजो रणे। अपि द्रक्ष्यामि भरतम् (o that I might see the banner —, that I might see Bharata).

1) The interchangeableness of present and optative in such relative sentences will be made clear by this. In Panc. I we have a series of ten çlokas (54—63) expounding what kind of people are fittest for attending on a king. All of these çlokas are framed on the same scheme, three pâdas being made up of a relative sentence, whereas the fourth makes up the apodosis, being the refrain स भवेद्राजवल्लभः. Now, in five çlokas out of the ten, the verb of the protasis is an *optative*, but in three it is a *present*, in one it is wanting. In the tenth the optative is employed *together with* the present (I, 55) प्रभुप्रसादजं वित्तं सुपात्रे यो नियोजयेत्। वस्त्राद्यं च दधात्यङ्गे स भवेद्राजवल्लभः.

c.) *possibility* and *doubt*. Panc. 282 धूर्तश्चिन्तयामास। किमहमनया..... करिष्यामि। किंच कदाप्यस्याः पृष्ठतः कोऽपि समेष्यति तन्मे महाननर्थः स्यात् (the rogue reflected: What shall I do with her? And perhaps somebody will come after her; then I shall get into great inconvenience). — Especially the future of the auxiliary, भविष्यति, often expresses *probability*. Mhbh. 1, 76, 32 व्यक्तं हतो मृतो वापि कचस्तात भविष्यति (I am sure, father, Kaca will have been injured or has died), Panc. 176 the deer Citrânga tells how himself has escaped the hunters, but मम यूथं तैर्लुब्धकैर्व्यापादितं भविष्यति (my flock is sure to have been killed by them).

Rem. 1. If such phrases, as »I blame," »I do not believe," »I cannot endure," »I wonder if (यदि)," »I suppose, surmise," »it is time" are added to the potential statement, लिङ् is idiomatic (see P. 3, 3, 147—150; 152—153; 168), the future being but rarely allowed, cp. P. 3, 3, 146 and 151 with comm. But if the said verbs are only implied, the future in °स्यति is used side by side with the optative. [1])

f.) *purpose*. Pat. I, p. 7 the master of the house comes to the potter and asks him कुरु घटं कार्यमनेन करिष्यामीति (make me a pot, that I may make use of it). Likewise R. 2, 54, 28 Bharadvâja says to Râma दशक्रोश इतस्तात गिरिर्यस्मिन्निवत्स्यसि (at a distance of ten *kroça* from here there is a mountain where you may dwell, cp. Lat. *mons in quo habites*). Cp. also न with fut. = lest" **405 R. 1.**

4*. Inversely a sanskrit optative may occasionally be rendered by a future. Mhbh. 1, 160, 1 Kuntî asks the brahman, at whose house she dwells, why he and his family are lamenting [दुःखं] विदित्वापकर्षेयं शक्यं चेदपकर्षितुम् (I will remove your pain, if possible, fr. *je chasserai votre douleur*). So Panc. 282, which example is quoted above, optative and future alternate; likewise Panc. 65 एवं कृते तव तावत्प्राणयात्रा क्लेशं विनापि भविष्यत्यस्माकं च पुनः सर्वोच्छेदनं न स्यात्.

4.** Even the future in °ता may sometimes express a subjunctive mood. As far as my information goes, this employment is limit-

---

1) The sûtra P. 3, 3, 146 is accepted too narrowly by the commentators. It enjoins the future in °स्यति for expressing the notion »to be sure, certainly," and s. 147 is to be considered an exception to it.

ed to the dominion of the potential mood. Mhbh. 4, 12, 3 अयं हयानीक्षति मामकान्दृढम्। ध्रुवं हयज्ञो भविता विचक्षणः (he examines my horses, he is sure to be a connoisseur in horses), Pat. I, p. 250 तथा विदूरे ऽव्यक्तमात्ररूपं दृष्ट्वा वक्तारो भवन्ति महिषी रूपमिव ब्राह्मणी रूपमिव (likewise, if at a distance one sees a person of whom one can only discern the outline, one is likely to say: it looks like the wife of a prince, it looks like the wife of a brâhmana).

345. लिङ् expressive of the *past* as well as the *present*.

Sanskrit makes no distinction between the different tenses of the subjunctive mood. The लिङ् expresses the past as well as the present. कुर्याम् may be occasionally = „I might, I would etc. *have done*." Ch. Up. 4, 14, 2 when the teacher asks his disciple »who has taught you, my dear?" सौम्य को नु त्वानुशशास, the other replies को नु मानुशिष्यात् (who should have taught me?), Gaut. 12, 1 शूद्रो द्विजातीनतिसंधायाभिहत्य वाग्दण्डपारुष्याभ्यामङ्गं मोच्यो येनोपहन्यात् (a çûdra, who has intentionally reviled twice-born men — shall lose the member, whereby he has offended), Mrcch. III, p. 124 Cârudatta speaks चिरयति मैत्रेयः। मा नाम वैक्लव्यादकार्यं कुर्यात् (Maitreya tarries; how, if, in his distress, he should have done some forbidden thing!). Yet an optative of the past may be made by adding स्यात् or भवेत् to the participle of the past, f. i. Kathâs. 27, 32 किं मयापकृतं राज्ञो भवेत् (in what can I have offended the king?).[1] Likewise, by putting them to the participle of the future one gets the subjunctive mood of the future.

For the rest, Sanskrit can hardly be said to possess something like *tenses* of the subjunctive mood.[2] Only a kind of op-

---

1) So already in the archaic dialect. Ait. Br. 1, 4, 1 यः पूर्वमनीजानः स्यात्तस्मै (to such a one, as has not sacrificed formerly), ईजान is the partic. of the perf. âtm. of यज्.

2) The Ṛgvedamantras, indeed, contain many optatives, belonging to the aorist, some also, which are made of the stem of the perfect. But they have early disappeared from the language. — In the archaic dialect the conditional may occasionally do duty of the past of the लिङ्, see **347** R. and cp. P. 3, 3, 140.

tative of the aorist has survived, but it is not what we should call a tense. It is rather a kind of mood, see the next paragraph.

346. Precative. The **precative** or **benedictive** (आशिषि लिङ्). This mood is restricted to benedictions, and even there it has a concurrent idiom: the imperative. Mâlat. VII, p. 91 विधेयासुर्देवाः परमरमणीयां परिणातिं। कृतार्थो भूयासम् (may the gods make the issue as happy as possible, may I obtain my desire), Utt. I, p. 5 किमन्यदाशास्महे। वीरप्रसवा भूयाः, Daç. 164 आचष्ट च हृष्टः कोशदासः। भूयासमेवं यावदायुरायतात्त्वि त्वत्प्रसादस्य पात्रमिति· [1]) P. 3, 3, 173.

347. Conditional. The so called **conditional** (लृङ्) is properly the past of the future in °स्यति. In classic Sanskrit its employment is limited to the expression of the so called *modus irrealis*, that is the mood significative of what would happen or have happened, if something else should have occurred, which really has not taken place. Then, mostly, both protasis and apodosis contain the conditional. [2])

Ch. Up. 6, 1, 7 यद्ध्येतदवेदिष्यन्कथं मे नावक्ष्यन् (for if they had known it, why should they not have told me so?), Panc. 237 तद्यदि तस्य वचनमकरिष्यन्नेते ततो न स्वल्पोऽप्यनर्थोऽभविष्यदेतेषाम् (for if they had done according to his words, then not the least misfortune would have befallen them), Daç 111 तौ चेद्राजपुत्रौ निरुपद्रवावेवावर्धिष्येतामियता कालेन तवेमां वयोवस्थामस्प्रक्ष्येताम् (if those two princes should have grown up without accidents, they would have reached your age by this time), Kumâras. 6, 68 गामधास्यत्कथं नागः..... आ रसातलमूलात्त्वमवालम्बिष्यथा न चेत् (how would the serpent [Çesha] bear the earth, if you [Vishnu] had not lifted it up from the bottom of hell?), Ch. Up.

---

1) Nala 17, 35 the precative ब्रूयास्त does the duty of an hortative imperative.

2) P. 3, 3, 139 लिङ्निमित्ते लृङ् क्रियातिपत्तौ·

140 भूते च. — Kâç. भूते च काले लिङ्निमित्ते क्रियातिपत्तौ सत्यां लृङ्प्रत्ययो भवति·

1, 10, 4 न वा अजीविष्यमिमानखादन् (forsooth, I should have died, if I had not eaten them). In the examples given, the conditional in the apodosis sometimes denotes a hypothetical past, sometimes a hypothetical present, but in the protasis it is always expressive of a past. I do not recollect having met with any instance of the conditional denoting the hypothetical present in both members; M. 7, 20 f. i. it is signified by the लिङ् in the protasis and by the conditional in the apodosis यदि न प्रणयेद्राजा दण्डं दण्ड्येष्वतन्द्रितः। शूले मत्स्यानिवापक्ष्यन्दुर्बलान्बलवत्तराः (if the king were not prompt to inflict punishment on those, who deserve it, the stronger would roast the weaker like fish on the spit). For the rest, it is everywhere allowed to use the लिङ् instead of the conditional, f. i. R. 2, 64, 22 यद्येतदशुभं कर्म न स्म मे कथयेः स्वयम्। फलेन्मूर्धा स्म ते राजन्सद्यः शतसहस्रधा (if you had not told me yourself this evil deed, your head would have fallen off in a thousand pieces), कथयेः and फलेत् = अकथयिष्यः and अफलिष्यत्.

Rem. In the archaic dialect the conditional had a larger sphere of employment. Though rarely used in its original meaning of a future's past (f. i. Ṛgv. 2, 30, 2 यो वृत्राय सिनमत्राभरिष्यत् »who was about to take away the provision of Vrtra"), it occurs there occasionally as the past of the लिङ्, even in not-hypothetical sentences. Maitr. S. 1, 8, 1 स तदेव नाविन्दत्प्रजापतिर्यदहोष्यत् (Praj. did not get what he could sacrifice)[1]), Çat. Br. 14, 4, 2, 3 तत एवास्य भयं वीयाय कस्माद्ध्यभेष्यत् (from that moment his fear vanished, for of whom could he have been afraid?)[2]).

---

1) Even here and in similar instances the conditional shows its origin. The sentence quoted from the Maitr. S. treats of an action put into the past, if it were a present one, the sentence would assume this shape न विन्दति यद्धोष्यति or जुहुयात्. In other terms, अहोष्यत् may here be considered as the past of होष्यति.

2) In a well-known passage of the Chândogya-upanishad (6, 1, 3) the conditional is hidden under a false reading उत तमादेशमप्राक्ष्यो येनाश्रुतं श्रुतं भवति etc. Çankara explains अप्राक्ष्यः by पृष्टवानसि, the Petr. Dict. accepts it as an aorist, though it is then a barbarism, for if aor., it would have been अप्राक्षीः. Replace अप्रक्ष्यः, and all is right »had you but asked the instruction, by which etc." Cp. P. 3, 3, 141.

IMPERATIVE.

348. *Imperative.* Sanskrit **imperative** (लोट्) comprises more than is conveyed by its European name. It is not only the equivalent of what *we* are wont to understand by this mood, but it is also expressive of wishes, possibility and doubt.

We will treat severally of its different employment:

I. The mood of precept and exhortation. I. The imperative, like ours, signifies an *order* or *injunction*, *permission*, *precept*, *exhortation*, *admonition.*

Examples: 2ᵈ person. Kathâs. 81, 56 अस्मत्स्वामिनीकृतं । भजस्वातिथ्यमुत्तिष्ठ स्नाहि भुङ्क्ष्व ततः परम् (enjoy the hospitality of our mistress, get up, take a bath, thereafter take food), Çâk. IV वत्सौ भगिन्याः पन्थानमादेशयतम् (my children, show your sister the way), Prab. V, p. 103 हा पुत्रकाः क्व गताः स्थ दत्त मे प्रतिवचनम्; — 3ᵈ person. Daç. 132 अपसरतु द्विरदकीट एष (let this wicked elephant withdraw), Nala 17, 32 प्रयतन्तु तव प्रेष्याः पुण्यश्लोकस्य मार्गणे (your attendants must try to find out Nala), Mâlav. V, p. 137 तौ पृथग्वरदाकूले शिष्टामुत्तरदक्षिणे (they may rule over —); — 1st person. Çâk. III यद्यनुमन्यसे तदहमेनां विशदां करवाणि (if you permit, I will make —), Mhbh. 1, 146, 29 चराम वसुधामिमाम् (let us wander over this country), Nala 7, 7 नलं वीरं पुष्करः परवीरहा दीव्यावेत्यब्रवीद् भ्राता.

Rem. In exhortations, some particles are often added to the 2ᵈ person, as अपि, अङ्ग, ननु etc. See **418**.

349. *courteous injunction.* In courteous injunctions and requests it is very common to use the imperative of the passive instead of the 2ᵈ person of the active. Then the agent is commonly not expressed (**10**). Ratnâv. IV, p. 100 king to messenger कथय कथामतिविस्तरतः, messenger to king देव श्रूयताम् (listen, Sire). Panc. 48 the barber enjoins his wife भद्रे शीघ्रमानीयतां क्षुरभाण्डम् (please, my dear, fetch me my razorbox). Vikram. I, p. 4 the apsarasas are bewailing their companion Urvaçî, carried off by the Dânavas, Purûravas intervenes and says अलमाक्रन्दितेन । पुरूरवसं मामेत्य कथ्यतां कुतो भवत्यः परित्रातव्या इति. — For the rest, भवान् is of course here likewise available (Mâlav. I, p. 4 त्वरतां भवान्) and when showing respect and reverence, one uses the title of the person addressed instead of it (**260**). So Panc. 86 तदद्य मां भक्षयित्वा प्राणान्धारयतु स्वामी is a more respectful mode of inviting, than स्वामिन् प्राणान्धारय, cp. ibid. 48 शृण्वन्तु भवन्तः सभासदः (v. a. I request the judges to listen).

350. Another manner of expressing polite request, equally frequent, is using the verb **अर्हति**. One says **श्रोतुमर्हसि** = **श्रूयताम्**, cp. our „deign to listen." Nala 3, 7 Nala says to the gods मां न प्रेषयितुमर्हथ (please, send not me), Çâk. V the door-keeper to the king कश्चिदेषामुपाध्यायसंदेशस्तं देवः श्रोतुमर्हति.

अर्हति when periphrasing the imperative.

Rem. The लिङ् and the future in °स्यति are concurrent idioms with the imperative, the former especially in exhortations and precepts (**343**, *a*), the latter, when giving instructions (**344**, *a*). The future does, however, not cease to be a future; in other terms, it is not used in orders or permissions to be acted up to immediately, but if two or more injunctions are given, then often the one prior in time is put in the imperative, the latter expressed by the future. Mâlav. III, p. 79 भद्रे यास्यसि। मम तावदुत्पन्नावसरमर्थित्वं श्रूयताम् (you may go, but first hear —). Hit. 108 the old jackal instructs the others, how to get rid of the blue jackal, their insolent kinsman. When giving the general precept, he uses the imperative कुरुत, but the future करिष्यथ, when giving the special injunction, to be acted up at a fixed point of time in the future [1]).

351. II. The imperative is expressive of *wishes* and *benedictions*.

II. Imperative expressive of wishes.

Examples: Such phrases as चिरं जीव, Hit. 118 गच्छ विजयी भव,

---

1) In this very meaning a few passages of the Mahâbhârata afford a 2ᵈ pers. plur. of the medial future in °ध्वम्, instead of °ध्वे, in other terms a formal difference, which stamps these forms as *imperatives of the future.* Bopp, *Vergl. Gr.* § 729 quotes three instances: Mhbh. 1, 17, 13; 3, 228, 8; 6, 27, 10, see Holtzmann, *Grammatisches aus dem Mhbhta* p. 33. To them I can add a fourth, Mhbh. 1, 133, 13: Drona being seized by a shark, calls upon his disciples for rescue ग्राहं हत्वा तु मोक्षयध्वं माम्.

Nâgân. IV, p. 61 विजयेतां कुमारौ (may the princes be victorious), Panc. 16 शिवास्ते पन्थानः सन्तु (v. a. God speed you on your way), Mudr. VII, p. 231 चिरमवतु महीं पार्थिवश्चन्द्रगुप्तः. — Here the precative (**346**) and the लिङ् are concurrent idioms.

Rem. It is to benedictions that the imperative in °तात् is limited in the classic language. Daç. 16 एनमायुष्मन्तं पितृरूपो भवानभिरक्षतात्. [1]) In the ancient dialect it had a wider employment, only see the series of precepts quoted Ait. Br. 2, 6, 13—16. [2])

P. 7, 1, 35

352. III. The imperative is a kind of potential mood, expressive of *possibility* and *doubt* (cp. **344**). It is especially used in interrogations.

III. Imperative expressive of possibility and doubt.

Examples are frequent of the 1st and 3d person. — Panc. I, 225 it says, a serpent even a not-poisonous one, is to be dreaded विषं भवतु मा भूयात्फटाटोपो भयंकरः (it may have poison or not, the swelling of a serpent's crest is dreadful), Mhbh. 1, 37, 8 अपि मन्त्रयमाणा हि हेतुं पश्याम मोक्षणे (perhaps by deliberation we may find some means for rescue), Mâlav. IV, p. 117 आः। कथं नु खल्वस्मात्संकटान्मोच्यावहै (how may we be rescued from this danger?), Utt. I, p. 21 प्रत्येतु कस्तद्भुवि (who on earth will believe it?), Vikram. V, p. 184 भो राजन्किं ते भूयः प्रियं करोतु पाकशासनः (say, king, what may Indra moreover do for you?), Hit. 118 कथमयं श्लाघ्यतां महासत्त्वः (how may this great-hearted man be praised [as he deserves]?).

353. IV. The imperative with मा or मास्म serves to express *prohibition*. Yet this idiom is comparatively little used, but instead of it *either* अलम् or कृतम् with the instrumental of a verbal noun, *or* the aorist without

IV. Imperative with मा and

1) Another instance is pointed out by prof. Kern as occurring in a Sanskrit inscription on a stone, originating from Java, which stone is now in the Museum of Antiquities at Calcutta. Vs. 4 of this metrical inscription has this close: स जयतादेर्लङ्गनामा नृपः (king Erlanga may be victorious). See Kern's paper in the *Bijdragen van het Instituut voor de Taal- Land- en Volkenkunde van Nederlandsch Indië*, 1885 (X, p. 1—21).

2) Delbrück, *Altindische Wortfolge*, p. 2—6 has endeavoured to prove that the imper. in °तात् did duty of an imperative of the future in the dialect of the brâhmana-works.

other constructions, expressive of prohibition. augment, preceded by मा or मास्म. „Do not fear" f. i. = अलं भयेन, कृतं भयेन or मा भैषीः P. 3, 3, 175.

Examples: 1. of imper. with मा and मास्म. Panc. 294 मा त्वं वैराग्यं गच्छ, Kathâs. 39, 233 यात मास्मेह तिष्ठत (go on, do not stay here); — 2. of अलम् and कृतम् with instrumental. Mudr. I, p. 46 अलमाशङ्कया (no hesitation more), ibid. p. 53 वत्सालं विषादेन (be not sorry, my dear), Panc. 64 अलं संभ्रमेण, Çâk. I कृतं संदेहेन; — 3. of aor. with मा. Daç. 143 मास्म भवत्यो भैषुः (do not fear, ladies), Mhbh. 1, 153, 34 मा चिरं कृथाः (do not tarry), R. 2, 42, 6 कैकेयि मामकाङ्गानि मा स्प्राक्षीः पापनिश्चये (do not touch my body, you evil-minded woman). Aorist with मा.

Rem. 1. अलम् is also construed with a gerund or an infin. Mudr. III, p. 124 अलमुपालभ्य (do not censure me any longer), Mṛcch. III, p. 106 अलं सुप्तजनं प्रबोधयितुम् (do not awake the sleeping people).

Rem. 2. In the epic dialect the augment is not always dropped in the aorist with मा. So in the famous imprecation R. 1, 2, 15 मा निषाद प्रतिष्ठां त्वमगमः शाश्वतीः समाः. Cp. Mhbh. 1, 37, 7 मा नः कालो ऽत्यगादयम्.

Rem. 3. With मास्म not only the aorist is allowed, but also the imperfect tense, of course without augment. R. 2, 9, 23 मा स्मैनं प्रत्युदीक्षेथा मा चैनमभिभाषथाः, Daç. 160 मास्म नाथ मत्कृतेऽध्यवस्यः साहसम्. P. 3, 3, 176.

Rem. 4. मा with optative is of course a concurrent idiom. In the prâkṛts also मा with future in °स्यति. Likewise in the epic dialect. Mhbh. 1, 30, 15 the three idioms are used side by side पुत्र मा साहसं कार्षीर्मा सद्यो लप्स्यसे व्यथाम्। मा त्वां दहेयुः संक्रुद्धा वालखिल्या मरीचिपाः.

354. The aorist with मा is not restricted to prohibition. It does occasionally duty as an optative with negation. Mṛcch. VIII, p. 280 वसन्तसेने। अन्यस्यामपि जातौ मा वेश्या भूस्त्वं हि सुन्दरि। चारित्र्यगुणसंपन्ने जायेथा विमले कुले, R. 2, 30, 19 मा वशं द्विषतां गमम्. It may even express a doubt (**352**): Kathâs. 42, 114 सहसा हि कृतं पापं कथं मा भूद्विपत्तये (how can a crime, recklessly perpetrated, fail to cause mishap?). Or anxiety: Pat. I, p. 418 मैवं विज्ञायि (lest one should decide thus).

355. In classic Sanskrit the 1st person of the imperative

Archaic conjunctive (लेट्).

is less used than the other two (cp. **356**). In fact, these 1st persons belong to another set of forms, viz. the so-called **conjunctive** (लेट्). In both dialects of vaidik compositions, in mantras as well as in brâhmaṇa-works, this conjunctive is still to be met with. But Pâṇini already qualifies it as archaic. In epic and classic Sanskrit, indeed, its 2d and 3d persons exist no more, whereas its 1st persons are the very forms considered to make part of the imperative (लोट्).

the 1st persons of the imperative belong to the लेट्.

This vaidik conjunctive shows a great relationship both in form and employment to Greek conjunctive, especially that of the Homeric dialect. It may express both, the hortative mood and the optative, and is much used in subordinate sentences, conveying a doubt or a purpose or having general bearing. Here are some instances of its use. Ait. Br. 2, 2, 5 यदि च तिष्ठासि यदि च शयासै द्रविणमेवास्मासु धत्तात् (whether you are standing or lying down, give us wealth), Ṛgv. 10, 85, 36 the marriage-mantra गृभ्णामि ते सौभगत्वाय हस्तं मया पत्या जरदष्टिर्यथासः, ibid. 39 दीर्घायुरस्या यः पतिर्जीवाति शरदः शतम् (may her husband have a long life, may he reach a hundred autumns), TS. 6, 5, 6, 2 योऽस्या जायाता अस्माकं स एकोऽसत् (who shall be born of her, must be one of us).[1]).

Rem. 1. Like न with optative in the epic dialect (**451 R. 1**), so नेत् with conjunctive in the vaidik works may be = »lest." Nir. 1, 11 नेज्जिह्मा यन्तो नरकं पताम (lest by going astray we shall go to hell), Ait. Br. 2, 12, 2 नेन्म इमेऽनभिप्रीता देवान्गच्छान् (lest they should go to the devas unsatisfied).

Rem. 2. Some few conjunctives, occurring in the archaic texts, belong to the system of the aorist, as कराम in Ṛgv. 10, 15, 6 मा

---

1) Instances from Ṛgv., AV., Çat. Br., Ait. Br. are brought together by Delbrück in his treatise *Der Gebrauch des Conjunctivs und Optativs im Sanskrit und Griechischen* Halle 1871, especially p. 107—190. — It may be observed, that the Chândogya-upanishad has not a single instance of the लेट् in the 2d or 3d person.

हिंसिष्ट पितरः केन चिन्नो यद्व आगः पुरुषता कराम (do us no injury, fathers, on account of any offence, which we, after the manner of men, may have committed against you).

356. *1st person of the present (लट्) employed as an imperative.* Instead of the 1st persons of the imperative, classic Sanskrit often uses the p r e s e n t (लट्), sometimes when having the nature of a hortative, as गच्छामः when = „let us go," but especially in dubitative interrogations: किं करोमि क्व गच्छामि (what shall I do, where shall I go?)

a.) present with hortative meaning. R. 2, 96, 20 अथवेहैव तिष्ठावः संनद्धावुद्यतायुधौ (let us stand still here —), Panc. 86 तस्यात्मशरीरदानं कुर्मः (let us present him with our body), Prabodh. II p. 29 भवतु। अस्मिन्नासने समुपविशामि [= °विशानि], R. 3, 61, 18 वनं सर्वं विचिनुवः (let us search through the whole forest).[1] — The idiom is regular with तावत्. Çâk. I भवतु। पादपान्तरित एव विश्वस्तां तावदेनां पश्यामि (well, I will look on her —), Mudr. IV, p. 138 Malayaketu to Bhâgurâyaṇa तन्नोपसर्पावः शृणुवस्तावत् (therefore, let us not approach, let us rather listen), Panc. 261 अत्रैव दुर्गे स्थितस्तावद्वेद्मि कोऽयं भविष्यति. Cp. यावत् with present **478** al. 2.

b) present in dubitative interrogations: Panc. 40 किं..... शस्त्रेण मारयामि किं वा विषं प्रयच्छामि किं वा पशुधर्मेण व्यापादयामि (shall I kill him with a weapon, or give him poison or put him to death as one kills a beast?), Hit. 95 क्व यामः किं वा कुर्मः, Mhbh. 1, 155, 42 किं करोम्यहमार्याणां निःशङ्कं वदतानघाः (friends, tell me frankly, what shall I do for you = किं करवाणि°). An instance of this idiom in the passive voice may be Panc. 37 तत्किं क्रियते [sc. आवाभ्याम्] »what shall be done by us?"

---

1) If these instances occurred only in verbs of the 1st conjugation, where the formal difference between the endings of the present and those of the imperative is a slight one, one could account for them in a satisfactory way by supposing errors of the copyists. But, in reality, instances being likewise found among the verbs of the 2d conjugation, it must be recognized, as we do, that the present instead of the imperative is idiomatic for the 1st person. Such phrases as कुर्मः, शृणुवः = कृणवाम and शृणवाव should have moved CAPPELLER in his edition of the

K TYAS.

357. *Krtyas.* The **krtyas**, as far as they do duty for finite verbs, may rank with the tenses, which are expressive of the subjunctive mood. They have the nature of Latin gerundivum, and, like this, they belong to the passive voice. But their sphere of employment is wider. They signify not only that, which one is *obliged* to do or what is *prescribed* to be done, but also what must happen *by necessity* or that which is *fit*, *expected*, *likely* to happen.

P. 3, 3, 163; 171; 172.

The many-sidedness of their employment. Examples: 1. *duty*, *precept* Yâjñ. I, 117 वृद्धभारिनृपस्नातस्त्रीरोगिवरचक्रिणां पन्था देयः (one must make room for an old man, one charged with a burden, for a king, a *snâtaka*, a woman, a sick man, a bridegroom and one in a carriage), Nala 1, 19 हन्तव्योऽस्मि न ते राजन् (do not kill me), Çâk. I आश्रममृगोऽयं न हन्तव्यः (— may not be killed), Panc. 269 शृगाल आह। अद्याप्येकवारं तवान्तिके तमानेष्यामि परं त्वया सज्जीकृतक्रमेण स्थातव्यम्. When substituting for these krtyas the active voice, one would get in the first example पन्थानं दद्यात्, in the second मा वधीः, in the third न कश्चिद्धन्तुमर्हति, in the fourth तिष्ठ.

2. *necessity*. Panc. 167 मयावश्यं देशान्तरं गन्तव्यम् (I must needs go abroad), ibid. I, 450 मूर्खाणां पण्डिता द्वेष्या निर्धनानां महाधनाः (blockheads are the natural enemies of the learned, the poor of the wealthy).

3. *probability*, *conjecture*, *expectation*, etc. Çâk. III अस्मिन् लतामण्डपे संनिहितया तया भवितव्यम् (she is sure to be in the neighbourhood of the bower), Panc. 240 सिंहश्चिन्तयामास। नूनमेतस्यां गुहायां रात्रौ केनापि सत्त्वेनागन्तव्यम् (the lion reflected: surely some animal will come into this hole to-night), Prabodh. V, p. 106 क्वचिदुपकृतिः कार्यमीभिः कृता क्रियतेऽथवा (are they likely to confer any benefit or have they done so before or are they doing so now?). The last example plainly shows, that the krtya borders upon the sphere of a participle of the future, कार्य being here almost = करिष्यमाण. Thus भवितव्य or भाव्य may be even = »future," भवितव्यता »the future."

Ratnâvalî in Boethlingk 's *Chrestomathy* to leave intact the presents of the kind, he has changed into imperatives.

4. Even *desert* and *ability* find their expression by them. Kâç. on P. 3 3, 169 gives this example भवता खलु कन्या वोढव्या = भवान्खलु कन्यां वहेत् = भवानेतदर्हेदिति, and on sûtra 172 भवता खलु भारो वोढव्यः = भवान्हि शक्तः. — The kṛtyas may be also expressive of *indignation* at some fact, not expected. Mudr. VII, p. 220 Râxasa, when hearing the glory of his foe Câṇakya proclaimed in the very streets of Pâtaliputra, exclaims एतदपि नाम राक्षसेन श्रोतव्यम् (and even this Râxasa must hear!); Daç. 78 the wretched Jaina monk deplores his misfortune and the necessity, he has been put to, to break with the faith of his fathers मम तु मन्दभाग्यस्य..... अफलं विप्रलम्भप्रायमीदृशमिदमधर्मवर्त्म धर्मवत्समाचरणीयमासीत् (thus, on such a road of disbelief, as this, which gives no fruit, but rather deception, I must walk, as if it were the true faith).

P. 3, 3, 169.

Rem. Some kṛtyas are restricted to »necessity," viz. those in °आव्य, cp. P. 3, 1, 125. — Other irregularities of meaning are caused by the improper employment of the passive voice, as दानीय, when denoting »the person who deserves a gift," संधेय »one fit to make an alliance with" (Panc. III, 8), उद्वेजनीय »to be dreaded" (ibid. III, 142). Some may have even an active meaning, see P. 3, 4, 68.

P. 3, 3, 113.

CHAPT. V. **Participles and participial idioms.**

358. When laying down the syntax of the participles, there must be distinguished between the participial forms and the participial employment.

Participles.

As to their form the **participles** are adjective nouns, derived by constant suffixes from any verbal root, and which are the proper exponents of participial employment. Sanskrit possesses 1. three participles for the continuous action, one in each voice (कुर्वन्, कुर्वाणः, क्रियमाणः), which are named *participles of the present* [1]), 2. two *participles for the future*, one in the

Different classes of them.

1) In Sanskrit, this term is less improper, than in many other languages, because its present has chiefly the character of expressing the durative (वर्तमान), see **326**.

active voice (करिष्यन्) and one serving both for the medial and the passive (करिष्यमाणः), 3. the *krtyas*, which are passive participles for the future, but with a special employment, see **357**, 4. two *participles for the past*, to signify what is done, achieved, completed as कृतः and कृतवान्, the latter of which has always an active meaning, as to the former see **360.**

It must be kept in mind, that the participles, unless they themselves do duty as finite verbs, denote the past, present or future only with regard to the time, involved by the chief verb of the sentence.

359. Additional remarks. — 1. As participles of the future in the active may be considered also *a.*) the krts in °उ, derived from desideratives, as चिकीर्षु (wishing to do, being about to do), cp. **52** *a*, f. i. Daç. 166 तत्र च स्वादु पानीयमेधांसि कन्दमूलफलानि संजिघृक्षवः..... अवातराम (and there [on that island] we descended, desiring to take sweet water, fuel, turnips, roots and fruits); *b.*) some in °इन्, mentioned by P. 3, 3, 3, as गमी ग्रामम् (one, who will go to the village), they do even duty as finite verbs: Kathâs. 35, 104 उत्तिष्ठ राजन्भावी ते वीरो वंशधरः सुतः (get up, my king, a son will be born to you —), Vikram. V, p. 181 सुरासुरविमर्दो भावी = °भविता; *c.*) those in °अक, when put close to the chief verb; they are expressive of a purpose, cp. **52** *c.* [1]).

2. Further there are the old participles of the past, formed with reduplication, such as चकृवान्, f. चक्रुषी, n. चकृवत् for the active voice, and चक्राणः for the passive. In classic Sanskrit they have almost wholly got out of use. Already Pânini restricts them to Holy Writ, with the exception of six, viz. सेदिवान्, ऊषिवान्, (P. 3, 2, 106—109.)

---

1) I was wrong, in doubting, on p. 39 N. 3 of this book, at the correctness of the example (Mhbh. 3, 73, 25 = Nala 21, 22) भवन्तमभिवादकः quoted by Whitney. When reading once more not only that passage, but the whole sarga, I clearly saw, that भवन्तम् cannot but depend here on अभिवादकः.

शुश्रुवान्, the compounds अनाश्वान्, उपेयिवान्, अनूचानः. The participle in °वान् (वांस्) is, however, oftener met with in the post-Pâninean literature, than would be expected by this rule, but it occurs chiefly in epic poetry and in kâvyas. Mhbh. 1, 44, 10 वितद्विवान्, R. 1, 26, 25 विनेदुषी, Kathâs. 25, 72 अनिदूस्य निषेदुषः, Kumâras. 2, 4 नमस्तुभ्यं..... भेदमुपेयुषे, ibid. 6, 72 पद्मातस्थुषा त्वया, ibid. 6, 64 इत्यूचिवांस्तमेवार्थम्, Kathâs. 81, 31, Çiçup. 1, 17 etc. That it may even do duty as finite verb, has been mentioned 338. But the participle of the past in °आन has wholly antiquated, and is only met with in the archaic dialect, see f. i. Çat. Br. 3, 9, 1, 1; 11, 1, 6, 8 etc.

360. *participles in °त passive or intransitive or active.*

Of the participles in °त the great majority have a passive meaning, hence it is customary to call the whole class the passive participle of the past. But some others are not passives, but intransitives, as गत (gone), मृत (died), भिन्न (split. Some again may be even transitive actives, as पीत (having drunk), प्राप्त (having reached), विस्मृत (having forgotten), विभक्त (having divided), in this case they may generally convey sometimes a passive, sometimes an active meaning. For instance:

आरूढ act. Daç. 138 आरूढश्च लोको यथायथमुच्चैःस्थानानि.	pass. R. 2, 83, 5 शतं सहस्राण्यश्वानां समारूढानि (the scholiast adds सादिभिः).

With this verb, the active meaning is the more common.

प्रसूत act. Utt. III, p. 38 तत्र दारकद्वयं प्रसूता [sc. सीता].	pass. Ragh. 1, 12 तदन्वये शुद्धिमति प्रसूतः..... दिलीपः.
अपराद्ध act. Çâk. I कथमपराद्धस्तपस्विनामस्मि (how, have I offended the holy men?)	pass. Kathâs. 17, 48 देव्या नैवापराद्धं ते (there is no offence done to you by the queen).
प्रविष्ट act. Vikram. II, p. 29 आदर्शनात्प्रविष्टा सा मे सुरलोकसुन्दरी हृदयम्.	pass. R. (Gorr.) 5, 56, 28 प्रविष्टं ते मया वक्त्रम्.
प्राप्त act. Mudr. I, p. 7 अभिमता भवनमतिथयः प्राप्ताः (welcome guests are come to my house).	pass. Hit. 24 पक्षिभिः..... तरुकोटरे ष्ववकाशस्थानि प्राप्तानि.

Moreover, in accordance to what has been stated above the neuter sing. of all intransitive participles may be employed also in a passive sense. Instead of अयं गतः, अयं मृतः, one says as well गतमनेन, मृतमनेन. Cp. Pat. I, p. 468. P. 3, 4, 72.

Rem. 1. If a participle in °त is used with intransitive meaning, then the transitive passive is commonly expressed by the corresponding part. of the causative. भिन्न means »split by itself" भेदित »split [by somebody]," प्रबुद्ध »awake" but प्रबोधित »roused," जात »born" but जनित »engendered," पतित »fallen" but पातित »thrown" etc.

Rem. 2. As far as I know, the participles in °न never convey a transitive active meaning; they are, as a rule, intransitives, as भग्न, भिन्न, मग्न.

361. Occasionally the participles in °त are used of the present. They are then expressive of an action achieved, completed, finished. So गत and स्थित when = „being," शक्त „able," मृत „dead," भग्न „broken." P. 3, 2, 187; 188.

362. *Participial employment.* II. We will now treat of the **participial employment**. Before defining it, abstraction is to be made of the case in which the participles are nothing more or less than simple attributive adjectives, as विरुद्धो धर्मः, when = „a forbidden law," or even substantives, as वृद्धः when = „old man," शिष्यः „when = disciple.[1]). Apart from this adjectival function, the participles serve to express attending circumstances or other qualifications

1) A special rule of Pâṇini (3, 3, 114) teaches the neuters of participles in °त to be admissible as nouns of action. So Mhbh. 1, 157, 41 सर्वैः सह मृतं श्रेयो न च मे जीवितं क्षमम् (it is better to die together, nor can I bear to live). Pat. I, p. 11 हिक्कितहसितकण्डूयितानि नैव दोषाय भवन्ति नाप्यभ्युदयाय (hiccoughing, laughing and scratching are neither sinful nor pious actions).

of the main action, whether temporal or local, causal, concessive, conditional, hypothetical, etc. In other terms, in Sanskrit, as elsewhere, the participles are a concurrent idiom of subordinate sentences, of which, indeed, they may be said to exhibit the rudimentary form.

Examples: 1. the participle equivalent to a simple relative clause. Panc. 2 अत्र च मद्दत्तां वृत्तिं भुञ्जानानां पण्डितानां पञ्चशती तिष्ठति (here are five hundred scholars, who enjoy a salary which I give them).

2. the participle denoting time, state, condition, circumstance. Panc. 268 शृगालः कोपाविष्टस्तमुवाच (the jackal being filled with anger, said to him), Bhoj. 17 एवं वित्तादिव्ययं कुर्वाणं राजानं प्रति कदाचिन्मुख्यामात्येनेत्थमभ्यधायि (now, as the king made such expenses of money etc., his first minister once addressed him thus), Mṛcch. VI, p. 222 वरं व्यायच्छतो मृत्युर्न गृहीतस्य बन्धने (better to die while showing prowess, than in fetters after having been seized).

3. the participle denoting cause, motive. Panc. 58 ते तथा कर्तव्या यथा पलायन्तो हन्यमानाः स्वर्गं न गच्छन्ति (they must be brought to such a pass as to be excluded from heaven, being killed in the flight), here the complex पलायन्तो हन्यमानाः points at the cause of their not reaching heaven; R. 1, 1, 99 पठन्रामायणं नरः प्रेत्य स्वर्गे महीयते (by reading the Râmâyana one gains heaven).

4. the participle equivalent to a concessive sentence. Panc. 304 भो निषिद्धस्त्वं मयानेकशो न शृणोषि (though I have dissuaded you several times, you do not listen to me). In this meaning, अपि is generally subjoined to the participle, see **423.**

5. the participle expressive of the protasis of a conditional or hypothetical sentence. Daç. 140 अस्य तु पाणिग्राहकस्य गतिमननुप्रपद्यमाना भवत्कुलं कलङ्कयेयम् (if I should not follow the path of my [deceased] husband, I should dishonour your family), Kathâs. 77, 92 अजल्पतो जानतस्ते शिरो यास्यति खण्डशः (if you do not say it, and know it, your head will fall off into a thousand pieces).

6. the participle denoting a purpose, aim, intention. Thus is the proper employment of the p a r t i c i p l e o f t h e f u t u r e. Kathâs. 38, 157 त्यक्ष्यन्ती तं देशं ब्राह्मणसादकृत वसतिं स्वाम् (being about to leave her country, she ceded her house to the brahmans),

Daç. 79 प्रकृतिस्थानमून्विधास्यन्कर्णोसुतप्रहिते पथि मतिमकरवम् (as I wished to bring them back to their natural state —) Mhbh. 1, 163, 16 वृक्षमादाय राक्षसः। ताडयिष्यंस्तदा भीमं पुनरभ्यद्रवद् बली (the giant took a tree and ran once more at Bhîma, that he might strike him).

363. As a rule, the mere participle suffices for this purpose. Now, as this is by far less done in modern languages, different connectives are to be added, when translating, as *when*, *if*, *though*, *because*, *as*, *while* sim. In short, participles in Sanskrit are as significant as they are in Latin and Greek.

The only particles added are इव, to denote comparison, and अपि, the exponent of a concessive meaning. Panc. 54 पश्यतास्या राजकन्यायाः पुरुषोपभुक्ताया इव शरीरावयवा विभाव्यन्ते (her body looks, *as if* she were —), ibid. 278 परितोष्यमाणापि न प्रसीदति (*though* she is being satisfied, she is not kind), ibid. II, 173 सकृत्कन्दुकपातेन पतत्यार्यः पतन्नपि (a noble-minded man falls as a ball does, *if* he should fall *at all*).

364. Nouns with participial employment. सन्त् added. The participial employment is not limited to the participles. Any adjective may be employed as if it were a participle. It is then usual to add to it the participle सन्त् (being). Yet, सन्त् is not indispensable and is often wanting, especially if it is a bahuvrîhi that has a participial employment.

Examples: *a.*) of सन्त् added. Çâk. IV वनौकसोऽपि सन्तो लौकिकज्ञा वयम् (though living in the forests, we know the world), ibid. III कुतस्ते कुसुमायुधस्य सतस्तैक्ष्ण्यमेतत् (how did you come by that sharpness, you, whose arrows are but flowers?), Kathâs. 24, 67 बाढं मया सा नगरी दृष्टा विद्यार्थिना सता। भ्रमता भुवम् (I saw that town, indeed, while I wandered about when a student), Panc. 44 कथं दृढबन्धनबद्धा सती तत्र गच्छामि (how can I go there, being tied with strong fetters?).

b.) of the mere adjective. Panc. I, 109 किं भक्तेनासमर्थेन किं शक्तेनापकारिणा (what is the use of a faithful [servant], if he be not able, what, of an able, if he be not faithful?), Çâk. II two young ascetics are approaching, the king, before their being ushered in, knows them by their voice and says अये धीरप्रशान्तस्वरैस्तपस्विभिर्भवितव्यम् (by the sound of their voice, which is strong and soft at the same time, they must be inferred to be ascetics), Hit. 91 तामाख्यातुकाम एव सत्वरमागतोऽहम् (wishing to tell it [sc. the news वार्ताम्], I have come here).

Rem. 1. Bahuvrîhis, the predicate of which is a participle, generally share the participial employment. Panc. 130 अथ तं दृष्ट्वा शङ्कितमना व्यचिन्तयत् (when he saw him, he became anxious and reflected), Ven. I, p. 25 देवि समुद्धतामर्षैरस्माभिरागतापि भवती नोपलक्षिता (Madam, by the angry mood I am in, I have not noticed your coming here), Mudr. III, p. 112 आर्येणैवं सर्वतो निरुद्धचेष्टाप्रसरस्य मम बन्धनमिव राज्यं न राज्यमिव (if mylord in this manner crosses my liberty of movement, my kingdom seems a prison to me, not a kingdom).

Rem. 2. सन्त्, however, is occasionally added even to real participles. Panc. 126 तेन मूर्खेण वानरेण क्रुद्धेन सता..... प्रहारो विहितः (now, that stupid monkey, being in an angry temper, gave a blow), ibid. 335 सोऽपि कर्कटस्तत्रैव स्थितः सन्सर्पप्राणानपाहरत् (while standing on that very spot, the crab etc.), Mhbh. 1, 166, 2 स..... पूर्वमेवागतां। सतीं ददर्शाप्सरसं तत्र, here सती added helps the understanding of the remote past. Cp. Panc. 248, l. 7.

Absolute cases.

365. Absolute cases. As the participle is an adjective noun, it needs must rest on some substantive, of which it is the predicate, and with which it is to agree in gender, number and case (**27**). We may call this substantive the *subject* of the participle. When being a pronoun, it is often not expressed (**10**), as little when a general subject. But, whether understood or expressed, it is likely to form part of the chief sentence, and by its noun-case, which is at the same time that of the participle, it marks the nature of the logical relation, which exists between the principal action and the subordinate one.

Yet, the participial employment is not restricted to

the case, that the subject of the participle occurs in the chief sentence. In Sanskrit, like many other languages, it extends also to the absolute cases, by which name one denotes the participle with its subject, if they are but loosely connected with the principal sentence, their noun-case not being grammatically dependent on any word or phrase in the chief sentence. Sanskrit has two absolute cases: the *locative* and the *genitive*. Of these, the former is the general one, the latter has a much narrower employment.

366. Absolute locative. The **absolute locative** is a very frequent idiom. It is the Sanskrit counterpart of the Latin absolute ablative and the like genitive of Greek. It shares the whole manysidedness of signification of the participial employment. In other terms, it is equivalent to any kind of subordinate sentence: temporal, modal, causal, conditional, hypothetical, concessive, etc. P. 2, 3, 37.

Examples: Kathâs. 5, 106 दिवसेषु गच्छत्सु (time going), ibid. 28, 134 एतस्मिन्मृते राजसुते कोऽर्थो ममासुभिः (that prince being dead, what care I for my own life?), Çâk. I पौरवे वसुमतीं शासति (*while* a Paurava rules the land), Daç. 118 तमसि विजृम्भिते..... उत्थिते क्षपाकरे..... यथोचितं शयनीयमभजे (*when* darkness had spread and the moon had risen, I went to bed), Çâk. I कर्णं ददात्यभिमुखं मयि भाषमाणे (she hearkens, *when I speak* in her presence), Hit. 96 एवमुक्तवति दूते (after the messenger had thus spoken), Nala 5, 33 वृते तु नैषधे भैम्या लोकपाला महौजसः..... नलायाष्टौ वरान्ददुः (Nala having been chosen by the daughter of Bhîma, —), Panc. 17 अथोपसृत्य दमनको निर्दिष्ट आसने पिङ्गलकं प्रणम्य प्राप्तानुज्ञ उपविष्टः.

367. It is not necessary, that the predicate of the absolute locative be a participle. It may be also a noun (adjective or substantive). Often, however, सन्त्, वर्तमान, स्थित etc. are added.

Examples of सन्त् etc. added to the participle or noun. Panc. 242 सूर्योदये ऽन्धतां प्राप्तेषूलूकेषु सत्सु (at day-break, when the owls had become blind) [cp. 364 R. 2], ibid. I, 310 रात्रौ दीपशिखाकान्तिर्न भानावुदिते सति (it is at night-time that the light of the lamp is pleasant, not when the sun has risen), ibid. 56 the king says to his daughter पुत्रि त्वयि दुहितरि वर्तमानायां नारायणे भगवति जामातरि स्थिते तत्किमेवं युज्यते यत्सर्वे पार्थिवा मया सह विग्रहं कुर्वन्ति (my child, as you are my daughter, and Lord Vishṇu my son-in-law, how etc.)

Examples of a nominal predicate without auxiliary. Panc. 62 एतत्सरः शीघ्रं शोषं यास्यति। अस्मिन् शुष्के..... एते नाशं यास्यन्ति (this lake will soon become dry, when it will be dry, they will perish), Bhoj. 12 राज्ञि धर्मिणि धर्मिष्ठाः पापे पापपराः सदा [viz. प्रजाः] (if the king be virtuous, the subjects will be virtuous, if wicked, they too will be fond of wickedness), Çâk. V कथं धर्मक्रियाविघ्नः सतां रक्षितरि त्वयि (— while you are the protector), Prabodh. II, p. 39 कामक्रोधादिषु प्रतिपक्षेषु कुतेयमुदेष्यति तथापि लघीयस्यपि रिपौ नानवहितेन जिगीषुणा भाव्यम् (as Love, Anger etc. are her adversaries, how will she [Vishnubhakti] march against them? Nevertheless, no one, who is desirous of victory, must be careless, even if his enemy is rather weak).

368. Occasionally the subject in the absolute locative is understood, as एवं सति ([this] being so), तथानुष्ठिते (after [this] had been performed in this way). Of course, it is always wanting with impersonal verbs, as Daç. 107 तेनाभ्युपगते (after his having consented), Mhbh. 1, 154, 21 गन्तव्ये न चिरं स्थातुमिह शक्यम् (since we must start, we cannot stay here long), ibid. 1, 150, 4 विदिते धृतराष्ट्रस्य धार्तराष्ट्रो न संशयः। दग्धवान्पाण्डुदायादान्.

369. *Absolute genitive.* Sometimes the **absolute genitive** is a concurrent idiom of the absolute locative. It is far from bearing the general character of the latter. It is limited, indeed, to the expression of some action not cared for while performing the main action. Sometimes the absolute genitive may be rendered by „though, notwithstanding, in spite of" and the like, sometimes it is simply pointing out, which action is going on at the time when the main action intervenes, then we may translate it by „while" or „as." Other restrictions of its employment are: 1. its predicate must have a durative meaning, and is therefore in most cases a participle of the present, or at least a partic. or adjective, which does duty as such; 2. its subject must be a person. Upon the whole, the absolute genitive is usually found in standing phrases [1]).

According to P. 2, 3, 38 the absolute genitive is expressive of some action not cared for, while performing the action of the chief sentence. The commentary illustrates this rule by the example रुदतः प्राव्राजीत्, which is interchangeable with रुदति प्रा°, because it means रुदन्तं पुत्रादिकमनादृत्य प्रव्रजितः (he has forsaken the world not ĉaring for the tears of his family). [2]).

---

1) These rules have chiefly been fixed by F. de Saussure in his valuable and exhaustive treatise *de l'emploi du génitif absolu en Sanscrit.*

The rule of the subject being a person is violated Kumâras. 1, 27 अनन्तपुष्पस्य मधोर्हि चूते द्विरेफमाला सविशेषसङ्गा (though spring has an immense variety of flowers, the rows of bees cling especially to the âmra-flower), unless it be supposed that Kâlidâsa means the personified Spring. — In this passage of the Râmâyaṇa (3, 11, 58) ततो भुक्तवतां तेषां विप्राणामिल्वलोऽब्रवीत्। वातापे निष्क्रमस्वेति a participle of the past in °तवन्त् is the predicate.

2) Pâṇini's sûtra runs thus: षष्ठी चानादरे. The precéding s. 37 यस्य च भावेन भावलक्षणम् enjoins the employment of the absolute locative. Now, s. 38 allows the genitive too, but only for the case, that there is to be expressed अनादर. One may ask, what is the exact meaning of this term. Does it mean »disregard," or has it rather a more general import, that of »indifference?" The former interpretation needs implies the participial action being known to the agent of the main action, but this is no requisite to the latter. If we consider the practice of Sanskrit phraseology, it becomes very probable, we must take अनादर in its widest sense. Then all cases of absolute genitive may range under it. In such phrases as R. 1, 60, 15 सशरीरो नरेश्वरः। दिवं जगाम काकुत्स्थ मुनीनां पश्यतां तदा। (under the eyes of the *munis*, the king [Triçanku] ascended to heaven) the *anâdara* is to be found in this, that the chief action is going on

Examples: 1. the gen. = *though*, *in spite of*, *notwithstanding*. Panc. 193 यदेते मया पृष्टाः सचिवास्तावदत्र स्थितस्यापि तव तत्परीक्षार्थम् (that I have asked them, though you were here, was but to make a trial), Mudr. III, p. 124 नन्दाः.... पशव इव हताः पश्यतो राक्षसस्य (— under the very eyes of Râxasa), Panc. 152 मूषकः] पश्यतो मे परिभ्रमन्, Mhbh. 1, 102, 70 विचित्रवीर्यस्तरुणो यक्ष्मणा समगृह्यत। सुहृदां यतमानानामाप्तैः सह चिकित्सकैः। जगाम..... यमसादनम् (Vicitravîrya became consumptive, when being young, and died in spite of the efforts of his friends and skilled physicians), R. 2, 100, 4 न हि त्वं जीवतस्तस्य वनमागन्तुमर्हसि (do not go to the forest during his lifetime [= *eo vivo*]). In the last example the notion of disregard appears, if one eliminates the negation: »the action of going to the forest though he is living, must not be done by you."[1]).

2. the gen. is expressive of a situation, existing at the time, when the main action intervenes, Eng. *while*, *as*. Panc. 131 एवं वदतस्तस्य स लुब्धकस्तत्रागत्य..... निभृतः स्थितः (while he was speaking thus, the said hunter came and concealed himself), ibid. 44 the barber's wife asks her friend नायं पापात्मा मम गताया उत्थितः (the rogue [she means her husband] has not risen [from his couch] during my absence, has he?), Kathâs. 18, 356 इति चिन्तयतस्तस्य तत्र तोयार्थमाययुः.... स्त्रियः (while he reflected thus, females came), ibid. 3, 11 तेषां निवसतां तत्र..... तीव्रो दुर्भिक्षः समजायत.

Rem. 1. Between these two different kinds of absolute genitive there are, of course, interjacent links. The *anâdara* of the action conveyed by the absolute genitive may be more than simple independence and less than full disregard. Mhbh. 1, 153, 7 ग्रहमेनं हनिष्यामि प्रेक्षन्त्यास्ते सुमध्यमे »I shall kill him, beautiful lady, and

---

quite independently of the circumstance, that the holy men were its spectators. Then, the term *anâdara* holds also good for the case, that the absolute genitive is merely expressive of the situation.

The Mahâbhâshya has no comment on our rule, the Kâtantra does not mention it at all, see Trilocanadâsa on Kât. 2, 4, 34 (p. 499 of EGGELING's ed.).

1) See DE SAUSSURE, p. 23. In the same book, p. 63—74 plenty of instances prove the frequency of the phrase पश्यतस्तस्य and the like.

even in your presence," here the absolute turn denotes the easiness of the enterprise.[1])

Rem. 2. The absolute genitive seems to be very rare in the archaic dialect.[2])

370. Apart from this absolute genitive, Sanskrit upon the whole shows a preference for employing genitives of the participle, either as dative-like genitives (**129**) or when depending on some substantive. The frequency of this turn makes it sometimes difficult to distinguish between the absolute and the not-absolute construction.

The semi-absolute genitive.

In some phrases both seem to mingle. For them we may use the term of s e m i - a b s o l u t e construction, for the logical relation between the genitive and the principal sentence, though not wholly wanting, is very loose, indeed.[3]) Here are some instances. Panc. 154 एवं चिन्तयतो महाकष्टेन स दिवसो व्यतिक्रान्तः (»he thinking so" or »for him as he thought so" the day passed slowly), Daç. 144 इह च नो वसन्तोनां द्वादश समाः समत्ययुः, and so regularly to denote »while somebody was doing so and so, some other arrived, the sun rose or set, time passed etc." See f. i. Panc. 56, l. 1, R. 3, 11, 68, Kathâs. 15, 123, R. 2, 62, 19, ibid. 85, 14. This idiom borders on that, treated **128** R. 2.

Of a somewhat different nature are such instances as Mudr. V, p. 180 चन्द्रगुप्तस्य विक्रेतुरधिकं लाभमिच्छतः। कल्पिता मूल्यमेतेषां क्रूरेण भवता वयम् (as Candragupta in selling them [the jewels], desired an ex-

---

1) DE SAUSSURE, p. 24 and 25 quotes a few passages pointing to the fact, that the absolute gen. occasionally may answer to fr. *pour peu que = for aught.*

2) The oldest instance of it, known to DE SAUSSURE, is Maitrâyaṇîyopanishad 1, 4 मिषतो बन्धुवर्गस्य महतीं श्रियं त्यक्त्वास्माल्लोकादमुं लोकं प्रयाताः. Another instance from the archaic dialect is Âp. Dharm. 1, 2, 7, 13 पश्यतोऽस्य, cp. the foot-note on p. 288 above.

3) See DE SAUSSURE p. 33—41.

orbitant profit, you, cruel man, have made ourselves the price), Panc. 162 तदेनं मुक्त्वा मम जीवन्त्या नान्यः पाणिं ग्रहीष्यति, Çâk. I करं व्याधुन्वन्त्याः पिबसि रतिसर्वस्वमधरम्, Nâgân. I, p. 8 तन्निवासयोग्यमिदं तपोवनं मन्ये भविष्यतीह वसतामस्माकं निर्वृतिः. In the first of these examples the genitive may be accepted as a dative-like one (**129**), in the remaining it depends on a noun (पाणिम्, मम understood, निर्वृतिः). Likewise Nala 24, 15, Panc. 57 यदि मम स्थानार्थमुद्यतस्य मृत्युर्भविष्यति, etc. etc. Cp. also the foot-note on p. 94 of this book.

Rem. The differences between the absolute and the semi-absolute genitives are sometimes very small, indeed. Panc. 156 एवं मे चिन्तयतस्ते भृत्या मम शत्रूणां सेवका जाताः, here the absolute turn would be doubtful but for the pronoun of the 1st person repeated. That in such phrases, as »while A. was doing this, B. arrived," the genitive is thought by Sanskrit-speakers an absolute one, is proved by this, that the absolute locative is used too. Mhbh. 1, 169, 1 वसत्सु तेषु प्रच्छन्नं पाण्डवेषु महात्मसु। आजगामाथ तान्द्रष्टुं व्यासः, Kathâs. 42, 165 अथैतस्यां च मयि च..... मरणाध्यवसायिन्योरागतस्त्वमिहाधुना.

371. The absolute turn admissible, even if its subject occurs also in the main sentence.

It is no hindrance to the absolute construction, if its subject is a word, occurring also in the main sentence. Panc. 67 एवं चिन्तयतस्तस्य शशको मन्दं मन्दं गत्वा प्रणम्य तस्याग्रे स्थितः, here तस्य, the subj. of चिन्तयतः means the lion, तस्याग्रे the same lion. Kathâs. 29, 77 कदर्थयति मामेषा तवाम्बा त्वय्यपि स्थिते, here the absolute loc. is used, though its subject त्वयि is also represented in the main sentence by तव. Cp. R. 3, 57, 2; Nala 5, 33.

372. Semi-absolute instrumental.

The semi-absolute employment must also be stated for the instrumental. Here are some instances. Kathâs. 29, 55 सखि भुक्तैः फलैरेतैर्जरा न ते भविष्यति (*by eating* these fruits you will enjoy eternal youth), R. 2, 64, 18 स चोद्धृतेन बाणेन सहसा स्वर्गमास्थितः (*as soon as* the arrow *had been drawn* out, he mounted to heaven), Panc. 57 सुभगे समस्तैः शत्रुभिर्हतैरन्नं पानं चास्वादयिष्यामि (my dear, I will not take either food or drink until *after having killed* all the enemies), ibid. 178 भद्र न भेतव्यमस्मद्विधैर्मित्रैर्विद्यमानैः (do not fear, *with* such friends as we are), Kathâs. 55, 213 तुष्टया विन्ध्यवासिन्या पत्नीपुत्रौ त्वमाप्स्यसि, Panc. 194 तैर्ज्ञातैः स्वपक्षः परपक्षश्च वश्यो भवति (Lat. *his cog-*

nitis et tui et adversarii tibi obnoxii erunt). In all of them the absolute locative might have been used. The instrumental represents the action, expressed by the participle, as the *cause* or *motive* or *means* of the main action, and in this respect it shows a close affinity to the Latin absolute ablative.

Other participial idioms.

373. Parti- ciple .dded to a erb of affec- on of nind.

Other participial idioms are:

I. The participle added to a verb, expressive of some affection of mind, to signify the motive of the affection. Panc. 149 किं न लज्जसे एवं ब्रुवाणः (do you not feel ashamed at speaking thus?), ibid. 147 शोचितव्यस्त्वं गर्वं गतः (one must pity you for having become proud), ibid. 112 अनयोर्विरोधं वितन्वता त्वया साधु न कृतम् (you have not done well by kindling discord between them), Mhbh. 1, 145, 9 तान्राज्यं पितृतः प्राप्तान्धृतराष्ट्रो न मृष्यते (Dhṛt. cannot endure their having obtained the kingdom from their father's side), Mahâv. I, p. 18 स्पृहयामि रामभद्रालङ्कृताय राज्ञे दशरथाय.

74. redi- ative cusa- e and omi- ative ress- by a rtici- or a oun d as ch.

II. The participle, which expresses the predicate of the object of the verbs of *seeing, hearing, knowing, thinking, feeling, conceiving, wishing* and the like. Since, of course, it must agree with the object, it is an accusative with the active voice, but a nominative with the passive of the chief verb (**6**). So it is said मां प्रविशन्तमपश्यत् (he saw me enter), pass. अहमनेन प्रविशन्दृश्ये. By using some other noun instead of the participle, we get the idiom, mentioned **32** c.), f. i. मां युवानमपश्यत् (he saw me being young = he saw, I was young).

This much used **accusative with participle** is the counterpart of Latin acc. with infinitive, which construction does not exist in Sanskrit (**390** R. 2). Concurrent idioms are the *oratio directa* with इति and relative sentences with the conjunctions यद् or यथा (491 foll).

Examples: *a.*) with an active chief verb. Panc. 51 काञ्चिद्राजकन्यां करेणुकारूढां..... समायातां दृष्टवन्तौ (they saw some princess approaching on elephant's back), Mudr. IV, p. 158 न मां दूरीभवन्तमिच्छति कुमारः (the prince does not desire my being far), Çâk. IV वेत्सि न मामुपस्थितम् (you do not know, I am near), Hit. 2 स भूपतिरेकदा केनापि पठ्यमानं श्लोकद्वयं शुश्राव (once the king heard somebody read two çlokas), Kathâs. 9, 74 शबरेण हठाक्रान्तमटव्यां सर्पमैक्षत, Çâk. VII अङ्गुलीयकदर्शनादूढपूर्वां तद्दुहितरमवगतोऽहम् (on seeing the ring, I remembered that I had wedded his daughter). As to the last examples cp. **14**, VIIly.

b.) with a passive chief verb. Mudr. III, p. 120 कस्मादार्येणापक्रामन्नुपेक्षितः (why have you overlooked his withdrawal?), R. 3, 67, 16 Jaṭâyu tells Râma, he has seen the carrying off of Sîtâ ह्रियमाणा मया दृष्टा रावणेन, Kathâs. 41, 4 मित्रेण कथितोऽधुना..... अमुष्य भ्राता देशान्तरे मृतः (a friend has now told him, his brother died abroad), Çâk. III गान्धर्वेण विवाहेन बह्व्यो राजर्षिकन्यकाः। श्रूयन्ते परिणीतास्ताः पितृभिश्चाभिनन्दिताः.

Predicative genitive.

Rem. If not a chief verb, but a nomen actionis is attended by the predicate of its object, both the object and its predicate are put in the genitive [110]. Panc. 67 the animals of the forest have engaged themselves to send every day one among them to the lion for food; when it was the turn of the hare, she went to the lion and said, she with four other hares had been sent by the animals मम लघुतरस्य प्रस्तात्वं विज्ञाय »as they knew me to be reputed [a] rather insignificant [animal]", Mâlav. I, p. 18 राज्ञः समक्षमेवावयोरधरोत्तरयोर्व्यक्तिर्भविष्यति (in the very presence of the king it will appear which of us is superior and which inferior).

375. Sanskrit possesses the turn *reges*

III. In translating Sanskrit participles, it is sometimes necessary to substitute for them infinitives or nouns of action. So the abs. locat. कृते शासने may be = »after performing the order." This idiom, the counterpart of Latin *reges exacti* = *exactio regum*, is not rare, *exacti = exactio regum.* especially in the instrumental[1]). So f. i. Nâgân. I, p. 5 किमनेनावस्तुना चिन्तितेन वरं तातान्नैवानुष्ठिता (do not reflect on this nonsense, better would it be to act after your father's injunction), Panc. I, 5 वरं जातप्रेतो वरमपि च कन्यैव जनिता..... न चाविद्वान् रूपद्रविणगुणयुक्तोऽपि तनयः (better is it, that he dies scarcely after being born, better is the birth of a daughter..... than an unlearned son etc.).[2]) So often the participle in °त with किम् or अलम्. R. 2, 36, 30 तदलं देवि रामस्य श्रिया विहतया त्वया (therefore cease to destroy Râma's happiness), Mṛcch. VIII, p. 244 किमनेन ताडितेन तपस्विना (why strike this poor fellow?).

PARTICIPLES ATTENDED BY AUXILIARIES.

376. *Periphrastic employment of participles.* Sometimes participles are expressive of the chief predicate. In this case, **auxiliaries** are often wanted to denote the person or the tense or the nature of the action. The combination of participle and auxiliary effects a kind of periphrastic conjugation, which sometimes has an emphatic character, and sometimes serves to express special shades of tenses or moods, not to be pointed out by mere flexion.

Rem. It is only the past participles, that may do duty as finite verbs by themselves, without auxiliary. But even this is only admissible, if the subject is evident from the context. For this reason, in the 1st and 2d person the absence of the auxiliary commonly necessitates the expression of the pronoun, and inversely. See **11**.

377. We may divide this periphrastic conjugation into the following classes:

---

1) See DE SAUSSURE, p. 94 N. 1.

2) An instance from the archaic dialect may be Ait. Br. 1, 13, 8 सर्वो ह वा एतेन [sc. सोमेन] क्रीयमाणेन नन्दति.

Periphrastic tenses and moods.

I. To the past participle the present अस्ति or भवति is added, f. i. Prabodh. V, p. 103 हा पुत्रकाः क्व गताः स्थ दत्त मे प्रतिवचनम्, Mâlat. IV, p. 65 अभ्युपपन्नवानस्मि. This idiom falls together with the employment of the sole past participle as a past tense, see **336**.

II. The past participle is attended by another tense or mood of अस्ति or भवति.

Here are some examples: Daç. 100 इत्थं च मयोपमन्त्रितोऽभूत् (and I addressed him with these words), Kathâs. 79, 132 राज्ञाप्युच्चलितो बभूव = राज्ञाप्युच्चचाल, Mhbh. 1, 42, 34 श्रुतं हि तेन तदभूत् (for he had heard this). — Çâk. V किमुद्दिश्य भगवता काश्यपेन मत्सकाशमृषयः प्रेरिताः स्युः, here the optative of the past is expressed by periphrase, Kathâs. 27, 32 किं मयापकृतं राज्ञो भवेत् (in what can I have offended the king?). From the archaic dialect I add Ait. Br. 1, 4, 1 यः पूर्वमनीजानः स्यात् (he, who has never before performed a sacrifice). Cp. **345**.

Rem. By putting भविष्यति to the past participle, the future perfect may be expressed. Mhbh. 1, 162, 21 अर्थौ द्वावपि निष्पन्नौ युधिष्ठिर भविष्यतः (both purposes will be performed), Prabodh II, p. 45 ततः... शान्तिरुपरता भविष्यति (then Çânti will have departed this life).

III. The participle of the future is accompanied by the auxiliary.

This idiom is almost limited to the archaic dialect. In the brâhmaṇas the participle of the future not rarely joins with भवति and स्यात्. Ait. Br. 2, 11, 6 तं यत्र निहनिष्यन्तो भवन्ति तदध्वर्युर्बर्हिरधस्तादुपास्यति (on which spot they are to kill [the victim], there the adhvaryut hrows sacred grass [*barhis*]), Çat. Br. 3, 2, 2, 23 यत्र सुप्त्वा पुनर्नावद्रास्यन्भवति (when he, after having slept, is not to sleep again), Âçv. Gṛhy. 1, 3, 1 यत्र क्व च होष्यन्त्स्यात्.

37 IV. The participle of the present with आस्ते[1]), तिष्ठति, वर्तते, अस्ति, भवति is expressive of a **continuous**

1) Cp. the similar employment of Homeric ἧσθαι. Il. α, 133 ἦ ἐθέλεις ὄφρ' αὐτὸς ἔχῃς γέρας, αὐτὰρ ἔμ' αὔτως | ἧσθαι δευόμενον.

The continuous action expressed by periphrase.

action and is to be compared with English *to be* with the partic. in *-ing*, चिन्तयन्नास्ते or तिष्ठति etc. „he is reflecting," चिन्तयन्नभूत् „he has been reflecting," चिन्तयन्नासीत् etc. — Panc. 42 कौलिकः..... स्वाकारं निगूहमानः सदैवास्ते (the weaver was always concealing his disposition), Kathâs. 42, 140 एषोऽनया क्रीडन्नास्त (he was sporting with her); Daç. 156 नृपात्मजा तु..... रुदन्त्येव स्थास्यति (but the princess will not cease weeping), Panc. 330 सा यत्नेन रक्ष्यमाणा तिष्ठति (she is being guarded carefully); Mhbh. 1, 11, 5 तस्याहं तपसो वीर्यं जानन्नासम् (I was knowing the power of his ascese), Utt. II, p. 34 एतत्तदेव हि वनं..... यस्मिन्नभूम चिरमेव पुरा वसन्तः (this is the very forest, where we formerly dwelled for a long time), R. 2, 74, 2 मा मृतं रुदती भव (do not weep for the dead one).

Rem. 1. The participle in °त or a verbal adjective, provided that they have the meaning of a present, may be similarly construed with आस्ते, तिष्ठति and the rest. Panc. 285 सर्वोऽपि जनः स्वकर्मणैव रतस्तिष्ठति (everybody is content with his trade), ibid. 283 महामत्स्यः सलिलान्निष्क्रम्य बहिः स्थित आस्ते (— is staying outside the water), ibid. 160 तस्य रजकस्य बृहत्कन्या तत्र शयने सुप्तासीत् (— was sleeping on that couch), ibid. 318 परिपूर्णोऽयं घटः सक्तुभिर्वर्तते (this pot is filled with porridge), R. 2, 75, 29 मा च तं..... द्राक्षीद्राज्यस्थमासीनम् (and may he never see him occupy the royal dignity), Vikram. IV, p. 131 नीपस्कन्धनिषण्णास्तिष्ठति (— is sitting —).

Rem. 2. In the same way verbs meaning *not ceasing to do* are construed with the participle. Panc. 65 [सिंहो] नित्यमेवानेकान्मृगशशकादीन्व्यापादयन्नोपरराम (the lion did not cease killing —), ibid. 275 सापि प्रतिदिनं कुटुम्बेन सह कलहं कुर्वाणा न विश्राम्यति.

Rem. 3. The archaic dialect expresses the continuous action also by the participle with the verb इ, occasionally चर् (cp. WHITNEY § 1075, *a* and *b*). Ait. Br. 1, 25, 2 तां [sc. इषुं] व्यसृजंस्तया पुरो भिन्दन्त आयन् (it was this, they shot off, and by which they destroyed the towns), Pancaviṃçabrâhmaṇa अदण्ड्यं दण्डेन घ्नन्तश्चरन्ति [1]).

1) Cp. this passage from a classic author (Panc. 282) सा [sc. भार्या] न कथंचिद्गृहे स्थैर्यमालम्बते केवलं परपुरुषानन्वेषमाणा परिभ्रमति.

Rem. 4. Note that the auxiliaries may also be put in the passive. See **32** *b*.

CHAPT. VI. **Gerunds.**

379. The gerunds hold a place somewhat intermediate between infinitive and participle. As to their etymology, they are petrified noun-cases, and for this reason they are not declinable.

Gerund in °त्वा (°य). Its original meaning.

I. **The gerund in °त्वा (°य)** is the petrified instrumental of a verbal noun. At the outset कृत्वा was, as it were, a kind of infinitive of the aorist. This original nature is discernible *a.*) when the gerund is construed with किम् and अलम्, *b.*) if the action conveyed by it has a general subject.

a.) With किम् and अलम्, the gerund serves to express a prohibition, cp. **353** R. 1. Daç. 137 किं तव गोपायित्वा (»do not conceal," liter. »what [profit should be] to you by concealing?"). R. 2, 28, 25 अलं ते वनं गत्वा (have done going to the forest.[1]).

b.) Panc. III, 107 वृक्षांश्छित्त्वा पशून्हत्वा कृत्वा रुधिरकर्दमम्। यद्येवं गम्यते स्वर्गो नरकं केन गम्यते (if by cutting down trees, by killing victims,

1) Something of the kind, indeed, is contained in a rule of Pâṇini (3, 4, 18) अलंखल्वोः प्रतिषेधयोः प्राचां क्त्वा »according to the eastern grammarians the gerund is to be put with अलम् and खलु, if they express a prohibition."

The following sûtra (3, 4, 19) उदीचां माङो व्यतीहारे has been wholly misunderstood by the commentators even up to Patanjali. Not the verbal root मा, but the particle of negation is meant. I am convinced, our sûtra does not contain a new rule, but it is the continuation and at the same time the explanation of the preceding, in other terms, it is an old vârttika. The eastern grammarians, it is said, teach the use of अलम् and खलु in prohibitions »*in exchange* for [= *instead* of] (व्यतीहारे) मा, prescribed by the Northern ones." In fact, अलं कृत्वा = मा कार्षीः. — Of खलु thus used I know no instances from literature.

by shedding streams of blood, if thus one goes to heaven, by what way does one go to hell?).

380. *It is employed almost as a participle of the past.* But in its most common employment the gerund may be said to do duty as a past participle of the active. Like the absolute locative and the other participial employment it enables the speaker to cut short subordinate sentences and to avoid the accumulation of finite verbs (**14**, I). Indeed, it has the full function of a participle. As a rule, it denotes the prior of two actions, performed by the same subject. Accordingly its subject is that of the chief action. So it usually refers to a nominative, if the chief verb is active, or to an instrumental, if it is a passive. Nothing, however, prevents its being referred to other cases, since the main subject may occasionally be a gen., locat., dative etc. P. 3, 4, 21.

1. Instances of the gerund referring to a nominative or to an instrumental are so common as to be found on almost every page. Panc. 3 अथासौ राजा तां प्रतिज्ञां श्रुत्वा..... तस्मै सादरं तान्कुमारान्समर्प्य परां निर्वृतिमाजगाम (then the king having heard this promise, entrusted the princes to him and was highly satisfied with this), here श्रुत्वा and समर्प्य refer to राजा; — Panc. 70 अथ तेन तं शत्रुं मत्वात्मानं तस्योपरि प्रक्षिप्य प्राणाः परित्यक्ताः, the gerunds मत्वा and प्रक्षिप्य refer to तेन.

2. Instances of the gerund referring to other noun-cases: 1. to an accus. R. 3, 41, 18 आत्मानं च हतं विद्धि हृत्वा सीताम् (be aware that yourself will be lost, when seizing Sîtâ); — 2. to a genitive. Nala 3, 14 तस्य दृष्ट्वैव ववृधे कामस्तां चारुहासिनीम् (his love increased as soon as he had beheld the fair one), Panc. 69 न युज्यते स्वामिनस्तस्य सामर्थ्यमविदित्वा गन्तुम् (it does not befit mylord to go before having explored his strength); — 3. to a dative. Kumâras. 2, 18 स्वागतं स्वानधीकारान्प्रभावैरवलम्ब्य वः।..... युगबाहुभ्यः (welcome to you, mighty ones, who uphold your offices by your power); — 4. to a locative. Panc. 125 वानरे व्यजनं नीत्वा वायुं विदधति, the loc. is the absolute one: »as

the monkey having brought the fan, was fanning". — The subject of the gerund is comparatively often a genitive or a locative, owing to the frequent employment of the dative-like genitive (**129**) and of the absolute locative. For the rest, it is only from the context, that the subject of a given gerund is to be known. That f. i. Bhoj. 96 एकदा राजा धारानगरे विचरन्क्वचित्पूर्णकुम्भं धृत्वा समायान्तीं पूर्णचन्द्राननां कांचिद् दृष्ट्वा..... प्राह the gerund धृत्वा refers to काञ्चित्, but दृष्ट्वा to राजा, can be learned no otherwise.

3. The gerund may even refer to a subject not expressed, but understood. Utt. IV, p. 72 स्वयमुपेत्य वैदेही द्रष्टव्यः, from the context it is plain, that त्वया is implied. Likewise Nâgân. V, p. 91 हा कुमार क्वेमं प्राणेभ्योऽपि वल्लभं जनं परित्यज्य गम्यते [sc. त्वया]. Or to a general subject, as f. i. R. 3, 48, 23. Cp. **379** *b*).

Rem. Like the participles, the gerund may serve to express different logical relations, as is evident from these examples. Daç. 149 नाहमिदं तत्त्वतो नावबुध्य मोक्ष्यामि भूमिशय्याम् (I shall not rise *before* having learned what this really is), R. 3, 21, 10 तान्भूमौ पतितान्दृष्ट्वा.... महांस्त्रासोऽभवन्मम (*when* I saw..... great fear arose within me), Panc. III, 77 उलूकं नृपतिं कृत्वा का नः सिद्धिर्भविष्यति (what profit shall we have, *if* we make the owl our king?). Cp. **362**.

381. *Gerund expressive of simultaneousness.* Not always the gerund can be said to denote a past action, done previously to the chief action. Sometimes there is simultaneousness. R. 3, 43, 9 एवं ब्रुवाणं काकुत्स्थं प्रतिवार्य शुचिस्मिता। उवाच सीता, here प्रतिवार्य and ब्रुवाणम् are simultaneous, »Laxmana thus speaking and dissuading her." Cp. Daç. 159 केन वा निमित्तेनोत्सवमनादृत्यैकान्ते भवानुत्कण्ठित इव..... तिष्ठति (by what cause do you keep apart, not caring for the feast, as if longing for somebody?), ibid. 182 अहं युष्मदाज्ञया पितृवनमभिरक्ष्य तदुपजीवी प्रतिवसामि (by your orders I guard the cemetery and in virtue of this function it is there that I dwell). — Cp. also the idiom, taught **203**.

Hence the gerund, in the same way as the participle of the present (**378**), may even attend such verbs as आस्ते, तिष्ठति, वर्तते, to signify a continuous action. Kumâras. 1, 1 पूर्वापरौ तोयनिधी वगाह्य स्थितः पृथिव्या इव मानदण्डः (extending to both oceans, the eastern and the western, [Mount Himâlaya] stands as the measuring stick of the earth). Daç. 177 सर्वपौरानतीत्य वर्तते (he is the foremost of all the townsmen [1]), M. 7, 195 उपरुध्यारिमासीत (he [the king] must keep the enemy invested).

Rem. Occasionally the gerund is even expressive of a predicative attribute. R. 3, 19, 4 कालपाशं समासज्य कण्ठे मोहान्न बुध्यते (he is unaware, he has fastened the rope of Death round his neck), Mâlav. V, p. 124 सखे। मदपेक्षामनुवृत्यानया धारिण्या पूर्वचरितैः सम्भाव्यत एवैतत् (my friend, you only think so from Dh. having acted up to my desire by her former actions!). R. 2, 73,4 अङ्गारमुपगुह्य स्म पिता मेनावबुद्धवान्.

382. Gerund in °अम्. II. The other gerund, that in °अम्, is as to its origin the acc. of a verbal noun. It denotes some concomitant action and is comparatively seldom employed. When put twice, it is expressive of repeated or uninterrupted action. P. 3, 4, 22. Daç. 30 लाटेश्वरो देशस्यास्य पालयितुस्तनयां तरुणीरत्नमसमानलावण्यं श्रावंश्रावमवधूतदुहितृप्रार्थनस्य तस्य नगरीमरौत्सीत् (the king of Lâta always hearing of the matchless beauty of the daughter of the monarch —), ibid. 95 आस्वादमास्वादम् (savouring without interruption [2]).

For the rest the gerund in °अम् is limited to standing phrases, at least in classic Sanskrit. Pânini (3, 4, 25—64) gives a list of them. Of the kind are P. 3, 4, 29 कन्यादर्शं वरयति (as soon as he sees a girl, he woos her), ibid. 52 शय्योत्थायं धावति (after rising from his couch he runs), ibid. 50 केशग्राहं युध्यन्ते (v. a. they fight seizing each other by the hair), Daç. 144 जीवग्राहमग्रहीषम् (I captured him alive) cp. P. 3, 4, 36, Mudr. II, p. 76 लोष्टघातं हतः (was killed by lumps of earth) cp. P. 3, 4, 37, Mhbh. 1, 154, 30 निष्पिष्यैनं बलाद् भूमौ पशुमारममारयत् (he pressed him violently to the earth and killed him as one slaughters a victim), Kumâras. 4, 26 स्तनसंबाधमुरो जघान (she beat her breast, injuring her bosom), cp. P. 3, 4, 55. Likewise

---

1) Cp. वर्तते with the instrumental **67** R. 1.

2) The same purpose is served by putting twice the gerund in °त्वा. Pat. *passim* उत्प्लुत्योत्प्लुत्य मण्डूका गच्छन्ति (frogs move by jumping). See P. 3, 4, 22 and cp. Panc. II, 100.

ज़ोषमास्ते = तूष्णीं भवति, see f. i. Viddhaç. II, p. 36. From the archaic dialect I add Ait. Br. 1, 21, 11 अङ्गसमाख्यायमेवास्मिंस्तदिन्द्रियाणि दधाति (he deposits in him the mental and motive powers, while calling each member by its name), cp. P. 3, 4, 58. In all these expressions the gerund is the final member of a compound. — Another idiom is the employment of it with पूर्वम्, प्रथमम् or अग्रे, then both the gerund in °अम् and that in °त्वा are available, as प्रथमंभोजम् (or भुक्त्वा) व्रजति (he eats first, then he goes).

P. 3, 4, 24.

Rem. Upon the whole the gerund in °अम् is oftener used in the archaic dialect of the brâhmanas, than afterwards, and it is even in such cases as are not specialized by Pâṇini. Ait. Br. 2, 19, 7 यद्वग्राहमनुब्रूयात् (if he pronounces them piecemeal), Çat. Br. 12, 8, 3, 7 अभिसंसारं दिदृक्षितार: (people will go and see in crowds). — Pân. 3, 4, 12 speaks of the gerund in °अम् with the verb शक् as a vaidik idiom. Maitr. S. 1, 6, 4 अग्निं वै देवा विभाजं नाशक्नुवन् = विभक्तुं नाशक्नुवन्. Cp. TBr. 1, 1, 5, 6.

CHAPT. VII. Infinitive.

383. Sanskrit **infinitive** is a much employed form. It serves to denote *aim* and *purpose*, almost to any extent and without restriction. As a rule, the infinitive in तुम् may be put to any predicate, just as the dative of the purpose, to which it is equivalent. In **87** we have quoted a striking instance of this equivalence, Çâk. I आर्तत्राणाय व: शस्त्रं न प्रहर्तुमनागसि. Other examples of the infinitive being expressive of the aim may be Mhbh. 1, 160, 15 न च मे विद्यते वित्तं संक्रेतुं पुरुषं क्वचित् (and I have no money to buy some man somewhere), R. 2, 52, 9 तव..... तर्तुं सागरगामिनीं नौरियम् (here is a ship for you to cross the river), Daç. 40 दुष्टहृदयमेनं निहन्तुं मृदुरुपाय: कश्चिन्मया चिन्त्यते (I devise some gentle means for killing that scoundrel), R. 1, 42, 24 तां वै धारयितुं राजन्नान्यं पश्यामि शूलिन: (I know no one but Çiva, to bear her [the Gangâ]).

Sanskrit infinitive. Its employment.

P. 3, 3, 10.

384. Sanskrit infinitive, like ours, acts in some degree as a complement to the main predicate. Pâṇini enjoins its being put to words of *being able*, *venturing*, *knowing*, *being irksome*, *being fit*, *undertaking*, *taking*, *going*, *tolerating*, *deserving*, *being met with*, those of *sufficing*, *being a match for*, and in such phrases as: there is *an opportunity*, *a time* for doing something. Of course, these injunctions do not exhaust the sphere of the infinitive's employment, and may easily be enlarged. With the verbs of *wishing* the infinitive is likewise mentioned by Pâṇini, but as he adds in express terms, provided that the subjects of both the infinitive and the verb of wishing are the same.

P. 3, 4, 65.

P. 3, 4, 66.

P. 3, 3, 167.

P. 3, 3, 158.

Examples: Mhbh. 1, 150, 23 गन्तुं न शक्नुमः (we cannot go), Panc. 70 कस्ते प्रतापं सोढुं समर्थः (who is able to sustain your splendour?), Kumâras. 4, 11 वसतिं प्रिय कामिनां प्रियास्त्वदृते प्रापयितुं क ईश्वरः (who, except you, my beloved [Kâma], has the power of conducting the loving maidens to their lovers?); — Ven. I, p. 36 संग्रामैकार्णवान्तःपयसि विचरितुं पण्डिताः पाण्डुपुत्राः (the sons of Pându are skilled in acquitting themselves on the battle-field); — Mrcch. VIII, p. 256 दुष्करं विषमौषधीकर्तुम् (it is difficult to change poison into medicine); — Panc. 315 अहं त्वां प्रष्टुमागतः (I have come to you in order to ask), R. 2, 96, 17 आवां हन्तुं समभ्येति (he approaches in order to kill us); — Panc. 195 सर्वे मन्त्रयितुमारब्धाः (all began to deliberate), Prabodh. I, p. 7 पृथिव्यामाधिपत्यं स्थिरीकर्तुमयमस्य संरम्भः (it is his intention to establish his sway on the earth), Daç. 112 भवानपारं शोकसागरमद्योत्तारयितुं स्थितः (you are decided to cross to-day the shoreless ocean of sorrow), R. 3, 9, 25 न कथञ्चन सा कार्या..... त्वया। बुद्धिर्वैरं विना हन्तुं राक्षसान् (you never should make up your mind to kill —); — R. 2, 44, 26 नार्हा त्वं शोचितुं देवि (you do not deserve to mourn); — Daç. 178 जीवितुं जिह्रेमि (I feel ashamed to live); — Kumâras. 5, 2 इयेष सा कर्तुम् (she wished to make); — Çâk. VI बाष्पस्तु न ददात्येनां द्रष्टुं चित्रगतामपि (my tears, however, do not allow me to see her even in a picture), Mâlav. II, p. 45 देव मदीयमिदानीं प्रयोगमवलोकयितुं प्रसादः क्रियताम् (Sire, do me the favour of looking now at my dramatic performance); — Daç. 203 स्नातुं भोक्तुं च लभते (he gets a bath and food).

With काल and the like, f. i. Nala 20, 11 नायं कालो विलम्बितुम्, Çâk. VII त्वामिन्द्रगुरवे निवेदयितुमन्तरान्वेषी भवामि (I am looking out for an opportunity of introducing you to the teacher of Indra), Vikram. V, p. 172 चरितं त्वया पूर्वस्मिन्नाश्रमपदे द्वितीयमध्यध्यासितुं समयः.

Rem. 1. Among the words of *sufficing*, the particle अलम् is to be noticed. It is used with infin. sometimes in its proper sense of »being enough," as M. 2, 214 अविद्वांसमलं लोके विद्वांसमपि वा पुनः। प्रमदा ह्युत्पथं नेतुम्, sometimes also अलम् with infin. expresses prohibition, just as अलम् with gerund (353, R. 1). R. 3, 59, 14 अलं विक्लवतां गन्तुम् (do not despair), Mrcch. III, p. 106 अलं सुप्तजनं प्रबोधयितुम्. In the same way किम् with infin. Mudr. III, p. 107 भवतः किं फलान्वेषणेन वाङ्मनसयोः खेदमुत्पादयितुम् (why should you worry your voice and mind by striving for success?).

Rem. 2. Instances of an infinitive with a verb of *remembering* may occur now and then. In this case the infin. is expressive of a *past* action, previously done by the same subject. [1]).

385. Its being used in compounds. When depending on a noun, the infinitive is not allowed to be compounded with it, save the nouns काम and मनः. Bahuvrîhis made up of infin. + either of them are often used. Mâlat. III, p. 49 किंचिदाख्येयमाख्यातुकामास्मि (I wish to tell something worth telling), Mhbh. 1, 146, 16 मामयं पापो दग्धुकामः पुरोचनः (P. desires to burn me), Panc. 71 किं वक्तुमना भवान् (what do you intend to say?).

386. Its character. The infinitive has preserved its original nature of being a noun-case. The only difference, that exists between it and the datives and locatives [2]) of nouns of

1) Of this idiom prof. KERN has pointed out to me some passages, borrowed from an inedited Buddhistic work, written in good Sanskrit, the *Jâtaka-mâlâ* (see HODGSON, *Essays* p. 17). Somebody, who has practised the virtue of *ahimsâ*, says of himself स्मरामि यत आत्मानं यतः प्राप्तोऽस्मि विज्ञताम्।नाभिजानामि संचिन्त्य प्राणिनं हिंसितुं क्वचित्. Another, famous for his munificence declares न हि स्मराम्यर्थितयागतानामाशाविपर्यासहतप्रभाणि। हिमानिलम्लापितपङ्कजानां समानदैन्यानि मुखानि कर्तुम् (v. a. I do not remember *to have disappointed* the expectation of those, who came to me as supplicants).

2) When depending on substantives, the noun of action may also be a genitive **(110)**, f. i. कालः प्रस्थानस्य or प्रस्थानाय or प्रस्थाने or प्रस्थातुम्.

action in °अन, °अ, °ति etc., is that the latter are construed with the genitive of their object, but the infinitive with the accusative. For the rest, they are synonymous. It is the same, whether one says अर्थं लब्धुं or अर्थस्य लाभाय पारयति, जयाय or जेतुं यतते.

Rem. A gen. of the kṛtya, doing duty as inf., is rare. Panc. 242 नायं वक्तव्यस्य कालः (it is now no time for telling it).[1]. Cp. वरम् with kṛtya 389 R.

387. *Infinitive joining passive verbs, and to be rendered by the passive inf. of English.* Like the nouns of action, the infinitive by itself neither belongs to the active voice nor to the passive. It may be construed with both classes of verbal forms, and seems to have an active meaning, when it is the complement of an active verb, but a passive, when of a passive. Panc. 258 we read कथं शक्यते तत्र गन्तुम्, sc. केनचित्, which is just as good as कथं कश्चिच्छक्नोति तत्र गन्तुम्; in the former sentence the subject is denoted by an instrumental, in the latter by a nominative, but in both it is the self-same infinitive, that completes the finite verb. Likewise it is equally correct to say मया कटः कर्तुं शक्यते as अहं शक्नोमि कटं कर्तुम्.

Instances of the infinitive attending in this manner a passive, are exceedingly frequent with शक्यते, शक्यः, शक्यम् (388), occasionally also with other verbs. Hit. 6 मया नीतिं ग्राहयितुं शक्यन्ते (by me they can be taught politics), R. 2, 86, 11 न देवासुरैः सर्वैः शक्यः प्रसहितुं युधि (he cannot be withstood by all the devas and asuras together); — Prabodh. VI, p. 119 कैः कैर्नाहम्.... ईहिता..... दासीकर्तुम्

---

1) The kṛtya doing duty as noun of action is an idiom not rarely found in the prâkṛts. Especially in the type, represented by this passage of Çâk. I का तुमं विसज्जिदव्वस्स रुंधिदव्वस्स वा (v.a. who are you, that you should dismiss me or stop me?).

(how many have not endeavoured to bring me into bondage?), Viddhaç. I, p. 15 धारयितुं न पारिता किं पुनरनुनेतुम् (I could not hold her, much less appease her). Cp. also Kumâras. 7, 57. This idiom is even used in such sentences, as Hit. 50 अत्राटवीराज्ये ऽभिषेक्तुं भवान्निरूपितः (it is you who have been chosen *to be anointed* king in this forest), and Mudr. III, p. 106: Candragupta has sent for his minister Cânakya. When arrived, the minister asks the king, for what reason he has been sent for; after hearing the reason, he replies वृषल। उपालब्धुं तर्हि वयमाहूताः (then I have been ordered here *to be upbraided*).

Rem. With those participles in °त, which have sometimes an active and sometimes a passive meaning, the infinitive is accordingly used in both senses. Cp (passive) Panc. 275 त्वया श्रियोऽर्थ एतत्कार्यमनुष्ठातुमारब्धम् with (intransitive) Panc. 276 अथ तौ जलं पीत्वा वनफलानि भक्षयित्वा गन्तुमारब्धौ. Of शक्, however, there exists a partic. शकित, which is exclusively to be used with an infinitive in the passive voice, whereas शक्त is always active[1]). Likewise यतित, not यत्त, is put to the infinitive, when bearing a passive meaning. Mhbh. 1, 154, 9 अपनेतुं च यतितो न चैव शकितो मया.

388. Infin. with शक्य. The krtya शक्य may be construed in two manners. It is equally correct to say स शक्यः —, सा शक्या द्रष्टुम् as शक्यं स (or सा) द्रष्टुम् „one can see him or her.'' In the latter case शक्यम् is a neuter and remains unchanged. There is even room for a third idiom, which is effected by construing शक्यम् with the instrum. of its subject and the accusat. of its object, as शक्यं मया तं (or तां) द्रष्टुम्.

Examples of the indeclinable शक्यम्: *a.*) with nom. Mâlav. III,

1) Kâç. on P. 7, 2, 17 teaches the form शकित for the passive, but he adds, that शक्त may also be used even then: सौनागाः कर्मणि निष्ठायां शकेरिटमिच्छन्ति विकल्पेन। शकितो घटः कर्तुम्। शक्तो घटः कर्तुम्, but when impersonal passive, one always says शक्त, ibid. भावे न भवत्येव। शक्तमनेन.

p. 85 एवं प्रणयवती सा न हि शक्यमुपेक्षितुं कुपिता (for, being so loving, she must not be disdained in her anger), Daç. 58 अशक्यं हि मदिच्छया विना.... दशनच्छद एष चुम्बयितुम् (these lips cannot be kissed against my will), R. 2, 62, 16 शक्यमापतितः सोढुं प्रहारो रिपुहस्ततः। सोढुमापतितः शोकः सुसूक्ष्मोऽपि न शक्यते; — *b*), with instrum. Pat. I, p. 39 तत्राशक्यं वर्णेनाप्यनर्थकेन भवितुम् (there not a single letter can be meaningless), R. 3, 40, 4 त्वद्वाक्यैर्न तु मां शक्यं भेत्तुं रामस्य संयुगे (but your words cannot withhold me from the struggle with Râma).

389. Another similar turn is the infinitive with युक्तम् (it is fit, it suits). If neither the subject nor the object of the action befitting is expressed, there is no difficulty; one should needs say f.i. न युक्तमिह स्थातुम्, no other turn of phrase being available. But when the subject or object or both of them are to be expressed, there is variety of idioms. 1. The object may be an *accusative*; 2. the object may be a *nominative* construed with युक्तम्; 3 the object may be a *nominative*, whose gender and number are transferred also to the adjective युक्त. As to the subject, it is put in the instrumental or in the genitive; [1]) the latter seems to be more frequent.

Infin with युक्त.

Examples: 1 of युक्तम् with an *accus.* Mudr. I, p. 30 न युक्तं प्राकृतमपि रिपुमवज्ञातुम् (it is not judicious to disdain even a mean enemy), Varâh. Bṛhats. 47, 2 भूयो वराहमिहिरस्य न युक्तमेतत्कर्तुम् (V. ought not to treat the same matter again), Mhbh. I, Paushyap. 118 न युक्तं भवतान्नमशुचि दत्त्वा प्रतिशापं दातुम् (it does not become you, after having given unclean food, to return the curse);

2. of युक्तम् with a *nomin.* Mhbh. I, Paushyap. 106 न युक्तं भवताहमनृतेनोपचरितुम् (it is not right that you should treat me with lies); [2])

1) Cp. the promiscuousness of gen. and instr. with the kṛtyas (**66** R.).

2) Cp. this prâkṛt-passage of Çâkuntala III जुत्तं से अहिलासो अहिणंदिदुं = skrt. युक्तमस्या अभिलाषोऽभिनन्दितुम्.

3. of युक्त agreeing in gender and number with the nomin. Kathâs. 22, 169 युक्ता परिणेतुमसौ मम (v. a. she suits me as a wife).

with न्याय्य; Rem. 1. In the same way न्याय्य with infinitive admits of two constructions. Sometimes it is a neuter with the acc. of the object, as R. (Gorr.) 6, 38, 28 न नप्तारं स्वयं न्याय्यं शप्तुमेवम् (it is not allowed to curse one's own grand-son in this manner), sometimes it is construed with a nomin. of the object, the gender and number of which itself adopts, and the instrum. of the subject, as Ragh. 2, 55 सेयं..... न्याय्या मया मोचयितुं भवत्तः (it is right she should be released from you by me).

with वरम् and असांप्रतम्. Rem. 2. With the turn युक्तम् with nomin. may be compared the nominative with infinitive, attending such adverbs as असांप्रतम् and वरम्. Kumâras. 2, 55 विषवृक्षो ऽपि संवर्ध्य स्वयं छेत्तुमसांप्रतम् (even a poisonous tree should not be cut down by him, who has reared it); — Mâlav. III, p. 55 उचितः प्रणयो वरं विहन्तुम् (it is better, that a love to which one is accustomed, should be repressed —), Daç. 94 वरमात्मा गोपायितुम् (it is better to defend ourselves). With वरम् one may also meet with the nom. of the kṛtya almost doing duty as infin., f. i. Nâgân. IV, p. 58 वरं राजपुत्र्याः सकाशं गन्तव्यम् (better is it to go to the encounter of the princess).

390. Character of Sanskrit infinitive. The original nature of the infinitive has not been obscured in Sanskrit. It has everywhere the character rather of an adverb, than of a noun[1]). Not only on account of its etymology, but also of its standing in some degree outside the common system of declension and conjugation, it may be called the counterpart of the Lat. supine[2]). It has no voices, no tenses. It nowhere serves to express the subject, predicate or ob-

---

1) In vernacular grammar the infinitive always ranks with the *avyaya*-class. Likewise the gerund.

2) Occasionally, even the employment of Latin supine borders on that of Sanskrit infinitive. Cp. such phrases as *venatum eunt*, *spectatum veniunt* with Skrt. व्रजति भोक्तुम्, आगतः क्रीडितुम्.

ject of a sentence [1]). In such sentences as „to give is better than to receive," Sanskrit avails itself of different idioms, chiefly by using nouns of action, but avoids using the infinitive [2]).

Rem. 1. Sometimes the 3d person of the present or the optative may be equivalent to our infinitive. Panc. II, 51 ददाति प्रतिगृह्णाति गुह्यमाख्याति पृच्छति। भुङ्क्ते भोजयते चैव षड्विधं प्रीतिलक्षणम् (to give, to receive, to tell one's secret, to ask it, to be guest and host, these are the six tokens of friendship). Cp. R. 3, 47, 17 दद्यान्न प्रतिगृह्णीयात्सत्यं ब्रूयान्न चानृतम्। एतद् ब्राह्मण रामस्य व्रतं धृतमनुत्तमम् (to give, not to receive, to speak the truth, not to speak falsehood, this is the sublime vow, o brahman, practised by Râma).

Rem. 2. Sanskrit has not the turn: accusative with infinitive [3]).

---

1) In such expressions as विद्यते भोक्तुम्, लभते भोक्तुम् we may speak of the infinitive as the subject and object of the finite verb, but this is only so from a logical point of view; and it is, indeed, *not considered so* by Sanskrit-speakers.

2) F. i. दानं प्रतिग्रहाद्विशिष्यते or यो ददाति यश्च प्रतिगृह्णाति तयोर्ददद्गरीयान् or वरं दानं न तु प्रतिग्रहः.

3) Jolly, *Geschichte des Infinitivs*, p. 253 sq. asserts its existence. He quotes but two examples: Kathâs. 20, 172 राजानं स्नातुं ददर्श and Sâv. 5, 10 = Mhbh. 3, 297, 102 मां च जीवितुमिच्छसि. In the latter passage both the Calc. and the Bomb. edition of the Mhbh. read मां च जीवन्तमि° and in the former स्नातुम् is an obvious misprint for स्नान्तम्. The participle is in both cases indispensable. So Kâç. on P. 3, 3, 158 after giving इच्छति भोक्तुम् (he wishes to eat) as an example of the infinitive, contrasts with this the participial idiom देवदत्तं भुञ्जानमिच्छति यज्ञदत्तः (Mr. B. wishes Mr. A. to eat). — Likewise R. 3, 24, 13 ed. Bomb. प्रतिकूलितुमिच्छामि नहि वाक्यमिदं त्वया the text is corrupt, the correct reading being प्रतिकूलितम्, nor is the infin. प्रतिकूलितुम् but प्रतिकूलयितुम्. A fourth instance would be Daç. 104 न चेदिमां वामलोचनामाप्नुयां न मृष्यति मां जीवितुं वसन्तबन्धुः (if I do not obtain this beautiful maiden, the God of Love will not suffer me to live), yet as मृष्यति is as a rule construed with acc. and *participle* (see but Mhbh. 1, 145, 9, M. 8, 346, Mhbh. 1, 95, 68, ibid. 4, 16, 28), I am convinced we have here likewise an error in the text, and जीवन्तम् must be put

Verbs of perceiving, thinking, telling etc. are construed with the accusative with participle (**374**).

391. *Old infinitives.* The infinitive in °तुम् is the sole remnant of a great many similar forms, which existed in the ancient language, especially in the old dialect of the Vaidik mantras. WHITNEY, *Sanskr. Gramm.* § 970 gives a detailed account of them. All of them are oblique cases of nouns of action. We call them infinitives, because they share the construction of the verb, from which they are derived. Most of them were obsolete as early as the period of the brâhmaṇa-works, some indeed survived, but adopted the construction of the nouns. In such passages f. i. as Ṛgv. 9, 88, 2 स ईं रथो न भूरिषाडयोजि महः पुरूणि सातये वसूनि (like a much-bearing chariot he has been horsed, the mighty one, to bring us abundant boons), we are inclined to call सातये an infinitive, for it has its object put in the *accusative*; likewise still Ait. Br. 2, 1, 1 यज्ञस्य किंचिदेषिष्यामः प्रज्ञात्यै, since किंचित् is the object of प्रज्ञात्यै. But in such passages as Ait. Br. 2, 17, 8 स्वर्गस्य लोकस्य समष्ट्यै (in order to gain heaven), the object is a *genitive*, and समष्ट्यै can no more be called infinitive. Now, the genitive with them is predominant in the brâhmaṇas and afterwards it is the sole idiom.

392. *Infin. in °तोः and °तवै.* Two old infinitives, however, are still employed in the brâhmaṇas, those in °तोः and in °तवै. Of the latter I have even met with an instance in a writer of so comparatively recent a date, as Patanjali [1]).

1. The infinitives in °तोः are either genitives or ablatives. When genitives, they are hardly found unless depending on ईश्वर [2]). The phrase ईश्वर with genitive in °तोः means »able to" or »liable to."

---

instead of ज्ञीव्रितुम्; I should not wonder, if the good reading were found in mss.

1) Pat. I, p. 2 तस्माद् ब्राह्मणेन न म्लेच्छितवै नापभाषितवै. The infin. is here equivalent to the kṛtya, according to what is prescribed by Pâṇini (3, 4, 14).

2) I know but one instance of a genitive depending on an other word. Ait. Br. 2, 20, 21 यशोऽर्तोर्बुभूषेत् ([if he] should strive after obtaining glory). In another passage Ait. Br. 6, 30, 7 the interpretation of the inf. प्रत्येतोः

It must be remarked that in this idiom ईश्वर sometimes agrees with its subject in gender and number, sometimes the masc. ईश्वरः is used irrespective of the gender and number of its subject, as if it were an indeclinable wood. Ait. Br. 1, 10, 2 ईश्वरा हैनं नि वा रोढोर्वि वा मथितोः (they are able to check him or to crush him), ibid. 1, 30, 11 ईश्वरौ ह वा एतौ यजमानं हिंसितोः; — ibid. 3, 48, 8 ईश्वरो हास्य वित्ते देवा अरन्तोः (it may be that the gods are not gratified by his offering), Çat. Br. 5, 1, 1, 9 तस्येश्वरः प्रजा पापीयसी भवितोः.

When ablatives, they are employed after the prepp. आ and पुरा. Then, however, they are commonly construed with the genitive of their object. Ait. Br. 2, 15, 9 पुरा वाचः प्रवदितोरनूच्यः [viz. प्रातरनुवाकः], ibid. 7, 2, 6 आ शरीराणामाहर्तोः.

2. The infinitive in °तवै is said by Pânini to be synonymous with the krtyas. This statement is confirmed by what we know about them from the ancient texts. In the Çatapatha they are much used, less often in similar works. Çat. Br. मूलान्युच्छेत्तवै ब्रूयात् (he must order the roots to be cut off.)

P. 3, 4, 14.

393. Both classes of infinitives also admit of an other construction. The subject etc. of those in °तोः and the object of those in °तवै may be put in the same case, which is represented by the infinitive, but difference of number, when existing, remains. Âpast. in Sâyaṇa's comment on Ait. Br. 2, 15, 15, p. 260 of AUFRECHT's ed. पुरा वाचः पुरा वा वयोभ्यः प्रवदितोः (— before the crying of birds), ibid. 2, 7, 6 ईश्वरो हास्य वाचो रक्षोभाषो जनितोः (verily, his voice is liable to become the voice of a raxas), ibid. 2, 1, 3 योऽस्य स्तृत्यस्तस्मै स्तर्तवै (to overthrow him, whom he is willing to overthrow [1]).

Rem. A *third* class of infinitives, those in °अः, which we are entitled to call infinitives of the aorist, as they are made of the most contracted form of the root, are occasionally construed in the same way, f. i. the vaidik phrase पुरा जर्तृभ्य आतृदः quoted by Kâç. on P. 3, 4, 17. Other instances may be met with in the Rgveda-mantras.

---

seems somewhat doubtful to me; the words प्रत्येतोर्हन्ताहम् are likely to mean »I am, indeed, able to understand", as if ईश्वरः should be supplied.

1) Cp. the well known idiom of Latin gerundivum. And even Latin affords instances of concord in gender and case, but disagreement in number. Cic. Philipp. 5, 3, 6 *facultas agrorum suis latronibus condonandi.*

SECTION V.

SYNTAX OF THE PARTICLES.

394 After treating the syntax of nouns and verbs, we now come to the words which are devoid of inflection. Part of them, indeed, have already been dealt with, viz. the adverbs in Ch. I of the Third, and the prepositions in Ch. IX of the Second Section. The rest are the so-called particles, most of them old little words as च, हि, वा, इव, अपि, whereas some others, as कामम्, तावत्, परम्, are petrified noun-cases. As to the employment of the particles, they serve different purposes, but they may be brought under two general heads: *modality* and *connection*. When modal, they are expressive of emphasis, negation, interrogation, exclamation and the like, when connective they are wanted to connect either whole sentences or parts of them. The distinction between these two classes of particles is, however, not an essential one. The same word may be sometimes a modal, sometimes a connective. So अपि may be a particle of interrogation, but also of copulation, वा commonly a disjunctive, serves occasionally to express emphasis. And so on.

Sanskrit likes putting together and even combining two or more particles.

CHAPT. I. **Particles of emphasis and limitation.**

395. Affirmative sentences do not want to be marked as such by special particles, as is necessary with negative and interrogative sentences. Yet, strong affirmation, so-called emphasis, is expressed by such words as

Emphatic particles. English *indeed*, *surely*, *verily*, viz. खलु, किल, नूनम्, बाढम्, नियतम्, सत्यम् or in full यत्सत्यम्. Of them, बाढम् and the rest rather bear the character of such adverbs, as „certainly, undoubtedly." Mudr. VII, p. 223 यत्सत्यं लज्जित इवास्मि, Daç. 93 त्वया नियतम्.... अहमपदेश्यः.

Rem. बाढम् is especially used in answers »yes, indeed". Kathâs. 24, 67 one asks कच्चित्त्वया सा कनकपुरी दृष्टा, the other answers बाढं मया सा नगरी दृष्टा. »Yes" is also तथा. Kathâs. 81, 19 the king asks his attendant to fetch him some water, the other answers तथा; in full, he would have said तथा क्रियते यथाज्ञापयति देवः, of which sentence all but तथा is understood. Sometimes the relative sentence यथाज्ञापयति etc. is expressed, but the rest understood. — अथ किम् is also = »yes" [1]). Mudr. II, p. 78 न खलु विदितास्ते निवसन्तश्चाणाक्यहतकेन। अथ किम् (Râxasa asks: the accursed Câṇakya does not know they dwell in Pâtalip., does he? Answ. Yes, he does).

396. नूनम्, ननु, खलु, किल, नाम are the most frequent emphatic particles. The last three of them are not put at the head, but नूनम् and ननु are usually the first word of the sentence, at least in prose. Daç. 130 नूनमसौ प्राणानिःस्पृहः किमपि कृच्छ्रं प्रपित्सते, Panc. 204 ननु स्वभावतोऽस्माकं शत्रुभूतोऽस्ति, Çâk. I आर्ये सम्यगनुबोधितोऽस्मि। अस्मिन्क्षणे खलु विस्मृतं मयैतत् (— but now, indeed, I did not remember it), ibid. I तपोवनसंनिहितसत्त्वरक्षणायै सज्जीभवन्तु भवन्तः। प्रत्यासन्नः किल मृगयाविहारी पार्थिवो दुष्यन्तः, Mudr. V, p. 173 अधिकारपदं नाम निर्दोषस्यापि पुरुषस्य महदाशङ्कास्थानम्.

ननु is properly an interrogative, which does duty as an emphatic [2]).

Rem. 1. The said emphatics are of course not wholly syno-

---

1) Literally, as it seems, »but how [do you doubt of it?]". Cp. Latin *Rogas?*

2) Yet ननु accompanies even the imperative. Kumâras. 4, 32 ननु मां प्रापय पत्युरन्तिकम्.

nymous, the slight differences which exist between them, making it occasionally necessary to use one and to avoid another. It is also to be observed, that sometimes and in some degree the emphatics may act as a kind of connectives, in as far as they, too, are a means for linking sentences together. In the example quoted from Panc. 204, ननु may be called with some right a causal particle, likewise खलु and किल in the two, quoted from Çâk. I. On the other hand, the connective हि is sometimes a mere emphatic.

Rem. 2. Emphatic particles are sometimes used in an ironical sense, especially नाम and किल. See f. i. Kumâras. 5, 32.

397. Ancient literature abounds in emphatic particles, many of which are obsolete in the classic dialect. Besides खलु, नाम, हि, we meet in archaic and epic works with वै, ह, स्म, नु, उ, उत, वा. Often these little particles only slightly strengthen the sense, and rather serve either to enhance the dignity of the style or to fill up the metre. Then we may call them expletives[1]). But they are not always used in this way, and each of them at the outset had its proper meaning.

Expletives

Accumulation of them is not rare, as ह स्म, ह वै, उ खलु etc.

Rem. 1. वै is especially used to lay stress on the word immediately preceding. It is excessively frequent both in liturgical and in epic writings. Still Patanjali used it sometimes. Pat I, p. 107 अकर्मका अपि वै सोपसर्गाः सकर्मका भवन्ति (nay, even intransitives become transitives, when compound). But afterwards it seems to be obsolete, at least in prose. — वा = वै is occasionally found in epic poetry.

Rem. 2. ह and उत are much liked at the end of a pâda, the former after a finite verb, उत in the phrase इत्युत. But they may

1) And so does vernacular grammar. Even as ancient an author as Yâska knows of particles which serve पादपूरणे.

also have other places; ह is very frequent in the brâhmana as well as in the epics. [1])

Rem. 3. Some, as खलु and वाव, are found in the brâhmanas, but not in the epics. The emphatic and also restrictive particle अह is often met with in the mantras and in the Çatapathabr., चित्, ईम् and कम् are restricted to the mantras.

398. एव. The enclitic एव is put after a word, in order to denote: even this, not anything else. We may, therefore, call एव a **restrictive.** It is exceedingly frequent, being hardly ever omitted, when any stress, however slight, is to be laid on a word. Panc. 212 अहमेव करिष्यामि (I myself will do it), Mâlav. I, p. 18 सप्रतिबन्धं कार्यं प्रभुरधिगन्तुं सहायवानेव (one is able to undertake a difficult task, only with a companion), Çâk. I दर्शनेनैव भवतीनां पुरस्कृतोऽस्मि (the very sight of the ladies honours me), Panc. 186 नित्यमेव निशागमे समेत्यास्मत्पक्षकदनं करोति, Mhbh. 1, 163, 11 Hiḍimba forbids Bhîma to eat, but the other, not caring for this, continues eating राक्षसं तमनादृत्य भुङ्क्त एव पराङ्मुखः, Kathâs. 30, 3 स तां दृष्ट्वैव रूपेण जगत्त्रितयमोहिनीम्। क्षोभं जगाम. As appears from the instances quoted, एव admits of manifold translations; it is often not translated at all. After pronouns it is sometimes = »the same, the very." Nala 2, 12 एतस्मिन्नेव काले (at that very time), Panc. 324 एकदैव (at the same time). Cp. **277.**

Rem. 1. In poetry एव is sometimes omitted. R. 3, 25, 39 नाददानं शरान्घोरान्विमुञ्चन्तं शरोत्तमान्। विकर्षमाणं पश्यन्ति राक्षसास्ते शरार्दिताः, here the scholiast is right in expounding विकर्षमाणमेव, »the râxasas did not see him charging his arrows nor discharging them, they saw him *only* keeping his bow bent [so swiftly Râma was shooting]." So Varâh. Yogay. 1, 18 भवति दैवयुतस्य सिद्धिः = भ° दैवयुतस्यैव सिद्धिः, cp. KERN's annot. in the *Ind. Stud.* X, p. 200.

1) P. 8, 1, 60 mentions ह, when denoting disapproval at some infringement on good manners. Kâç. illustrates this rule a. o. by the example स्वयं ह रथेन याति। उपाध्यायं पदातिं गमयति. In this sense also अह is used [P. 8, 1, 61], moreover, when orders are given to different persons at the same time, f. i. त्वमह ग्रामं गच्छ। त्वमहारण्यं गच्छ (Kâç.).

Rem. 2. In the mantras ईम्, इत्, चित्, अह may do the duty of एव.

399. (केवलम् and परम्.) The other restrictives are केवलम्, परम्, कामम् and तावत्. Of these, केवलम् and परम् are = „only, at least, but." Panc. 312 न वेत्सि त्वं गीतं केवलमुन्नदसि, Kathâs. 32, 143 योगबलेन चेत्।एषा राज्ञा नवा भार्या हन्यते तन्न युज्यते।.... तस्माद् बुद्धिबलेनैषा राज्ञो विश्लिष्यतां परम्.

(कामम्.) कामम् mostly announces some adversative particle, being almost = »to be sure" (**442**, 1°). It is but seldom used without adversative sentence. Daç. 126 यद्यप्सरोभिः संगच्छसे संगच्छस्व कामम् (if you have intercourse with apsarases, so).

(तावत्.) तावत् has a peculiar employment. Properly it is an elliptical phrase, for at the outset it must have meant something like this: „as much [is certain]." Accordingly it advances a statement which is asserted „at all events" or „at least" or „before others." As it is often an enclitic, the said translations are generally too forcible. In expositions of many links one likes to put तावत् to the first of them, then it may be compared with fr. „d'abord," cp. **439**. It is also much used in exhortations and with imperatives.

Examples: Kathâs. 28, 60 अहो केयमसंभाव्यवपुर्भवेत्। न तावन्मानुषी (o! who may this beautiful woman be? She is, *at all events*, not a mortal). Panc. 318 a brahman thus reflects परिपूर्णोऽयं घटस्तावत्सक्तुभिर्वर्तते।तद्यदि दुर्भिक्षं भवति तदनेन रूपकाणां शतमुत्पद्यते (*well*, this pot is filled with porridge, now if there should be a famine, then —), ibid. 37 Damanaka says to Karataka आवां तावदप्रधानतां गतौ। एष पिङ्गलकः..... स्वव्यापारपराङ्मुखः संजातः।सर्वोऽपि परिजनो गतः।तत्किं क्रियते (*in the first place* we have lost our influence, next our king has become averse to his duty, and finally all his attendants are gone, what is to be done in these circumstances?), ibid. 23 तत्तावज्जानामि कस्यायं शब्दः (therefore, I will know *at least*, whose voice it is). Mudr.

III, p. 114 यत्नल्लेख्यपत्त्रं तावद् दीयताम् (only, give up the letter). Çâk. VI the king eagerly exclaims धनुस्तावत् (my bow! = »I want to have my bow and to have it soon"); likewise Mâlav. I, p. 20 the king greets the dancing-masters स्वागतं भवद्भ्याम्, then turning to his attendance he continues आसने तावदत्रभवतोः, cp. Vikram. V, p. 180 अर्घोऽर्घस्तावत्.

जातु. Rem. जातु, an old emphatic particle, seems to be restricted to poetry and almost to negative and interrogative sentences: न जातु »not at all." Sometimes it may be almost = »perchance, perhaps." Kathâs. 25, 24 जानीयात्स वृद्धो जातु तां पुरीम्. Sometimes चित् is affixed to it, see **402**.

Chapt. II. **Negation**.

400. Negative particles. Sanskrit has three negative particles: **न**, **मा** and the prefix **अ(न्)**°. Of these the last mentioned is only used in compounds, **मा** is the special particle of prohibition.

401. न. Its place in the sentence. The general negation is **न**. It negatives as well single words or notions as whole statements. In the former case it is put immediately before the word denied. Panc. 147 परिज्ञातस्त्वं सम्यङ् सुहृत् (I have clearly experienced you to be an unfriend).

When denying the whole statement, one is tolerably free where to put the negation. Commonly, two places are preferred: either at the head of the whole sentence — so regularly for rhetorical purposes, as in the case of antithesis, epanaphora, also in emphatical denials — or just before the verb. Yet, as has been said, any other place is admissible and very often met with, especially in poets.

Examples: न heading the sentence. Panc. 26 न दीनोपरि महान्तः कुप्यन्तीति न त्वं तेन निपातितः (as men of superior rank do not feel angry towards a wretch, he has not killed you), Mudr. IV, p. 137 न मया सुचिरमपि विचारयता तेषां वाक्यार्थोऽधिगतः (though I have been reflecting on it quite a while, I do not understand what it is, they speak of); — of न just before the verb: Panc. 48 नापितो वक्तुं न शशाक, Hit. 95 कोऽप्युपायो ऽस्माकं जीवनाय नास्ति.

anaphora: Panc. I, 4 न सा विद्या न तद्दानं न तच्छिल्पं न सा कला। नार्थार्थिभिर्न तत्स्थैर्यं धनिनां यन्न गीयते (no knowledge, no munificence, no skill, no art, no perseverance can be imagined which is not praised in the wealthy by those who desire profit of them); — emphatic denial: Panc. 54 the weaver, who acts the part of Vishṇu says to the princess सुभगे नाहं दर्शनपथं मानुषाणां गच्छामि.

Instances of another place, than at the head or before the verb: Daç. 198 तमलमस्मि नाहमुद्धर्तुम् (I am not able to rescue him), Hit. 9 अहं.... न कथं विश्वासभूमिः, Kumâras. 5, 5 सुतां शशाक मेना न नियन्तुमुद्यमात्, Panc. I, 27 किं तेन जातु जातेन..... आरोहति न यः स्वस्य वंशस्याग्रे ध्वजो यथा; ibid. II, 168 वाञ्छा निवर्तते नार्थैः = नार्थैर्वाञ्छा नि°; Kathâs. 24, 171 तत्किं त्वमेव मूल्येन गृह्णास्याभरणं न तत्.

Rem. न is sometimes by itself the whole predicate, the verb being implied. Daç. 156 तस्मै चेयमनुमता दातुमितरस्मै न (she was destined for him, not for another), Panc. 116 साधोः शिक्षा गुणाय संपद्यते नासाधोः (education turns to advantage in a good man, but in a wicked one not so).

402. *न combined with other particles.* The combinations of न with indefinite pronouns or pronominal adverbs to express *none*, *no*, *neither*, *nowhere* and the like are treated **282** and **288** R. 3.

When accompanying connective particles, न precedes them as a rule, as नच [cp. Latin *neque*), न वा, नापि, नहि, न तु, न पुनः, नो [= न + उ]. Cp. **429**. With नु it becomes the interrogative particle ननु (**413**).

„Not even" is न.... अपि, न.... एव; „not at all" न जातु; „not indeed" न खलु, न नूनम्, न सत्यम् etc.; „not yet" न तावत्. Panc. 30 न रात्रावप्यधिशेते (even at night he did not find his rest); — M. 2, 94 न जातु कामः कामानामुपभोगेन शाम्यति

(lust is by no means quenched by enjoyment); here चित् is not rarely added, as Mhbh. 1, 49, 4 कल्याणं प्रतिपत्स्यामि विपरीतं न जातु चित्; — Çâk. I न खलु न खलु बाणाः संनिपात्योऽयमस्मिन्मृदुनि मृगशरीरे; — R. 2, 30, 35 न सत्यम्; — Mhbh. 1, 24, 14 न तावद् दृश्यते सूर्यः (the sun is not yet visible).

Rem. 1. नो at the outset served to signify the negation + the adversative particle = »but not", yet उ having almost got obsolete in the classic dialect, नो is sometimes considered almost a synonym of the simple न and is used chiefly in poetry instead of it either as an emphatic negation, or for metrical purposes. See f. i. Mrcch. IV, p. 135 नो मुष्णाम्यबलाम् etc; ibid. IX, p. 314; Panc. II, 153; V, 24.

Rem. 2. The archaic dialect possessed a negation नेत् = न + इत्. It is sometimes a mere negation, but commonly it is = »lest", then it is construed with the conjunctive mood (लेट्), cp. **355** R. 1.

403. अ° or अन्°. The negation अ° — अन् — is only used as the first member of compounds, both bahuvrîhis, and tatpurushas, see **218** and **223** *c*). In tatpurushas its force is not always the same. अमित्र f. i. not only denotes „not a friend" but also the very opposite of मित्र, viz. „foe." Of the latter kind are sundry common words, as अनल्प (much), अनेक (many), अयशः (dishonour). The former type involves identity of meaning with the separate negation न, f. i. Daç. 69 ऐहिकस्य सुखस्याभाजनं जनोऽयम् (I am no vessel for wordly pleasure), Panc. 62 तेषां वियोगं द्रष्टुमहमसमर्थः = °न समर्थः, Daç. 199 कदाचिदप्यवितृष्णो गुणेषु (not a single moment [he was] not thirsting for virtue).

Further अ° in tatpurushas may denote »all except this," अब्राह्मणः = »anybody but a brahman." M. 5, 18 in the list of eatable animals it is said भक्ष्यान्.... आहुरनुष्ट्रांश्चैकतोदतः, Kull. comments तयोष्ट्रवर्जितानेकदन्तपंक्त्युपेतान्.

Rem. न is not wholly excluded from compounds, but it is rarely used so, f. i. नचिरेण = अचिरेण (soon) etc.; नातिदूरे (not far), नपुंसक (eunuch; [the] neuter [gender]).

404. अ° may be compounded with verbal forms, viz. participles, gerunds and infinitives. Panc. 67 अनिच्छन्नपि (though not wishing it); Kum. 1, 37 Pârvatî being taken in his arms by Çiva, is said to ascend his shoulder अनन्यनारीकमनीयमङ्कम् (— not to be cherished by other women); — Panc. 69 न युज्यते स्वामिनस्तस्य सामर्थ्यमविदित्वा गन्तुम् (it does not befit my master to go without having experienced his strength), Daç. 75 स्वभवनमगत्वैव तमृषिमभाषत; — R. 2, 48, 11 नैनं शक्ष्यन्त्यनर्चितुम् (they cannot help honouring him), Pat. I, p. 230 अयमपि योगः शक्यो ऽवक्तुम् (this rule, too, might have remained unsaid). Of अ° with inf. I know no instances except such as are construed with the verb शक्.

Rem. A vârtt. on P. 6, 3, 73 allows अ° also put to the finite verb, provided that it be intended to express blame, as अपचसि त्वं जाल्म, as if we should say: »you miscook" = »you do not cook well."

405. मा. मा is the proper negation to be used with the imperative and its concurrent idioms; in other terms it expresses *prohibition*, or in a wider sense *the desire to keep off*. Examples of its employment with imperative, optative, aorist without augment have been given **353** and **354**. A strong prohibition is not rarely expressed by the sole मा or by मैवम् (not so) with ellipsis of the verb; मा तावत् signifies reprobation, as Mâlav. I, p. 3.

With imperative मा is also used, if the imperative expresses doubt or uncertainty. Mhbh. 14, 6, 8 गच्छ वा मा वा (you are free to go or not [as you like]). In the same meaning also with लिङ्, as Panc. I, 225 विषं भवतु मा भूयात् (there may be poison or not). Moreover मा with लिङ् may express solicitude. Mrcch. III, p. 124 अये चिरयति मैत्रेयः। मा नाम वैक्लव्यादकार्यं कुर्यात् (Maitreya tarries long, in his distress I hope he will do nothing unbecoming). As to मा with the future in epic poetry and in the prâkrts, see **353** R. 4.

Rem. 1. When subjoined to some chief sentence, मा admits of being translated by »lest," as Mhbh. 5, 37, 45 मा वनं छिन्धि सव्याघ्रं मा व्याघ्रा नीनशन्वनात् (do not destroy the forest with tigers, lest the tigers should disappear from the forest), cp. ibid. 1, 30, 15 quoted

353 R. 4.[1]). In other terms, मा with लिङ्, aorist or future may be synonymous with यथा न or येन न. — In epic poetry न with optative is also used = »lest;" instances are not rare. Mhbh. 1, 154, 35 शीघ्रं गच्छाम भद्रं ते न नो विद्यात्सुयोधनः (let us go instantaneously, lest Duryodhana should know of us), ibid. 1, 56, 23 तन्ने दद्यां वरं विप्र न निवर्तेत्क्रतुर्मम, R. 2, 63, 43 तं प्रसादय·न त्वां शपेत्, Nala 14, 14 etc.[2]).

Rem. 2. न, not मा, is the negation to be used with the potential mood, in hypothetical sentences, in general precepts and with the लिङ् taught **343** *e.*).[3]). Nala 13, 42 Damayantî says the conditions upon which she will be a maid-servant: उच्छिष्टं नैव भुञ्जीयां न कुर्यां पादधावनम्।न चाहं पुरुषानन्यान्प्रभाषेयम्, here न, not मा, is in its place.

406. Two negations in the same sentence are equivalent to a strong affirmation. Ch. Up. 4, 4, 5 नैतदब्राह्मणो विवक्तुमर्हति (no one but a brahman can thus speak out), R. 2, 30, 31 न खल्वहं न गच्छेयम् (I cannot but go, indeed), ibid. 2, 32, 46 न तत्र कश्चिन्न बभूव तर्पितः (there was no one there but was made content), Mâlav. epilogue आशास्यमीतिविगमप्रभृति प्रजानां संपत्स्यते न खलु गोप्तरि नाग्निमित्रे, comm. न खलु संपत्स्यत इति न।अपि तु संपत्स्यत एव[4]).

Two negations equivalent to a strong affirmation.

407. If two or more negative sentences are to be connected, the negation is often put but once. So

---

1) Panc. 325 मा = »lest" is construed with a *present*: दूरागच्छामि मा कश्चिन्ममाप्यनर्थो भवति. Instead of भवति one would rather expect भवेत्.

2) Sometimes न is construed so even with the future in °स्यति. Mhbh. 1, 146, 30 भौमं च बिलमद्यैव करवाम सुसंवृतम्।..... न नस्तत्र हुताशः संप्रधक्ष्यति.

3) मा..... यदि = »if not" I have met with Mâlat. IX, p. 160: अकरिष्यदसौ पापमतिनिष्करुणैव सा।माभविष्यमहं तत्र यदि तत्परिपन्थिनी. But माभ° may be a false reading instead of नाभ°.

4) R. 3, 47, 8 नाद्य भोक्ष्ये न च स्वप्स्ये न पास्ये न कदाचन is an instance of emphatic denial by means of repeating the negation, unless the reading be false and we must read न पास्ये च कदाचन. — In Panc. 116 the words मम वचनमशृण्वन्नात्मनः शान्तिमपि न वेत्सि are erroneously resolved thus अशृण्वन् नात्मनः°, they are = अशृण्वन् + आत्मनः.

Negation when omitted?

न..... च may be = „neither..... nor, not.... nor"; न.... अपि = „not.. . not even;" न.... वा = „not... nor". This omission of the negation in the second link is necessary in the idiom न.... यथा or इव „not.... no more than." R. 2, 59, 8 पुष्पाणि... नातिभान्त्यल्पगन्धीनि फलानि च यथापुरम् (the flowers do not glisten..... *nor* do the fruits as before), M. 4, 56 नाप्सु मूत्रं पुरीषं वा ष्ठीवनं वा समुत्सृजेत् (neither..... nor..... nor), Panc. IV, 53 माता यस्य गृहे नास्ति भार्या च प्रियवादिनी। अरण्ये तेन गन्तव्यम्; — Bhoj. 15 न तं राजानमिच्छन्ति प्रजाः षण्डमिव स्त्रियः (such a king is not desired by his subjects, no more than a eunuch is by women); R. 3, 47, 37 नाहं शक्या त्वया स्प्रष्टुमादित्यस्य प्रभा यथा (— no more than the sunshine).

But, in asyndetical connection of negative sentences the negation is always repeated, cp. Panc. I, 4 in **401**.

CHAPT. III. **Interrogations**.

408. Interrogations.

Interrogative sentences are twofold. Sometimes it is the whole action or fact, which is put in question, as „is he gone?", sometimes it is not the fact itself but one of its elements, that is asked after, as: „where does he dwell? who has seen him?" Questions of the latter type are introduced by interrogative pronouns or adverbs, those of the former 1st by particles, which partly are also derivatives from the interrogative pronoun, 2ly the interrogation is signified by the mere mode of pronouncing.

Interrogative pronouns and adverbs.

I. The interrogative pronoun is क, the interrogative adverbs, as क्व, कुतः, किमिति (why?), are its derivatives. As a rule they head the sentence, at least in prose; in poetry they may be put anywhere. Panc. 126 केनोपायेनैषां धनं लभे, Daç. 82 कासि वासु क्व यासि, Pat. I, p. 427 कति

भवतो भार्याः; — Mrcch. IX, p. 302 अथेदानीं वसन्तसेना क्व गता; Panc. II, 4 अत्रैश्चापि युधिष्ठिरेण सहसा प्राप्तो ह्यनर्थः कथम्.

Rem. Like other pronouns the interrogative may be part of a compound. Mrcch. IX, p. 302 किंनामधेयं तस्या मित्रम् (v. a. what is the name of her lover?), Daç. 74 जन्मनः प्रभृत्यर्थकामवार्तानभिज्ञा वयं ज्ञेयौ चेमौ किंरूपौ किंपरिवारौ किंफलौ च (as long as I live, I have been unacquainted with the course of [those two objects of human pursuit] Profit and Pleasure, and I should like to know what is their shape, who are their attendants and what fruit they yield), Pat. I, p. 6 कथञ्जातीयक उत्सर्गः कर्तव्यः कथञ्जातीयको ऽपवादः (rule and exception being wanted, what is the nature of either?).

409. Other remarks on the interrogative pronoun and its derivatives. — 1. They may depend on participles, gerunds and the like, also subordinate sentences. Mhbh. 1, 162, 11 तस्य व्यवसितस्त्यागो बुद्धिमास्थाय कां त्वया (v. a. what motive has made you decide to abandon this [man]?), Mudr. I, p. 28 यदि किं स्यात् (if what would be?).

2. Nothing precludes the presence of more interrogatives, referring to different things, in the same sentence. Pat. I, p. 241 केष्वर्थेषु काञ्शब्दान्प्रयुञ्जते (what sounds do they employ [and] in what meanings?), Kathâs. 41, 37 कोऽर्थी प्रार्थयते कः किं कस्मै किं दीयतामिति (who is indigent? who begs [and] for what? to whom should be given [and] what?).

3. Some particles, viz. वा, स्वित्, इव, नु, उ, नाम, are subjoined to them, in order to express some interest taken in the question by the speaker. Cp. the like duty of Lat. -*nam* and *tandem*, Greek ποτέ, French *donc*. Çâk. I मानुषीषु कथं वा स्यादस्य रूपस्य संभवः (is it then possible, that such a beauty should be of human origin?); Mhbh. 1, 91, 8 कति स्विदेव मुनयः कति मौनानि चाप्युत। भवन्तीति तदाचक्ष्व श्रोतुमिच्छामहे वयम्; R. 2, 38, 8 अपकारं कमिव ते करोति जनकात्मजा (what possible injury can Janaka's daughter do you then?); Ch. Up. 4, 14, 2 ब्रह्मविद इव सौम्य ते मुखं भाति। को नु त्वानुशशास (friend, your face shines like that of one who knows Brahman; who has taught you?); Kathâs. 16, 9 किं नाम न सहन्ते हि भर्तृभक्ताः कुलाङ्गनाः.

4. Note the phrase कोऽयम् (who is it, that — here?), f. i. Hit.

21 ततस्तमायान्तं दृष्ट्वा पक्षिशावकैर्भयार्तैः कोलाहलः कृतः। तच्छ्रुत्वा जरद्गवेनोक्तं। ऽयमायाति·

5. किम् may do duty as a particle, see **412**, 3°.

410 *Rhetorical questions.* Sanskrit has a pronounced predilection for rhetorical questions (**14**, VI). Hence, the interrogative pronouns and adverbs are often to be translated rather freely. Here are some examples: R. 2, 44, 7 किं न प्राप्तस्तवात्मजः = सर्वं प्रा°, Hit. 22 जातिमात्रेण किं कश्चिद्वध्यते पूज्यते क्वचित् (v. a. nobody is punished or honoured anywhere on account of his birth alone), Kathâs. 28, 10 बुद्धेन च परस्यार्थे..... आत्मापि तृणवद्दत्तः का वराके धने कथा (the Buddha has given up his own self like a grass-blade for the benefit of his neighbour, how, then, can there be question about [giving up] wretched riches?). Cp. Mhbh. 1, 74, 27, Çâk. I, vs. 19 etc. Cp. also अथ किम् = »yes," किं तु = »but" (**441**), किं च = »moreover" (**437**).

कथम् and कुतः In a similar way **कथम्** and **कुतः** frequently precede the cause, reason or motive, when expressed by a new sentence. For this reason, one may sometimes render them by »indeed." Mudr. V, p. 157 अहो विचित्रतार्यचाणक्यनीतेः। कुतः the reason is given in the strophe, which immediately follows, ibid. I, p. 29 कस्य परिज्ञाने नियुक्तो निपुणक इति न ज्ञायते। आ ज्ञातम्। अये कथमयं प्रकृतिचित्तपरिज्ञाने नियुक्तो निपुणक इति·

क्व च... ...क्व च· Rem. The idiom **क्व च.... क्व च** serves to denote a great discrepancy between two things. Daç. 77 क्व तपः क्व च रुदितम् (v. a. to be an ascetic and to weep are incompatible), R. 2, 106, 18 क्व चारण्यं क्व च क्षात्रं क्व जटाः क्व च पालनम्, Çâk. I क्व बत हरिणकानां जीवितं चातिलोलं। क्व च निशितनिपाताः सारपुङ्खाः शरास्ते· Cp. Kathâs. 28, 6, R. 3, 9, 27 etc.

411. *Interrogatives and relatives in indirect questions.* In *indirect questions* the interrogatives are employed, but instead of them the relatives are also admissible. Kathâs. 39, 174 पश्यैनं वञ्चये कथम् (see, how I delude him), Panc. 55 ज्ञायतां किमेते कञ्चुकिनो वदन्ति (be informed of what these guards are telling). On the other hand Kathâs. 39, 87 तस्यै सर्वम्..... अब्रवीत्। योऽसौ यन्नामधेयश्च यस्य पुत्रो महीपतेः (he told her everything, who he was, of what name, whose king's son), the direct question would have been कस्त्वं किंनामधेयश्च कस्य पुत्रः. Likewise Mâlat. II, p. 39 पितैव ते जानाति योऽसौ यादृशश्च, R. 2, 52, 60 शृणु. . . . . यदर्थं त्वां प्रेषयामि पुरीमितः.

412. *Interrogative particles.* II. In such interrogative sentences, as put the whole fact into question, interrogative particles are sometimes added, sometimes omitted. When they are omitted, the verb mostly heads the sentence. When added, it is they that are usually put at the head. The said particles are अपि, उत, किम् and कच्चित्.

a). Examples of questions *without* interrog. particle: Panc. 21 भो दमनक शृणोषि शब्दं दूरान्महान्तम् (say, Dam., do you hear a noise distant and great?), ibid. 326 अस्ति तस्य दुरात्मनः प्रतिषेधोपायः कश्चित् (is there any means for checking that scoundrel?), Mâlav. IX, p. 159 कथय जीवति मे प्रिया (say, does my sweetheart live?).

b). Examples of questions *with* interrog. particle:

1. अपि. — Panc. 35 अपि भवतः शिवम् (v. a. are you in good health?), ibid. 25 अपि सत्यम् (is it true?), Kathâs. 24, 208 अपि जानीथ (do you know?), Vikram. IV, p. 142 अपि दृष्टवानसि मम प्रियां वने.

2. उत, in simple questions very rare and obsolete, it seems. Kâç. on P. 3, 3, 152 उत दण्डः पतिष्यति (will the stick fall?). As to its use in alternatives see **414**.

3. किम्. — Daç. 170 शक्नोषि किम् = Lat. *potesne?*

4. कच्चित्. — R. 1, 52, 7 कच्चित्ते कुशलं राजन्. . . . . कच्चित्ते विजिताः सर्वे रिपवः (are you in good health, king?. . . . . have you subdued all your enemies?), Mhbh. 1, 5, 1 पुराणमखिलं तात पिता तेऽधीतवान्पुरा। कच्चित्त्वमपि तत्सर्वमधीषे, cp. Nala 4, 24, Kathâs. 75, 93 etc.

Rem. Like the other interrogatives (**409**, 3°) the said particles may be strengthened by adding to them some other particle as इव, वा, नु, उ, नाम. Of the kind is अपि नाम, किं नु, किं नु खलु, किमिव and the like. — Çâk. I अपि नाम कुलपतेरियमसवर्णाक्षेत्रसंभवा भवेत् (can she have been born to the chief of the family from a wife of a different caste?); ibid. VII किं वा शकुन्तलेत्यस्य मातुराख्या (is Çak. perhaps the name of his mother?); Bhoj. 64 ततः कविर्व्यचिन्तयत्। किमु राज्ञा नाश्रावि; Mhbh. 1, 151, 28 किं नु दुःखतरं शक्यं मया द्रष्टुमतः परम् (what can I see more unhappy than this?); Mhbh. 1, 162, 11 कच्चिन्नु दुःखैर्बुद्धिस्ते विलुप्ता गतचेतसः.

412*. Many times the particle किम् may be compared to Latin *num*, as it makes a negative answer to be expected. Kathâs. 28, 7 निरस्येनापि किं त्यक्तं विश्वामित्रेण जीवितं। मेनकायां प्रयातायां प्रसूयैव शकुन्तलाम् (Lat. *num Viçv. vita excessit* —?), Mudr. I, p. 27 किं भवानस्मदुपाध्यायादपि धर्मवित्तमः (are you even more learned than our teacher?).

413. On the other hand, न put into the question announces an affirmative answer, like Latin *nonne*. It generally attends some interrogative particle, viz. अपि or किम्, but may also be used by itself. By combining न and नु one gets ननु which is to be considered a new particle, fully answering to Lat. *nonne*, Greek *οὐκοῦν*, and which for this reason has also the force of an emphatic (**396**). Examples: Ch. Up. 1, 10, 4 न स्विदेतेऽप्युच्छिष्टा इति (were not these [beans] also left [and therefore unclean]?); — R. 2, 72, 5 अपि नाध्वश्रमः शीघ्रं रथेनापततस्तव (are you not tired with the long way, having driven quickly?); — Ratn. III, p. 79 किं पद्मस्य रुचिं न हन्ति नयनानन्दं विधत्ते न किम् [viz. वक्त्रेन्दुस्तव] (does not [the splendour of your face] outshine the brilliancy of the white lotus and does it not cause delight to the eyes?); — R. 2, 22, 22 ननु दैवस्य कर्म तत् (is not that the effect of Destiny?).

Rem. Yet, न put to कच्चित् = किम् *num*, since कच्चित् alone may be rather = *nonne*. R. 2, 72, 44 कच्चिन्न ब्राह्मणधनं हृतं रामेण कस्यचित्, cp. ibid. 1, 74, 21; 2, 57, 7; Mhbh. 1, 23, 10.

414. *Disjunctive interrogations.* Disjunctive interrogations are characterized by a great variety of particles. Commonly the former member begins with किम्, but there are many other combinations. Here are some instances:

1. In the former member किम्, in the latter वा or किं वा or

अथवा or उत or आहो or उताहो. — Daç. 149 किमयं स्वप्नः किं विप्रलम्भो वा (is this a vision or is it delusion?), Panc. 230 किमेनमुत्थाय हन्म्यथवा हेलयैव प्रसुप्तौ द्वावप्येतौ व्यापादयामि (shall I rise and kill him or shall I slay both of them while sleeping?), Mrcch. III, p. 113 किं लक्ष्यसुप्तमुत परमार्थसुप्तमिदं द्वयम् (are these two men sleeping indeed, or counterfeiting sleep?), Çâk. I वैखानसं किमनया व्रतमा प्रदानात्..... निषेवितव्यम्। अत्यन्तमेव..... आहो निवत्स्यति समं हरिणाङ्गनाभिः (must she keep the vow of chastity up to her marriage or is she to dwell with the antelopes of the hermitage for ever?). — To either member or to both another particle may be subjoined, f. i. instead of किम् one may say किमु, किं नु, in the second member instead of उत, आहो or उताहो, also किमुत, उतस्वित्, आहोस्वित् etc. Mrcch. X, p. 367 किं नु स्वर्गात्पुनः प्राप्ता..... किमुतान्येयमागता (is she come back from heaven, or is she another [Vasantasenâ]?), Panc. 202 किं केनापि पाशेन बद्ध उताहोस्वित्केनापि व्यापादितः (has anybody caught him in a snare or has anybody killed him?).

2. The former member contains some other particle, not किम्. So f. i. नु..... नु Kumâras. 1, 46 तया गृहीतं नु मृगाङ्गनाभ्यस्ततो गृहीतं नु मृगाङ्गनाभिः (has she borrowed it from the antelopes, or the antelopes from her?); — कच्चित्..... वा Mhbh. 1, 162, 3; — उत..... वा Kumâras. 4, 8; — वा..... वा Pat. I, p. 6 एतत्प्राधान्येन परीक्षितं नित्यो वा स्यात्कार्यो वेति [sc. शब्दः].

3. The former member is without particle. Of the kind are Panc. 294 सत्योऽयं स्वप्नः किं वाऽसत्यो भविष्यति न ज्ञायते; Çâk. V मूढः स्यामहमेषा वा वदेन्मिथ्या (either I must be out of my wits or she must lie); Çâk. I धावन्ति वर्त्मनि तरन्ति नु वाजिनस्ते.

Rem. If the second member is »or no," one says न वा. Panc. 329 किं प्रतिविधानमस्ति न वा (is there any remedy or no?), Daç. 140 एष मे पतिस्त्वापकर्ता न वेति दैवमेव जानाति. — »Yes or no" is वा न वा. Nala 18, 24 नहि स ज्ञायते वीरो नलो जीवति वा न वा.

415. Disjunctive interrogations of three or more members of course show a still greater variety of interrogative particles. Kumâras. 6, 23 किं येन सृजसि व्यक्तमुत येन बिभर्षि तत्। अथ विश्वस्य संहर्ता भागः कतम एष ते (v. a. are you Brahmâ, Vishnu or Çiva?); Panc. 332 किं मम वधोपायक्रमः कुब्जस्य वोताहो अन्यस्य वा कस्यचित् (is it I, against whom the plot is laid or is it the hunchback or anybody else?); Daç.

89 किं विलासात्किमभिलाषात्किमकस्मादेव न जाने; Çâk. VI स्वप्नो नु माया नु मतिभ्रमो नु क्लिष्टं नु तावत्फलमेव पुण्यम् (was it a dream or a delusion or perplexity of mind or was indeed the store of my good works exhausted?); Panc. 177 किं सिंहादिभिः क्वापि व्यापादित उत लुब्धकैरथवाऽनले प्रपतितो गर्तविषमे वा नवतृणलौल्यात्; Kathâs. 72, 185; Pat. I, p. 5, l. 14 किम्..... आहोस्वित्.... आहोस्वित्; Panc. 48, l. 19; etc. etc.

Chapt. IV. Exclamation.

416. Exclamations and particles of exclamation. Exclamation is *either* signified by simple interjections, as हा (alas), बत (ah), अहह (oh!) आः, अहो both expressive of surprise and strong emotion, धिक् (fy), and nouns used as such, as कष्टम् (it is a pity, alas), दिष्ट्या (thanks to God), साधु (well done), आश्चर्यम् (marvellous), शान्तम् or शान्तं पापम् — see Rem. on **2** — *or* expressed by a full sentence, commonly beginning with one of the said interjections or exclamative particles.

Exclamative sentences, introduced by interrogative pronouns or pronominal adverbs are, not nearly so often met with in Sanskrit as in our language. Still, the idiom exists. Daç. 67 king Râjahamsa rejoices when seeing again his comrades and exclaims कथं समस्त एष मित्रगणः समागतः को नामायमभ्युदयः Ven. I, p. 25 Sahadeva to Bhîma का खलु वेला तत्रभवत्याः प्राप्तायाः (how long it is, indeed, since Mylady is here!).

Here are some examples of exclamatives: Panc. 25 अहो शोभनमापतितम्, here अहो is expressive of joy, but R. 2, 115, 3 गतश्चाहो दिवं राजा it expresses sorrow; — R. 2, 12, 73 वैदेही बत मे प्राणान्शोचन्तो क्षपयिष्यति; — Kumâras. 3, 20 अहो and बत together: अहो बतासि स्पृहणीयवीर्यः; — Mhbh. 1, 157, 41 अहो धिक्कां गतिं त्वद्य गमिष्यामि; Panc. 158 धिङ्मूर्ख त्वं° (for shame, you blockhead, you —); — Mudr. III, p. 104 आ ज्ञातम् (o I remember); Prabodh. *passim* आः पाप (o, you rascal!); — Mudr. II, p. 84 दिष्ट्या दृष्टोऽसि तत्परिष्वजस्व माम्.

417. अहो and धिक् are often construed in a particular

अहो with nomin. manner. अहो is apt to be used with the nominative of an abstract noun, expressive of the fact which causes the astonishment. But धिक् — or, in full, धिगस्तु — is attended by the accus. (sometimes also, but not so often, the nomin.) of the person or thing, which causes the indignation or anger.

धिक् with accus.

Examples: 1. of अहो with nomin. — Nala 3, 17 Damayantî, when seeing on a sudden the beautiful appearance of Nala, exclaims अहो रूपमहो कान्तिरहो धैर्यं महात्मनः, Mudr. I, p. 38 Cânakya takes the letter, glances over it and says praisingly अहो दर्शनीयताक्षराणाम् (an excellent hand indeed), Panc. 92 the Ocean disapproving the words of the bird, which he has overheard, exclaims अहो गर्वः पक्षिकीटस्यास्य, Mudr. VI, p. 197 Râxasa, when entering the old garden, being sad with grief, laments अहो जीर्णोद्यानस्य नाभिरमणीयता (how little charm this old garden has!).

2. of धिक् with acc. Mhbh. 1, 131, 23 धिगेतां वः कृतास्त्रताम् (shame over your skill at arms!), R. 2, 49, 4 राजानं धिग्दशरथं कामस्य वशमास्थितम्, ibid. 2, 47, 4 धिगस्तु खलु निद्रां ताम् (v. a. cûrsed sleep!), Kâd. I, p. 18 धिग्विधातारमसदृशसंयोगकारिणम्; — of धिक् with nom. Panc. 156 धिगियं दरिद्रता, ibid. I, 174 धिगर्थाः कष्टसंश्रयाः.

Rem. 1. Occasionally धिक् occurs with a gen. Hariv. 8722 स्त्रीस्वभावस्य धिक्खलु.

Rem. 2. Pat. I, p. 443 हा देवदत्तम् affords also an instance of हा, construed with the accus.

18. Some particles are used in exhortations. They of course attend imperatives and such tenses as have the meaning of imperatives. The principal of them are अङ्ग, हन्त both = „well, come,” Lat. *age* and *agedum*. Kathâs. 24, 143 हन्त प्रसीदानय तम्. With the 1st person = fr. *allons*. Ch. Up. 5, 11, 2 तं हन्ताभ्यागच्छामेति तं हाभ्याजग्मुः (»Well, let us go to him.” Thus speaking, they went to him); R. 2, 96, 15 अङ्गावेक्षस्व सौमित्रे (come, look here, Laxmaṇa). — Among others, ननु and अपि, as Kumâras. 4, 32 ननु मां प्रापय पत्युरन्तिकम् (do, bring me together with

अङ्ग, हन्त etc.

my husband), Kâç. on P. 1, 4, 96 अपि सिञ्च, cp. Kâç. on P. 8, 1, 33 अङ्ग पठ (pray, read). — Like our »come," the imperat. एहि may assume the nature of a particle, f. i. Kathâs. 37, 200 एहि तस्यान्तिकं.... याव (come, let us go to him) and so already at so remote a period as when the marriage-mantras have been composed. Âçv. Grhy. 1, 7, 6 तावेहि विवहावहै प्रजां प्रजनयावहै.

Rem. Neither अङ्ग nor हन्त are however limited to this employment. Occasionally they accompany also the indicative mood. Kâç. on P. 8, 2, 96 अङ्ग देवदत्त मिथ्या वदसि (I say, my friend, you say the thing that is not), Mudr. I, p. 38 हन्त जितो मलयकेतुः. When addressing some person, while offering him something, one uses हन्त, fr. *voilà*. Schol. on P. 8, 2, 99 गां मे देहि भोः। हन्त ते ददामि.

419. *अयि and रे.* All interjections readily join with vocatives. Two, अयि and रे, are especially employed so, since they serve to draw the attention of the person addressed, in a word, like भोः the vocat. of भवान् (259) — and Lat. *heus*. Kumâras. 4, 28 अयि संप्रति देहि दर्शनं स्मर (come, Kâma, show yourself now), Hit. 9 व्याघ्र उवाच। शृणु रे पान्थ. — अयि is especially fit for gentle address »prithee [1]".

---

1) अयि is also asserted by lexicographers to be a particle of interrogation. I greatly doubt the correctness of this statement. अयि may easily be confounded in mss. with अपि, and, in fact, it is not rarely a various reading of the interrogative अपि, see the passages of Çâk. quoted by the Petr. Dict. s. v. अयि 2). The Petr. Dict. adds five more instances: *a*) three from the Kumâras., *b*) one from the Mṛcch., *c*) one from the Pancatantra. Of them, *a*) Kumâras. 4, 3 अयि जीवितनाथ जीवसि, though Mallin. comments thus on it अयि प्रश्नानुनययोरिति विश्वः। अयि जी° जी° प्राणिषि कच्चिदिति, it is by no means necessary to accept here अयि as an interrogative, better it is to keep to its duty as an interjection अयि जीवितनाथ »o, my Lord" जीवसि »are you alive?" So Mallin. himsel explains Kumâras. 5, 62 अयीति कोमलामन्त्रणे As to the remaining passage ibid. 5, 33—35, the edition of Prof. Târanâtha has अपि, not अयि. — *b*) In the two editions of the Mṛcch., I have at hand, the particle अयि is wanting, instead of अयि जानीषे they have भद्र जानीषे. — *c*). As to

A cognate particle is अये, sometimes = अयि, sometimes expressive of astonishment. Çâk. VI king Dushyanta, when perceiving on a sudden the charioteer of Indra standing near, exclaims अये मातलिः. Cp. Mṛcch. I, p. 17 अये सर्वकालमित्रं मैत्रेयः प्राप्तः.

420. Vocative. As to the vocative, it is generally put at the head, at least in prose, for poets may give it any place, according to the exigencies of the metre or rhythm.

In flowery style the vocative is not rarely attended by epithets, as Mâlat. VI, p. 87 आ दुरात्मन्मालतीनिमित्तं व्यापादितास्मद्गुरो माधवहतक (accursed Mâdhava, thou who hast murdered our teacher because of the wretched Mâlatî). In ordinary prose they are avoided.

CHAPT. V. **Connective particles.**

421. Connective particles. The most important connective particles are five monosyllables: च, वा, उ, तु, हि, and four dissyllables अथ, अपि, इव and उत. Of these, च, अपि, अथ and उत have the most general bearing, as they are simply copulating words = „and, also, further," though they often admit of some special modification of meaning, so as to get the force of adversatives, concessives etc. For the rest, वा is the disjunctive, तु and the archaic उ are adversatives, हि is causal, इव is the particle of comparison.

In the classic language उ and उत are no more used alone, but in some combinations they are, cp. **402** R. 1; **442**, 2° and 4°. That अपि, उ and उत may also be interrogative particles, has been shown above **412** and **414**.

Side by side with the said connective particles one

Panc. p. 38, 6, quoted by the Petr. Dict. = p. 44, last line of Vidyâsâgara's ed., this editor signifies by his very interpunction, that he considers अयि an exclamative, not an interrogative, as he has अयि! शिवं भवत्याः (my dear, has no harm befallen you?).

uses several adverbs, serving the same purpose, as अपरम् and अन्यत् or अन्यच्च „further, moreover," परम् „but, yet," तथा „likewise, and," the conclusives तत् and तस्मात् „therefore," the causal यतः „for," पुनः „on the other hand, again, but." They have completely assumed the nature of conjunctions.

Combinations of these particles either with each other or with other particles are excessively frequent. So च and अपि, अथ and वा, परम् and तु are very often combined, एव is often added to च, अपि, वा, तु. Some of them may be considered as units, as अथवा when = „indeed," तथापि „nevertheless."

422. As the connection of sentences is the subject-matter of the last Section of this Syntax, it will here suffice to give a succinct account of the connective particles severally, especially with regard to their linking together words within the compass of one and the same sentence.

च. 1. च is the copulative particle *par excellence* „and." It is as a rule subjoined to the word annexed, as रामो लक्ष्मणश्च, but if it annexes a complex of words or a whole sentence, it is affixed to the first word, as पिता मातुश्च स्वसा (father and mother's sister). Panc. 225 चौरेण। कश्चिद् दृष्टः। दृष्ट्वा च तं..... चौरोऽब्रवीत्. This order is seldom inverted in prose (f. i. Panc. 126 राज्ञो वक्त्रो द्विधा जातं राजा मृतश्च instead of मृतश्च राजा), oftener in poetry. Nala 1, 22 निपेतुस्ते गरुत्मन्तः सा ददर्श च तान्गणान्, Kathâs. 44, 3: the preceding sentence is स पितुर्गृहे..... अवसत्सुखम्, then there follows एकदा पितुरास्थाने स्थितश्च पुरुषं..... ददर्श सः.

Sometimes in poetry च is put between the two links connected by it. Mhbh. 1, 148, 2 अथ युधिष्ठिरः। भीमसेनार्जुनौ चोभौ यमौ प्रोवाच (then Yudh. addressed Bhîm., Arj. and the twins), M. 9, 322 इह चामुत्र वर्धते (he becomes great in this world and in the other).

In poets, च is not rarely put to each of the members connected, also in archaic prose; see f. i. Ch. Up. 1, 3, 2, and cp. τε..... τε of Greek poets. But if it is necessary to state that the same thing is endowed with different qualities etc. at the same time, this idiom is also used in prose. Pat. I, p. 430 याज्ञिकश्चायं वैयाकरणश्च (he is an accomplished sacrificer as well as a grammarian), Prabodh. I, p. 15 मोदं जनयति च संमोहयति च (it procures joy and perplexes at the same time). — As to च..... च expressive of simultaneousness, see **438** R. 2.

Rem. 1. If three or more terms are to be connected, च is generally put but once, and with the last of them. Panc. 6 भिक्षया नृपसेवया कृषिकर्मणा विद्योपार्जनेन व्यवहारेण च (by begging, by attending on the prince, by agriculture, by turning one's learning into money, and by trade), Daç. 78 सुभगेन च मया स्वधनस्य स्वगृहस्य स्वगणस्य स्वदेहस्य स्वजीवितस्य च सैवेश्वरी कृता. Then च is rarely wanting, sometimes in rhetorical style, as Pat. I, p. 431 अहरहर्नयमानो गामश्वं पुरुषं पशुम्, R. 3, 69, 32 कराभ्यां विविधान्गृह्य ऋक्षान्पक्षिगणान्मृगान्, and in some phrases, as Mrcch. I, p. 20 भाग्यक्रमेण हि धनानि भवन्ति यान्ति (v. a. as soon as they have come, they disappear), Bhoj. 10 जरां मृत्युं भयं व्याधिं यो जानाति स पण्डितः.

Rem. 2. Sometimes च must be translated by a more energetic particle than »and." It may be = »even." R. 1, 1, 4 कस्य बिभ्यति देवाश्च (of whom are even the gods afraid?), it may be a slight affirmative and even have adversative power, cp. **441**.

423. अपि. 2. **अपि** may be 1. = „and, too, moreover, also," 2. = „even," 3. = „though". Like **च**, it is commonly subjoined to the word — or first of the words — connected by it; in poets, it not rarely precedes. Examples of 1. Pat. I, p. 125 तवाश्वो नष्टो ममापि रथो दग्धः (your horse is lost and my chariot is burnt). Panc. 246 the king of the frogs mounts on the back of the serpent Mandavisha; seeing this, the others too do so शेषा अपि यथाज्येष्ठं तत्पृष्ठोपरि समारुरुहुः; Çâk. I अस्ति नः सच्चरितश्रवणलोभादन्यदपि

प्रष्टव्यम् (v. a. — I would ask you once more); — of 2. Mudr. I, p. 30 न युक्तं प्राकृतमपि रिपुमवज्ञातुम् (it is not advisable to despise a foe, not even a mean one); — of 3. Kathâs. 42, 28 अन्वगात्स च तं तुष्णीमनिच्छन्नपि (and, though reluctantly, he followed him).

In poetry however, अपि occasionally precedes the word it attends instead of being subjoined to it. Mhbh. 1, 76, 52 कं ब्रह्महत्या न दहेदपीन्द्रम् (whom would not the hurting of a brahman consume? even Indra), Kumâras. 6, 59 Himavân says अपि व्याप्तदिगन्तानि नाङ्गानि प्रभवन्ति मे (my limbs though stretching in all directions, have no power —), Panc. III, 92 अपि स्वर्गे instead of स्वर्गेऽपि etc. Another instance of poetical license is such an arrangement as we have Nala 1, 30 त्वमप्येवं नले वद instead of त्वमेवं नलेऽपि वद (speak in this way also to N.).

Rem. Apart from being a connective, अपि has many more meanings. It may be *a*) an interrogative particle, see **412**; *b*) with imperative it strengthens the exhortation, see Kâç. on P. 1, 4, 96 अपि सिञ्च (do, pour out); *c*) it often precedes the लिङ्, when doing duty as an optative (**343**, *b*) or in the idiom mentioned **343** *c*) 5°. In these cases अपि heads the sentence. — In other meanings again it is used, when subjoined to nouns of number (**298**), or when put to the interrogative pronouns and adverbs, see **281** and **288**.

Moreover अपि, when of time, may be = 1. »only, but," as मुहूर्तमपि प्रतीक्षस्व (wait but for a moment), 2. »still," f. i. Kathâs. 3, 18 बालोऽपि »when still a boy."

424. उत. 3. **उत** is almost a synonym of **अपि**. In the classic language it is obsolete. As to its employment as an interrogative particle see **412**, 2° and **414**, with optative it is also used like अपि, see **343** *c*) 5°, and cp. P. 3, 3, 152. — As a connective it is found in the old liturgical and epic literature. Mhbh. 1, 90, 24 मानाग्निहोत्रमुत मानमौनं मानेनाधीतमुत मानयज्ञः. At the close of verses or pâdas, उत and अप्युत are rather emphatics or mere expletives. — In classic prose one uses किमुत (**442**, 4°) and प्रत्युत (**442**, 2°).

425. अथ. 4. **अथ** serves to introduce some new element (person, thing or fact). It may be wholly = **च**, and connect even single words, f. i. Panc. V, 11 व्याधितेन सशोकेन चिन्ताग्रस्तेन जन्तुना। कामार्तेनाथ मत्तेन दृष्टः स्वप्नो निरर्थकः, here अथ is equivalent to च. Occasionally अथ may be a disjunctive, as Kathâs. 79, 24 ज्ञानी शूरोऽथ विज्ञानो भर्तास्मद्दुहितुर्मतः.

Its most common employment, however, is to annex a new sentence, especially if there be a change of subject; hence it is not rarely an adversative. Sometimes it introduces the apodosis, sometimes it has a temporal meaning „afterwards," 1) moreover it may do duty as a conditional conjunction, as will be more fully explained in the last Section of this book.

Note its employment at the beginning of a book or chapter or section, where it is the traditional opening-word in profane writings, like the syllable ओम् in Holy Writ. Pancatantra IV f. i. commences अथेदमारभ्यते लब्धप्रणाशं नाम चतुर्थं तन्त्रम् (now begins the 4th tantra —).

In prose it is the first word, but in poetry it may hold any other place.

426. अथ combines with other particles. So we have अथापि, अथ च, अथो (= अथ + उ), see f. i. Âçv. Gṛhy. 1, 1, 3; R. 3, 11, 74; Panc. IV, 73. But the commonest of those combinations is अथवा which is almost looked upon as a unit. It is used for the sake of correcting one's self. It introduces, therefore, a statement more exact than the preceding one; in accordance with the nature of the contrast between the two, one may translate अथवा

अथवा.

---

1) Especially in the archaic dialect. Ait. Br. 2, 25, 1 तेषामार्त्तिं यतामभिसृष्टानां वायुर्मुखं प्रथमः प्रत्यपद्यताथेन्द्रो ऽथ मित्रावरुणावथाश्विनौ (of them — Agni reached the aim the first, *after him* Indra, *then* Mitra and Varuṇa, *then* the Açvins).

by „or rather" or „on the contrary" or „no" or „but," f. i. Panc. 23 अन्यतो व्रजामि। अथवा नैतदुच्यते (I will go to another place. But that will not do), R. 3, 60, 29 नैव सा नूनमथवा हिंसिता चारुहासिनी (surely, it is not she, no, she has been hurt, my graceful lady).

As to अथ किम्, see **395** R.

427. तथा. तथा „so," when = „likewise" that is „and, too," may also be reckoned among the connectives. This employment is chiefly poetical.

For the rest, अपि, च and तथा may be strengthened by एव and may mingle together. Hence arises a great variety of combinations, especially in verse, as अप्येव, अपि च, चापि; चैव, एव च; तथैव, तथा च etc.

428. वा. The enclitic वा, like च, is subjoined to the word which it annexes. It is the disjunctive particle „or." अहं त्वं वा „I or you." „Either..... or" is वा..... वा. M. 3, 26 पृथक्पृथग्वा मिश्रौ वा विवाहौ (the two modes of marriage either performed severally or conjoined), Kathâs. 31, 39 न हि पश्यति तुङ्गं वा श्वभ्रं वा स्त्रीजनोऽग्रतः। स्मरेण नीतः.

Rem. Instead of वा..... वा one says also वा यदि वा. R. 3, 11, 90 नात्र जीवेन्मृषावादी क्रूरो वा यदि वा शठः। नृशंसः पापवृत्तो वा (here no liar can live, nor a cruel man, nor a rogue, nor a barbarous one nor an evildoer), cp. R. 2, 109, 4, Panc. I, 118. — Likewise one uses वा... अपि वा or वापि, etc. As to वा in interrogations, see **409**, 3° and **412** R., on its force as an emphatic **397** R. 1.

429. तु, हि and उ. तु, हि and the enclitic उ are, like च and वा, subjoined to the first word of the sentence. हि was at the outset an emphatic, a weak „indeed," but generally it is a causal particle, at least in prose; तु and उ are adversatives „but; on the other hand." उ is no more used in the classic dialect, save when added to some other particle, as नो = न + उ, अथो = अथ + उ, cp. 402 R. 1.

430. इव. इव „like, as" is the particle of comparison. It is always put after the standard of comparison, सिंह इव बलवान् (strong like a lion). Mṛcch. I, p. 48 अन्धस्य दृष्टिरिव पुष्टिरिवातुरस्य मूर्खस्य बुद्धिरिव सिद्धिरिवालसस्य। स्वल्पस्मृतेर्व्यसनिनः परमेव विद्या। .... सा प्रनष्टा (she has disappeared, like the sight of the blind, like the health of the sick, like the wisdom of the fool, like the prosperity of the sluggard, like the learning of the dull and dissipated), Çâk. VI कच्चिदहमिव विस्मृतवानसि त्वम् (have you perhaps forgotten it, as I have?). If the standard of comparison or the simile consists of more words, इव likes to be put in the midst of them. Çâk. VII किं नु खलु बाले ऽस्मिन्नौरस इव पुत्रे स्निह्यति मे मनः. Exceptions as to the place of इव may occasionally be found in poets.

यथा. The other particle of comparison is the relative यथा. It is especially used, if the standard of comparison is expressed by a full sentence, but it does the same duty as इव.

Rem. 1. It is a matter of course, that इव and यथा have no influence at all on the case of the noun they are construed with. Both the noun compared and the standard of comparison are put in the same case. Kumâras. 4, 25 तैः परिदेविताक्षरैर्हृदये दिग्धशरैरिवाहतः (struck by those lamentations, as if they were poisoned arrows); Nala 2, 28 तं दृष्ट्वा.... भ्राजमानं यथा रविम् (on seeing him who was bright like the sun).

Rem. 2. Note the idiom आभासत इव »he appears like," f. i. Kumâras. 7, 3 [तत्पुरं] स्वर्ग इवाबभासे.

Rem. 3. इव and यथा are often used in similes. In this case they may be strengthened by adding to them such epithets as साक्षात् (in person), विग्रहवन्त् or विग्रहिन् (embodied), स्वयम्, अपर (cp. Lat. *Mars alter*) and the like. Nala 1, 4 the hero is said to have been an excellent archer and ruler of his subjects साक्षादिव मनुः स्वयम् »as if he were Manu himself," Daç. 116 a beautiful woman is called रतिरिव विग्रहिणी (the goddess Rati embodied), Mhbh. 1, 85, 5 ययातिः पालयामास साक्षादिन्द्र इवापरः. Cp. Kumâras. 6, 11, Ragh. 2, 16, Mâlav. I, p. 24, Kâm. 3, 30, etc.

431. Moreover, **इव** is used to soften some expression, in the same way as German *etwa*, our *rather*, *almost*, *as if it were*. Mudr. II, p. 58 विफलमिव राक्षसप्रयत्नमवगच्छामि (I perceive that the exertions of R. are almost fruitless), R. 2, 85, 7 इयं ते महती सेना शङ्कां जनयतीव मे.

432. Our „as," when not expressing likeness, is not rendered at all in Sanskrit or by **स्थाने** with gen. But „as" = „for instance, namely" is **तद्यथा**. Mudr. III, p. 117 वृषल इह खलु विरक्तानां प्रकृतीनां द्विविधं प्रतिविधानं तद्यथानुग्रहो निग्रहश्चेति (well, Vrshala, there are two means to be put into effect against disaffected subjects, viz. favour and force).

तद्यथा.

SECTION VI.

ON THE CONNECTION OF SENTENCES.

433. In Section II—V we have treated of the different constituent elements of the sentence. This last part of the Syntax will deal with the various ways, in which sentences are linked together. Two main categories are here to be distinguished, 1. coordination, when — grammatically speaking — there is equality of rank between the sentences conjoined, 2. subordination, that is such a union, as makes one of the links depend upon the other, so as to constitute a period made up of a chief sentence and a clause or subordinate sentence. The former class is generally characterized by such particles as have been dealt with in the last chapter of the preceding Section, the latter class by relatives.

Occasionally Sanskrit prefers coordination in such cases in which our language would rather use the other mode of junction, and inversely.

Example of coordination in Sanskrit, subordination with us: Mṛcch. III, p. 116 एतद्गर्हितं कर्म निन्दामि च करोमि च (though blaming it I do it).

Example of subordination in Sanskrit, coordination with us: Daç. 30 रत्नं तत्रैकमद्राक्षम्। तदादाय गत्वा कंचनाध्वानमम्बरमणेरत्युष्णतया गन्तुमक्षमः..... किमपि देवायतनं प्रविष्टः etc. In translating such sentences as this there is, as a rule, a greater deal of coordination in English, f. i. »I saw there [in the water] a jewel, I took it and went on, until being tired by the exceeding glow of the sun, I entered some temple." Cp. 14, I.

CHAPT. I. **Coordination**.

434. Coordination, though chiefly expressed by little particles, as च, is not exclusively signified by them. The demonstrative pronoun, especially स, may be a fit instrument for annexing a new sentence. Sometimes both particle and pronoun are wanting, and sentences are simply put together: the so-called asyndeton.

Coordination by means of:

435. I. As to the **demonstrative**, some instances have been given **275**. I add one more from the beginning of the Pancatantra अस्ति दाक्षिणात्ये जनपदे महिलारोप्यं नाम नगरम्। तत्र..... अमरशक्तिर्नाम राजा बभूव। तस्य त्रयः पुत्राः..... बभूवुः. Nothing prevents the employment of both dem. pronoun and particle together. So often सोऽपि.

1. the demonstrative.

The acc. neuter तत् and the abl. neuter तस्मात्, when = „therefore, for this reason," have wholly got the nature of particles. Likewise तेन.

436. II. The **asyndeton** is mostly met with either in short statements, to express antithesis, or for rhetorical pur-

2. the asyndeton.

poses, especially where the speaker is excited. Panc. 26 अस्त्येवं स महात्मा वयं कृपणाः (so it is, he is a Lord and we are wretches), ibid. 113 न ते दोषो ऽयं स्वामिनो दोषः (it is not your fault, but that of your master), Mudr. III, p. 106 अनुभूयत एवैतन्नाशास्यते (this is already a real possession, not an expected one), Daç. 16 किं करोमि क्व गच्छामि भवद्भिर्न किमदर्शि (what shall I do? whither shall I go? have you not seen [him]?). Panc. 134 सत्वरमागच्छ गुरुतरं प्रयोजनमस्ति, here the second sentence enunciates the reason of the former one, but there is no causal particle. In a similar way वा is omitted in the passionate declaration of Damayantî (Nala 4, 4) यदि त्वं भजमानां मां प्रत्याख्यास्यसि मानद। विषमग्निं जलं रज्जुमास्थास्ये तव कारणात्, likewise Kumâras. 6, 12 स्त्री पुमानित्यनास्थैषा वृत्तं हि महितं सताम् (whether man or woman, it matters not —).

437. III. When treating of sentences connected by **particles** it is best to keep apart the logical categories.

3. particles.

Copulative particles.

Mere copulation is denoted by च, अपि, अथ — either single or combined, as अपि च, चापि, अथापि —, by किं च, अपरम्, अन्यच्च, by ततः and ततश्च. They answer to English *and*, *also*, *likewise*, *moreover*, *further*, *then*, *thereupon* etc. They are not quite synonymous, and each of them may have its proper sphere (as ततः to subjoin what is subsequent in time, किं च, अपरम्, अन्यच्च to signify the importance of what is added, अथ to import a change of the scene, of the action, of the actors etc.), yet it is neither easy nor necessary to draw the boundary-lines sharply between them.

Examples: 1. च. Daç. 83 निशि वयमिमां पुरीं प्रविष्टा दृष्टश्च ममैव नायको दवीकरेण; — 2. अपि. Mudr. II, p. 69 प्रियंवदक.... विश्रम्यतां परिजनेन। त्वमपि स्वमधिकारमशून्यं कुरु (Priy., my attendants may keep their rest and you, discharge your duty); — 3. अथ. R. 3, 14, 4 स तं पितृसखं मत्वा पूजयामास राघवः।.... तस्य कुलमव्यग्रमथ पप्रच्छ नाम च, Panc. 3 the king first spoke to Vishnuçarman, »*then* the other replied" अथ विष्णुशर्मा

तं राजानमूचे; — 4. किं च. Panc. 214 किमत्र चिन्त्यते। अविचारितमयं हन्तव्यः the reasons, why he is to be killed are then given: यतः..... किं च..... उक्तं..... श्रूयते च (for..... moreover..... then one says.... it is also taught); — 5 अपरम्. Panc. 135 मदाश्रयाः सर्वा एते वराकाः। अपरं स्वकुटुम्बं परित्यज्य समागताः (all these poor fellows are depending on me, besides they have left their families in order to join me), ibid. IV, 65 मित्रं ह्यमित्रतां यातमपरं (secondly) मे प्रिया मृता गृहमन्येन च (moreover) व्याप्तम्; — 6. अन्यच्च. Panc. 168 a heavenly being prevents Somilaka from suicide, and says मैवं साहसं कुरु..... तद्गच्छ स्वगृहं प्रति। अन्यच्च भवदोयसाहसेनाहं तुष्टः; — 7. ततः. Daç. 138 अहं तु..... त्वया प्रवेशयिष्ये। ततः पितरमुज्जीव्य तदभिरुचितेनाभ्युपायेन चेष्टिष्यामः (you must make me enter, then recall our father into life and act in the way that shall please him).

Rem. 1. अथ is not seldom = »now", fr. *or*. Panc. 94 कस्मिंश्चिज्जलाशये..... त्रयो मत्स्याः सन्ति। अथ कदाचित्तं जलाशयं दृष्ट्वा गच्छद्भिर्मत्स्यजीविभिरुक्तम् (in some pond there were three fishes. *Now*, one day fishermen passed, looked at that pond and said).

Rem. 2. च, अपि, अथ are sometimes to be rendered by *but*, *yet*, *nevertheless*. See **441**.

438. च..... च, अपि..... अपि, च..... अपि etc. = „as well as;" „not only..... but also." Utt. II, p. 29 विसृष्टश्च..... मेध्यो ऽश्व उपकल्पिताश्च यथाशास्त्रं तस्य रक्षितारस्तेषामधिष्ठाता लक्ष्मणात्मजश्च..... साधनान्वितो ऽनुप्रहितः (not only the sacrificial horse has been loosed to roam at will, but also guards have been appointed to it according to the ritual, and Laxmana's son has been sent after it).

Rem. 1. The archaic dialect has also the combination उत.... उत. The old verse उत त्वः पश्यन्न ददर्श वाचमुत त्वः शृण्वन्न शृणोत्येनाम् is commented on by Yâska in this way अप्येकः पश्यन्न पश्यति वाचमपि च शृण्वन्न शृणोत्येनाम् (see Nir. 1, 19).

Rem. 2. A repeated च may occasionally denote *simultaneousness*. Kumâras. 3, 58 उमा च शम्भोः समाससाद प्रतिहारभूमिम्। योगात्स च.... उपारराम (Umâ reached the entrance of Çiva's hermitage, and at the same time Çiva ceased his mystic exercises), cp. ibid. vs. 66, Ragh. 3, 40; 10, 6; Kathâs. 18, 120.

439. The foresaid particles are also used to connect three or more links. In enumerations, it is regular to put तावत् in the first link (cp. **399**). Panc. 281 एकस्तावद्गृहभङ्गो ऽपरस्त्वद्विधेन मित्रेण सह चित्तविश्लेषः (in the first place the loss of my dwelling, then the alienation of such a friend as you). The complete set of particles is: एकं तावत्, आदौ तावत् or प्रथमं तावत् in the first link, अपरम् or अथ or ततः or अन्यच्च etc. in the second and other links. Panc. 67 the lion chides the hare, who has been despatched to him by the other animals एकं तावत्त्वं लघुः प्राप्तो ऽपरं वेलातिक्रमेण, Panc. 181 आदौ तावद्वित्तनाशस्ततः परिवारभ्रंशस्ततो देशत्यागस्ततो मित्रवियोगः, Mudr. III p. 173 the three links of an argumentation are marked by तावत्, ततः and अतः.

440. Disjunction. Disjunctive sentences are characterized by वा, or वा..... वा, वा यदि वा, अथवा. See **428** and **426**.

Another kind of disjunction is that represented by „some..... others..... others again" and the like. Here indefinite pronouns are to be employed, as केचित्..... केचित्; केचित् or एके..... अपरे, अन्ये etc. Likewise the adverbs made of them. Mudr. IV, p. 138 मन्त्रभङ्गभयाद्राज्ञां कथयन्त्यन्यथा पुरः। अन्यथा विवृतार्थेषु स्वैरालापेषु मन्त्रिणः.

441. Antithesis. Antithesis may be variously denoted. In the first place it may be expressed by adversative particles, viz. तु (**429**), परम्, पुनः, also by such combinations as किं तु, परं तु, परं किं तु. Further च, अपि, अथ may be = *on the other hand*, *on my-*, *your-*, *his part*, *again* etc., or if stronger antithesis is implied, = *but*, *yet*. Nor is the asyndeton rare, in which case it is the mere arrangement of the two contrasting ideas, by which the antithesis appears, see **436**.

Examples: *a.*) antithesis expressed by adversative particles. — तु. Mṛcch. IV, p. 141 स्त्रियो हि नाम खल्वेता निसर्गादेव पण्डिताः। पुरुषाणां तु पाण्डित्यं शास्त्रैरेवोपदिश्यते (womankind, indeed, are wise by nature, but to men wisdom is to be taught by manuals); — परम्. Panc. 315 अस्त्येतत्परं तथापि गृहिणीं पृच्छामि (it is so, yet I will ask my wife nevertheless); — किं तु. Hit. 106 दुर्गं तावदिदमेव चिरात्सुनिरूपितमास्ते महत्सरः। किं त्वेतन्मध्यद्वीपे भक्ष्यवस्तूनां संग्रहः क्रियताम् (well, this great lake has been very aptly chosen to be our fortress, but you must lay up provisions in the island in the midst of it); — परं तु. Panc. 304 शास्त्रपारं गताः परं तु बुद्धिरहिताः; — परं किं तु. Panc. 16 सत्यमेतत्परं किं तु° (this is true, but —); — पुनः. Panc. 72 अयं शष्पभोजी देवपादानां पुनः शत्रवो मांसाशिनः (he is an herbivorous animal, but your enemies are carnivorous).

Rem. 1. पुनः, like तु, is generally subjoined to the first word of the sentence. It must be kept in mind that its adversative power is but secondary; properly it means »again," and may be used in the weakened meaning of »on the other hand, yet," just as *again* in English [1]).

Rem. 2. Of the adversative उ instances are often met with in such works as the Aitareyabrâhmana and the Chândogyopanishad, occasionally even in the epic poems. It mostly joins with some particle or relative. Ait. Br. 2, 39, 11 यावतां वै स ज्ञातानां वेद ते भवन्ति। येषामु न वेद किमु ते स्युः (— but those, of whom he has no knowledge, what is to become of them?), Ch. Up. 6, 4, 6 यदु.... यदु, ibid. 4, 15, 3 एष उ »but he." Sometimes it is almost = च, for it has less adversative force than तु.

b). च, अपि or अथ = *but*, *yet*, *nevertheless*. Nala 1, 5 Bhîma bears the epithet of प्रजाकामः, to which are added the words स चाप्रजः »beloved of his subjects [and at the same time »desiring to have children"], *yet* childless". R. 3, 37, 2 सुलभाः पुरुषा राजन्सततं प्रियवादिनः। अप्रियस्य च पथ्यस्य वक्ता श्रोता च दुर्लभः (they who always speak things pleasant to be heard are easy to be found, *but* it is as difficult to meet with one who speaks an unpleasant yet wholesome word, as with one who listens to such a one), Mudr. III,

1) Yet, like »again," it may occasionally head the sentence. Panc. 3 नाहं विद्याविक्रयं शासनशतेनापि करोमि। पुनरेतांस्तव पुत्रान्मासषट्केन यदि नीतिशास्त्रज्ञान्न करोमि ततः स्वनामत्यागं करोमि; Daç. 181, l. 14.

p. 105 Câṇakya to the chief of the eunuchs अहो राजपरिजनस्य चाणाक्यस्योपरि विद्वेषपक्षपातः। अथ क्व वृषलस्तिष्ठति (the king's attendants are indeed Cânakya's enemies. *But* where is the çûdra-king?). Likewise अथवा, cp. **426.**

442. Observations on the adversative particles.

Adversatives answering to limitatives

1. To emphasize the antithesis, a limitative particle may precede in the foregoing sentence. Then we have the type of Greek μέν..... δέ, Latin *quidem*..... *sed* or *vero*. Such limitative particles in Sanskrit are तावत्, खलु, केवलम्, कामम्, किल, सत्यम्, परम्. Panc. 313 अहं तावत्क्षेत्रपालमवलोकयामि। त्वं पुनः स्वेच्छया गीतं कुरु (I will look out for the farmer, but you —), ibid. 195 अस्माकं तावद्वैनतेयो राजा। स च..... न कामपि चिन्तामस्माकं करोति (it is true, we have a king, Garuda but he does not care for us), Mhbh. 1, 48, 6 कामं च मम न न्याय्यं प्रष्टुं त्वां कार्यमीदृशं। किं तु कार्यगरीयस्त्वात्ततस्त्वाहमचूचुदम् (to be sure, it does not befit me to ask you about such a matter, but owing to its great importance I have ventured to urge you), Panc. III, 171 स निनिन्द किलात्मानं न तु तं लुब्धकं पुनः (he accused himself, but not the fowler), Kathâs. 39, 21 वयसा परं कनिष्ठः सो ऽभवत्तेषां गुणैर्ज्येष्ठतमस्त्वभूत्.

अपि तु and प्रत्युत.

2. If the preceding sentence is negative, the adversative particle must be rather strong. Such strong adversatives are किं तु, परं तु, अपि तु and प्रत्युत "on the contrary." Panc. 203 न तवेदं गृहं किं तु ममैव, Daç 77 न वपुर्वसु वा पुंस्त्वमूलमपि तु प्रकृष्टगणिकाप्रार्थ्ययौवनो हि यः स पुमान् (neither external beauty nor riches are the result of manhood, no, he is a man who is loved by the foremost courtesan), ibid. 100 राजा त्वां....नोच्छेत्स्यति प्रत्युत प्रापयिष्यत्येव यौवराज्यम् (he will [not only] not kill you; but he will even make you heir-apparent).

3. न केवलम् in the former, च, अपि etc. in the latter member are = च.... च "not only..... but also." Panc. I, 33 न केवलमसंमानं लभते च विडम्बनाम्, Nâgân. V, p. 85 अयं वत्सो जीमूतवाहनो न केवलं ध्रियते प्रत्युत कृताञ्जलिना गरुडेन शिष्येणेव पर्युपास्यमानस्तिष्ठति (not only my son Jîm. here is alive, nay he is even respected by Garuḍa, as a pupil reverences his teacher), Ragh. 3, 31 न केवलं तद्गुरुरेकपार्थिवः क्षितावभूदेकधनुर्धरोऽपि सः. — Similarly न परम्..... अपि or च or प्रत्युत sim., see f. i. Kathâs. 33, 138. As to न परम्..... यावत् see **480.**

Rem. If on the other hand न precedes and केवलम् or परम् introduce the second sentence, these particles may be almost = »but." Panc. 122 न भवसि त्वं सज्जनः केवलं पापबुद्धिरसि (you are not an honest man, you are but an evil-minded fellow), Prabodh. IV, p. 84 क्लमो न वाचां शिरसो न शूलं न चित्ततापो न तनोर्विमर्दः। न चापि हिंसादिरनर्थयोगः श्लाघ्या परं क्रोधजये ऽहमेका (in the subduing of anger not fatigue of voice, nor head-ache etc., but I [forbearance] alone am to be praised).

किमु, किं पुनः and the like. 4. The phrases किमु, किं नु, किं पुनः, किमुत and कुतः have the meaning of Lat. *nedum* »how much more" or »how much less," when heading the second member of a complex sentence. This idiom is much liked in Sanskrit. Utt. III, p. 39 ननु त्वामवनिपृष्ठवर्तिनीम्..... वनदेवता अपि न द्रक्ष्यन्ति किं पुनर्मर्त्याः (not even to the deities of the forest you will be visible, how much less to men?), R. 2, 30, 21 इमं हि सहितुं शोकं मुहूर्तमपि नोत्सहे। किं पुनर्दश वर्षाणि त्रीणि चैकं च दुःखिता (I cannot bear this sorrow not even for a moment, how much less for fourteen long years), Hit. 2 एकैकमप्यनर्थाय किमु यत्र चतुष्टयम् (even each of them by itself suffices for mischief, how much more to him, who possesses them all four), R. 2, 48, 21 न हि नो जीवितेनार्थः कुतः पुत्रैः कुतो धनैः.

443. हि, the causal particle. The causal particle is हि (429). It may be compared with Greek γάρ, since like this it has a rather general employment when annexing sentences which contain some motive, reason, cause or even a mere illustration of that which precedes. For this reason, it may sometimes be rendered by „for" or „because" or „since," sometimes with less emphasis, sometimes it is not to be translated at all. At the outset it was, indeed, a mere affirmative particle. Viddhaç. I, p. 7 श्रियः प्रदुग्धे विपदो रुणाद्धि यशांसि सूते मलिनं प्रमार्ष्टि। संस्कारशौचेन परं पुनीते शुद्धा हि बुद्धिः किल कामधेनुः (pure wisdom is indeed a cow of plenty; it milks blessings, it repels mishap, it produces glory, it cleanses the dirty, etc.) Kâd. I, p. 20 the king has declared his astonishment at the great

gift of speech of the parrot which has been offered to him; in reply to this he is to d किमत्र चित्रम्।एते हि शुकशारिकाप्रभृतयो विहङ्गविशेषा यथाश्रुतं वाचमुच्चारयन्ति (why wonder at this? since parrots, magpies and the like birds well repeat the words they have heard), Hit. 4 आहारनिद्राभयमैथुनं च सामान्यमेतत्पशुभिर्नराणाम्।धर्मो हि तेषामधिको विशेषो धर्मेण हीनाः पशुभिः समानाः.

For the rest, if it be necessary to signify the cause or motive as such, the relatives यतः and यस्मात् are used. See **467**.

444. Conclusive particles. As conclusive particles we may consider the demonstratives तत् and तस्मात्, ततः, अतः, तर्हि „therefore, hence, for this reason." Hit. 5 पूर्वजन्मकृतं कर्म तद् दैवमिति कथ्यते। तस्मात्पुरुषकारेण यत्नं कुर्यादतन्द्रितः.

445. Conclusive force of the pronoun स. Especially तत् is exceedingly frequent, and in drawing inferences it is always added.

Rem In the archaic dialect many other accus. neuters of demonstrative pronouns were to some extent used as particles: एतत्, अदः, इदम् almost = एवम्, इत्यम्, इति. See f. i. Ait. Br. 1, 9, 6; 14, 6; Ch. Up. 4, 2, 1; 6, 8, 3.

Even the pronoun स, when conjoined with another pronoun, especially a personal one, may import a conclusive meaning. Mhbh. 1, 146, 29 Yudhishthira advising his brothers that it is necessary to keep themselves hidden from Duryodhana, concludes thus ते वयं मृगयाशीलाश्चराम वसुधामिमाम् etc. (let us *therefore* ramble over this country, being intent on hunting), Çâk. II Dushyanta is requested by his mother to return to his capital, but he wants to remain in the hermitage, to defend which from the evil spirits he has been entreated by the hermits; now he decides to stay there himself and to send his vidûshaka home in his stead, with these words सखे माधव्य त्वमप्यम्बाभिः पुत्र इव गृहीतः स भवानितः प्रतिनिवृत्य.... तत्रभवतीनां पुत्रकार्यमनुष्ठातुमर्हति (friend M., my mother treats you too as a son, *therefore*, do you go back home —),

Utt. I, p. 11 Sîtâ perceives the portrait of the deity Gangâ; Râma praises the deity and concludes सा त्वमम्ब..... सीतायां शिवानुध्यानपरा भव (be, *then*, mother, propitious to Sîtâ). Another instance illustrative of this idiom is Ragh. 1, 5, but it is too long to be quoted, for to translate it correctly the whole passage would have to be given. Cp. also Mhbh. 1, 153, 4.

Rem. Occasionally स is used so, even without the personal pronoun added. Daç. 141 पुत्र मयासि जातमात्रः पापया परित्यक्तः। स किमर्थमेवं मामतिनिर्घृणामनुगृह्णासि (I have abandoned you, my son, as soon as you were born, why, *then*, do you welcome thus your cruel mother?). Cp. f. i. Ait. Br. 1, 7, 3 सा वै वो वरं वृणै.

446. तथापि. *Nevertheless*, *however*, *yet* is **तथापि**. It commonly introduces the apodosis after a concessive protasis (**483**), but sometimes it may usher in a new sentence, as Panc 332 भोः सत्यमेतद् दैवानुकूलतया सर्वं कल्याणं संपद्यते।तथापि पुरुषेण सतां वचनं कार्यम् (it cannot be denied, that every success occurs according to Destiny, *nevertheless* a man ought to perform the prescriptions of the good), cp. 315, l. 22.

447. Connecting negative sentences: *a*) with affirmative ones. When connecting a negative sentence with an affirmative one, the negation, as a rule, precedes the connective particle. Therefore, **न च** = Lat. *neque*, **न वा**, **न तु**, **नहि**, **नापि** etc., likewise **नो** = **न** + **उ**, **न ह**, **नोत**. Nala 3, 16 प्रशशंसुश्च सुप्रीता नलं ताः [sc. परमाङ्गनाः]..... न चैनमभ्यभाषन्त (the women praised Nala, but did not address him), Panc. 241 एकैकां वनकाष्ठिकां दिने दिने प्रक्षिपति न च ते मूर्खा उलूका विजानन्ति (day after day he throws down a little piece of wood, the stupid owls not being aware of it); [1]) M. 2, 87 कुर्यादन्यन्न वा कुर्यात् (he may

1) Occasionally this order is inverted: च न or च.... न. Panc. 285 सर्वलोकानां चिरन्तनाश्चतुर्भूमिका गृहाः सन्ति मम च नात्र (— but not so have I), R. 2, 26, 3 वैदेही चापि तत्सर्वं न शुश्राव

act otherwise or not); Daç. 141 सैव सदृशकारिणी। नहि मादृशो जनो तवार्हति कलप्रलापामृतानि कर्णाभ्यां पातुम् (she has done well, for a person like me does not deserve —); Vikram. IV, p. 148 उर्वशीगात्रस्पर्शादिव निर्वृतं मे हृदयं न पुनरस्ति विश्वासः (— my heart is content, yet I cannot believe it to be true); M. 9, 270 न होढेन विना चौरं घातयेद्धार्मिको नृपः (indeed, a righteous king must never put to death a thief, unless the stolen objects [are found with him]). Cp. न चेत् 485.

448. *b.) with negative ones.* If the sentences connected are both negative, the negation of the latter may be omitted. Yet the negation is often retained; and, if there is some antithesis between the two links, moreover in causal and in conclusive sentences, it may not be wanting. One needs says न..... न तु and नहि and न पुनः.

Examples of negation omitted are given **407.** To them may be added M. 2, 98 न हृष्यति ग्लायति वा (is neither rejoiced nor sad). This idiom is especially employed, if two or more negative sentences precede, to annex a last link. Nala 1, 13 न देवेषु न यक्षेषु तादृग्रूपवती क्वचित्। मानुषेष्वपि चान्येषु दृष्टपूर्वाथवा श्रुता (neither among gods nor among yaxas nor among men and others such a beauty had been seen or heard of).

Examples of negation retained: Panc. 44 अद्यप्रभृति गृहान्निष्क्रमणं न करोषि न च परुषं वदसि (from this day forth you shall not be a gadding nor speak harsh words), ibid. 29 न कोऽपि तादृक्केनापि चतुरो दृष्टो नापि श्रुतो वा.

Examples of न..... नहि, न..... न तु etc. Panc. I, 48 यो न वेत्ति गुणान्यस्य न तं सेवेत पण्डितः। नहि तस्मात्फलं किंचित्, Daç. 91 धनादृते न तत्स्वजनो ऽनुमन्यते। न तु धनदायासावभ्युपगच्छति (her kinsmen do not cede [her] unless for money, but she does not accept [a lover] who buys her for money).

Examples of asyndeton न..... न »neither..... nor.” M. 4, 55 नाश्नीयात्संधिवेलायां न गच्छेन्नापि संविशेत्। न चैव प्रलिखेद्भूमिं नात्मनो ऽपहरेत्स्रजम्, Panc. III, 98 नाच्छादयति कौपीनं न दंशमशकापहम्। शुनः पुच्छम् (a dog’s tail neither covers the privy parts nor does it propel the vermin).

Chapt. II. **Subordination. Periods and clauses.**

449. When subordinating some fact or action to some other one, there are two different manners for bringing this relation to grammatical expression, either by synthesis or by analysis. The synthetic expression takes up the clauses into the frame of the chief sentence, while denoting them by verbal nouns or nominal forms of the verb, as participles, gerunds, infinitives and the like. Then, the sentence contains but one finite verb significative of the principal action, the other actions appearing in the shape of nouns and nominal forms which by their noun-cases and modalities are to represent the relations existing between the main action and the secondary ones. By the analytic structure, on the contrary, both the principal and the subordinate fact are evolved into full sentences, either of them containing its finite verb. Then, the clause is marked by a relative, which by its form or its referring to some demonstrative, or even by the place occupied by it, points out the chief sentence on which it depends. A relative sentence by itself is nonsense, it demands some main sentence to depend upon, of which it is logically but a detached link.

Exactly speaking, it is the analytic expression alone that constitutes *subordination of sentences.* The synthetical expression of clauses does not create new sentences. For this reason, the participles etc. are no subject-matter of this chapter, and have been dealt with in Section IV.

In Sanskrit both modes haye been used from time

immemorial. We have no evidence to decide which may be the oldest. For the rest, the relative system stands to participles, infinitives etc., almost as prepositions to noun-cases, as auxiliaries to verbal flection.

450. Sometimes the logical equivalence of a gerund, a participle etc. to the protasis of a period is grammatically expressed by a subsequent अथ or ततः. Ch. Up. 6, 13, 1 लवणमेतदुदके ऽवधायाथ मा प्रातरुपसीदथाः (v. a. place this salt in water, and then wait on me in the morning), Kathâs. 13, 144 सापि प्रव्राजिका तस्माद्वणिक्पुत्रचतुष्टयात्.... आदायैकमथाययौ, Nala 5, 10 तान्समीक्ष्य.... अथ वैदर्भी नाभ्यजानान्नलं नृपम्. (as Damayantî contemplated them, she did not recognize king Nala), ibid. 2, 14 तावर्चयित्वा मघवा ततः कुशलमव्ययं।पप्रच्छानामयं चापि तयोः, M. 11, 91 तया स्वकाये निर्दग्धे मुच्यते किल्विषात्ततः (by this [penance] such a one, when his body is wholly burnt, is then released from sin).

451. *The relative system.* Subordinate sentences, then, are characterized by **relatives.** By this name I designate the pronoun य with all its derivatives, whether they may be called pronouns as यः (who), यावान् (Lat. *quantus*), यादृशः (Lat. *qualis*), or pronominal adverbs as यतः (whence), यत्र (where), यथा (as), and conjunctions as यदि (if). They have in common the property of referring to some demonstrative, either expressed or implied in the main sentence. Such a couple of relative and demonstrative, standing one in the clause the other in the main sentence, may be compared to a system of hook and eye holding together two different parts of a piece of cloth. Of the kind are यः..... स, यादृशः..... तादृशः, यत्र..... तत्र, यदा..... तदा, यदि..... ततः or तदा or अथ etc.

452. From observing the practice of Sanskrit authors the following general rules about the relative sentences may be laid down.

Its properties.

1. The demonstrative is chiefly the pronoun स, सा, तत् and its derivatives, as तत्र, तथा, तदा, ततः. Yet, it must be kept in mind that relative adverbs do not necessarily require demonstrative adverbs of the same category; in other terms, one is not compelled to use the type यतः..... ततः, यत्र..... तत्र alone, but sometimes some other demonstrative, f. i. a noun-case of the pronoun may answer to the relative adverb, as यत्र त्वमवसः स देशो रमणीयः (it is a charming country where you dwelled).

2. Sanskrit likes to put the relative sentence first. In this case we have a period consisting of a **protasis** or former member, which is the relative sentence, and an **apodosis** or latter member, the principal sentence. This order is the regular one and much more used than inserting the relative sentence in the main one, as is generally done in modern European tongues. The demonstr. is commonly expressed, sometimes it is understood.

Examples: Panc. II, 20 यस्माच्च येन च यदा च यथा च यच्च यावच्च यत्र च शुभाशुभमात्मकर्म। तस्माच्च तेन च तदा च तथा च तच्च तावच्च तत्र च विधातृवशादुपैति (good and evil works of the individual are so requited by the Divine Power as to reach [the performer] by the same cause, by the same agent, at the same time, in the same way, at the same spot, and to be of the same quality and quantity), M. 1, 42 येषां तु यादृशं कर्म भूतानामिह कीर्तितं। तत्तथा वो ऽभिधास्यामि (now, what duties are assigned to the different beings in this world, I will tell you), Utt. III, p. 42 यत्र द्रुमा अपि मृगा अपि बन्धवो मे। यानि प्रियासहचरश्चिरमध्यवात्सम्। एतानि तानि बहुनिर्झरकन्दराणि। गोदावरीपरिसरस्य गिरेस्तटानि, Panc. 48 तदस्य यद्युज्यते तत्क्रियताम् (do to him that which is fit to be done).

Sometimes, however, the relative sentence follows after the principal one. In this case, the demonstrative is often omitted. Mrcch. I, p. 19 एतत्तु मां दहति यद्गृहमस्मदीयं। क्षीणार्थमित्यतिथयः परिवर्जयन्ति (this ails me, that —), Nala 2, 25 सर्वे [sc. लोकपालाः]. . . . विदर्भानभिजग्मुस्ते यतः सर्वे महीक्षितः (all of them went to Vidarbha, whither all princes were on their way).

3. Like the interrogative (**280**), the relative may be part of a compound. Mrcch. III, p. 111 यद्विस्मयं यान्ति पौराः = यस्य विस्मयं°, Ch. Up. 4, 4, 2 साहमेतन्न वेद यद्गोत्रस्त्वमसि (I do not know of what gotra you are), Ven. II, p. 44 तदादेशय तमुद्देशं यत्रस्था भानुमती.

4. Nothing prevents the relative depending on a gerund, participle or absolute case. Ch. Up. 5, 1, 7 ते ह प्राणाः प्रजापतिं पितरमेत्योचुर्भगवन्को नः श्रेष्ठ इति। तान्होवाच यस्मिन्व उत्क्रान्ते शरीरं पापिष्ठतरमिव दृश्येत स वः श्रेष्ठ इति (the [five] senses went to their father Prajâpati and said: »Sir, who is the best of us?" He replied: »he by whose departure the body seems worse than worst, he is the best of you"), Bhoj. 26 नगरं विलोक्य कमपि मूर्खममात्यो नापश्यद्यं निरस्य विदुषे गृहं दीयते (the minister looked about the town, but did not find any illiterate person to expel from his house, in order to give it to a man of learning). — Kumâras. 1, 3 the pronoun यस्य is to be construed with the former part of a tatpurusha यस्य हिमं न सौभाग्यविलोपि जातम् (v. a. whose happiness [of Himavân] is not disturbed by the snow), Mrcch. III, p. 111 the thief speaks: तत्कस्मिन्देशे दर्शयाम्यात्मशिल्पं। दृष्ट्वा श्वो यं यद्विस्मयं यान्ति पौराः (on what spot, then, shall I show my skill, which the citizens will admire to-morrow when looking at it?).

5. In prose, the relative is, as a rule, the first word of the relative sentence. Panc. 53 यत्र कन्यान्तःपुरे वायुं मुक्त्वा नान्यस्य प्रवेशो ऽस्ति तत्र°, ibid. 62 यैः सहाहं वृद्धिं गतः सदैव क्रीडितश्चैते° (they, with whom I always stayed, with whom I grew up and played —). In poetry it may be put anywhere. Varâh. Brh. 32, 4 the Earth says to the Creator भगवन्नाम ममैतत्त्वया कृतं यदचलेति तन्न तथा (o Lord, the name of firmness which thou hast bestowed upon me, is vain). The çlokas I, 54-63 of the Pancatantra, which have been quoted

for a different purpose on page 266 of this book, may also give some illustration of the poetical license in putting the relative; in one çloka (vs. 62) the relative heads the sentence, in two it is wanting, the seven others exhibit the utmost variety.[1]) Panc. I, 414 the relative sentence runs thus: नराधिपा नीचजनानुवर्तिनो बुधोपदिष्टेन पथा न यान्ति ये. R. 2, 28, 26 we have this order वनं तु नेतुं न कृता मतिर्यदा बभूव रामेण तदा महात्मना। न तस्य सीता वचनं चकार instead of यदा तु रामेण वनं नेतुं मतिर्न कृता तदा सीता तस्य वचनं न चकार. Cp. f. i. Kathâs. 29, 183.

453. As the demonstrative स may have a general meaning (**276**), य may have it likewise and of course also the derivatives of both. Accordingly यः..... स is not seldom = „who or whosoever.... [he]." There are, however, various ways for emphasizing the generality of import, which are mentioned above (**287**).[2])

454. In general propositions, the relative sentence is not rarely characterized by two or more different relatives placed close together. When translating them, all of them, or at least all but one, become indefinites or must be rendered in some different way. Panc. V, 9 यस्य यदा विभवः स्यात्तस्य तदा दासतां यान्ति (if a person is wealthy for some time, they become his servants for so long), M. 7, 96 यो यज्जयति तस्य तत् (that which one captures, is one's own), Pat. I, p. 123 गावो दिवसं चरितवत्यो यो यस्याः प्रसवो भवति तेन सह शेरते (the cows when having grazed by day-time, lie during the night each with her

1) vs. 54. °करोति निर्विकल्पं यः स भवेद्राजवल्लभः
55. प्रभुप्रसादजं वित्तं सुपात्रे यो नियोजयेत्..... स°
56 अन्तःपुरचरैः सार्धं यो न मन्त्रं समाचरेत्.... स°
57. यूतं यो यमदूताभं..... पश्येत्.......... स°
etc.

2) To the instances given **287** I add Panc. I, 389 येन केनाप्युपायेन..... उद्धरेद् दीनमात्मानम्, cp. the note on p. 215.

own calf), Panc. I, 48 यो न वेत्ति गुणान्यस्य न तं सेवेत पण्डितः (a wise man must not attend on such a one, as does not know his qualities), Hit. 106 यो यत्र कुशलः कार्ये तं तत्र विनियोजयेत्.

CHAPT. III. **Relative sentences, introduced by pronouns.**

455. *Precedence of the relative pronoun.* The general rules laid down in **453** for all kinds of relative sentences are especially applicable to those whose relative is the pronoun य itself. It is, therefore, regular to make the relative precede. In Sanskrit, as a rule, it is not the demonstrative which is the antecedent of the relative, but inversely. Panc. 319 मेष] एको.... महानसे प्रविश्य यत्पश्यति तत्सर्वं भक्षयति। ते च सूपकारा यत्किंचित्पात्रं पश्यन्ति तेनाशु ताडयन्ति, Mudr. V, p. 180 य आर्यस्तं पृच्छ वयमिदानीमनार्याः संवृत्ताः (ask one who is a honourable man, not me who have now turned dishonest), Bhoj. 9 ये मया नियमा उपवासाश्च त्वत्कृते कृतास्ते ऽद्य मे विफला जाताः (the penances and fasts which I have performed in your behalf, have now proved fruitless).

This precedence is, indeed, but the consequence of the entire employment of relative pronouns in Sanskrit composition. They are not used, as in many other languages, where the relative sentence may be a concurrent idiom of participles and adjectives and a means for paraphrasing. But in Sanskrit only such attributes as are of importance to the understanding of the main sentence, are fit for analytical expression by means of relative sentences. [1])

456. Sometimes the relative protasis + demonstrative apo-

---

1) DE SAUSSURE *de l'emploi du génitif absolu*, p. 38: »la proposition relative, en effet, contient toujours en sanscrit une donnée importante, et modifie foncièrement la portée de la proposition principale."

dosis, even serves the purpose of emphasizing a simple sentence. In this case, the relative sentence is but the paraphrase of the main subject. Instead of **सोऽश्वो मे मृतः** (my horse has died) it may be said **यो मेऽश्वः स मृतः**. This periphrastic idiom is especially employed in giving definitions, and in general, if the chief predicate is nominal, it is a fit means for distinguishing the subject from the predicate by pointing out the former as something already known. The archaic monuments offer plenty of instances of this idiom. In classic literature, though far less common, it is however not wanting. Examples: *a.*) from archaic texts. Ch. Up. 1, 3, 3 यः प्राणापानयोः संधिः स व्यानो यो व्यानः सा वाक्. Çat. Br. 14, 7, 1, 33 अथ ये शतं मनुष्याणामानन्दाः स एकः पितॄणां जितलोकानामानन्दः, Muir O. S. T. I, p. 46 translates this passage thus: »now a hundred pleasures of men are one pleasure of the Pitris who have conquered the worlds." Mhbh. I, Paushyap. Uttanka asks his teacher about some strange apparitions he has come across, while executing the orders of his teacher. The other answers ये ते स्त्रियौ धाता विधाता च (the two women [you have seen] were the Dhâtr and the Vidhâtṛ) ये च ते कृष्णाः सितास्तन्तवस्ते रात्र्यहनी (and the black and the white threads [they were weaving] were day and night) and so on: यः पुरुषः स पर्जन्यः। योऽश्वः सोऽग्निः। य ऋषभः..... स ऐरावतो नागराट्। यश्चैनमधिरूढः पुरुषः स चेन्द्रः; — *b.*) from classic literature. Panc. 62 अत्र पुनः सरसि ये जलचरास्ते निश्चिन्ताः सन्ति (but in this lake the aquatic animals are brainless), Mudr. V, p. 172 यत्तदलङ्करणत्रयं क्रीतं तन्मध्यादेकं दीयताम् (give me one of these very three ornaments you have bought).

457. Inverted order. If the relative sentence *follows*, the inverted order may be accounted for by some special reason. Mrcch. IV, p. 138 अपण्डितास्ते पुरुषा मता मे ये स्त्रीषु च श्रीषु च विश्वसन्ति (I hold those unwise, who rely on women and fortune), here the stress laid on the predicate अपण्डिताः has caused the chief sentence to be placed before. Likewise Kumâras. 2, 51 the gods entreat Brahmâ

तदिच्छामो विभो स्रष्टुं सेनान्यं तस्य (sc. तारकस्य) शान्तये.... गोप्तारं सर्वसैन्यानां यं पुरस्कृत्य गोत्रभित्। प्रत्यानेष्यति शत्रुभ्यो वन्दीमिव जयश्रियम्. The opening-line of the Kumârasambhava is अस्त्युत्तरस्यां दिशि देवतात्मा हिमालयो नाम नगाधिराजः etc., the glory and the magnificence of Himavân are extolled in the following sixteen çlokas (1, 2—17) each of them adding a new ornament to his splendour. In all of them it is the relative alone, which connects the different links of the eulogy, referring as it does to the preceding हिमालयः of the chief sentence in çl. 1. And so often, if somebody or something is characterized by a series of clauses, the relative sentences follow after the main sentence. In the last instances quoted the demonstrative in the main sentence is wanting and it is the noun alone that does duty as what we are wont to call the relative's antecedent. Sometimes, however, it may happen that there is no other antecedent to be supplied than just the wanting demonstr. R. 3, 19, 7 न हि पश्याम्यहं लोके यः कुर्यान्मम विप्रियम् (I am not aware of [anybody] in the world, who can do evil to me).

458. The relative pronoun may have a causal character etc.; यः = "that he."

458. The relative pronoun must follow the main sentence, if it introduces a clause of a special character, especially a causal one, yet it may also import a *consequence*, a *disposition*, or even a *purpose*. In other terms, the relative pronoun is sometimes used, where one would expect a relative adverb or conjunction, यः being almost = यत्स (that he) or = यथा स (in order that he), or = यादृशः (such as to —). Cp. Lat. *qui* = *quum is* and *qui* = *ut is*.

a.) The relative clause implies a cause, motive or reason. So especially after such verbs and nouns as signify a disposition either glad or sad, either benevolent or malevolent, either content or discontent, and the like. Panc. 250 भाग्यवांस्त्वमेवासि यस्यारब्धं सर्वमेव संसिध्यति (you are fortunate, indeed, for whatever you undertake succeeds), Daç. 90 सैव धन्या गणिकादारिका यामेवं भवन्मनोऽभिनिविशते (she is to be congratulated that it is she, who is the object of your love), Çâk. I अहो असाधुदर्शी तत्रभवान्कण्वो य इमां वल्कलधारणे नियुङ्क्ते (it is ill-judged of the Reverend Kaṇva to order her —), Panc. 55 तस्य कृतान्तः कुपितो येनैतदेवं क्रियते, Daç. 135 अहमेव मूढो ऽपराद्धो यस्तव.... समादिष्टवान्वधम्.

Rem. Note the idiom योऽहम्, यस्त्वम् in such causal clauses. R. 2, 59, 32 अशोभनं योऽहमिहाद्य राघवं दिदृक्षमाणो न लभे सलक्ष्मणम् (it is a pity that I do not find Râma and Laxmaṇa), Mṛcch. III, p. 125 नाहं दरिद्रः।यस्य मम विभवानुगता भार्या सुखदुःखसुहृद्भवान्..... (I am not poor, since I have —), R. 2, 44, 26 नार्हा त्वं शोचितुं देवि यस्यास्ते राघवः सुतः. Likewise य एष. Çâk. VII अये सेयमत्रभवती शकुन्तला। यैषा वसने परिधूसरे वसाना..... मम दीर्घं विरहव्रतं बिभर्ति. Cp. the kindred idiom सोऽहम् etc. (**445**)[1]).

b) the relative clause imports an ability, consequence or design. Panc. 192 तदत्रैव स्थितेन त्वया कश्चित्समर्थः समाश्रयणीयो यो विपत्प्रतीकारं करोति (v. a. you must apply to somebody, who is able to defend you), ibid. 91 का मात्रा समुद्रस्य यो मम दूषयिष्यति प्रसूतिम् (what is the Ocean, that he should hurt my offspring?). In these examples from the classic dialect the present is used or the future. In the old and epic style such clauses require the optative mood (लिङ्) cp. **344** *f*). Mhbh. 1, 157, 25 नहि योगं प्रपश्यामि येन मुच्येयमापदः (I see no means, indeed, how to get rid of distress), R. 1, 54, 3 परित्यक्ता वसिष्ठेन किमहं सुमहात्मना। याहं राजभृतैर्दीना ह्रियेय भृशदुःखिता (why has V. left me, to be captured by the king's attendants?), ibid. 3, 13, 11 व्यादिश मे देशं सोदकं बहुकाननम्। यत्राश्रमपदं कृत्वा वसेयं निरतः सुखम्.

Rem. The pronoun य, therefore, may even be correlative to a preceding ईदृश, एवंभूत and the like. In all such cases the clause

---

1) The combination यः स serves different wants. Sometimes it generalizes the relative, so as to make it an indefinite = सर्व, see **287** *c.*) and Mṛcch. X, p. 360 यत्र तत्र स्थिता »staying anywhere." Sometimes it is to be resolved into स (the »renowned" or the »well-known" etc.) यः, as Mhbh. 1, 67, 71 धनुर्वेदे च वेदे च यं तं वेदविदो विदुः।वरिष्ठम्. In the same way य एष, य असौ are to be resolved. Mudr. III, p. 115 यावेतौ गजाध्यक्षाश्वाध्यक्षौ..... एतौ खलु etc.

bears a consecutive character more or less expressed. Hit. 6 अस्ति कश्चिदेवंभूतो विद्वान्यो मम पुत्राणाम्..... नीतिशास्त्रोपदेशेन पुनर्जन्म कारयितुं समर्थः (is there any learned man so clever, *as to* —), Mudr. V, p. 166 कीदृशं तत्कार्यगौरवं यद्राजशासनमुल्लङ्घयसि (of what nature are those important affairs, *that* you should transgress the king's orders?), Mhbh. 1, 157, 14 एतावान्पुरुषस्तात कृतं यस्मिन्न नश्यति.

459. Some other special idioms may be noticed:

1. the idiom यत्सत्यम् v. a. »surely", cp. **395**. Ven. I, p. 19 यत्सत्यं कम्पितमिव मे हृदयम् (my heart trembles, indeed);

type: यः etc. = »considering."

2. the type, represented by R. 2, 44, 14 या श्रीः शौर्यं च रामस्य या च कल्याण सत्त्वता। निवृत्तारण्यवासः स्वं क्षिप्रं राज्यमवाप्स्यति (considering Râma's happiness, his heroism and his virtue, he will soon recover his kingdom), cp. Latin *quā erat clementiā Caesar, victos conservavit hostes* and the like;

यः = यदि कश्चित्

3. यः = यदि कश्चित्, as M. 2, 95 यश्चैतान्प्राप्नुयात्सर्वान्यश्चैतान्केवलांस्त्यजेत्। प्रापणात्सर्वकामानां परित्यागो विशिष्यते; here the repeated यः = »if somebody" and »if some other," cp. Mhbh. 1, 79, 6. In this and similar constructions the noun or the demonstrative referred to are understood. Cp. यावत् = »as far as" and the like (**460** R. 1).

य after the demonstratives तावन्त्, तादृश and the like.

460. The pronominal adjectives **यावन्त्, यादृश** and the like, are as a rule used along with their demonstratives **तावन्त्, तादृश** etc. Kathâs. 78, 130 यादृशास्तन्तवः कामं तादृशो जायते पटः (one may judge a cloth from its constituent threads v. a. *ex ungue leonem*), Mhbh. 1, 167, 34 स पुत्रः..... इष्यते यद्विधो राजन्भविता ते तथाविधः (such a son as you wish will be born to you), M. 8, 155 यावती संभवेद्वृद्धिस्तावतीं दातुमर्हति (he must pay as much interest as appears [from the documents]).

Rem. 1. यावत्, when subst. neuter, is sometimes employed in a somewhat elliptical way, f. i. Vikram. V, p. 181 इयं चोर्वशी यावदायुषस्ते सहधर्मचारिणी भवतु (and Urvaçî here will be your wife for the whole time of your life), Daç. 74 परिवारस्त्वस्य यावदिह रम्यमुज्ज्वलं च (and its train consists of all that is charming and splendid here on earth)." Cp. Lat. *quantum est hominum venustiorum* and the like. Cp. also the turn इति यावत् (as much as), frequent with commentators.

Rem. 2. A counterpart to the idioms mentioned in **459**, are यादृश and यावन्त् when connected rather loosely with the main sentence. R 3, 24, 6 यादृशा इह कूजन्ति पक्षिणो वनचारिणः। अग्रतो नो भयं प्राप्तम् (considering the shouts of the birds here, some danger is near us). So especially यावत् and यावता = »as far as, in as much as," cp. **479**.

Rem. 3. If the relative sentence import *a reason*, *a consequence*, *a purpose*, it is the pronoun य that is the correlative of तादृश, not यादृश and its synonyms. See **458**, *b*) and **466**.

Chapt. IV. Relative adverbs and conjunctions.

461. Relative adverbs. Some noun-cases of य may be used quite adverbially and even assume the nature of conjunctions, as यत्, येन, यतः and यस्मात्, moreover यावत् and यावता. With them rank such as are derived by means of adverbial suffixes, यथा, यदा, यदि. All of them serve to introduce various kinds of clauses and subordinate sentences. If we except यदा, restricted to temporal clauses, and यदि exclusively employed in conditional and hypothetical protases, we cannot say that each of the named conjunctions has its own logical sphere of employment. So for instance, यत् may sometimes express a reason, sometimes a circumstance, now it points to a purpose, now it merely paraphrases a fact. Similarly यावत् may be time-denoting or it may indicate a proportion. And so on.

1. Relative noun-cases used as conjunctions.

a.) यत्; येन; यतः and यस्मात्.

462 यत्. यत् and the rest have nearly the character of such conjunctions as Lat. *quod* and *quo*, Engl. *that*. At the outset they were cases of the neuter of the pronoun. Compare f. i. these two sentences: Kumâras. 4, 9 यद्वोचस्तद्वैमि कैतवम् (that which you said, I understand it to be falsehood) with Çâk. V यन्मिथः समयादिमां मदीयां दुहितरं भवानुपायंस्त तन्मया प्रीतिमता युवयोरनुज्ञातम् (that you have wedded my daughter by mutual agreement, I forgive it both of you). In the former, यत् is the acc. of the pronoun and expresses the object of the relative sentence, in the latter it is a mere conjunction serving to introduce the periphrase of the subject of the main sentence, expressed by the demonstr. तत्, but it is no *essential* element of the proposition.

463. Its employment. The **conjunction** यत् is chiefly employed to paraphrase a fact, especially if this fact be an important element of the main sentence: subject or object. As a rule, the demonstrative is added.

Panc. 147 नैतद्वेत्सि यत्त्वया..... नरकोपार्जनं कृतम् (you are not aware you have deserved hell), Vikram. I, p. 18 ननु वज्रिण एव वीर्यमेतद्विजयन्ते द्विषतो यदस्य पक्षाः (it is, forsooth, the glory of the Thunderer, that his warriors triumph over his adversaries), Mhbh. 1, 150, 23 इतः कष्टतरं किं तु यद्वयं गहने वने। दिशश्च न विजानीमो गन्तुं चैव न शक्नुमः (what can be more miserable than this, that —), Panc. 56 किमेवं युज्यते यत्सर्वे पार्थिवा मया सह विग्रहं कुर्वन्ति (is this right, that all kings are making war against me?), Çâk. II उत्कर्षः स च धन्विनां यदिषवः सिध्यन्ति लक्ष्ये चले (it is the highest glory for an archer, that his arrows hit a moving aim). [1]). — In the following instances, the relative

---

1) In the archaic dialect the indeclinable यत् occasionally serves, like the pronoun य, for the periphrastic expression of simple nominal predicates (**456**). Ch. Up. 1, 1, 8 एषो एव समृद्धिर्यदनुज्ञा, Max Müller translates »now permission is gratification". Cp. also the passage of Mahâv. quoted **466** R.

sentence precedes. Panc. 113 यत्त्वं मन्त्रित्वमभिलषसि तदप्ययुक्तम् (that you covet the rank of minister, this too is unbecoming), Nala 18, 10 यत्सा तेन परित्यक्ता तत्र न क्रोद्धुमर्हति (she must not be angry, that he has left her).

464. The object of the words of *saying*, *thinking*, *believing* etc. is often paraphrased by a clause, introduced by the conjunction यत्. Cp. **494**. Likewise by यथा (**472**) or यतः.

Examples: Panc. 58 तस्मिन्हते सर्वो जनो वदिष्यति यत्प्रभूतक्षत्रियैर्मिलित्वा वासुदेवो गरुडश्च निपातितः (he being killed, people will say that Vâs. and Gar. have been killed in a battle with a great number of warriors), ibid. 201 किं न वेत्ति भवान्यन्मम परिग्रहोऽयम् (you know, indeed, that these are my subjects), Ch. Up. 4, 10, 5 विजानाम्यहं यत्प्राणो ब्रह्म (I understand that breath is Brahman), Çâk. VI न किल श्रुतं युवाभ्यां यद्वासन्तिकैस्तरुभिरपि देवस्य शासनं प्रमाणीकृतम् (have you not heard, indeed, that even the trees of Spring obey to the order of His Majesty?).

Rem. The well known Greek type οἶδα τὸν ἄνδρα ὅτι δίκαιός ἐστι is also good Sanskrit. Panc. 280 ज्ञातस्त्वं मया प्रथममेव यत्त्वं स्त्रीवश्यः स्त्रीजितश्च, Nala 17, 40 स नरः सर्वथा ज्ञेयः कश्चासौ क्व च वर्तते, R. 3, 3, 3 त्वां तु वेदितुमिच्छावः कस्त्वं चरसि दण्डकान्, Mhbh. 1, 168, 9 अनुजांस्तु न जानामि गच्छेयुर्नेति वा पुनः (but of my brothers I do not know, whether they will go or not).

465. Sometimes the sentence introduced by यत् has a more or less causal character. When thus employed, यत् is sometimes = *that*, f. i. after such phrases as *I am happy*, *glad*, *sad*, *it is good*, *I wonder* etc., *what have I done to you?* and the like, sometimes it is = *because*, *since*, *as*. Cp. the pronoun य with causal meaning (**458**).

यत् a causal particle.

Examples: Panc. 143 धन्योऽहं यद्भवतापि सह तत्र कालं नयामि (I am happy that I shall still pass the time there in your company), here यत् = योऽहम् (**458**, *a* R.), Panc. 203 न त्वया सुन्दरं कृतं यन्ममावसथस्था-

ने प्रविष्टोऽसि (you have not done well to have entered my dwelling-place), Mrcch. V, p. 188 जलधर निर्लज्जस्त्वं यन्मा दयितस्य वेश्म गच्छन्तीं स्तनितेन भीषयित्वा धाराहस्तैः परामृशसि (cloud, thou art cruel, as thou frightenest me first by thy thunder, then layest violent hands on me, attacking me with showers of rain, while I am going to my sweetheart), R. 2, 113, 16 नैतच्चित्रं..... यदार्यं त्वयि तिष्ठेत् (it is no wonder, that —), ibid. 2, 63, 38 किं तवापकृतं राजन्वने निवसता मया।..... यदहं ताडितस्त्वया (in what have I offended you that you should have slain me?), ibid. 2, 61, 9 वज्रसारमयं नूनं हृदयं मे न संशयः। अपश्यन्त्या न तं यद्वै फलतीदं सहस्रधा (certainly, my heart is of the hardest stone, since it does not burst into a thousand pieces now that I do not see him [my son]), Mudr. II, p. 79 किं शेषस्य भरव्यथा न वपुषि क्ष्मां न क्षिपत्येष यत्। किं वा नास्ति परिश्रमो दिनपतेरास्ते न यन्निश्चलः ([may it be inferred that] Çesha does not suffer from his burden, because he does not throw off the earth, or [that] the Sun does not feel tired, because he is not motionless?). R. 2, 68, 2 यत् (since) precedes, तत् (for this reason) follows.

Rem. Occasionally येन and यतः are used like यत् in such phrases as »I am happy that" and the like. Prabodh. IV, p. 81 धन्योऽस्मि येन स्वामिनाहमेवं संभावितः (I am happy, that my master has in this way honoured me), Panc. 296 किं वयं ब्राह्मणसमाना यत आमन्त्रणं करोषि (are we the equals of brahmans, that you call us to dinner?).

यतः is occasionally put to verbs of *knowing*, *saying*, etc. (**464**).

466 यत्, when final or consecutive.

यत्, common as it is as a causal particle, is somewhat rarely found as a final or consecutive conjunction, *that* = »in order that," or = »in consequence of which." Panc. 199 क्रियतां तेषां कृते काचिद्विभीषिका यत्कथमपि दैवान्न समायान्ति (frighten them in some way or other, that perchance they may not return somehow), Kâç. on P. 3, 2, 36 explains असूर्यंपश्या राजदाराः in this way एवं नाम गुप्ता यत्सूर्यमपि न पश्यन्ति (being indeed so closely guarded as not to see the sun), Kumâras. 1, 37 एतावता यत् (in so much that). Cp. Mrcch. V, p. 201, where Cârudatta exclaims वर्षशतमस्तु दुर्दिनमविरतधारं शतह्रदा स्फुरतु। अस्मद्विधदुर्लभया यदहं प्रियया परिष्वक्तः (let the rain descend incessantly and let the lightning flash for ever, in consequence of which I hold my beloved in my arms, her who was unattainable to somebody like me).

Rem. Mahâv. II, p. 21 the râxasa says अनर्थ एव वो यत्कन्येयमन्यस्मै दीयत इति, the literal sense of which is »to give her to another is mischief to you," but when translating more freely »woe to you, *if* she should be given to another." In the archaic dialect यत् is occasionally a full synonym of यदि. Only see these passages of the Chândogya-upanishad: 5, 15, 2 संदेहस्ते व्यशीर्यद्यन्मां नागमिष्यः (your body would have perished, if you had not come to me), and 6, 11, 2 यदेकां शाखां जीवो जहात्यथ शुष्यति (if the life leaves one of the branches [of the tree], that branch withers).

In this passage of Âçval. Gṛhyas. (3, 4, 7) तस्य द्वावनध्यायौ यदात्माशुचिर्यद्देशः (the cases of prohibition to study Holy Writ are two-fold: impurity of person and impurity of place) यत् may be accepted = »if," but one may also account for it by referring to the idiom mentioned in the foot-note on p. 358.

467. यतः and यस्मात्. Of यतः and यस्मात् the causal employment is more strongly marked than of यत्. They not only denote the reason, but also the efficient and material cause: *for*, *because*. The period is sometimes expressed in full यस्मात्..... तस्मात्, यतः..... ततः sim., sometimes the demonstrative is not added. Panc. III, 105 अहिंसापूर्वको धर्मो यस्मात्सद्भिरुदाहृतः। यूकमत्कुणदंशादींस्तस्मात्तानपि रक्षयेत् (*since* the wise have declared clemency the highest virtue, one must protect even the smallest insects), ibid. p. 107 यतस्ते शङ्कुसदृशौ कर्णौ ततः शङ्कुकर्णो नाम भविष्यति, ibid. 72 तदस्मान्न सिध्यति यतः° (this does not hold good, because —), cp. Kathâs. 30, 39. — Both यतः and यस्मात् are excessively frequent, when adding the causes to facts already mentioned before. Then they are concurrent with हि, and like this, they may be said to serve for coordination rather than subordination. F i. Panc. 241 अहो कल्याणमस्माकमुपस्थितं यद्रक्ताक्षो गतः। यतः स दीर्घदर्श्येते च मूढमनसः (it is good for us, that Ṛaktâxa is gone, for he is wise but these [others] are stupid).

Rem. With the same function are used the full phrases येन कारणेन, यस्मात्कारणात्, यत्कारणम् and the like. Panc. 216 अस्माकं मध्ये त्वया न वर्तितव्यं येन कारणेनास्माभिर्गृहीतं तत्सरः (you must not stay with us, for we have taken possession of this lake), ibid. 218 यत्कारणं शरणागतो न वध्यते = Lat. *nam* supplex non interficitur.

468. येन. The conjunction **येन** is chiefly expressive of purpose or intention. One might, therefore, expect it to be construed with the optative or the future, and indeed so it is, yet the present is oftener employed, especially in simple prose. The same applies to **यथा**, when a final particle, see **471**:

1. with लिङ्: Kathâs. 36, 106 तदिदानीं वनं गत्वा हरिं शरणमाश्रये। येन स्यां नैव दुःखानां भाजनं पुनरीदृशाम् (therefore I will retire to the forest now and pray to Hari, that I may never more be exposed to such misfortunes); — 2. with future: Panc. 329 द्रुततरं गच्छामि येनैष न मम पृष्ठमेष्यति (I will go more swiftly, that he may not overtake me); — 3. with present: Panc. 327 प्रेषय मां येन गृहं गच्छामि (dismiss me, that I may go home), ibid. 52 यत्किंचिद् दुःखकारणं तद्वद येन प्रतीकारः क्रियते.

When the demonstrative precedes, the sentence introduced by येन may be also a consecutive one, as it points to the direct consequence of the action signified by the main sentence. Kathâs. 12, 100 तथा कुरु येन सः। गृहान्मम निवर्तेत (act *so that* he will retire from my house), Hit. 10 the tiger speaks मम चैतावाँल्लोभविरहो येन स्वहस्तस्थमपि सुवर्णकङ्कणं यस्मै कस्मैचिद् दातुमिच्छामि (I am *so* free from covetousness, *as* to wish to give —).

469. On the other hand, **येन** — as it properly signifies „by the which" — may introduce also a *causal* sentence. Kathâs. 36, 121 येनाहं भवताहतः। तादृक् श्वेतो गजो भूमौ भवानुत्पद्यतामिति (*because* you have struck me —), Panc. 274 किमहमेताभ्यां हीनो येन मामुपहसतः (am I inferior to them, that they should laugh at me?). Cp. **465** R.

b.) यथा.

470 यथा. The employment of **यथा** bears a great resemblance to that of Latin *ut*. Like this, **यथा** has originally been a particle of comparison „as," the correlative of which is the demonstrative „so, thus." Yet its duty is not limited to the expression of equation, but extends to many other logical relations, chiefly *consequence* and *purpose* or *aim*, though it may answer sometimes our causal or merely epexegetical „that."

a.) When used in its proper sense for the sake of comparison, the parallelism of **यथा..... तथा** or its synonyms (**एवम्, इत्थम्**) is frequent, although the omission of the demonstr. is not excluded. Pat. I, p. 51 यथेच्छसि तथास्तु (be it so, as you desire), Utt. II, p. 27 वितरति गुरुः प्राज्ञे विद्यां यथैव तथा जडे (the teacher bestows his learning on his sluggish disciple just as he does on the keen-witted one), R. 3, 19, 18 इमामवस्थां नीताहं यथाऽनाथाऽसती तथा (I am reduced to this state, as [if I were] a woman of bad conduct who has no protector), Hit. 108 एवमनुष्ठेयं यथा वदामि; — demonstr. omitted: Nala 22, 4 ब्रूयाश्चैनं कथान्ते त्वं पर्णादवचनं यथा (speak to him as Parnâda spoke), Mhbh. 4, 2, 5 मंस्यन्ते मां यथा नृपम् (they will consider me like a king).

Rem. 1. यथा may also be = »in so far as." R. 3, 5, 18 Râma admires the knightly attitude and the vigour of Indra and his men, who appear like youths of twenty-five, रूपं बिभ्रति says he to Laxmaṇa सौमित्रे पञ्चविंशतिवार्षिकम्..... यथेमे पुरुषव्याघ्रा दृश्यन्ते प्रियदर्शनाः (they bear the shape of youths of twenty-five, in so far as we may judge from their outward appearance). Hence न तथा..... यथा = Lat. *non tam..... quam*, 1. »not so much..... as," f. i. Kumâras. 5, 37 तथा न गाङ्गैः सलिलैर्दिवश्च्युतैः। यथा त्वदीयैश्चरितैरनाविलैर्महीधरः पावित एष सान्वयः, 2. »not exactly..... but," f. i. M. 2, 96 न तथैतानि [sc. इन्द्रियाणि] शक्यन्ते संनियन्तुमसेवया। विषयेषु प्रजुष्टानि यथा ज्ञानेन नित्यशः.

Rem. 2. In protestations and oaths यथा..... तेन सत्येन = »as sure as..... so surely." R. 2, 64, 40 अपापोऽसि यथा पुत्र निहतः पापकर्मणा। तेन सत्येन गच्छाशु ये लोकास्त्वस्त्रयोधिनाम् (as sure as you being sinless have been killed, my son, by an evil-doer, so surely may you go swiftly to the abodes of the warriors), cp. Nala 5, 16-20.

Rem. 3. यथा with लिङ् may be = »as if" (**343**, *d*). Ch. Up. 5, 24, 1 यथाङ्गारानपोह्य भस्मनि जुहुयात्तादृक्तत्स्यात् (this would be *as if* a man were to remove the [live] coals and pour his libation in [dead] ashes. R. 3, 51, 34 the vulture Jaṭâyu is said to have fallen upon Râvaṇa in the same way »as if some mahaunt mounts a wicked elephant" अधिरूढो गजारोहो यथा स्याद् दुष्टवारणम्.

Rem. 4. यद्वत्..... तद्वत् are equivalent to यथा..... तथा. With optative यद्वत् is also = »as if." Varâh. Brh. 2, 19 नगरद्वारलोष्टस्य यद्वत्स्यादुपयाचितम्। आदेशस्तद्वदज्ञानाम् (a prediction by ignorant men is as useless as if one were to question a clod of earth at the town-gate).

471. *b) final and consecutive.* *b.*) यथा points to the result, either effected or aimed at. The *result effected* is set forth by यथा construed with a past tense and preceded by तथा. The *result aimed at* or (what is often identical) the *purpose* is expressed by यथा construed with an optative (लिङ्), a future or, as is oftener done, a present (cp. **468**). In both categories of sentences the demonstrative तथा is generally added.

Examples: 1. यथा points to the result effected. Kathâs. 25, 120 क्रमेण च ययौ तत्र प्रकर्षं स तथा यथा। अजीयत न केनापि प्रतिमल्लेन भूतले (and by degrees he became *such* a master in this art [boxing], *that* no adversary on earth could vanquish him), Panc. 318 एवं तेन ध्यानस्थितेन तथैव पादप्रहारो दत्तो यथा स घटो भग्नः (as he was thinking so, he gave the pot *such* a kick *that* it broke). See also Kumâras. 5, 15.

2. यथा signifies the result aimed at, the purpose. Here the present usually follows. Panc. 2 यथा मम मनोरथाः सिद्धिं यान्ति तथानुष्ठीयताम् (act *so as to* cause my wishes to be fulfilled), Kathâs. 26, 42 युवां मे कुरुतं तथा यथाहमद्य पश्यामि तां युष्मत्स्वामिनीमिह (cause me to see your queen to-day), Panc. 151 अहं तथा भक्षयामि यथा बहून्यहानि मे प्राणयात्रा भवति (I will eat [of it] *in such a way*, *as to* be supported by it for many days), Çâk. I आश्रमबाधा यथा न भवति तथाहमपि यतिष्ये (I too will take care, *that* there may be done no harm to the hermitage), Hit. 108 यथायं नश्यति तन्मया विधेयम्. — Yet, the optative (लिङ्) is also found, especially in ornate style and in ancient literature. Mhbh. 1, 163, 3 यथा त्विदं न विन्देयुर्नरा नगरवासिनः। तथायं ब्राह्मणो वाच्यः (but this brahman

should be warned, that the townsmen may not become aware of it), Kathâs. 13, 55 स चापुत्रो बहून्विप्रान्संघाट्य प्रणतोऽब्रवीत्। तथा कुरुत पुत्रो मे यथा स्याद्चिराद्दिति, Vikram. II, p. 38 तदुपायश्चिन्त्यतां यथा सफलप्रार्थनो भवेयम्. — Instance of the future: Fanc. 105 मयान्योन्यं ताभ्यां.... भेदस्तथा विहितो यथा भूयोऽपि मन्त्रयन्तावेकस्थानस्थितौ न द्रक्ष्यसि (I have made them so discordant that you will see them never more deliberate together).

The future is of course wanted, if the main sentence has a future. Nala 1, 20 दमयन्तीसकाशे त्वां कथयिष्यामि नैषध। यथा त्वदन्यं पुरुषं न सा मंस्यति कर्हिचित्. Likewise the optative, if the main sentence has an optative. Daç. 138 तथा विषं स्तम्भयेयं यथा मृत इत्युद्वास्येत (I will arrest the poison, but in such a manner, that he will be left for dead).

Rem. 1. If the demonstrative is not added, यथा = »[in order] that." Panc. 56 संबोध्योऽद्य त्वया निजभर्ता यथा मम शत्रून्व्यापादयति (you must exhort your husband, that he may kill my enemies). Cp. Nala 1, 20.

Rem. 2. Instead of यथा न with optative, epic poets often use the simple न (**405** R. 1). Moreover, मा may be = »lest," when it agrees with aorist or with optative, in epic poetry even with the future, cp. **405** R. 1. — In affirmative sentences the omission of यथा is very rare, yet there are instances of it. R. 1, 39, 11 तत्तथा क्रियतां राजन्यज्ञोऽच्छिद्रः कृतो भवेत् (make the sacrifice to be accomplished without flaw).

472. *c.)* **यथा** serves to paraphrase the object of *knowing*, *saying*, *declaring* etc. just as **यत्** (**464**). Kumâras. 4, 36 विदितं खलु ते यथा स्मरः क्षणमप्युत्सहते न मां विना (you know, certainly, that Kâma cannot be without me, even for a moment), Mâlat. IV, p. 69 अयि भवानमंस्त यथा भूरिवसुरेव मालतीमस्मभ्यं दास्यति (say, did you believe that it was Bhûr. who will give me Mâlatî?), Panc. 200 ज्ञानात्येव भवान्यथार्थवादिनो दूतस्य न दोषः करणीयः, Mhbh. 1, 42, 34 Kâçyapa starts to the rescue of king Parixit श्रुतं हि तेन [sc. काश्यपेन] तद्भूद्यथा तं राजसत्तमं। तक्षकः पन्नगश्रेष्ठो नेष्यते यमसादनम्.

c) यथा paraphrases the object.

Rem. In the first and the last of the instances quoted we are free to translate यथा by »how." Indeed, this employment of यथा does not lie very far from that, mentioned **411**.

473. *d.)* Finally, **यथा** may sometimes have the nature of

d) यथा, when a causal particle.

d) यथा, a causal particle. This seems to have been more usual in ancient literature, than afterwards. Ch. Up. 6, 13, 1 तद्धावमृश्य न विवेद यथा विलीनमेवाङ्ग (he [the son] having looked for it [the salt, he had placed in the water] did not find it, *for*, of course, it was melted), R. 3, 57, 19 Râma surmises, Sîtâ will have incurred some harm. सर्वथा जनकात्मजा। विनष्टा भक्षिता वापि राक्षसैर्वनचारिभिः॥अशुभान्येव भूयिष्ठं यथा प्रादुर्भवन्ति मे (— as it is chiefly prognostics of evil, that appear to me).

This causal meaning of यथा is sometimes indicated by adding हि, the exponent of causality. R. 3, 11, 47 एतदेवाश्रमपदं नूनं तस्य.... अगस्त्यस्य मुनेर्भ्रातुर्दृश्यते..... यथा हीमे वनस्यास्य ज्ञाताः पथि सहस्रशः.... द्रुमाः.

In the instances quoted the clause with यथा follows the main sentence. If it precedes, we may translate it by *as much as, considering*, etc. Nala 21, 8 यथासौ रथनिर्घोषः पूरयन्निव मेदिनीम्। ममाह्लादयते चेतो नल एव महीपतिः (*considering* the joy, which causes to me the sound of the chariot, I know it is Nala).

c.) यदा AND यावत्.

474. यदा. यदा is a temporal conjunction = our „when." Its demonstrative which is generally not omitted, is तदा „then." Panc. 303 यदा रामो राजासीत्तदाहम्.... अनेन पथा समायातः, Mṛcch. I, p. 55 यदा तु भाग्यक्षयपीडितां दशां नरः कृतान्तोपहितां प्रपद्यते। तदास्य मित्राण्यपि यान्त्यमित्रतां चिरानुरक्तोऽपि विरज्यते जनः.

यदा repeated is of course = »whenever." Kathâs. 25, 216 तस्मान्निशि च भूयोऽपि त्वमेष्यसि यदा यदा। तदा तदा वटतरोर्मूलात्प्राप्स्यसि मामितः. — यदैव »at the very time that." Ven. I, p. 24 कुरुषु तावद्संधेयता तदैव निवेदिता यदैवास्माभिरितो वनं गच्छद्भिः सर्वैरेव कुरुकुलस्य निधनं प्रतिज्ञातम्. — यदाप्रभृति »since." R. 2, 116, 13 त्वं यदाप्रभृति ह्यस्मिन्नाश्रमे तात वर्तसे। तदाप्रभृति रक्षांसि विप्रकुर्वन्ति तापसान् (for the hermits are being vexed by the râxasas since the time, that you stay here).

475. यावत्. यावत् is chiefly used of time. Then the parallelism यावत्..... तावत् is generally expressed in full. Two cases are here to be distinguished. Either *simultaneousness* of the two actions is denoted, or the action with तावत् is *precedent* to the other.

यावत् .... तावत् = while.

I. If यावत्..... तावत्, or inversely तावत्..... यावत् are expressive of simultaneousness, यावत् properly = *as long as*, *while*. Yet, it is also expressive of *at which time*, *when*, sometimes it may even be rendered by *as soon as*.

1. यावत् *as long as*, *while* [1]). In this meaning it is construed with the present, even when expressive of past facts, cp. **327.** Hit. 68 देव यावदहं जीवामि तावद्भयं न कर्तव्यम् (as long as I live, you ought not to fear), Panc. V, 64 तावत्स्यात्सुप्रसन्नास्यस्तावद्गुरुजने रतः। पुरुषो योषितां यावन्न शृणोति वचो रहः. In both instances यावत्..... तावत् = »during which time..... during that time." But not rarely its meaning is »during which time..... in the meanwhile." Panc. 290 यावदसौ [sc. शृगालः] तद्देहकृतद्वारेण किंचिन्मांसं भक्षयति तावदतिसंक्रुद्धोऽपरः शृगालः समाययौ, ibid. 42 यावद् देवदत्तमुद्दिश्य व्रजति तावत्तद्भर्ता संमुखो मदविह्वलाङ्गः समभ्येति (as she is going to her sweetheart, she comes across her husband [2]).

2. यावत् *at which time*. Panc. 277 यावत्तां[पेटाम्]उत्पाटयति तावत्तं पङ्गुं ददर्श (as he opened the basket, he saw the paralytic), Kathâs. 4, 36 यावत्किंचिद्गता तावन्निरुद्धा सा पुरोधसा (as she went on a little, she was stopped by the priest).

3. यावत् *as soon as* Panc. 313 यावद्रासभो दृष्टस्तावल्लगुडप्रहारैर्हतः (as soon as the ass was seen, he was beaten with sticks).

476. II. If the sentence introduced by यावत् is expressive of an action, subsequent in time to that expressed by the main sentence, two cases are possible:

---

1) Cp. the similar employment of यावत्, when preposition (**54** R. 2 and cp. **169**).

2) यावद्यावत्.... तावत्तावत् = »for every time.... for this time" (cp. **252**, 3°). Mudr. IV, p. 143 यावद्यावन्निरपेक्षश्चाणाक्यहतकश्चन्द्रगुप्ताद् दूरीभवति तावत्तावदस्य स्वार्थसिद्धिः

यावत् =until.

a.) **यावत्** = *till what time, until.*

यावत् *until* is generally construed with the लिङ् or with its equivalent, the present (**468**). Then it expresses the *intention*, but when stating a *fact*, past tenses are admissible (cp. **471**).

Examples: 1. with लिङ्. Daç. 156 सैषा भवद्भुजतरुच्छायायामखण्डितचारित्रा तावदध्यास्तां यावदस्याः पाणिग्राहकमानयेयम् (therefore you must protect her, until I bring her husband here), Mudr. V, p. 167 ताड्यतां तावद्यावत्सर्वमनेन कथितं भवेत् (let him be beaten until he has confessed the whole); 2. with the present. Panc. 276 यावदहं भोजनं गृहीत्वा समागच्छामि तावदत्र त्वया स्थातव्यम् (you must stay here, until I return with food), ibid. 286 तावत्त्वयैतौ यत्नेन रक्षणीयौ यावदहमपरामुष्ट्रीं नीत्वा समागच्छामि; 3. with the future. Daç. 72 प्रतीक्षस्व कानिचिद् दिनानि यावदियं सुकुमारी.... प्रकृतावेव स्यास्यति; — 4. with past tense, stating a fact. Kathâs. 4, 58 सो ऽपि पुरोहितः] तावच्चेटिकाभिर्विमोहितः। यावत्तृतीये प्रहरे दण्डाधिपतिरागमत् (the maid-servants beguiled the priest, until at the third *prahara* the judge came).

477. यावत् + न = before, *priusquam.*

b.) it is simply stated that the action of the main sentence has happened *before* the other. This is done by the phrase **तावत्..... यावत्** with negation, the literal meaning of which is: one action happened, *as long as* the other did *not* happen. It is to be noticed, that **न** has no fixed place, but may precede **यावत्** or follow it, either close to or separated from it by other words.

Examples: of यावन्न = *before*, Lat. *priusquam.* Panc. 74 यावन्न कश्चिद्वेत्ति तावच्छीघ्रं गम्यताम् (go away soon, before anybody knows of it), Mhbh. 1, 202, 11 यावन्न कृतमूलास्ते पाण्डवेयाः..... तावत्प्रहरणीयास्ते (you must strike them, before they have taken root); — यावत्..... न. Nâgân. II, p. 37 न तावन्मुञ्चामि यावन्मम हृदयवल्लभां शिलायामालेख्यगतां न पश्यसि (I do not let go [your hand], before you see my sweetheart painted on the stone), Panc. 67 सत्वरं निवेदय यावन्मम दंष्ट्रान्तर्गतो न भवान्भविष्यति (tell it me quickly, before I make a bite of you), M. 2, 172 शूद्रेण हि समस्तावद्यावद्वेदे न जायते (before he is born in the Veda, he is equal to a çûdra); — न यावत्. Panc. 320 the chief monkey gives to his

band the counsel of fleeing away न यावत्सर्वेषां संक्षयो भवति तावदन्तद्रा-
ष्ट्रगृहं संत्यज्य वनं गच्छामः, ibid. II, 191 एकस्य दुःखस्य न यावदन्तं गच्छाम्यहं पारमिवार्णवस्य। तावद् द्वितीयं समुपस्थितं मे.

Rem. Another word answering to Latin *priusquam* is पुरा. Indeed, like our »before," पुरा is sometimes a preposition, sometimes an adverb, sometimes a conjunction (cp. **324** R. 1.). In the classic dialect it is almost obsolete.

478. यावत् = [in order] that. *c*). When construed with the 1st person of the present, यावत् may also denote the *purpose*. In this case, the main sentence which generally precedes, is only expressive of some preparatory action to be completed „about the time" at which the action purposed is intended to take place; तावत् is as a rule omitted. Çâk. I सूत आश्रमोपरोधो मा भूत्तदिहैव रथं स्थापय यावदवतरामि (charioteer, in order to avoid disturbing the hermitage, you must stop here, *that* I may descend), Kathâs. 16, 38 परमान्नं पचेः शीघ्रं स्नात्वा यावदुपैम्यहम् (cook an excellent meal for me, quickly, [that I may take it] when I come here after bathing), Vikram. V, p. 162 king to charioteer तदुपश्लेषय शरं यावन्निन्नपयामि.

Rem. In this passage यावत् is construed with the 3d person of the imperative. Mhbh. 3, 72, 4 निगृह्णीष्व.... हयानेतान्....। वार्ष्णेयो यावदेनं मे पटमानयतामिह.

479. Not rarely the purpose is set forth by यावत् in an almost elliptical way, no main sentence being expressed. In other terms, यावत् with the 1st pers. of the present is used in self-exhortations, such as are explained **356**. Sometimes we may translate it by „in the meanwhile." Mudr. II p. 59 यावदहममात्यराक्षसं पश्यामि (well, let me wait on Minister Râxasa), Çâk. I यावदेताश्छायामिमामाश्रित्य प्रतिपालयामि, Vikram. IV, p. 114 यावदस्मिन्कानने प्रियां प्रनष्टामन्वेषयामि.

480. यावत् is not always time-denoting, it is also a conjunction of manner = *as far as*, *in so much as*, as is,

यावत् = in so far as. indeed, evident from its etymology. **Mâlat. III, p. 50** यावदश्रृणवं मालत्येव..... हेतुरिति (in so far as I have heard, M. was the cause), Kâthas. 5, 136. In this meaning यथा is also available, see **470** R. 1.

Rem. 1. Note these phrases: 1. न तावत्..... यावत् »not so much..... but rather.” Kâthas. 26, 23 न तावत्सा च कनकपुरी दृष्टा मया पुरी। अपदे नश्यता यावद् दाशेन्द्रोऽप्येव नाशितः (v. a. »instead of seeing that Gold-city, I myself am lost and I have made the chief of fishermen to perish also,” liter. I have not so much seen Gold-city, but I have rather —); — 2. न परम् or न केवलम्..... यावत् »not only..... but also.” Kathâs. 28, 160 व्रणास्तस्य दिने दिने। न परं न रुरोहैव यावन्नाडीत्वमाययौ (not only the wound did not heal, but it became even a fistula), Panc. 36 न केवलं सेवका इत्थंभूता यावत्समस्तमप्येतज्जगत्परस्परं भक्षणार्थं सामादिभिरुपायैस्तिष्ठति (it is not only the attendants, who are so natured, but the whole of the creatures of this earth stand to each other in some relation, friendly or otherwise, for obtaining food), cp. **470**, R. 1.

Rem. 2. Pat. I, p. 9 सन्तीति तावद् ब्रूमो यदेताञ्शास्त्रविदः शास्त्रेणानुविदधते (we say: they exist, only *in so far as* they who know the theory [of grammar] employ them in their theories) affords an instance of तावत्..... यत् instead of तावत्..... यावत्. For analogous phrases see **458** *b*).

480*. In both acceptations, of time and of manner, one will meet occasionally with यावता = यावत्. Instances of यावता = »as far as” are found especially in Patanjali, of यावता = »whilst; as,” यावता न = »before” in the Bhâgav. Pur. and elsewhere.

d.) यदि.

481. यदि after verbs of *doubting, inquiring* etc. यदि (if) is chiefly employed in the protasis of conditional periods. This main function will be treated in the following chapter. But, moreover, like our „if,” Greek εἰ, Lat. *si*, यदि serves to introduce the relative sentence which is the object of verbs of *doubting*, *inquiring*, *observing*, *expecting*, *telling* and the like. पश्यामि यदि = „I will see if (whether).”

Examples: Panc. 200 अन्विष्यतां यद्यस्माद् व्यसनात्सुनिर्मुक्तिः (inquire, if there is any opportunity of being relieved from this misfortune), ibid. 121 कथय मे यद्यस्ति कश्चिदुपायस्तद्विनाशाय (tell me if —), Mhbh. 1, 154, 4 यदि वास्य वनस्य त्वं देवता यदि वाप्सराः।आचक्ष्व मम (tell me whether you are the deity of this forest or an apsaras), Çâk. VI विचार्यतां यदि काचिदापन्नसत्त्वा तस्य भार्यासु स्यात् (reflect if not one of his wives may be in the family-way), Kumâras. 5, 44 वद प्रदोषे स्फुटचन्द्रतारका विभावरी यद्यरुणाय कल्पते (say, if the splendour of the evening-sky illumined by moon and stars, does befit Aruṇa). — Sometimes यदि and यत् are equally available, f. i. with चित्रम् (wonder), and with such phrases as *I cannot bear*, *I do not believe*. Çâk. III किमत्र चित्रं यदि विशाखे शशाङ्कलेखामनुवर्तेते (what wonder is it, that the two stars of the asterism Viçâkhâ join the crescent?), R. 2, 51, 14 नाशंसे यदि जीवन्ति सर्वे ते (I do not think, they are alive), ibid. 2, 86, 15 we have the like sentence, but the verb is an optative (जीवेयुः). Cp. also R. 2, 73, 8 दुष्करं यदि जीवेताम्, and the like.

P. 3, 3, 147 with vârtt.

Note also यदि with verbs of *swearing*, *cursing* and the like. Panc. 75 मम देवगुरुकृतः शपथः स्याद्यदि तदास्वादयामि (I may be cursed by gods or parents, if I taste of it).

482. Sometimes the clause with यदि is used in a somewhat elliptical way, viz. without apodosis. Çâk. VII Dushyanta considers whether he shall ask the boy, whom he already suspects to be his son, about the name of his mother: यदि तावदस्य शिशोर्मातरं नामतः पृच्छेयम् (if I should ask now the name of his mother?). In a similar way, if hope is uttered. R. 2, 59, 3 आशया यदि मां रामः पुनः शब्दापयेदिति (hoping: »perhaps Râma will again address me"), ibid. 3, 54, 3 Sîtâ when being carried away by Râvana casts off her upper-garment and her jewels among a little band of apes यदि रामाय शंसेयुरिति (perhaps they will show them to Râma).[1]). Such sentences require the optative (लिङ्) because of the nature of their contents.

A different character is displayed by such ellipsis, as is shown R. 3, 17, 21, where Çûrpanakhâ says to Râma रावणो नाम मे भ्राता

---

1) Cp. the similar employment of Latin *si*, f. i. in the *Aeneid*, book VI, vs. 187 *si nunc se nobis ille aureus arbore ramus ostendat nemore in tanto.*

यदि ते श्रोत्रमागतः (my brother is named Râvaṇa, whom perhaps you will have heard of).[1]).

483. यद्यपि. By adding अपि to यदि, we get यद्यपि, the concessive particle *though*, *although*. Its correlative in the apodosis is तथापि *nevertheless*, *however*, *yet*, either expressed, or omitted. Panc. 37 यद्यपि त्वदीयवचनं न करोति तथापि स्वामी स्वदोषनाशाय वाच्यः (even if he does not listen to your words, yet you must blame your master that he may amend his faults), Kathâs. 52, 375 वत्स यद्यपि शूरस्त्वं सैन्यमस्ति च ते बहु। तथापि नैव विश्वास्या जयश्रीश्चपला रणे (my child, though you are valiant and have a great army, you must never trust to the victory in battle, since it is inconstant), Çâk. I वाचं न मिश्रयति यद्यपि मे वचोभिः। कर्णं ददात्यभिमुखं मयि भाषमाणे (though she does not join in the conversation, yet she listens attentively, while I am speaking).

Rem. अपि यदि instead of यद्यपि is poetical, as f. i. Prabodh. I, p. 10 अपि यदि विशिखाः शरासनं वा कुसुममयं ससुरासुरं तथापि। मम जगदखिलम् (though my [Kâma's] bow and arrows are made of flowers, nevertheless the whole creation with gods and demons is mine).

Chapt. V. The conditional period.

484. Conditional period. The conditional period is a compound sentence, made up of a protasis and an apodosis. The protasis contains the condition, whereas the apodosis states what will happen under the said condition. The grammatical exponents of the protasis are यदि or चेत्. Of these, यदि since it is a relative, heads the sentence, at least in prose. But, as a rule, चेत् is not put at the head, it is often the last word of the sentence; yet, स, एष, न sim. being used, it is put close after them.

यदि and चेत्.

In the apodosis no correlative is necessary. Yet it is

1) Cp. Lat. *si*, f. i. *Aeneid*, book II, vs. 81.

Corre-lative emon-strati-es in he apo-dosis.

often expressed, viz. **ततः** or **तदा** or **तत्** or **तर्हि**, occasionally **अथ.**

Examples of यदि and चेत्: *a.*) without correlative in the apodosis. Daç. 105 यद्यहमस्मि तस्करो भद्रा बध्नीत माम् (if I am a thief, fetter me, gentlemen), Daç. 72 यदीह भगवत्पादमूलं न शरणं शरणमस्तु मम कृपणाया हिरण्यरेताः (if Your Holiness does not afford me protection, the god of fire must be my refuge); — Kathâs. 25, 19 भगवान्वक्तु वेत्ति चेत् (say it, Reverend, if you know it), Kumâras. 5, 40 न चेद्रहस्यं प्रतिवक्तुमर्हसि (answer me, prithee, if it is no secret).

b.) with correlative. Hit. 23 यद्यन्नं नास्ति तदा सुप्रीतेनापि वचसा तावदतिथिः पूज्यः (if food is wanting, one must entertain one's guest at least with kind speech), Daç. 90 साचेदियं प्रकृतिमापद्येत तदा पेशलं भवेत् (if she should be brought to reason, that would be charming); — Mhbh. 1, 43, 1 Taxaka says to Kâçyapa यदि दष्टं मयेह त्वं शक्तः किंचिच्चिकित्सितुं। ततो वृक्षं मया दष्टमिमं जीवय काश्यप; — Panc. 334 अवश्यं यदि गन्तव्यं तदेष कर्कटोऽपि सहायः (if [you] are obliged to go, even this crab may be your companion), Kathâs. 24, 146 न चेत्कुप्यसि तत्किंचित्प्रभो विज्ञापयाम्यहम् (if you are not angry, I have something to entreat of you); — Panc. 16 यद्येवमभिमतं तर्हि शिवास्ते पन्थानः सन्तु; — Çâk. VII न चेन्मुनिकुमारोऽयमथ कोऽस्य व्यपदेशः (if he is not the son of a muni, what, then, is his name?).

Rem. 1. In most cases the protasis precedes. Sometimes, however, the main sentence is put first, f. i. Daç. 91 अजिनरत्नं मया तुभ्यं देयं यदि प्रतिदानं रागमञ्जरी (I am bound to deliver you the magic skin, provided that Râgamanjarî be given in return to me), Kâd. I, p. 101 श्रूयतां यदि कुतूहलम्.

Rem. 2. R. 3, 43, 19 यदि.... तु = »if..... at least." Sîtâ to Râma जीवन्न यदि तेऽभ्येति ग्रहणं मृगसत्तमः। अजिनं नरशार्दूल रुचिरं तु भविष्यति। निहतस्यास्य सत्त्वस्य (even if the precious deer should not be taken alive, its skin at least will be a beautiful spoil). — यदि परम् = »if but." Ratn. III p. 81 the king throws himself at the feet of his queen: the reddish glow of your feet, says he, caused by painting, I will take off with my bent head, but the glow of anger on your cheeks I am able to drive away यदि परं करुणा मयि स्यात् »only in case, that you show mercy to me." Another instance is Kathâs. 34, 261.

Rem. 3. The combination यदि चेत् is sometimes found in epic poetry, f. i. R. 2, 48, 21, Mhbh. 1, 104, 37. In fact, चेत् has not been at the outset a conjunction, nor is it a relative, though in the classic dia ect it may bear this character. It is properly a combination of च + इत् the emphatic particle (**398** R. 2)[1]. In the archaic dialect even the simple च does occasional duty as a conditional particle[2].

485. न चेत्. न चेत् is rather to be looked upon as a unity, like Latin *nisi*. Daç. 97 न चेदजिनरत्नं प्रतिप्रयच्छसि न चेद्वा नागरिकेभ्यश्चोरितकानि प्रत्यर्पयसि द्रक्ष्यसि पारमष्टादशानां कारणानामन्ते च मृत्युमुखम् (if you do not give back the magic skin, or if you do not restore to the townsmen the objects, you have stolen from them, you shall pass through the eighteen kinds of torture and finally you shall see the door of Death).

नो चेत्. Instead of न चेत् it is also said नो चेत्, that is न + the advers. उ + चेत्, but the adversative force of उ is not always conspicuous. R. 3, 40, 26 नो चेत्करोषि मारीच हन्मि त्वामहमद्य वै (if you do not do it, forsooth, I'll kill you to day).

Rem. 1. Note नो चेत् making up the whole protasis. So it is especially used in threatening like Lat. *si minus*, Germ. *widrigenfalls*, f. i. Panc. 76 एवं ज्ञात्वा त्वयैष वध्यः। नो चेत्त्वां व्यापादयिष्यति (you must kill him, otherwise he will kill you). For the rest, अन्यथा is equally good. Panc. 124 समर्पय मे सुतमन्यथा राजकुले निवेदयिष्यामि (surrender me my son, otherwise I will prefer charges with the king's court).

Rem. 2. The very opposite of नो चेत् is यद्येवम्, which is likewise often used by itself. It expresses concession and assent »if that is so" v. a. »in that case." Daç. 101 यद्येवमेहि.... त्वामहं मोचयिष्यामि (in that case, come, I will set you free).

486. When proposing an alternative, it may be said यदि ....

---

1) Cp. नेत् (**355** R. 1) = न + इत्.

2) P. 8, 1, 30 it is termed चण्. Kâç. comments: चण् णिद्विशिष्टोऽयं चेदर्थे वर्तते। अयं च मरिष्यति। अयं चेन्मरिष्यतीत्यर्थः. See *Petr. Dict.* II, p. 905, s. v. च 8).

Alter-natives. यदि, like Latin *sive.... sive*, or यदि + adversative particle. But commonly the relative is wanting in the second protasis, and instead of it the adversative is employed alone, especially अथ or its compounds (अथवा, अथ तु, अथापि). In other terms, अथ etc. are virtually the Sanskrit expression of *but if*, Lat. *sin*.

Examples of 1. यदि retained in the second protasis. Panc. 85 स्वामिन्यद्यभयप्रदानं दत्त्वा वधः क्रियते तदेष दोषो भवति। पुनर्यदि देवपादानां भक्त्या स आत्मनो जीवितव्यं प्रयच्छति तन्न दोषः (Lord, if you kill him, to whom you have granted security, it is a sin, but if from attachment to your Lordship he offers you his own life, it is not a sin), cp. Panc. 45, l. 13 यदि.... अथवा यदि.

2. अथ etc. = »but if, and if." Pat. I, p. 8 यदि सन्ति नाप्रयुक्ता अथाप्रयुक्ता न सन्ति सन्ति चाप्रयुक्ताश्चेति विप्रतिषिद्धम् (if they are, they [can]not [be said to be] not employed, and if they are not employed, they are not; [to say,] they are and at the same time one does not employ them, is a self-contradictory statement); — Çâk. V यदि यथा वदति क्षितिपस्तथा त्वमसि किं पितुरुत्कुलया त्वया। अथ तु वेत्सि शुचि व्रतमात्मनः पतिकुले तव दास्यमपि क्षमम् (if thou art what the king says, what will thy father care for thee, who hast disgraced thy family? But if thou knowest thyself chaste and pure, even slavery in thy husband's house is to be borne by thee); — Panc. 172 यदि ते धनेन प्रयोजनमभक्षितेन ततस्त्वामपि गुप्तधनं करोमि। अथवा दत्तभोग्येन धनेन ते प्रयोजनं तदुपभुक्तधनं करोमि (if you want riches not to enjoy them, I will make you [like] Guptadhana, but if you want riches which give enjoyment, I will make you [like] Upabhuktadhana).

Rem. Sometimes in an alternative the former assumption is not expressed in the shape of a conditional period. Yet even then अथ = *but if*, Lat. *sin* is nevertheless available. R. 2, 60, 3 Kausalyâ, the mother of Râma, entreats his charioteer Sumantra to conduct her into the forest to Râma, Sîtâ and Laxmaṇa, अथ, she adds, तान्नानुगच्छामि गमिष्यामि यमक्षयम् (but, if I do not reach them, I will die). Çâk. VII Dushyanta being informed by the nurse: »nobody except his father, his mother or himself is allowed to take up the magic herb of the boy Sarvadamana," asks अथ गृह्णाति (and if one should take it up —).

487. Asyndetic construction. Occasionally the protasis of a conditional period is not introduced by any particle at all. This asyndetic construction is not very common, but it exists in Sanskrit, as it does in many other languages. Just as we say: *should he have done it* = *if he should* etc., or as the Latin poet HORACE (Epp. 1, 1, 33) *fervet avaritia miseroque cupidine pectus: sunt verba et voces, quibus hunc lenire dolorem possis*, so the Sanskrit poet, quoted Hit. 98, writes खलः करोति दुर्वृत्तं नूनं फलति साधुषु (should a rascal do evil, the consequences will certainly be felt by honest people [1]).

2. Another type of asyndetic connection is that exemplified Mṛcch. V, p. 184 मेघा वर्षन्तु गर्जन्तु मुञ्चन्त्वशनिमेव वा। गणयन्ति न शीतोष्णं रमणाभिमुखाः स्त्रियः (the clouds may pour out rain, thunder and lightning, women who are going to their sweethearts do not care for the weather). Here the protasis is expressive of the possible obstacles and still the chief action passes. The imperative in the protasis is, it seems, not necessary, cp. Panc. V, 25 शूरः सुरूपः सुभगश्च वाग्मी शस्त्राणि शास्त्राणि विदांकरोति। अर्थं विना नैव यशश्च मानं प्राप्नोति मर्त्योऽत्र मनुष्यलोके (suppose one to be gallant, well-shapen, happy in love, eloquent, a master at all kind of arms and in all branches of learning, yet, without money no man on earth will achieve glory or honor).

3. A third type of asyndetic construction is an imperative followed by a future, when exhorting to an action and foretelling its result, f. i. *do so and you will be happy* = do so, [for if you do so] you will be happy. So R. 1, 46, 5 Kâçyapa says to Diti शुचिर्भव तपोधने। जनयिष्यसि पुत्रं त्वं शक्रहन्तारमाहवे.

488. As to the tenses and moods, employed in the conditional period, it is to be kept in mind that the conditional period does not import an absolute statement, but rather an assertion in such a manner, that its correct-

---

1) Compare Pat. I, p. 31 एकोऽन्धो दर्शनेऽसमर्थस्तत्समुदायश्च शतमप्यसमर्थम् »one blind man being unable to see, a collection of blind ones will likewise be unable."

Tenses and moods in conditional periods.

ness is made to depend upon the correctness of some other statement presupposed. Now, we must distinguish according to the intention of the speaker, between three cases: 1. the speaker neither affirms nor denies the reality of the fact supposed, 2. he presupposes something known to himself and to his audience to be a real fact, 3. he assumes something impossible or at least improbable, at all events something not real. Hence it follows, from a logical point of view there are three categories of conditional periods:

1°. those, whose protases contain a condition, which the speaker leaves undecided whether it be correct or not;

2°. such as warrant the correctness of the main assertion by the well-known correctness of the protasis;

3°. those, whose protases import an evident untruth, in other terms, such as affirm what would happen if some fact occurred or had occurred, which however cannot or will not occur or have occurred.

In the first and second categories the fact *presupposed* is put in the same tense or mood, as would be required, if it were really *asserted.* In other terms: the employment of past, present and future tenses, of indicative, imperative and लिङ् is determined by the *general* character of their significance and idiosyncrasy, which has been treated in Chapt. III of the fourth Section. That the present often, sometimes also the optative (लिङ्), are used instead of a future tense, can scarcely be said to be an exception, cp. **468** and **324**, 1°.

489. Conditional periods of the third category require the employment of the optative (लिङ्); if they are, however, expressive of a supposition, which cannot be realized because the proper time has already passed, the conditional is also available, cp. **347**.

Examples: 1st category. Çâk. V यदि यथा वदति क्षितिपस्तथा त्वमसि किं पितुरुत्कुलया त्वया।अथ तु वेत्सि शुचि व्रतमात्मनः पतिकुले तव दास्यमपि क्षमम्, here the present tense is expressive of present time: »if you really are....., but if you are knowing;" — Panc. 278 the minister's wife makes this condition to her husband यदि शिरो मुण्डयित्वा मम पादयोर्निपतसि तदा प्रसादाभिमुखी भवामि (if you fall at my feet with shaven head, I will be kind again), here the present tense signifies something to be fulfilled in the future. But ibid. 113 यदि त्वमस्य मन्त्री भविष्यसि तदान्योऽपि कश्चिन्नास्य समीपे साधुजनः समेष्यति (if you shall be his minister, then no other honest man will come near him) the future tense is used of future action. Likewise Nala 20, 15 कामं च ते करिष्यामि यन्मां वक्ष्यसि बाहुक।विदर्भान्यदि यात्वाद्य सूर्यं दर्शयितासि मे there is a future in both the conditional clause and the main sentence. Cp. 341*.

Rem. In conditional periods of this category the लिङ् is wanted, if for some accessory reason there be a tendency for employing it, f. i. in suppositions of a general bearing (**343** *e*), as Varâh. Yog. 1, 4 स्याच्छिद्रमेकमपि चेत्तत एव सर्वं नाशं प्रयाति (if but one [of the aforesaid conditions for the success of a prince] be deficient, the whole perishes).

2d category. Mhbh. 3, 297, 98 Sâvitrî prays यदि मेऽस्ति तपस्तप्तं यदि दत्तं हुतं यदि। श्वश्रूश्वशुरभर्तृणां मम पुण्यास्तु शर्वरी (if I have done penance, bestowed gifts and poured out libations — [and so I have] — this night may be propitious —), Mṛcch. III, p. 121 यदि तावत्कृतान्तेन प्रणयोऽर्थेषु मे कृतः।किमिदानीं नृशंसेन चारित्रमपि दूषितम् (if thou hast loved till now my fortune only, why, destructive Fate, hast thou now without mercy profaned my virtuous name?).

3d category. Mṛcch III, p. 113 दीपं चापि न मर्षयेदभिमुखं स्याल्लक्ष्यसुप्तं यदि [sc. द्वयम्] (nor would they bear the light being brought near to them, if they only feigned to sleep), R. 2, 67, 36 अहो तम इवेदं स्यान्न प्रज्ञायेत किंचन।राजा चेन्न भवेल्लोके विभजन्साध्वसाधुनी (darkness as it were would be on earth, and nothing would be discernible, if no king were in the world, to discriminate between good and evil),

Kumâras. 6, 61 कर्तव्यं वो न पश्यामि स्याच्चेत्किं नोपपद्यते (I know nothing, I could do for you; if there should be, all is granted). Other instances of लिङ् see **343** *d*), instances of conditional **347**.

490. Sometimes the protasis is implied in a participle(**362**, 5°). Panc. I, 32 निवसन्नन्तर्दारुणि लङ्घ्यो वह्निर्न तु ज्वलितः (the fire may be passed when hidden in the wood, not, when blazing). — Likewise in an adjective which does duty as a participle. Mhbh. 1, 8, 221 त्वत्तोऽपत्यवतो लोके चरेयं धर्ममुत्तमम् (if I had a child by you, I should walk the highest path of duty). Or the protasis may be an absolute locative. Panc. II, 198 it is said of a friend that he is प्राप्ते भये परित्राणम् »a shelter, if danger have appeared."

CHAPT. VI. The direct construction ; इति.

491. Direct construction. A special kind of subordination is the so called indirect construction, representing words uttered or reflections made by another, not in the shape they originally did bear, but transformed according to the speaker's point of view. This mode of quoting speech or thought of another, although it is not wholly unknown in Sanskrit, is not idiómatic. As a rule the Sanskrit speaker avails himself of the **direct construction**, that is, he does not change the outward form of the words and ideas quoted, but he reproduces them unaltered, just as they came from the mouth or arose in the mind of their authors. Instead of saying, as we do, *you have said you would come*, one says rather in this way *I will come, so you have said* आगमिष्यामीत्यवादीद्भवान्.

It is but one idiom, the *accusative with participle*, that can be set apart for the indirect construction, see **374**. As to the subordinate sentences, introduced by यत्, यथा, येन or यतः = »that," यदि = »if" (**481**), in a great many cases here will be no formal difference whatever between the direct and the indirect construction, owing among others to the faculty of expressing the predicate by a noun; where there may be such a difference, the direct construction is, as a rule, employed, cp. **494**.

492. इति. The direct construction is characterized by the particle इति generally added to the words or the thought quoted: आगमिष्यामीत्यवादीः (you have said you would come), न मां कश्चित्पश्यतीति चिन्तयति (he thinks nobody sees him).

इति is properly a demonstrative adverb, meaning »thus, so, in this manner"[1]) and for this reason a synonym to इत्थम्, एवम्. Ṛgv. 10, 119, 1 इति वा इति मे मनो गामश्वं सनुयामिति (so indeed, so is my thought, that I may obtain kine and horses); Ratn. III, p. 70 the parting sun taking his leave from the white lotus is represented by the simile of a lover, who goes away from his beloved, to come back the next morning यातो ऽस्मि पद्मवदने समयो ममैष सुप्ता मयैव भवती प्रतिबोधनीया। प्रत्यायनामयमितीव सरोरुहिण्याः सूर्यो ऽस्तमस्तकनिविष्टकरः करोति (I go, lily-face, it is my time, [yet] it is I who will awake you out of sleep, in almost this way the sinking sun comforts the water-lily). But as इति is almost exclusively employed for quoting one's thought or the utterance thereof[2]), it is often not to be rendered at all. Moreover we often use the indirect construction. Nala 3, 1 तेभ्यः प्रतिज्ञाय नलः करिष्य इति (Nala promised them, he would do so —). Sometimes इति abounds even in Sanskrit, the pleonasm इत्येवम् and the like being allowed, cp. **496** R.

493. In short, the direct construction with इति is not only necessary, when quoting one's words spoken or

---

1) Lat. *ita* is both formally and as to its meaning the same word as इति.

2) I recollect but one instance of इति = »so, thus," used as a pure demonstrative, viz. Panc. 327 वानरो ऽपि तिष्ठति यथा भवानिति (the monkey stood, just as you do). Note also the employment of इति at the close of literary compositions, f. i. इति शाकुन्तले प्रथमो ऽङ्कः (here ends the first act of the Çâkuntala), just as अथ is used in the beginning.

Employment of इति. written, but it is also idiomatic to express by it the object of knowing, thinking, believing, reflecting, doubting, rejoicing, wondering and the like, to expound the fact which acts as a cause or motive, to signify the object of purpose and wish, etc.

Examples of the direct construction with इति: *a.*) when quoting words spoken or otherwise uttered. Mâlat. I, p. 11 कथितमवलोकितया मदनोद्यानं गतो माधव इति (A. had told me, M. was gone to the grove of Kâma); Daç. 68 अङ्गेषु.... कश्चिदस्ति तपःप्रभावोत्पन्नदिव्यचक्षुर्मरीचिर्नाम महर्षिरिति कुतश्चित्संलपतो जनसमाजादुपलभ्य (as I heard from some people conversing, there was in the country of Anga —); Mudr. I, p. 37 न चाख्येयमस्मै चाणाक्यो लेखयतीति (he must not be informed that it is Cânakya who has it written by him); Mṛcch. VIII, p. 242 धन्यस्त्वं पुण्यस्त्वमिति भवन्तं स्तौति.

b.) when expressive of the contents of one's thought. Mhbh.1, 74, 29 मन्यते पापकं कृत्वा न कश्चिद्वेत्ति मामिति (after doing some evil one thinks, nobody knows me as such), Panc. 8 स्वामिन्मृतोऽसौ संजीवकोऽस्माभिस्तु सार्थवाहस्याभीष्ट इति मत्वा वह्निना संस्कृतः (master, that [bull] Saṃjîvaka has died; now, as we thought the merchant liked him, we have consumed his body by fire), Hit. 24 अनन्तरं च तेनैव जरद्गवेनास्माकं शावकाः खादिता इति सर्वैः पक्षिभिर्निश्चित्य मिलित्वा गृध्रो व्यापादितः (after this, all the birds, understanding that it was Jaradgava himself who had devoured their young ones, killed the vulture by joint exertion), Çâk. V मूढः स्यामहमेषा वा वदेन्मिथ्येति संशये (I am at a loss whether I am perhaps astray, or that she lies), Panc. I, 222 पुत्रीति जाता महतीह चिन्ता कस्मै प्रदेयेति महान्वितर्कः। दत्त्वा सुखं प्राप्स्यति वा न वेति, Nâgân. V, p. 80 कदाचिन्नायं नाग इति [मां] ज्ञात्वा परित्यजेन्नागशत्रुः.

c.) when setting forth the motives of emotions (*rejoicing*, *wondering* and the like) and of judgments (*approbation*, *disapproval*), the contents of a *bargain*, a *convention* etc., in short, in all such cases as also admit of being expressed by a clause introduced by यत्. Hit. 11 न धर्मशास्त्रं पठतीति कारणम् (that he reads the law-books, is not the cause), Panc. V, 26 पुरुषः स एव बाह्यः क्षणेन भवतीति विचित्रमेतत् (it is singular, that the very same man [having lost his wealth] should forthwith become a stranger), Çâk. I तत्रभवान्कण्वः शाश्वते ब्रह्मणि

वर्तेत इयं च वः सखी तस्यात्मजेति कथमेतत् (how is it, that, Kaṇva observing a holy life for ever, your friend should be his daughter?), Hit. 10 व्याघ्रो मानुषं खादतीति लोकापवादः (that the tiger eats the man is slanderous gossip), Daç. 116 ताभ्यां..... कृतः समयोऽभूदावयोः पुत्रवत्याः पुत्राय दुहितृमत्या दुहिता देयेति (the two [queens] made this bargain, that if one of them should become mother to a son, and the other to a daughter, they would make their children marry each other).

d.) when signifying a purpose or a wish. Here it is clear, the reflections quoted are put in the imperative, the future, the optative (लिङ्). Nala 26, 6 पुनः प्रवर्ततां द्यूतमिति मे निश्चिता मतिः (I am decided to take up the game again), Panc. 301 वयं तत्र यास्यामो यत्र धनाप्तिर्मृत्युर्वा भविष्यतीत्येष निश्चयः (we have made up our minds to go to a country where we have the chance of getting either money or death); — Pat. I, p. 76 कार्याणि न सिध्यन्ति। इष्यन्ते च स्युरिति (what is to be done does not succeed, yet it is wished to be done).

e.) as to इति, when expressive of motive or cause, see **497**.

494. As it appears from the instances quoted, the direct construction may precede the chief predicate as well as follow it. In the latter case, the relative conjunctions यत् or यथा, like our „that," may introduce it, but its *direct character remains unchanged* by them. For this reason even when using यत् or यथा, इति may be retained[1]). Panc. 159 सा सखी तत्सकाशं गत्वा प्रोधमब्रवीत्। यदहं चन्द्रवत्या तवान्तिकं प्रेषिता भणितं च त्वां प्रति तया यन्मम त्वद्दर्शनान्मनोभवेन पश्चिमावस्था कृता (the friend went to him and hastily said to him: »Candrâvatî has sent me to you and tells you, Kâma has almost made her die with love by causing her to see you"), ibid. 102 तं वद यदन्यो भृत्यो वाहनायास्मत्स्थाने क्रियताम् (tell him, he must appoint some other of his servants, instead of me, to be his carrier); — Mudr. VII, p. 229 विदितमेव यथा वयं मलयकेतौ किंचित्कालान्तरमुषिताः (it is certainly known [to you] that I stayed for some time with Malaya-

1) Compare the similar employment of Greek ὅτι with the direct construction.

ketu), Mṛcch. II, p. 82 कथितं च मम प्रियवयस्येन शर्विलकेन यथा किलार्यकनामा गोपालदारकः सिद्धादेशेन समादिष्टो राजा भविष्यतीति.

Rem. 1. Occasionally also येन or यतः are used for this purpose. Panc. 266 गत्वा तत्सकाशम्.... अन्विष्य मम संदेशं कथय येनागम्यतामेकाकिनापि भवता द्रुततरम्.

Rem. 2. In a similar way इति may be added to relative or interrogative sentences, depending on some word of *saying* or *knowing* (411). Çâk. I ज्ञास्यसि कियद्भुजो मे रक्षति मौर्वीकिणाङ्क इति (you will know how mighty my arm is to protect etc.), Nâgân. V, p. 73 तत्त्वरितं विज्ञायागच्छ किमसौ स्वगृहमागतो न वेति.

495. As a rule, in prose इति is put immediately after the direct construction. But sometimes an other arrangement is preferred, especially in poets and for metrical reasons. So in epic poetry such phrases as इत्युवाच, इत्युक्तः sometimes precede the words quoted, sometimes they follow after them. F. i. R. 1, 47, 8 the line उवाच प्राञ्जलिर्वाक्यमितीदं बलसूदनः precedes the very words quoted, Daç. 191 the sentence दिशि दिश्युत्यकीर्त्यत जनेन »in all regions this was told of me" precedes, the contents of the rumour follow. Cp. Kumâras. 4, 27 इति चैनम् [sc. वसन्तम्] उवाच दुःखिता। सुहृदः पश्य वसन्त किं स्थितम्, etc. — On the other hand, R. 1, 27, 26 it has been said first what was spoken to Râma, then follows who said so. Nor is it rare to put इति in the midst of the words quoted. Panc. III, 160 मा चास्मै त्वं कृथा द्वेषं बद्धानेनेति मत्प्रिया = अनेन मत्प्रिया बद्धेति »be not moved with anger towards him [while thinking]: it is he, who caught my sweetheart." R. 1, 55, 11 स पुत्रमेकं राज्याय पालयेति नियुज्य च। पृथिवीं क्षत्रधर्मेण वनमेवाभ्यपद्यत, here the direct construction is पालय पृथिवीं क्षत्रधर्मेण.

496. *Synonyms of इति, etc.* इति, though it is the commonest contrivance for expressing the direct construction, is by no means indispensable. Other demonstratives, as एवम्, इत्थम्, the pronouns एष, अयम्, ईदृश may likewise serve that purpose. Nothing, too, forbids quoting without using any demonstrative at all.

Examples: *a.*) of the direct constr. set forth by a demonstrative other but इति. Panc. 18 स्वाम्येवं वदति चिराद्दृश्यते (my master speaks thus: »it is long ago since I saw you"), ibid. I, 302 अहं हि संमतो राज्ञो य एवं मन्यते कुधीः। बलीवर्दः स विज्ञेयो विषाणपरिवर्जितः. R. 2, 61, 1 कौसल्या रुदती चार्ता भर्तारमिदमब्रवीत्, vs. 2-26 contain the very words of the queen, vs. 27 इमां गिरं दारुणशब्दसंहितां निशम्य..... ततः स शोकं प्रविवेश पार्थिवः, here इदम् and इमाम् point to the words spoken, not इति.

Rem. The pleonasm इत्येवम्, इत्येष etc. is frequent. See Mhbh. 1, 119, 38, Kathâs. 35, 50, M. 2,15, etc. etc.

b.) neither इति nor any other demonstrative is used. So very often in dialogues स आह..... सोऽप्याह and the like. Nala 8, 7 तास्तु सर्वाः प्रकृतयो द्वितीयं समुपस्थिताः। न्यवेदयद्भीमसुता न स तत्प्रत्यनन्दत (Damayantî informed Nala, that his officers had come to him a second time, but he did not care for it), Panc. I, 150 यो मोहान्मन्यते मूढो रक्तेयं मम कामिनी। स तस्या वशगो नित्यं भवेत्, R. 3, 7, 15 भवान्सर्वत्र कुशलः सर्वभूतहिते रतः। आख्यातं शरभङ्गेन (that you are etc., has been told by Çarabhanga). As to such constructions as कामो मे (or इच्छामि) भुञ्जीत — or भुङ्क्तां — भवान् (I wish you to eat), न संभावयामि तत्रभवान्नाम वृषलं याजयेत् (I do not believe, indeed, I do not, he will sacrifice for a çûdra) etc. see Kâç. on P. 3, 3, 145, 153 and 157.

497. Elliptical construction.

It is of frequent occurrence that the verb of *speaking*, *knowing*, *thinking*, *deliberating* etc. is not expressed, but इति alone is the exponent of the direct construction. In this case, इति is of great importance for the sense, and its translation is various, according to the relation which exists between the main action and the contents of the direct construction inserted. For instance, if it happens that some motive is denoted by it, then इति may be translated by *because*, *since* or by *therefore*, *for this reason*. Another time the direct construction may be expressive of something to be done, then इति requires being rendered by *in order that*, sim. Sometimes again this somewhat elliptical idiom serves only to enhance the vividness of the style.

In full, one says also इति कृत्वा (lit. „thus doing)" = „thus thinking, considering, reflecting."

Examples: R. 1, 55, 11 स पुत्रमेकं राज्याय पालयेति नियुज्य च। पृथिवीं क्षत्रधर्मेण वनमेवाभ्यपद्यत, here इति नियुज्य = »with these words he appointed him". — Mṛcch. I, p. 38 Câruḍatta apostrophizes Poverty दारिद्र्य शोचामि भवन्तमेवमस्मच्छरीरे सुहृदित्युषित्वा (»in this way I mourn, Poverty, for thee, who hast dwelled with me as a friend", lit. considering me your friend). — Mudr. III, p. 126 चाणक्यतः स्खलितभक्तिमहं सुखेन जेष्यामि मौर्यमिति संप्रति यः प्रयुक्तः। भेदः किलैष भवता (the dissension you have plotted, thinking you would easily vanquish Candragupta, if his faith in Cânakya should be shaken). Mhbh. 1, 153, 42 पुनर्भीमो बलादेनं विचकर्ष महाबलः। मा शब्दः सुखसुप्तानां भ्रातॄणां मे भवेदिति (again, the strong Bhîma shook him [but in such a way], that no noise might awake his brothers who slept quietly), R. 3, 10, 3 क्षत्रियैर्धार्यते चापो नार्तशब्दो भवेदिति (the warriors carry their bows in order to rescue the distressed), R. 2, 52, 28 न चाहमनुशोचामि लक्ष्मणो न च शोचति। अयोध्यायाश्च्युताश्चेति वने वत्स्यामहेति वा (neither I nor Laxmaṇa mourns for our having been expulsed from Ayodhyâ or for having to dwell in the forest), Mṛcch. I, p. 19 गृहमस्मदीयं क्षीणार्थमित्यथितयः परिवर्जयन्ति (guests shun my dwelling, because wealth has vanished from it), Pat. I, p. 99 न हि भिक्षुकाः सन्तीति स्थाल्यो नाधिश्रीयन्ते न च मृगाः सन्तीति यवा नोप्यन्ते (we do not abstain from cooking, considering there are beggars, nor do we abstain from sowing, considering there are antelopes), Utt. I, p. 2 वैदेशिकोऽस्मीति पृच्छामि (as I am a stranger to this country, I question [you]), Mâlav. I, p. 3 पुराणमित्येव न साधु सर्वं न चापि काव्यं नवमित्यवद्यम् (not every old poem is to be approved only for its age, nor is new poetry to be blamed only because it is new); — Çâk. II दर्भाङ्कुरेण चरणः क्षत इत्यकाण्डे तन्वी स्थिता कतिचिदेव पदानि गत्वा (when she had gone some steps, she stopped on a sudden feigning her foot was hurt by a blade of grass), Kathâs. 62, 49 नीडो मे तव नेत्येवं विवाद उदभूद् द्वयोः (a quarrel arose between them on account of the nest, lit. »[both of them saying] the nest is mine, not yours"), and compare the altercation, which is found in the opening stanza of the Mudrârâxasa, and is intended to display the cunning of Çiva:

धन्या केयं स्थिता ते शिरसि शशिकला किं नु नामैतदस्याः
नामैवास्यास्तदेतत्परिचितमपि ते विस्मृतं कस्य हेतोः
नारीं पृच्छामि नेन्दुं कथयतु विजया न प्रमाणं यदीन्दु-
र्देव्या निह्नोतुमिच्छोरिति सुरसरितं शाठ्यमव्याद्विभोर्वः

the last pâda signifies: »may the craft of the Lord protect you, [who] desirous of concealing Gangâ from Devî, his wife, [acted] thus," how he acted is set forth in pâda 1—3, containing the questions of Umâ and the answers of Çiva.

Rem. 1. Among the most common applications of this freer construction, note तथेति to express consent, lit. »[saying] yes," किमिति »why?" lit. »[asking] what?" — Comments and glosses are marked by इति (इति यावत्, इति भावः etc.), quotations by इति with the name of the author or his work. Objections, which may be made, are represented by इति चेत् — in full इति चेद्वदेत् —, f. i. Sây. on Ait. Br. 1, 20, 3 नाभिशब्दवाच्यत्वं कथमिति चेत्। तदुच्यते (now, as one might ask why it [the navel] is denoted by the word *nâbhi*, etc.) And so on.

Rem. 2. इति is also used when imitating sounds, as पटिति करोति. Nala 2, 4 न नक्तं न दिवा शेते हा हेति रुदती पुनः. cp. P. 6, 1, 98.

Rem. 3. Pânini teaches: The 2d person *sing.* of the imperative put twice with इति may be added to the narrative tense of the same verb, in order to denote the action being done with intensity or repeatedly लुनीहि लुनीहीत्ययं लुनाति। लुनीहि लुनीहीतीमे लुनन्ति. Likewise this singular number of the imper. repeated may express the performing of several actions at the same time. Kâç. exemplifies it by this instance भ्राष्ट्रमट मठमट खटूरमट स्थाल्यपिधानमटेत्येव त्वमटसि। युवामटथः। यूयमटथ, to represent the hurry and bustle of people occupied in the kitchen. Instead of the same verb put twice, also synonyms may be used. Çiçup. 1, 51 पुरीमवस्कन्द लुनीहि नन्दनं मुषाण रत्नानि हरामराङ्गनाः। विगृह्य चक्रे नमुचिद्विषा बली य इत्थमस्वास्थ्यमहर्दिवं दिवः. P. 3, 4, 2-5.

For the rest, it is not the repetition of imperatives alone, that serves to bring forward the idea of tumultuary action. In such cases as Panc. 62 अथ ते तत्र विश्वासमापन्नास्तात मातुल भ्रातरिति ब्रुवाणा अहंपूर्वमहंपूर्वमिति समन्तात्परितस्थुः, the repeated words अहं पूर्वम् serve the same purpose. And so often.

498. Nominative with इति. Since इति quotes or pretends to quote speech or thought, the direct construction, which is distinguished by it from the main framework of the context, is a sentence or a complex of sentences, not a mere complex of words. Yet, these sentences are not always given in full, they are sometimes elliptical and may even consist of one single word. When a noun, this is of course a **nominative.** So f. i. Nala 16, 8 तां..... तर्कयामास भैमीति (her she guessed to be the daughter of Bhîma, lit. she guessed [thinking: „she is] the daughter of Bhîma"). There is a predilection for using such a nominative with इति, in order to express the predicate of the object of verbs of *calling*, *styling*, *considering*, *holding for* and the like (**32**, *c*). Nala 2, 20 विदर्भराज्ञो दुहिता दमयन्तीति विश्रुता, Panc. 1 तस्य त्रयः पुत्राः परमदुर्मेधसो बहुशक्तिरुग्रशक्तिरनन्तशक्तिश्चेतिनामानो बभूवुः, Mhbh. 1, 155, 9 अर्हसि कृपां कर्तुं मयि..... मत्वा मूढेति (show mercy to me, think I am out of my wits), Prabodh. VI, p. 115 निग्रह इति वक्तव्ये कथमनुग्रहः पृच्छ्यते (it is of punishment you ought to have spoken and you ask about her reward), Kumâras. 5, 28 वदन्त्यपर्णेति च ताम् (they call her Apar$_n$â), Panc. 103 कथं ज्ञेयो मयासौ दुष्टबुद्धिरिति (how can I know him to be evil-minded?), Mhbh. 1, 34, 3 सखेति कृत्वा तु सखे पृष्टो वक्ष्याम्यहं त्वया (— but considering you as my friend, I will tell it you in reply to your question), cp. ibid. 1, 77, 17.

499. Anacoluthon. Similarly nominatives with इति may specify general terms (cp. **493**, *c*). Pat. I, p. 411 the essential qualities of a brahman are thus enumerated तथा गौरः शुच्याचारः पिङ्गलः कपिलकेश इत्येतानप्यभ्यन्तरान्ब्राह्मण्ये गुणान्कुर्वन्ति.

Now, as according to **496** इति may be wanting here, we get also a kind of a n a c o l u t h o n, nominatives agreeing with oblique cases. Kâm. 2, 19 याजनाध्यापने शुद्धे विशुद्धाच्च प्रतिग्रहः। वृत्तित्रयमिदं प्राहुर्मुनयो ज्येष्ठवर्णिनः here the nom. याजनाध्यापने and प्रतिग्रहः are the specification of the accus. वृत्तित्रयम्. Panc. III, 220 कुलं

च शीलं च सनाथता च विद्या च वित्तं च वपुर्वयश्च। एतान्गुणान्सप्त विचिन्त्य देया कन्या बुधैः, M. 5, 133 मक्षिका विप्रुषश्छाया गौरश्वः सूर्यरश्मयः। रजो भूर्वायुरग्निश्च स्पर्शे मेध्यानि निर्दिशेत्. A similar character is displayed by the nominatives, which periphraze a partitive case. One instance has been given in the chapter on the genitive (**117**, 1°), here is another: Mhbh. 13, 22, 14 अश्वमेधसहस्रं च सत्यं च तुलया धृतम्। नाभिजानामि यद्यस्य सत्यस्यार्धमवाप्नुयात् = »these two put in a balance, a hundred açvamedhas and Truth, I am not sure whether the sacrifices would reach half the weight of Truth."

500. *मन्ये, जाने etc. inserted.* Some verbal forms as मन्ये (I think), जाने (I know, I think), शङ्के (I guess), आशंसे (I trust), पश्य (look) often have no influence at all on the sentence even when put in the midst. Likewise such phrases as न संशयः, नात्र संशयः v. a. „undoubtedly, no doubt."

Kathâs. 25, 166 सुप्ता जाने स्त्रिया स्वप्ने कयाप्युक्तास्मि दिव्यया (a heavenly woman, methinks, spoke to me, when asleep), Nâgân. II, p. 35 कुसुममपि विचेतुं यो न मन्ये समर्थः। कलयति स कथं ते पाशमुद्बन्धनाय (this [hand] of yours, which hardly I think would gather even a flower, how can it serve to put a halter round your neck?), R. 2, 84, 18 आशंसे स्वाशिता सेना वत्स्यत्येनां विभावरीम् (I trust the army being well supplied with food, will stay [with me] for the night), Çâk. VI शङ्के संहरति स्मरोऽपि चकित-स्तूणार्धकृष्टं शरम् (even Kâma, I believe, draws back his arrow), Kathâs. 26, 13 ब्रह्मन्विनाशकालोऽयं ध्रुवमस्माकमागतः। यदकस्मात्प्रवहणं पश्यात्रैव प्रयात्यधः, Panc. 48 the wife of the barber cries पापेनानेन मम सदाचारवर्तिन्याः पश्यत नासिकाछेदो विहितः.

Rem. मन्ये, जाने and the like not seldom express irony, in which case may be applied what is taught by Pâṇini (1, 4, 106 and 8, 1, 46) about एहि मन्ये with the 2d person of the future एहि मन्य ओदनं भोक्ष्यसे »now, indeed, you will eat rice," if the meaning of the speaker is: »you think you will, but it cannot be, there is no rice to be eaten. [1])"

1) The explication of Pâṇini, मन्ये is used *instead of* मन्यसे, cannot be accepted. The idea »you think falsely" is not purported by मन्ये, but it is implied by the ironical form of utterance. In sentences of the kind मन्ये has almost got the character of a particle.

INDEX OF SANSKRIT WORDS.

The numbers refer to the paragraphs.
